PRICE RATIOS

11. Dividend yield *(Chapter 20)*

$$= \frac{\text{Dividend per share}}{\text{Price per share}}$$

12. Sales per dollar of common at market value *(Chapter 20)*

$$= \frac{\text{Sales}}{\text{Weighted average shares outstanding x stock price}}$$

13. Price-to-book value *(Chapter 20)*

$$= \frac{\text{Price per share}}{\text{Book value per share}}$$

PROFITABILITY RATIOS

14. Return on capital *(Chapter 20)*

$$= \frac{\text{Net income} + \text{minority interest} + \text{tax-adjusted interest}}{\text{Tangible assets} - \text{short-term accrued payables}}$$

15. Capital turnover *(Chapter 20)*

$$= \frac{\text{Sales}}{\text{Tangible assets} - \text{short-term accrued payables}}$$

16. Earnings margin *(Chapter 20)*

$$= \frac{\text{Net income} + \text{minority interest} + \text{tax-adjusted interest}}{\text{Sales}}$$

17. Return on capital before depreciation *(Chapter 20)*

$$= \frac{\text{Net income} + \text{minority interest} + \text{tax-adjusted interest} + \text{depreciation}}{\text{Tangible assets} - \text{short-term accrued payables}}$$

18. Return on common equity *(Chapter 20)*

$$= \frac{\text{Net income} - \text{preferred dividend requirements}}{\text{Common equity} - \text{goodwill} - \text{most intangibles} + \text{deferred tax liability}}$$

GROWTH RATIOS

19. Growth in sales *(Chapter 20)*

$$= \frac{\text{Sales in final period}}{\text{Sales in base period}}$$

20. Growth in total return *(Chapter 20)*

$$= \frac{\text{Net earned for total capital in final period}}{\text{Net earned for total capital in base period}}$$

Graham and Dodd's
Security Analysis

Graham and Dodd's
Security Analysis

Fifth Edition

Sidney Cottle

President, FRS Associates
Coauthor of *Security Analysis*, Fourth Edition

Roger F. Murray

S. Sloan Colt Professor Emeritus of Banking
and Finance
Columbia University Graduate School of Business

Frank E. Block

Member of Financial Accounting Standards Board,
1979–1985 (retired)
Past President of FAF and ICFA

With the collaboration of

Martin L. Leibowitz

Managing Director, Bond Portfolio Analysis Group
Salomon Brothers, Inc.

McGraw-Hill Book Company

**New York   St. Louis   San Francisco   Auckland
Bogotá   Hamburg   London   Madrid   Mexico
Milan   Montreal   New Delhi   Panama
Paris   São Paulo   Singapore
Sydney   Tokyo   Toronto**

Library of Congress Cataloging-in-Publication Data

Cottle, Sidney.
  [Security analysis]
  Graham and Dodd's security analysis/Sidney Cottle, Roger F.
Murray, Frank E. Block, with the collaboration of Martin L.
Leibowitz.
    p. cm.
  Rev. ed. of: Security analysis/Benjamin Graham. 4th ed. 1962.
  Includes index.
  ISBN 0-07-013235-6
  1. Investment analysis. 2. Securities — United States. I. Roger
F. Murray. II. Block, Frank E. III. Graham, Benjamin, 1894–
Security analysis. IV. Title. V. Title: Security analysis.
HG4529.C675 1988
332.63'2 – dc 19   87-19990

    16 17 18 19 20 DOC/DOC 0 9 8 7 6 5 4 3 2

ISBN 0-07-013235-6

This book is printed on recycled, acid-free paper containing a minimum of 50% recycled de-
inked fiber.

The editors for this book were Martha Jewett and Barbara B. Toniolo,
the designer was Naomi Auerbach, and the production supervisor was
Dianne Walber. This book was set in Baskerville. It was composed by the
McGraw-Hill Book Company Professional & Reference Division
Composition unit.

Printed and bound by R. R. Donnelley and Sons Company

The authors wish to express their deep appreciation to Autranet and Donaldson, Lufkin, & Jenrette for the grant which provided important support for the fifth edition of this book. This grant is an expression of the interest in and dedication of these two organizations to advancing the effectiveness of the investment process.

Contents

Part 3   Analysis of Fixed-Income Securities

Part 4   Valuation of Common Stocks and Contingent Claims

Part 5   Impact of Security Analysis

Preface

The Graham and Dodd concept of security analysis, with its emphasis on value, does not need a revised edition. The principles of fundamental analysis articulated in all four of the previous editions still serve their adherents well. Indeed, many investment managers use terms such as "value based" and "a Graham and Dodd approach" interchangeably to describe their method of security selection. This Fifth Edition, therefore, is not the revision of principles but an updating of techniques used in their application. Moreover, an era of acquisitions, leveraged buyouts, and restructurings requires the intensive analytical effort to determine the value of companies which a Graham and Dodd approach provides.

Studies of market efficiencies, modern portfolio theory, and the insights from financial economics argue that for *all* investors or for the *average* investor there are no consistent returns to be earned from security analysis. Supposedly, the market's pricing mechanism, fueled by the efforts of capable analysts, is too efficient to afford opportunities even for *some* investors to earn superior returns from security selection. The Graham and Dodd approach, however, takes the view that the market's pricing mechanism remains based to such a degree upon faulty and frequently irrational analytical processes that the price of a security only occasionally coincides with the intrinsic value around which it tends to fluctuate.

Since the conceptual framework of security analysis, the quality of financial information, and the analytical processes applied to it each deserve careful examination, this edition, like its predecessors, starts in Part 1 with an exposition of the role of security analysis in investment decision making, a definition of intrinsic value, and the analytical dependencies involved in the selection of securities. The concept of a margin of safety is presented.

Part 2 addresses the analysis of financial statements in the search for reliable estimates of company earning power, as distinguished from periodically reported "earnings." The adjustments required for the consistency and comparability of company and industry ratio analysis are almost completely new because of the many changes in accounting, tax, and disclosure rules since the Fourth Edition in 1962.

Part 3 provides a comprehensive perspective on the market for fixed-income securities and standards for their selection. The determination of an issuer's creditworthiness is addressed in terms of the financial statement analysis principles developed in Part 2.

The valuation approach to common stock selection is presented in Part 4. The significance of earning power, dividends, growth, and assets is developed in the course of arriving at the capitalization rate for establishing a company's intrinsic value. Options, warrants, and convertibles are covered in a chapter's treatment of contingent claims.

Issues of corporate governance with which the security analyst is concerned are addressed in Part 5.

Throughout this edition, the authors have sought to sustain the traditional Graham and Dodd respect for the facts, to distinguish genuine accomplishment from hopes and expectations, and to reach sound principles of valuation. The conservatism inherent in the Graham and Dodd approach raises serious questions about the level of stock prices illustrated by a Dow Jones Average of 2400 in early 1987. A reasonable set of value standards is presented for acceptance, rejection, or modification by the reader.

This restatement of Graham and Dodd principles seeks to reflect such dynamics of change as the present role of institutional investors in the securities markets, the development of new financial technology, an extensive array of contingent claims, and major revisions in financial reporting practices. Specific criteria for the valuation of corporate securities have been refined to reflect the flow of research in financial analysis. In the face of these changes, the principles defined by Graham and Dodd have proved durable and continue to provide the structure for security analysis as a discipline.

This book is a living tribute to the analytical genius of the late Benjamin Graham. The first four editions were source books for members of the Financial Analysts Federation and for the Institute of Certified Financial Analysts, for which Graham was an original inspiration and advocate. An important result of his leadership has been the emphasis on ethical standards and continuing education which these two organizations now provide. As a result, continuing progress in the discipline of security analysis is assured.

This Fifth Edition is the collaborative product of three authors. Sidney Cottle, co-author of the Fourth Edition, has provided many years of specialized research and investment consulting to large corporate clients and institutional investors. Dr. Cottle was formerly Director of Finance at Stanford Research Institute and a member of the faculty of the Graduate School of Business, Stanford University. Frank E. Block, CFA, brings to this edition 30 years of investment experience in bank trust departments and on Wall Street. As a recent board member of the Financial Accounting Standards Board, Mr. Block has been immersed in financial statement accounting developments. Roger F. Murray, S. Sloan Colt Professor Emeritus of Banking and Finance, Columbia University Graduate School of Business, managed money as a vice president of Bankers Trust Company and an executive vice president of Teachers Insurance and Annuity Association and College Retirement Equities Fund. A past president of the American Finance Association, Dr. Murray is the originator of the Individual Retirement Account concept and taught countless Columbia Business School students from two previous editions. We are indebted to Martin L. Leibowitz, Managing Director, Bond Portfolio Analysis Group, Salomon Brothers, Inc., for his authorship of Chapter 23 on the bond investing environment.

The magnitude of undertaking this new edition after 25 years is not to be minimized. Those many individuals whose ideas and assistance have contributed to the completion of this book already know of the authors' deep appreciation. A special debt of gratitude is owed to Nancy C. Doolittle for many timely criticisms, searching questions, and correct answers.

Falmouth, Maine   *David L. Dodd*
April 1987   Professor Emeritus of Finance
                                            Columbia University

PART 1

Financial Analysis and Approach

1

Financial Analysis, Investment Decision Making, and Security Analysis

This book focuses on that major aspect of financial analysis which has been labeled "security analysis" since that term was given currency by the title of this book in its first 1934 edition.[1] Security analysis examines and evaluates individual securities to estimate the results of investing in them. Financial analysis in general and security analysis in particular must be viewed within the context of the total process of investment

---

[1] Previously, leading financial institutions had statistical departments in which statisticians pored over railroad traffic density maps and calculated the pace of treated tie replacements and the adequacy of railroad equipment maintenance. In those cases where meaningful financial data were available for industrial companies, the statisticians attempted to make comparisons between leading companies but contributed little to the investment decision-making process. Benjamin Graham's first course offering at Columbia University in 1929 was titled "Investments." David Dodd's careful notes and examples from that course were the rich ore from which was mined that first 1934 edition. *Security Analysis*, with the passage of time, migrated from a book title to the generic name for a major financial discipline. Statistical departments became analysis departments and, eventually, investment research functions.

decision making. The place of these disciplines in that process is the subject of this chapter.

Financial Analysis

Financial analysis is the informative and predictive function in investing. It provides information about the past and present, and it quantifies expectations for the future. Capital-budgeting decisions, corporate financial policies, and informed selections of securities for investment are all products of financial analysis. Analytical resources mobilized for these purposes include economic, capital market, sector, and specific-security analyses.

Economic analysis provides both near-term (next four to eight quarters) and longer-term (next five years or more) projections for the total economy in terms of the nation's output of goods and services, inflation, profits, monetary and fiscal policy, and productivity. It thus provides the foundation for capital market, sector, industry, and company estimates of the future.

Capital market analysis develops value and return estimates primarily for the stock and bond markets. Stock market estimates are developed for the market as a whole, as represented by established indexes. Bond market estimates pertain to the general level and term structure of interest rates and to return differentials which may be reflected in expected returns as a result of exposure to price variability and default risk.

Security analysis examines the industries and securities of individual companies primarily to develop value and return expectations for securities and thus to distinguish overpriced securities from underpriced ones.

Between capital market analysis and security analysis, with some characteristics of each, is sector (also called "common factor") analysis. Broader than industry and company analysis, sector analysis may be viewed as a bridge between capital market analysis and security analysis. In the stock market context, sectors consist of major groupings of stocks (e.g., according to economic sector, growth rate, or cyclicality in earnings) that either cut across or combine several industries.

Individual and Institutional Investors

Current emphasis on the increasing role of institutions has focused on the form rather than the substance of the investment decision-making process. The similarities and identities of the steps taken both by institutions and by individuals therefore deserve recognition at the outset of this volume. The common goal of all investors is to acquire assets that are at least fairly priced and preferably underpriced. Should such assets become overvalued, the investors' goal is to recognize the fact and to dispose of them. Since this valuation relates to unknown future events, its accuracy may depend as much on the economic, capital market, sector, and industry factors at work as on specific company performance. Individual investors make implicit forecasts or assumptions about these factors without elaborate reports, because they have no need to communicate beyond the purchase or sale order to their brokers. An institution, however, must develop a deliberative process for reconciling different views and a communication system to make the conclusions uniformly applicable. Also, a staff of security analysts must have for their use a consensus of economic and other factors for application to individual companies so that their work is based on consistent expectations for the future.

A large institution's policy committee minutes may, then, require extensive reports and supporting materials to keep a defined investment strategy in place. The individual need not prepare any formal studies because a simple one-line note may serve to preserve the basis of a decision for future reference. The absence of a "paper trail" does not differentiate the individual's from the institution's process in reaching decisions.

Top-Down and Bottom-Up Approaches

Given the formal apparatus of analytical assignments to economic, capital market, and sector forecasts, one would expect that all institutions would be "top-down" investors, that is, those who begin with the economy, both domestic and international, and proceed to capital markets, sectors, and industries, in making specific security selections. Individuals, in contrast, might be "bottom-up" investors, who screen large numbers of stocks in their search for cases of undervaluation, giving barely a nod to the environmental factors. In fact, however, many very large institutional investors use a bottom-up approach, and many individuals of modest resources proceed from the top down.

It follows that the security analyst may have different types of audiences for findings. Top-down portfolio managers will seek assurance that they and a security analyst are both working from common assumptions, whereas the bottom-up manager may be interested principally in company-specific information. The uses to which the security analyst's effort is put, then, can differ widely, but this does not change the analysis discipline or course of inquiry. Valuation takes into account all the characteristics of a company and its business to determine the suitability of a security for a particular portfolio structure.

Investing as a Discipline

Investing, like medicine, law, and economics, lies somewhere between an art and a science. Certain aspects of investing lend themselves to the scientific approach. Moreover, the creation of computerized data banks and advances in quantitative techniques and computer skills have accelerated the use of scientific methods. However, corporations are business enterprises subject to the vagaries of human management and operate in a highly dynamic and competitive environment. Furthermore, many compete in both international and domestic markets. As a result, for the security analyst, the number of variables remains almost infinite, and the judgment factor still dominates investment decisions.

It is doubtful that investing will ever be classified as a science. Nevertheless, research, training, and experience have developed investing into a discipline. *Discipline* refers here to a structured, consistent, and orderly process without rigidity in either concept or method. Such a process will minimize the impact of human emotions at market peaks and troughs. In other words, investing should be conducted systematically. For investors, there is no single, momentous, and everlasting decision regarding either a single security or a portfolio, because the investment environment is highly dynamic. The fortunes and market valuations of individual companies and entire industries change markedly and sometimes rapidly. As a result, only the most unusual securities are purchased as permanent holdings. To illustrate, recall that, measured in growth and profitability, steel was once one of the leading industries in the United States. However, from 1982 to 1986, eight large integrated steel companies suffered an aggregate loss in excess of $4 billion.

Many will also recall when the aluminum industry was one of the favorites in the marketplace. Alcoa sold at more than 40 times earnings in 1960 compared with a 1979 average of 3.7 times earnings and 8.1 times consensus estimated earnings per share (EPS) of $3.85 in early 1985.

More recently, Coleco Industries (a manufacturer of swimming pool and water products, toys, dolls, and consumer electronic products) rose from a low of 3 in 1979 to a high of 65 in 1983 when Cabbage Patch dolls were at a premium. In 1985, Coleco traded below 10. Some issues currently considered highly attractive undoubtedly will be considered equally unattractive at some future date.

Comparative Selection

Comparative selection among alternative investment opportunities requires appraisal of securities so that their relative attractiveness in terms of return and risk can be judged at any time. This purpose can be accomplished only if consistent analytical procedures are employed and industry and company forecasts are based on an internally consistent set of economic and capital market projections. If Dow Chemical is selected for purchase, it must be considered more attractive than Union Carbide, Hercules, Monsanto, or other issues with comparable investment characteristics. Thus isolated analysis and evaluation of an individual security is impractical and inappropriate. One security cannot be effectively appraised apart from other securities or apart from the general investment climate.

Consistency and comparability are so important that they should be the twin goals of the security analyst. Consistency applies to data for an individual company across time, whereas comparability seeks valid data on companies for each time period. Without consistency and comparability, the investor cannot exercise sound judgment in identifying instances of overvaluation and undervaluation. For example, Amoco Corporation (formerly Standard Oil of Indiana) does not include excise taxes in "sales and other operating revenues," whereas Chevron and Mobil include them. As the data in Table 1.1 indicate, adjustment for this fact is necessary in comparing the three companies.

In 1985 excise taxes equalled 6 percent of "net sales" for Amoco, 5 percent for Chevron, and 6.3 percent for Mobil. This item is therefore large enough to affect the comparability of the expense

Table 1.1. Adjusting Sales for Comparability
(In Millions of Dollars)

	1985	1984	1983
Amoco (Standard Oil of Indiana)			
Net sales (as reported)	26,922	26,949	27,635
Excludes excise tax	1,615	1,555	1,557
Chevron			
Sales (as reported)	43,845	46,173	28,411*
Includes excise tax	2,103	1,957	1,069
Net sales excluding tax	41,742	44,216	27,342
Mobil			
Sales (as reported)	59,458	59,492	57,996
Includes excise tax	3,498	3,445	3,389
Net sales excluding tax	55,960	56,047	54,067

*Prior to acquisition of Gulf Oil.

and profit ratios of Amoco relative to the other two companies. Moreover, since the excise tax was not the same percentage of sales for the individual companies over the 1983 to 1985 span, it would have some impact on the percentage drop in sales for each company.

Investment Decision Making

Investment decisions can best be viewed as an integrated process to which security analysis makes its unique contribution. Portfolio management, dealt with exclusively in other books, requires the consistent application of economic, capital market, and sector analysis to the definition of objectives and the measurement of performance. Security analysis serves the investment decision maker by identifying the fairly priced or underpriced securities which are most likely to produce the desired results.

The decision maker, whether a portfolio manager or the alter ego, the analyst, is shopping in the discount store for attractive merchandise. The analyst, like a good salesperson, provides information on the relative merits of the store's different offerings. The discussion relates to quality, durability, service features, and especially to price. Without carrying the analogy too far, it is clear that a knowledgeable shopper will have well-defined specifications for the desired product, and the salesperson will be well-informed on comparative values and quick to identify a bargain.

The Security Analysis Discipline

In making valuation judgments about securities, the analyst applies consistently a process which will achieve the following:

- A true picture of a company as a going concern over a representative time span
- A carefully prepared estimate of current normal earning power
- A projection of future profitability and growth with an informed judgment as to the reliability of such expectations
- A translation of these conclusions into a valuation of the company and its securities which on average will prove to be more reliable than that of the marketplace

A discipline requires diligence, thoroughness, and consistency of method to ensure reliability of the output. Nothing should be taken for granted, nor should the analyst ever lose a skeptical view of the world.

When circumstances do not permit the assembly and analysis of a sufficient body of reliable information, the analyst must question the validity of any conclusion. A disciplined approach also requires that judgments be reached with the least possible influence from those with an interest in the outcome.

Conditional Forecasting and Risk

Conditional forecasting recognizes that the profitability of all business enterprises and the market value of their shares are to some degree affected by (or conditional on) external factors—principally the economy and the stock market.

In analyzing and valuing companies, security analysts have always sought to appraise such risk factors as product obsolescence, intensity of competition, operating leverage, financial leverage, and earnings volatility. It is setting forth risk in more definitive terms that is a new dimension of security analysis. Risk characteristics of a security by itself or in combination with others can be measured in a way that will assist the investment decision maker in portfolio construction. The security analyst should be prepared to supply such information.

Analysts must be prepared to specify in some definitive form what uncertainty is attached to their forecasts. For example, the form could be ratings such as 1 through 5 or the range for estimates of earnings or values indicated. The estimation of risk is considered at several points in subsequent chapters, particularly those concerned with financial statement analysis, projections of earnings and dividends, and common stock valuation.

Security Analysis in Perspective

With the evolution of portfolio theory and new methods of addressing investment management problems, more is expected of the security analyst. The perennnial challenge is to identify instances of mispricing in markets which are being made more efficient by better trained security analysts. In addition, the analyst is called on to provide estimates of both current and prospective normal or trend line earning power for units of ownership called "shares of stock" for the obvious reason that the portfolio manager makes purchases or sales in these terms, not in fractions of the value of an enterprise.

In providing valuation judgments to investors, the security analyst must, of course, be able to communicate with them in meaningful terms.

The analyst evaluates companies, not stock certificates, which have constantly changing backing in the form of assets and earning power, but so intent are the demands of clients that the analyst can easily be diverted from the task. It is essential, therefore, for the security analyst to adhere to a disciplined approach. When fundamental analysis of the company is completed and a judgment reached as to value, it may then, and only then, be timely to consider how the enterprise is being financed and how the expected returns will be divided among security holders.

2
Securities and Security Markets

Chapter 2 deals with security analysis from three standpoints:

1. An overview of the nature of the vast array of securities that lie before the practitioner for possible analysis
2. The behavior of the stock and bond markets
3. The efficient market hypothesis

In regard to item 3, the chapter articulates the authors' position on this controversial issue and outlines the price concepts on which are based everything subsequently said about common stocks analysis and investments.

The Array of Securities

Ignoring unusual and ambiguous cases, securities can be divided into two main groups: (1) government obligations and (2) bonds and stocks of corporations. Mortgage-backed securities, limited partnerships, and real estate vehicles derive their characteristics from the underlying assets, most of which do not qualify as securities having common features for analysis.

Government Obligations

Government obligations are those of nations, states, municipalities, and their agencies. Many such obligations may be subjected to a specialized and frequently elaborate form of analysis. Others—mainly the huge bulk of U.S. government obligations—are rightly considered to be as sound as the paper money in which all debt is now payable. Thus, there is no need to analyze U.S. obligations to determine their safety. The types of government obligations that were extant in 1985 are summarized in Table 2.1.

Table 2.1. Government Obligations Outstanding in 1985
(In Billions of Dollars)

Type		Amount at par
U.S. government marketable securities		1423.5
Bills (up to 1-year maturity)	399.9	
Notes (1-to-10-year maturity)	812.5	
Bonds	211.1	
Federal and federally sponsored credit agencies*		263.9†
Credit market instruments of state and local governments		674.49††

*Federal agency major debt issuers include the Federal Housing Administration, Government National Mortgage Association, and Tennessee Valley Authority. Federally sponsored agencies include Federal Home Loan Banks, Federal National Mortgage Association, Federal Home Loan Mortgage Corporation, Farm Credit Banks, and Student Loan Marketing Association.

†This figure excludes mortgage pool securities of $368.9 billion which are not direct liabilities of the issuing agencies but are, rather, contingent liabilities.

††This figure represents total tax-exempt liabilities—i.e., direct state and local governments, households and nonprofit organizations, and nonfinancial corporate business (industrial revenue bonds). All these are direct liabilities of the issuing governmental body.

SOURCES: Board of Governors of the Federal Reserve System, Washington, D.C., *Federal Reserve Bulletin*, December 1986, table 1.41, "Gross Public Debt of U.S.Treasury," p. A30, and *Flow of Funds Accounts, Assets and Liabilities Outstanding*, September 1986, "Credit Market Debt Owned by Financial Sectors," p. 2, "Tax Exempt Securities and Loans," p. 40.

Corporate Securities

There are approximately 2.7 million active corporations in the United States. Each has shares and possibly bonds outstanding, and any of these companies could theoretically be referred to a security analyst for study. However, the large majority of companies are private, "closed corporations" that do not come within the purview of analysis for widespread use. Companies that are the primary focus of analysis are those that have securities with a quoted market price. About 3100 such enterprises have bonds or stocks that are traded on security exchanges.[1] In addition, over-the-counter (or OTC) issues include as many as 25,000 corporations. For many of these latter concerns, however, the market is so inactive that it is virtually nonexistent.[2]

[1]According to the Securities and Exchange Commission's *52nd Annual Report of the Securities and Exchange Commission* (Washington, D.C. 1986, p. 138) 3133 companies have securities traded on exchanges.

[2]Fewer than 18 percent of the OTC stocks have daily quotes appearing in the automated quotations of the National Association of Securities Dealers. See NASDAQ in Table 2.2.

A broader census of securities subject to analysis may be taken from such investment services and manuals as Standard & Poor's and Moody's. These include companies for which statistical data are regularly made public. Figures for 1986 relating to these companies as well as to OTC securities and NASDAQ companies are given in Table 2.2.

Table 2.2. Census of Companies with Public Securities

Moody's manuals	
Public utilities	500
Transportation	600
Industrials	1,800
Banks and finance	12,000
Standard & Poor's Monthly Guides	
Bonds	6,500
Stocks (preferred and common)	3,250
OTC (portion of companies quoted in NASDAQ)	2,250
OTC companies quoted in the National Association of Security Dealers (NASDAQ) automated tracking system	4,400
OTC daily sheets of National Quotation Bureau (on an average business day)	
Bonds	5,100
Stocks	11,800

Primary Common Stocks. A distinction exists between primary (or "first-line" or "standard") and secondary common stocks. As in most distinctions of quality or degree, establishing a clear-cut dividing line is difficult. Primary common stocks are those of large and prominent companies. The companies generally have good records of earnings and continued dividends, and their stocks have substantial marketability. They are considered eligible, somewhat as a matter of course, for inclusion in widely diversified portfolios of financial institutions. There are some 500 to 600 issues of this type about which there would be little dispute. In any given period perhaps another 100 enter and leave the select circle or are recognized as primary by some authorities and not by others. The primary group is well represented by the companies included in the *Fortune* 500 and Standard & Poor's Composite Index of 500 stocks (S&P 500).

Secondary Common Stocks. Many more common stocks are marginal, that is, they are regarded as nearly primary grade and are expected by many purchasers eventually to reach that status. Other stocks are thought by their particular adherents to be "just as good" as the typical primary stock.

(This is often an error in judgment made under conditions of speculative enthusiasm.) However, some 75 percent of listed stock issues and perhaps 90 percent or more of unlisted issues clearly belong in the secondary category. This placement influences their market price behavior in significant ways that the analyst must not fail to consider.

Behavior of the Security Markets

A competent analyst should be sufficiently familiar with important price patterns of the securities markets to draw intelligent conclusions about probable price movements of different types of security issues. These conclusions should take into account the broad pattern of price fluctuations that is likely for the issue considered.

High-Grade Corporate Bonds

There is no widely accepted division of bonds into high-grade and secondary issues. Therefore, high-grade bonds are somewhat arbitrarily defined herein as those issues classified by Moody's and Standard & Poor's in the first three ratings (Aaa through A).[3] In spite of definitional differences, the intent is clear: High-grade bonds are those exempt from present and presumably future doubt as to prompt payment of interest or principal. Putting aside for the moment considerations arising from call provisions, the price of high-grade bonds is mainly a function of the going rate of interest for their maturity bracket. If the basic interest rate declines, the price of a high-grade bond should rise so as to bring down its yield

Table 2.3. Yield and Price of High-Grade Bonds

Selected periods	Yield on Moody's Aaa corporate bonds (monthly average)		Price of Madison Gas & Electric Co. (Minn.) first 4¾s Aa bonds (due 1991)	
	Low	High	High	Low
1960–1964	4.19%	4.61%	108 ⅝	100¾
1965–1969	4.41	7.72	104 ⅝	64
1970–1974	7.08	9.27	73 ⅛	53
1975–1979	7.92	10.76	70 ⅞	56
1980–1984	10.58	15.49	69 ¾	46

Sources: Compiled from Moody's *Industrial Manual* and *Public Utility Manual*, Moody's Investors Services, Inc., New York, N.Y.

[3]Salomon Brothers classify high-grade bonds as the first two rating categories (Aaa and Aa), whereas some regulatory agencies treat the first four categories (Aaa through Baa) as investment-grade issues.

accordingly. Conversely, the price should fall when interest rates advance. This principle is illustrated in Table 2.3.

In considering bonds of this quality, the future course of interest rates is the principal factor to anticipate. As it happens, this factor does not lend itself well to security analysis. Because today's interest rates reflect expected changes in relevant economic factors, particularly expectations as to future inflation, a forecast that future rates will be higher or lower than present rates is more a matter of economic and capital market analysis than of security analysis.

Accordingly, in the field of high-grade bonds, the security analyst is ordinarily concerned not with price anticipations but rather with careful determination of the quality of the issue, that is, with its creditworthiness. In this regard, the role of the analyst is critical, because in recent years the pace of change in bond ratings has increased[4] and because a reduction of the credit rating on a bond can significantly impact its market price. The analyst's assignment is, of course, to anticipate changes of credit ratings.

Price fluctuations attributable to changes in interest rates rarely affect confidence in an individual issuer's ability to meet interest and principal payments when due and to pay off or refund the issue at maturity. However, the amplification of these price fluctuations in recent years, especially in the form of price declines, has threatened the solvency of financial institutions. To minimize these untoward effects, banks and insurance companies, which make up the largest body of owners, are permitted by law to ignore market variations in investment-grade issues when presenting their annual statements of condition.[5]

As Table 2.3 indicates, the modest changes in interest rates during the 1960 to 1964 period had limited impact on the price of Madison Gas & Electric Company's first mortgage at 4¾s. However, as interest rates rose over the next four 5-year spans, the price decline reflected the relatively long duration of this issue. (See Chapter 23 for discussion of duration as a measure of the sensitivity of price to interest rate changes.)

Table 2.4 compares the price movements of three sinking fund (SF) debentures, each of which was offered at approximately 100 in the 1966 to 1967 period, had a long duration, and had (and still has) an Aaa rating by Moody's.

---

[4]During the 10-year span from 1971 to 1980, only 1 bond out of the 20 industrial bonds rated Aaa by Moody in 1971 was dropped from its top rating. In contrast, over the 5-year span from 1981 to 1985, 48 bonds out of the 78 rated Aaa in 1981 suffered reduced ratings.

[5]Instead, they can show these at "amortized cost"—i.e., at a cost increased or decreased to reflect the gradual approach of repayment at par on the maturity date. This action does not change the reality of the price movements in the marketplace.

Table 2.4. Prices of Three High-Grade (Aaa) Debentures (1967 to 1986)

	Price		
Issue	High 1967	Low 1981	End 1986
General Electric SF debenture 5.30s due 1992, offered 1967	98	51	91⅛
Exxon SF debenture 6s due 1997, offered 1967	100¼	47	88¼
Amoco SF debenture 6s due 1991, offered 1966	109½	55⅛	96¼

SOURCES: Moody's *Industrial Manual*; Standard & Poor's *Bond Guide*.

High-Grade Preferred Stocks

Table 2.5 sets forth the cyclical high and low dividend yields over the 19 years from 1968 to 1986 on high-grade preferred stocks, as measured by Moody's high-grade, low-dividend industrials. To illustrate the erosion of capital values attributable to a rise in yields, Table 2.5 relates Moody's high-grade preferred dividend yield to the price of DuPont's $4.50 preferred stock over the same 19-year span.

The security analyst is responsible here, as well as in the case of top-grade corporate bonds, for a careful appraisal of the quality of the preferred stock, leaving the appraisal of the attractiveness of high-grade preferred stock yields to those undertaking interest rate projections.

Table 2.5. Yield and Price of High-Grade Preferred Stock

Selected years	Yield on Moody's low dividend series monthly average (percent)		Price of DuPont $4.50 preferred stock (dollars)	
1968	5.47	(low)	82½	(high)
1970	7.31	(high)	60½	(low)
1971	6.18	(low)	77¾	(high)
1975	8.08	(high)	53⅞	(low)
1977	7.00	(low)	66¾	(high)
1982	12.54	(high)	34½	(low)
1983	9.57	(low)	47⅜	(high)
1984	10.42	(high)	39	(low)
1986	7.54	(low)	64½	(high)

SOURCE: Compiled from Moody's *Industrial Manual*.

Second-Grade Senior Securities

Second-grade senior securities are here defined as bonds and preferred stocks classified by Moody's and Standard & Poor's ratings as below the first four ratings (Aaa through Baa). Such issues, because of their credit (default) risk, quite properly offer a risk premium. Even within the first four ratings, the annual yield spread between Moody's Aaa and Baa corporate bonds averaged 1.46 percent from 1975 through 1986. Investors' conceptions of the credit risk differential between corporate Aaa and Baa bonds can change markedly as economic conditions change, as is demonstrated in Figure 2.1, which presents the annual yield spread between Moody's Aaa and Baa bonds over the 12-year span. Typically, the yield spread narrows during prosperous periods and widens during recessionary periods. For example, over the 12-year period, the yield spread ranged from a low of 0.72 percent (July 1978) to a high of 2.69 percent (September 1982).

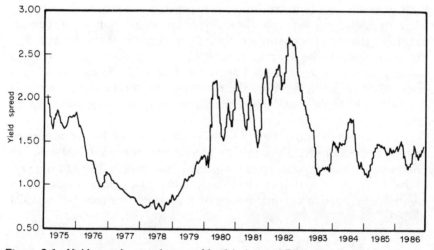

Figure 2.1 Yield spread means between Moody's Aaa and Baa corporate bonds. (*Source: Compiled from* Moody's Industrial Manuals, *Moody's Investors Services, Inc. New York, N.Y.*)

Common Stocks

The expected return from holding a common stock for investment is likely to come more from capital appreciation than from dividend payments. Price at time of purchase and at time of sale will be the real determinant of investment accomplishment. Since the long-term future of share prices cannot be reliably predicted, it is essential to avoid paying too much for a company. This is the origin of the familiar statement that "price is the the analyst's best friend." A major component of an investment's margin of safety must always be avoidance of paying too much for the asset. In this respect, the consideration is price in an absolute, not a relative, sense.

Role of Past Price and Return Performance.   In anticipating future price behavior, one begins with an examination of the history of the fluctuations and cycles which have occurred in the returns on common stocks. The past requires interpretation as a starting point for the formulation of expectations as to the future, but accepting any mechanical extrapolation of the past as a forecast of the future is extremely hazardous. Consideration must also be given to existing and emerging social, political, and economic forces of change that can be expected to affect the level and variability of common stock returns.

The total rate of return for common stocks depends, of course, on both price change and dividend payments. In the more remote past, when dividend payout typically represented more than 60 percent of earnings, dividends constituted the major portion of the return. For the last 15 years, the average payout ratio has been 44 percent for a broad group like Standard & Poor's 400 Industrial Stock index. As a result, the valuation given by the marketplace to retained earnings is the more important and more variable component of total equity returns.

Over shorter periods, the change in stock prices will be the dominant factor. For example, although dividends for the S&P 500 rose 16 percent over the six-year span from the beginning of 1969 to the end of 1974, the sharp 1973 to 1974 decline in stock prices resulted in a *negative* average annual total return of 3.4 percent for the 1969 to 1974 period.

Long-Term Stock Price Behavior.   To provide perspective and assist in anticipating the future, two summary reviews of the long-term movements of common stock prices are presented. The first covers the secular trend in annual prices, and the second covers the amplitude of price cycles using monthly average data.

Figure 2.2 presents an overview of the annual movements in stock prices over the period from 1887 through 1986. The chart includes a mathematically fitted trend line representing the average annual compound rate of price increase for the entire 100-year span. This view brings out two basic characteristics of the behavior of stock prices: (1) their underlying long-term upward thrust resulting from economic growth and reinvestment of earnings and (2) their cyclical nature, marked by great variability in the extent and duration of the intermediate fluctuations. Note that the departures of actual prices from the trend line are so substantial and extend over such long periods that the annual average rate of increase is of doubtful value as either a yardstick of the past or an indicator of the future.

The following tabulation shows the average annual rate of price increase (dividends not included) for the 100-year span and for each of the four 25-year periods. The differences in the annual rates for the 25-year periods indicate how rates can vary over long periods. A mathematical test indicates that the trend line for the full span fits the data better than that for any 25-year period.

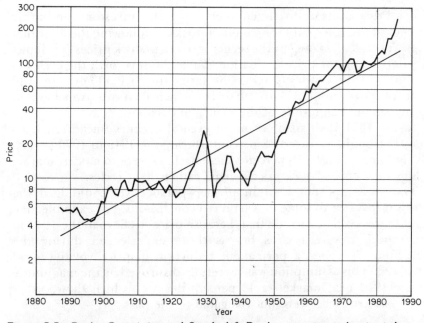

Figure 2.2 Cowles Commission and Standard & Poor's composite stock price index, yearly averages of monthly prices, 1887–1986. (*Source: For the early years, the price series is based on the annual data of the Cowles Commission and subsequently on the S&P 500. Alfred Cowles, 3rd and Associates, Cowles Commission for Research in Economics, Common Stock Indexes, Monograph No. 3, Principia Press, Inc. Bloomington, Ind. 1939, pp. 66–67, Standard & Poor's Statistical Service, Security Price Index Record, 1986, p. 110, and Current Statistics, January 1987, p. 40.)*

1887–1986	3.8%
1887–1911	3.2
1912–1936	2.4%
1937–1961	8.3%
1962–1986	3.6%

It is reasonable to conclude that in the future (as in the past) there will be secular growth in the prices of a comprehensive cross section of investment-quality common stocks. However, the typical investor should not take much comfort from the highly probable expectation as to future growth, because the secular increase in stock prices is exceedingly erratic. As a result of the substantial volatility in stock prices, extended periods have been characterized by no secular growth, limited growth, dramatically high growth, or growth somewhere in between.[6] (Note that these data take no account of inflation or deflation representing as they do nominal prices.)

Stock Price Cycles. Even genuinely long-term investors can hardly disregard the price paid for common stocks by following the logic that they will be "bailed out" by the secular growth in stock prices. To depict the importance of price evaluation, Table 2.6 sets forth the cycles in the price of the Cowles Commission series and S&P 500 over the full span of 116 years (1871 to 1986) for which data are available and examines the magnitude of the principal declines.

In the 1871-1949 span, 12 major cyclical declines (measured from peak to trough) averaged 38 percent. During the 1949 to 1970 period, six declines averaged 18 percent; these declines were so modest that we designate them as "stock price swings" rather than "cycles."[7]

These data, if not kept in proper perspective, could lead the postwar investor to some unwarranted conclusions. For example, one might incorrectly conclude that, because price declines in the 1949 to 1970 period were not as big as those experienced during the preceding 78 years, a permanent reduction in price volatility had occurred. This assumption was forcefully disproved by the magnitude of the 1974 bear market (a 43 percent decline), which showed that stock market cycles were not relegated to the past.

---

[6]An extreme example: the S&P 500 peaked at 31.92 in September 1929 and did not recover to that level until 25 years later, in September 1954.

[7]For a different point of view, see R. R. Officer, "The Variability of the Market Factor of the New York Stock Exchange," *Journal of Business*, July 1973, pp. 434–453. Officer's conclusion is that the apparent postwar decline in market-factor variability observed by other studies was shown to be more accurately described as a return to normal levels of variability after the abnormally high levels of the 1930s.

Table 2.6. Major Stock Price Movement, 1871–1986
Cowles Commission and Standard & Poor's Composite Stock Price
Series, Based on Monthly Averages

Trough		Peak		Percent change	
				Rise	Decline
Date	Low price ($)	Date	High price ($)	from low	to next low
Jan.1871	4.44	Apr. 1872	5.13	16	47
June 1877	2.73	June 1881	6.58	141	36
Jan. 1885	4.24	May 1887	5.90	39	22
Dec. 1890	4.60	Aug. 1892	5.62	22	32
Aug. 1896	3.81	Sept. 1902	8.85	132	29
Oct. 1903	6.26	Sept. 1906	10.03	60	38
Nov. 1907	6.25	Dec. 1909	10.30	65	29
Dec. 1914	7.35	July 1919	9.51	29	32
Aug. 1921	6.45	Sept. 1929	31.30	385	85
June 1932	4.77	Feb. 1937	18.11	280	45
Apr. 1938	9.89	Nov. 1938	13.07	32	40
Apr. 1942	7.84	May 1946	18.70	139	25
June 1949	13.97	Jan. 1953	26.18	87	11
Sept. 1953	23.27	July 1956	48.78	110	17
Dec. 1957	40.33	July 1959	59.74	48	10
Oct. 1960	53.73	Dec. 1961	71.74	34	22
June 1962	55.63	Jan. 1966	93.32	68	17
Oct. 1966	77.13	Dec. 1968	106.50	38	29
June 1970	75.59	Jan. 1973	118.40	57	43
Dec. 1974	67.07	Sept. 1976	105.50	57	16
Mar. 1978	88.82	Nov. 1980	135.70	53	19
July 1982	109.40	Oct. 1983	167.70	53	10
July 1984	151.10	*			

*The price series at the end of 1986 was 248.61—a rise from the low of 65%.

SOURCES: *Security Price Index Record*, 1976 and 1986 and Current Statistics, January 1987, p. 40; Standard & Poor's Corporation, New York.

Two significant conclusions can be drawn from the 1973 to 1974 price decline: (1) An appraisal of the price level of the stock market is essential in the evaluation of investment opportunities in individual securities, and (2) the amplitude and character of future stock market price movements cannot be anticipated simply by extrapolating historical data.

Edgar Lawrence Smith's conclusion in the early 1920s that there should be a long-term rise in the value of a well-diversified list of quality stocks was—and continues to be—sound.[8] However, over the postwar

[8]Edgar Lawrence Smith, *Common Stocks as Long Term Investments*, Macmillan, New York, 1924. See also Winthrop B. Walker, *A Re-examination of Common Stocks as Long Term Investments*, thesis for the Graduate School of Banking at Rutgers University, Anthoesner Press, Portland, Maine, 1954.

period until early 1973, many investors misinterpreted this concept, purchasing premium-quality, high-growth stocks at almost any price—to their subsequent regret.

Total Return.   Price behavior may also be analyzed from the standpoint of total return. The research of others shows that annual total returns for common stocks (based on the S&P 500) were negative (measured from the beginning of a year to the end of the same year) in 19 out of the last 59 years (from 1926 through 1984). Furthermore, the compound total rate of return for common stocks (the S&P 500 with dividends reinvested) purchased at the beginning of 1965 and held until the end of 1984 (7.8 percent) was only slightly above the return on Treasury bills (7.1 percent) over the same period.[9] Figure 2.3 indicates that over the 20-year span, in only 11 holding periods did the total return for stock equal or exceed the return for Treasury bills. The price

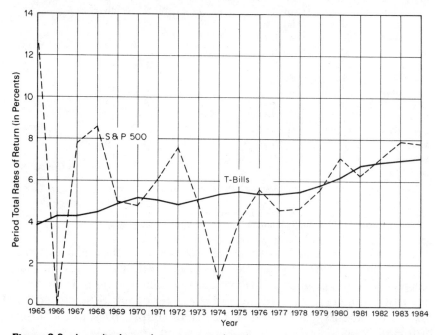

Figure 2.3 Annualized cumulative compound total rates of return: S&P 500 and Treasury Bills. Stock investment beginning 1965, with returns on year-end basis, 1965–1984. (This period of measurement was prior to the dramatic subsequent increase in stock-holding period returns.) (*Source: Compiled by FRS Associates from Ibbotson Associates, Stocks, Bonds, Bills, and Inflation: 1984 Yearbook, Chicago, 1985.*)

[9]R. G. Ibbotson Associates, Inc., *Stocks, Bonds, Bills, and Inflation: 1984 Yearbook,* Chicago, 1985, pp. 90–91, 98.

appreciation from the beginning of 1965 to the end of 1984 was at a compound annual rate of only 3.3 percent.

The Efficient Market Hypothesis

In its various forms, the efficient market hypothesis (EMH) has different implications for the discipline of security analysis.[10]

Weak Form

One statement of the so-called weak form of the EMH is simply that prices of common stocks are independent, that is, past prices have no predictive power for future prices. In general, we agree with this proposition. Market analysis or technical analysis of price behavior is not, in our judgment, an adequate substitute for fundamental analysis in the selection of individual issues.

This independence of stock prices has given the market the descriptive term a *random walk*. Elaborate tests of the correlation of successive prices, runs, and filter rules find some weak relationships, but they are not sufficient to generate trading profits after taking account of transaction costs. Buying on relative strength and attempting to catch the "January effect" from year-end tax selling are among the frequently explored avenues to successful stock selection without analytical effort. Compared with all the fortunes made from long-term investing based on in-depth security analysis, the absence of large cumulative additions to wealth from market analysis is a striking commentary.

However, another dimension of the behavior of share prices should not be ignored: the investment community's entrancement with fads or the pseudo-rationalization of "new insights." We do not need to return to experiences with the South-Sea Bubble or Tulipmania from the pages of Charles Mackay's *Extraordinary Popular Delusions and the Madness of Crowds* (1841); we can consult the records of periodic "hot new issue" speculation, one-decision investing in quality growth stocks in the 1960s, the popularity of real estate investment trusts in the 1970s, and the merger mania of the 1980s. All these waves of enthusiasm are propelled by persistent price trends right up to the hour of their reversal. B. Rosenberg and A. Rudd

---

[10]For a comprehensive and insightful overview of the efficient market hypothesis, its forms, and specific research see B. L. Boldt and H. L. Arbit, "Efficient Markets and the Professional Investor," *Financial Analysts Journal*, July–August 1984, pp. 22–33; also E. J. Elton and M. J. Gruber, *Modern Portfolio Theory and Investment Analysis*, 2d ed., John Wiley & Sons, New York, 1984, pp. 394–402. An excellent discussion of the evidence developed from accounting data relative to the semistrong and strong forms is provided in W. H. Beaver, *Financial Reporting: An Accounting Revolution*, Prentice-Hall, Englewood Cliffs, N.J., 1981, chaps. 5 and 6.

argue, for example, that the serial correlation of certain components of monthly returns permits adding to return by portfolio rebalancing.[11]

Semistrong Form

The semistrong form of the EMH is simply that all public information is reflected in the market price. Because a changing mix of favorable and unfavorable information about companies, industries, the capital market, and the economy is constantly arriving at the marketplace in a random fashion, prices, broadly viewed, should behave in an equally random pattern as the information is translated into share prices. New information, numerous tests have demonstrated, is rapidly incorporated in the security price. Given the broad access to wire services and news releases, the speed of transmission is not surprising; however, rapidity is not always equivalent to accuracy.

One astute observer of markets, Jack Treynor, observes that in addition to information which is clear in its significance, there are "slow" ideas. The diligent analyst may accumulate a number of discrete pieces of information used to construct a mosaic which provides an unfolding picture of a company very different from the consensus view. At a trade show, the analyst observes that Company A has operational and deliverable chemical pumps, whereas Company B, seeking to meet the same market demand, displays only a mock-up. Since neither pump has actually been tested in use, the difference in orders, sales, and earnings will not show up on the broadtape for some months. Other "slow" ideas may emerge from apparently unrelated developments which investors will not relate to a particular company for an extended period.

In essence, there are extramarket returns from analysts' greater diligence and superior understanding which are independent of the timing or breadth of distribution of the information. The trained, knowledgeable analyst can, and frequently does, interpret information with materially better judgment than that expressed by the consensus in the marketplace. To the extent that this occurs, the semistrong form of market efficiency has not been validated.

An example which demonstrates that extramarket returns can result from the superior use of public information is the Value Line Timeliness Ranking Model. This model is based on publicly available information from which are derived relative earnings and prices, an earnings and price momentum factor, and an earnings surprise factor for each of the 1700 stocks in the Value Line universe. Through the use of multiple

---

[11]B. Rosenberg and A. Rudd, "Factor-Related and Specific Returns of Common Stocks: Serial Correlation and Market Inefficiency," *Journal of Finance*, May 1982, pp. 551–552.

regression analysis, the stocks are classified by expected price performance over the next 12 months so that Group 1 is expected to have the best performance and Group 5, the poorest. As shown, the 20.5-year record (April 1965 to December 1986) of the rankings indicates that this fact-based model using historical data trends can produce above-average risk-adjusted returns, thus refuting the semistrong form of market efficiency:[12]

Ranking group	Price change (percent)
1	2071
2	1103
3	495
4	166
5	24
Dow-Jones industrial average	109

Strong Form

The strong form of EMH states that security prices fully reflect all knowable information. Furthermore, intensive analysis will not enable the analyst to reach judgments different from the market's prices with enough consistency to earn additional returns. The EMH fully recognizes security analysts' contributions—their fruitless efforts to identify mispricings are what make the market efficient. In this view, security analysis is a public service which assists markets in the optimum allocation of resources, but it need not be rewarded with more than civil service compensation scales, nor should investors replace their dart boards with this volume. Instead investors can participate in low-cost market index portfolios which can track the selected index with a small margin of error and minimum transaction costs.

The "evidence" offered of market efficiency is derived in part from analysis of the performance of actively managed portfolios, and mutual funds frequently are used.[13] The average performance of the average mutual fund manager may be expected to fall short of his or her universe by the costs of transactions; safekeeping and accounting functions; distribution, legal, and auditing services; shareholder records

---

[12]"Selection & Opinion," *The Value Line Investment Survey*, January 23, 1987, p. 719.

[13]See such historic studies as W. F. Sharpe, "Mutual Fund Performance," *Journal of Business, Security Prices, A Supplement*, January 1966, pp. 119–138; M. C. Jensen, "The Performance of Mutual Funds in the Period 1945–64," *Journal of Finance*, May 1968, pp. 389–416; I. Friend, M. Blume, and J. Crocket, *Mutual Funds and Other Institutional Investors: A New Perspective*, McGraw-Hill, New York, 1970; P. J. Williamson, "Measuring Mutual Fund Performance, *Financial Analysts Journal*, November/December 1972, pp. 78–84.

and reporting; and management fees. Actually different groups of funds outperform their universes of stocks for extended periods. We believe that the fact that some funds outperform their market sectors consistently by the decade is not by chance but is instead evidence that disciplined security analysis applied across different markets has a logic which can be tested and validated.

There can be little doubt that improvement in analytic techniques and in the recognition of sound principles has increased the efficiency of the market. Gross disparities between economic values and market prices have been substantially reduced since the first edition of this book in 1934. We hope that this edition will make a contribution to further reducing the inefficiency of analysts and thereby to increasing the efficiency of security pricing, but our fundamental conviction is that market prices, like a stopped clock, are a correct representation of value twice in an investor's day.

Despite the gains in market efficiency, careful study has shown the existence of *anomalies*,[14] including the small-company effect, the low prices-to-earnings multiple undervaluation, and similar phenomena which challenge the accuracy of the market's pricing mechanism. One knowledgeable observer's view is expressed in this provocative editorial in the *Financial Analysts Journal*:

> The rush of these new-found anomalous market characteristics is large enough to warrant its own buzzword.... It's idiosyncratic.... Enter an abundance of idiosyncrasies—small firm effect, turn-of-the-year effect, low price-earnings ratio, junk bonds (stocks?), low-priced stocks, the Value Line phenomenon, weekend effects, performance of low beta portfolios, sector rotation, and information coefficients. Documented

[14]The following list is indicative of the scope and nature of the research: E. F. Renshaw, "Stock Market Panics: A Test of the Efficient Market Hypothesis," *Financial Analysts Journal*, May–June, 1984, pp. 48–52; D. A. Goodman and J. W. Peavey, III, "Industry Relative Price-Earnings Ratios as Indicators of Investment Returns," *Financial Analysts Journal*, July–August, 1983, pp. 60–66; R. F. Vandell and G. W. Kester, *A History of Risk-Premia Estimates for Equities: 1944 to 1978*, Financial Analysts Research Foundation, Charlottesville, Va., 1983, p. 135; M. R. Reinganum, "Abnormal Returns in Small Firm Portfolios," *Financial Analysts Journal*, March–April 1981, pp. 52–57; C. P. Jones, R. J. Rendleman, Jr., and H. Latane, "Stock Returns and SUEs during the 1970s," *The Journal of Portfolio Management*, Winter 1984, pp. 18–22; C. M. Budwell, III, "A test of market efficiency: SUE/PE," *The Journal of Portfolio Management*, Summer 1979, pp. 53–58; R. Ferguson, "An efficient stock market? Ridiculous!" *Journal of Portfolio Management*, Summer 1983, pp. 31–37; K. P. Ambachtsheer and J. L. Farrell, Jr., "Can Active Management Add Value?," *Financial Analysts Journal*, November–December 1979, pp. 39–45; K. P. Ambachtsheer, *The Predictive Accuracy of the Value Line and Wells Fargo Stock Advisory Services*, Canavest House, Toronto, Canada, November, 1976.

idiosyncratic market phenomena, like crocuses, herald a new season. The question is: How long can the EMH continue, unrevised, against the burgeoning list of idiosyncratic phenomena?[15]

Finally, if all stocks are efficiently priced, as EMH maintains, the proven necessity for broad diversification would be eliminated. One would only need to match the variability characteristics of handful of issues with the owner's tolerance for uncertainty of returns. A further implication of EMH is that there is comfort in the thought that it is difficult to do worse than the returns provided by one's risk class, because shares are so efficiently priced. Our thoughtful judgment is simply that one should not assume efficient pricing but should undertake to verify it by disciplined security analysis.

3

Scope and Limitations of Security Analysis

Analysis is the careful study of available facts so that one can understand and draw conclusions from them on the basis of established principles and sound logic. Identification and examination of relevant past and present factors for estimating the future inevitably entail substantial uncertainty and the need to exercise judgment. Consequently, individual analytical skill and discretion are important in determining success or failure. This chapter discusses the scope and limits of analysis and some of the judgments it requires.

Financial Analysis

Rational decisions for the valuation of securities require a series of forecasts. Using the top-down approach, they comprise forecasts for:

- The economy
- Stock and bond markets
- Sectors of the market
- Industries
- Individual companies

Analytical Dependencies:
The Chain of Forecasts

These series of projections are interdependent and help generate forecasts of earnings, dividends, growth, and stability for an individual company. Chapters 5, 6, and 7 are devoted to economic, capital market, and sector analysis, respectively. Industry analysis is discussed in Chapter 9. At this juncture, dependency of the analytical process on economic trends, industry considerations, and company issues are illustrated for a specific company as we broadly examine the factors determining General Motors Corporation's sales and profits, operating income, and measures of profitability.[1]

Factors Affecting Sales and Profits.   Many industries depend on the domestic and world economies. Sales of most business corporations—particularly major ones—are significantly affected by what happens to that corporation's industry. In turn, results are influenced by forces internal to the enterprise, such as product mix and management quality.

To project future sales and income for General Motors, analysts will focus on factors such as overall economic trends:

- U.S. and foreign GNP growth
- Unemployment levels
- Trends in consumer savings and borrowing
- Consumer confidence levels and buying plans
- Trends in consumer durable expenditures
- Tax changes as they affect disposable income
- Consumer loan interest rates and availability

Automotive industry considerations might include:

- Degree of industry maturation relative to GNP growth
- Import restraints on foreign autos

---

[1]A full-scale company valuation is the scope of this entire book, whereas the purpose of this example is restricted to showing how the various levels of analysis are interdependent. Properly conducted valuations require adjustments to reported earnings and examination of more than one year of historical data. For General Motors, issues such as the huge investment tax credit's impact on its 1985 effective tax rate, consolidation of its captive finance company (GMAC), goodwill items, and identification of nonoperating income sources are essential to complete analysis.

- Fuel availability and prices
- Car price increases relative to inflation
- Used car prices and scrappage levels
- Average age of cars on the road and assumptions about the replacement cycle
- Trends in raw material and labor costs

Some company specific issues would be:

- Diversification into nonautomotive areas
- Product mix by geographical and product areas
- New-product introduction and market share trends
- Profitability trends
- Depreciation and tooling expenses
- Nonoperating sources of income such as nonconsolidated equity in subsidiaries and affiliates
- Balance sheet issues such as financial leverage, shares repurchased, new- equity offerings
- Tax rate variances from the statutory rate
- Changes in management or management focus (e.g., a major cost reduction program)

Operating Income.   Income numbers are prerequisites to the analysis of a company and the development of projections. Table 3.1 shows that General Motors' operating income in 1985 was $4.2 billion. After allowing for equity in earnings of nonconsolidated subsidiaries and associates, other income and expenses, and income taxes, reported net income was $4 billion. However, these numbers alone provide only partial insight into the profitability of an enterprise.

Measures of Profitability.   The analyst must now relate these operating income figures meaningfully in order to derive essential measures of profitability. Such measures include capital turnover, the ratio of net available for total capital (NATC) to sales (earnings margin), return on average total capital (ROTC), and return on average common stockholders' equity (ROE). For General Motors, 1985 was a good year. Capital turnover, as calculated for its basic automobile business, was 2.7× and net available for total capital was 4.9 percent of sales. The product of these two figures—return on total capital—was 13.2 percent, a higher figure

Table 3.1. General Motors Corporation Consolidated
Income Account, Year Ended December 31, 1985
(In Thousands of Dollars)

Net sales	96,371,700
Cost of sales	81,654,600
Selling, general, and administrative expenses	4,294,200
Depreciation	2,777,900
Amortization of special tools	3,083,300
Amortization of intangible assets	347,300
Total operating expenses	92,157,300
Operating income	4,214,400
Equity in unconsolidated	
subsidiaries and associates	1,008,000
Interest received	1,328,300
Miscellaneous income	143,600
Total income	6,694,300
Interest and other expenses	1,065,000
Income before taxes	5,629,300
Income taxes (foreign, U.S., and state)	1,630,300
Net income	3,999,000
Plus interest adjusted for tax offset	689,100
Net available for total capital	4,688,100

than achieved in any recent year except 1984. The return on common
equity (ROE) was 15.0 percent.

Interpretation of Company Profitability Ratios. The year 1985 reflected generally favorable economic conditions and industry trends, and
General Motors' worldwide unit sales of automobiles, trucks, and buses
increased 13 percent. Domestic sales produced 77 percent of the total and
91 percent of net income. The decline of 2 percent in net income from
its 1984 level in the face of this increase in volume reflects an industry
factor of price competition from imports. Company cost increases were
incurred in the installation of new computerization systems and in up-
grading manufacturing efficiency. A related company-specific development was the integrating of Electronic Data Systems into the corporate
structure.

With the aid of these key profitability measures, the analyst is
prepared to address the impact of economic, industry, and company
factors on the profitability of a company. Are 1985 results normal and
recurring or distorted by special circumstances? What factors stimulate
growth in earning power? How sensitive is the firm to the economic

environment, both international and domestic? How stable can the investor expect earning power to be over a three- to five-year span? A single year's observations may or may not be representative, but they have their place in identifying trends and, most important, disclosing signs of change in fundamental investment characteristics of the company.

Level of Uncertainty.   The foregoing example broadly demonstrates the series of forecasts entailed in estimating the current earnings of an enterprise. Projections at each level—economy, industry, and company—carry their own margin of error. Since projections at one level bear on projections at the next, the error factor can increase as the projection process moves step by step from the economy, to the industry, to the company. A single figure for net available for common equity (NACE) and other similar estimates are clearly the analyst's most probable estimates, within some range of reason. Accordingly, analysts should indicate the degree of uncertainty in their forecasts with either an estimate range or a subjective confidence rating scale (such as 1 through 5).

A forecast of earnings and dividends is not the analyst's last task in arriving at a value estimate for a stock. The final step is to select a capitalization rate for earnings or dividends. The term *capitalization rate* in its generic sense denotes the factor used to determine the present value of either forecast normalized earnings (a multiplier) or an estimated stream of dividends (a discount rate).

In the final instance, investors are concerned with the returns that result from the purchase and sale of individual issues. Thus, most investment research is directed toward examination and evaluation of individual securities.

Security Analysis

Security analysis develops and presents the important facts regarding corporate stocks or bond issues in a manner that will be most informative and useful to the investor. Such analysis also seeks dependable conclusions, based on the facts and applicable standards, as to the intrinsic value and risk characteristics of a security.

From this information and assumptions as to the time interval for the convergence of price and value, the return expected from a stock at its current market price can be determined, and analysts can gain some idea as to the probability that the expected return will actually be attained. In this manner security analysis provides the basis for selecting individual issues to buy or sell from among available choices.

Confronting Market and Informational Challenges

The importance and prestige of security analysis have increased over the years, roughly paralleling the steady improvement in corporate reports and other statistical data that are raw material for such analysis. However, despite the contribution of analysts to market efficiency, the pendulum will continue to swing toward undue market pessimism in periods of recession and undue market optimism in periods of extended prosperity. These swings will be exaggerated in the behavior of the glamor stocks of the moment, such as the small technology stocks in the 1983 to 1986 span. Pervasive optimism was also evident in the early and late 1960s and in all of 1972 and part of 1973. Nevertheless, security analysis, *when properly performed*, has met these market challenges satisfactorily.

However, security analysis is not always *properly performed*. One of its most flagrant failures was the Penn Central debacle; there was plenty of evidence in advance of 1970 for those who searched for it.[2]

The opportunities for effective analysis continue to improve. In recent years, substantive changes have taken place in accounting procedures and in the reporting practices of corporations. Enactment of various laws administered by the Securities and Exchange Commission (SEC) and continuing pressure from the SEC and such others as the Accounting Principles Board (APB), and its successor the Financial Accounting Standards Board (FASB),[3] and the Financial Analysts Federation's Financial Accounting Policy Committee and its Corporate Information Committee for full disclosure have significantly improved the quality and quantity of published corporate data.[4] Likewise, the increased attention given by many corporations to

[2]On this subject, see B. Graham, *The Intelligent Investor*, 4th ed., Harper & Row, New York, 1973, p. 234. See also R. F. Murray, "The Penn Central Debacle: Lessons for Financial Analysis," *The Journal of Finance*, May 1971, pp. 327–332.

[3]The scope of the activity of the FASB and the SEC are effectively summarized in William H. Beaver, *Financial Reporting: An Accounting Revolution*, Prentice-Hall, Englewood Cliffs, N. J. 1981, pp. 1–2. For an extensive study of financial disclosure, see *Report of the Advisory Committee on Corporate Disclosure to the Securities and Exchange Commission*, November 3, 1977, U.S. Government Printing Office, Washington D.C., 1977.

[4]For a brief review of what has happened to financial accounting over much of the postwar period and some explanation as to why it happened by a person who had a role in shaping some of it, see William C. Norby, "A 35-year Review of Financial Accounting and Reporting to the Investor," *Financial Analysts Journal*, July-August 1982, pp. 33–35.

their annual reports has significantly improved the reports' informational value.[5] These improvements have increased the scope and dependability of security analysis. At the same time, the rapid pace of change has reduced the year-to-year consistency of accounting information, presenting the analyst with new challenges.

Three Functions of Security Analysis

The three functions of security analysis detailed in the following sections may be categorized as follows:

- Descriptive
- Valuation
- Critical

Descriptive Function

Descriptive analysis marshals, analyzes, and interprets the important facts relating to an issue and presents this information in a coherent, readily intelligible manner. There are gradations of accomplishment and of related skill in this descriptive function.

The most elementary descriptive analysis is found in the familiar and indispensable statistical presentations of the various security manuals and similar descriptive services. In these instances, the analyst acts more as a reporter than analyst. For large companies, the material is essentially as taken directly from reports filed with the SEC (primarily the company's annual and 10-K reports). In some instances, because of the time factor, the latest year's statement may be contained in the annual report to stockholders.[6]

A penetrating descriptive analysis must go beyond merely presenting the reported figures. In many cases, the analyst will need to make various kinds of adjustments to provide more consistent and meaningful operating results across the span of years covered and to make the data for a number of companies more comparable. The scope of this analysis is the subject of Part 2.

Descriptive analysis requires a thorough probing of companies to understand the causes of past and present profitability and to interpret their relationship to future profitability. This analysis includes such important factors as:

[5]For a critical opinion see D. G. Sutliff, "Annual Reports Today," *Financial Analysts Journal*, May–June 1984, p. 10.

[6]Increasingly companies are issuing to shareholders a combined annual report and 10K form. Thus both become available simultaneously.

- Acquisitions and mergers
- Shifts in product mix
- Expansion of market areas
- Changes in market share
- Intensity of foreign competition
- Capacity utilization

Detailed comparisons of companies in the same industry or industries are also included. Most important, descriptive analysis projects earning power or dividend-paying capacity, based on a specific set (or sets) of economic assumptions.

Valuation Function

The second function of security analysis is to develop value estimates for stocks and bonds. Experienced analysts should be prepared to express judgments on the relative investment attractiveness of securities under review.

Many of the laity believe that experienced security analysts worth their salt will be able to develop reliable value estimates for any stock or bond issue at any time; this belief is far from true. Certain times and security situations are propitious for sound analytical judgment. Analysts may be only modestly qualified to handle others. Still others may be so speculative that an analyst's study and conclusions, although better than nothing, may be subject to such a high degree of uncertainty as to be of little dependable value.

Valuation of Senior Securities.   Analysis and valuation of investment-grade bonds have traditionally followed well-established principles.[7] The object is to make it as certain as possible that the earning power of the corporation will ensure meeting interest and principal payments in the future. The generally accepted method requires an ample margin of safety in the past which, supported by earnings projections, can be expected to protect against possible adverse developments. Although the techniques and standards used in this work are by no means uniform, one competent analyst's practical conclusions are not likely to differ strikingly from another's. These conclusions may include determination of a suitable price and yield for the issue, which will bring it in line with the

---

[7]The term *investment grade* typically refers to the top *four* ratings (Aaa through Baa); we reserve the term *high-grade bonds* for the top *three* ratings.

current expected return for its class. In general, investment-grade preferred stocks are dealt with in the same manner as bonds.

When the fourth edition of this book was written in 1962, the amount of second-grade bonds outstanding was modest. In contrast, as of the fourth quarter 1986, $124.7 billion of publicly offered corporate bonds with credit ratings below the top four categories are outstanding. As a result, the analysis of second-grade bonds has become a major aspect of fixed-income security analysis. The price levels of such bonds (and preferred stocks) at their extreme points will usually offer interesting and rewarding opportunities for value analysis

Valuation of Private Placement Issues.   From an analytical standpoint, a substantial volume of interest-paying securities lie outside the above two categories of investment-grade bonds and second-grade bonds. These securities consist principally of direct (private) placements that lack liquidity. For this reason, they require a more probing analysis of the longer-term outlook for the company than do marketable investment-grade issues. Gross proceeds from privately placed corporate bonds were over $42 billion in 1984, equivalent to 88 percent of publicly offered corporate bonds. Bank term loans belong in this same category.

Valuation of Common Stocks.   The analysis and valuation of common stocks are the most fascinating aspects of the valuation function. The purpose is to provide the investor with explicit estimates of return and risk. These estimates form the basis for identifying from a list of stocks those that are priced at less than their value (and therefore are candidates for purchase) and those that are priced in excess of their value (and therefore are candidates for sale).[8] Part 4 deals with the factors which analysts will consider in developing their valuation estimates.

Three Approaches to Analysis and Valuation

There are three broad concepts or approaches to the analysis and valuation of common stocks. The first and oldest approach places primary emphasis on anticipated market performance. In the true sense, this approach is not based on a valuation concept, because it does not seek to value a stock apart from the market. Hence, we term it the

---

[8]The following discussion relates to the valuation of an enterprise as a "going concern." In recent years, the extensive acquisition and merger movement has resulted in valuing firms considered to be acquisition candidates in terms of their "takeover value." In this perspective, there may be consideration of liquidating value.

"anticipation" approach. The second and third approaches clearly rest on valuation—one on *intrinsic* values, the other on *relative* values.

Anticipation Approach.   The *anticipation approach* is typified by the many published lists suggesting stocks that will "outperform" the market over some specified time span such as the next 6 or 12 months. This approach ordinarily assumes that the present market price is, by and large, an appropriate reflection of the present situation of a stock, including the general opinion (consensus view) of its future. However, the price, say, a year from now, will probably be quite different from today's price, although it will be appropriate for the general conditions and expectations a year hence. Such price forecasts are speculative ventures for which an analytical discipline is of little assistance.

The function of the security analyst is to anticipate the new situation and to appraise the extent to which the company's market price will benefit or suffer through a detailed study of the business position and near term prospects of the company. The presumption is that the analyst's work and skill in examining publicly available data will produce a more accurate projection of future company results than is generally held (the consensus view) and already implicit in the present market price. This approach, clearly, does not seek to establish what a stock is worth. It does not determine the value of a stock—a determination that we consider to be essential.

Intrinsic Value Approach.   The second approach contrasts markedly with the anticipation approach, attempting to value a stock independently of its current market price. The *intrinsic value approach* is a normative concept that seeks to determine *what a stock is worth*, that is, the price at which it should sell if *properly* priced in a normal market. This approach underlies our views on security analysis and is the subject of Chapter 4.

This independent value has a variety of names, the most widely used and thus the most familiar of which is intrinsic value.[9] It may also be called "indicated value," "normal value," "investment value," "reasonable value," "fair value" (in some legal proceedings), and "appraised value."

In view of its widespread adoption, the term *intrinsic value* is used throughout this book. However, if an alternative term were now being selected, we would prefer the more descriptive *central value*, because it

---

[9]We do not know when the term *intrinsic value* was first applied to investments, but it was referred to in a pamphlet published in 1848, *Stocks, and Stock-jobbing in Wall Street* by William Armstrong, p. 12.

constitutes the central tendency in value about which actual price is expected to fluctuate.

Relative Value Approach. The third approach is concerned with *relative* rather than intrinsic value. Instead of accepting the complete independence of intrinsic value from the current level of stock prices, in this approach analysts more or less accept the prevailing level for the general market and seek to determine the relative value of a stock in terms of it. For example, they may develop the capitalization rate for an individual issue relative to the rate at which the earnings or dividends for a cross section of the market, such as the S&P 500, is being capitalized or relative to the current capitalization rate for a specific industry or other group, such as a comparable group of high-growth stocks that typifies the market for the individual share being evaluated.

For example, suppose an analyst concludes that, because the expected growth and quality are higher for a specific issue than for the S&P 500, the issue is entitled to a multiplier equivalent to 120 percent of that for the S&P 500. Let's say that the price index for the S&P 500 is 240, a representative earnings forecast is $17 for the next 12 months, and the resulting market multiplier is 14.1×. Accordingly, the relative multiplier for the above stock would be 16.9× (120 percent of 14.1×).

Acceptance by the relative value approach of the prevailing level of stock prices can prove to be hazardous. For example, in January 1973 the market was at a cyclical peak. If, at that time, an investor had purchased a cross section of those issues that were considered to be relatively most attractive, the portfolio would have suffered a substantial decline, even though it did not bear the full brunt of the severe 1973–1974 bear market that brought a 43 percent overall drop in prices.

The Corporate Critic Function

The analyst as a corporate critic stands apart from the valuation and selection of securities. In this role, the analyst is a financial leader concerned with the contribution that can be made to finance and to the financial community. Broad experience in the analysis and appraisal of securities should provide the analyst with insight into financial practices and policies of corporations and corporate governance. Moreover, in guiding the investment of funds directly or indirectly, the analyst is concerned with these practices and policies as they affect the investor. For example, the security analyst is interested in seeing that securities, especially bonds and preferred stocks, be issued with adequate protective provisions, and—more important still—that appropriate methods of enforcement of these covenants be part of accepted financial practice.

Since fair presentation of the facts is particularly important, analysts must be highly critical of accounting methods and disclosure practices. Finally, the analyst must be concerned with all corporate policies affecting the security holder, since the value of the issue being analyzed may depend largely on the acts of management in the expected economic and competitive environment. Some important facets of corporate policies are:

- Questions of capital structure
- Dividend and expansion policies
- Managerial capacity and compensation
- Bylaw provisions
- Continuation or liquidation of unprofitable business

Part 5 considers these matters of considerable import to the senior analyst.

4
Intrinsic Value

Intrinsic value is the investment concept on which our views of security analysis are founded. Without some defined standards of value for judging whether securities are over- or underpriced in the marketplace, the analyst is a potential victim of the tides of pessimism and euphoria which sweep the security markets. Equally destructive of satisfactory investment are the fads and herd instincts of major participants in the marketplace. For security analysis to contribute positively to the investment decision-making process, the discipline must provide a basis for resisting the pressure to be either a passive follower of prevailing sentiment or a mindless contrarian committed simply to thinking in opposite terms from the consensus.

As observed in Chapter 2, market prices across time will tend to coincide with the value of the enterprise on occasion, in the course of fluctuating above and below the intrinsic or central value. This convergence of price and value may be illusive as to its timing but must eventuate if markets are reasonably efficient and adequately informed. Indeed, a valuation of a company which is out of line with price behavior over a full market cycle is automatically suspect.

The traditional definition of intrinsic value emphasizes the role of facts: *the value which is justified by assets, earnings, dividends, definite prospects, and the factor of management.*

Valuation Factors

These four earnings factors are the major components of the intrinsic value of a going concern:

1. Level of normal earning power and profitability in the employment of assets as distinguished from the reported earnings, which may be, and frequently are, distorted by transient influences
2. Dividends actually paid or the capacity to pay such dividends currently and in the future
3. A realistic expectation about the trend line growth of earning power
4. Stability and predictability of these quantitative and qualitative projections of the future economic value of the enterprise

In capitalizing these earning power components, the valuation process involves the derivation of a risk premium, relative to an assured flow of returns, based on the following:

1. Variability of expected returns around trend line returns, reflecting industry factors, operating and financial leverage, creditworthiness, and nonfinancial elements
2. Positive value of growth potential derived from definite prospects such as new products, new markets, and external economic and social developments
3. Informed and experience-based appraisal of management's ability to cope with the uncertainties and unpredictable events of the long-term future

In essence, the intrinsic value of the firm is its economic value as a going concern, taking account of its characteristics, the nature of its business(es), and the investment environment.

Normative and Dynamic Aspects

This definition of intrinsic value is both normative and dynamic. It is a normative concept in that it is based on expected average relationships and thus seeks to estimate what price *should be* in terms of worth in contrast to what actual price may be.

Although the primary objective of defining intrinsic value is to emphasize the distinction between value and current market price, an aura of permanence is not imputed to this value. In reality, the computed intrinsic value will change from year to year, as earnings, dividends, and the other factors governing value change.[1] Although the reported earnings per share of nearly all companies grow at variable rates, normal earnings ordinarily increase steadily. Intrinsic value is therefore dynamic in that it is a moving target which can be expected to move forward but in a much less volatile manner than typical cyclical or other gyrations of market price. Thus, if intrinsic value is accurately estimated, price will fluctuate about it.

Acceptance of Concept

In general, investment practitioners now concede the existence of an intrinsic value that differs from price. Otherwise, the merit of substantial expenditures by both Wall Street and investment management organizations for the development of value estimates on broad lists of common stocks would be highly questionable.

Price and Value

Central Tendency in Price

As suggested earlier, perhaps a more descriptive title for this estimated value is *central value*. A typical investment-quality issue has a central tendency in price that has a meaningful relationship with the normal level and expected growth of earnings and cash dividends and the degree of risk inherent in those expectations. It is this relationship that provides the essential basis for selection of a multiplier for projected earnings or a discount rate for projected dividends and thus for derivation of a central value estimate. Therefore, intrinsic value is in essence the central tendency in price. Viewed in this manner, the actual coincidence between market price and the more stable central tendency in price will usually be brief. Typically, they will coincide when an advancing price reaches and passes through value and when a declining price drops to and falls below value.

---

[1]Irrespective of the total projection span used, most investment organizations project earnings and dividends for a company on a fiscal year basis and then review these projections quarterly. Therefore, unless a fundamental change occurs within a 12-month period, as reported in quarterly or other data, intrinsic value is usually computed on an annual basis.

Coincidence of Price and Value:
An Example

Since the intrinsic (central) value of a stock changes gradually, the fact that market price does not coincide for long with value may be readily established by examining the price gyrations of a cross section of 12 randomly selected investment-quality companies with different rates of growth and degrees of stability in earnings.

Table 4.1 sets forth the percentage price changes for the 12 companies over the 1978 to 1986 span, roughly in terms of the cyclical swings of the S&P 500. To provide perspective, the fluctuations of the S&P 500 are included. Note that the extent and range of the price rises for the 12 companies from their 1978 lows to their 1979–1980 highs are substantial. The same is true for the declines to their 1981–1982 lows and their subsequent rises to 1985–1986 highs.

The recession, accelerating inflation (for a portion of the six-year span), and other events had a substantial impact on the earnings outlook for many of these companies and on their capitalization rates. Can one conclude that (1) the earning power (or dividend paying capacity) of a representative group of quality U.S. companies has a "yo-yo" characteristic or that (2) the normal capitalization rate for this earning power or dividend-paying capacity could change to the extent implied by these price changes? Clearly, the answer is no. Furthermore, even in these relatively short market swings, finding that market prices bracket intrinsic values would not be surprising.

Price Behavior Factor in Selecting
a Multiple

One additional aspect of the price behavior of common stocks requires comment. Departure of the market multiples of individual issues, or groups of stocks, from prior levels for extended periods requires the analyst to interpret with care use of the past price record as a guide to the future. For example, Table 4.2 compares the price-to-earnings (P/E) ratios for high-growth and average-growth stocks over the 1968–1986 period. Note from the table that over the six-year span 1968 to 1973, high-growth stocks sold at high multiples (P/E ratios). The 1968–69 annual average was 30.0× and the 1971–1973 average was even higher at 33.6×. In the market rise from 1970 to 1973, the P/E ratio went from a 1970 low of 24.1× to a 1972 high of 40.3×. In marked contrast, the 1971–1973 composite P/E ratio for 15 investment-quality average growth companies was below the 1968–1969 level (13.9× versus 15.6×). The compression in market multiples which followed in subsequent years through 1985 represents an unprecedented bear market in growth as a component of stock value.

Table 4.1. Price Fluctuations in Individual Common Stocks

Issue	1978 low ($)	1979–1980 high ($)	Percent rise	1981–1982 low ($)	Percent decline	1985–1986 high ($)	Percent rise
Avon Products	44	56	27	19	66	36	89
Black & Decker	14	25	79	12	52	27	125
Coca-Cola	12	15	25	10	33	45	350
Colgate-Palmolive	16	20	25	14	30	47	236
IBM	59	81	37	48	41	162	238
American Brands	10	22	120	17	23	53	212
R. R. Donnelly & Sons	11	19	73	15	21	80	433
RJR Nabisco	10	19	90	16	16	55	244
Caterpillar Inc.	45	64	42	33	48	55	67
General Motors	54	66	22	34	48	89	162
PPG Industries	6	10	67	7	30	39	457
Weyerhaeuser	21	38	81	23	39	41	78
Average			57		37		224
S&P 500	89	136	53	109	20	254	133

NOTE: Prices and percentages are rounded. Prices are adjusted for stock splits and stock dividends.

SOURCES: Compiled from *The Value Line Investment Survey* and Standard & Poor's *Statistical Service*, *Security Price Index Record* and *Current Statistics*.

Table 4.2. Comparative Price/Earnings Ratios of High-Growth Stocks and Average-Growth Stocks, 1968-1986

	High-growth stocks			Average-growth stocks		
	High	Low	Avg.*	High	Low	Avg.*
1968	32.2×	27.0×	29.9×	16.9×	14.3×	15.6×
1969	31.7	27.9	30.1	17.1	15.0	15.7
1970	30.3	24.1	26.4	14.6	12.2	13.3
1971	34.0	28.3	31.2	15.9	14.1	15.0
1972	40.3	33.1	36.9	15.3	13.2	14.6
1973	37.0	25.8	32.8	13.9	10.3	12.2
1974	25.0	14.5	20.5	11.3	7.6	9.4
1975	21.8	15.6	18.7	10.1	8.6	9.5
1976	18.4	14.1	16.5	9.9	8.4	9.1
1977	13.0	11.0	12.1	9.1	7.7	8.5
1978	12.7	9.9	11.0	8.4	7.3	7.8
1979	11.0	8.5	10.0	8.0	6.7	7.7
1980	9.9	8.1	9.1	7.9	6.2	7.1
1981	9.7	8.3	8.9	7.2	6.3	6.7
1982	10.8	7.9	8.8	7.9	6.1	6.8
1983	12.4	9.9	11.3	9.9	7.9	8.9
1984	10.2	8.9	9.4	8.3	7.5	7.9
1985	11.9	9.8	10.3	10.2	8.4	9.5
1986	14.8	11.9	13.6	13.3	10.1	12.1

*Twelve-month-end averages.

SOURCE: FRS Associates, *Structure of the Market Studies.*

If conditions of this nature prevail for a relatively extended period (such as two or three years or longer), does the security analyst adjust upward the multiple used in arriving at the intrinsic value for a high-growth issue and downward for an average-growth issue on the logic that a revaluation has taken place? If so, what standards should be used in establishing the new multiples?

In retrospect, the answer is easy. An upward multiple revaluation instituted for high-growth stocks based on the experience of 1971 to 1973, would have had devastating results in 1974. The low P/E ratio in that year (14.5×) was 64 percent below the 1972 high P/E ratio (40.3).

Suppose the reverse situation: The average multiple for the 15 high-growth stocks in 1978 was 11.0×. The composite P/E ratio was thus down 67 percent below the 1971–1973 level of 30.0×. What should the analyst do? One step is clear: The quality of the issues must be carefully checked to determine that the fundamentals still prevail. If they do, security analysts would naturally ask themselves: Has the market overdone it? To complete the analysis, the 1978 P/E ratio for average stocks was 7.8× or down only 44 percent from the 1971–1973 level (13.9×). The next step would be to ask this question: Are growth stocks underpriced relative to average stocks?

Let us see what the outcome would have been if the analyst had decided that growth stocks were underpriced. In terms of price appreciation, an investment in 15 growth stocks at the average price in 1978 would have shown an increase of 53 percent at the average market price in 1984, whereas a like investment in 15 average stocks would have increased 114 percent. Although the 1973–1978 decline in the multiplier for growth stocks was tremendous, the market apparently still considered the decline inadequate.

Our findings are confirmed by an independent study of large capitalization growth companies for the period 1973 through 1981: "Unfortunately, the group became so popular that they became overpriced. Also, slower earnings growth companies seemed to benefit relatively more from accelerating inflation. The large capital growth stocks substantially underperformed the general market between mid-1973 and year-end 1981."[2]

These excesses of the stock market present the analyst with both basic opportunities and practical difficulties and frustrations. Excesses present discrepancies between price and value for the security analyst to discover. However, if optimism or pessimism increases unduly and continues for an extended period, the security analyst's labors may appear useless. Conceivably, the time lag in vindicating value conclusions may be so great as to destroy the viability of such analysis. Our own experience and observations lead to a contrary conclusion. With the appropriate combination of skill, prudence, and patience, the valuation approach—as contrasted with the market movement (anticipation) approach—should yield a satisfactory annual return with moderate risk.

Convergence of Price on Value

As previously emphasized, investment returns are realized from purchases and sales in the marketplace, not from analysts' skillful derivations of intrinsic value. It is a basic assumption, therefore, that price may be expected to converge on intrinsic value. The key questions, therefore, are: Will price and value converge? If so, when?

Soundness of the Valuation

The definition of a sound valuation is not theoretical or conceptual; it is pragmatic. A *sound valuation* is eventually validated in an efficiently functioning marketplace. It is axiomatic, therefore, that price will

[2]William S. Gray, III, "Portfolio Construction: Equity" in J. L. Maginn and D. L. Tuttle, *Managing Investment Portfolios*, Warren, Gorham & Lamont, Boston, 1983, p. 386.

converge on a sound determination of intrinsic value. Sound valuations should be most attainable when there is a continuity and consistency in the company's earning power as a reflection of the inherent stability of its business. For example, net income of Abbott Laboratories recorded an average annual growth rate of approximately 22 percent from 1972 through 1985. The year-to-year growth was extremely stable, with only a slight bulge during the inflationary 1975–1980 years, as shown in Figure 4.1 by the closeness of each year's net income to the calculated trend line.

Unseasoned companies in new fields of activity, in striking contrast, provide no sound basis for the determination of an intrinsic value. The risks inherent in the business, an untested management, and uncertain access to additional capital combine to make an analytical determination of value unlikely if not impossible. Analysts serve their discipline best by

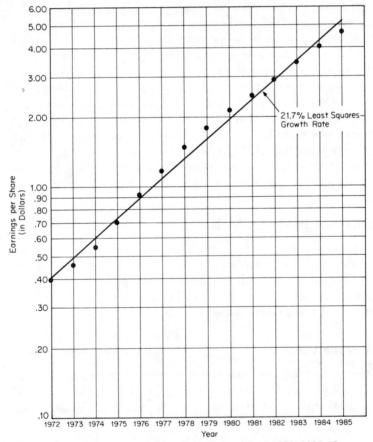

Figure 4.1 Abbott Laboratories: Net income growth rate, 1972–1985. (*Source: Compiled from Value Line, Inc., The Value Line Investment Survey.*)

identifying such companies as highly speculative and by not attempting to value them, even though we recognize that there will be pressure to make valuations of initial public offerings (IPOs) and other unseasoned issues.[3] The buyer of such securities is not making an investment but a bet on a new technology, a new market, a new service, or an innovation in established product markets. Winning bets on such situations can produce very rich rewards, but they are in an odds setting rather than a valuation process. Recognizing these limitations of the valuation approach may prove as useful as almost any other aspect of the analyst's efforts.

Timing of Convergence

The investor who purchases a consistent, growing stream of earnings and dividends at a price which provides a satisfactory investment position can, of course, ignore the failure of the marketplace to recognize fully the merits of a selection. Being out of phase with the market because it is engaging in one of its surges of enthusiasm elsewhere, however, is frustrating and quite possibly an opportunity loss. The reward for identifying underpriced securities, after all, is to earn the superior return from the market's subsequent upward revaluation to a price consistent with intrinsic value.

Attempting to predict the timing of this convergence of price on value is not a fruitful or appropriate undertaking for the analyst. Accurate predictions obviously depend on one's ability (or luck) in forecasting a change in the preferences and expectations of an unknown body of investors reacting to an unknown future environment. Students of the diversity of market cross currents may be of some assistance, perhaps using measures of relative price strength.[4]

Inability to predict the timing of convergence is not a serious defect of the valuation approach. Experience shows that the convergence does

---

[3]*Forbes* magazine conducted a study of 1922 initial public offerings (IPOs) that went public at $1 a share or more in the United States from January 1975 through June 1985. This study revealed that, based upon June 30, 1985, prices, almost 60 percent were below their initial offering price and about four percent ended in bankruptcy. Relative to the S&P 500 during the same period, approximately 13 percent were down at least 95 percent and approximately half were down at least 50 percent ("Why New Issues Are Lousy Investments," *Forbes*, December 2, 1985). The 1986 study found that 61 percent of the IPOs underperformed the S&P 500 ("New Issues: Who's Hot, Who's Not," *Forbes*, March 19, 1987).

[4]The ratio of the price of an individual stock or group of stocks to the price of a broad market index is plotted as a measure of relative strength. A ratio declining for six months or a year may indicate that investors are persistently unimpressed with the idea that this is a case of undervaluation. A static or persistently advancing ratio, however, may suggest a receptiveness to recognition of possible cheapness.

occur. Diversification is the investor's logical means of averaging favorable and unfavorable surprises in the emerging components of value and in the early and late convergences of price on value.

5
Economic
Analysis

Return expectations for the stock and bond markets and sales, cost, and profit projections for industries and nearly all companies necessarily embody economic assumptions. It is the exceptional case for which this is not true.[1]

Economic forecasts need to be considered in terms of the individual analyst's requirements and must be viewed from the standpoint of both their usage and their preparation. Accordingly, this chapter:

- Describes the nature of economic forecasts required by the security analyst
- Discusses the need for longer-term (secular) forecasts as well as near-term (cyclical) forecasts and explains the conceptual differences between the two
- Points out the need to understand the interrelationships among macroeconomic variables and to develop linkages between these variables and the performance of capital markets, economic sectors, industries, and companies
- Provides a discussion of projection methodology and illustrations of key underlying assumptions

Economic assumptions may be explicit or implicit. For an investment organization, explicit forecasts are necessary for effective communication throughout the organization. Individual investors may assimilate

[1]Several exceptional cases are noted at the end of this chapter.

from review of a series of forecasts an implicit and intuitive set that is satisfactory for their purposes.

In all instances, investors using such forecasts should have clearly in mind the time span (or spans) for which they want projections and the key cyclical or secular assumptions underlying the forecasts used.

Economic Forecasts in Perspective

Economic forecasts provide essential underpinning for stock and bond market, industry, and company projections. The outlook for stock and bond markets depends on the outlook for such basic economic factors as:

- The growth rate for real GNP and GNP in current dollars
- The supply of funds coming principally from business and personal saving, including pension funds[2]
- The demand for funds arising from financing expenditures by consumers, business, and governments
- The inflation rate and anticipated inflationary pressures
- Corporate profits

Similarly, the outlook for industries and companies depends on the outlook for those economic factors that affect demand for their products and the cost of labor, material, and capital. The accuracy and consistency of analysts' projections for industry and company sales, expenses, and earnings lie in the closer knitting of economic and security analysis. This requires establishing internally consistent economic projections on which all other forecasts should depend.

Large organizations with in-house economists develop their own forecasts. In the process, they examine the projections of others (such as brokerage houses and banks) and frequently subscribe to one or more forecasting services, such as Data Resources, Inc., Chase Econometrics, and the Wharton Econometric Model. Computer access to these models allows for testing of alternative assumptions and otherwise modifying the "standard" projections produced by the forecasting services.

Small investment organizations and individual investors typically rely on external forecasts as provided by brokerage houses and subscription

---

[2]For several years, some state and local governments have had an operating surplus, which is also a source of gross savings. Foreign capital inflows are an additional source of funds.

services as mentioned above. These smaller organizations are less likely to have computer access to an econometric model and will rely primarily on the memoranda and reports issued at regular intervals (quarterly or more frequently).

Cyclical and Secular Forecasts

Investment decisions should be based on longer-term as well as near-term projections. Indeed, institutional investment decisions are increasingly made on a longer-term basis.[3]

On the one hand, investment theory tells us that the worth of a common stock is the present value of its entire future earnings or dividend stream. However, the uncertainty of projections rises as futurity is lengthened and the present value of distant earnings or dividends is small. Therefore, explicit long-term projections are impractical.

On the other hand, the earning power or dividend-paying capacity of an enterprise and thus the central tendency in its price cannot be judged adequately on the basis of a one- or two-year outlook. The normal current price level, longer-term growth, stability of earnings, and the dividend payout ratio of the typical company cannot be effectively appraised in terms of what may happen in the next year. Likewise, it would be purely coincidental if the future growth rate of industries, the stock market, or the total economy were meaningfully indicated by the near-term outlook. Undue emphasis on the near-term can produce distorted investment decisions.

The conceptual differences between near-term cyclical predictions and longer-term secular projections are as pronounced as the differences in the projection spans. These differences must be understood because they involve substantially different appraisals of the future.

Near-Term Forecasts

In general, near-term projections comprise the next four to eight quarters and are typically designated as "forecasts" by business economists. These projections represent definitive estimates of what will happen in a given time frame. They are predictions of the specific level

---

[3]Unfortunately, too frequently investors pressure for gains in short-term (quarter-by-quarter) profitability. This places undue emphasis on near-term forecasts and may prove disadvantageous in the long run.

and nature of economic activity on a quarter-by-quarter basis, and thus they map out the cyclical path that the economy is expected to follow.

Quarterly Demand Forecasts. Near-term forecasts are primarily "demand" forecasts.[4] The level of business activity in the short run is determined more by changes in income and expenditures than by changes in capacity. Accordingly, although careful consideration must be given to the relationship of demand to the nation's existing output capacity (whether little or substantial "slack" exists in the economy), demand rather than capacity can change significantly over the near term.[5]

Putting aside such major disruptive events as war, severe droughts, or an oil embargo, economic change in the near term is almost entirely the result of changes in the incomes and expenditures of individuals, the level of corporate profits and business expenditures, and monetary and fiscal policy designed to influence incomes and expenditures. Accordingly, near-term forecasts are primarily the result of economic forces; that is, forces generated within the economic system itself. For this reason, economic models are particularly vital to near-term forecasts.

Economic Models. These models are derived from extensive systematic analysis of the past behavior of key economic variables and delineate in general terms the behavior patterns and interrelationships within the economic system of households, businesses, governments, and foreigners—the principal classes of economic units. Whether they are preparing a set of mathematical (econometric) forecasts with extensive sectoral detail or only simplified judgmental forecasts, economists develop models systematically within a given conceptual framework.

The practical use of models lies in answering such questions as the following: What are the implications of a reduction of income taxes on the level and pattern of personal consumption expenditures? What effect on business plant and equipment expenditures can be expected from an increase in the investment tax credit? What will be the impact of a significant increase in federal expenditures on aggregate demand? What will an increase in the gasoline tax do to fuel consumption?

[4]See Geoffrey H. Moore, *Business Cycles, Inflation, and Forecasting*, National Bureau of Economic Research, Studies on Business Cycles, no. 24, 1980.

[5]However, it is to be recognized that, as a result of economic recovery, accelerated depreciation, and tax reduction, considerable capacity was added in 1983 and 1984.

Articles and books dealing with the methods and techniques of near-term economic forecasting exist in profusion.[6] An overall knowledge of the workings of the economy is essential in analyzing industries and companies as well as in reaching effective investment decisions.

Longer-Term Projections

Longer-term predictions are frequently referred to as "projections."[7] No consensus exists as to the length of the longer term, since the projection span beyond the next two years cannot be forecast as confidently as the near term. For in-depth analysis and a comprehensive set of projections, the optimum longer-term span is considered to be 5 to 10 years. A period much shorter than 5 years is unduly affected by cyclical forces; whereas for the longer span, projections are considered more in terms of secular forces and structural changes. An interval much longer than 10 years raises an increasing number of uncertainties, particularly in regard to social, political, and technological change.

Use of a five-year span is suggested in most instances. Because the U.S. and world economies are highly dynamic, an in-depth analysis is more manageable when restricted to five years. Furthermore, the duration of the business cycle in the postwar period (measured from trough to trough) has averaged between four and five years.[8] Thus, a five-year projection span covers the typical business cycle and is also a reasonable period for measuring the investment performance of security analysts and portfolio managers.

Our suggestion that in-depth analysis of secular growth be limited to five years is not meant to confine an organization's horizon. Also needed is a notional (less specific) longer-term idea of the social, political, and economic environment in the form of a skeletal set of projections

[6]For example, see L. Klein and R. M. Young, *An Introduction to Econometric Forecasting and Forecasting Models*, Lexington Books, Lexington, Mass., 1980. Also, a comprehensive collection of 32 papers on the many aspects of forecasting by an impressive list of practitioners is contained in *Methods and Techniques of Business Forecasting*, edited by W. F. Butler, R. A. Kavesh, and R. B. Platt, Prentice-Hall, Englewood Cliffs, N.J., 1974. A summary discussion by two of the editors, Kavesh and Platt, entitled, "Economic Forecasting," is in S. N. Levine, ed., *Financial Analyst's Handbook I*, Dow-Jones-Irwin, Homewood, Ill., 1975, pp. 928–943. Related subjects exist in Part V of the *Handbook*: "Economic Analysis and Timing." Another comprehensive undertaking is a two-volume study by B. G. Hickman, ed., *Econometric Models of Cyclical Behavior*, Studies in Income & Wealth, no. 36, National Bureau of Economic Research, Columbia University Press, New York, 1972.

[7]The terms *forecasts* and *projections* are used interchangeably. The context indicates whether the predictions are for the near or longer term.

[8]For the 1945–1981 span, the average duration was 60 months. If the two extremes (34 and 117 months) are eliminated, the average is 53 months (based on a National Bureau of Economic Research reprint from the *Business Conditions Digest*, July 1982, p. 105).

covering such key variables as the growth rate for real GNP, inflation, GNP in current dollars, and corporate profits. Forecasts beyond five years primarily indicate whether the investment environment will be significantly different from that expected on a secular basis, develop consistency in industry and company projections by security analysts, and provide inputs for the "steady state" or "terminal" stage of a dividend discount model. These projections are more directional than dimensional. For example, inflation was probably the most disruptive economic force experienced by investors from the late 1960s to the early 1980s. It adversely affected economic activity, reduced corporate profits, drove interest rates up and stock prices down, and distorted relative returns in the capital markets. Indeed, for a portion of the 1970s, the return on Treasury bills exceeded the return on both stocks and bonds. Thus, when investing in long-term assets such as stocks or bonds, one must evaluate the economic and investment climate beyond that expected for the next five years.

Secular Average Projections.   Longer-term projections ordinarily take the form of annual rather than quarterly forecasts and are primarily secular rather than cyclical. They should not predict either the actual level of activity for each year over the five-year span or the actual change from one year to the next. Instead, longer-term projections abstract from cyclical variations and represent basic trends and levels in the economy that underlie cyclical swings. Fluctuations in demand cause cyclical oscillations around the trend.

Long-term projections provide specific estimates for a particular future (terminal) year that is ordinarily considered to be a midcycle or representative "average" year. The level of employment and nature of activity in the initial year are also assumed to be those of an average year. The terminal year is thus basically the culmination of forecasts of expected *average* annual changes for the intervening span of years. Use of this averaging concept, which relies on good and poor years offsetting one another, makes secular projections less reliable as the projection span is shortened. This is another reason why longer-term projections should not cover a span less than five years.

Supply Projections.   Longer-term projections of real GNP (output in physical terms, inflation adjusted) are primarily "supply" forecasts. Accordingly, they give particular attention to demographics—the increase in population, age distribution, and growth in the labor force. Capital formation, innovation, and increased productivity (output per worker-hour) are also important. Thus longer-term projections take as their point of departure estimates of growth in the nation's output potential—the average annual increase in the volume of goods and services (output in constant dollars) that the United States could produce if operating at a stipulated level of employment.

These initial estimates are then modified for the expected growth and nature of demand over the projection span to provide "best guess" estimates. Experience establishes that, in their most useful form, these modified projections consider a number of factors in addition to the secular forces of growth and structural change in the economy:

- The relationship of the current and expected near-term level of economic activity to the nation's output potential
- Expected government economic policy, including monetary and fiscal policy
- International political and economic developments
- The nature and amplitude of business cycles over the projection span; the severity of recessions
- The probability of rampant inflation

Resolution of these issues is highly uncertain; however, their consideration is essential to preparing longer-term projections for the economy and security markets.

Conditional and Interdisciplinary.   Longer-term projections are much more conditional than near-term predictions. They are affected substantially more by noneconomic factors. Over a span of years, social, political, technological, and international forces can critically affect both the demand for goods and services and the ability to produce them. Accordingly, effective longer-term economic forecasts are interdisciplinary undertakings to a surprising extent.

Importance of Longer-Term Projections.   The primary importance of these longer-term projections does not lie in the specific numbers generated, which principally represent orders of magnitude. Rather, it lies in the research findings and reasoning on which the numbers are based and in the benchmarks and relationships they establish. It would be coincidence if the projections were an exact anticipation of the future; nevertheless, explicit forecasts are necessary for the mental discipline, logic, and cross-checks required in drawing definitive conclusions.[9]

---

[9]The discipline and key considerations in making a longer-term forecast are effectively set forth by W. S. Gray III in "Developing a Long-Term Outlook for the U.S. Economy and Stock Market," *Financial Analysts Journal,* July–August 1979, pp. 29–39.

In-depth estimates of the longer-term future provide critical insights into the underlying growth and structural changes in the economy that cannot be seen from near-term forecasts. They also provide essential perspective in judging the near term. It is unlikely that the initial year will actually be at midcycle (an average or equilibrium year). The longer-term (secular) projection will thus provide a benchmark for judging the extent of the current departure from the secular trend.[10]

Long-term projections provide security analysts with information to estimate the growth rates of both industries and companies. Longer-term growth in earnings is the major determinant of the multiplier of investment-quality common stocks. Therefore, it is regrettable that so much research effort is devoted to forecasting the next four to eight quarters and that only limited—albeit increasing—effort is devoted to the longer term.

Linkage between Economic and Security Analysis

Linkage with Near-Term Forecasts

There are well-established methodologies for forecasting the near-term outlook for the economy or analyzing the past experience of companies and predicting the future. However, the greatest difficulty exists and the least has been accomplished in tailoring economic forecasts to provide maximum assistance to security analysts.

Finding Stable Relationships.   The challenge is to find reasonably stable relationships between specific macroeconomic variables and such factors as industry and company sales, costs, and profits. Although such a task is not easy, security analysts can increase their judgment factor and reach more effective investment decisions by consistently considering a given set of macroeconomic variables.

Institutions should review and discuss quarterly the economic projections of such macroeconomic variables as real GNP, inflation, nominal GNP, and selected expenditure components. The significance of individual variables will change from time to time, and the amount of attention devoted at a specific time to any one will vary.

---

[10]As a result, the current returns from investment asset classes will probably differ from forecast equilibrium returns.

Judging Risk of Forecasts.   The risk (likelihood of being wrong) involved in any set of forecasts must be judged. This estimation should take place at all levels in the hierarchy of forecasts, beginning with the outlook for the economy, progressing through the securities markets, sectors, and industries, and terminating with the outlook for individual issues. Accordingly, the probabilities associated with the economic projections adopted as the "most probable" forecast should be assessed.

Two approaches can be employed in subjectively estimating such probabilities. One is to develop alternative scenarios that bracket a range of reason and indicate more optimistic and more pessimistic possibilities than the most probable forecast.

The other approach is to use as a base either a consensus forecast obtained from external sources or the output of a comprehensive model (such as Data Resources' model). This base set of projections can then be modified to the extent that an organization has strongly differing opinions. The probabilities assigned in this case can be judged not only by appraising the degree of conviction held relative to the modifications of the control model but also by examining the range of forecasts prevailing among other forecasters, such as several Wall Street economists.

A summary of key macroeconomic variables in a set of near-term forecasts is provided in the following pages, together with examples illustrating the relationship of sales for two industries to a major economic variable.

Key Macroeconomic Variables Identified.   The mass of data pertaining to the U.S. economy can be segregated into two principal categories—income and expenditure (the latter is the so-called product category). The overall level of economic activity is considered in terms of its major expenditure components and is illustrated in Table 5.1.

The summary of key macroeconomic variables provides the minimum amount of information needed in terms of expenditures. How much further disaggregation is required will depend on the depth of analysis within an organization. For example, personal consumption expenditures for nondurable goods can be further disaggregated in terms of clothing and shoes, food, fuel oil and coal, gasoline and oil, and other expenditures.

Table 5.1 shows that the realized increase in expenditures from 1984 to 1985 was significantly different from one major component to another. For instance, among personal consumption expenditures, the rate of increase for services was substantially more than that for nondurable goods. In similar fashion, the increase in business expenditures for investment in structures exceeded that for any other component. These and other obvious differences in sectoral expenditures carried important implications for the growth in sales and profits of industries and companies in 1985.

Table 5.1. Summary of GNP and Major Expenditure Components Percentage Change between 1984 and 1985

	Year (in billions of dollars)		Percent
	1984	1985	change
GNP (1982 dollars)	3,489.9	3,585.2	2.7
GNP deflator (1982 = 100)	107.9	111.5	3.3
GNP (current dollars)	3,765.0	3,998.1	6.2
Personal consumption expenditures	2,428.2	2,600.5	7.1
Durable goods	331.2	359.3	8.5
Nondurable goods	870.1	905.1	4.0
Services	1,227.0	1,336.1	8.9
Gross private domestic investment	662.1	661.1	(0.2)
Fixed investment	598.0	650.0	8.7
Nonresidential (business)	416.5	458.2	10.0
Structures	139.3	154.8	11.1
Producers durable equipment	277.3	303.4	9.4
Residential	181.4	191.8	5.7
Change in business inventories	64.1	11.1	(82.6)
Net exports of goods and services	−58.7	−78.9	
Exports	382.7	369.8	(3.4)
Imports	441.4	448.6	1.6
Government purchases of goods & services	733.4	815.4	11.2
Federal	311.3	354.1	13.7
National defense	235.0	259.4	10.4
Nondefense	76.2	94.7	24.3
State and local	422.2	461.3	9.3

SOURCE: U.S. Department of Commerce, *Survey of Current Business*, December 1986, tables 1.1, 1.2, and 7.4, pp. 3, 13.

Retail Store Sales and Nondurable Goods Expenditures.   The next step is to examine the relationship between particular industries and an expenditure component. Table 5.2 illustrates the close relationship between retail store sales and personal consumption expenditures for nondurable goods. Although the 10-year span saw little cyclical fluctuation, no year was far from the period average of 14.6 percent. Thus, a reliable forecast of this major economic variable would have helped a security analyst responsible for the retail trade sector.

Table 5.2. Relation of Retail Store Sales to Personal Consumption Expenditures for Nondurable Goods, 1976–1985

Year	Personal consumption expenditures (in billions of dollars)	Retail store sales (in billions of dollars)	Retail sales as percent of personal consumption expenditures
1976	452.0	63.6	14.1
1977	490.4	68.7	14.0
1978	541.8	75.8	14.0
1979	613.2	82.0	13.4
1980	681.4	95.5	14.0
1981	740.6	105.9	14.3
1982	771.0	108.3	14.0
1983	817.0	125.2	15.3
1984	872.4	139.8	16.0
1985	912.5	153.4	16.8

SOURCES: Council of Economic Advisors, *Economic Report of the President 1986*, p. 252. Industry data compiled from *The Value Line Investment Survey*, Retail Store Industry studies.

Toiletries and Cosmetics Sales and Nondurable Good Expenditures. An even closer relationship (both relative and absolute) exists between toiletries and cosmetics industry sales and personal consumption expenditures. The range of cyclical fluctuation over the 10-year average of 1.4 percent was within plus or minus 0.1 percent. Sales as a percentage of personal consumption expenditures for nondurable goods are shown in Table 5.3.

Table 5.3. Sales as Percentage of Personal Consumption Expenditures for Nondurable Goods, 1976–1985 (Toiletries and Cosmetics)

Year	Percent	Year	Percent
1976	1.3	1981	1.5
1977	1.3	1982	1.5
1978	1.4	1983	1.4
1979	1.5	1984	1.4
1980	1.5	1985	1.4

SOURCES: Council of Economic Advisors, *Economic Report of the President 1986*, p. 252. Industry data compiled from *The Value Line Investment Survey*, Toiletries/Cosmetics Industry studies.

Linkage with Longer-Term Projections

There are numerous approaches to developing secular projections. The following pages summarize one approach providing a definitive analytical framework for the considerations entailed. This summary gives a set of illustrative assumptions for the key macro variables that underlie longer-term projections for the U.S. economy. This summary is not intended to indicate a preference for a specific method.

First Causes. Domestic, social, political, and international forces are first causes underlying economic developments. Their complex interaction creates both the climate within which business operates and the position of the United States in major international markets. Analysis of these first causes provides the foundation for specific estimates of the economy.

A purely national approach to economics is a fragmentary concept no longer valid in this expanding world market and evolving system of internationalized production. Analysts must consider the world political outlook, the interdependence of nations, and the increasing importance of other nations besides the "superpowers."

Analysts must also identify social forces expected to dominate in the United States over the projection span and appraise the major changes expected to result from these forces. These include changes occurring in values held by Americans as the result of age, education, employment, and affluence. They also entail growing recognition of the power of interest groups and collective action, the extent of federal government involvement, and the impact of changing occupations on people's income and expenditure patterns.

Longer-term estimates should be trend or secular projections representing average ("normal") annual growth rates from an estimated current midcycle year to a midcycle year five years hence. Both the initial and terminal years are estimated to be average from the standpoint of composition of GNP as well as price level.

Key Trend Projections. Since trend projections are based on the growth in supply or output capability of the economy, critical assumptions must be made about the following:

- Trend growth rate in the labor force. This rate is a measure of the increase in the supply of labor. It is a function of the age, sex distribution, and participation rate (percentage of those of working age seeking employment) of the population.

- Trend rate of increase in productivity (output per worker-hour). This increase is determined by such key factors as the amount of business fixed investment (capital-labor ratio), technological progress, shifts in the proportions employed in different occupations, and the age, education, and level of experience of the work force.

- Average unemployment rate for the projection span. Given the supply capability of the economy, this rate is the primary determinant of the level of GNP in real terms (the volume of output).

- Trend growth rate in real GNP. This rate measures the increase in the nation's output potential—in the supply capability of the economy—and is principally the sum of growth in the labor force (giving consideration to the employment rate) and the increase in productivity.

- Average annual inflation rate for the period. This assumption makes it possible to convert GNP in real terms to nominal terms (output valued at market prices).

Two sets of projections will serve as examples: Example 1 is for the five-year span 1984 to 1989 and was developed by a financial institution. Example 2 is a set of assumptions and projections for the five-year span from 1973 to 1978 and was prepared in 1974 by FRS Associates. Each example is generally representative of prevalent assumptions and projections held at the time the projections were made. Example 2 demonstrates the extent to which outcomes depart from expectations in longer-term projections and, through comparison with the forecasts in example 1, illustrates the extent to which expectations can change in a 10-year period.

Example 1. This illustrative set of key projections by a financial institution are for the period 1984 through 1989:

Trend growth rate in labor force	1.3%
Trend rate of increase in productivity	1.5
Trend growth rate in real GNP (1.013 × 1.015)	2.8
Increase in inflation (GNP deflator)	5.0
Trend growth rate in nominal GNP (1.028 × 1.05)	7.9

The above real GNP estimate assumes an average unemployment rate of 7 percent for the five-year span. One must estimate that level of output (real GNP) which, in the last year for which actual data are available, is consistent with 7 percent unemployment. This estimation is usually accomplished by deriving a production function that considers the size of the employed labor force, capital stock, productivity, and so forth.

With real GNP estimated for the base or initial year, the trend values for GNP over the next five years can be calculated using the growth rate established above. The value for real GNP in 1984 was estimated at $3395 billion (by coincidence approximately the actual of $3490 billion). Using a growth rate of 2.8 percent, the trend value for real GNP in 1989 would be $3898 billion ($1.028^5 \times \$3395$).

Real GNP for 1989 can be readily translated into nominal GNP by accepting the GNP deflator in 1984 and then increasing it at a stipulated rate. In this instance, it is an estimated compound rate of 5 percent. In 1984 the deflator stood at 107.9 with 1982 equalling 100. Compounded at 5 percent ($1.05^5 \times 107.9 = 137.7$), nominal GNP in 1989 would be $1.377 \times \$3898$, or $5368 billion.

Example 2. Table 5.4 summarizes the key FRS economic projections for the 1973 to 1978 span, sets forth the supporting logic as stated in 1974, and cites the subsequent actual experience.

Two points are to be stressed. First, although most of the foregoing projections were directionally correct, the margin of error in the individual economic variables producing nominal GNP was substantial. Actual and estimated nominal GNP were close only because of offsetting errors in the projections. Second, as shown in Table 5.5— a tabulation of the estimates prepared in 1974 and 1984—over the 10-year span marked changes have occurred in prevalent expectations about the longer-term performance of the economy.

Given the margins of error, should longer-term economic projections be avoided? Not at all. They are essential to the analytical and decision-making process and must be made. The error factor, however, does require that some concept of the degree of uncertainty surrounding any given set of projections is needed.

Leads and Lags

In most instances, a change in GNP or some specific economic variable will not bring a coincidental and proportional response in the sales and profits of an industry or company. There will be inevitable leads and lags. For example, the dynamics of the inventory cycle are well known.

A pronounced slowdown in consumer spending will cause inventories to become excessive and thus have a compounding impact on retail sales and profits and, in turn, on the manufacture of consumer goods and, with a lag effect, on the raw material producer.

Table 5.4. Economic Secular Projections for the 1973–1978 Span and Actual Results

Projected average	Actual average
Trend growth rate in labor force: The labor force will continue to increase at a rapid rate. The 1.7 percent annual increase over the span will exceed the 1947–1973 average of 1.5 percent, but will be below the 1968–73 average of 2 percent.	2.7 percent (the expected deceleration in the number of women entering the labor force did not take place)
Average unemployment rate: The continued addition of young people and women to the labor force (due to high job turnover rates) will result in an unemployment rate of 4.5 percent over the span rather than the 4 percent used earlier by the government.	7.0 percent (much higher than projected)
Rate of increase in productivity (output per worker-hour): The rate will be 2.2 percent per year for the total economy. Fewer workers shifting out of agriculture, the short supply and high price of energy, and increased investment to improve the environment will deter increases in aggregate productivity.	1.2 percent (due to sluggish growth of the economy)
Trend growth rate in real GNP: The growth in real GNP will be 3.9 percent per year. This span will have a more rapid increase in the labor force and a slower increase in productivity. Because actual output in 1973 was slightly below the high employment potential, the growth rate from actual output in 1973 to the high employment estimate in 1978 will be 4.2 percent per year.	2.8 percent (well below the estimated potential)
Average annual inflation rate: The average inflation will be 6.1 percent, as measured by the GNP deflator—significantly above the 1968–1973 average of 4.7 percent. The deflator will continue to be affected by the momentum of the present rate of inflation, as substantially increased costs work their way through the nation's entire pricing system and wage-rate structure.	7.3 percent (even higher than projected)
Average annual GNP—current dollars (market value of the nation's output of goods and services): The average GNP will be 10.2 percent per year.	10.3 percent (the proximity of the projection to actual outcome is due to the higher inflation rate, because the level of economic activity was less than expected)

Table 5.5. Comparison of 1974 and 1984 Estimates

| | Five-year rate of increase (%) | |
	1974 projections	1984 projections
Labor force	1.7	1.3
Productivity	2.2	1.5
Real GNP	3.9	2.8
Inflation	6.1	5.0
Nominal GNP	10.2	7.9
Level of unemployment	4.5	7.0

However, it is possible to construct an internally consistent set of macroeconomic projections that provide the security analyst with an essential guide to the future. These projections make possible a level of comparability for company forecasts that otherwise could not be attained.

Exceptional Cases

In stressing the significance of finding linkages between the growth and profitability of industries and companies and economic factors, we do not imply that in most instances there will be a consistent and readily discernible relationship waiting to be discovered. Too many potential variables exist to permit tight correlations in most instances. It is equally important to recognize those industries and companies whose fortunes have little or no meaningful relationship to macroeconomic variables. In these instances, the analyst's assignment shifts to identifying the nonexistence of linkages and to preparing different and independent bases for predictions of the future. The following examples in which noneconomic factors dominate illustrate our point.

Technological Factors

The explosive demand in the early 1980s for computer software programs was not the critical factor in appraising a company in this field. Rather, what was critical was the company's capacity to deliver the most cost-efficient software package and to integrate new features providing competitive equality or advantage. In the case of personal computers, the critical factor was the capacity to be first and become the industry standard, to have a product easily understood by novice users, or to be promoted by heroic advertising. The program itself could be far from perfection.

The demand for defense electronics is derived essentially from new-product development and by the nation's defense posture and, to this extent, is relatively independent of the economic environment.

The market for individual drugs and for whole courses of medical treatment depends on the results of clinical tests and Federal Drug Administration (FDA) approval rather than on economic demand factors.

Regulatory Factors

Despite a probable substantial potential for cellular radio communication services, the granting of licenses will be the critical determinant of company growth, and thus this industry is dominated by regulatory considerations. Some other examples include electric utility companies that have abandoned large nuclear power projects. These companies will find their earnings determined less by the demand for electrical power than by the extent to which they are allowed to recover huge costs through rate adjustments. Another example is financial institutions whose future growth will be significantly affected by whether they are permitted to continue broadening their range of services. Finally, deregulation in the air transport industry has intensified competition and has caused both a shakeout and some industry consolidation.

Political and International Factors

The price of copper may be more influenced by Chilean balance-of-payment problems than by the level of world economic growth—this assessment of the copper industry must consider political and international factors. At the time when world petroleum prices were set more by the OPEC cartel than by free-market forces, world business conditions were not the primary determinant of prices. (Business conditions subsequently have had a substantial impact on the cartel and prices.)

Another example is health care: the federal government policies on cost containment of health services may be more relevant to the industry than the surging social demand for health care.

Global excess capacity caused by worldwide political interference, governmental subsidies, and protectionism have created critical conditions in an increasing number of industries (such as autos, steel, computers, semiconductors, heavy equipment, textiles, and chemicals). Such conditions can dwarf the value of economic correlations based solely on U.S. economic data.

6
Capital Market Analysis

Interrelationship of Stocks and Bonds

In appraising the attractiveness of individual issues, the security analyst must consider the expected capital market environment as well as the economic environment. Although the capital market consists of several security or financial markets, the new issue market for bonds and the secondary market for corporate stocks are of primary interest.[1]

There are few institutions or individuals that cannot consider—up to some point—bonds and stocks as alternative investments, although there are constraints on the percentage of some institutional portfolios that can be invested in either equities or fixed income securities. Since so many possess the option of moving freely between the two markets, the stock and bond markets are interrelated. The relationship is complex and in some past periods has been exceedingly tenuous. In fact, judging from the price-to-earnings (P/E) ratios that

---

[1]For a broad-based review of bonds and money market instruments, see D. M. Darst, *The Handbook of the Bond and Money Markets*, McGraw-Hill, New York, 1981, and Marcia Stigum, *The Money Market*, rev. ed., Dow Jones-Irwin, Homewood, Ill., 1983.

have prevailed in the upper reaches of some bull markets, stock investors at such times seem to have become oblivious to bond yields.[2]

Chapter 6 suggests an effective analytical approach to the bond and stock markets by setting forth those factors that need to be appraised in determining the relative attractiveness of the bond and stock markets. In this connection, illustrative forecasts by others are used as examples.

Bond Market

An adequate valuation of the stock market is not possible unless the analyst has reached some conclusions about the bond market. Investment judgments are more meaningful when developed from a comparative analysis of the returns on the two types of securities.

Outlook for Interest Rates

For two reasons it is appropriate to begin our discussion with the bond market. First, assuming creditworthiness is established, the overriding consideration in bond market analysis is a single factor—the outlook for interest rates. (The other principal factors are maturity, coupon, and quality spreads and sector differentials, such as those among utility, industrial, and government bonds.) Interest-rate forecasting is a difficult and hazardous task.

Second, the outlook for interest rates—hence the expected return on bonds—is an important consideration in deciding the return to be sought from stocks. The holding-period return expected from bonds is essential for deciding the total return (dividend yield plus appreciation) desired from common stocks and thus in deciding on the appropriate price to be paid for stocks—that is, in selecting a multiplier for earnings or a discount rate for dividends.

---

[2]For example, in the fourth quarter of 1972 the S&P 400 sold at a high P/E ratio of 19.3 × with a dividend yield of only 2.4 percent. At the same time, the yield on the S&P AAA bond index was 7.1 percent. To provide a total return from stocks in excess of that prevailing for top-quality bonds, it would have been necessary, from the existing high price, for stock prices to rise at an annual rate of nearly 5 percent. If the high P/E were maintained and there were sufficient growth in earnings, this rise could have resulted. There was some growth in earnings. However, the P/E ratio collapsed to 7.1 × by 1974 and has not since recovered to the 1972 high. The price index for the S&P 400 dropped more than 45 percent and did not climb back to the 1972 level until 1980.

Dimensions of the Bond Market

The substantial dimension of the bond market may be readily seen from the volume of publicly held issues. The aggregate amounts outstanding on December 31, 1985 by type of bond are shown in Table 6.1.

Table 6.1. Aggregate Bond Amounts Outstanding on December 31, 1985

Type of bond	Amount outstanding (in billions of dollars)
Corporate bonds (publicly offered straight issues)	464.7
U.S. government bonds and notes (coupon issues publicly held)	1023.6
Federal agencies (coupon issues)	632.8[*]
Municipal bonds and notes	674.4
Total	2795.5

[*]This figure includes mortgage pool securities of $368.9 billion.

SOURCES: *Prospects for Financial Markets in 1987*, Salomon Brothers, New York, Dec. 16, 1986, pp. 54, 57–59; Board of Governors of the Federal Reserve System, "Gross Public Debt of U.S. Treasury," *Federal Reserve Bulletin*, December 1986, "Credit Market Debt Owed by Financial Sectors, and Tax Exempt Securities and Loans," *Flow of Funds Accounts, Financial Assets and Liabilities Year-End, 1962-85*, September 1986.

Indicators for the Level of Interest Rates

High Grade Bond Series

It is possible to think of the "general" or "overall" *level* of long-term interest rates as the yield of Moody's or Standard & Poor's highest-grade bond series. These indexes are composed of representative top-quality and seasoned industrial, rail, and utility bonds. (Another broad measure of the entire bond market is the Shearson Lehman Government and Corporate Bond Index.)

The bond yield can be taken as an appropriate comparative rate of return yardstick for analyzing the past and projecting the future return on common stocks. The attractiveness of this expected return is judged by a common stock investor in terms of the return available on alternative investments, giving due consideration to the relative risk.

Market Rate of Interest: Example

The rate of interest observable in the marketplace is the nominal rate for a bond with a fixed coupon and maturity. The quotation of price and yield to maturity take into account the premium or discount to be amortized or accrued during the term to maturity. For example, a General Mills 8⅞s debenture maturing in 1995 and selling at its 1984 low of 71 is said to provide a yield to maturity of 13.5 percent. This estimate assumes that all the semiannual coupons will be reinvested at 13.5 percent. In fact, only the accrual of the discount is assured at that rate. When offered at par in 1970, this bond had a duration of 11 years, ignoring the effect of the sinking fund.[3] At the 1984 low, the bond's duration had shortened to 6.6 years. Since duration indicates the rough measure of price change for each 1 percent change in interest rates, we can observe how the passage of time and a dramatic rise in interest rates greatly altered the sensitivity of this bond to fluctuations in the market rate of interest. Actual prices of the bond during a recent 12-year span were as shown in Table 6.2.

Table 6.2. General Mills' 8⅞s Debenture Due 1995

	High	Low
1975	103½	92¼
1976	103½	98
1977	102½	97
1978	102¾	97
1979	94¾	83
1980	86½	65
1981	71⅛	61
1982	82	62⅝
1983	87½	78⅜
1984	83½	71
1985	95⅞	81
1986	107	92⅛

Price fluctuations in bonds and other debt instruments attributable to interest rate changes have provided a strong stimulus to extensive research on the history (*what* happened)[4] and on the theory (*why* it happened) of interest rates.

Theory of Interest Rates

Theory provides the conceptual structure on which analysis rests. In modern times, Irving Fisher was one of the early and leading theoreticians. More than 75 years ago, Fisher first held that observed market

[3]Duration, expressed in years, is the weighted present value of the future cash receipts promised by the bond contract.

[4]One of the outstanding authorities, the late Sidney Homer, wrote *A History of Interest Rates*, 2d ed., Rutgers University Press, New Brunswick, N.J., 1977.

(nominal) rates of interest have two components: (1) a real rate of interest (constant purchasing power) determined fundamentally by the supply of and the demand for funds plus (2) a premium based on expected inflation.[5] This construct assumed—from a credit standpoint—risk-free securities. If a credit risk were entailed, a further premium would be added.

Today, there is widespread acceptance of the Fisherian view that the level of interest rates is determined by:

- The supply of savings
- The demand for funds
- Inflationary expectations[6]

However, disagreements and problems arise as soon as one moves from this explanation of the market rate in its basic formulation to identification of the factors directly bearing on each of the determinants of the market rate and to the measurement and description of their relationships.

In addition to the rate of inflation, such factors as growth in GNP, corporate profits and financing requirements, volume of consumer credit, Federal Reserve policy, federal budget deficits, the nation's trade deficit, and capital inflow from abroad are considered.

Real Rate of Interest

In accepting Fisher's basic principle that the market interest rate consists of two parts, the challenge is to apply this simple principle to forecasting. If it were possible to determine inflationary expectations with meaningful accuracy, the real rate could be readily derived. If the real rate changed slowly, as was generally true until the late 1970s, then the market rate of interest could be projected based primarily on the expected future rate of inflation.

However, real interest rates fluctuated substantially in the latter part of the 1970s and the early 1980s. The real rate recorded in 1985 of approximately 7 percent was about twice the long-term average. The increased rate is attributed to the increased volatility of fixed-income securities because of fluctuations in

---

[5]Subsequently amplified in Irving Fisher, *The Theory of Interest*, Macmillan, New York, 1930.

[6]To illustrate the impact of inflation, in 1965, on the eve of the inflation that still troubles nations, portfolio managers bought long-term, high-grade corporate bonds yielding 4.5 percent or less. By mid-1970, when the annual rate of inflation approached 5.5 percent, the real return on these bonds proved to be less than zero. In the United States, we subsequently had double digit inflation. As a result, inflation had a dramatic effect on interest rates, as the annual price range over the 1975 to 1986 span for General Mills' sinking fund debentures establishes (cited earlier in this chapter).

the nominal rate, changes resulting from financial market deregulation, large federal budget deficits, pressure from the U.S. dollar's changes in value, and greater variability of money growth.[7] The concept of a real rate is helpful because it emphasizes that the supply of and demand for loanable funds, as well as inflationary expectations, must be carefully analyzed in projecting the market rate of interest.

Projecting the Interest Rate

The person responsible for analyzing and projecting the interest rate (that is, the "capital market analyst") has, within the context of economic projections, three principal tasks:

- To examine past and present flows of personal and corporate savings and to forecast flows over the selected future period
- To examine the past and present demand for funds by corporations, households, and governments and to forecast demand for the period
- To forecast the inflation rate and its impact on the nominal interest rate

In developing the above estimates, the analyst will appraise the possible impact of expected government monetary and fiscal policy on both the supply of and demand for funds. International economic factors and capital flows must also be considered, since they can have a substantial impact. For example, in a Salomon Brothers study, *1985 Prospects for Financial Markets*, the authors predicted a "massive" inflow of foreign capital: "An enormous, unprecedented gap has emerged between the levels of production and expenditure in the U.S. economy. On one side, it has created an unexpected trade deficit, and on the other, a surprising capital inflow—both of which will grow further in 1985."[8]

There are varied and often conflicting views as to the relationship between economic and other factors and the supply of funds—for example, whether higher interest rates cause people to save more or less. Furthermore, although texts are replete with theoretical discussions of consumers' consumption-saving propensities, capable researchers have had difficulty explaining quantitatively the specific level of personal saving (the ratio of personal saving to disposable income) that has

---

[7]Supporting studies include Z. Bodin, A. Kane, and R. McDonald, "Why Haven't Nominal Rates Declined?" *Financial Analysts Journal*, March–April 1984, pp. 16–27. P. S. Holland, "Real Interest Rates: What Accounts for Their Recent Rise?" *Review*, Federal Reserve Bank of St. Louis, December 1984, pp. 18–29.

[8]H. Kaufman, J. McKeon, and N. Kimelman, *1985 Prospects for Financial Markets*, December 11, 1984, p. 5.

existed in the United States over a period of time. To illustrate, the personal saving ratio averaged 6.8 percent of disposable income in the United States over the 1965 to 1984 period. However, the range over this 20-year period was from 5.0 percent to 8.6 percent.[9]

In addition, there are an extensive number of studies on the net productivity of capital and other factors underlying the demand for funds. In the case of such factors of production as labor and land, the amount that business can pay for capital must across time be related to its productivity. Similarly, in a sense, the amount that people can pay in the form of interest on such borrowings as home mortgages or automobile loans is determined by the value of the services provided by those assets.

Clearly, interest rate forecasting is difficult and hazardous. The capital market analyst needs to develop a consistent method for coping with the uncertainties and substantial conceptual problems involved. Some specific factors that the capital market analyst needs to examine and appraise in predicting the supply of and demand for funds are discussed below.

Level of Savings Flow. The expected level of personal saving will be largely a function of disposable personal income, which will be affected by (1) a continually greater proportion of families supported by more than one income, (2) wage earners aged 25 to 34 receiving an increasing share of income, and (3) per capita disposable income increased by the larger fraction of the population working.

Other factors are also important. Public and private pension funds are growing rapidly and are another significant source of savings. Viewed from a flow-of-funds standpoint, corporate saving is equivalent to retained cash flow. Accordingly, attention must be given to depreciation and deferred income taxes as well as corporate profits and cash dividend payments to stockholders.

In terms of budget receipts and expenditures, past experience makes it doubtful that there will be federal government saving. The battle is, rather, how to trim and finance deficit budgets. However, saving does occur in the form of the increase in government insurance and pension reserves, including the Civil Service Employees Retirement and Railroad Retirement accounts as well as state and local government employee retirement funds. Also, at times the receipts of some state and local governments exceed expenditures.

Level of Demand for Funds. The cause-and-effect relationship between expenditures by households, corporations, and governments and the financial requirements of these sectors is much clearer than how the savings rate for individuals relates to other economic factors. For example, external financing by corporations will be influenced by plant and

---

[9]U.S. Department of Commerce, *Survey of Current Business*, February 1986, p. 25.

equipment expenditures. Accordingly, given the expenditure projections developed through economic analysis, the capital market analyst can probably estimate the demand for funds by household and corporate sectors with more confidence than the aggregate supply of funds. Because of its political features, the federal deficit and thus the government's demand for funds cannot be predicted with equal confidence.

Interest Rates and Inflation.   The basic relationship between interest rates and the inflation rate is worth reemphasizing. Inflation is a critical factor affecting the supply of and demand for funds. If money's purchasing power is depreciating and this trend is expected to continue, lenders will add an inflation premium to the interest rate they demand. At the same time, the borrower will be prepared, up to a point, to pay a higher rate because of the potential depreciation in money.

Stock Market Valuation

Having developed (or obtained) a forecast of the level of interest rates, the capital market analyst is in a position to undertake the valuation of the stock market. To accomplish this task effectively, they must decide at the outset what key factors to predict and how to use these factors in determining the intrinsic value of a selected index for the stock market, such as Standard & Poor's Composite Index of 500 stocks (S&P 500) or 400 industrial stocks (S&P 400). In this analysis, attention can be concentrated on the dominant considerations in the appraisal of the stock market.

Valuation models for the market can be fashioned after those for individual stocks. Investment value is determined basically by the current normal level, growth, and stability of earning power, and the normal payout rate.[10] The three principal steps in valuing the stock market are: (1) forecasting earnings, (2) estimating the dividend payout ratio, and (3) selecting a capitalization rate.

Earnings for Market Index

Several methods may be used in forecasting earnings for the selected stock market index. (Chapter 29 applies market index projections in the progression from macroeconomic forecasts to individual company earnings estimates.) Three methods of forecasting index earnings are described in the following discussion.

---

[10]The term *stability* embraces all the factors of variability that make it difficult to predict the normal level, secular growth, and cyclical volatility of a company's earnings.

Aggregate Profits Linked to Corporate Profits after Taxes. One approach is to link aggregate profits for, say, the S&P 400 industrial companies to total corporate profits after taxes using data compiled by the Department of Commerce in connection with the GNP accounts.[11] Earnings for the S&P 400 can then be derived from these aggregate estimates. Alternatively, earnings for the index may be estimated directly through computing the percentage that earnings for the index are per billion dollars of total corporate profits.[12] Data for both techniques are set forth in Table 6.3. Another technique is to relate the aggregate profits for the S&P 400 to total corporate profits through regression analysis.

Table 6.3. Aggregate Profits and Earnings of S&P 400 Industrial Companies as Percentage of Total Corporate Profits after Tax, 1976–1985

Year	Corporate profits after tax ($ billions)	Amount* ($ billions)	Percent of corporate profits after tax	Index earnings	Earnings per billion dollars of corporate profit after tax
		Aggregate profit of S&P 400			
1976	102.5	49.4	48.2	10.68	10.4
1977	122.0	54.3	44.5	11.57	9.5
1978	145.9	62.0	42.5	13.12	9.0
1979	165.1	78.7	47.7	16.21	9.8
1980	149.8	79.5	53.1	16.13	10.8
1981	140.0	85.0	60.7	16.70	11.9
1982	106.5	68.8	64.6	13.21	12.4
1983	130.4	80.3	61.6	14.73	11.3
1984	140.3	92.7	66.1	17.98	12.8
1985	131.4	78.4	59.7	15.28	11.6

*Income before extraordinary items and discontinued operations.

SOURCES: Compiled from U.S. Department of Commerce, *Survey of Current Business*, table 1.14, "National Income by Type of Income"; Standard & Poor's *Statistical Service— Security Price Index Record*; Standard & Poor's Compustat Services, Inc., *Financial Dynamics*.

Sales–Profit Margin. A second method for forecasting earnings for the stock market we term the "sales–profit margin" approach. Aggregate sales for the S&P 400 industrial companies can be related to GNP over selected spans of years. In turn, profits after taxes can be related to sales

[11]As an alternative, profits after tax for nonfinancial corporations could be used. However, this series does not include profits from foreign operations, and the relationship to the aggregate profits of the 400 is slightly less stable.

[12]These data are not for net income available for total capital, as would be preferred, but for net income after the deduction of interest and lease payments.

to obtain a ratio representing the profit margin on sales for the S&P 400. Table 6.4 provides data for GNP, sales, and net income and their relationships over the 10-year span from 1976 to 1985. By analyzing the past and present relationships of sales to GNP and after-tax profits to sales, aggregate profits for the 400 companies can be estimated within the context of overall projections for the U.S economy. Using this profit estimate the analyst can then derive an earnings forecast.

Table 6.4. Relationship of Aggregate Sales of S&P 400 Companies to GNP and Net Income to Sales, 1976–1985

Year	GNP ($ billion)	S&P 400 sales ($ billion)	Sales/ GNP(%)	S&P 400 net income ($ billion)	Net income/ sales(%)
1976	1782.8	901.5	50.6	49.6	5.5
1977	1990.5	1021.5	51.3	54.4	5.3
1978	2249.7	1160.4	51.6	62.3	5.4
1979	2508.2	1376.6	54.9	78.8	5.7
1980	2732.0	1583.8	58.0	80.4	5.1
1981	3052.6	1729.5	56.7	86.3	5.0
1982	3166.0	1716.5	54.2	68.4	4.0
1983	3401.6	1777.4	52.3	74.2	4.2
1984	3774.7	1904.1	50.4	92.2	4.8
1985	3992.5	1972.2	49.4	76.0	3.9

SOURCES: *Economic Report of the President*, February 1986, National Income or Expenditure Table B-1 p.232; Standard & Poor's Compustat Services, Inc., *Financial Dynamics*, Industry Composite, October 1986.

Return on Equity.   The third method for forecasting earnings is based on an analysis of rates of return on book value of the common stock equity (ROE).[13] Book value increases over time as a result of retained earnings and typically the sale of new equity at more than book value. Because of substitutions (dropping one company and adding another) in the list of corporations making up the 400, shifts in accounting practices, new equity financing and share repurchases, and other factors, the actual increase in book value of the S&P 400 in any one year may differ from the amount of retained earnings in that year, adding an additional margin of error in predicting the increase in book value over a span of years. Another complicating factor is that book value is an historic figure, but earnings are expressed in current dollars. Moreover, changes in capital structure can decrease or increase the leverage on the common equity and thus affect the ROE.

[13]The aggregate profit and sales–profit margin approaches discussed above can be applied to the S&P 500 as well as the S&P 400. However, book value data are not compiled for the S&P 500, and thus, the rate of return method cannot readily be used with the S&P 500.

Accordingly, the ROE method is necessarily rough. Nevertheless, as Table 6.5 illustrates, ROE is a meaningful ratio in spite of the uneven effects of inflation. It provides additional insights into the projection of earnings.[14]

Table 6.5. Return on Average Common Stock Equity for S&P 400, 1976–1985

Year	Average book value ($ billion)*	Earnings ($ billions)	Return on equity (%)
1976	73.55	10.68	14.5
1977	79.24	11.57	14.6
1978	85.97	13.12	15.3
1979	94.22	16.21	17.2
1980	103.51	16.13	15.6
1981	112.20	16.70	14.9
1982	117.35	13.21	11.3
1983	120.46	14.73	12.2
1984	122.80	17.98	14.6
1985	124.74	15.28	12.2
1976–1980			15.4
1981–1985			13.0

*Average of beginning and end of year.

SOURCE: Standard & Poor's Statistical Service, *1986 Security Price Index Record* and *Current Statistics*, November 1986.

An analysis of these ratios and the outlook for growth in sales and for profit margins can provide the basis for a judgment of both a near-term and a "normal" rate of return on book value. The projected normal rate can then be used with a projected average (normal) retention rate (1 minus the cash dividend payout rate) to provide a useful approximation of the secular growth rate in earnings. The use of averages assumes that index earnings grow at a constant secular rate and that book value is not distorted by changes in accounting practices or by substantial sales or repurchases of stock at prices significantly different from book value. It also assumes that leverage caused by capital structure remains relatively constant over the projected span. This is a questionable assumption in the 1980s.

The forecast of secular earnings growth rate derived from the return on book value times the retention rate can then be compared with growth rates developed by the two preceding methods. These

[14]ROE can be analyzed in greater detail by relating sales and profit margin data to book value over a decade or more. Return on equity can be expressed as the product of (1) sales per dollar of book value (turnover) and (2) the profit margin per dollar of sales. The analysis and projection of ROE can then be structured in terms of separate considerations of turnover and profit margin.

different methods provide valuable checks. Careful examination of any significant differences in the results allows a final decision on the growth rate (or range of rates) to be employed.

Dividend Payout Ratio

The proportion of a corporation's earnings that is paid out in cash dividends depends primarily on management's judgment regarding:

- Expected financial requirements of the corporation resulting from growth in sales, asset expansion, and other factors
- Expected profitability (including cash flow)
- The degree of access to the capital markets and the cost of externally raised capital
- The effect of a change in dividend policy on the market price of the stock, which will require consideration of the possible impact on the type of investor to whom the stock appeals

The growth and profitability of major U.S. corporations, their financial requirements, and thus their cash dividend policies are significantly deter-

Table 6.6. Earnings, Dividends, and Payout Ratio for S&P 400, 1966–1985

Year	Earnings ($ billions)	Dividends ($ billions)	Dividends as percent of	
			Earnings	Cash flow
1966	5.89	2.98	51	30
1967	5.66	3.01	53	30
1968	6.15	3.18	52	29
1969	6.17	3.27	53	29
1970	5.43	3.24	60	30
1971	6.02	3.18	53	28
1972	6.83	3.22	47	26
1973	8.86	3.48	39	23
1974	9.69	3.72	38	23
1975	8.55	3.78	44	24
1976	10.68	4.25	40	23
1977	11.57	4.96	43	24
1978	13.12	5.35	41	24
1979	16.21	5.98	37	22
1980	16.13	6.55	41	23
1981	16.70	7.00	42	23
1982	13.21	7.18	54	26
1983	14.73	7.37	50	25
1984	17.98	7.43	41	22
1985	15.28	7.74	51	24

SOURCE: Standard & Poor's Statistical Service, *1986 Security Price Index Record*, pp. 120–121; Standard & Poor's Compustat Service, Inc., *Financial Dynamics*, Industrial Composite, October 1986.

mined by the outlook for the U.S. economy, and therefore macroeconomic forecasts are important.

Table 6.6 provides earnings and dividend data for the S&P 400 over the 20-year period from 1966 to 1985.[15] Note that in the last half of the 1960s, the amount of earnings paid out in cash dividends was slightly in excess of 50 percent, whereas, throughout most of the 1970s, the payout was close to 40 percent. In this period of pronounced inflation and thus high capital requirements, corporations retained more earnings. The more meaningful relationship of dividends to cash flow shows a pattern more consistent with these factors.

Anyone valuing the S&P 400, or any other broad market index, must account for the impact of the expected payout ratio on such key factors as growth in earnings and capital structure changes.

Capitalization Rate

The selection of a capitalization rate also involves deciding on an appropriate total return requirement for the market. Several different methods may be employed in selecting the capitalization rate.

Intrinsic value is determined by the expected level, growth, and stability of earnings and by the dividend payout ratio. However, the rate at which earnings (through a multiplier) or dividends (through a discount rate) are to be capitalized is not determined solely by these factors.

Return differentials in the capital markets are determined by the continuous trade-off between risk and return. Accordingly someone selecting a capitalization rate for the market should add a risk differential to the expected interest rate to obtain the expected rate of return for common stocks.

There is merit in looking at the record as one considers the appropriate risk differential for common stocks. The average annual compound rates of return that were actually realized for the principal classes of securities over the 60-year span from 1926 to 1985 are shown in Table 6.7.[16]

---

[15]The average payouts for the S&P 400 and the S&P 500 were almost identical for the following periods:

Period	S&P 400	S&P 500
1966–1970	53.6%	55.1%
1971–1980	42.3	42.5
1981–1985	47.7	49.4

SOURCE: Standard & Poor's Statistical Service, *Security Price Index Record*.

[16]Total return with reinvestment monthly of dividends or interest as calculated by Ibbotson Associates, Inc. in *Stocks, Bonds, Bills, and Inflation: 1986 Yearbook*, Chicago, Ill., February 1986. pp. 90, 94, 96, 98. This annual publication is a recognized source of capital market information.

Table 6.7. Rates of Return for the Principal Classes
of Securities, 1926–1985

Security	Average annual return
U.S. Treasury bills	3.4%
Long-term U.S. government bonds	4.1
Long-term corporate bonds	4.8
Common stocks	9.8

SOURCE: Ibbotson Associates, Inc., *Stocks, Bonds, Bills, and Inflation: 1986 Yearbook*, Chicago, Ill., February 1986, pp. 91, 95, 97, 99.

The departures from these long-term averages are both dramatic and extended. As shown in Table 6.8 an investment in common stocks at the beginning of any year in the first half of the 1970s and held until the end of 1979 would have had a total return less than that for Treasury bills. Indeed, for the 1973 to 1979 span, stocks were the lowest and Treasury bills were the highest return investment.

In a recent five-year period (1980 to 1984), stocks once again provided the highest returns. Note in Table 6.9, however, that Treasury bills outperformed long-term government bonds.

Table 6.8. Comparative Holding Period Total Returns
on Stocks, Treasury Bills, and Bonds for Selected Periods,
1970–1979

Holding period	Common stocks	Treasury bills	Government bonds	Corporate bonds
1970–1979	5.9%	6.3%	5.5%	6.2%
1971–1979	6.1	6.3	4.8	5.0
1972–1979	5.1	6.5	3.8	4.2
1973–1979	3.2	6.9	3.5	3.8
1974–1979	6.6	6.9	4.3	

SOURCE: Ibbotson Associates, Inc., *Stocks, Bonds, Bills, and Inflation: 1985 Yearbook*, Chicago, Ill., February 1985, pp. 91, 95, 97, 99.

Table 6.9. Rates of Return for the Principal Classes
of Securities, 1980–1984

Security	Average annual return
Common stocks	14.8%
Long-term corporate bonds	11.1
U.S. Treasury bills	11.0
Long-term U.S. government bonds	9.8

SOURCE: Ibbotson Associates, Inc., *Stocks, Bonds, Bills, and Inflation: 1986 Yearbook*, Chicago, Ill., February 1986, pp. 91, 95, 97, 99.

Valuation for the S&P 400—
An Illustration

The following valuation by a professional investor illustrates how a valuation for the S&P 400 was developed through a set of 10-year (1978 to 1988) forecasts of earnings, a dividend payout ratio, and a capitalization rate. The example also shows how GNP, corporate profits, and inflation projections provided underpinning for the forecast.[17] The sequel to this illustration of methodology is an appraisal of the forecasts midpoint in the projection span, that is, the degree of accuracy is reviewed with the benefit of five years of hindsight.[18] The stock valuation model used holds that stock prices are determined by:

- The current dividend yield
- An expected dividend growth rate
- An expected total return that provides a satisfactory risk premium over the yield to maturity on longer-term bonds

This model is made operational by the series of projections set forth in Table 6.10.

Table 6.10. Projected S&P 400 Common Stock Prices 1988

Current conditions (October 1978)			
Price Index: 113			Dividends: $5.45*

	Projected conditions (October 1988)		
	Least favorable	Most likely	Most favorable
Growth rates, 1978–1988			
GNP (nominal)	10%	9%	8%
S&P 400 earnings	11	10	9
S&P 400 dividends	12	11	10
1988 conditions			
Inflation rate	8.0%	6.0%	4.0%
Long-term interest rate	11.0	9.0	7.0
Dividend growth rate	9.5	9.0	8.5
Dividend payout	44.0	44.0	44.0
Price index			
Risk premium (1988)			
5.5%	241	280	352
4.5%	281	343	469
3.5%	337	441	704

*Later revised to $5.31 for 12 months ending September 30, 1978.

[17]These forecasts were made in 1978 by W. S. Gray and appeared in "Developing a Long-Term Outlook for the U.S. Economy and Stock Market," *Financial Analysts Journal*, July–August 1979, pp. 29—39.
[18]See William S. Gray, "The Stock Market and the Economy in 1988," *The Journal of Portfolio Management*, Summer 1984, pp. 73—80.

The following summarizes how the projections in Table 6.10 were derived, sets forth what actually happened from 1978 to 1983, and indicates where midcourse corrections were necessary:

Growth Rates, 1978–1988

- *Nominal GNP.* The most likely forecast of 9 percent was the product of a 3 percent growth in real GNP and a 6 percent inflation rate. Actual 1978 to 1983 growth in real GNP was only 1.3 percent. However, since the inflation rate averaged 7.4 percent per year, nominal GNP grew at an annual rate of 8.8 percent, or close to the projected "most likely" 9 percent for the 10-year span. With this additional five years of record to draw on, the 3 percent real growth was still considered appropriate for the remaining five years.

- *S&P 400 earnings.* Since business management had adjusted to inflation, corporate profits as a percentage of GNP were expected to recover somewhat. Consequently, earnings for the S&P 400 were forecast to increase at an annual rate of 10 percent. Actual 1978–1983 growth rate was 2.4 percent. The severity of the 1981–1982 recession had not been anticipated.

- *S&P 400 dividends.* The forecast 11 percent rate, which was higher than for earnings, was based on an expected increase in the payout ratio. Actual 1978–1983 growth rate in dividends was 6.6 percent. Again, it was not expected that the recession of 1981–1982 would be as long or severe. Midcourse correction was to revise the 11 percent growth rate to 9 percent for the 1983–1988 span.

Forecasts of 1988 Conditions

- *Inflation.* The inflation rate was expected to be less than the then-prevailing rate and in the 6 to 7 percent range. It was felt that inflation had become such an urgent problem that the political climate was ripe for a solution. Although actual inflation for 1978 to 1983 averaged 7.4 percent per year, it was expected that it would remain between 5 and 7 percent for 1983 to 1988.

- *Long-term interest rate.* Assuming a 3 percent real rate, the estimated range of 7 to 11 percent, with 9 percent being the most likely, was in tandem with inflation projections. On October 15, 1983, the yield on Aa industrial bonds was about 12.1 percent in the secondary market. It was anticipated that more normal rates would return and thus would increase the most likely figure by only 1 percent (from 9 to 10 percent).

- *Dividend growth rate.* The range for 1988 was anticipated to be 8.5 to 9.5 percent with most likely set at 9 percent. This factor remains unchanged after the 1983 review.

- *Dividend payout.* The dividend payout was set at the single figure of 44 percent in the table. The 44 percent figure represented an upward adjustment in the then existent payout ratio. Actual payout from 1978 to 1983 averaged 45 percent. In the 1983 review, the 1988 estimate is increased to 46 percent.

- *Risk premium.* The projected range was 3.5 to 5.5 percent over the S&P Composite Bond yield, with 4.5 percent selected as the most likely. The forecast of the risk premium in 1988 was based on an appraisal of the following five factors: (1) an economic system characterized by increased stability of final demand, (2) more financial leverage resulting from an increase in the percentage of long-term debt in corporate capitalization structures and higher interest costs, (3) growing institutionalization of common stock holdings which has permitted greater diversification and resulted in reduced specific risk, (4) less favorable tax treatment of both ordinary investment income and capital gains, and (5) the changed structure of expected returns from stocks with less return coming from dividend yield and more from capital appreciation. The conclusion was the premium forecast of 4 to 4.5 percent cited above. In the 1983 review, it was concluded that the premium forecast made in 1978 was in the right direction (less than for the 1926 to 1976 period) but that 3 to 3.5 percent was more appropriate for 1983 to 1988. The primary reason for this conclusion was the probability of rising inflation, which increases the risk of fixed-rate bonds and thereby reduces the return spread (risk premium) between stocks and bonds.[19]

Table 6.11 compares the 1978 set of projections for a most likely value for the S&P 400 in 1988 with the revised set of projections as of 1983.

---

[19]For additional research on this subject, see B. Copeland, "Inflation, Interest Rates, and Equity Risk Premia," *Financial Analysts Journal*, May–June 1982, pp. 32–43. A comprehensive analysis is provided in a monograph by R. F. Vandell and G. W. Kester, *A History of Risk Premia Estimates for Equities: 1944 to 1978*, Financial Analysts Research Foundation, Charlottesville, Va., 1983.

Table 6.11. Comparison of Original and Revised
Projections of 1988 Conditions for S&P 400

	Projections made in	
	1978	1983
Dividends, 1988	$15.47	$13.45
Interest rate, 1988	9.0%	10.0%
Risk premium	4.5%	3.5%
Discount rate	13.5%	13.5%
Dividend growth rate beyond 1988	9.0%	9.0%
Dividend yield, 1988	4.5%	4.5%
Value S&P 400 in 1988	343	299

This example demonstrates a disciplined approach to analyzing and valuing the market. It also illustrates the uncertainties involved in forecasting the performances of the stock market. The merit of using a range of estimates is clear.

7
Stock Market Sector Analysis

Sector Analysis Defined

As pointed out in Chapter 1, sector analysis is not an independent type of analysis but rather functions as a bridge between capital market analysis and security analysis. It has some of the characteristics of both. It transcends industries and provides insights into the stock market, thus, sector analysis is an important factor in broad policy decisions.

Management of investment portfolios includes increased selection of stocks from a universe that extends substantially beyond the traditional S&P-500 type of large, well-known, quality issues. The purpose is to improve diversification and to find sectors of the market that are priced less efficiently than larger capitalization stocks. In addition analysts recognize that the stock market consists of numerous large market sectors or segments that—in terms of group price movements and total return results—are characterized by disparate performance.

A variety of approaches deals with the reality that the market is not monolithic. Investors are interested in alternative ways of segmenting the market. There are four principal bases for forming stock market sectors:

- Financial characteristics of individual issues, such as P/E ratios, dividend yields, and size (market capitalization)
- Economic sectors, such as consumer nondurable goods, consumer durables, capital goods, transportation, finance, and technology
- Total return behavior of stocks (statistically formed homogeneous groups), based on the degree of correlation between stock returns
- Fundamental characteristics of firms, such as groups formed on the basis of growth, cyclicality, and stability of earnings

The following analyses of different market sector performances provide valuable insights into stock market behavior. Moreover, separating the market into sectors assists in the development of logical analytical specialization.

SEI Homogeneous Groups

One method for forming market sectors that has received substantial attention is combining stocks that in the past have had similar total return patterns.[1]

Using this method, SEI Corporation divides stocks into four sectors (homogeneous stock groups) based on historical total rate of return patterns. Specifically, SEI removes the impact of the market on each stock (using regression analysis) and groups the stocks on the basis of distinctive residual return patterns. Groups are formed so that the average correlation (comovement) between residual returns for any two stocks in the same group is high, whereas the correlation between any two stocks in two different groups is low.

Formation of the groups was initially undertaken by A. G. Becker, Incorporated, and was based on a statistical analysis of monthly total returns of the individual stocks over the 114-month period from December 31, 1962 through June 30, 1972.[2] Before the correlation coefficients between the individual stocks were calculated, the effects of the market (S&P 500) were deducted from each stock's monthly total return figures. These groups were formed through cluster

---

[1] For an early study of stock groups, see B. F. King, "Market and Industry Factors in Stock Price Behavior," *Journal of Business*, vol. 39, special supp., January 1966, University of Chicago Press. Subsequent well-known studies include: E. J. Elton, and M. J. Gruber, "Improved Forecasting through the Design of Homogeneous Groups," *Journal of Business*, October 1971, pp. 432–450; and J. L. Farrell, Jr., "Analyzing Covariation of Returns to Determine Homogeneous Stock Groupings," *Journal of Business*, April 1974. pp. 186–207.

[2] Becker maintained the series until November 1983, when it was acquired and is now produced by SEI Corporation.

analysis.[3] After their formation, the groups were judgmentally deter-mined to have growth, stable, or cyclical total return characteristics.

To ensure that the stock groups continue to exhibit appropriate return characteristics, a clustering of updated residual returns is repeated every six months, and the groups are thus periodically reformed. Such continuing analysis of the groups has produced substantial changes in composition.

As part of the update, a fourth group, energy, was identified and added in June 1981. Once the group was identified, the composition and return characteristics of this group were backdated from 1972 on.

Cumulative total return wealth indexes for the four homogeneous stock groups were developed beginning with December 31, 1972. These indexes were created by setting each of the four groups equal to 100 on the beginning date and multiplying each previous month's value by 1 plus the subsequent month's percentage change in total return, as weighted by market capitaliza-tion.

The value-weighted indexes in Figure 7.1 show that for the December 31, 1972 through December 31, 1986 period, the energy group had the largest cumulative total return, followed by the stable, cyclical, and high-growth groups. The lagging performance of the high-growth group is, in part, a result of the starting date. The impressive increase in growth stock values during the 1970–1972 period is not recorded. Instead, the indexes begin at the cyclical peak of the 1970–1972 market advance.

Figure 7.1 shows that, measured in terms of cumulative wealth indexes, the energy and stable groups increased more than fivefold (555 and 528 percent respectively) over the 14-year span. They significantly exceeded the index for the cyclical group (390 percent). The growth-stock group (244 percent) was far outperformed by all other groups, and, in fact, the group did not recover to its year-beginning 1973 level until late in 1982. The compound annual returns for the four groups over the entire span were as follows:

Energy	13.0%
Stable	12.6
Cyclical	10.2
Growth	6.6

Because this range is determined by the accident of the starting (and finishing) date, it should not be taken as an indication of relative values at a particular point in time.

---

[3]Cluster analysis is a statistical method of combining stocks into meaningful groups. By combining the two most highly correlated stocks and averaging their returns, the sample size is reduced by one stock. The averaged returns of the two combined stocks are then regressed on all the other stocks. This method is continued until the correlation falls below a required level.

90

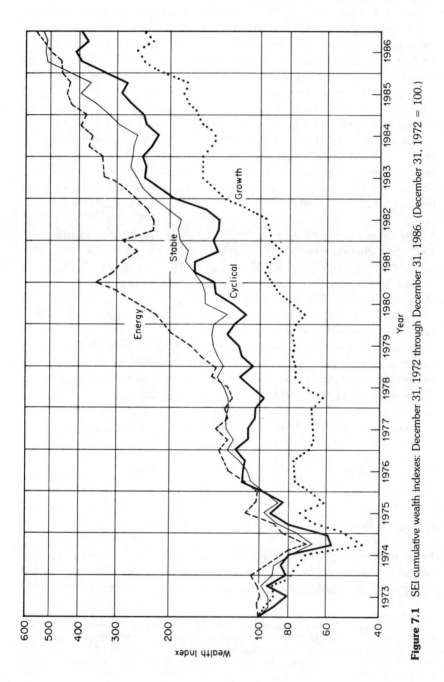

Figure 7.1 SEI cumulative wealth indexes: December 31, 1972 through December 31, 1986. (December 31, 1972 = 100.)

Table 7.1 compares the cyclical total return movements of the SEI groups with the S&P 500.[4] This table is more helpful, since it includes eight market peak and trough points for the measurement of returns.

Table 7.1. Comparative Cyclical Total Return Performance for S&P 500 and SEI Homogeneous Groups

	S&P 500	Growth	Stable	Cyclical	Energy
Dec.1972–Sept.1974	−42.7%	−53.5%	− 33.1%	− 42.9%	− 29.7%
Sept.1974–Dec.1976	+86.3	+60.0	+ 90.0	+109.3	+ 93.2
Dec.1976–Feb.1978	−14.2	−16.5	− 3.2	− 21.2	− 11.6
Feb.1978–Nov.1980	+86.6	+45.2	+ 22.9	+ 54.3	+ 220.6
Nov.1980–July 1982	−17.2	+ 6.4	+ 19.1	− 7.2	− 45.8
July 1982–Nov. 1983	+65.9	+61.4	+ 52.6	+ 85.3	+ 55.6
Nov.1983–July 1984	− 6.8	− 7.5	− 5.6	− 13.2	+ 2.8
July 1984–Dec. 1986*	+77.4	+70.3	+103.7	+ 79.8	+ 66.1

*Not a market peak.

NOTE: S&P 500 peaks and troughs based on cumulative month-end total returns.

Two principal conclusions can be drawn from the total return characteristics of the SEI homogeneous groups. First, performance differentials among major stock market sectors spanning cyclical advances and declines are striking. Second, on a cycle-by-cycle basis, over the eight cyclical swings, no clearcut group superiority existed.

FRS Industrial Groups

To demonstrate further the vastly different performance characteristics of stock market sectors, we analyze the cyclical price performance of a different set of sectors. In this instance stocks are grouped according to their earnings characteristics.

A number of fundamental company characteristics can be used to classify stocks into sectors. One variable almost universally selected is growth in earnings per share (EPS). FRS Associates has formed market sectors using both growth and cyclicality in earnings per share. Four industrial stock groups—composed of major corporations—were formed late in 1972.

The industrial groups are equally weighted and rebalanced monthly.[5]

[4]In a number of instances, the dates for the S&P 500 cyclical turning points and the percentage changes are different than those in Table 2.6 (Chapter 2). Table 7.1 shows total returns (price change plus dividends) rather than prices only. Furthermore, month-end prices, rather than daily close prices, are used in calculating total returns. In this manner, the data for the S&P 500 and the SEI groups are made comparable.

[5]The FRS groups differ from the SEI groups which are statistically derived homogeneous groups, market-value weighted, and reconstructed every six months (FRS Associates, Los Altos, California).

By analyzing historical EPS growth rates and other company characteristics over a 10-year span, groups of 15 stocks were placed in the following categories: high growth, above average growth, average growth, and major cyclical. Stocks initially chosen have been kept in their respective groups, except for a limited number of changes due to mergers. Accordingly the returns subsequent to late 1972 have no postselection bias. These groups are well diversified in terms of industries except for the average growth group, which has 40 percent of its companies in the food processing industry.

At the time of construction, to qualify for the high-growth group, stocks were required to have EPS compound annual growth rates of 11 percent or more over the previous 10-year span. Above-average-growth stocks had rates between 9 percent and 11 percent, and average growth stocks had rates between 4 percent and 9 percent. The fourth industrial sector, major cyclicals, was restricted to stocks with EPS growth patterns with pronounced cyclicality.

If the price performance of a group is to be meaningful, there must be reasonable consistency (correlation) in price movements of individual stocks constituting the group, and the performance of the group must be distinguishable from those of other groups. Statistical tests were undertaken over the 1974–1979 span to determine the validity of the four FRS stock groups. The research concluded that the price performances of the groups were sufficiently distinctive to represent different sectors of the stock market.

It is to be seen from Figure 7.2 that, based on price performance for the 1972–1986 span, the average-growth group far outperformed the other three groups by the end of the 14-year span. In contrast, the high-growth group did not recover to its December 1972 level until late 1984. Based on December 1972 equalling 100, the following are the relative price indexes as of the end of December 1986:

Average-growth stocks	372.54
Above-average-growth stocks	244.36
Major cyclicals	216.01
High-growth stocks	154.12

Table 7.2 shows the cyclical price movements (based on month-end prices) in the period from December 1972 to December 1986 for the S&P 500 and the four FRS industrial stock groups. The cycles are, again, in terms of the S&P 500. The pronounced differences in price performance in four market cycles among the FRS groups and in comparison with the S&P 500[6] are to be seen.

[6]Note that the S&P 500 is market-value weighted, whereas the FRS series are equal-value weighted.

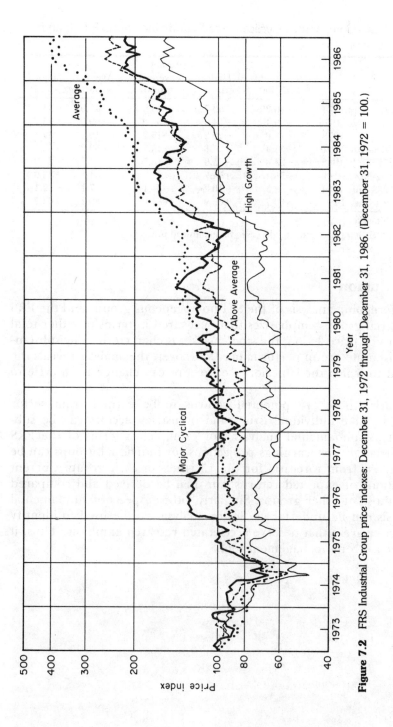

Figure 7.2 FRS Industrial Group price indexes: December 31, 1972 through December 31, 1986. (December 31, 1972 = 100.)

Table 7.2. Comparative Cyclical Price Performance of S&P 500 and FRS Industrial Groups

	S&P 500	High-growth	Above-average growth	Average growth	Major cyclicals
Dec. 1972–Sept.1974	−46.2%	−53.7%	−43.5%	−41.0%	−33.8%
Sept. 1974–Dec. 1976	+69.1	+54.0	+65.0	+69.9	+95.7
Dec. 1976–Feb. 1978	−19.0	−22.2	−15.7	−10.1	−34.1
Feb. 1978–Nov. 1980	+61.4	+27.8	+29.7	+52.2	+42.3
Nov. 1980–July 1982	−23.8	− 5.6	+18.7	− 4.3	−25.0
July 1982-Nov. 1983	+55.4	+54.7	+16.2	+61.5	+86.0
Nov. 1983–July 1984	− 9.5	−10.2	− 4.1	− 7.1	−22.1
July 1984–Dec. 1986*	+60.7	+65.9	+81.0	+89.1	+63.7

*Not a market peak.

NOTE: S&P 500 peaks and troughs based on month-end prices.

Conclusion

The foregoing analysis of the SEI homogeneous groups and the FRS industrial groups emphasizes that, measured in terms of either total returns or price action, the stock market is characterized by substantial disparate group performance. Moreover, the analysis reveals the extent to which the superiority of groups can change from cycle to cycle.

Clearly, there are potential returns to be earned from sector analysis. Like individual issues and industries, sectors can be subjected to fundamental analysis. For example, in terms of the FRS industrial groups, earnings projections for individual groups can be generated from forecasts for the 15 issues in each group. Current valuations of expected returns can then be derived and compared with those of other groups. Similarly, other aspects of fundamental analysis can be undertaken. Sector analysis can be used to identify attractive areas that deserve accelerated research emphasis. Thus, it can be a strong management tool.

8

Nature and Sources of the Analyst's Information

Major Sources of Information

Most corporate data used by the security analyst will come from four major sources. Two may be called "original" parallel sources: information sent by the company to its stockholders and the press and material filed by the company with a regulatory body—most often the Securities and Exchange Commission (SEC).

The third source is broad-based financial services, such as Moody's or Standard and Poor's, which reproduce or summarize nearly all the information from the original sources as it becomes available. For many analytical purposes, it is reasonable to rely on the material as restated in the various manuals, supplements, or current information services of these organizations.[1] Another independent subscription source is *The*

---

[1] Such publications include Moody's Investors Service, *Industrial, Public Utility, Bank & Finance*, and *Transportation* manuals as well as the *Bond Record*; and Standard & Poor's Statistical Service publications of the *Security Price Index Record*, the monthly *Current Statistics*, and *Basic Statistics*. To understand the implications of changes in accounting requirements on financial statements, analysts refer to publications such as the FASB's Accounting Standards *Original Pronouncements* and *Current Text*, Miller's

Value Line Investment Survey, which conducts a systematic review of 1700 companies in 92 industries. When doing in-depth primary research, however, the analyst generally should consult original sources to ascertain that nothing of importance is overlooked.

The fourth source of information are the recent and rapidly expanding computerized databases accompanied by software programs ("packages" or "systems") for analyzing and arraying the data. There are many vendors in this field, and the number is ever increasing. In some instances, the databases represent compilations ranging from several hundred to several thousand companies and cover a span of up to 10 or 20 years. Because of the impact on company-reported data of such factors as acquisitions and mergers, changes in accounting procedures, discontinued operations, and extraordinary items, the analyst will need to check the consistency of databases that extend over a number of years. Since the data will be neatly arrayed on the computer screen in the vendor's format with the ratios computed, accepting such "processed" data with inadequate analysis can be tempting.

In addition to these four distinctive sources remains the vast heterogeneous grouping of information not easily categorized, including a panoply of publications, ranging from trade journals to government publications. These sources provide important information relative to specific industries, economic sectors, and U.S. and foreign economies. Many companies regularly provide supplemental statistical and other data to security analysts and others that request it. This source includes important information provided by corporate officers at meetings of Societies of Security Analysts. Field trips by analysts to corporate headquarters and discussions with management supplement published information. In addition, analysts gain insights through discussions with suppliers, competitors, customers, unions, and distributors. Another source of information is the body of expectational data providing consensus earnings forecasts prepared by security analysts. Suppliers in this field include Lynch, Jones and Ryan's IBES, Zacks, and S&P's Earnings Forecaster, which combined cover more than 8000 equity securities.

The amount of material available from all sources varies widely. At one extreme are small, privately held corporations that are subject to practically no regulatory requirements but typically issue audited financial statements to their stockholders. As long as such companies do not (1) issue securities to be publicly offered or sold in interstate commerce or through the mail, (2) register securities on a national securities exchange, or (3) have at least $3 million in assets and 500 or more

---

GAAP Guide, and *Accounting Trends & Techniques* by the AICPA. An additional source of analytical information is the wealth of research publications prepared by the large brokerage firms.

stockholders, they are not required to submit financial statements and other information to the SEC.

At the other extreme are corporations with publicly listed securities that must fulfill all SEC financial reporting requirements for reports filed with the Commission and follow generally accepted accounting principles (GAAP)—as determined by the Financial Accounting Standards Board (FASB)—in audited statements provided stockholders and the general public.[2]

Reports to Regulatory Bodies Other Than the SEC

Some companies in industries subject to regulation by public agencies are required to file with those agencies financial statements that are available for public inspection. Most of these reports are considerably more elaborate than the average published statements.

Public Utilities

In every state, public utility companies are subject to comprehensive regulation by state public service commissions. In general, these regulatory bodies have jurisdiction over rates, issuance of securities, property acquisitions, standards of service, accounting methods for purposes of regulatory reporting, and so forth. These companies must file comprehensive and detailed annual reports, which are open to inspection by the public at the commissions' offices. As mentioned, these reports usually contain substantially more detailed financial and operating statistics than are found in annual reports to stockholders. In some cases monthly operating statements are also filed and are available for public inspection.

In addition to submitting information to state commissions, all interstate electric and natural gas companies file similarly detailed annual reports with the Federal Energy Regulatory Commission. These reports

---

[2]Generally accepted accounting principles (GAAP) consist of a set of standards covering the preparation of financial statements. These standards have been developed and promulgated primarily by three bodies over a span of 45 years. The first was the Committee on Accounting Procedure (1939 to 1959) which issued *Accounting Research Bulletins*. It was superseded by the Accounting Principles Board (APB), which from 1959 to 1973 issued *Opinions*. In 1973, the APB was, in turn, succeeded by the Financial Accounting Standards Board (FASB), which issues *Statements of Financial Accounting Standards*. The pronouncements of the FASB and its predecessors do not have statutory standing; their authority rests on their acceptance by the accounting profession, state CPA licensing boards, corporate management, and financial analysts, and on SEC-required use of FASB standards. SEC regulation S-X, Rule 4-01 requires that financial statements filed with the commission comply with GAAP.

can be inspected at the commission's headquarters in Washington, D.C., and, in certain cases, at its regional offices.

Although virtually all the material included in these commission reports is interesting and important, its presentation usually requires considerable interpretation to reveal the investment significance. Certain financial services assemble these data together with the appropriate ratios and unit figures for various periods of years.

Insurance Companies

Insurance companies file detailed annual statements of uniform character (the so-called convention reports) with the insurance department of each state in which the concern does business. In addition, every three years the state of domicile (with the participation of other state departments) audits. These audit results are open to inspection and are the source of the underwriting experience compiled by *Best Reports*, although they provide no insight into the quality of investment portfolios.

Railroads

Railroads file detailed quarterly statements with the Interstate Commerce Commission (ICC) and even more complete annual reports are required by the Commission. Many of the data so furnished are reproduced in the annual *Transportation Statistics of Railways in the United States* (the "blue book") published by the ICC. The uniform system of accounts prescribed by the ICC is not ordinarily very useful to the security analyst but will provide maintenance and other operating information. Accounting practices prescribed by the ICC do much to obscure the health and profitability of carriers.

Companies Subject to SEC Regulation

Most companies studied by the analyst will have securities listed on a registered securities exchange, will have had a public offering of securities since 1933, or both. In such cases, four sorts of material are available to the analyst:

- Basic registration statement or prospectus
- Annual reports (including the Form 10-K Report)

- Interim reports (10-Q Reports)
- 8-K event-oriented reports

The Basic Registration Statement (or Prospectus)

The basic registration statement provides a detailed description of the company's business and properties and often serves as a starting point for detailed analysis.[3] This is the primary disclosure document that serves the objectives of SEC rule 10(b)–5. In the case of long-established concerns, much of the financial data contained in the registration statements for earlier years can be obtained from the security manuals (such as Moody's or Standard & Poor's).

Proxy Statement

Proxy statements sent to shareholders to solicit their votes at annual and special meetings are another source of information for the analyst's study. They disclose the terms of executive employment, incentive and retirement programs, shareholdings of directors, and all proposals dealing with corporate performance.

How officers and directors respond to shareholders' recommendations dealing with social responsibilities and government issues tells a great deal about the "corporate culture." Compensation plans and inside ownership may also be indicative of the extent to which management and shareholder interests coincide. "Golden parachutes" and employment contracts are also disclosed in the proxy statement. If the proxy statement is concerned with mergers or acquisitions, the information equals that of a prospectus.

Annual Data

Data included in a company's annual report to stockholders are, within the latitude of GAAP, subject to considerable management discretion. However, annual reports now contain much more information than formerly and thus are more helpful to the analyst. In fact, the distinction between the information included in annual reports (as stipulated by the SEC) and that filed on form 10-K has been reduced.

Data filed with the SEC are mandatory. Each corporation with listed securities must file annually with the SEC a Form 10-K that contains

[3]Form S-1, 17 CFR (Code of Federal Regulations) 239.11.

several important exhibits of financial data in prescribed detail and additional material helpful in analyzing and understanding a company's performance.

The Form 10-K contains four parts: Part I is principally a description of the company's business activities, including information regarding industry segments. Part II covers the market for the company's common stock, selected financial data, discussion and analysis by management of the company's financial condition and operating results, and financial statements. Part III pertains to directors and executive officers, compensation, stock options, related party transactions, and similar matters. Part IV consists primarily of supplementary financial statements and financial statement schedules, such as property, plant, and equipment, and accumulated depreciation.

The 10-K report contains the following financial statements and supplementary data:

1. Lines of business for the past three years in terms of sales and income before extraordinary items and income taxes; the data cover those product lines that contributed 10 percent or more to the total sales or income before taxes and extraordinary items

2. Balance sheets for the past two years

3. Income statements for three years

4. A statement of changes in financial position

The latter two financial exhibits must be in comparative columnar form for the close of the three latest fiscal years. In addition, the statements have to be audited and prepared according to generally accepted accounting principles.[4]

Some companies required to file Form 10-K with the SEC send copies to stockholders along with their annual reports or include the 10-K as part of the printed annual report document. All companies will provide copies of this report if requested in writing.

In addition, each company publishes an annual financial statement for distribution among stockholders and the general public. These reports are somewhat similar in format and must have the financial statements required in the 10-K reports along with other data. In totality, they normally contain slightly less financial data than the 10-K, but they often exhibit financial histories for as much as the past five or ten years that highlight certain vital financial information. The major items shown in 10-K reports but not in annual company reports are certain detailed footnote disclosures and extensive information on the board of

---

[4]See SEC rules 17 CFR 210.3-01, 210.3-02, and 210.4-01 (a)(1).

directors. Companies are allowed by the SEC to incorporate by reference from their annual reports to their 10-K reports to avoid duplication.

Interim Reports

Interim information is uniformly available for publicly listed companies. These concerns supply quarterly financial statements to all stockholders and interested parties, but quarterly SEC reports (10-Q) must be requested. The analyst needs to weigh carefully investment judgments based on quarterly reports, because they contain estimates that are not used in the annual report and year-end adjustments can be substantial.

Quarterly reports are usually unaudited, although auditor involvement is increasing through the review process. Certain quarterly data required in 10-Q reports must be included in the company's annual report.[5]

The development of the 10-Q report is an example of the increased information available to modern investors. As of the first fiscal quarter of 1970, reports on Form 10-Q became an SEC requirement for those companies that had previously filed semi-annual 9-K reports. In place of the 9-K report, the SEC required quarterly financial reports for the first three quarters of the fiscal year.[6] This information did not have to be supplied to stockholders.

Subsequent to 1970, the SEC issued several releases on interim reporting requirements. In a major statement concerning this issue, the SEC published *Accounting Series Release No. 177* (September 1975). Under this ruling the following items became 10-Q report requirements:

1. The most recent quarter's condensed income statement compared with that for the same quarter of the previous year and the year-to-date figures for both years

[5] As stated in Accounting Series Release 177, Sept. 10, 1975, "Notice of Adoption of Amendments to Form 10-Q and Regulation S-X Regarding Interim Financial Reporting," *SEC Docket*, in a company's annual stockholder report: "...Disclosure of net sales, gross profit, income before extraordinary items and cumulative effect of a change in accounting, per share data based upon such income, and net income for each quarter within the two most recent fiscal years and any subsequent fiscal period for which income statements are presented, is appropriate for the protection of investors in the case of large companies whose shares are actively traded."

[6] "Securities Exchange Act of 1934 Release No. 9004, October 28, 1970," *SEC Docket* (Adoption of Form 10-Q, Rescission of Form 9-K and Amendment of Rules 13a–13 and 15d–13).

2. The recent quarter's condensed source and application-of-funds statement on a year-to-date basis for the current and previous year

3. The recent quarter's condensed balance sheet[7]

4. Pro forma information on business combinations stated as a purchase

5. Conformity with the generally accepted accounting principles governing interim financial reports

6. Increased disclosure relative to accounting changes[8]

These changes forced independent public accountants to become more involved in interim financial reports.

8-K Current Report

The 8-K report must be filed with the SEC within 15 days of the occurrence of a specified event. The most important events covered by the 8-K report are:

1. Changes in control of the registered company

2. Acquisition or disposition of assets

3. Bankruptcy or receivership

4. Changes in certifying accountant

5. Resignation of a director or directors

6. Other materially important items

7. Financial statements and exhibits of acquired business or real estate properties of significant size

---

[7]According to SEC rule 10–01 (c)(1), 17 CFR 210.10–01 (c) (1), a condensed balance sheet for the corresponding quarter of the preceding fiscal year needs to be provided if necessary for understanding the impact of seasonal fluctuations of the company's financial condition.

[8]"Accounting Series Release No. 177, September 10, 1975," *SEC Docket*, September 1975 (Notice of Adoption of Amendments to Form 10-Q and Regulation S-X Regarding Interim Financial Reporting). One of the more controversial issues of this release is that concerning the "preferability" of accounting changes. Release No. 177 stated: "In connection with accounting changes, a letter from the registrant's independent public accountant is required to be filed in which the accountant states whether or not the changes are to an alternative principle which in his judgment are preferable under the circumstances." Arthur Andersen & Co. challenged the legality of the SEC to require public accountants to issue a statement of "preferability" when an accounting change occurred. However, the courts upheld the provisions of ASR #177 (and ASR #150) and rejected the Arthur Andersen motion for a preliminary injunction against the SEC. (See "Arthur Andersen Is Set Back in Bid to Bar SEC Ruling," *The Wall Street Journal*, Sept. 7, 1976, p. 18.)

When items such as these are reported in 8-K reports, the timeliness of the data can help investors see the latest developments with respect to the financial affairs of the business.

Unlisted Companies

The original pressure both for detailed annual reports to stockholders and for the publication of interim financial statements came largely from the New York Stock Exchange and thus related to listed companies. This pressure paved the way for the SEC's regulations in this area. However, unlisted companies, with $3 million or more of assets and 500 or more stockholders must file with the SEC the same kinds of reports as listed companies. Furthermore, their annual reports to stockholders must comply with GAAP as promulgated by the FASB.

Segment Reporting and Other Disclosures

The improvement in corporate reporting has been far-reaching. Some areas in which there has been an increase of available information include the breakdown of sales by products or product lines (segment reporting) and by consuming industries, research and development costs, long-term lease arrangements, wages and salaries ("employee statistics"), foreign operations, capital expenditures, inventory valuation, and depreciation.[9] Of these improvements, segment reporting has proved to be the most valuable.[10]

Production, Property, and Capital Budget Data

The dollar figures supplied in the balance sheet and income account should be supplemented where relevant by certain additional qualitative information. The analyst would like to have the following material if available:

---

[9]There have been suggestions that companies should supply information pertaining to fixed and variable costs so that analysts might more accurately estimate profit at various levels of activity. Clearly, such information would be helpful to the skilled analyst, particularly if the analyst is concerned primarily with projecting earnings on a quarter-by-quarter or year-by-year basis. Prevailing on corporate management to provide these data may prove to be a long range undertaking, but this should not deter the effort.

[10]Another development was adjustment of historical cost data for inflation. Inflation has recently subsided some in the United States, but the marked inflation of the 1970s and early 1980s resulted first in the SEC and then the FASB requiring about 1200 large companies to disclose certain effects of changing prices on their financial position and operating results. These requirements became voluntary starting in 1987.

1. Orders booked and unfilled orders (when this information is material to an understanding of the company's business, it is required in the company's 10-K report)

2. Productive capacity where relevant

3. Production in units where relevant

4. Description of property owned and amount and quantity of any mineral properties

5. Capital expenditure projections (capital budget) and research and development budgets

6. Patent and lease expirations

Most of this information is contained in registration statements relating to security offerings, in proxy material bearing on mergers and the like, or in 10-K reports. It is not so frequently supplied in the annual reports themselves.

Computerized Databases and Software Systems

A major objective of security analysis is to derive information from data. This requires gathering data, putting them into usable form, and analyzing them in a systematic manner. The advent and widespread availability of the personal computer has important implications for how the security analyst performs these steps.

Databases

Data can be gathered from computerized databases (or data banks) available on a time-sharing basis, on magnetic media, or by optical storage. Although many such bases exist, our focus is on financial statement databases for use in fundamental analysis.

Reported versus Adjusted. Databases differ importantly in terms of the universe of companies covered and the period of years for which data are compiled. They also differ in regard to the extent to which the data are taken *as reported* by individual companies in their financial statements and the extent to which they are *adjusted and restated* by security analysts. Practically all data banks are adjusted for stock splits and significant stock dividends. However, in those instances where there have been acquisitions and mergers or major changes in accounting, the differences in reported and adjusted data over a span of years can be substantial and thus important. Accordingly, in using a computerized data bank, the security analyst should understand whether the data are as reported or adjusted.

Both reported and adjusted data are of interest to the security analyst. Reported earnings data help in analyzing past price performance, whereas adjusted data are essential for a consistent picture of a company's growth and profitability across a number of years. Adjusted data are also essential in effectively comparing the performance of companies.

Computerized databases are secondary sources of information. In a sense, databases that are on a reported basis are comparable to Moody's and Standard & Poor's manuals. Accordingly, the same caveat applies to them as to information provided in the manuals: Original sources should be consulted when doing primary research. For data banks on a reported basis, analysts need to make the aforementioned adjustments for such factors as acquisitions and mergers, changes in accounting procedures, and discontinued operations. For those data banks that are on an adjusted basis, analysts will need to understand fully the nature of the adjustments made to determine whether they are consistent with their organization's practices.

The differentiation between reported and adjusted data becomes a generic basis for categorizing data banks. The following descriptions give a snapshot of some current products being continually up-dated.

"As-Reported" Databases. The following represent primarily the "as reported" category:

- *Value Line Data Base II.* Covers comprehensive financial data derived from annual and 10-K reports for approximately 1700 major industrial, transportation, utility, and financial companies. Annual data begin in 1955 and quarterly data in 1963. An extensive series of ratios and relationships are calculated. Prior years' figures are not restated for acquisitions and mergers. Lines of business are restated if the company does so. The Value Line earnings and projection file provides annual and quarterly earnings projections by Value Line's research department as well as stock timeliness rankings.

- *Disclosure II Data Base.* Contains business and financial information from reports filed with the SEC for more than 10,000 companies. Three years of income statement data and two years of balance sheet figures are made available. No ratios are computed.

- *Media General Financial Services.* Provides 10 years of financial data on 5000 companies. The data are compiled from company annual reports, SEC 10-K, interim reports, SEC 10-Q, and wire releases. Included are income, balance sheet, revenues, earnings (on a quarterly basis), and industry information. Fundamental ratio analysis, as well as price and trading volume data, are provided.

Adjusted Database. *Standard & Poor's Compustat Services (Compustat) Data Base* is the major supplier of an "adjusted" database that consists of up to 20 years of annual information and 10 years of quarterly figures for more than 6000 industrials and in excess of 500 utilities, telephone companies, and banks. These data are extracted from annual reports to stockholders and filings with the SEC. "Standardized data definitions and collection procedures" are employed to provide comparability among companies.

The potential for developing electronic data systems for compiling and retrieving information on public companies is illustrated by SEC experimentation with its effort bearing the acronym EDGAR. Another information retrieval product is the National Automated Accounting Research System (NAARS), sponsored by the AICPA, which has 5 years of on-line annual reports (full text), footnotes, and 10-K supplemental schedules on 4200 companies. Also included are inflation-adjusted information and earnings-per-share exhibits. Acronyms representing accounting concepts facilitate the user's search for specific information.

Future growth in the market for comprehensive databases will depend largely on further technological developments that reduce the cost of getting and manipulating data. Although the demand remains high for anticipated earnings, dividends, and payout ratio information, there is also a trend toward the compilation of specialty databases with emphasis on industries such as energy and health care.[11] Other trends include the further integration of macroeconomic, industry, and company databases and expansion of databases to keep pace with the movement toward international diversification in portfolio management, although this move is fraught with the problems of accounting data inconsistency.[12]

[11]Based on an interview with D. Berman, Executive Vice-President, and S. Chamberlin, partner, of Lynch, Jones & Ryan, New York.

[12]One of the leaders in adjusting international indices for comparability is the Morgan Stanley Capital International Perspective personal computer version which provides over 400 data items on approximately 2000 of the largest companies in 19 countries. Another product is offered by IBES International with information on 3800 stocks in 22 countries. International databases are also being developed for some 3000 industrial companies in 24 countries as Worldscope Industrial Company Profiles, a published and time-sharing service, by Wright Investors' Service of Bridgeport, Connecticut.

Software Programs

Putting data in usable form for analysis involves not only formatting financial data derived from reports to stockholders, the SEC, and other regulatory agencies but also calculating the ratios, relationships, and growth rates considered necessary for analytical purposes. In addition, analysts must establish a consistent framework for the comparative analysis of companies.

In this burgeoning and highly competitive field of endeavor a host of vendors are providing computer programs for accomplishing this step. The programs differ greatly in scope and nature. They reflect the analytical and valuation logic of the designer and seek to cope with today's information explosion. It is a fast-paced business requiring incorporation of distinctive features to meet specific analytical needs.

Purchase of software programs requires examination of the spectrum available to determine which programs will perform analytical requirements most effectively and will be compatible with other software packages in use. Selection should be based on the best complement to an institution's analytical and valuation process.

Suppliers in this field constitute a heterogeneous group composed of brokerage houses, specialty software organizations, investment managers (such as banks), and investment consulting firms. Some originate databases; others obtain data from an originating organization and add unique software systems to create proprietary products.

Although the many software programs on the market vary widely in terms of capability, they all typically sort and screen data, calculate ratios and other relationships, and construct reports. They provide for downloading of data to electronic spreadsheets as designated by the program or by the analyst to meet specific needs. Examples of software systems include the following:

- *Salomon Brothers' Stockfacts.* This time-sharing system provides access, for those who subscribe independently, to Compustat, Value Line, IBES, and Zacks. Balance sheet, income statement, sources and uses of funds, and restated financial data are available on both an annual and a quarterly basis. The software system centers on a unique fundamental factor model and a dividend discount model, two models used in deriving five-year growth rates for sales and earnings, determining economic factor sensitivities and line of business breakdowns, and forecasting returns for more than 4500 companies. Growth projections are in terms of a base-case economic scenario and an input-output model. The program is interactive, allowing the analyst to alter the economic scenario and to insert projections into the dividend discount model. Forecasts by Salomon's industry analysts are also included.[13]

---

[13]For an in-depth account of the development of the fundamental factor model, see *The Evolution of a New Approach to Investment Risk*, Salomon Brothers, New York, May 1984. Further changes are anticipated in the *Stockfacts* software system.

- *FactSet Data Systems.* The *FactSet* software system presently uses Compustat, IBES, Value Line, and Zack's databases. A proprietary feature is the display and analysis of a company's financial statements, profitability ratios, growth rates, and stock valuation. The results for the last 12 months are superimposed on a 10-year record. Another proprietary feature is an iterative and interactive forecasting model which recognizes the complex interactions among corporate asset investment decisions, financing of these investments, management of them, and growth in earnings. The model allows analysts to test a range of assumptions and sensitivities and generates pro forma financial statements.[14]

- *Drexel Burnham Lambert's Decision Analysis Investment Systems (DAIS).* The *DAIS* system covers more than 8000 companies. The fundamental databases are comprised of financial statement information from Compustat, Value Line, and data covering approximately 600 companies developed by Drexel Burnham Lambert (DBL) analysts. The expectational databases consist of forecasts compiled by Zacks, IBES, and earnings, dividend, and value estimates by DBL analysts. Valuation is based on the firm's dividend discount model and on "historical models" which analyze a stock universe in terms of such relative valuation measures as price-earnings and price-to-book ratios. The system is interactive and enables users to simulate alternative scenarios. Sensitivity analysis can be undertaken on the dividend discount model to determine the impact of changed assumptions on a company's implied rate of return.

- *Shearson Lehman Brothers' Finstat.* The on-line portion of this software system employs the Interactive Data Corporation's (IDC) database of price and related information, Zack's Investment Research, and IBES data on expectational earnings, and Compustat Financial Data Bases. The system provides company annual and quarterly formats, industry composites, and business segment analysis. The system also employs a proprietary database of over 2600 large market capitalization companies with an average of 11 years of annual data and over 5 years of quarterly data for over 2000 companies. This database, for use with monthly diskettes, includes adjustments made to company-reported data by the firm's data processors primarily for nonrecurring and extraordinary items. It provides profitability and other ratios, growth rates, capital structure proportions, and a percentage breakdown of assets.

---

[14]Based on an interview with Howard Wille, President, Factset Data Systems, New York.

- *Interactive Data Corporation.* The company's PC Screen product accesses Compustat, IBES, and other financial data on over 6500 companies and provides a spectrum of financial data for fundamental analysis. The *DataSheet* product enables analysts to massage data accessed from Compustat, IBES, Extel (international data), and the Value Line universe.

- *Lotus Development, Lotus One Source.* This software system incorporates Compustat, Value Line, Media General, IBES, daily stock prices, Ford Investor Services, and *Disclosure II*. The system makes it possible to manipulate and integrate databases to undertake comprehensive analysis of industries and companies. Substantial ratio and performance analysis is also available.

- *Shaw Data Services Inc., Research Services.* In terms of fundamental analysis, this software system uses four databases: Shaw's Security Evaluation Service (S/EV), Merrill Lynch Data Service, IBES, and BARRA Beta Coefficients. Detailed financial information and comparative analysis of companies and industries are provided.

The personal computer, with a database and the appropriate software system, becomes a powerful tool for security analysts. It frees them to analyze the data, develop projections, and value individual companies, because they can spend less time collecting, arraying, and processing data. To facilitate detailed analysis, companies can be aggregated more readily, traditional industry financial series can be created, and broader sector or homogeneous group data can be assembled. Growing use of personal computers will also allow greater flexibility in running calculations and testing alternative sets of forecasts.[15]

The analyst must, however, not lose an essential inquisitive and skeptical view of all financial statements just because they come in large quantities convenient for further processing. *Whether adjustments are required for consistency and comparability will not be disclosed without the application of informed judgment to the raw figures.*

Other Information Sources

Supplementary Economic Information

Security analysts use a substantial amount of noncompany information dealing with the economy as a whole, with a particular segment of it, and

---

[15]However, use of the personal computer by the analyst will not be without its challenges. In this regard see J. Kolman, "Is the Microcomputer Becoming a Menace for Analysts?" *Institutional Investor*, August 1985, pp. 245–246.

with industries. Much material may be found in the weekly and monthly publications of the Department of Commerce, and the monthly *Survey of Current Business* and *Business Conditions Digest* are indispensable. Also available are the *U.S. Industrial Outlook*, Department of Agriculture crop reports, and the Bureau of Mines output data. Other important sources are the *Economic Report of the President* and the *Federal Reserve Bulletin*(s) and *Flow of Funds Accounts* prepared by the Board of Governors of the Federal Reserve System. These are but a few of the government and governmental agencies publications pertinent for examination.

Trade Journals

Many important summary industry figures are published at frequent intervals in the various trade journals. In these publications will be found a continuous and detailed picture of the current and prospective state of the industry. Thus, analysts can usually acquire without undue difficulty a fairly complete knowledge of the history and problems of the industry with which they are dealing. Sometimes analysts can obtain unofficial data relating to individual concerns. For example, various trade papers carry the weekly output (estimated) of each automobile company, the current rate of production of the major steel and copper companies, or an estimate of the season's crop for each sugar producer.[16]

Official Documents

In times past, when many corporations were highly secretive about their affairs, the wide-awake analyst was often able to unearth little-known information in various kinds of official documents. (Examples were reports of the Federal Trade Commission and the U.S. Coal Commission.) Today, new information may be found in the elaborate hearings and lengthy opinions of such government organizations as the SEC and the ICC.

Requests for Direct Information from the Company

Published information may often be supplemented to an important extent by private inquiry or interviews with the management. There is

---

[16]Much of this type of data is republished in the *Wall Street Journal*. For a comprehensive listing of industry trade journals as well as an excellent listing of investment information sources, see J. B. Cohen, E. D. Zinbarg, and A. Ziekel, *Investment Analysis and Portfolio Management*, 4th ed., Richard D. Irwin, Homewood, Ill. 1982.

no reason why stockholders should not ask for information on specific points, and in many cases all or part of the data asked for will be furnished. Never forget that a stockholder is an owner of the business and an employer of its officers. The investor is entitled not only to ask legitimate questions but also to have them answered, unless there is some persuasive reason to the contrary.

Increasingly, managements are giving frank and adequate answers to pertinent queries. This includes the explanation of obscure or unusual items in the financial statements. Excellent working arrangements have been established between security analysts and corporate executives through the activities of the more than 50 analyst societies that are members of the Financial Analysts Federation. The luncheon meetings of these organizations are addressed each year by scores of company heads, who often give insights into the operations, problems, and prospects of their corporations. Company-sponsored presentations by entire management teams, often on site, provide additional opportunities for analysts to gain a sense of management philosophy.

Direct corporate contacts provide less-filtered information than is frequently available from brokerage reports. Analysts can focus on issues pertinent to their organization's investment criteria and time horizons. Analysts must be careful, however, that they are not simply reporters of management's expectations. They must adhere to their own views of the company's strengths, product position, financial control, and growth prospects. Where possible, analysts should talk with several branches of the management structure to obtain necessary in-depth information.

9

Qualitative and Quantitative Factors in Security Analysis and the Margin of Safety Concept

After analysts have learned what information is available and where to find it, they face the harder question of how to use it. Analyzing a security involves an analysis of the business. Such a study could be carried to an unlimited degree of detail, hence practical judgment must be exercised to determine how far the process should go. Naturally, the circumstances will bear on the decision. A buyer of a $10,000 bond would not consider as thorough an analysis as would a large insurance company considering the purchase of a $5 million block of stock. The latter's study would still be less detailed than that made by investment bankers underwriting an issue. From another angle, a less intensive analysis is needed in selecting a high-grade bond yielding, say, 9 percent, than in seeking a well-secured issue yielding 10.5 percent or an unquestioned bargain in the field of common stocks.

Extent of Analysis and Value of Data

The analyst must exercise a sense of proportion in deciding how deep to delve. In choosing and dealing with the materials of analysis, one must consider not only inherent importance and dependability but also accessibility and convenience. The analyst must not be misled by the availability of a mass of data (e.g., in the reports of the railroads to the Interstate Commerce Commission) into making elaborate studies of nonessentials.

However, it is frequently necessary to resign oneself to the lack of significant information because it can be secured only by expenditure of more effort than can be spared or the problem will justify. This would be true of some of the elements involved in a complete business analysis—for instance, the extent to which an enterprise depends on patent protection or geographical advantages or favorable labor conditions which may not endure.

Most important, the analyst must recognize that the value of particular kinds of data varies greatly with the type of enterprise being studied. The five-year financial statements of a stable company, such as a utility, large chain-store enterprise, or a food company will provide, if not a conclusive basis, at least a reasonably sound one for measuring the safety of the senior issues and the attractiveness of the common shares. But the earnings statements for the same period of a small manufacturing enterprise in an intensely competitive or high technology field (e.g., electronics) may have so slight a bearing on the future earnings as to be virtually valueless. The same, of course, applies to any other type of speculative enterprise. (Nevertheless, at times the shares of innumerable small concerns have been offered to the public on the strength mainly of a satisfactory three- to five-year sales record but only a few quarters of profitability.)

Quantitative versus Qualitative Elements in Analysis

It is convenient at times to classify the elements of an analysis under two headings: the quantitative and the qualitative. The former might be considered the company's statistical exhibit. Included in it would be all the useful items in the income account, balance sheet, and funds statement, together with such additional specific data as production, unit prices, costs, capacity, unfilled orders, and pension liabilities. The various items may be subclassified under the headings: (1) capitalization, (2) earnings and dividends, (3) assets and liabilities, and (4) operating statistics.

The qualitative factors, however, deal with such matters as the nature of the business; the relative position of the individual company in its industry and the intensity of competition in the marketplace (this factor verges on the quantitative because of the significant amount of data that can be developed and analyzed); the business' physical, geographical, and operating characteristics; the character of the management; and, finally, the longer-term outlook for the company, including the trend in future earnings for the industry, and for business in general. Today, questions of this sort are addressed in company annual reports more than in the past. However, for fuller answers the analyst needs to look to miscellaneous sources of information of greatly varying dependability—including a large admixture of mere opinion.

Broadly speaking, the important quantitative factors lend themselves to much more precise consideration in appraising a specific company than do the qualitative factors. Pertinent data about the former are more easily obtained and better suited to the forming of definitive conclusions. Furthermore, the financial results in themselves epitomize such qualitative elements as the ability of a reasonably long-entrenched management. This point of view does not minimize the importance of qualitative factors in appraising the performance of a company, but it does indicate that a detailed study of them—to be justified—should provide sufficient additional insight to assist significantly in valuing the company. Such a study should keep the analyst from confusing hopes with facts.

Qualitative Factors

The qualitative factors most scrutinized are the nature of the business, the character of management, and the trend of future earnings. These elements are exceedingly important and difficult to assess.

Nature and Prospects of the Business in an Industry Analysis

The concept of the nature of a business includes a general idea of future prospects. If analysts (or investors) are so situated that industry analysis can be undertaken in depth, they will find that a substantial amount of valuable data can be compiled. However, for two principal reasons this subject is considered a qualitative factor. First, investors' notions of a "good business" are often based on surmise and bias as well as on a knowledge of the specific facts and conditions in the industry. Second, substantial judgment is involved in predicting the influence of broad industry conditions on the future performance of an individual company.

Role of Industry Studies. The specific role that industry studies should play in investing is a much debated subject. At one extreme is the view that industry selection is all-important and company selection almost inconsequential. At the other is the view that not only is company selection by far the dominant consideration but also industry data are of doubtful significance because of such factors as the growing multi-industry character of many major corporations.[1] Nevertheless, one approach to investment in common stocks is first to select the most promising industry or industries and then pick out fairly valued or undervalued companies in those industries.

The existence of an attractive industry outlook, however, is not a sine qua non for the purchase of a specific common stock. Well-known examples exist of companies which, over a period of years, have moved counter to the experience of their industry. For this reason, beware of overemphasizing the general outlook for an industry in selecting individual issues. Not all the companies in an industry with a particularly bright outlook will necessarily enjoy its good fortunes, nor will all the firms in an industry with a dark prognostication suffer a decline.

For example, the aerospace industry enjoyed a rising rate of return over the last decade, but Boeing had a declining rate until its recent reversal. In contrast, the machinery industry suffered a declining rate of return, but Ex-Cell-O (a diversified manufacturer of machine tools, package machinery, automotive components, etc.) had a rising rate prior to its acquisition by Textron in 1986.

---

[1]Ever-widening product diversification and, in recent years, a host of acquisitions and mergers have changed an increasing number of corporate enterprises into multi-industry undertakings. Consequently, the classification of complex corporate entities by industries is becoming more difficult—the acquisition of General Foods by Philip Morris, Nabisco Brands by R. J. Reynolds, and Carnation by Nestlé are examples. (See "The Brand-name Mergers" story in *Business Week*, Oct. 21, 1985. pp. 108–116.) The extent of this trend is also indicated by incorporation in *The Value Line Investment Survey* of a "multiform" industry of 42 diversified companies. Nevertheless, within most industries of primary importance, there remains across time a core of companies that, from an investment standpoint, are reasonably comparable. Therefore, if industry data are used as broad—rather than exact—indicators of the earnings and financial patterns of the principal segments of the U.S. industrial structure, they constitute helpful analytical tools.

Regardless of the differences of opinion as to the place of industry studies in common-stock investing, clearly a company's performance cannot be completely or permanently isolated from the economic climate of the industry (or industries) within which the major portion of its activities occur. Consequently, industry information has an essential role to play in the evaluation of individual companies.

Depth of Industry Analysis. If industry data are important, does it follow that industry studies are of equal importance? The basic utility of that mass of industry studies which represents primarily a "warm-over" of readily available and usually familiar data is questionable. Insofar as these studies relate to the past, the elements dealt with have already influenced the results of the companies in the industry and the average market price of their securities. The risk in overemphasizing the favorable or unfavorable position of the industry, in addition to the high or low company earnings produced by this position, involves counting cause and effect as two factors in the valuation instead of one, as they really are. Insofar as they relate to the future, these studies generally assume that past characteristics and trends will continue. These forward projections of the past are misleading at least as often as they are useful.

To make a significant contribution to common stock investing, industry analysis must be undertaken in sufficient depth to generate new information and to reveal more fully than before the anatomy of the industry. Moreover, comparative analysis is at the heart of both industry studies and company studies. Therefore an industry's performance should be examined in terms of the experiences of other industries. Industry studies of this type provide clearer insight into the forces operative in an industry and bring into better focus the relative performance of an industry, allowing a more accurate appraisal of the future.

Such studies are particularly valuable when they lead to well-founded conclusions differing from those in vogue. Typically, these conclusions would forecast the *reversal* of a condition or trend that had been so long continued as to be accepted as permanent on Wall Street. Reversals of this kind are surprisingly frequent, as is illustrated in Table 9.1, which shows average return on total assets in 1976 to 1980 and 1981 to 1985 for 17 industries. Over this short span of ten years, note particularly the sharp drop in relative profitability of the machinery and forest products industries. In contrast, the relative profitability of the electrical products and aerospace industries improved markedly. Moreover, out of the 17 industries only 2 had the same ranking in the last half of the span as in the first half.

Compilations of composite sales, assets, earnings, and other financial data for the major companies in individual industries are available from

Table 9.1. Average Return on Total Assets for 1976 to 1980 and for 1981 to 1985

	1976 to 1980			1981 to 1985	
Rank	Industry	Percent return	Rank	Industry	Percent return
1	Cosmetics	11.35	1	Drugs	11.28
2	Drugs	11.23	2	Computer/bus. equip.	9.08
3	Computer/bus. equip.	10.58	3	Electronics	8.28
4	Oil well equip. & serv.	10.04	4	Cosmetics	8.22
5	Electronics	9.23	5	Electrical products	8.21
6	Foods	8.01	6	Foods	8.00
7	Machinery	7.92	7	Oil well equip. & serv.	6.34
8	Oil, domestic	7.84	8	Aerospace	6.23
9	Paper	7.54	9	Oil, domestic	6.11
10	Forest products	7.43	10	Oil, international	5.85
11	Oil, international	7.37	11	Paper	5.48
12	Electrical products	7.41	12	Chemicals	4.43
13	Building materials	6.72	13	Retail stores	4.12
14	Chemicals	6.70	14	Forest products	2.78
15	Aerospace	6.08	15	Building materials	2.74
16	Retail Stores	5.60	16	Machinery	.43
17	Steel	2.66	17	Steel	-1.92

SOURCE: Based on data compiled by Salomon Brothers, Inc., *The Composite Financial Statements of the S&P 400 and Selected Industry Groups—1986*, August 29, 1986.

brokerage houses, investment services, and other sources. These compilations, together with descriptive material, will assist the analyst in understanding the nature of a company's business. An intensive examination of an individual security should include consideration of the industrywide conditions that have contributed to the specific company's performance. (Industry analysis will be dealt with in more detail in Chapter 22.)

Nonfinancial Factors

Some important determinants of a business nature cannot be derived from corporate financial statements or extensive industry data. Cigarette manufacturers, for example, face a public acceptance of maintained or even increased high excise taxes on their product, as do distilled liquor producers. Demand is affected by the increases in retail prices as well as restrictions on advertising. By quantitative standards, equity securities of companies in these industries appear to be constantly undervalued in the marketplace. The responses by corporate managements have been steps to diversify lines of business by R. J. Reynolds (now RJR Nabisco), Philip Morris, and American Tobacco (now American Brands). Liggett Group and P. Lorillard have become parts of multi-industry companies, and Seagram Company became a 22.5 percent owner of duPont.

Regulatory Developments. Trends in regulatory policies and practices may drastically change competitive and cost factors; witness the banking, broadcasting, drug, health care, insurance, public utility and telecommunication, thrift, and transportation industries. Reliable estimates of present and future earning power are impossible without informed qualitative judgments about future regulatory developments.

The evolution of government regulation is not dictated simply by economic factors; political pressures may be equally relevant. Protection of markets and industries, nuclear power, farm price supports, and entry to financial service lines of business are all debatable on economic grounds, but the outcomes may be dictated more by regional and political pressures which are difficult to predict. As a result, the security analyst faces an array of possibilities whose consequences must be assessed.

Social Issues. Equal employment opportunities, the controversial concept of comparable worth, labor relations, employee safety standards, product quality, and marketing practices are issues raised by the public in relation to perceived or advocated standards of social responsibility. Because of the predominance of value judgments in many such issues, the security analyst's clear preference is to refer such matters to the investor for evaluation and decision.[2]

In certain instances, however, these abstract questions of corporate conduct turn out to have major consequences. Manville Corporation (asbestos) and A. H. Robins (Dalkon Shield) filed bankruptcy petitions under Chapter 11 when product damages to health surfaced on a broad scale. Employee safety was the issue emerging from Union Carbide's Bhopal, India, plant disaster. For some years, infant formula marketing practices in the third world and overseas drug labeling were issues for shareholder resolutions. In the case of Nestlé, a consumer boycott of products in domestic markets spread until the company agreed to the World Health Organization's standards for infant formula promotion.

---

[2]The Investor Responsibility Research Center (IRC), a not-for-profit research center in Washington, D.C., was originally established by educational and foundation endowments to provide objective information about the whole range of social responsibility issues facing shareholders. Subsequently, banks, insurance companies, pension funds, and other investment managers became subscribers. In addition to the general range of social issues, IRRC now provides South Africa and corporate governance services. Among activist organizations addressing social and ethical issues are the Council of Economic Priorities, Inform, and Interfaith Center on Corporate Responsibility, all located in New York. An institutional perspective on social investing is provided in Dan M. McGill, ed., *Social Investing*, Richard D. Irwin for the Pension Research Council, Homewood, Ill., 1984.

Some investors refuse to own securities of companies manufacturing space or other weapons. Whether such investor boycotts affect valuations seems very doubtful. The tendency of large defense contractors to sell at lower multiples of earnings may simply reflect the risks associated with the concentration of orders in a single customer, the Department of Defense.

South Africa. The role of U.S. companies doing business in South Africa is another social or ethical issue for investors. Advocates of withdrawal argue that the mere presence of a major company shows support and acceptance of the white minority's repugnant practices of racial discrimination. Signatories of the Sullivan Principles, opponents of withdrawal argue, have been forces of constructive change which are essential to undermining the social and economic deprivation of nonwhite South Africans. Later versions of the Sullivan Principles even pressed U.S. companies to work actively for civil rights such as freedom of movement, home ownership, and education. Such steps were taken by some companies right up until the time of their withdrawal from the country.

For most major companies, less than 1 percent of sales and a smaller fraction of profits were being generated from South African operations. Sale of a line of business, therefore, seldom presented the analyst with a valuation adjustment problem. The threat of boycotts by the purchasing departments of major government units, however, is a different matter. Similarly, bank financing in South Africa became a presumptive reason for some to close their deposit accounts in lending banks.

The intensity of controversy over investment in South Africa inevitably raised questions about doing business with governments behind the Iron Curtain, labor relations in Northern Ireland, and human rights in Chile.

Environment. Air and water pollution from processes such as paper, cement, steel, and chemical operations have long been the targets of environmental complaints. Toxic waste disposal problems have surfaced in many areas, and the widespread threat of acid rain has raised interstate and international (with Canada) issues of how to allocate the costs of reduction.

Closings of old paper mills where processes could not be economically modified to reduce damage to the environment were tangible evidence that the analyst had to know more about this dimension of plant capacity. Cleaning up past instances of careless handling of waste materials is an expense without possible contribution to efficiency and productivity. The modernization of steel capacity, for example, was loaded with the additional cost of pollution control.

Implications for Analysis.   These kinds of external, nonfinancial factors can easily distract the analyst from measurable quantities like sales and the components of earning power. To some extent, of course, they should. But more important than a particular complicated issue may be the manner in which management deals with the controversy. How management deals with major policy decisions within the four walls of the boardroom will seldom if ever be fully known to the security analyst, but valuable insights into this process can be obtained from close observation of management's dealings with employees, customers, public bodies, media, analysts, and shareholders. Insensitivity, inflexibility, and ignorance of the environment in which the company operates are almost infallible signs of potential frictions and failures in the effective management and motivation of key employees.

   If analysts accept the dictum that "the business of business is business," they will regard social and community responsibility issues as either irrelevant or, worse, a diversion of resources from the almighty bottom line. Such a myopic view ignores the reality that the U.S. business system, like all of the major institutions in our society, must earn acceptance every day by accountability and responsible behavior. The corporate statement that "we have to do well if we are to do good" is completely valid, but the public will insist that the predicate not be forgotten.

Management

Many consider picking a company with good management even more important than picking a company in a promising industry. Little tangible information is available about management. Objective tests of managerial ability are few and rather unscientific. In most cases the investor must rely on a reputation which may or may not be deserved. The most convincing proof of capable management lies in a superior comparative record over a period of time, but that brings us back to quantitative data.

   There is a strong tendency in the stock market to value the management factor twice in calculations. Stock prices reflect the large and growing earnings which the good management has produced, plus analysts add a substantial increment for "good management" considered separately. This amounts to "counting the same trick twice" and is a frequent cause of overvaluation.

The quantitative record alone would indicate that most drug and newspaper companies have good managements, whereas farm machinery and large steel companies are poorly managed. Yet the true causes of the good and bad records may be traced to currency price trends and foreign competition. The recent record, moreover, is often the result of management decisions made five or ten years ago by a different management group.

Thus the management factor does assume quite independent importance when a significant change therein has recently taken place or is considered probable. In such cases, future results may be very different from those of the past. Typically, but by no means always, changes in management are for the better; they often occur because results are so unsatisfactory as to demand a drastic shake-up. In this area, particularly, the analyst may profit from personal contacts with the new directing heads. These investigations may lead the analyst to expect future results that are not already discounted in the current price.

Trend of Future Earnings

The trend of earnings is a key factor in current analysis and appraisal of common stocks. A record of increasing earnings is a favorable factor and should be given full weight in a valuation.[3] If a graphic array of the sales, earnings, or other financial data for a company or industry reveals reasonably consistent growth, measuring this growth through either a visually or mathematically fitted trend line is both appropriate and desirable.

Thus the use of trend lines is commended. At the same time, the fundamental difference between the use of a trend line to measure past performance and its extrapolation as a measure of future performance must be stressed. To estimate future earnings by projecting the past trend and then accepting that projection as a basis for valuing a common stock may be sound in a few specific instances, but it must be used with extreme caution. The analyst must be fully aware of the implications of extrapolating a trend line.

A mathematically fitted trend to past data is a fact, but a projected trend is only an assumption. Factors of economic adjustment and readjustment that militate against the maintenance of abnormal prosperity or depression in the economy as a whole are equally opposed to

---

[3]A survey of 2000 members of the Financial Analysts Federation showed that an overwhelming proportion gave much more consideration to the growth of earnings over the next five years than to the short run change in earnings (L. C. Chugh and J. W. Meador, "The Stock Valuation Process: The Analysts' View," *Financial Analysts Journal*, November–December 1984, pp. 41–48).

the indefinite continuation of the same for either an individual company or industry.[4] By the time a trend seems to be firmly established, conditions may well be ripe for a change.

For example, over the span from 1960 through 1973, the earnings per share of Avon Products grew at the annual rate of 17.4 percent. Note from Figure 9.1 the consistency of this growth. This made Avon one of the most revered issues of the growth stock era. A brief pause in this growth in EPS occurred in 1974. Nevertheless, from 1974 through 1979 the annual growth rate was, again, close to 17 percent. However, since 1979 Avon's earnings have seen a pronounced decline, and 1984's results were 48 percent below the 1979 high. In 1984 the price fell to 14 percent of its 1972 high.

A trend represents the relationship of the individual data in a time series. Thus, like any statistical measure, it is derived from the data for the period selected and is, of course, subject to any fundamental distortions which exist in the data. To illustrate, a trend fitted to the aggregate net income of a group of five international oil companies for the period from 1970 through 1980 reveals an average annual growth rate of 16.6 percent. However, in 1981, an analyst should have had serious doubts about extrapolating this trend. The growth rate was significantly influenced by the formation of OPEC and its pricing policy and by the world demand for oil. As a result of these forces aggregate net income for the five companies increased 122 percent between 1972 and 1974 and 128 percent between 1978 and 1980.[5] The increase in net income was therefore characterized more by a step function than a trend. In addition, in 1981, the analyst would have been concerned about flat oil prices, reduced demand resulting from worldwide economic weakness, energy conservation, expanded exploration, and internal differences in OPEC and its loss of market share. The analyst's primary role is to anticipate change when others are extrapolating the past.

Trends are certainly one of the tools which analysts should have in their analytical kit. But they are only *one* of the tools and, therefore, should take their place along with *individual* and *average* figures of the

[4]In a well-known study on this subject by J. G. Craig and B. G. Malkiel, "The Consensus and Accuracy of Some Predictions of the Growth of Corporate Earnings," *The Journal of Finance*, March 1968, pp. 67–84, the authors conclude "Evidence has recently accumulated that earnings growth in past periods is not a useful predictor of future earnings growth." The classic paper on this subject by Ian M. D. Little bore the title "Higgledy Piggledy Growth" (1962) and showed that in Great Britain corporate earnings were serially independent, i.e., historical changes in earnings were useless in predicting future changes. John Lintner and Robert Glauber, together with other researchers, confirmed that the same conclusion applied to U.S. companies.

[5]Survey reports on individual companies used in this illustration are Exxon Corporation, The Royal Dutch/Shell Transport Group, Chevron Corporation, Mobil Corporation, and Texaco Incorporated, *The Value Line Investment Survey*.

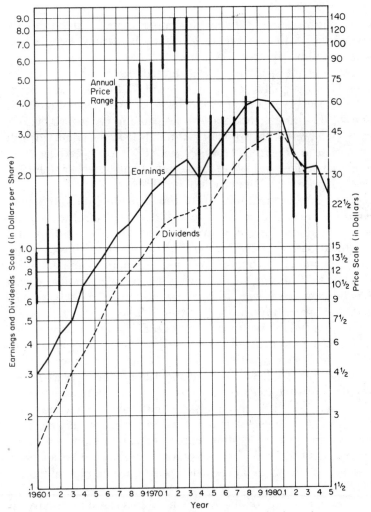

Figure 9.1 Avon Products, Inc.: Annual earnings, dividends, and price range, 1960–1985. (1985 earnings before discontinued operations.)

past. The analyst must not take comfort from the fact that they can be computed according to mathematical formulas. Not only does their use involve a number of subjective decisions (period for which computed, type of trend, etc.), but also situations will occur where trend analysis is of questionable value.

A trend projection has an air of definiteness which may mislead the unwary; it should be used only as a rough index of what may be expected from the future. Furthermore, a trend projection—which can be indefinitely extended—should not be allowed to obscure a financial condition which, in terms of past experience and present earnings levels, appears to be unsatisfactory. This important point may be clarified by the following example from the distant past.

In 1929 nearly all public utility holding-company systems showed a continued growth of earnings, but the fixed charges of many were so heavy—by reason of pyramidal capital structures—that they consumed nearly all the available earnings. Investors bought bonds of these systems freely on the theory that the small margin of safety was no drawback, since earnings were certain to continue to increase. They were thus making a clear prediction as to the future, upon the correctness of which depended the justification of their investment. If their prediction was wrong—as it proved to be in 1931 to 1932—they were bound to suffer serious loss.

Other examples from the same era are the bonds of railroads and steel companies which, because of very favorable past trends in earnings, had high ratings. As a result, the conservative investor following conventional wisdom, as well as the leveraged speculator, encountered severe losses in the Great Crash of 1929 to 1932 and the accompanying depression.

The recent investor experience with Real Estate Investment Trusts (REITs), however, shows that the appeal of high leveraging accompanied by presumed persistent growth did not expire with the Great Depression experience. REITs were launched by the Congress in 1960 to provide a vehicle for the small investor to participate in real estate lending and equity investing. The resulting structure could not have been more skillfully designed to create an accident on the way to occurrence. The Internal Revenue Service insisted that there be no reserves accumulated for possible losses. The incentives to increase leverage and the pressure to invest immediately ensured a financial position which only a vigorous and uninterrupted increase in real estate prices could possibly rescue from disaster.

By the end of 1969, REITs had $2.5 billion of assets and $1.6 billion of equity. At the peak in mid-1974, assets had increased to almost $21 billion but net worth only to $6.6 billion. When trees failed to grow to the sky, dividends to shareholders declined by 79 percent from the 1974 peak to mid-1977, and an index of share prices declined 75 percent from the 1972 level. The few REITs which survived were those with a greater proportion of sound equity investments and less reliance on leverage.[6]

---

[6]M. E. Polakoff and T. A. Durkin, *Financial Institutions and Markets*, 2d ed., Houghton Mifflin, Boston, pp. 194–195.

Qualitative Factors Resist Appraisal

A projected trend is, in fact, a statement of future prospects. Again, it is a qualitative, not a quantitative, factor in security analysis. In similar fashion, conclusions as to the nature of the business and the abilities of management have their chief significance in their bearing on the company's outlook. These qualitative factors are therefore all similar in general character. They all involve the same basic difficulty for the analyst, that is, judging how far they may be properly reflected in the price of a given security. The hazard is the tendency to overemphasize them. The same influence is constantly at work in the general market. The recurrent excesses of its advances and declines are due fundamentally to the fact that, when values are determined chiefly by the outlook, the resultant judgments are not subject to any mathematical controls and are almost inevitably carried to extremes.

Importance of Qualitative Factors in Analytical Thinking

Note the strong opinion in this book that security analysis should be primarily a process of *measurement*—either of safety, in the case of a typical bond, or of value, in the case of a typical common stock. This view led to a preference for the valuation approach rather than the anticipation approach, as stated in Chapter 3. This view now leads to a word of caution. Do not place *undue* emphasis on nonmeasurable factors of quality in analyzing and valuing companies. This is a very important point. It was this undue emphasis on quality that in the 1960s and beginning of the 1970s led to the dictum, "Make sure of the quality and price will take care of itself." This concept produced some disastrous results for the holders of quality growth stocks (so-called one-decision stocks) in the 1973–1974 market decline. The price performance of the following four stocks illustrates the extent of the decline:

	1972–1973 High	1974 Low	Percent decline
Control data	39⅝	4¾	88
Honeywell	85⅜	8¾	90
IBM	91¼	37⅝	59
RCA	45	9¼	79

Qualitative factors are, of course, important considerations in analyzing and valuing a security. The findings of the previously mentioned survey of 2000 members of the Financial Analysts Federation revealed that researchers concluded that the predictive process is based primarily on qualitative factors.[7] The difference today, compared to the early 1960s, is the increased availability of quantitative data for probing and appraising these factors. The result should be a fuller assessment of qualitative factors in the valuation process.

Security Analysis and the Future

Estimated values are, of course, based on expectations. These value expectations are most reliable when a company's record represents a reasonably reliable guide to the future. In this regard the analyst's approach is diametrically opposed to that of the speculator, who is seeking to cope with highly uncertain future developments in which the past is not a reasonable guide to the future. Analysts treat the future as a hazard which their expectations must encounter and attempt to guard against.

Offsets to the Hazards of the Future. The hazards of the future may be met by security analysts in several ways. Analysts may place prime emphasis upon the presence of a large margin of safety for the security to absorb whatever adverse developments are reasonably likely to occur. In such cases, the analyst will be prepared to see unsatisfactory earnings for the issue during recession periods, but will expect that the company's *financial strength* will carry it unharmed through such a setback and that its *average earnings* will be enough to justify fully the bond or stock purchase being recommended.

In other cases, the analyst may emphasize the factor of *inherent stability*. Here the nature of the industry or the company is supposedly such as to immunize it in large measure from the recurring adversity that befalls most enterprises.

Finally, the analyst may properly give considerable weight to the *prospects* themselves, favoring companies that have better-than-average prospects. In common stock selections, the analyst will value such concerns more liberally than others. However, beware of carrying such liberality to the point of enthusiasm, for at that point the sober moderation that distinguishes the investment approach from the speculative one will be lost. The security analyst is on safest ground when favorable expectations are treated as an added reason for a purchase which would not be unsound if based entirely on the past record and the present situation.

Inherent Stability. The factor of inherent stability has particular appeal

[7]Chugh and Meador, "Stock Valuation Process," pp. 41–48.

to the security analyst, because it minimizes the risk that new conditions will upset calculations derived from the past record. Stability, like trend, may be expressed in quantitative terms—for example, by stating that over the 15-year 1970 to 1984 span the return on total capital of Winn-Dixie, Incorporated never dropped below 16.6 percent nor rose above 20.1 percent. Moreover, average returns for the last two 5-year periods were nearly identical (17.7 and 17.2 percent, respectively). In similar manner, the EPS of United States Tobacco Company have grown at an almost constant rate of 15.1 percent over the last 20 years, and the EPS of Capital Cities Communications, Incorporated experienced an almost constant 18.6 percent growth rate over the 20 years ended in 1984. But stability is really a qualitative trait, because it derives in the first instance from the character of the business and not from its statistical record. A stable record suggests that the business is inherently stable, but this suggestion may be rebutted by other considerations.

For example, over the 10-year span from 1970 through 1980, Texas Instruments enjoyed an increase in earnings every year except 1975; EPS rose from $1.36 to $9.22, an average annual rate of nearly 24 percent. The share price increased from a low of 31 in 1970 to a high of 151 in 1980. However, since 1980, earnings have been on a far-from-steady course. In 1981, EPS dropped 50 percent, recovered some in 1982, and became negative in 1983. After a sharp rebound in 1984, a deficit was again reported in 1985 and the stock in that year sold as low as 86, a loss of 43 percent from the 1980 high. In this span the company was buffeted by its withdrawal from the home computer field and by the low demand, overcapacity, and fierce competition in the semiconductor business.

Quantitative Factors

Margin of Safety as the Basic Quantitative Factor

The presence of a margin of safety is the distinguishing characteristic of true investment. In like manner the margin of safety may be considered the most fundamental quantitative concept in security analysis. In the case of a bond, this margin is determined by the excess of earning power over interest requirements and the value of the enterprise above the senior claims against it. Thus a given bond will be approved as a safe investment because it has an adequate safety margin. The margin is expressed quantitatively by the analyst and is compared with specific quantitative criteria.

In the case of a common stock, it would be represented by a goodly margin of calculated intrinsic value over the current market price. However, in the selection of primary or leading common stocks for conventional investment, such a margin between value and price has not typically been present. In these instances the margin of safety is contributed to by such qualitative factors as the firm's dominant position in its industry and product markets and expected growth in earnings. Thus in valuing common stocks, the analyst will need to consider carefully qualitative factors as well as quantitative. Other factors that contribute to a margin of safety include assets carried in land and property accounts at amounts substantially below their current market value (e.g., timberland or mineral reserves) and cash flows that provide a degree of financial flexibility and therefore allow a business to withstand adversity, to add to or change product lines, and to take other action that will improve the competitive position of the company. At the same time, a primary stock would be recommended only if its price were within or below the intrinsic value range (e.g., fairly valued).

In the case of secondary stocks, there is much more uncertainty and unpredictability in a company's performance. Accordingly, the analyst would look for a compensating margin of safety between price and value.

Summary

This discussion of qualitative and quantitative factors can be summed up with the dictum that the analyst's conclusions must always rest on the figures and on established tests and standards. However, these figures alone are not sufficient; they may be completely vitiated by qualitative considerations of an opposite import. A security may make a satisfactory statistical showing, but doubt as to the future or distrust of the management may properly impel its rejection. Again, the analyst may correctly attach prime importance to the qualitative element of inherent stability, because its presence means that conclusions based on past results are not so likely to be upset by unexpected developments. Also, the analyst will be far more confident in the selection of an issue if an adequate quantitative exhibit can be buttressed with unusually favorable qualitative factors.

However, when the investment decision depends to a major degree on these qualitative factors—that is, whenever the price is considerably higher than the figures alone would justify—the analytical basis of approval is lacking. Thus, a satisfactory statistical exhibit is a necessary though by no means sufficient condition for a favorable decision by the analyst.

PART 2
Analysis of
Financial
Statements

10

Overview of Financial Statement Analysis

A major activity of security analysis is the analysis of financial statements. This analysis includes two steps: First, the financial statements must be adjusted to reflect an analyst's viewpoint, that is, the analyst changes the published numbers, eliminates some assets and liabilities, creates new ones, alters the allocation of expenses to time periods, and, in effect, creates a new set of financial statements. Second, the analyst processes the new information by the calculation of averages, ratios, trends, equations, and other statistical treatment.

The Accounting Environment

The Accounting Revolution

The dramatic way in which generally accepted accounting principles (GAAP) and accounting standard-setting have changed over the past quarter century in the United States has been called "an accounting revolution."[1] The rules have been expanded from a few thin pamphlets

---

[1] William H. Beaver, *Financial Reporting: An Accounting Revolution.* Englewood Cliffs, New Jersey: Prentice-Hall, 1981.

to a massive 2000 pages of opinions, standards, and other pronouncements. There are other new authoritative publications, such as the many industry *Audit Guides* issued by the Auditing Standards Board and the *Statements of Position* on industry and transaction accounting issued by the Accounting Standards Executive Committee of the American Institute of Certified Public Accountants (AICPA). The accounting standard-setting structure has evolved from a part-time, largely volunteer committee of the AICPA to a full-time independent Financial Accounting Standards Board (FASB) sponsored jointly by the AICPA, the Financial Executives Institute, the Financial Analysts Federation, the National Association of Accountants, the American Association of Accountants, and the Securities Industry Association.

The Authority of the Financial Accounting Standards Board

The FASB's authority is derived not from its independence but from recognition by outside organizations. In and of itself, the board has no powers. However, the ethics rules of the AICPA,[2] recognition and acceptance by the Securities and Exchange Commission[3] which is empowered by Congress to set accounting standards for registrant companies, and recognition by the various state licensing bodies that admit certified public accountants (CPAs) to public practice give the FASB its power to make effective accounting rules. In addition, the board's power is ensured by the general acceptance of FASB-established standards by preparers, users, accountants, regulatory bodies, governments, courts, and foreign accounting standard-setting bodies.

Better Rules and Worse Compliance

The improvements arising from the pronouncements of the Accounting Principles Board (APB) and the FASB include the elimination of many accounting alternatives for economically similar transactions, thereby enhancing the comparability of accounting figures among companies

[2]American Institute of Certified Public Accountants, *AICPA Professional Standards*, Rule 203, New York, N.Y. This ethics rule forbids departures from an accounting principle which has been established by the FASB or its predecessor, the Accounting Principles Board, unless the auditor is able to demonstrate clearly that following GAAP would result in misleading financial statements. The departures must be clearly explained and the auditor must stand ready to defend his departure.

[3]Securities and Exchange Commission, *Accounting Series Release 150*, December 20, 1973, Washington, D.C. In this release the Commission states that the standards and practices promulgated by the FASB in its statements and interpretations will be considered as having authoritative support, and those to the contrary to have no such support.

and industries, ensuring greater consistency of accounting through time so that trends and variability can be identified, and providing a codified set of definitions and concepts underlying U.S. accounting.

At the same time, the inflation that began in the early 1970s significantly harmed the corporate capital structure. Inflation requires more capital to produce the same physical volume of goods or units of service. This capital could not be obtained by retained earnings alone, and dilutive effects made sale of stock at depressed prices even more unattractive than borrowing at high interest rates. The logic was that the high interest costs were tax deductible (even 18 percent interest costs only 11.88 percent after a 34 percent tax deduction!), and the debt could be refunded later when rates declined. This view led to an increase in the ratio of debt to equity, which increases the risk of corporations. Additional financial leverage occurred because the new debt was issued at high interest rates and therefore interest claimed a larger share of operating income and cash flows.

The inflation put pressure on true profit margins—that is, margins after deducting inventory profits and the current cost of depreciation. Thus, a shortfall of cash flows made the balance sheet risk even more apparent, which led many investors to become more risk averse. Investors sought companies having lower rather than higher risks, which put some pressure on managements to improve at least the appearance of the balance sheet if not the underlying risk. Company managers also were putting pressure on portfolio managers to produce near-term investment performance in pension portfolios, and they were focusing heavily on quarterly measurements. The focus on immediate pension fund investment results led portfolio managers to seek companies that had favorable short-term earnings results, leading both company financial officers and investment managers to complain that the other was forcing an unrealistic time horizon on them.[4] This situation is now changing, particularly as corporate financial officers become more sophisticated in measuring the investment performance of their portfolios and accept that valid judgments of performance require longer periods. Perhaps this will relieve some of the pressures on the companies to report near-term earnings. These pressures were thought by many to have fostered the increase in transactions designed to achieve accounting results that are not justified by the economic substance. The "front ending" of earnings, removing debt from the balance sheet and writing up or down assets, has become something of a problem that mars the overall picture of accounting rules that are steadily improving.

In 1984 the FASB set up the Emerging Issues Task Force to identify questionable transactions and to suggest the appropriate accounting for them.

---

[4]"The Folly of Inflating Quarterly Profits," *New York Times*, Mar. 2, 1986, pp. 2, 8.

The Committee was formed partly because of SEC concerns whether the accounting community was addressing abusive transactions promptly enough to keep them from spreading.

Adjustments by the Analyst

Implicit versus Explicit Adjustments

The security analyst has two avenues to follow in making adjustments to accounting information. The explicit approach changes the actual numbers in the income statement and balance sheet. The alternative approach makes an implicit adjustment to the earnings multiplier or to the discount rate used to value the security. Since the explicit adjustments can be made with considerable accuracy and the implicit adjustments are simply "Kentucky windage," analysts should make the explicit changes whenever possible. The situation is analogous to processing low-grade ore: Accounting includes estimates and allocations which are not very accurate, but analysts can increase the information content of accounting. The cumulative effect of a number of small explicit adjustments can make the information more accurate and complete. Thus the information content, like the few ounces of gold in several tons of ore, must be extracted to the fullest extent.

Mandatory, Situational, and Judgmental Classes of Adjustments

Analyst adjustments break down into three classifications:

1. *Mandatory adjustments.*   Standard rules, to be applied in every case, for example, the adjustment of all previous per-share figures for a stock split .

2. *Situational adjustments.*   Those made only when appropriate or specific conditions exist—intangibles that are salable or bring in income stay on the balance sheet; all others are removed .

3. *Judgmental adjustments.*   Those applied by the analyst through a combination of experience, common sense, and observation of the practices of other analysts considered to be knowledgeable and experienced

Why Make Adjustments at All?

Presenting economic reality is impossible, through accounting or any other process. Economics is not an exact science; rather it is a social science in which value judgments play a major role. It would be wonderful if accounting were one of the exact sciences that observes all variables, measures them with whatever degree of accuracy is needed, and presents a final number that all would agree was "economic reality." Unfortunately, it is not even possible for two persons to agree on what economic reality is. Economic activity manifests itself in many ways that are not subject to scientific observation and measurement. Accounting cannot observe directly the economic effects of a competitor going bankrupt or an expanded training program. Good management is an asset and bad management a liability, but accounting has no way to put reliable numbers on the balance sheet to reflect such values. Accounting takes a commonsense approach to such problems—it simply measures what it *can* observe and measure, which is mostly exchange transactions in which the company was a party.

The analyst may be able to capture a more faithful picture of reality by adding to or adjusting this information in ways not permitted by accounting rules. Analysts make adjustments to accounting information for a variety of reasons. Perhaps the most important is to adjust the numbers to reflect the analysts' notions of income and capital maintenance, where those notions disagree with the notions used in accounting.

For some transactions, accounting borrows from economics certain simplifying assumptions which most analysts reject: for example, the assumption of perfect, interchangeable, frictionless, costless markets in which participants happily exchange their goods at fair (rather than advantageous) prices, the assumption that markets are always rational or that changes in interest rate differentials fully explain changes in the relative prices of foreign currencies. The analyst may be able to compensate to reflect different beliefs about such matters.

Security analysis is not restricted by the rules of accounting and therefore can use a more flexible approach in dealing with the accounting numbers and the facts garnered from nonaccounting sources. Where accounting allows alternatives for the same transaction or where management judgments allow different presentations for the same facts, the analyst can compensate for these differences, thereby improving comparability, accuracy, and completeness. Analysts can remove the effects of transactions that are narrowly within the rules of accounting but outside the boundaries of economic substance or of common sense.

Analysis requires the ability to discriminate, to separate the ordinary from the unusual, and to detect change. These require disaggregation, enhancement, and reconstruction of accounting information to prepare it for further processing.

Income and Capital Maintenance Notions

Perspectives on Earnings

Economists' Views. One cannot determine income or "earnings" unless one also determines that the original capital has been maintained. This notion was well expressed by J. R. Hicks in a discussion of a series of income and capital maintenance notions.[5]

E1. Well-Offness. Hicks's first definition of income was the amount that one could consume and still be as well off at the end of the period as at the beginning.

E2. Ability to Consume. Hicks also expressed income in expectational terms suggesting that income was the amount one could consume and still expect to continue consuming that much in the future.

E3. Real Consumption. A third notion of income emphasized goods and services in real rather than nominal terms.

E4. Social Welfare Utility Added. Hicks also multiplied his number of definitions by two when he mentioned that the amounts ideally should be adjusted for the utility of the goods and services that the income could buy. He pointed out that utility was impossible to quantify. Hicks's conclusion was that these notions are all useful but fragile, and, with tongue in cheek, he admonished economists to avoid discussions of income whenever possible.

Accountants' Views. Capital maintenance has been the subject of much debate among accountants over the years.

A1. Financial Capital. The objective of financial capital maintenance is to maintain the amount of net worth on the balance sheet. This is a pure *net asset* view that looks to the carrying amounts of assets less liabilities, with some favoring current costs and others historical. Since the balance sheet excludes the assets and liabilities that cannot be measured, this capital-maintenance notion is incomplete.

A2. Physical Capital. Accounting also has considered various physical-capital maintenance notions, generally expressing the idea in terms of

[5]John Richard Hicks, *Value and Capital*, 2d ed., Oxford, Clarendon Press, 1950, pp. 171–188.

either replacement costs or of operating capability, that is, the ability to produce a fixed amount of goods or services.

A3. Distributable Income. The physical-capital maintenance notion can be adjusted to produce an income number known as "distributable income," which is akin to Hicks's first definition of the amount that can be consumed without being worse off at the end of the period.

A4. Purchasing Power. Accounting also offers methods to express each of those forms of capital maintenance in real terms rather than in nominal terms, in general, by adjusting for changes in the general price level (but not, of course, for changes in utility).

Security Analysts' Views. Security analysts also have thoughts about capital maintenance and counterpart income ideas.

S1. Investor Wealth. Some believe that a company does not really earn money unless it maintains the market value of the common stock, and thus their approach does not measure the company's operating performance. It measures investor wealth, hardly a matter to include in the company's accounts.

S2. Earning Power. A second view is that a company earns income only after it has maintained the previously existing earning power.

S3. Expected Dividends. A third income notion used by security analysts is the excess income after the company has maintained the expected future dividend stream.

S4. Distributable Income. Some analysts favor the "distributable income" notion developed in Great Britain. That is the amount a company could distribute after making necessary capital expenditures, providing for working capital needs, and using available borrowing capacity.

S5. Liquidating Value. Still another concept is an asset value notion that requires maintaining the liquidating value of the company before any increment of earnings can exist. This is the accountants' net asset view rather than an investment value approach.

Which Income Notion Should Analysts Use?

All of the notions mentioned are useful in that they help us think about the performance of a corporation. For an *ongoing* firm, the S2 and S3 security analyst income notions of maintaining earning power and maintaining the expected future stream of dividends are best because they lead most directly to the pricing of securities. In the case of mergers, buy-out candidates, bankruptcies, and other asset-oriented analyses, the liquidating value income notion is often very useful.

Asset Values and Investment Values

An important distinction is found in the security analysts' S2 and S3 notions of income when compared with the notions used by accountants. Most accounting income notions use *asset values* (although some values may be out of date). It is implicit that the asset values minus the liabilities (or the value of the liabilities) will provide a net worth number that "represents" the value of the firm. That number is likely to tell the approximate amount at which assets could be sold and the liabilities settled, one by one.

The analyst is looking for another value—investment value. Investment value is concerned not with what the assets could be sold for but with what they can be *used* for—what they will generate in future earnings that can be paid out as dividends or added to the company's growth. Most security analysts' favorite calculations of investment value are (1) capitalized earning power, or (2) the capitalized stream of future dividends.

Fundamentalists' Beliefs

The fundamental analyst believes that stock market prices fluctuate around the underlying investment value and that the two coincide occasionally. This belief rejects the idea that, normally, stocks are priced correctly in the market, and it even implies doubt that the market behaves rationally most of the time. Because stock prices move randomly with only a weak gravitational pull toward intrinsic value, the coincidence of price and value occurs infrequently, like Halley's comet. This means that the "convergence time" is long—perhaps three to five years. The analyst using the techniques recommended in this book must have a relatively long time horizon and considerable patience. The approach is that of a "fundamentalist" or value-oriented analyst. Value-oriented analysts are not traders, but rather, they are long-term investors who look on investing as being something more like marriage than like a mere flirtation. Investment value involves forecasts of future earnings and dividends that must begin to come true before the market is likely to appreciate them. It is therefore important to understand that the value sought in this book is not the asset value, and it is surely not the market price.

Consider the following hypothetical scene: A company manager tells an analyst that the company earned $8 a share and paid out $2 in dividends. The analyst inquires why the dividend payout was only 25 percent while most other companies in that industry are paying out well over half of their earnings. The manager answers "We needed the $6 to buy more efficient machines, so that our costs and pricing would be as low as our competitors'. Our old machines were out of date." From an analyst's perspective, how much did the company earn? The retained $6 was not earnings, but made up for a short fall of depreciation, or perhaps a write-off of obsolete machinery. The "retained earnings" were not available for dividend payments, and they added nothing to the future earning power of the company. In what sense were they earnings at all? The example can be broadened into a principle: *Retained earnings that cannot result in subsequent increases in earning power are not true earnings from a security analyst's viewpoint.*

The Nature and Limitations of Accounting

Accounting grew out of a need to know, to remember, and to decide. The Industrial Revolution required the gathering of capital from many sources under a single management to gain economies of scale. The separation of ownership and management clearly required some accountability for the stewardship of capital and the profitable use thereof. Not all analysts are aware that the financial statements they receive are prepared not by auditors but by the management of companies. The philosophy of the financial reports was for many years management's statement of its stewardship of the shareholders' assets. In effect, the statements were an annual management report card in which management graded itself on the success of its activities. As a result, the annual report often focused more on operating performance and market performance than the analyst would prefer, sometimes at the expense of the clearest picture of corporate profitability. Although the stewardship notion still prevails in the minds of many management people, the direction of accounting in recent years has been more toward the needs of users.

Management Information System

The foundation or information base of accounting is the management-control and decision-making system. Such a system is designed to present what management needs to know, given the decisions it will make in dealing with individual assets and liabilities. The manager has access to these assets and liabilities, whereas ordinarily the outside investor or creditor does not. Management also needs an accounting system for tax records, regulatory reporting, SEC requirements, and other reasons. Investor needs differ from management needs in some respects because investors must make different decisions.

The Orderly Character of Accounting

Accounting is a distinctive information set in a number of respects. Its orderliness makes it subject to systematic evaluation.

Articulation.   The statements articulate both the statics and the dynamics of a company, that is, they present state and change of state.

Single Measuring Unit.   Accounting is quantified in a single measuring unit—the dollar, in the case of the United States.

Reliability.   Accounting has considerable reliability because it is audited and because it deals with transactions and events after the fact and attempts to minimize the injection of subjective estimates of the future. Unfortunately, at least some estimates have to be made, such as the useful lives of long-lived assets.

Representational Faithfulness.   Accounting is representationally faithful—it is what it purports to be. Accounting does not purport to present the actual asset, which might be a desk or a computer or a building. However, it does make representations that it will provide specific information such as unrecovered cost, fair value, or some other attribute, and this can be useful information about the desk, computer or building.

Relevance.   Much of the relevance of accounting information comes about because it is "entity specific"—emphasis is on the completed exchange transactions of the entity.

Consistency and Comparability.   Accounting provides considerable consistency through time and comparability between companies, industries, and sectors. Of course, the consistency and comparability are not perfect, because accounting cannot be applied with perfect consistency, alternatives exist, and the rules of accounting are often changed, interrupting some of the continuity.

Accrual Accounting

Today's model of accrual accounting links cause and effect by matching causal costs with resulting revenues in the same time period. The mere cataloging of cash transactions would provide far less information about the income of a period, and therefore a certain amount of matching must be provided. Accrual accounting is far more predictive of future cash flows than is the direct observation of the cash flows of a single period.[6] For example, the purchase of a major new piece of equipment in a particular period might cause a reduction in cash and the appearance of negative income, even though the equipment will be used to produce revenue for many years. Its costs should be allocated to all those periods rather than merely the one in which the equipment was purchased.

The Cash Cycle

Accrual accounting is very descriptive of the "cash-to-cash" cycles of business. Business organizations start with cash, invest in raw materials, labor, services, and parts and end up with an entirely new product or service to offer to the public. For those goods and services the company receives cash, or accounts receivables, which in turn are ultimately converted back to cash again, completing the round trip from cash outlay to cash receipt. It would be nice if all companies liquidated to an all-cash position at the end of each year and satisfied all their liabilities— there would be few quarrels about the amount of profits. Unfortunately, many cash cycles are still going on at the end of the year. Some of them are quite short cycles, and others extend over many years. Thus, accrual accounting is designed to record as well as possible the performance of the company, using various conventions that capture the part of each cash cycle that was completed during the period.

Matching, of course, can be abused. It is easy to cross the line from matching to smoothing, and the temptation is to "make it look good" rather than to "tell it like it was." The auditor must see that management's statements tell it like it was, within the confines of accounting rules and conventions. It is the analyst's job to go the rest of the way and "tell it *all* like it really *was*."

The Conservatism of Accounting

By and large, accounting has considerable conservatism built into it. Accounting tends to wait until there is reasonable assurance before recognizing revenue and profits and to reflect losses quite promptly. This is a helpful offset to the natural optimism of management.

---

[6]Financial Accounting Standards Board, *Reporting*, Nov. 1978, paras. 44–48. Concept No. 1, *Objectives of Financial Reporting*, Nov. 1978 paras. 44–48.

Conservatism is of great importance to analysts, because it contributes to their margin of safety in buying and selling securities.

Realization Principle

Accounting contains a realization principle that says revenue should not be recognized until (1) the company has performed all the activities necessary to "earn" its income and (2) the company has "realized" cash in hand or has assurance of receiving future cash. The creation of a high-quality account receivable is usually considered sufficient for the latter test.

Cash Inflows

Thus, the overall view of accounting is that it is well-structured for the analyst's further processing. Investors look to the company for cash inflows to themselves. Investor cash inflows depend totally on the company's holdings of cash and the company's ability to generate cash inflows. Recall that about all an investor gets from the company is dividend checks and financial reports. Since the market for used annual reports is modest, it is the stream of dividends to which investors look for their rewards. They have a choice of continuing to receive the stream of dividends or selling the stock in the marketplace. They do not have direct access to the assets and liabilities, as does the management of the company. The timing of the investors' cash inflows will be somewhat different from the cash picture of the company.

The Auditor's Opinion

A traditional saying of security analysts is "Read the auditor's opinion, the footnotes, and only *then* the financial statements. That way you won't forget the first two." There is much confusion about the auditor's involvement with financial statements. The auditor does not ordinarily prepare them. *Financial statements are the representations of management who actually prepare the statements.* It is the auditor's job to do certain checking and sampling, to examine the management control system, and to determine that the accounting principles followed are in accordance with generally accepted accounting principles. The auditor's qualification of an opinion is often important in determining whether a company may be looked upon as a going concern, or one likely to go into liquidation or bankruptcy. Auditors can "qualify" their opinions when they are uncertain whether the statements may be relied upon, and they can subsequently withdraw those qualifications.

Example. Coopers & Lybrand qualified the 1982 annual report of General Refractories Company with the following words: "Although certain goals of the company's 1982 business plan were achieved, the company's 1983 business plan continues to reflect the need to reduce operating losses, sell its domestic building products division, obtain additional working capital, successfully renegotiate its raw materials purchase agreement, and meet its obligations and restrictive covenants pursuant to the most recent loan agreement." By the time of the 1983 annual report, many of those uncertainties and problems had been resolved or ameliorated, and Coopers & Lybrand withdrew their qualification, stating "Accordingly, our present opinion on the 1982 and 1981 consolidated financial statements is different than that expressed in our previous report."

Limitations of Accounting

Accounting, of course, has a variety of imperfections which the analyst should know and guard against. As mentioned earlier accounting cannot measure or even observe many events and circumstances. Accounting is not a pure model in that it is not entirely based on historical cost, nor on recoverable investment, nor on current value, nor any of the other single measures that purists would love to have. For pragmatic reasons of cost and benefit and of understandability, accounting uses a mixture of attributes in measuring assets and liabilities. Yet, the end result is usable for those who understand and learn to deal with accounting's limitations.

Accounting is full of judgmental decisions and is therefore highly subjective. Someone has to determine the appropriate depreciation pattern, costs must be allocated, say, between period expenses and capitalizable inventory, and it is difficult to prove whether such decisions are right or wrong. Human frailty enters into this type of decision making, and not surprisingly self-interest, pride, inherent optimism, and other characteristics of management incline some to be biased toward reporting greater amounts of income now at the expense of lower amounts later on. For this reason, the majority of the adjustments made by analysts tend to reduce today's reported earnings and report larger earnings in the future.

Reported Earnings and "True" Earnings

Analysts' activities are somewhat schizophrenic, for they want to know two sets of earnings: reported earnings and "economic" earnings. The latter is the analysts' view of true income—income that can be (1) distributed without diminishing capital or (2) reinvested to produce greater future income. Nevertheless, the analyst would like to estimate accurately *what the company will report* as earnings for the next period. This is important because reported earnings have at least a short-term impact on the market price of a stock. A number of investing techniques have been developed using reported earnings alone, without adjustments by the analysts. *Value Line Investment Service* has been studied many times because of the consistent favorable investment results of the service's stock ranking system.[7] The two most important ingredients in the Value Line methodology are earnings momentum and price momentum. The earnings used are *reported* earnings. Many academic studies also have used reported earnings to test the speed with which information is absorbed by the market. Tests of the "price earnings" effect—a belief that low-price-earnings stocks provide higher total returns than do high-price-earnings stocks—have been published. These studies use reported earnings. Kisor studied the effects of relative earnings changes on stock prices and found that relative changes in reported earnings correlated with relative total returns over various time periods.[8]

At the same time, analysts know that dividends are paid out of the true economic earnings and not whatever was reported as earnings. Thus they have to estimate economic earnings to generate an expected stream of future dividends. Economic earnings are also essential in developing an estimate of "earning power." Earning power is more a capacity to pay dividends and increase the size of the earnings base than an accrual accounting system would report. Economic earnings that are retained always result in increased earning power if they are properly invested by management.

Some analysts lose the distinction between these two earnings, perhaps because they have misconceptions about the accuracy of earnings reports. Reported annual earnings may not be within 10 or 20 percent of the adjusted earnings that an analyst would consider to be the year's true results. Quarterly earnings reports are prepared using the so-called integral method, which makes them largely a reflection of management's estimates for the full year results. It is remarkable that the stock market reacts violently to interim earnings that are a few percentage points greater or less than expected, when the accuracy of quarterly earnings depends so heavily on subjective estimates of what

[7]Fischer Black, "Yes, Virginia, There Is Hope: Tests of the Value Line Ranking System," presented at a seminar of the Center for Research in Security Prices, Graduate School of Business, University of Chicago, May 1971.

[8]Manowm C. Kisor and Van A. Messner, "The Filter Approach to Earnings Forecasts," *The Financial Analysts Journal*, Jan-Feb 1969, 109–115.

subsequent quarters will be. This market vulnerability to earnings reports that are contrary to expectations is particularly pronounced in the case of glamorous growth stocks, where so much of the price is based on hopes and dreams and so little on assets and demonstrated earning power.

The evidence that the market reacts to reported earnings is quite powerful, but a large body of evidence indicates that the market "sees through" mere accounting differences and makes proper adjustments therefor. For example, the market will adjust the stock price of a company that uses LIFO inventory accounting so that it is in keeping with stocks of other companies that use FIFO. Similarly, the market will equalize the price of companies that use different depreciation methods.[9] We are persuaded that if the market understands the accounting differences and has the information necessary to make the adjustments, it will adjust prices properly. The effects of the market's adjustments will tend to persist over time, whereas the effects of reported earnings tend to be relatively short-lived, normally expiring in a matter of days or a few months. The importance of the adjusted earnings, which the analyst attempts to bring as close to "true" earnings as possible, is to provide a valid beginning point for forecasts of the future.

Finally, some areas of specialized accounting present very soft and subjective numbers. Outstanding examples are the percentage-of-completion method of contract accounting, and accounting for motion pictures and cable television. In each of these areas, accounting accepts the value of timeliness in exchange for a reduction in precision, rather than face the alternative of no financial information. The difficulty is not a frailty of accounting but rather the innate uncertainty in business affairs.

The Use of Adjusted Accounting Numbers

Analysts adjust the financial statements to get closer to their own notions of income and capital maintenance. These income notions may be selected partly for the decision to be made. In some cases they are devised to compare companies in an industry or a sector. All must be put on a common basis, to the degree that information is available to do so. Adjustments prepare the statements for subsequent processing and

[9]W. H. Beaver and R. E. Dukes, "Tax Allocation and Depreciation Methods," *The Accounting Review*, July 1973, pp. 549–555; see also R. E. Dukes, "An Investigation of the Effects of Expensing Research and Development Costs on Security Prices," in M. Schiff and G. Sorter eds., *Proceedings of the Conference on Topical Research in Accounting*, New York University, New York, 1976, pp. 147–193; G. Foster, "Valuation Parameters of Property-Liability Companies," *Journal of Finance*, June 1947, pp. 823–836; Raymond J. Ball, "Changes in Accounting Techniques and Stock Prices," University of Chicago, 1971.

analysis, which often consist of calculating ratios to determine which relationships are stable and which ones are variable. The analyst may adjust to find the true level of an item at a point in time, or what the normal level is over the business cycle. These processes require changing the accounting numbers to improve their accuracy, comparability, and consistency before measuring a trend, calculating a ratio, or taking the average of a number of years. Increasingly, analysts are using statistical techniques and mathematical models, as the profession grows more sophisticated. The most frequently used model is a financial model of the company. This is a full set of past statements, trends, ratios, equations, and relationships. These form a base for projections several years into the future. The future is where money is made—or lost.

11
Analysis of the Income Statement

All security analysis involves the analysis of financial statements. True, the weight given to the financial material may vary enormously, depending on the kind of security studied and the basic motivation of the prospective purchaser. The standing of investment-grade bonds and preferred stocks is decisively controlled by the financial record. These bonds and stocks must meet specific tests of safety, which turn upon such criteria as:

- Relation of past earnings to fixed charges (and preferred dividends)
- Dividend record
- Relation of funded debt to the property account
- Working-capital position
- Volume of business done

Although qualitative factors may be important in analyzing stocks and bonds, they cannot be used to determine risk without support from the actual figures.

Pertinence of the Past Record to the Future

In the selection of common stocks, future expectations are the primary basis of attractiveness and value. In theory these expectations may be so different from past performance that the latter could be virtually irrelevant to the analysis, but this separation of the future from the past rarely occurs. A tendency toward an underlying continuity in business affairs makes the financial record the logical point of departure for any future projection.

Most companies and industries have certain identifiable financial characteristics that remain stable or change only slowly over time, and only the trader on market movements or the heedless speculator following tips or hunches will ignore the financial results—the statistical showing—of a common stock. The investment approach to every kind of security—which is the analytical approach—requires the proper application of analysis to the financial statements.

In Chapter 2 we pointed out that the descriptive function of security analysis involves marshaling the important facts relating to an issue and presenting them in a coherent, readily intelligible manner. Analysis of financial statements plays a major part in this descriptive function, and Part 2 details such analysis up to the point where the indicated results are actually to be used in the evaluation and the choice of securities.

The Typical Pattern of an Analytical Study

Every reasonably complete analysis of a corporate issue has three major divisions:

1. A description of the company's business and properties (perhaps including some historical data and some details about the management)

2. Financial material: the capitalization, the record of earnings and dividends for a considerable number of years, a funds flow analysis, and one or more recent balance sheets

3. Prospects of the enterprise in the form of projected future financial statements and the merits of the security

The Written Report

We cannot overemphasize the importance of the preparation of a written report as a discipline for the practicing analyst. This activity enhances orderliness of thought, greater attention to detail, and emphasis on facts rather than assumptions. Communication is improved and ambiguity reduced. A conclusion must be reached and a record established for future review. The good investment organization reviews its past successes and failures and learns from them. The individual analyst or advisor should do no less.

Uses of the Income Statement

The indications furnished by the income statement may be analyzed and discussed from various angles, including the average results for the period, the minimum for any year,and the trend and variability over the years. In many common stock write-ups considerable and perhaps excessive attention is paid to the current figure, which may be misleading. Well-trained analysts use past income statements primarily as a guide to formulating estimates of future earnings, or earning power, which will serve as the chief basis of their conclusions respecting the merits of a common stock. A level of earnings which has been achieved in the past is a more credible prospect than a projection of new record-high results.

Three Aspects of Income Statement Analysis

The importance attached to the income statement in security analysis makes discerning study of the published figures doubly essential. A really good job of income statement analysis may be anything but a simple matter. Many complications may have to be unraveled, many quirks or special entries guarded against, many variations between companies equalized. The broad study of corporate income statements may be classified under three headings:

1. *Accounting.* The leading question here is, "What were the true earnings for the past periods studied?".

2. *Business.* The leading question is, "What indications does the earnings record carry as to the future earning power of the company?".

3. *Security valuation.* For security valuation, the leading question is, "What elements in the earnings exhibit should the analyst take into account and what standards should be followed, in endeavoring to arrive at a reasonable valuation of the shares?"

Chapters 11 through 19 deal with the accounting aspect of statement analysis, treating the income statement, its relationship to the funds statement, and the balance sheet. Discussion of the business aspect is presented in Chapters 29 and 30. Valuation is discussed in Chapters 31 through 34.

Basic Procedures for Arriving at True Operating Earnings

Fraudulent and Other Misrepresentative Transactions

Analysts must start, of course, with the assumption that the figures they are studying are not fraudulent, that the various assets and liabilities in the balance sheet are honestly stated as they would appear on the books without omissions or fictitious entries. Analysts must also assume that where discretion is used in valuing assets or estimating liabilities, such estimates are based on management's informed and honest judgment.

The published annual reports of companies registered with the SEC have been audited by independent public accountants and bear their certification. This is now a requirement of law. The auditing procedures have been tightened up considerably since 1933, partly through the efforts of the accountants themselves and partly at the insistence of the SEC. Not only have the possibilities of outright fraud been greatly reduced, but—of more practical importance—analysts are now supplied with the year's results in sufficient detail and with enough explanatory comment to permit intelligent interpretation of the figures.

Prior to the SEC legislation, which began in 1933, semifraudulent distortions of corporate accounts were not unusual. The misrepresentation was almost always to make the results look better than they were, and it was generally associated with some scheme of stock market manipulation in which management was participating. Although the incidence of such practices has receded, the analyst must continue to be vigilant for cases of misleading financial statements and outright fraud.

Good Analysis Can Help to Avoid Investment in Fraudulent Companies

Security analysts are unlikely to uncover fraud, but they do have tools to reveal unusual patterns that are difficult to rationalize. A stock should never be recommended unless the analyst knows and understands the company. Companies involved in fraud or in questionable transactions are at least occasionally avoided by careful analysts who conclude that the numbers simply don't make sense.

The good securities analyst does not stay in touch merely with those companies that are candidates for purchase. Competitors, unions, trade associations, vendors, customers, and a host of other sources provide information and insights about trends, technical developments, share of market, trade gossip, and the like. It is through such channels that the analyst often first hears of unusual transactions or suspicious circumstances.

The analyst uses a number of sensitive ratios, particularly the activity ratios (asset turnover, inventory turnover, accounts receivable turnover, and the like) that are designed to give the earliest possible warning that something is changing in a company. Evidence of change almost always initiates inquiries to management about the causes of change. Where management explanations are inadequate, the analyst's suspicions may be aroused.

The analyst has a number of ways to predict the rate at which a company grows. Some techniques are oriented toward the company's ability to finance growth. When the reported growth exceeds that which the analyst projected the company was capable of financing, there is cause for concern.

An analyst familiar with the insurance business would know that rapid growth demands tremendous amounts of capital because of the heavy initial cost of putting business on the books. In the case of Equity Funding Corporation, an analyst might not have recognized that fraud was taking place, but the analysis of capital needs did at least turn some analysts away simply because they could find no reasonable way for the company to finance its growth goals.

Accountants' and Analysts' Results

Since the reports of nearly all companies are honestly compiled and are certified by their auditors as conforming with generally accepted accounting principles (GAAP), why should the security analyst need to meddle with the figures? A major reason is that accepted accounting principles allow considerable leeway in the statement of results. This leeway permits the company to report its earnings on a basis that may not reflect the true operating results for the year (including its interest in affiliated companies) as the analyst would present such results.

Comparability of Inventories and Depreciation. In particular, accounting permits considerable latitude in the basis of reporting inventories and depreciation. Adjustments are necessary to permit valid comparisons. The analyst must restate and interpret the figures, not so much in accordance with permissible practices of accounting as in the form most enlightening to the investor.

Consistency Through Time.   While the increased number of accounting standards has improved comparability between companies engaging in similar transactions, the accounting changes themselves have created some problems with consistency through time. Most accounting standards become effective prospectively: That is, past transactions do not have to be restated to reflect the new requirements, for several reasons, including the cost of restatement, availability of the necessary data, questions of whether the company would have engaged in the transaction had the new rule been in effect, and concern that the credibility of accounting is harmed when previously issued statements are altered. From the analyst's viewpoint the frequent changes result in trends and averages that include transactions that are accounted for using both old and new rules. Such discontinuities and inconsistencies are a small price to pay for significantly improved accounting information. If the analyst stays aware of rule changes, they can usually be dealt with.

Professional versus Practical Implications of Analysts' Adjustments.   A distinction needs to be drawn between the importance of financial statement analysis as a matter of necessary procedure by the professional analyst and its importance in leading to the most successful selection of securities—particularly common stocks. If the practitioner is to use the past record as the starting point for a study, the figures must be presented adequately and accurately. Analysts who fail to make the corrections required by sound techniques do a bad professional job of analysis. From that point of view, a comprehensive training in financial statement analysis is an essential part of the practitioner's education.

Statement Analysis Less Helpful in Selecting Stocks Than Bonds.   Competent marshaling of the figures can usually be depended on to lead to successful choices of bonds and preferred stocks. Here the overriding question is whether the issue meets certain minimum standards of safety based on past performance. But in the common stock field, values depend to a significant extent on expectations as to the rate of future growth of earnings. Consequently, the following four factors will largely determine the success of a common stock purchase:

Whether the analyst's expectations are more accurate than the market's

Whether such expectations are fulfilled

3. Whether current expectations about future growth rate are more or less favorable than earlier ones

4. Changes, up or down, in the market's basis of capitalizing such expectations

These determinants of market value and the success of common stock purchases are by no means closely related to the past record. In view of the present preoccupation with the tempo of the future, much of the analyst's work in an accurate presentation of the past may appear rather irrelevant and of little practical value when applied to the choice of common stocks. It would be unrealistic not to recognize that the emphasis of common stock investing is on the future.

Nonetheless, the analyst should continue to do this searching and critical analysis of the past—for several reasons. First, professional standards must be maintained in whatever the analyst does, even though the market may, at times, seem to pay little heed to such presentations. Second, it is still true that in a number of individual instances this critical analysis will lead to worthwhile conclusions as to the overvaluation of certain issues and, particularly, the undervaluation of others. Often the analysis of earnings merely confirms that the earnings figures presented by the company are reasonably accurate and the net adjustments are so small as to be insignificant. Very often this is an indication that the market is dealing with the correct earnings number and that there is little likelihood that the stock will be priced other than in line with the market. It is just as important to eliminate fairly priced stocks from consideration as potential purchases as it is to discover those that are undervalued or overvalued. Third, regardless of the valuation model used—a multiplier of earnings, dividend discount model, or whatever—the current level of earnings is the starting point of the calculations and projections. To project properly for a given company, the current earning power must be determined as accurately as possible. Earning power might be called "the capacity to earn," and this capacity is not found solely in the accounting records. Leading questions are whether the company has the physical, manufacturing, distribution, managerial, financial, and other capabilities necessary to achieve the projections. If a company does not have those capacities in place, can the company acquire them? If the company has "done it before," the projections of the future have been demonstrated to be at least reasonable. Finally, the stock markets of the future will reflect periods of optimism during which a price is willingly paid for expected future success far exceeding the past—and more pessimistic times when even proven accomplishments can be bought at miserly prices.

Overview of the Seven Steps in the Analysis of Income Statements

To arrive at the indicated earning power for the period studied, the analyst should follow a standard procedure consisting of seven steps (the first two are discussed at length in this chapter):

1. *Deal properly with nonrecurring items.* The analyst must eliminate nonrecurring items from a single-year analysis, but include them in most long-term analyses.

2. *Eliminate unjustified income recognition.* Analysts need to eliminate any reported income that is not justified by economic substance. For example, if a company awards key officers and employees compensation in the form of stock options that have economic value but are not considered to be compensation by accounting rules, the analyst should record the estimated value of the option as compensation expense, less its tax effect, and thereby reduce the company's earnings. (Proper income recognition is indirectly a subject of all chapters on financial statement analysis, i.e., Chapters 10 through 20.)

3. *Direct entries to surplus.* Earnings must be adjusted to include inappropriate direct entries to surplus (Chapter 12)

4. *Use comparable inventory and depreciation methods.* The analyst should place the inventory valuation (Chapter 13) and the depreciation and amortization expense (Chapter 14) on a common basis, suitable for comparative study. (This may not always be possible.)

5. *Consolidate affiliates.* Analysts adjust earnings for the operations of subsidiaries and affiliates (Chapter 16) e.g., joint ventures, grantor trusts, investments carried on a cost basis, to the extent they are not included but available. Determining whether a legal entity is an affiliate should be based on the economic substance of the arrangement, and not its legal form.

6. *Provide for income taxes.* The analyst must now adjust the income tax expense to place it in proper relationship to the adjusted earnings before tax (Chapter 17).

7. *Record absent assets and liabilities.* The analyst should include the effects of certain unrecorded assets and liabilities, such as operating leases, some operating loss carryforwards, and some unconsolidated subsidiaries (Chapters 18 and 19).

Nonrecurring Items

Events That Occurred in Past Years

As is evident from the name, nonrecurring gains or losses arise for reasons outside the regular course of the business. The entries are of two main types. The first type relates entirely to events that occurred in past years, such as the following:

Tax Adjustments and Tax Forgiveness. Payments of back taxes or tax refunds, not previously provided for, and interest thereon (sometimes accompanied by adjustments in depreciation reserves), and tax forgiveness are nonrecurring items.

Example. The Tax Reform Act of 1984 included several areas of tax forgiveness. As a result, the 1984 annual report of Archer Daniels Midland Company showed a $12 million reversal of deferred taxes previously provided on unremitted Domestic International Sales Corporation (DISC) earnings; the new law had eliminated all income taxes on unreversed timing differences outstanding on December 31, 1984.

Example. Similarly, the 1984 income statement of Aetna Life and Casualty Insurance Company carried a $65 million "fresh start adjustment" as an income tax credit resulting from the 1984 Act's requirement for a recomputation of policy reserves with permanent forgiveness of the taxes that otherwise would have resulted from that recalculation.

Litigation, Claims, and Renegotiation. Results of litigation or other claims (e.g., renegotiation, damage suits, public utility rate controversies) are nonrecurring items that relate to prior years. *Accounting Trends and Techniques* (1985)[1] showed that 339 out of 600 companies showed loss contingencies as a result of pending litigation. In the vast majority of cases, no liability number was shown, as is customary in the case of litigation. Litigation is by far the largest cause of loss contingencies.

Example. AM International, Inc., in the year ended July 31,1984, settled a lawsuit with Richard B. Black, former chairman of the board, by certain stock transactions (the value of which was not clear) and by canceling a note of $1,668,750 owed by Black to the company.

Changes in Accounting and in Accounting Estimates. Another nonrecurring item is the cumulative effect of an accounting change or a change in an estimate (for the latter see the Bethlehem example in Chapter 14).

[1]AICPA, *Accounting Trends and Techniques*, New York, 1985, p. 52.

Example. In the year ended September 30, 1984, Ashland Oil, Inc., changed the actuarial cost method used in calculating its pension obligations to one that "more closely resembles the method of accounting for pension costs proposed by the Financial Accounting Standards Board." This change decreased the net loss by $6,262,000 ($0.23 per share) in 1984. The pension footnote also indicated that the company's 1984 estimated accumulated plan benefits were calculated based on an 8.9 percent interest rate in 1984 as compared with 10.1 percent interest rate in 1983, resulting in an actuarial loss that would be spread over future years. No figures were given for the effects of the interest rate change.

Prior Period Adjustments and Restatements

Example. Statement 52, *Foreign Currency Translation,*[2] required adjustment of the opening balances to the new requirements by applying current exchange rates to certain foreign subsidiaries. Abbott Laboratories' 1985 form 10-K includes a footnote which states "Translation adjustments for 1983 include opening balance adjustments of $49,376" (thousands).

Events That Occurred in the Current Year

The other type of special transaction originated in the current year but is nonetheless of an exceptional character which sets it off from the ordinary operations. The following are examples of this category:

Sale of Assets.   Profits or losses on the sale of fixed assets—or of investments, for a noninvestment company—are such nonrecurring items.

Major Asset Sale Programs

Major asset sales programs often involve sums that dwarf the ordinary activities of the company. That is, the gain or loss on sale of a major portion of the business may be several times the company's ordinary earning power. The most frequent and important nonrecurring items arise from the sale or other disposition of productive assets—plant or equipment. Such dispositions are often related to sale or discontinuation of a division, product line, or subsidiary. Other expenses of terminating employees, loss on inventories, and the like may be provided for at the same time if the sale is part of a major restructuring.

[2]Financial Accounting Standards Board, Statement 52, *Foreign Currency Translation,* Stanford, Conn., 1981.

The standard accounting treatment, as for other similar transactions, is to show the pretax amount in the income account before (ordinary) net income. The item qualifies for treatment by the analyst as "extraordinary."

Allocating the Gain or Loss to the Proper Years

Allocating such gains to the proper years is often difficult. In most cases, attribution to a single year does not give the right answer. In some cases the loss will be event-oriented, such as an environmental protection ruling, a new law, an abrupt decline of the dollar in the foreign exchange markets, a technological breakthrough, or some other event that is specific and can clearly be identified with a single time period. More often, restructuring, plant shutdowns, product abandonments, and the like are brought about by steadily deteriorating conditions over a relatively long period. Similarly, many gains on sales of assets resulted from price appreciation that occurred over 10 or 20 years, but the gain is recognized in accounting when the sale takes place. The analyst must make a decision, once the time period has been identified: What pattern of spreading the gain or loss best describes the economics of the situation? Although straight-line spreading is the easiest to calculate, the economics may dictate some other attribution of the gain or loss to individual years. The analyst must remember that the pattern of gains or losses that was recorded— all in one period—is the least appropriate one, because it is almost certainly the wrong pattern.

The gain or loss on such dispositions may be excluded from the income account by the analyst, but any related tax effects resulting from the excluded gain or loss should also be excluded. Care must be taken to use the proper tax rate (ordinary income, foreign, state, or U. S. rates).

Example. Ideal Basic Industries, during a period of restructuring, made provisions for shutdowns, write-downs, and gains and losses on facilities sold in the amounts of a $15,000,000 loss in 1980, $15,000,000 loss in 1981, $11,768,000 loss in 1983, and a $940,000 gain in 1984. The analyst should exclude these items from the results of each individual year but would probably choose to include them in calculating a five-year average. In 1983 and 1984, the company showed extraordinary gains on early extinguishment of debt in the amounts of $4,663,000 and $4,198,000, respectively. During the years 1982 to 1984, new debt was issued well in excess of the amounts retired in the extinguishment. As a result, interest expense rose rapidly from $32 million in 1982 to $46 million in 1984. There appears to have been no economic gain on the extinguishment, and the gains should be excluded from the income of the individual years. Treatment of such gains over longer periods is arguable, but, in general, they should be excluded.

In the middle 1980s many financial institutions, in an effort to improve their capital ratios, sold off office buildings which had appreciated substantially over the years and leased them back for extended periods. Such sales are not expected to recur, and give little insight into the earning power of the company. They should be excluded from ordinary earnings. In contrast, auto rental companies, such as Hertz, Avis, and National, optimize their use of automobiles by selling them when they reach either a specified age or mileage. Those companies operate their own used car lots, and the sale of cars is clearly a part of the ordinary recurring operations of those companies.

Write-up or Write-down of Investments.   Another nonrecurring item involves adjustments of certain investments to market value, for a non-investment company, or write-down of nonmarketable investments. An example of the latter was the 1985 write-down by American Can Company of its holding of New TC Preferred Stock by $40 million because of losses of the mortgage insurance subsidiary of New TC.

Adjustment of Foreign Assets.   Write-downs or recoveries of foreign assets are also nonrecurring items. In 1979 ITT Corporation made a provision for a $305 million loss on its Quebec pulp mill, "with no tax benefit."

Losses on foreign operations have frequently arisen through both political and financial (foreign-exchange) disturbances. Formerly, many companies with diversified foreign interests set up reserves, usually by charges to income, to absorb possible future losses of this kind. The income statement was thus spared if and when the loss arose. Statement No. 5, *Accounting for Contingencies*,[3] issued in March 1975, bans general reserves of this sort. A provision is made only when the loss becomes "probable," as defined, and it must go through the income statement rather than directly to surplus.

Life Insurance and Other Insurance Gains.   Proceeds of life insurance policies collected are for most companies an irregular source of cash inflows, and not a part of the ordinary activities of the company. Certain other insurance gains are nonrecurring in character. The 1985 annual

---

[3]Financial Accounting Standards Board, Statement No. 5, *Accounting for Contingencies*, Stamford, Conn., 1975.

report of Fluorocarbon Company showed as an extraordinary item $966,000 of insurance collected in excess of the carrying amount of its Birmingham, Alabama, fluid sealing plant which burned in August, 1984. Although fires are a recurring part of the business scene, gains on insurance coverage that exceed the carrying amount of plant and equipment should not be considered a part of the normal operating earnings of a company.

Discontinued Operations. Income from discontinued operations will not recur, although some capital may remain from the discontinued activity. That capital can be reinvested in other profitable operations.

Unusual or Infrequent Items

In general, today's accounting calls for an all-inclusive income statement, with rare exceptions (e.g., certain gains and losses from foreign currency fluctuations, pensions, and marketable securities). The term *extraordinary* has long been restricted to those events that are *both* infrequent and unusual. Extraordinary items are presented below the line called "Net Income" and are presented "net of tax." At the same time events that are *either* unusual or infrequent, but not both are shown separately on the face of the income statement, above net income, and must be shown without the tax effect. Footnotes usually reveal the related tax effect. The analyst will generally conclude that items that are either unusual or infrequent should be treated as nonrecurring.

Twofold Status of Nonrecurring Items in Analysis

Most nonrecurring items play a double and contradictory role in security analysis. They should be excluded from the results for a single year, but they should be included in the overall results for a period of years. A substantial refund of overpaid taxes, for example, has nothing to do with the current year's operating profit, and it is a misuse of language to call it part of the "earnings" of the year in which it was received. Because the analyst is interested in trends, the results of events need to be placed in the years in which the events occurred. If a tax refund is received in 1987 for overpayment of taxes on income earned in 1984 and 1985, the analyst should restate the taxes for 1984 and 1985 and eliminate the refund from 1987.

In a 7- or 10-year analysis of average earnings, a tax refund pertaining to the period belongs in the picture just as much as the profits or losses against which it accrued. In a long-range analysis of past results, the best rule is to take in every real profit or loss item unless it is quite unrelated to the normal operations of the business. Voluntary markups or markdowns of capital items, such as plant or intangibles, should not be considered a real gain or loss.

Analysts frequently encounter factors that influence income favorably or unfavorably for the short term, but that will change significantly during the period for which they are projecting income. Examples might include:

- Low-cost debt that will mature in a few years
- A favorable lease that is soon to expire
- The near-term expiration of patents, royalties, and supply and other contracts

Analysts will adjust projections to reflect, say, that the old 4 percent bonds which mature in two years are likely to be refinanced with 10 percent bonds.

Rules for the Treatment of Nonrecurring Items

Clearly, where substantial nonrecurring items exist there cannot be any completely satisfactory statements of earnings by single years, for neither the inclusion nor the exclusion of such items will do full justice to the situation. It is doubtful, in any event, that really worthwhile indications of earning power and intrinsic value could be obtained from a study of the current year's results alone. Fuller consideration of this point must be reserved for the discussion of the significance of the earnings record in Chapter 29.

However, the security analyst does face the problem of properly interpreting, and perhaps restating, the earnings reported for relatively short periods. A logical and consistent approach to the various kinds of nonrecurring items is needed. The analyst may be helped by the following three suggestions for the treatment of nonrecurring items in the income statement:

1. Small items should be accepted as reported. For convenience, *small* is defined as affecting net income by less than 5 percent. If a number of items are involved, the cumulative effect shall be considered in applying the 5 percent rule.
2. When an item is excluded, a corresponding adjustment must be allowed for in the income tax deduction.

3. Most nonrecurring items excluded from the single year's analysis must nevertheless be included in a statement of long-term or average results.

Gains and Losses on the Company's Securities

Gains and losses on the early extinguishment of debt raise two issues. A gain may reflect a recent rise in interest rates or perhaps a decline in credit rating that occurred over many years. The economic cause of the gain must be determined to identify the year or years in which the gain should be placed—if any.

A second issue is whether the gain should be included at all. An appropriate question is whether the company is really any "better off." If the company is merely substituting a smaller face amount of high-coupon bonds for a larger face amount of low-coupon bonds, the cost of capital stays about the same for the ongoing firm. What was gained in the face amount of bonds outstanding will be lost in the higher coupons which will be paid in future years. (The present value of the new and old bonds is the same.) Yet, for a firm facing near-term liquidation, the gain is very real because it will be available for distribution to shareholders.

Whatever the source of funds for the extinguishment, a cost of capital or an opportunity cost was incurred at the same market level as that at which the debt was extinguished. For the ongoing firm, gains and losses from all capital transactions are best excluded at least from the current year's results.

A particularly troublesome transaction is a gain on extinguishment of debt when it is accomplished by a swap for the company's equity securities. The tax effects of extinguishment of debt through use of the company's stock are somewhat unusual. Any gain is considered income by the IRS, but the income can be avoided by electing to reduce the tax-cost basis of depreciable assets, if any exist. Thus, although the income will be free from immediate taxation, the reduction in depreciation in future years will increase future taxable income by exactly the same amount, so that income taxes will be paid in subsequent years. Thus, deferred income taxes should be provided on the gain.

A key question is whether the company sold stock at a favorable or unfavorable price. Gains on the extinguishment of debt often occur because interest rates have risen. When interest rates are high, it is likely that stocks are depressed. Thus, the analyst may wish to determine whether management has made a wise decision under the circumstances. The company, of course, could have sold stock without paying off the debt, which suggests that the fact that they paid off the debt is somewhat irrelevant. For purposes of determining earning power, such "internal" transactions are irrelevant. Yet the longer-term record should include the tax expense, because it probably will become payable.

Capital Gains and Losses of Financial Companies

Financial companies are those whose assets are almost exclusively in the form of cash, receivables, and securities. They include:

- Banks
- Insurance companies
- Investment companies and mutual funds
- Holding companies that do not report on a consolidated basis
- Credit or finance companies

In all but the latter group, investment in marketable securities is a major or at least a significant part of the business. Gains or losses from the investment portfolio, both realized and unrealized, will usually be significant in relation to what is called its ordinary or operating income. Should such changes in portfolio values be viewed as recurring or nonrecurring items in the analysis of income accounts of financial companies?

The question has no categorical answer. These gains and losses are certainly recurring in the sense that they occur every year in a greater or lesser amount, and they are without doubt related to the regular business operations. But they are not recurring in the sense that under normal operating conditions the business would be geared to make a certain normal profit out of security price movements. The year-to-year fluctuations in prices of equity securities are much larger than the expected annual average capital appreciation, and will not give a representative number, even if averaged over several years. Thus, their inclusion is likely to give misleading signals about the future. In contrast, the interest and dividend income from the securities owned is reasonably stable and predictable.

There seems to be a sharp distinction between realized and unrealized profits or losses. The former are necessarily entered on the books; they have income tax consequences; in the case of most investment funds, realized profits result in corresponding distributions to stockholders.[4]

---

[4]Under the tax code, regulated investment companies may reduce or avoid income tax by distributing their income and realized security profits in a prescribed manner.

However, a change in market value may be left unrecognized or is perhaps mentioned only in a footnote to the balance sheet or as a direct entry to equity, depending on the industry. Whether a security profit or loss is "real" until it is realized is a less important issue than it appears—the real distinction is between the overall long-term results, which are of major significance, and the more or less fortuitous changes in security values during a single year.

In a single-year analysis, the analyst should group together the realized and unrealized portfolio gain or loss. (This is done in the standard or conventional form of reporting the income statement of insurance companies.) The figures for the 12 months should be presented in two parts: (1) ordinary income and (2) portfolio profit or loss. Comparatively little significance will attach to the latter component because it is governed mainly by security-market conditions in the year, but the former may serve as a guide to future projections.

In a long-term analysis the portfolio results must always play a part; for investment funds, portfolio results are particularly significant in determining the relative accomplishment of the management. Former editions of this book suggested that the period taken for study be one between substantially equal levels of the stock market (the "equal level method"). For such a span the portfolio profit and loss would properly enter into the analysis on a par with the other components of earning power, providing a measure of the skill of the management in this important part of the operations of a financial company.

Because markets move to new record high levels, such comparisons are not always available—the ending level may be far above any useful starting point. An alternative is to calculate (or estimate) portfolio betas and use them to adjust the observed returns for market risk. Comparisons of risk-adjusted returns over time are as useful as results from the equal level method. In either case the time period should be at least five years, preferably longer.

Such comparisons of portfolios should seek to bring together companies with similar general policies, objectives, and portfolio compositions. It is obvious, for instance, that an all-stock fund would be expected to show better results during a rising stock market than would a balanced fund with a substantial bond component.

12

Effect of Reserves, Contingencies, and Valuation Accounts on the Income Statement

Use of Reserves Restricted

Reserves have played a prominent but not always helpful part in corporate accounting. The unhelpful type of reserves consisted of arbitrary amounts of income set aside by management to provide for general and unspecified contingencies. Such reserves were set up in good years, and the amounts brought back in poor years, thereby smoothing the earnings trend. The word *reserves* continues in use today, but FASB Statement No. 5, *Accounting for Contingencies*,[1] eliminates most questionable uses. This statement requires that a loss contingency be accrued by a charge to income if

1. It is probable that an asset has been impaired or a liability has been incurred at the date of the financial statements

2. It is probable that future events will occur confirming the fact of the loss

3. The amount can be reasonably estimated

[1]Financial Accounting Standards Board, Stanford, Conn., 1975.

If the amount cannot be determined, disclosure is required.

The recognition of gain contingencies in income is forbidden. Current accounting eliminates reserves for general or unspecified business risks and many remote contingencies such as:

- Guarantees of indebtedness of others
- Standby letters of credit
- Guarantees to repurchase receivables
- Self-insurance

The write-down of operating assets was specifically excluded from Statement 5. Special problems of write-offs resulting from restructurings are treated in separate sections of this chapter, as are postemployment benefits and foreign currency translation.

Three Classes of Reserves Generally

The word *reserves* is commonly used to describe three types of accounting items:

- Valuations accounts
- Liabilities
- Reserves against future developments

Valuation Accounts.   The standard reserves to reduce assets in valuation accounts are those against:

- Receivables, for uncollectables
- Fixed assets, for depreciation and other amortization
- Marketable securities to mark down to current price
- Other investments and net foreign assets to estimated current value or recoverable amount
- Inventories, to a figure below cost
- Loans and mortgages, for doubtful accounts

Liabilities.   Some routine liabilities arising from the past are called reserves, usually when the liability is *noncurrent and uncertain as to timing or amount*. Liabilities include reserves for taxes, for renegotiation, for pensions (especially where "book reserve" pension accounting is used), for claims in litigation, and for similar liabilities.

Other liability reserves are especially important in specific industries, for example:

Industry	Reserve
Insurance	Unearned premiums
	Policy reserves
	Loss reserves
Credit	Unearned finance charges
Transportation	Injuries and damages
Shipping	Recapture of subsidy
Public utilities	Rate adjustments and refunds

All these may be called reserves, simply because of uncertainties of timing or amount, but they are really liabilities.

Reserves against Future Developments.   Reserves to provide for probable losses include: plant impairments and similar costs for proposed plant restructuring, closure or abandonment, and discontinuation of a product line.

Balance Sheet Treatment of Reserve Items

The reserve type of transaction appears in the income statement under such titles as "Provision for Plant Shutdown," "Special Charge," or "Reserve for Rationalization." In each case, there will be a balance sheet effect:

1. An asset will be eliminated or reduced.

2. A liability will created or increased.

3. Stockholders' equity will be reduced.

Special Rules for Treatment of Certain Reserve Items

Small Items.   Reserve items that effect net income by less than 5 percent when all such items are aggregated should be accepted as they appear.

Deferred Taxes.   Deferred income taxes should be considered ordinary deductions from current income, unless they relate clearly to a nonrecurring item or have some other special characteristic.

Discussion of Frequently Used Reserves

The following paragraphs discuss a few reserve items because of their frequency or because of some peculiar characteristic. However, reserves relating to inventory accounting (Chapter 13), depreciation (Chapter 14), and deferred taxes (Chapter 17) are of such importance and complexity that we shall deal with them separately.

Reserves for Bad Debts

Reserves for bad debts are nearly always accepted as stated for nonfinancial companies. Certain financial institutions, such as banks, have special optional rules which may require adjustment by the analyst. The 10-K usually provides charge-off-information that is useful in judging the adequacy of bad debt reserves which are tax-deductible for some companies. Many bank analysts use the actual charge-offs in preference to the "provision for loan losses" (now being phased out for tax purposes for banks having assets of $500 million or more). Those analysts consider such reserves to be a device for smoothing earnings. For companies in installment selling or in the lending business, credit losses are important and may require special scrutiny.

The Treatment of Loan Loss Reserves of Banks

The loan loss reserves of banks can be used both as a device to smooth earnings and as a hidden reserve. As a result, bank analysts often eliminate changes in the reserve for loan losses from the income statement and substitute therefor the actual charge-offs and recoveries of the individual years. This results in more volatile income statements that are probably more reflective of what actually happened in a particular year. Averaging the actual charge-offs and recoveries gives a better picture of earning power than averaging the loan loss reserve as a percentage of loans. At times, bank stock analysts will make major adjustments to the loan loss reserves of these institutions. For example, in the middle 1980s, the reserves were clearly inadequate for banks operating in the "oil patch" to the extent that they were involved heavily in real estate loans and in oil drilling loans. Similarly, analysts made significant adjustments for expected losses on loans to less developed countries.

High-Risk Industries

Certain industries, from time to time or regularly, are at high risk of credit losses. Their loan loss or bad debt provisions require the analyst's special attention. For example, the credit losses of gambling casinos are highly variable from year to year. The shell home business typically makes sales with a very small down payment, and the risk is substantial that buyers will "walk away" from their loans. Those savings and loan associations that face massive withdrawal of deposits may have to sell substantial amounts of mortgages to raise the necessary funds. If the mortgages are under water or of doubtful quality, the ordinary loss provisions may be inadequate.

Allowance for Marketable Securities

These valuation accounts are not tax deductible until losses are actually realized (except for security dealers). FASB Statement No. 12, *Accounting for Certain Marketable Securities*, requires recognition in income of unrealized gains and losses in portfolios of marketable equity securities that are classified as current assets. *Realized* gains and losses are included in income of the period regardless of the current or noncurrent classifications; some, but not all, *unrealized* gains and losses of noncurrent portfolios of equity securities are shown in the equity section of the balance sheet, but they bypass the income statement. Certain industries have specialized accounting for marketable securities.

For nonfinancial companies, changes in such reserves should be regarded as nonrecurring, but they are rarely important enough to require adjustment of the income account. In the analysis of financial companies, distinguishing between unrealized depreciation (or "quotational losses") on portfolio securities and losses actually taken does not seem practicable.

Example. In 1982 Resorts International, Inc., reported a net gain of $16.7 million from marketable securities. This number included $42.2 million from the sale of U.S. Treasury bond futures contracts and certain Treasury bonds, losses of $6 million from the sale of marketable equity securities, and dividend income of $2.7 million. The gain triggered recognition of the benefit of $4.2 million of tax loss carryforwards. In addition, working capital was enhanced by $45 million by reclassification of marketable securities to current assets. Although the company's primary business is hotels and casinos, it has had an interesting history of investing in interest rate and metals futures contracts as well as fixed income and equity securities. The investing activities have been sufficiently large to justify the analyst marking the portfolio to market and calculating annual investment results.

Reserves Against Other Investments

In general, reserves for investments apply to subsidiary or affiliated companies. Valuation accounts are applied to subsidiaries and affiliates under several sets of circumstances. If management has determined to sell or liquidate a subsidiary, a loss may be recognized based on the estimated proceeds, net of expenses. Occasionally foreign subsidiaries will be nationalized with inadequate compensation, and the compensation may be in dispute, involving either negotiations or litigation. Under those circumstances, an estimate of the loss is made, and the carrying amount of the investment is reduced to reflect the expected loss.

Renegotiation and Litigation Reserves

A significant source of the reserve type of liability is the various amounts that are set aside or should be, for renegotiation of contracts in dispute and for the outcome of litigation. Some examples are:

- Disputes in defense contracts
- Disapproval by the commissioner of insurance premiums charged
- Refund order by a state utility commission
- Litigation over a force majeure cancellation of contract
- Litigation over a tax dispute
- Litigation over application of price control regulations

Example. The 1985 Exxon Corporation annual report showed a line item in the income statement titled "Hawkins provision" in the amount of $948 million, with a footnote on the face of the statement that the amount, net of related taxes, was $545 million. This case concerned a price dispute about oil produced in the East Texas Hawkins Field. Disclosure was suitable throughout the years of litigation. An analyst would normally spread a loss of this sort over the years in which the oil was produced. We know now that the earnings of those years were overstated.

Property and Casualty Insurance Reserves

In the fire and casualty insurance business, damage claims—both those litigated and those settled peaceably—are a basic part of operations. The results for any year and the equity shown for the stockholders will depend in large measure on the method followed in computing reserves for unsettled and unreported losses. The regulatory bodies require that specific formulas be followed in setting up the minimum reserves for personal injury claims in automobile insurance and for workers' compensation claims. (If the company's own estimate, on a "case basis," indicates a larger liability, that figure must be used instead.) Liability under other types of claims is a matter for management to determine, subject to a triennial or quadrennial check by insurance commission examiners. There is room for a considerable degree of either overestimation or underestimation in this field.

Unearned-Premium Liability. Analysts give credit in the income statement for certain unearned premiums. Today these are always "short-tailed" policies in which all claims are fully reported shortly after the expiration of the policy. The following formula is used by some analysts to calculate the value of these policies, representing approximately the cost of putting the business on the books.

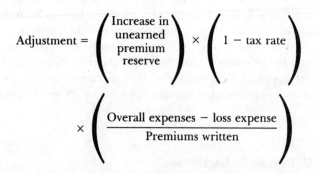

$$\text{Adjustment} = \begin{pmatrix} \text{Increase in} \\ \text{unearned} \\ \text{premium} \\ \text{reserve} \end{pmatrix} \times \begin{pmatrix} 1 - \text{tax rate} \end{pmatrix}$$

$$\times \begin{pmatrix} \dfrac{\text{Overall expenses} - \text{loss expense}}{\text{Premiums written}} \end{pmatrix}$$

Analysts must use only the increase in unearned premiums for the particular types of policies for which they wish to give credit, using information from the Commissioners' Standard Report. Once the adjustment is calculated, the resulting number is compared with the prices acceptable to reinsurance companies for insuring the same liability. This procedure is recommended.

The previous practice of including in income 35 to 40 percent of the unearned premium on long-tailed policies, such as product liability, has proved to be a poor practice because of failure to make the proper tax adjustment and because of a tremendous underestimation of the cost of claims in an era of inflation. Very few analysts or financial services continue this previously popular procedure. It is interesting that the Tax Reform Act of 1986 embraced this repudiated form of income for the first time, subjecting 20 percent of the increase in unearned premiums to taxation.

Other Common Reserves

Reserve for Unearned Finance Charges

The accounting for finance charges "paid" by the borrower in advance—by having them added to his debt—is essentially identical with that for insurance premiums paid on issuance of the policy. A reserve is set up for that portion of the finance charges that has not been earned by the passage of time. The amount is properly deductible from the receivables themselves on the asset side along with the bad-debt reserve.

Undoubtedly the stockholders have some equity in these unearned finance charges, since they partly reflect expenses incurred in putting the business on the books, as do the unearned-premium reserves of insurance companies. It is not customary to allow for such an equity in any official calculation of earnings or net worth. Caution would suggest that such values be used as additional motivation for purchasing a stock already considered undervalued rather than putting them into the valuation calculation itself. Our conservatism is bolstered by the current abuses of somewhat similar fee income by some financial institutions.

Reserve for Unexpired Subscriptions

The liability of newspaper and magazine publishers for unexpired subscriptions is similar to that for unearned premiums. Unexpired subscriptions offer an interesting example of an unbooked asset. Subscriptions are liabilities to pay money or deliver the publication, yet the liability is more than offset by the value of the customer list. When a magazine ceases publication, other publishers are pleased to purchase the customer list for cash and, in addition, assume the liability for the subscriptions. The acquiring publisher then offers the old subscribers the choice of a new publication or return of the remaining portion of the subscription price. Since most subscribers choose the new publication, the purchase is an attractive and inexpensive way of increasing circulation. Again, we would not be anxious to include in the accounts any value for the unexpired subscriptions, but they are an incentive in the decision to buy a stock already determined to be reasonably priced. The analyst has no way to value a subscription list because that would require knowledge of subscriber demographics, such as age, location, income, wealth, and hobbies.

Reserve for Rate Adjustments

Public utility companies have frequently been subject to regulatory proceedings looking to reduce rates and charges. In some cases such reductions, if ordered, will be retroactive. Many of these rate cases result from plant abandonments due to excess capacity, to construction delays which increase the interest costs of plants, and to unexpected inflation. Consumer groups and others often vigorously resist the resulting increase in the cost of utility products and services. Rate commissions have disallowed some costs as being imprudently incurred; in some cases both return on investment and recovery of investment have been disallowed. Utility companies have been extremely reluctant to write down the assets in question, because they believe that once they do so the rate commission will be far less likely to grant them recovery. Thus, they would prefer to maintain the old carrying values until the final judicial appeal has been turned down. This, of course, can extend over several years in the case of appeals that must go through several levels of the court system. This delayed recognition of losses when they become probable is not justifiable. In such cases, analysts should attempt their own estimates of an appropriate adjustment and treat it as a nonrecurring item.

Valuation Accounts for Loan and Mortgage Portfolios

Portfolios of loans and mortgages held by thrift institutions, such as savings and loan associations and mutual savings banks, are ordinarily carried at cost, adjusted for amortization of premiums and accretion of discounts. A loan loss reserve is provided. However, that loan loss reserve is an estimate of credit losses and has nothing to do with the market value of the portfolio. Under some circumstances, the thrift institution may be forced to liquidate a significant portion of its portfolio in order to raise cash either to pay interest or cover the withdrawal of deposits. Since accounting does not require these portfolios to be carried at market value, it is incumbent upon the analyst to make an estimate of market value and of the degree of invasion of the portfolio that is likely to take place when a thrift institution gets into trouble. Such a calculation is not necessary, of course, if the institution is profitable and the maturities of its loan portfolio are reasonably well matched against the maturities of outstanding deposit instruments.

Provision for Losses on Major Restructurings

Major Write-Downs

Discontinuation of a product line, sale of a segment, reorganization of a division, or other restructuring, are nonrecurring items which usually require that a provision be set up for expected losses. These write-downs and write-offs are presented in the accounts with a variety of descriptive titles, some of which tend to soften the negative aspects and sometimes leave the impression that the whole affair is a bit of good news. Losses are recognized based on a management decision to dispose of assets and activities and the amount is a management estimate, usually based on a written plan that has been approved by the Board of Directors. The problem is that plans do change, and the program may ultimately turn out to be much larger or smaller than originally thought. In general, accounting for management intentions is a perilous activity. Analyzing such accounting is equally perilous and analysts often find themselves waiting for the other shoe to drop. The bookkeeping entries may include both a reduction in the carrying amounts of assets and setting up a liability. A major cost is the various termination benefits given to employees. These amounts include early retirement incentives, aid in finding employment, counseling, moving and traveling expenses, and special separation bonuses and are often more significant in amount than the losses on inventory and plant. The analytical issues include both the estimation of the loss and its treatment as a nonrecurring event.

Table 12.1. Armco, Inc.
(In Millions of Dollars)

Year	Income from continuing operation	Oil field equipment	Steel operations	Fabricated products and services	Nickel	Other	Gain on sale	Total
			Nonrecurring items					
			Special charges					
1986	(361.6)*	(108.0)	(235.0)	—	—	7.4	—	(335.6)
1985	(143.2)*	25.1	(110.0)	69.9	—	42.0†	167.9‡	55.9
1984	(249.3)*	(190.0)	(10.0)	(10.0)	—	(135.0)§	(172.5)¶	(172.5)
1983	(506.2)	—	(235.9)	—	—	(60.8)	—	(296.7)
1982	(359.8)	—	(300.0)	—	(71.9)	(88.4)	—	(460.3)
1981	220.9	—	—	—	—	—	—	—

*As restated in 1986.
†Includes $58 tax benefit of loss carryforward.
‡Aerospace and strategic materials and $33.2 gain on sale of tax benefits.
§Includes $120 provision for future losses of Armco Financial Services Group.
¶Coal operations.

Example. Table 12.1 shows the series of special write-offs, provisions for losses, gains on sales, and related nonrecurring transactions resulting from Armco, Inc.'s efforts to restructure nearly all of its operations during the years 1982 through 1986. Several characteristics of such restructurings are shown in the table and deserve mention. First, the initial write-off, write-down, or loss provision is generally a round number, indicating that it is a rough estimate rather than a realized gain or loss. Second, it is not uncommon for a company to discover that the first cut was not deep enough, and that additional write-downs and loss provisions are necessary. This is seen in the company's steel operations in which a sizable provision was made in 1982. In 1983 there was an additional loss that probably represented realized losses, such as sale of assets, payments to terminated employees, and the like (a nonrounded number of $235.9 million). Then, again, further losses were provided for in the subsequent two years (round numbers), with the final resolution lying yet ahead. Fabricated Products and Services is somewhat similar. An initial $10 million provision was made, a round number, followed by a more precise $69.1 million loss. Income from continuing operations has been restated for the years 1984 to 1986 to include the losses of Armco Financial Services Group. Earlier Armco had announced intentions to dispose of that group, but has concluded that another five years will be necessary before those operations can be sold.

Allocation by the Analyst

What should analysts do in situations such as Armco's? It seems clear that the amount of special items shown in each of the years does not pertain purely to the year in which it was reported. Simply adding up all of the gains and losses of the nonrecurring nature and spreading them evenly over some arbitrary period would be an improper technique. The correct technique is to place each gain or loss in the year or years in which it is believed to have occurred. The proper procedure is to examine each loss or gain, seek its cause, and deal with it individually.

Profits in the steel industry peaked in 1979 and, overall, turned into losses for the years 1982 to 1986. An analyst might spread the steel operation losses over the years 1982 to 1986 or perhaps start a year or so earlier.

In the case of the oil field equipment loss and gain, the numbers should be combined and applied to the years when that industry turned unprofitable. Profits in the oil service industry peaked in 1981, losses began in 1983, and by 1985 losses and large charge-offs were pervasive. Given industry conditions, the analyst might spread the net oil field equipment loss over the years 1983 to 1986, admitting that a case can be made for going back as far as 1982.

The outright sale of the coal operations and the aerospace and strategic materials division resulted in gains that were realized in the years they were reported. They should be excluded from estimates of normal earnings, but included in longer term averages. The proceeds of such a sale are, of course, available to earn profits and will add to future earning power.

The loss on the nickel operation probably belongs in 1982, which is about the time that industry turned unprofitable.

Clearly, the benefits of the tax loss carryforwards, which were realized in 1985, came about through the losses accumulated from 1982 through 1985. They should be spread over that period. The tax benefit appears to be a part of normal earnings for those years, in contrast to the other nonrecurring items in the table.

One of the most interesting and unusual of the nonrecurring items in Table 12.1 is the $33.2 million gain on sale of tax benefits. In effect, 1985 net income was credited with an amount which ordinarily would have been tax deductions for subsequent years. Ideally, to place it properly in terms of a normal earnings calculation, it should be spread evenly over future years rather than taken in 1985, although normally the issue is one of spreading nonrecurring items over past years rather than future years.

Analysts also must make decisions about the pattern of allocation among years. They may choose to spread an amount evenly or in proportion to some factor (such as spreading the tax loss carryforward in proportion to the past losses), or even choose an accelerating pace, putting the larger amounts in the later years and smaller amounts in the earlier years.

Cash Flow Timing May Differ

The paragraphs above have encouraged putting the gain or loss in the proper year, but have not addressed the question of cash flows. One of the interesting characteristics of write-offs and provisions for restructuring is that the cash flow may not take place in the year the loss is recorded. Often it occurs the following year or over a period of several years. The analyst should be alert to this fact, since what appears to be a healthy net current asset position may not have received any of the impact of the provision, and an examination of the facts may indicate that liquidity will undergo some strain when the cash outflows actually take place.

Big Bath Accounting

An equally difficult aspect of these major write-offs is so-called big bath accounting. Big bath accounting does not occur when an unprofitable activity is sold or liquidated. It comes about when the activity is continued, but the inventory, plant, and equipment have been written down, resulting in lower subsequent expenses.

Including the Kitchen Sink. Once it is decided to take a major write-down, there is little additional embarrassment in charging off every possible doubtful asset, thereby preparing the way for accounting prosperity. In subsequent years, cost of goods sold and depreciation will be reduced proportionately, so that the company may show excellent profits and a fine return on capital. The cause of the earnings recovery is still clearly visible in the first year after the write-down, because the analyst can see more than one year's financial statements in the annual report. However, a few years after that, the bath may no longer be visible and the analyst is apt to conclude that the company is highly profitable. The dangers of being misled by big bath accounting make it necessary for the analyst to review financial statements covering a history of at least 5 to 10 years before reaching a conclusion about the profitability of a company, the quality of its management, the efficiency of its operations, and similar matters.

Example. In 1969 and 1970 Lockheed Corporation made an aggregate provision of $340 million for losses on Department of Defense contracts. Depreciation expense dropped $8.5 million from $56.3 million in 1970 to $47.8 million in 1972. The lower depreciation, and probably lower cost of goods sold, made an appreciable contribution to 1972 profits of $13.0 million.

Foreign Currency Translation Adjustments

The most frequent cause of changes in dollar-carrying amounts of the assets and liabilities of foreign subsidiaries whose functional currency is the local currency is the fluctuation of the dollar value of that currency. When the foreign currency declines relative to the dollar the beginning net worth of the subsidiary and its earnings during the period will be reduced accordingly, but the loss will bypass the income statement and be shown in an account in equity, generally entitled "Foreign Currency Translation Adjustment." *Adjustment*, in this case, is a nice but misleading term for real gains and losses. Most of them should be included in income.

Transactions and Translation Adjustments

Transactions.   An important but sometimes misunderstood technical difference exists between foreign currency *transactions* and foreign currency *translation adjustments*. Transactions result in gains and losses when an entity holds monetary assets (cash, receivables and the like) or owes liabilities which are denominated in a currency that is different from the currency in which the entity measures its results and, before settlement, the relative values of the currencies change. For example, an entity which uses the peso as its *functional currency* will suffer a transaction loss if it owes French francs while the franc rises relative to the peso.

Translation Adjustments.   Translation adjustments arise in the process of converting the foreign affiliate's financial statements from the local currency into the parent company's home currency. If the currency of the parent is the same as that of the affiliate, no translation adjustment arises. However, if the currencies of the parent and the affiliate are not the same, gains or losses which appeared in the affiliate's statements will usually be different when remeasured in the parent's currency. A subsidiary's gain may even turn out to be a parent company loss, or vice versa. Thus, remember that translation is the process of *remeasuring* the results so that they reflect what happened in terms of the parent's currency—that in which the parent's dividends and borrowings are paid. Remeasuring reveals real gains and losses for those who expect to be paid in dollars— not merely a mechanical "adjustment."

The Importance of a Dollar Perspective. The most fundamental decision in measuring anything is selecting the appropriate unit. When measuring a U.S. company's ability to pay dividends and debt, obviously the measuring unit must be the dollar. Investors and creditors from the United States cannot make decisions other than in terms of the number of dollars they expect to receive. An extreme example will make it obvious why translation adjustments reflect real gains and losses.

Example. Assume that a British subsidiary owns a $100 bill. At the beginning of the year 1 pound is selling at $2. From the viewpoint of the British manager, the company has an asset worth 50 pounds. At the end of the year the pound has dropped to $1. The British manager then calculates that bill is worth 100 pounds, resulting in a 50-pound foreign currency transaction profit, which must be reported in the subsidiary's income statement. This amount will be translated into dollars as a $50 transaction gain. It will appear in the parent's income statement.

The translation process, which converts the statements from the local (pound) perspective to a dollar perspective, recognizes that the $50 transaction gain does not exist in a dollar world and that the $100 bill has not changed in dollar value. Therefore the parent must enter a $50 foreign currency translation adjustment (loss) to wipe out the nonexistent gain. The problem for the analyst is that translation adjustments go directly to equity, leaving the economically nonexistent gain in income. Thus, if the translation adjustment is not recognized for what it is—a loss—income will be overstated. Obviously in this case the analyst would subtract $50 translation adjustment loss from the income statement to offset the incorrect gain that would otherwise be reported.

Are All Translation Adjustments Gains and Losses? It is less obvious what to do when the assets of that subsidiary include, say, a building. The analyst will ask the questions: "If the pound declines, will the parent really suffer a loss on this building? Is it likely that the future flows of dollars from the building will decline?"

The Answers Are Situational. If the building were a warehouse leased to someone for 20 years at a rent of 10,000 pounds per year, it does appear clear that the dollar flows to the parent company and its U.S. stockholders would go up and down with the pound.

However, if the building is a manufacturing plant that produces parts for a product that is sold in the United States for dollars, fluctuations in the pound would not appear to affect very much the expected future dollar cash flows generated by the plant. Thus in the second case the translation adjustment is probably not an economic loss and should not enter income (or the balance sheet either, for that matter). Unhappily, most situations are not nearly so clear as these two examples. The effects of exchange rate changes on plant and equipment will rarely be subject to reliable analysis.

The Difficulty for Analysts Is Lack of Information.   To a security analyst, foreign currency translation adjustments are among the most difficult of the reserve types of transactions to analyze with confidence. Often the necessary information is simply not available.

The Answers Lie in Each Asset and Liability.   The gains and losses that arise as a result of foreign currency fluctuations do so because *individual* assets are owned and liabilities owed and because particular revenues and expenses occur. Exchange rate changes have widely differing economic consequences for different types of assets and liabilities. For a given rate movement, one asset may become more valuable and another less valuable.

Individual Assets and Liabilities Are at Risk—Not the Affiliate's Net Worth.   Yet, many companies, and even accounting itself, take the view that it is the net worth of a foreign subsidiary that is at risk to currency fluctuations, and not the individual assets and liabilities that make up that net worth. As a result, many companies do not keep track of the sources of their various translation gains and losses. Instead, they simply calculate the total amount for the year using a simple short cut formula.[2] Companies that hold that particular viewpoint and use the short-cut method may not be able to answer the analyst's questions about how much of their foreign currency translation adjustment came from the plant account or how much from long-term debt. Clearly foreign currency is not only difficult to analyze, but also lacking in consistent and organized disclosure of the desired details.

---

[2]Setting aside certain adjustments for hedging transactions, the foreign currency translation adjustment equals (1) the opening net worth multiplied by the change in the rate of exchange from the beginning of the year to the end of the year plus (2) net income times the difference between the average rate and the year-end rate. Other companies simply observe the discrepancy between net income and the change in net worth on the balance sheet after both have been translated into dollars. That difference is added to or subtracted from the adjustment balance and though of as a sort of errors and omissions account.

A Compromise Adjustment Technique

Adjustments Arising from Working Capital Should Be Included in Income. The values of short-term monetary items, such as cash, receivables and payables, fluctuate with the value of the foreign currency in which they are denominated. If they are classified as current, they will soon be converted into cash, and the gains and losses will be realized. Similarly, since inventory will be sold in a relatively short time—probably before there is a major change in exchange rates—their adjustment gains and losses should also be included in income. Ideally, gains and losses from working capital items, adjusted of course for tax consequences, are the *minimum* the analyst should include in income.

The Assumptions Behind the Working Capital Recommendation . Several assumptions were made in our recommendation to recognize the translation gains and losses from current assets and liabilities. They should be examined carefully. The inventory assumption is important and it is not inconsistent with today's accounting model. Evidence of the rapid turnover of inventories is abundant. The assumption that inventories can and will be sold is required to justify existing carrying amounts. And the assumption that today's foreign exchange rate is the best estimate of tomorrow's is the basis for recognizing transaction gains and losses on those same assets and liabilities.

Funds Statement May Tell. There is a technique which will often permit the analyst to determine the gains and losses from working capital items. The information is often found in the funds statement. Many funds statements reconcile to changes in working capital. Foreign currency translation adjustments are among the contributors to changes in working capital, which is further evidence that the adjustments are likely soon to become realized gains and losses. This method will not always work because of the flexibility available to management in the presentation of the funds statement. Sometimes they give precisely the number that is wanted: the effect of foreign currency translation on working capital. In other cases, it may be possible to divine the desired number by working back and forth between the two balance sheets and the funds statement.

Current Effects Equal Total Effects Minus Noncurrent Effects. An alternative method is available for estimating the translation effects from working capital if the funds statement fails to tell the story. Since we know the total foreign currency translation adjustment (the year-to-year changes in the amounts in equity), we may be able to estimate the portion from noncurrent items and subtract that from the total to obtain the current portion. The principal noncurrent items are

1. Plant and equipment
2. Long term debt
3. Deferred taxes

   The effect of currency fluctuations on plant, property, and equipment is often shown in Schedules V and VI of the 10-K report, or can be estimated from the segment disclosures and other sources. The amounts and currencies of long term debt are usually available in sufficient detail for estimating their exchange rate gains and losses. Deferred taxes are less significant abroad than in the United States because the books are usually kept on the tax basis. Unless the company is forthcoming, the analyst probably will not have enough information to estimate the effects arising from deferred taxes.

   The exclusion from income of gains and losses from the noncurrent items may not be particularly harmful to the analysis of a company. First, the realization of those gains and losses, even if exchange rates remain exactly where they were at the end of the year, will take place over a long period of time as plant and equipment are used up and as interest and principal of obligations are paid. Second, the extreme difficulty of determining whether translation gains and losses on plant and equipment represent economic gains or losses raises questions whether the analyst has the ability to deal with them. As a result, in the ordinary case, it is adequate to include in income those translation adjustment gains and losses that arise from working capital only.

Inconsistent Treatment of Translation Effects in the Funds Statement

Table 12.2 presents the treatment by four companies of foreign currency translation adjustment effects in the funds statement. The four companies are similar in certain respects:

- Each had an aggregate foreign currency translation adjustment gain.

- Each reconciled to cash and equivalent.

The treatment of the foreign currency translation adjustment and the funds statement was dramatically different for the four companies.

   The presentation by American Brands was ideal. The description of the number was perfectly clear and the analyst would simply add the $24.1 million, less an appropriate provision for income taxes, to net income.

Table 12.2. Foreign Currency Translation Adjustments from 1985
Funds Statements

Company	Funds statement reconciles to	Total foreign currency translation adjustment ($million)	Adjustment— Method of presentation and amount ($ million)
American Brands	Cash	75.3 gain	"Effect of foreign currency rate changes on work capital..............................24.1"
Abbott Laboratories	Cash	28.2 gain	"Cash used in operations: Translation adjustment (28.2)"
IBM	Cash	1,482.0 gain	"Sources ⋮ Uses ⋮ Translation effects..........677.00"
United Technologies	Cash	74.4 gain	Not mentioned

Abbott Laboratories listed its entire foreign currency translation adjustment from both current and noncurrent sources under the broad title "Cash Used in Operations." A subordinate line entitled "Translation Adjustment" gave as the amount a negative $28.2 million. The implication would be that, because it was a negative number, it was a *source of cash* from operations. Probably only a small amount of the adjustment gain was a source of cash and equivalent holdings, and there was no hint of what portion might have come from current or from noncurrent assets and liabilities. The information is useless and misleading.

IBM presented "Translation Effects" in the amount of $677 million as a separate line item below the items referred to as "Sources" and as "Uses." Some addition and subtraction had to be done to determine that it was a gain. Comparative analysis of the balance sheets and the funds statement showed that the amount was the gains from holdings of cash and equivalent items. Other information from the 10-K and annual report permitted an estimate of the gains on noncurrent assets and liabilities, but too many assumptions and guesses were needed to permit a reliable estimate. The analyst should adjust income *at least* for the known gain on cash items.

United Technologies Corporation did not mention the foreign currency effects in its funds statement, although they were doubtless present in some form.

Funds statements that reconcile to working capital have a much better batting average in providing information on the gains and losses from working capital items than do the funds statements reconciling to cash. However, either method can be inconsistent and confusing.

Pensions and Other Postemployment Benefits

Defined Contribution Pension Plans Present No Analysis Problems

Defined contribution plans present no particular problems for the analyst. If the company has made the contribution, it has no liability for any further payments. If a contribution has not been made, the amount is shown on the balance sheet as a current liability. In either event, the cost of pension expense will have been properly reflected in income.

Multiemployer Pension Plans and the Withdrawal Liability

Multiemployer plans become complex only if the company is likely to withdraw from the plan and thereby generate a withdrawal liability under the Employee Retirement Income Security Act of 1974 (ERISA). Once the withdrawal liability is known or becomes estimable the recommended procedure is for the analyst to see that any additional liability (less its tax effect) is recorded as a loss in the income statement, but treated as a nonrecurring item. The balance sheet, too, should be restated.

Defined Benefit Pension Plans

Uncertainty of Pension Liability.   The pension benefit obligation falls in the broad category of reserves for a noncurrent liability of an uncertain amount and timing of payment. Estimations of the size of the pension obligation and its proper present value are a staggering exercise. A 20-year-old man may be working for a company with at least some probability of receiving pension payments 60 years from now. The amount of the payments may depend upon his salary 45 years from now. The actuary must discount using estimates of interest rates over as much as 80 years.

Different choices of salary progression and interest rate assumptions can give defendable answers of which some are five times as large as others.

Opinion 8 Was Too Flexible.   The costs and liabilities of defined benefit pension plans were not comparable under Accounting Principles Board (APB) Opinion No. 8 because almost any actuarial cost method, except "pay-as-you-go" and "terminal funding," was acceptable for purposes of funding and for determining pension expense. In addition, great freedom was available in the selection of actuarial assumptions and in changing them. Comparability of pension expense between companies occurred only by happenstance. The most popular actuarial funding method was "entry age normal," largely because it provided the company with the greatest flexibility in tax planning. Entry age normal is one of the more conservative funding methods, although it can be and often is used with very unconservative methods of dealing with actuarial gains and losses. It calculates the actuarial benefits expected to be paid and then solves for that constant percentage of projected payroll that will fund the benefits by the time they come due. This procedure tends to stabilize profit margins and thereby reduce fluctuations in earnings.

Disclosures Have Been a Stopgap Answer.   Since 1980 footnote disclosure of the actuarial present value of vested and nonvested accumulated plan benefits, plan assets at market value, and the interest rate assumption have been available. The first of these items gave a rough approximation of the liability which would be owed under ERISA if the plan were terminated. No information was given on salary projections, which are a necessary component of the ultimate liability of a final pay plan for an ongoing firm.

New Pension Accounting Required by Statement 87.   In December 1985, the FASB issued Statement No. 87, Employers' Accounting for Pensions. For most of the requirements of Statement 87, the effective date is the first fiscal year beginning after December 15, 1986. That is, for calendar year companies most of the requirements will be in place for the 1987 annual report, although the requirement for recognition of certain pension liabilities is deferred for two additional years.

Ongoing Firm Rather Than Liquidation Approach.   Statement 36 had called for information on accumulated benefits, which are simply the benefits earned to date based on the present salary level. Accumulated benefits are the amount workers would be entitled to if they stopped working for the company at the date of the financial statements—a liquidation notion. Statement 87 calls for a number that is more suitable for the ongoing firm with a final pay plan—the benefits earned for the services rendered to date based on future pay rates—not today's level.

Projected Unit Credit Includes Salary Progression. All companies will be required to use the same actuarial method—the "projected unit credit" (also called "unit credit with service pro rate") actuarial cost method, which includes the salary progression that results from inflation, promotions, and productivity gains. In addition, limitations are put on the freedom to select actuarial assumptions. The interest rate assumption must give consideration to rates of return currently available on existing plan assets and reasonable estimates of the rates at which future contributions, dividends, interest, rent, and maturities will be reinvested. There is an additional admonition that the company should consider rates at which the liability for pensions could be extinguished by purchase of annuities. Here again, the requirements force more realistic and more comparable interest rate assumptions than are commonly used. The salary progression number must be consistent with the interest rate assumption, which should eliminate some game playing in the spread between the interest rate and the salary progression. These two are the most important assumptions in pension calculations. Consistency would require that both incorporate the same inflation assumption.

Prior Service Obligations Arise from Plan Changes

Prior service obligations come about when a plan is initiated or amended and gives benefit credits for previous service. The new accounting calls for amortization of prior service costs and of actuarial gains and losses over the remaining service lives of the existing employees rather than the more typical 30 or 40 years. This forces a more consistent pattern of amortization than has existed in the past. Previous practice for amortization of prior service costs and actuarial gains and losses delayed the larger portion of such effects for unreasonably long periods of time. The amortization period for prior service cost often extended well beyond the work lives of the workers benefited.

Pension Plan Can Be Consolidated by Analysts

Components of Pension Expenses. There will be an extensive set of disclosures, including the following components of pension expense:

1. Service cost
2. Interest cost
3. Actual return on assets
4. Net total of the other components
   a. Net asset gain or loss during the period deferred for later recognition
   b. Amortization of the net gain or loss from earlier periods
   c. Amortization of unrecognized prior service cost
   d. Amortization of any transition net asset or liability existing at the date of initial application of the statement

Income Statement Consolidation

First Method. Given this information plus pension balance sheet information, the analyst may take at least two routes toward consolidating the pension results into the income statement. In one method, the net periodic pension cost for the period would be subtracted from compensation expense, and the service cost component and the various amortization items are added to compensation costs:

- The interest cost is added to the company's other interest expense.
- The return on plan assets is added to the company's "other income."
- Income tax expense is adjusted.

This approach views the pension plan as (1) an investment, with an investment return, (2) a borrowing from the employees, with an interest cost of that borrowing, and (3) a labor cost that includes the amortization of various gains and losses and prior service costs.

Second Method. A second approach to consolidation subtracts the net periodic pension cost for the period from labor expenses and substitutes the service cost component. The interest cost and the investment income are treated as above, but the actual gains and losses for the year are reflected in the income statement as "pension gain or loss" or under some similar title. Taxes would be adjusted. The second method introduces into income all the gains and losses, including investment portfolio results. There are no deferrals or smoothing.

Pension Plan Balance Sheet. All the information needed to construct a pension fund balance sheet will be shown in footnotes including the fair value of plan assets, the pension liability, and details of the unrecognized prior service cost, gains and losses, and the like.

Balance Sheet Consolidation. Simply knowing the pension assets and liability permits setting up a pension fund balance sheet, since the difference between the assets and liability is the net worth or net deficit. If desired, the analyst can consolidate the pension fund's balance sheet into that of the plan sponsor. First, any pension liability or asset shown on the sponsor's balance sheet should be removed and equity adjusted for its removal. Then, the plan assets are added to the assets of the sponsor, the pension liability is added to the sponsor's liabilities, and the difference between the two (the net worth or net deficit of the pension fund) is added to or subtracted from the net worth of the sponsor, less the tax effect. The tax liability would be adjusted for the consolidation.

Such consolidation is encouraged for some purposes, such as analysis of fixed-income securities or the potential to withdraw excess pension assets. However, consolidation can be misleading because of limitations on the prompt access to pension assets, inaccuracy in the estimated pension liability, and the inherent volatility of marketable securities. The analyst is cautioned against consolidation of the pension fund in studies that attempt to determine normal earning power. Fluctuations in the market value of plan assets or a change in a single actuarial assumption might wipe out or double a company's earnings for a particular year. The effects of such fluctuations may distract analysts from more significant matters, such as the company's basic operating activities.

How to Treat Prior Service Cost

A broad question for the analyst is whether payments for the account of past services under a pension plan should be considered a discharge of a past obligation, a nonrecurring charge against earnings, or an ordinary operating expense. What is the practical significance of each choice?

The Creation of Prior Service Liability. A liability for prior service cost occurs when a plan is initiated or amended and gives credit for services that were rendered in previous years. (This book uses the terms *prior service cost* and *past service cost* interchangeably, as does Statement 87.) In effect, the company has an immediate liability, and the worker could walk away the next day, render no more services, and be entitled to the increased benefits under the plan formula. Under ERISA, prior service obligations resulting from plan amendments are phased in over a five-year period for purposes of calculating the ERISA termination liability.

Spreading Prior Service Cost. However, whether or not there is an immediate legal liability, accounting has generally viewed prior service cost as an expense that should be spread over subsequent years.

Recognizing the entire prior service liability as a charge to income at once could result in a noncharacteristic level of earnings.

Past Service as an Ordinary Charge Against Income. Both practical and logical reasoning suggest that the annual pension contributions resulting from past service be included as an ordinary charge against income. Such payments are allowed as annual deductions for tax purposes and are not subject to capitalization in inventories, as are other pension expenses. Past service costs are the result less of events in the distant past than of a voluntary or union-enforced decision to pay out sums in the future. They will represent actual and regular cash disbursements over a period of years, not offset by additional assets for the company. Thus they come much closer to being an ordinary and current expense than the discharge of a past debt, such as the paying off of a serial bond issue.

Nonrecurring Treatment Is Contradictory. The effect of treating the annual payments as a nonrecurring charge is contradictory: They are ignored in the true earnings for a single year but are deducted from the long-term results. Obviously, any *regular* charge that figures in the long-term analysis should also be deducted in a single year's analysis. Otherwise the result is simply to create an unnecessary difference between the successive short-term and the long-term results. (It is only the *irregular* nature of large nonrecurring items that makes it preferable to exclude them from a single-year analysis.)

Actuarial Gains and Losses

Nature of the Gains and Losses. The amortization of actuarial gains and losses is another difficult analytical problem. Actuarial gains and losses are really not quite like ordinary gains and losses. They are not measured from zero but rather from the actuarial assumption. If the assumption is that the portfolio will earn 6 percent and the year's return is 4 percent, an *actuarial loss* equal to 2 percent is multiplied by the opening balance of the plan assets. Obviously, the pension fund did not actually lose money—it made 4 percent. It may turn out that the average rate of return for the next 100 years will be precisely 4 percent, which really means that the actuary and the company should have agreed on 4 percent as their assumption of return on plan assets. In such a case the problem is not that the performance of the plan assets fell short but that the actuarial estimate was too high. Similar arguments can be made for the various other actuarial estimates, whether they be salary progression, turnover, mortality, or whatever.

Changes in Assumptions Are Called Gains and Losses. A change in an actuarial assumption changes the liability, and this is also called an "actuarial gain or loss." It is the peculiar nature of the actuarial gains and losses that appears to justify spreading them over some reasonable period, such as the working lives of the employees, rather than recognizing them at once. In addition, immediate recognition of actuarial gains and losses would tend to inject into the income statement the full effect of the fluctuations of the stock and bond markets. Although those fluctuations are important, they should be studied separately from operating earnings.

Settlements, Curtailments, and Termination Benefits

In recent years it has not been unusual for a company to terminate its pension plan, purchase annuities covering all the company's pension obligation, and take down some of or all the excess assets from the plan. Previous accounting would permit recognition of a gain on the "asset reversion" only if the company did not start up a new defined benefit pension plan. Statement No. 88, *Employers Accounting for Settlements and Curtailments of Defined Benefit Plans and for Termination Benefits*, requires recognition of a gain to the extent that assets are taken down by the plan sponsor. Plan sponsors can leave assets in the pension fund and recognize only part of the gain if they choose. For example, in 1984 AMAX Corporation had about $150 million of excess plan assets but chose to take down only about $100 million in its asset reversion. This left a voluntary $50 million reserve—in effect, prepaid pension expense that is not shown on the balance sheet. The analyst can recognize a gain on *all* the excess assets resulting from a plan termination, treating it as a nonrecurring item, or recognize no gain at present, but instead project lower pension expense in future years as a result of the excess assets left in the plan. Your authors are not of one mind on this matter.

Other Postemployment Benefits

Disclosure of the annual costs of other *post*employment benefits (OPEB) is required. These benefits consist primarily of health and life insurance that are continued after the employee has reached retirement age. Often the spouse is covered. The amounts are potentially very large. In 1985 the average cost of medical care for persons over age 65 was about $4800 per annum. Medicare paid for approximately 60 percent of that number, leaving the rest to be paid by the elderly people and/or their previous employers. The amount and nature of coverage, the deductibles, caps and other characteristics of the plan will vary from company to company, but there is little doubt that many companies are obligated for very substantial amounts of health benefits for many years into the future. Accrual accounting would seem to call for recording the liability and the expense for those benefits over the working lives of the employees rather than on a pay-as-you-go basis (the current practice). The recommended procedure for accruing an OPEB balance sheet liability is to multiply the annual expense number by a factor between 10 and 15, with the factor rising with the age of the work force. Annual changes in the liability should be added to the reported expense number, with an appropriate tax adjustment.

Example. The following data are based on information provided by a company which has a large number of divisions, nearly all of which offer postretirement health care and life insurance benefits. The benefits are generally similar, but not identical for all divisions. Table 12.3 shows the benefits in 1985 in a typical division.

Table 12.3. Other Postemployment Benefits

Postemployment Medical Benefits	
Eligibility	Retirees and dependents
Hospitalization	100% of reasonable and customary charges
Surgical	$500 schedule
Deductible	$100–$150 per individual (based on pay)
	80–100% after $1000 employee
	out-of-pocket expense
Maximum	$25,000 per 3 years
Integration with Medicare	Carve-out
Part B Reimbursement	$12.26
Employee contributions	None
Dental benefits	None in 1985

Postemployment Death Benefits (Nonpension)		
	Company-paid	Contributory
Benefit at retirement	$1,000–5,000	None
Ultimate benefit	Same	None
Employee contributions	—	None

In 1985 the company's pay-as-you-go expense amounted to $5,740,000. If the company were to reflect the expense of benefits earned to date (the equivalent of the unit credit method) and amortize the accumulated benefits over 10 years, the expense would rise to $23,104,000, assuming 9 percent inflation in medical costs and a 9 percent investment return. A projected unit credit approach would raise the expense item to $36,364,000. The balance sheet liability for all accumulated liabilities would be $110,000,000, and the projected benefit obligation would be $195,000,000. Use of the projected unit credit method would have reduced profits and net worth by about 5 percent. The average age of the work force was in the low thirties.

13
Inventory Valuation and Cost of Goods Sold

From the standpoint of security analysis, the problems of inventory accounting and of depreciation accounting have a generic relationship. Both can have an important bearing on reported earnings, and in both cases the amounts are determined in accordance with principles and theories rather than as the simple result of cash or credit transactions during the year under review. Chapter 13 discusses inventory and depreciation accounting briefly before concentrating on inventory valuation.

Methods of Valuing Inventories and Calculating Depreciation

The standard method of valuing merchandise inventory is to carry it "at cost or market, whichever is lower." The standard method of calculating depreciation (and other amortization) is to write down each depreciable item from cost to salvage value by regular charges against income extending over its expected life. Until recently the chief job of the security analyst in these fields has been to make sure that the standard accounting practices were followed in the corporate reports examined.

In general, the departures were in the direction of overstatement of income, e.g., by failure to mark down inventory to market or by omitting or skimping the depreciation charge. Less frequently, the income and assets were understated by an overconservative policy in valuing inventory or figuring depreciation and amortization.

Since the end of World War II, the questions of inventory valuation and depreciation policy have taken on a somewhat different complexion. Many corporate managers have thought that the standard accounting practice was not well-suited to a protracted period of rising prices. On the one hand, profits were increased by a nonrecurring and probably illusory gain arising from the marking up of inventory values to their ever-higher replacement levels. On the other hand, the tax-allowed depreciation, based on cost, was becoming grossly inadequate to provide for the replacement of worn-out facilities at these same higher price levels. When the tax laws were changed to permit faster depreciation, many companies changed their accounting practices to minimize the impact of inflationary forces upon the income statement. The issues involved here have implications beyond the area of accurate reporting to the stockholders. They have led to a vigorous demand for the right to charge higher depreciation against earnings for tax purposes during inflationary times, and they have also figured prominently in labor disputes where the "real" profits of business and its consequent "ability to pay" have been in controversy.

Inventory Profits and Inflation

The Recent History

The post–World War II years could be divided (somewhat arbitrarily) into five phases of inflation. The 1947–1957 period reflected pent-up inflationary forces, held down by wage and price controls during World War II, and the effects of the Korean War. The 1958–1965 years signaled peace and moderate growth, accompanied by relatively moderate inflation and virtually no inventory profits. Deficits from the Viet Nam War and large social spending and turmoil in the international monetary markets led to an acceleration of inflation and inventory profits in the years from 1966 to 1972. The fourth period ends abruptly in 1983 because the awesome inflationary effects of the OPEC oil cartel and the collapse of the Bretton Woods Agreement (fixed exchange rates) seem to have run their course and then abated. The 1984–1986 period benefited from declines in oil and other commodity prices and a stronger dollar. Table 13.1 demonstrates the expected pattern—high inventory profits tend to accompany high inflation rates, and the opposite holds true for lower inflation.

Table 13.1. Inflation and Inventory Profits, 1947–1986

Period	Average annual inflation rate (%)*	Corporate profits before tax ($ billion)	Inventory mark-up ($ billion)	Mark-up as percent of corporate profits
1947–1957	2.6	40.3	1.7	4.2
1958–1965	1.4	56.5	0.2	0.3
1966–1972	4.2	85.5	4.4	5.1
1973–1983	7.8	187.4	23.3	12.4
1984–1986	3.0	196.1†	−1.1†	0.0†

*Compound annual rates of change in the Consumer Price Index for all clerical and factory workers, prepared by the Department of Labor.

†Fourth quarter of 1986 reflects preliminary figures.

SOURCES: Corporate Domestic Product of the National Income and Products Accounts is prepared by the Department of Commerce. Data taken from Department of Commerce, *Business Statistics*, 1984, p. 201; *Business Conditions Digest*, April 1984, pp. 95, 99; *Survey of Current Business*, February 1987, pp. 5–6.

It is clear from Table 13.1 that inventory profits tend to follow the pattern of acceleration and deceleration of price changes in the economy. The nineteenth-century economic history of the United States shows that prices sometimes follow a downward course for extended periods. The effects on profits would be just the opposite under such circumstances, since they would result in inventory mark-downs rather than mark-ups.

Security Analyst's Approach to Inventories and Depreciation

Adjust to Normalize Expense. The security analyst is interested in these matters from two practical standpoints. First, analysts must decide what treatment of inventory and depreciation will help in calculating the normal earning power and—less important—the actual asset values.

Seek Comparability. Second, to the extent possible, the analyst must develop a means of placing all companies in a given industrial group on the same accounting basis, as regards inventories and depreciation, to permit a proper comparative analysis.

Inflation Accounting

From 1976 to 1986 most large companies were required, first by the SEC and then by the FASB, to report the effects of inflation on their inventories and plant accounts. In 1987 the information became voluntary, but some companies may continue to provide it. The FASB requirements included presentations in a constant-dollar mode, using dollars of constant purchasing power, which made the information more complex.[1] Analysts could prepare constant-dollar numbers from the annual report without the help of the companies, but none thought it worthwhile. The current cost and replacement cost numbers are potentially useful. They permit analysts to place FIFO companies on a LIFO inventory basis, which we consider to be a better measure of earning power.[2] The current cost and replacement cost information on the plant account and on depreciation may be helpful in estimating the costs of new plant and equipment, but these figures are not very accurate.

Analysts' Resounding Apathy Is Not Justified

Although the inflation accounting information has enjoyed little interest among users of financial statements,[3] we encourage the analyst at least to consider the implications provided by the information for

- Converting FIFO income statements to LIFO
- Estimating future capital expenditure levels
- Working capital requirements
- Liquidating values
- Potential as takeover candidates

---

[1] For many years accountants have worried about the unstable nature of the dollar, or any other currency, as a measuring unit when its purchasing power changes. Many feel that accounting has an obligation to measure in inflation-free units. If analysts were to use such dollars of constant purchasing power in their projections, the mathematics of the process would require that they forecast future earnings and dividends in constant dollars. This would require a correct forecast of future inflation. Even worse, the dividends would have to be discounted to present value using the *real* interest rate, which has been hypothesized but never observed. Analysts bypass this problem by dealing in nominal dollars and nominal interest rates, which already have an inflation premium built into them.

[2] LIFO and FIFO methods are discussed extensively in the next section of this chapter.

[3] William C. Norby, "Application of Inflation-Adjusted Accounting Data," *The Financial Analysts Journal*, March–April 1983, pp. 33–39; Robert H. Berliner, "Do Analysts Use Inflation-Adjusted Information? Results of a Survey," *The Financial Analysts Journal*, March–April 1983, pp. 65–72.

Inventory Calculation

FIFO and LIFO

The two most important ways of calculating inventory costs are known as *first-in, first-out* (FIFO) and *last-in, first-out* (LIFO). Both are subject to the "lower of cost or market" requirement. FIFO is based on the usually correct *flow assumption* that a company will deliver the oldest inventory first, before "moth and dust doth corrupt." LIFO inventories must also be carried at cost, but cost is calculated using the assumption that the newest inventory is sold.

The basic difference between FIFO and LIFO is generally illustrated by a company's coal pile. If the coal bought is piled on top and the coal used is taken from the bottom, we have a typical case of first-in, first-out. The old coal is used up first, and the stock remaining would naturally be valued on the basis of the most recent purchases. But if the coal used is taken off the top, the physical flow would be the typical last-in, first-out situation. The coal on hand at the inventory date would include some old or original purchases which would be valued at an unchanging price from year to year.

During a period of sharply rising prices, FIFO calculations mark up inventories to about current replacement cost. Hence computed earnings are increased by a special profit (called "holding gains" by accountants) arising from the sale of older and cheaper materials at advancing quotations. Under the same circumstances, the LIFO method will hold down the carrying value of a given quantity of inventory to its original low level and thus exclude year-to-year inventory profits from the reported earnings.

Increased Use of LIFO

Annually, the publication *Accounting Trends and Techniques* compares many of the accounting practices of 600 companies. The number of companies using LIFO accounting for a significant part of their inventories rose from 194 (32 percent) in 1960 to 400 (67 percent) in 1984.[4] The first-in, first-out method was widely used before the recent inflation, because it seemed to correspond to the actualities of business.

Use of Multiple Methods

LIFO accounting is not acceptable for tax or reporting purposes in most foreign countries, and for that reason most multinational companies

[4]American Institute of Certified Public Accountants, *Accounting Trends and Techniques*, 1961 and 1985.

carry foreign inventories on a FIFO basis. Diversified companies often use specialized inventory accounting techniques ordinarily employed by the industries in which they operate. Thus, a conglomerate that owns a retailing operation is likely to include the retail method among its inventory accounting methods. Subsidiaries engaged in the production of agricultural commodities or precious metals will usually mark such inventories to market prices instead of carrying them on a cost basis. Still other companies use several different inventory accounting methods because they have made acquisitions and either have not had time to change the subsidiary's inventory method or have not found it worth the trouble. In the footnote on accounting policies, companies list the principal inventory cost methods used, but they do not always give much information on how large or small a part of the total inventory is carried on a particular method.

The Economic Logic of LIFO

In continuous production or merchandising, older goods are normally sold first if possible so that those remaining on hand may be fresh and up to date. The newer LIFO idea is thus in reality a somewhat artificial concept, which recommends itself, however, because of its stabilizing effect on corporate results. Beyond this, it has the support of economic theory. For instance, calculations of national income by the Department of Commerce exclude gains or losses from inventory valuation, as unrelated to the actual production and distribution of goods. (Similarly the Department includes a capital consumption adjustment from corporate profits to reflect inadequate depreciation charges, similar to the effects of using replacement cost depreciation.) Finally, the LIFO method is a permitted method of accounting, subject to certain limitations, under the Internal Revenue Code.

Example. The difference between the FIFO (formerly the standard) and the LIFO methods of computing cost of goods sold and inventory on hand can be illustrated by the following simplified and hypothetical example (see Table 13.2): A company starts with 10 million pounds of copper, buys 10 million pounds each year for three years, and sells the same amount each year at a 2-cent advance above current cost price. The initial cost is 10 cents; the average and closing cost price is 15 cents the first year, 20 cents the second year, and 10 cents the third year. We assume that the company has no operating expenses.

Obviously the company ends up where it started in inventory and has made a continuous profit of 2 cents per pound. Common sense would insist the company has made $200,000 each year. But the standard or

Table 13.2. FIFO and LIFO

	First year		Second year		Third year	
		FIFO				
Proceeds of goods sold......................		$1,700,000		$2,200,000		$1,200,000
Cost of goods sold:						
Opening inventory.........	$1,000,000		$1,500,000		$2,000,000	
Purchases.............	1,500,000		2,000,000		1,000,000	
Totals...........	$2,500,000		$3,500,000		$3,000,000	
Less closing inventory (lower of cost or market) ...	1,500,000	1,000,000	2,000,000	1,500,000	1,000,000	2,000,000
Gross profit............		$ 700,000		$ 700,000		$ (800,000)
		LIFO				
Proceeds of goods sold......................		$1,700,000		$2,200,000		$1,200,000
Cost of goods sold (same as purchases during year)......................		1,500,000		2,000,000		1,000,000
Gross profit............		$ 200,000		$ 200,000		$ 200,000
Closing inventory...		1,000,000		1,000,000		1,000,000

FIFO method of accounting would show a profit of $700,000 in the first year, the same in the second year, and a loss of $800,000 in the third year. In general, operating losses can be carried back 3 years or forward 15 years for tax purposes. Thus, the $800,000 operating loss would be carried back against the profits of the previous two years, resulting in a tax refund.

However, by the last-in, first-out method, the profit would work out as $200,000 each year—the sensible figure, and income tax would be payable on this amount in the proper years.

LIFO Problems and Issues

The example we have given places the LIFO method in a particularly (and misleadingly) favorable light, because it excludes two complicating factors: (1) the triggering of profits by layer invasion, and (2) use of questionable versions of LIFO.

The Liquidation of LIFO Cost Layers

Most companies either grow or simply go out of business. Those that grow do an increasing volume of business, which requires a larger volume in inventory. Thus, a company may have 100 units of inventory at the end of year 1 and 175 units at the end of year 2. If prices are rising, the 100 units bought in year 1 will have a lower cost than those bought in year 2. These yearly increments are referred to as "layers." Over a period of time, a company will accumulate many layers in a given pool of products, each at a different price. If a year comes along when the physical volume of inventory declines, the first layer invaded is the most recent one, and if the volume decline is large, additional layers will be invaded, which means that older and older costs are leaving the balance sheet and entering into the costs of goods sold. Since in inflationary times these older costs are presumably lower costs, they increase the profit margin.

IRS Conformity Rules

One of the original requirements for use of LIFO accounting for tax purposes was that the company report its costs of goods sold to shareholders precisely the same way as to the Internal Revenue Service (IRS). This was called the "LIFO Conformity Rule." In addition, the IRS has been rather strict about the size of the LIFO pools (groups of related products) it would accept for tax purposes. Naturally, the companies wanted tax pools that were as all-encompassing as possible, and the IRS was anxious to keep the pools as small as possible to ensure accidental invasion of lower-cost layers, which would result in the larger amounts of tax revenue.

Pools and Puddles

Internal Revenue Service LIFO conformity rules have been relaxed so that companies now can report large "pools" for tax purposes and small puddles to stockholders. Layer invasion occurs less frequently when the inventory pools are large; small pools give management an opportunity to report larger profits almost at will by deliberately reducing the physical volume of certain pools at year end or, say, by setting up pools by model year. The footnote reconciling income taxes with the statutory rate will reveal if a company is using significantly different LIFO pools for tax and stockholder reporting purposes. The footnote on inventories will reveal the amount of LIFO reserves and the amount by which income was increased as a result of invasion of layers. Layer invasion does not always result in an increase in profits. Some older layers have *higher* costs rather than lower costs.

Often, layer invasion occurs by accident, or because a company is discontinuing certain product lines or reducing its size in a restructuring.

Example. Firestone Tire & Rubber Company reported reductions in inventory quantities during 1983 resulting from a partial liquidation of LIFO costs. The effect of this partial liquidation was to decrease cost of sales by $55 million in 1983. Net income for 1983 was $111 million.

Example. The Deere & Company 1985 annual report reported: "During the last three years, the company inventories have declined due mainly to lower levels of production and increased emphasis on inventory reduction. As a result, lower costs which prevailed in prior years were matched against current year revenues, the effect of which was to increase net income. . . ." Of the $158.7 million total income for the three-year period, $151.2 million came about through inventory layer invasion. Yet, at the end of fiscal 1985 the company still had $971 million of LIFO reserves.

Variations of LIFO Calculation

LIFO calculation is not a single method, but rather a family of methods that can give a wide variety of results. Some methods are so misleading that they are not permitted by the SEC. The analyst should realize that management has great flexibility in determining just what expenses shall be capitalized as inventories or written off as period expenses. Accounting requires that at least some factory overhead be included in inventories. The rule may be "If it's here in town it's SG&A (selling, general, and administrative expense), and if it's out at the plant, it's inventory." Thus if the personnel department were located in town, its activities would be expensed; if it were located at the plant, at least part of its expenses would be capitalized as inventory. Conservative managements lean toward capitalizing direct expenses and as few additional costs as possible. More liberal managers capitalize anything related to production, a view encouraged by the 1986 Tax Reform Act. If the procedure is not patently misleading, there is really no way to prove that one inventory judgment is right and another wrong.

Do not automatically assume that a company using LIFO has more conservative accounting than one using FIFO. In certain industries in which costs are dropping dramatically, such as semiconductors and computers, placing the latest costs in inventory decreases costs rather than the opposite. It is interesting that in 1984 only 38 percent of the industry groups that include computers and semiconductors were using LIFO, although the average for all industries was 67 percent. For companies with declining costs, FIFO calculation produces lower profits as well as lower taxes, thereby yielding the traditional advantage of LIFO accounting.

LIFO Reserves

For practical reasons most companies keep their internal inventory records on a FIFO basis and calculate the LIFO numbers only when the financial statements are prepared. Most use pools of dollar value and make the adjustments by applying internal price indexes to the dollar amounts rather than to physical units.

The dollar difference between the LIFO and FIFO inventory amounts is often called the "LIFO reserve," "the excess of current cost over the carrying amount of inventories," and similar terms. A few companies show the reserve on the balance sheet, but most companies using LIFO figures reveal either the reserve or the FIFO amount in footnotes.

Example. Norton Company reported in its inventory footnote for 1984, "If the average or standard cost (first in, first out) method of inventory evaluation (which approximates replacement costs) had been used for all inventories by the company, inventories would have been $62,115,000 higher than reported at December 1, 1984 ($61,327,000 at December 31, 1983)." Note that the LIFO reserve increased only $788,000 as a result of using LIFO during 1984, whereas net income for the year was $60,425,000. The difference in inventory method would have changed earnings by only 1 percent, yet the LIFO reserve was about 10 percent of total shareholders' equity.

Inclusion of LIFO Reserves in Calculating Certain Ratios

The Norton example does call attention to an issue involved in calculating such ratios as return on equity and return on invested capital (discussed in Chapter 20). LIFO inventories are sometimes stated at absurdly low numbers on the balance sheet, and the sorts of ratios just mentioned attempt to relate the amount of return earned to the amount of capital employed to earn it. That capital should include the LIFO reserve less an appropriate tax provision. The increment should simply be added to stated capital in the denominator, whether the income in the numerator is LIFO- or FIFO-based. This procedure will make the return on equity of companies using FIFO and LIFO accounting much more comparable, because the denominator will be the same and the numerators are normally not very different.

Other Inventory Methods

The Base Stock or Normal Stock Method

The base stock method of inventory valuation is a variation of LIFO accounting; it is applied to some minimum level of raw materials, usually metals or agricultural commodities, and the rest of inventories are accounted for on some other basis. Because past practice was to write the base stock down to nominal amounts, some companies had significant hidden assets. The method is based on the theory that the company must regularly carry a certain physical stock of materials and that there is no more reason to vary the value of this normal stock from year to year—because of market changes—than there would be to vary the value of the manufacturing plant as its price or level of operations rises or falls.

When part of a normal stock inventory is sold, bringing the amount on hand below the basic requirement, earnings have to be charged with a reserve for the replacement of the deficiency. In effect this cancels out the large profit made on the sale. Thus, base-stock figuring differs from the LIFO method in the matter of layer invasion profits.

On the whole, the base stock method probably produces more conservatively stated and more stable earnings over an extended period than does the LIFO method.

The Average and Standard Methods

The average cost method is used by about 39 percent of companies for at least part of their inventories. Since the average includes both older and newer inventory, the expense tends to fall somewhere between LIFO and FIFO figures, but it is closer than either to the actual cost of specific items.

Standard cost is usually applied to work in process and finished goods based on past patterns of cost and productivity. Unusual costs are thus excluded from the carrying amount and are, therefore, expensed. Except for the expensing of unusual costs, the standard cost method's results are close to average cost results.

The Retail Method

An accepted method of valuing retailers' inventories, including those of department stores and chain stores, starts with the current retail selling price of each item and deducts an appropriate "mark-on." The resulting value gives a calculated replacement cost which corresponds to the expected realization less normal expense and profit. This figure is regarded as more closely reflecting the true value of each inventory item to the store than either the actual recorded cost of each item or its current quotation in the wholesale market.

LIFO For Retailers

Retail stores that follow the LIFO method use a special technique based on an official index of retail prices. The inventory in each department is first valued according to the retail method, and then the cost is reduced in inverse proportion to the advance in the official index number. The IRS makes an exception here to its normal rule of requiring the LIFO indexes to be internally derived.

The Security Analyst and Inventory Valuation Methods

LIFO or FIFO?

If, in a period of inflation, there are two generally similar companies and one reports on the LIFO and the other on the FIFO basis, the second will probably show somewhat larger earnings than the former. Should the analyst accept both earnings statements as correct? If not, what adjustments should be made?

Comparability

Two companies cannot be fairly compared unless a substantially similar method of inventory valuation is applied to each. For this purpose either the LIFO or the FIFO method could properly be used, if the data are available. Since most companies are now at least partly on a LIFO basis, adjusting the inventories and earnings of those using FIFO methods to conform with the majority might seem wise. However, this will be possible only if the FIFO companies report current cost of inventory and costs of goods sold under Statement 33 or are willing to release the needed information to the analyst. Too often that information will not be available, and the analyst will have to adjust the LIFO-based companies to FIFO figures. Disclosure of the LIFO reserve and/or the FIFO inventory amount is required by the SEC for the 10-K and these figures are almost invariably in the annual report. Even per-share figures are often given. Thus, comparable figures are almost always available on a FIFO basis.

Adjusting Formulas. The adjustment to either method from the other is straightforward using these formulas:

Formula 1. Beginning inventory plus purchases minus ending inventory equals cost of goods sold

Formula 2. LIFO inventory plus LIFO reserve equals FIFO inventory

Note that no special adjustment to these formulas is needed when there is LIFO layer invasion.

Table 13.3. Selected Data from the 1985 Annual Report
of the Maytag Company
(In Millions of Dollars)

	1985	1984
1. LIFO reserve	37.3	39.1
2. Inventories (LIFO)	78.5	77.7
3. Total = FIFO inventories	115.8*	116.8*
4. Cost of sales	432.9	421.5
5. Stockholders' equity (LIFO)	256.6	228.9
6. Stockholders' equity (FIFO)	276.7†	250.0†
7. Net income (LIFO)	71.8	63.1
8. FIFO net income	70.8‡	

* From Formula 2.
† FIFO stockholders' equity = [(1 − tax rate) × (LIFO reserve)] + LIFO stockholders' equity. The tax rate was 46% at the time of this example.
‡ FIFO net income = [(1985 LIFO reserve − 1984 LIFO reserve) × (1 − tax rate)] + 1985 LIFO net income.
NOTE: Years ended December 31.

Example. The 1985 annual report of Maytag Company, highlighted in Table 13.3, provides a useful example. The table includes certain FIFO numbers which are footnoted to show how they were calculated from the other information in the table. Since we have the beginning and ending inventory numbers and the cost of goods sold, we can easily calculate, using Formula 1, that the purchases during the year were $433.7 million ($432.9 + $78.5 − $77.7 =$433.7). The amount of purchases is independent of the inventory method.

The third line of the table is simply the result of applying Formula 2. Having the beginning and ending FIFO inventories and the purchases for input in Formula 1 permits calculation of the FIFO cost of goods sold of $434.7 million ($116.8 + $433.7 − $115.8 = $434.7). This is $1.8 million more than the LIFO cost of goods sold and is the same as the decline in the LIFO reserve. FIFO after-tax income is $1.8 million × (1 − tax rate), or $1 million less than the LIFO after-tax income. Note that the tax rate was 46 percent at the time of this example—not 34 percent.

The U.S. income tax rate should be used for these LIFO-related adjustments, because LIFO inventories are usually domestic. For some purposes analysts should consider the effects on available tax loss carryforwards, the percentage limitation on the investment tax credit, and other aspects of the ever-changing Tax Code and regulations.

Which Basis Should the Analyst Prefer?

Use FIFO on the Balance Sheet. In balance sheet studies the current cost or the replacement cost of inventories are often the most informative figures for the analyst to use. Using FIFO inventories or including the LIFO reserve and an appropriate tax adjustment for LIFO-based companies gives a better picture of the net current assets and the capital at work by putting all companies in the same industry in a comparable position and avoiding price levels related to dates arbitrarily selected in the past. If the analyst believes the current price level is vulnerable, allowances can be made for any expected degree of decline.

Use LIFO in the Income Statement. However, the use of LIFO cost of goods sold in the income statement analysis has its own advantages. The most recent costs give information that is useful in predicting the next year's costs. LIFO accounting does not suffer the problems of a full current cost accounting system. The dynamics of the going firm are expressed in the completed cash-to-cash cycles. Conservatism is well served by maintaining the realization principle and avoiding inventory profits. Requiring that the earnings process be complete before earnings are reported reduces opportunities to overstate operating results.

Problems of Using Both Methods at Once

There are problems in the simultaneous use of LIFO in the income statement and FIFO on the balance sheet. First, the income statement and the balance sheet no longer articulate. That is, changes in equity are no longer explained by the income statement. Second, inventories are marked up by the LIFO reserve, less appropriate taxes, but sooner or later, layer invasion will cause the unrealized gains to become realized and flow through the income statement to equity. Since those gains have already been reflected in equity, care must be taken to see that they do not get counted twice. This problem has been referred to by accountants as the "recycling" or the "reclassification of equity" problem. If the analyst calculates a growth rate of book value per share using FIFO inventories on the balance sheet, the trend will include FIFO profits—

not LIFO ones. The exercise is further complicated by the need to provide deferred taxes for the inventory write-up.

Limit the Use of Mixed Measurements

Clearly, there are advantages to treating inventories differently in the income statement and the balance sheet. At the same time, the inconsistent measurement system strongly suggests that the analyst should not treat the statements as if they were integral. It is recommended that the FIFO inventory adjustment should be limited to use (1) in balance sheet ratio calculations, and (2) in balance sheet analyses that are oriented toward liquidating values or asset values, rather than "going concern" or earning power values. The distinction between the analysts' investment value approach and accounting's asset value approach must be kept in mind. The use of LIFO cost of goods sold in the income statement offers considerable useful information for estimating earning power, the cornerstone of investment value.

14
Effect of Depreciation and Amortization on Taxes and Income

Expenses That Must Be Allocated Over Time

Depreciation, depletion, and amortization have a common characteristic: They involve costs or expenses that must be allocated to a number of periods rather than be absorbed in a single period.

A critical analysis of an income statement must pay particular attention to the amounts deducted for depreciation and other noncash charges. These items differ from ordinary operating expenses in the following ways:

- They do not usually signify a current and corresponding outlay of cash.

- They represent the estimated shrinkage in the value of the fixed or capital assets, due to wearing out, to technological or economic obsolescence, to using up, or to their approaching extinction for whatever cause.

- They ensure that the capital invested in the asset is returned in cash from the revenue stream.

- They create timing differences between amounts that are tax deductible and amounts that are reported to shareholders as expense, resulting in deferred taxes.

Depreciation and Amortization

Leading Questions Regarding Depreciation and Amortization

The accounting theory that governs depreciation charges appears simple enough. If a capital asset has limited life, provision must be made to write off the (unsalvaged) cost of that asset by charges against earnings distributed over the asset's useful life. But behind this simple theory lie five complications:

Accounting rules themselves permit a value other than cost as the basis of the amortization charge.

Companies have wide latitude as to the choice of allocation method and the length of an asset's life.

Certain companies may not follow accepted accounting practice in stating their amortization deduction in the income statement.

In most cases a company will use one permitted basis of amortization in its tax returns and another in its published statements.

Sometimes an allowance that is justified from an accounting standpoint is not justified from an investment standpoint.

Apart from these technical issues, some tend to regard the depreciation deduction as in some sense an "unreal" expense and to concentrate attention on earnings before depreciation and amortization, or so-called cash flow.

The Analyst's Basic Approach to Depreciation and Other Amortizations

In this rather complex area we suggest that the analyst be guided by the following basic principles:

The analyst should make certain that the amortization provision is adequate by conservative standards.

The analyst should seek, as far as possible, to apply uniform measures of depreciation, making the necessary adjustments in comparative studies.

3. The analyst must maintain a sense of proportion—avoiding those items that might have no appreciable influence on the conclusions reached.

Amortization Charges in Corporate Accounts

The attention that the analyst will give to depreciation will vary with its significance. If a poor choice of depreciation method or the length of useful lives has only a small effect on net income, the depreciation question needs little attention. Where the customary relationship requires, say, a dollar of investment in plant to generate a dollar of annual sales, the analyst will study the depreciation question with great care. If a company has a relatively small amount of fixed assets, its amortization charge will have only a minor influence on its profits. This situation will be found generally in the major divisions of financial, trade, and service enterprises. In the manufacturing field the plant investment and associated depreciation is less important for light operations of the assembly type than for the heavy and integrated operations of basic industries. In mining, chemicals, oil and gas production, and the public utility and railroad industries, the fixed assets bulk very large, and amortization is correspondingly important.

Industry Depreciation Characteristics

The relationship between the depreciation tax deduction and other major financial elements for various industry groups is summarized in Table 14.1. The data are taken from 1983 Corporation Income Tax forms, the latest released by the Internal Revenue Service (IRS). Observe that for manufacturing companies generally the amortization charge was more than 9.5 percent of depreciable assets, about 3.9 percent of sales and 47 percent of taxable income before such deduction. The right column illustrates the wide divergence between industries as to the importance of depreciation in its impact on profits. Clearly, where the ratio is high, a very small error in estimating the useful lives of plant and equipment assets could result in a very large error in the income number. (Note that the taxable income shown in Table 14.1 is before foreign, state, local, and U.S. possession income taxes, totalling about $25 billion for all corporations in 1983.) Profits before amortization were divided fairly evenly among depreciation, all income taxes, and final net income.

Table 14.1. Corporate Tax Depreciation Rates, 1983[*]

	Total receipts (millions)	U.S. income taxes after credits (millions)	Taxable income[†] (millions)	Depreciable assets (millions)	Depreciation deduction (millions)	Ratio of depreciation to assets	Ratio of depreciation to taxable income
All corporations	$7,135,494	$51,862	$218,686	$2,730,372	$241,492	8.8%	110%
Sectors							
Mining	132,420	722	4,623	85,787	7,786	9.1	168
Construction	290,799	1,393	5,505	57,711	6,281	10.7	101
Manufacturing	2,552,831	24,961	113,610	1,051,144	99,416	9.5	88
Transportation and utilities	657,421	5,430	25,612	901,874	56,162	6.2	219
Wholesale and retail trade	2,119,445	10,653	33,503	246,665	27,667	11.2	83
Finance, ins., real estate	902,822	5,697	22,470	193,098	19,654	9.9	88
Services	416,462	2,674	11,840	162,395	21,194	13.1	179
Selected industries							
Metal mining	50,701	25	47	6,118	370	6.0	787
Coal	15,669	115	256	10,995	1,014	9.2	396
Oil and gas production	103,637	489	4,049	60,221	5,806	9.6	143
Food and kindred products	305,288	2,581	9,434	78,572	8,502	10.8	90
Paper and allied products	69,614	707	1,159	43,441	3,290	7.6	284
Printing and publishing	93,783	1,980	5,509	33,374	4,120	12.3	75
Chemical and allied	236,327	2,631	14,013	122,298	10,463	8.6	75
Petroleum refining	511,125	3,722	30,092	220,043	18,223	8.3	61
Machinery (except electrical)	179,634	2,210	11,271	82,237	9,266	11.3	82
Electrical and electronic	202,754	2,077	8,036	78,676	9,284	11.8	116
Motor vehicle	171,176	1,178	5,678	65,054	7,911	12.2	139
Transportation	235,696	1,535	5,954	176,993	14,749	8.3	248
Telephone	120,585	525	5,732	235,491	20,097	8.5	351
Electric and gas utilities	281,028	2,911	12,565	478,062	19,736	4.1	157

[*]Department of Treasury, Internal Revenue Service, *Statistics of Income—1983, Corporate Income Tax Returns,* pp. 16–21.
[†]Income before U.S. Possessions', Foreign, State, and Federal Taxes.

The figures in our table demonstrate that for most industries the depreciation and amortization allowance is of major importance in relation to net income. Consequently analysts must determine what is normal or adequate depreciation for companies generally and for industrial groups, and they must detect and evaluate individual or group departures from these norms.

Standard Methods of Computing Depreciation

The Diversity of Depreciation Practices— An Analyst's Challenge

Four theoretical approaches to the writing off of property during its useful life are found in current account practice. In addition, the useful lives used by different companies for stockholder reporting purposes cover an extremely wide range, and these differences can produce dramatic results. For example, a chemical company had been using conservative useful lives for its chemical plants but changed its accounting to use the same useful lives as prevailed among its principal competitors. The effect of this change in estimate was a doubling of the company's earnings in comparison to the amount it would have reported under the old depreciation schedule.

Straight-line

For many decades the usual approach to depreciation has been the *straight-line method*, which charges off the same dollar amount each year. That amount is the difference between book cost and estimated salvage, divided by the estimated years of useful life.

Accelerated Methods

A more conservative approach assumes that an asset loses a larger portion of its economic value in the earlier years of use than in the later years, and with this method the depreciation charge diminishes over the asset's life. These accelerated methods include *double declining balance, 150 percent declining balance,* and *sum-of-the-years' digits.* At present companies may depreciate, for tax purposes, assets placed in service between 1980 and 1986 using the modified *accelerated cost recovery system* (ACRS) schedules. Assets placed in service after 1986 may be depreciated for tax purposes using straight-line, 150 percent, or 200 percent declining balance methods depending on the asset class life and other factors. The present class life asset depreciation range (CLADR) system provides ranges of useful lines that are shorter than the economic lives but not as conservative as either ACRS lives or the ADR lives that apply to assets put in service between 1970 and 1981. ACRS was designed to offset the effects of inflation by permitting the use of special depreciation schedules with very short useful lives. Use of even the less liberal modified ACRS of the Tax Reform Act of 1986 for financial reporting purposes would still overstate depreciation expense by a good margin in the early years and have no depreciation charge at all in the later years. Even the present CLADR system tends to have that effect, but to a lesser degree.

Calculating the Sum of the Years' Digits.   Mechanically, most accelerated depreciation methods are fairly straightforward. In the case of the sum of the years' digits, a piece of four-year equipment would have a sum of the digits of $1 + 2 + 3 + 4 = 10$. Thus, in the first year, the depreciation would be $\frac{4}{10}$ of cost-minus-salvage value, the next year $\frac{3}{10}$, and so on.

Declining Balance Calculations.   The double declining balance method first calculates straight-line depreciation as a percentage of cost-minus-salvage and then doubles that percentage as the first year's depreciation. The second year's depreciation will be that same doubled percentage multiplied by the remaining balance to be depreciated. At some point, the formula's depreciation reaches an amount less than straight-line depreciation and for the asset's remaining life the straight-line method is used. Other declining balance methods are calculated similarly.

Unit of Production

The third commonly used method is based on the principle that wear and tear is a function not only of the passage of time but also of the use made of the facilities. Companies using this approach will vary the depreciation rate in some proportion to the rate of operations during the period. This calculation, usually called the *unit-of-production* method, tends to smooth earnings.

   Example.   In 1983, Bethlehem Steel Corporation changed its depreciation policies. The new depreciation method is a base of straight-line depreciation with adjustments not to exceed 25 percent in either direction for the level of operation of the plants. Bethlehem also adopted the policy of capitalizing the cost of relining blast furnaces and depreciating the capitalized cost on a unit-of-production basis. A footnote explained that the management believed the changes would provide a better matching of revenues and expenses and bring Bethlehem's accounting practices in line with those predominant in the steel industry. The depreciable lives were also lengthened. The changes were mainly applicable to facilities producing steel and raw materials.

Mortgage or Sinking Fund Methods

A fourth approach to depreciation permits *smaller* deductions in the earlier years than in the later ones. This amortization charge is set aside —sometimes just for purposes of computation—and will earn compound interest until the property is retired. This method has been considered appropriate for public utility companies by a few utility commissions in the western United States. Proposals of similar so-called sinking fund or mortgage methods for other industries have been resisted by accountants.

Depreciation on the Phase-in of New Utility Plants

The FASB is currently considering the appropriateness of phase-in depreciation for newly completed nuclear electricity plants. These phase-in plans are meant to reduce the shock of the large rate increases needed to pay for the plants. Some of these plans in effect book *negative* depreciation in the early years through writing up the plant by an amount greater than the reported depreciation. Such procedures may be suitable for rate-making purposes, but they are totally unjustified for accounting use by any reasonable notion of wear and tear, obsolescence, or return of capital. (Oddly, a staff paper of the California Public Service Commission calls such a calculation "economic depreciation"!)

The Portfolio Problem

Portfolio problems arise when companies have a choice of levels of aggregation at which to measure depreciation. At one extreme, an entire factory and its machinery can be considered a single asset and depreciated using one of the accepted methods. This large portfolio of individual assets could have been broken down into smaller portfolios such as, say, individual production lines. These in turn could have been broken down into individual machines and pieces of equipment. Or all machines of a similar type could be aggregated into a portfolio of, say, machine lathes. The large aggregation, such as the entire plant, allows accountants to expense some expenditures immediately as "maintenance" rather than capitalizing and then amortizing them over a period of years. Large aggregations can also obscure obsolescent equipment that rightfully should have been written down to salvage value. Thus, in comparing depreciation expense, analysts should consider not only the method and the assets' useful lives but also how the method is applied. In general, information on the latter is not provided in the financial reports and must be obtained by discussions with management. Maintenance expense is often given in 10-K and certain regulatory reports, and can sometimes give useful clues about internal operations, depreciation, and the like.

Depreciation and Current Values

When plant and equipment are written up or down, depreciation expenses usually rise or fall proportionately. In the first third of this century, write-ups were a widely used method of stock manipulation, and a source of the expression *watered stock.* In the early thirties, write-downs were common as companies sought to relieve their income statements of the depreciation burden.[1]

Capitalization of Interest and AFUDC

The capitalization of interest as a cost of acquiring plant and equipment presents a difficult analytical problem. Once accounting formally endorsed interest capitalization, it quickly became a requirement for income tax purposes. For tax purposes the capitalized interest is an asset amortizable over a period up to 10 years rather than an investor's return when the asset was earned and paid for.

Interest Cost Is a Return on Investment— AFUDC Is Not

The analyst should consider the cost of capital in terms of the distinction between return *on* capital and return *of* capital. Interest is a return on capital, since it is the reward earned for use of capital. Surely no bondholder would imagine that an interest check received is a return of the original investment. Yet, capitalized interest never appears as such

---

[1] Many political historians believe that the testimony of Professor Soloman Fabricant on the practices of writing assets up or down to current value, and the unfortunate results for investors who were misled by such accounting, was the persuasive evidence of stock manipulation that led Congress to pass the 1933 Act creating the SEC.

on the income statement. The absence of the interest expense results in immediately higher reported income and higher taxable income. That higher reported income, of course, will be offset over the years by higher depreciation expense of the overstated asset that was acquired.

Capitalized interest is shown in a footnote each year. In subsequent years the reader of income statements sees only *depreciation*, which is, by definition, a return *of* capital. Thus, the capitalized interest never appears in the financial statements as a return *on* capital. Unless the interest is adjusted by the analyst, the company's return on invested capital over the years will be permanently understated. The return on equity will be front-ended, although total earnings over the years will be exactly the same for the common stock.

The allowance for equity funds used during construction (AFUDC) has even less justification than capitalized interest. It is merely direction from a utility commission to a public utility to make bookkeeping entries—to record a profit and an imaginary asset—*without any transaction!* In effect, the commission is saying "It's bad politics to raise utility rates right now, but you must *seem* profitable to survive, so report a profit, and maybe we can raise rates later on." If nonutilities reported profits on such fantasies, some would accuse them of fraud.

It is a matter of some difficulty to unwind the accounting. To do so perfectly would require information on the useful life and depreciation method applied to the specific assets acquired and the amount of interest and AFUDC included in their carrying amounts. Depreciation could then be adjusted to exclude those amortizations, and the capitalized interest could then be shown properly as return on capital in the year paid. Lacking such detailed information, the analyst should use the company's normal depreciation rate expressed as a percentage of gross plant and equipment, or some other reasonable approximation, to eliminate the amortization of the capitalized interest and AFUDC.

Adjustment for Capitalized Interest

The following hypothetical example may help explain the effects of interest capitalization and why the analyst must adjust for it. Assume that a company takes two years to construct a machine. The out-of-pocket costs of building the machine are $100, the average investment in the acquired equipment during the acquisition period is $50, and the applicable interest rate is 10 percent; 10 percent interest for two years on $50 amounts to $10. Thus, interest will be capitalized to the extent of $10, and the initial carrying amount of the machine will be $110. During the two-year acquisition period, interest will be capitalized rather than run through the income statement as an expense. Thus, over the two years, the apparent earnings for the common shareholders will be increased by $10 before taxes or $6.60 after a 34 percent income tax rate.

If the machine has a five-year useful life and zero salvage value, the annual depreciation will be one-fifth of $110, or $22. Without interest capitalization, the depreciation would have been $20 a year. This $2 of additional depreciation a year brings the total pretax earnings for the common stock down by $10, or $6.60 after taxes during the depreciation years. Thus, the increase in earnings during the acquisition period is exactly offset by a decrease in earnings during the depreciation period.

The potentially misleading effect arises because the interest cost never appears on the income statement. Thus, an ordinary calculation of return on investment will never show that $10 of return unless the analyst makes an adjustment for it. The appropriate adjustments would be to return the $10 of interest expense to the income statements in the years in which it was paid out and to reduce taxes paid or payable by $3.40 over the two years. In the subsequent five years the analyst would reduce depreciation by $2 per year and increase tax expense and the deferred tax liability by $0.68 each year (34 percent of $2).

On the surface, reconstruction of such transactions seems hardly worth the effort, until one considers that in capital-intensive industries, especially those whose plants require many years to construct, the interest numbers can become enormous. The interest component on a nuclear power plant can easily approach half of the total cost. If a company's construction program is large, its entire interest expense for the year may disappear from the income statement, with 66 percent of that amount flowing to net income. This can easily increase net income by 25, 50, or 100 percent in the years of interest capitalization.

The old accounting adage "You make money selling things—not by buying them!" seems most appropriate to this situation. Accepting badly distorted earnings and a permanent error in a company's historical rate of return on investment are too high a price for the analyst to pay for avoiding work. The analyst must restate the record to eliminate the capitalized interest, its amortization, and the related tax effects (see "Depreciation" in Chapter 17).

Deferred Taxes and Accelerated Depreciation

The Statement of Depreciation Policy

The depreciation policies of the more important companies are summarized in the detailed descriptions appearing in the financial manuals.

They must be set forth in a registration statement and prospectus covering the sale of securities, in proxy statements relating to mergers and similar transactions, and in annual reports. In recent years the depreciation footnote in many annual reports has diminished to a statement that a particular method is used "over the estimated useful lives." Many companies used to give more useful ranges of lives for the major classes of assets.

Example. The International Paper Company's 1984 annual report was more helpful than most. It provided the following information about useful-life estimations for company assets:

Buildings	2.5 percent
Machinery and equipment	5 to 33 percent
Woods equipment	10 to 16 percent
Start-up costs	5 years
Timberlands	As timber is cut
Roads and land improvements	Over economic lives

Investment Tax Credit

To encourage the construction of new plant and equipment, the Congress from time to time during the post–World War II period has allowed tax credits equal to a specified percentage, usually 10 percent, of the cost of certain plant and equipment. Two methods are acceptable for accounting for the investment tax credit. The most widely used is *flow through*, which reflects the full value of the credit in net income in the year taken. The *deferral* method, used primarily by public utilities, defers the credit and amortizes it over the life of the asset. Those in favor of the flow through method argue that the credit is *earned* by acquiring the asset. Those who favor deferral and amortization believe that the tax credit is a subsidy that merely *reduces the cost* of the asset and should be deferred and amortized in the same fashion as the asset itself. The Tax Reform Act of 1986 eliminated the investment tax credit.

Post-SEC Practices

Between, say, 1935 and 1954 the vast majority of companies used the straight-line method of depreciation applied to the cost (less salvage) of their assets, as required on tax returns. The year 1954 marked the beginning of the trend toward more liberal tax depreciation. For a time companies tended to change their financial reporting depreciation toward these faster tax methods. That trend has been reversed because the earnings penalty was too painful. In 1984, 567 of 600 companies used straight-line for some of or all their depreciable assets; 60 used unit-of-production calculations; 54, declining balance; 15, sum-of-the-years' digits; and 76, unspecified accelerated methods.[2] Companies that used more than one depreciation method did so because they had recent acquisitions, because they were fulfilling foreign accounting requirements for certain subsidiaries, or because they wanted to keep certain divisions in accord with the practices of the industry in which they operated.

Deferred Tax Effects

Book-Tax Timing Differences. The use of accelerated depreciation and of ACRS for tax purposes are the largest causes of the difference between the taxable income recorded on the tax form and the profits shown in the published financial reports. A survey of sources of book–tax depreciation timing differences of 600 companies in 1984 showed that 488 had timing differences due to depreciation.[3] No other type of timing difference was nearly as widespread nor as large in magnitude.

Contribution to Cash Flow. Since in recent years the deferred tax effect has been one-third to one-half of the difference between book depreciation and tax depreciation, deferred income taxes have become a very important contributor to a company's cash flow. Even at a 34 percent tax rate and using the new asset depreciation range lives, the impact is large.

Normalization of Reported Earnings

Taxes are deferred when a company reports faster depreciation on the tax form than in the financial statements. The simple example in Table 14.2 may help explain why the recording of a deferred income tax liability improves the reporting of after-tax income to investors and also has favorable cash flow consequences.

Assume that the company has only one asset, a machine with an expected useful life of six years. The machine cost $300. The company has annual revenues of $100, and no expenses other than depreciation and taxes. Assume also that the tax laws permit such a machine to be depreciated straight line over a period of three years.

---

[2] American Institute of Certified Public Accountants, *Accounting Trends and Techniques*, 1985, New York, p. 268.

[3] American Institute of Certified Public Accountants, *Accounting Trends and Techniques*, 1985, New York, p. 275.

Table 14.2. Comparison of Shareholder and Tax Reporting

		As Reported to Shareholders				
Year	Revenue	Depre-ciation	Pretax income	Tax expense at 34% rate	After-tax income	Cash flow
1	$100	$50	$50	$17*	$33	$100
2	100	50	50	17*	33	100
3	100	50	50	17*	33	100
4	100	50	50	17†	33	66
5	100	50	50	17†	33	66
6	100	50	50	17†	33	66

		As Reported on the Tax Form		
Year	Revenue	Depre-ciation	Pretax income	Taxes paid at 34% rate
1	$100	$100	$ 0	$ 0
2	100	100	0	0
3	100	100	0	0
4	100	0	100	34
5	100	0	100	34
6	100	0	100	34

*Additions to the deferred tax liability.
†The deferred tax account is reduced by this amount.

The report to shareholders reflects accurately the economics in the after-tax income column. The six years of revenue are charged with a reasonable allocation of the cost of the $300 machine. The tax expense shown in the report to shareholders represents annual increases of $17 in the company's deferred tax liability for the first three years. At the end of the third year the company would have a $51 tax liability related to the machine. During each of the final three years $17 of deferred tax liability would "mature," and $17 of new tax expense would come about from operations, so the company would have to make tax payments in the amount of $34 in each of those three years. (Accountants refer to this maturing phenomenon as a "reversal of book-tax timing differences.")

The cash flows of this company in each year equal the sum of net income plus depreciation plus the increase (or minus the decrease) in the deferred tax liability.

A Comparison of Depreciation Rates and Methods

The Renaissance of Straight-Line.   Table 14.3 shows depreciation rates and methods for 29 major industrial companies in 1984 and selected earlier years. The average depreciation rate as a percentage of gross plant advanced from 5.0 percent in 1949 to 5.6 percent in 1959 and to 6.6 percent in 1984. The effect is a reduction in reported earnings of about 10 percent over the 25 years, and the question is whether the newer depreciation rates are appropriate.

By themselves, the depreciation methods give little evidence about the adequacy of the depreciation amount or the effect of the related deferred income taxes. The letters SD, DB, and AM all represent accelerated methods that give more rapid depreciation than straight-line in the early years and less in the later years, and are thus considered to be conservative. A switch from any of those three methods to straight line would appear to be a move away from from conservatism. Nine of the companies switched from one of those three accelerated methods to the straight-line method between 1959 and 1984. In five of the cases, depreciation as a percentage of gross plant declined, but, in the other four, the ratio *increased.* Presumably in those cases the movement to a less conservative method was offset by more conservative useful lives, although this cannot be said with certainty because the mix of assets held might have changed. Overall, the 1984 rate of 6.6 percent appears to have risen more through use of significantly shorter lives than through change of method. This probably occurred because most companies prefer to use the same lives for both tax and reporting purposes.

Units-of-Production Growing in Popularity
An interesting trend between 1959 and 1984 was the shift toward depreciation methods that reflected levels of activity—the units-of-production method—that occurred in raw materials industries such as steel, oil, and paper.

Proper Useful Lives, Properly Applied

Depreciation Rate Is the Reciprocal of the Useful Life.   If the rate of depreciation to gross plant is 5 percent, it is implicit that the average fixed asset, excluding land, has an expected life of 1 divided by 5 percent, or 20 years. A decline in the depreciation rate suggests that longer useful lives are being estimated. This is not necessarily nonconservative because the mix of depreciable assets can shift considerably over time. In contrast, obsolescence, whether competitively or technologically caused, can shorten the lives of assets considerably. A decline in foreign competition due to a weak dollar can lengthen the life of a piece of equipment otherwise near retirement.

Table 14.3. Comparative Depreciation Allowances for Twenty-Nine Companies

	1984		1959		1948	
	Ratio to gross plant	Method	Ratio to gross plant	Method	Ratio to gross plant	Method
Allied Signal	7.1%	SL	5.4%	SD	3.7%	SL
Alcoa	5.3	SL	4.8	SD	2.3	SL
American Brands	7.8	SL	4.2	SL	4.0	SL
American Can	6.7	SL	4.4	SL	3.6	SL
American Tel. & Tel.	7.2	SL	4.7	SL	3.4	SL
Bethlehem Steel	3.8	UP	4.3	DB	2.7	SL
Chevron Corp.	6.1	UP	4.5	SL	5.5	SL
Chrysler*	9.9	SL†	6.3	SL	9.3	SL
Du Pont	6.3	SD	7.5	SL	8.3	SL
Eastman Kodak	7.0	AM	6.0	SD	5.1	SL
Exxon	6.3	UP	5.3	SL	4.9	SL
General Electric	7.5	SD	7.5	SL	7.7	SL
General Foods	6.1	SL	6.3	SD	4.3	SL
General Motors*	11.9	AM	6.7	AM	6.3	SL
Goodyear	5.3	SL	6.3	SD	5.9	SL
INCO Ltd.	3.8	SL	2.5	SL	2.8	SL
International Paper	4.6	UP	6.3	DB	4.7	SL
Manville	5.2	SL	5.5	SD	4.4	SL
Navistar Int'l	7.0	SL	6.0	SL	4.7	SL
Owens Illinois	5.9	SL	5.0	SD	4.8	SL
Procter & Gamble	4.9	SL	3.8	SL	3.3	SL
Sears Roebuck	4.9‡	SL	5.5	SD	7.5	SL
Swift Independent	7.7	SL	4.5	SD	4.4	SL
Texaco	7.7	UP	6.7	SL	6.7	SL
Union Carbide	4.6	SL	6.2	SL	4.0	SL
U.S. Steel	5.5	UP	3.2	UP	3.9	UP
United Technologies	7.7	AM	9.9	SD	7.4	SL
Westinghouse Electric	7.8	SL	6.2	SL	4.3	SL
Woolworth	12.1	SL	6.1	SL	5.8	SL
Average	6.6		5.6		5.0	

NOTE: These companies were in the Dow-Jones industrials average in 1959. Anaconda has been omitted due to its acquisition by another company. SL=straight line, SD=sum of the years' digits, DB=declining balance, AM=accelerated method, UP=units of production or activity related.

*Includes amortization of special tools.
†An accelerated method is used for assets acquired before 1980.
‡Merchandising division only.

Useful Lives Are Affected by Shifts in the Economy.   The U.S. economy has been characterized in the postwar years by a shift away from the old basic industries and toward new technological products and the service industries. Both areas include higher technology content, which suggests that the new sectors might see an increasing influence of technological obsolescence in the lives of assets.

Decline of Basic Industries: Are Write-Downs a Suitable Substitute for Adequate Depreciation?   Part of the problem in the old basic and raw materials industries has been the growth of those industries in the stronger third-world countries. Those countries have low wages and, in some cases, more modern equipment than their U.S. counterparts. The average depreciation rate in the basic industries probably should have been more rapid in the past to reflect the economic obsolescence. Yet the record shows very low depreciation rates. It is in those industries that we observe today the largest number of plant write-downs, plant closings, abandonments, restructuring of product lines, and the like. The average depreciation rate in 1984 for the loss-ridden steel industries was 4 percent, which implies a 25-year useful life. A leading question therefore is: Are large write-downs of obsolete plants a suitable substitute for adequate depreciation?

Intra-Industry Depreciation Ranges Should Be Narrowed by the Analyst.   In contrast to the integrated steel companies, the average depreciation rate of a dozen electronics companies in 1984 was 10 percent, implying a 10-year average life for plant and equipment. Given the short life cycle of new products in the electronics industry, this rapid depreciation may well be justified. Regardless, the analyst should be uncomfortable with the *range* of depreciation rates in the electronics industry (from 7 to 16.1 percent) and in the steel industry (from 2.6 to 5.5 percent).

Are Depreciation Charges Adequate?

At least two sources of useful information provide background on the reasonableness of depreciation lives for the entire corporate sector: current cost data and the National Income and Product Accounts.

Current Cost Information.   Statement 33 required, through 1986, that some 1200 companies present current cost depreciation in their annual reports. The difference between the current cost and historical cost amounts represents the additional amounts needed to replace at current prices the operating capability used up during the year. Current cost depreciation exceeded historical cost depreciation by 37 percent in 1980 and averaged 31 percent from 1980 to 1983.[4] These figures suggest a serious short fall in the provision for replacement.

National Income and Product Accounts. The National Income and Product Accounts include Table 1.12, Gross Domestic Product of Corporations. This is a partial income statement of the domestic business of U.S. corporations, and the table includes a capital consumption adjustment (CCA), which is the amount necessary to bring depreciation to a current cost number. In 1985 the capital consumption allowance was $197.4 billion before adding the capital consumption adjustment of $71.8 billion. This suggests that historical cost depreciation should have been increased by 36 percent to cover the current costs of consuming fixed assets in 1985.

Although both the current cost data and the National Income and Product Accounts information paint a gloomy picture, there are some offsetting factors. Many companies use the IRS class life asset depreciation ranges (CLADR) for their ordinary depreciation, which place the useful lives on a significantly conservative basis. Second, although technological change has undoubtedly increased obsolescence, at the same time it has brought significant increases in efficiency and improvement in product quality which are not reflected in the replacement cost prices. The industries in which depreciation has seemed the most inadequate are the ones which have taken large write-downs and write-offs over the last few years and which have shown the poorest profit histories. Their share of the economy is declining, making their depreciation practices less significant on an overall basis. History will tell us the truth of it, but on balance today's depreciation rates are probably adequate if inflation stays under, say, 5 percent.

Adjust for Comparability

An Example of the Recommended Procedure

The recommended way of dealing with disparate depreciation methods and lives is to put all companies that are to be compared on a comparable basis. A method recommended for its simplicity places all companies in an industry on a straight-line basis, using the industry-average depreciation rate which is calculated as the ratio of depreciation expense to gross plant. Straight-line calculation is the easiest method because the

---

[4]Price Waterhouse & Co., *Inflation Accounting*, New York, 1981.

assets' ages are not needed; the amount of depreciation is simply gross plant divided by a conservative useful life.

Airline Depreciation Rates

Table 14.4 shows the depreciation rates for seven large airlines in 1984 (the year to June 30, 1985, in the case of Delta Airlines). To make the depreciation figures for these airlines more comparable, the analyst might calculate the average ratio of depreciation to gross plant, which in this case turns out to be 6.82 percent. That average percentage would be multiplied by the gross plant of each airline to determine whether

Table 14.4. Major Airline Depreciation Rates, 1984

	AMR Corp.	Delta	Eastern	NWA Corp.	PanAm Corp.	Trans- Air	UAL Inc.
Gross plant ($ million)	4759	4423	4505	2643	2762	3428	6714
Depreciation ($ million)	307.7	346.5	287.7	167.2	207.7	224.1	445.6
Net income ($ million)	233.9	175.6	37.9(d)	56.0	206.8(d)	29.9	282.4
Depreciation to gross plant (percent)	6.47	7.83	6.39	6.33	7.52	6.54	6.54
Depreciation adjustment to 6.82% after 46% tax ($ million)	+9.0	+24.1	−10.5	−7.0	+10.5	−5.2	−6.5
Adjusted net income ($ million)	224.9	199.7	48.4(d)	49.0	196.3(d)	24.7	275.9

Sources: *Moody's Transportation Manual*, New York, 1985: *Standard & Poor's Corporation Records*, New York, 1985.

reported depreciation was above or below average. If, as in the case of Delta Airlines, the company appeared to be overdepreciating, a depreciation adjustment would be calculated:

$$(7.83\% - 6.82\%) \times \$4423 \times (1 - 46\%) = \$24.1$$

The excess depreciation, expressed as a rate, is multiplied by gross plant and equipment and the result is tax-adjusted at the 1984 tax rate of 46 percent to obtain the proper adjustment to net income. Similar adjustments for the other airlines result in some increases and decreases which change earnings by a significant percentage.

The precision of such adjustments would be greatly improved by a more detailed analysis of each company. Some of these companies operate hotels, reservation systems, automobile rental subsidiaries, and the like. The conscientious analyst would seek separate financial statements for these divisions and affiliates to calculate more precise weighted average depreciation adjustments.

Amortization Charges of Mining and Oil Companies

These important sectors of the industrial field are subject to special factors bearing on amortization. In addition to ordinary depreciation on buildings and equipment, they must allow for depletion of their ore, oil, and similar nonrenewable reserves. Mining companies also incur exploration and development expense; the corresponding charges for oil and gas producers would come under the headings of unproductive leases, dry holes, and drilling costs in which "intangible drilling costs" have a special accounting and tax status. These items are significant in their bearing on the true profits, and they are often troublesome to the analyst because different enterprises use varying methods to deal with these figures in their accounts.

Depletion Charges—A Recovery of Costs

Depletion represents the using up of exhaustible capital assets, mainly underground, by turning them into products for sale. It applies to companies producing oil and gas, metals and many other minerals, sulphur and other chemicals from deposits, clay, limestone, and other similar materials. Timber companies also face depletion costs, although their wasting asset is above ground and may be renewed by reforestation. As the holdings, or reserves, of these products are exhausted, their cost must be gradually written off through charges against earnings so that the original capital will be returned. In a company's own accounts such charges are made by deducting that percentage of the cost of the property which the mineral extracted bears to the total mineral content. This units-of-production method can be applied also to depreciation of oil and gas wells and other equipment, the service life of which is governed by the same factors. For tax purposes, however, an important departure from the standard method of computing depletion has been permitted—percentage depletion.

Percentage Depletion Is a Tax Rule— Not a Recovery of Costs

The concept of percentage depletion arose because searching for minerals and hydrocarbons underground is highly risky, and most exploration efforts fail to discover economically useful deposits. To make the reward commensurate with the risk, Congress allowed a special tax deduction, which was calculated as a specified percentage of the sales value. The percentage differed according to the mineral in question. The overall effect of this incentive was that successful explorers would receive profits and cost recovery on their own investments, plus an additional bounty equal to recovery of the unsuccessful explorers' costs and their expected returns. Exploring for minerals would then, in the aggregate, be economically attractive—a positive sum game. Regardless of the merits of the concept behind percentage depletion, it has sparked much political controversy. As a result, Congress has reduced the tax benefits in recent decades. Table 14.5 shows the percentage of sales value allowed under the tax codes in 1954 and in 1987 for a few minerals.

Table 14.5. Percentage Depletion Deductions

	Percentage depletion allowed	
	1954	1987
Oil and gas	27.5	0 *
Sulphur and uranium	23	22
Gold, silver	15	15
Metal mines	15	14
Coal	10	10
Clay, shale	5	5–22[†]
Gravel, peat	5	5

*For producers who are also refiners or marketers and for production over 1000 barrels per day of oil or 6000 mcf of gas per day.
†Depending on grade and location.
SOURCE: *Internal Revenue Code of 1986*, vol. 1, Commerce Clearing House, Chicago, 1986, pp. 5310–5311.

The percentage depletion allowance is limited to not more than 50 percent of net income before depletion for each producing property. Thus, the overall allowance can exceed 50 percent of a company's *total* net income if other operations of the company are losing money. For tax purposes, the company must take the larger of percentage depletion or the ordinary cost-based depletion. In the past, percentage depletion was almost always larger than cost-based depletion and over time accumulated amounts in excess of the cost of finding and developing deposits. Typically, reports to stockholders include only cost-based depletion, and the amortization of intangible drilling costs is also significantly lower than the amounts expensed on the tax return.

Note that any excess of percentage depletion over book depletion is a *permanent* tax-timing difference that will not reverse. That is, that difference will never appear in the statements issued to stockholders, nor will a time come when reported depletion expense will be less because of that difference. The effect of the excess percentage depletion is the same as the permanent difference that exists on interest from tax-exempt bonds: Permanantly tax-exempt income is created, and the analyst need make no provision for deferred taxes.

Oil Accounting Practices

Two basic accounting methods are used in the oil and gas industry:

- *Successful efforts.* Capitalize only the wells which discover oil and gas.
- *Full cost.* Capitalize all the costs of a field or area if at least some wells are successful enough to ensure recovery of the costs.

Some full-cost companies define the field or area very narrowly, and their results are close to successful efforts in accounting. In other cases, the area of interest may be an entire country or a large area such as "off-shore United States." Nearly all small exploration companies use full-cost calculations, although many large companies remain on successful efforts accounting. It is very difficult for the analyst to put companies using these two accounting methods on a comparable basis.

Reserve Information—More Important Than the Accounting Method. Although the lack of comparability is frustrating, the analyst should not lose sight of a much more important fact; usually, the oil-producing company's largest asset, oil and gas underground, is not on the books at all. The books show only the costs of wells that lead to the oil, plus other equipment. Information about the reserves, including the quantities, quality, and locations, and the "standardized measure" of discounted future net cash inflows are important information. The latter discounts expected future net cash inflows from proved reserves, based on year-end prices and costs, using a 10 percent discount rate. The oil analyst is probably better served pursuing information about existing reserves and their future cash inflows than by spending the same amount of time trying to untangle the accounting differences.

Accounting for Intangible Drilling Costs. Intangible drilling costs represent the labor and overhead costs incurred in drilling oil and gas wells, as distinguished from the cost of pipe and other tangible materials. The income tax law gives the option of capitalizing and amortizing the costs or immediately writing them off. Companies normally take the immediate write-off for the tax benefits. The active and expanding producers have always kept ahead of the tax collector in their increasing intangible drilling accounts, a cause of frequent debate in Congress.

Oil Royalties. Taxes paid to foreign governments result in credits that reduce U.S. taxes. Payments to foreign governments as oil production occurs can be described with many captions—for example, royalties, severance taxes, or income taxes. From the company's viewpoint, payments as foreign income taxes are desirable to get the foreign tax credit rather than a mere deduction. The more payments are structured to look like income taxes, the greater the concern of the foreign government about the transfer price at which the oil or gas is sold to the company's refinery or pipeline in another country. Thus, political developments both at home and abroad can overwhelm the statistical record, as can the more obvious risk of nationalization of foreign reserves. In underdeveloped countries, nationalization usually occurs when the government ceases to need the company's capital and skills.

Depletion of Mining Companies

Depletion is no longer an important item in the published accounts of mining companies. Some have written off their exploration costs when incurred or over too short a period and have no costs left to amortize. Others show a deduction based on the cost of their mining properties, but this figure is almost always comparatively small. In former years some concerns deducted the percentage depletion allowed by the tax law, and the analyst had to restore such amounts to net income and deduct instead a cost depletion amount to recover the actual investment.

At one time financial services used to state the per share earnings of mining companies "before depletion." That unfortunate practice is no longer common. Failure to recover the investment in reserves is failure to maintain the capital of the company. Income is not properly stated without such a charge.

Income Effects of Operating Leases and Capital Leases

Operating Leases

A major development of the past quarter century has been the growth of assets accounted for as operating leases. The reported expense is the rental cost, a level expense that tends to smooth earnings. (See Chapter 18.)

Capital Leases

Under a capital lease, a liability is shown on the balance sheet and the asset is presented separately from other plant and equipment. The asset is depreciated, usually straight-line. The interest component of the borrowing is reflected using the mortgage or interest methods. The effect is to reduce the early years' net income and to increase income in the later years of the lease.

Amortization of Intangible Assets

Intangible assets fall into various classes, depending on how they may be amortized in the tax returns and on the varying treatment accorded them in corporate accounts. These items usually have a small effect on reported earnings, but there are exceptions, particularly when goodwill is large. (Intangible drilling costs are not really intangible and are invariably carried in the balance sheet as part of the tangible property account.) Four classes of intangibles are discussed below, based on their tax or accounting treatment.

Items to Expense or Amortize

Exploration Costs and Mine-Development Expense. Exploration costs and mine development expenses are almost always written off for taxes, but their treatment on the books varies. Productive exploration and development expense is regularly capitalized and amortized over the life of the property.

Research and Development Costs. Research and development costs must be charged to current expense. Most research and development is unsuccessful, and there is no consistent relationship between (1) the value of the discovery, process, or product, and (2) the amount of money spent. Clearly, when successful, research and development are a real economic asset. However, analysts rarely have the information to determine the cost of that asset or to estimate the useful life over which it should be amortized. Setting up such an asset would require company guidance regarding the allocation of research and development costs between expense and the cost of successful products.

Much of what is called research and development is ordinary engineering related to cost reduction, styling, and production—the ordinary engineering application of known processes and materials to some existing function or part. These ordinary and recurring expenses should be charged to expense as incurred. It is in the exploratory research of the sort found in drugs, electronics, and biotechnology that analysts have attempted to reflect in some way the results of successful research efforts. For example, analysts following the drug industry have devised such adjustments as adding back half the cost of research to reported earnings for purposes of comparing companies. Another method is to adjust earnings upward or downward by a figure that represents the amount the company's research expenditures (expressed as a percentage of sales) deviate from the industry average.

Items to Amortize on Tax Returns

Intangibles which are amortized on the tax return include:

- Patents
- Licenses
- Royalties
- Motion pictures and television programs
- Sound recordings
- Costs of leases

(Leasehold improvements—often buildings erected on leased land—should be considered the equivalent of tangible assets with lives coterminous with the leases involved.) In the past most companies "conservatively" wrote off the cost of patents against *surplus* and thus relieved future earnings of the usually small amortization charge. Today the cost of patents and licenses is regularly amortized against income. Regardless of the treatment of such items on the tax return, the analyst should follow the general rule of eliminating intangibles and their amortization unless they are known to be marketable or to have a direct stream of revenue attributable to them. In many cases, it will be obvious to the analyst that the intangible asset has great value. For example, RCA pioneered in radio and television and continues to receive substantial royalty income for use of its patents. The film libraries of the movie companies generate substantial income from leases to television stations and reissue of old classics—note, for instance, the $1.5 billion paid by Turner Broadcasting System for MGM Entertainment Company. However, usually the intangibles have little or no value, but that information is seldom revealed to the security analyst unless management is asked specifically about it.

Development Items to Expense on Tax Returns

Development items include advertising, start-up costs, early deficits, and the like. In some rather varied cases these have been capitalized in the accounts, increasing the reported earnings. If such items appear on the balance sheet, analysts should eliminate them and their amortization. The magnitude of these items is sometimes proportionate to the ineptitude with which the expenditures were incurred.

Purchased Goodwill and Other Doubtful Debits

The fourth group of intangibles includes those which may be neither expensed nor amortized on the tax returns. Chief of these is goodwill, especially the important element of "purchased goodwill," which arises when a business is acquired at a cost exceeding the fair value of its net assets in a business combination accounted for as a purchase rather than a pooling of interests.

Warren Buffett, a student and associate of Ben Graham, has commented, "An analyst can live a rich and fulfilling life without ever knowing about goodwill or its amortization." By this, he meant that goodwill and its amortization are void of information and should be eliminated by the analyst. Thus goodwill should be written off, and its amortization should be removed from the income statement. If no asset existed economically, no economic cost was incurred in using it. The analyst should not allow its amortization to affect current or future earnings. No tax adjustment is required because amortization of goodwill is not tax deductible.

Goodwill is a premium paid in excess of fair value of net assets. It represents the acquiring company's estimate of the excess of *investment value* over *asset value*. However, this estimate is soon out of date, reflecting projections of earnings under the new ownership. If the company has financial difficulties, the goodwill evaporates quickly. Thus goodwill is not a reliable asset.

Accounting requires that purchased goodwill be amortized over no more than 40 years. Its immediate write-off is forbidden. At times, even amortization over 40 years can result in significant amounts in the income statement. For example, Manufacturers Hanover Bank acquired goodwill of $626 million in 1984 in its acquisition of CIT Financial Corporation. Amortization will be over 34 years, or $18.4 million per year.

15

Analysis of the Funds Flow Statement

In Chapter 14 we discussed a number of aspects of depreciation, depletion, and other amortization, as these items appear, either actually or ideally, in the company's accounts. We are now ready to extend the discussion into the concept of cash flow, which is currently an important part of Wall Street's thinking. Two approaches are offered in preference to the conventional funds statement, and the uses and interpretation of cash flow statements are discussed.

Some Funds Statement Definitions

Reconciliation to Cash or Working Capital

A funds statement, officially called the "statement of changes in financial position," attempts to explain many changes in the balance sheet from one period to the next, from various causes in addition to net income. For simplicity we will use more familiar terms such as *funds statement* or *cash flow statement*. The bottom line is either *net changes in cash and equivalent*, or *net changes in working capital*, but many other balance sheet changes, including investing and financing activities, are included. (*Cash equivalents* typically include U.S. Treasury bills, commercial paper, certificates of deposit, and other short-term high-quality temporary investments of cash.)

Operating, Financing, and Investing Activities

Since little official guidance is given for funds statements, they vary widely. Some practices are quite common, such as presenting the statement in three categories: operating, financing, and investment activities. Since there are currently no official definitions of these categories, similar items are classified differently, based on judgments or preferences of different managements.

Direct and Indirect Methods

Discussions of the funds statement are hampered by loose usage of terminology—particularly the phrases *direct method* and *indirect method*. In this book an indirect method is any method that does not look to actual cash flows as a starting point. For example, as defined here, the typical funds statement uses the indirect method when it considers the sum of the following as sources of "cash from operations":

- Net income
- Depreciation
- Other noncash charges
- The increase (or minus the decrease) in deferred taxes

It is possible to have all those items and still have no cash inflows. Those four items are merely an approximation of net cash inflows, because they are income or expenses that are assumed not to require any current cash outflow. Implicit assumptions here are that cash revenues exist, and that the above list of items would not make any demands upon those cash inflows.

The direct method looks to direct sources of cash. Direct cash inflows include:

- Sales for cash
- Collection of receivables, rent, interest, and dividends
- Receipt of tax refunds
- Sales of securities
- Other transactions

Similarly, the direct method looks to actual cash outflows, using currency, checks, wire transfer, and the like to make payments to others, rather than to accrual bookkeeping entries.

Indirect Method Is Normally Used

Unfortunately, even though companies have the information to prepare direct cash flow statements, the custom is to use an indirect method in the funds statement. Often what is actually presented in the funds statement is a combination of *some*

- Year-to-year changes in balance sheet items (such as depreciation of equipment)
- True flows of cash (for example, cash purchase of supplies)
- Accrual entries (such as setting up a warranty reserve for products sold)

Some items are gross amounts and others are net of tax or expense.

Using a funds flow statement based on accrual accounting as a check on the accrual income statement is a sort of self-fulfilling prophecy. Misleading information about cash flows in one is liable to show up undetected in the other.

The Importance of Cash Flows

Investors and creditors can receive cash only if the company has holdings of cash or net inflows of cash. As a result, investors examine the relationship between the accrual income reported in the income statement and the related cash flow from revenues and for expenditures. Over the life of a company, use of accrual accounting or cash accounting does not matter, since income turns out to be the same. In any one year cash inflows and outflows may deviate from accruals by a wide margin. Over a period of several years a cash-based income statement should begin to approach the numbers presented in the regular accrual income statement. Some analysts use a rule of thumb that if the earnings estimated from the funds statement are within 15 or 20 percent of the reported earnings of the income statement over a five-year period, the latter number is "validated."

Bank credit officers in particular are aware that loans must be repaid with cash. They, too, would like to know whether a company generates cash from its operations in amounts sufficient to service debt, pay rental obligations, and maintain operating capability without strain. The user of financial statements can do most of the job of preparing an ordinary funds flow statement from the existing income statement, balance sheet, footnotes, and knowledge or estimates of the amount of capital expenditures. The desirability of cash flow information is clear when one considers that bankers are known to have prepared cash flow statements as early as 1863.

Dividends and Cash Flow

The security analyst is interested in cash inflows for a variety of reasons. One, of course, is the stream of dividends which constitutes a major portion of return. While the reason may not be immediately obvious, there is a much higher correlation between dividends and cash flow than there is between dividends and earnings. This occurs partly because earnings are highly volatile—much more so than cash flow—and companies attempt to pay a relatively stable pattern of dividends. Usually dividends are not cut because of what are considered to be temporary declines in earnings; often, all or most of the dividend will be continued even during a period of two or three years of deficits. The dividend will not be continued, however, if the decline in cash flow is great enough to encroach on debt service and necessary capital expenditures. Thus, the prediction of future dividends is heavily influenced by the analyst's projection of future cash flows from operations and mandatory cash outflows.

Dividend Policy

Companies budget future dividend payments the same way that they budget any other cash outflow such as debt service requirements, capital expenditures, or any forecastable demand for cash. As a result, when a board of directors sets a general dividend policy, it is often in terms of and always in consideration of projected cash flows—not earnings. Thus, the internal policy might well be described as 20 to 25 percent of average cash flow, even for companies that express their dividend policy publicly in terms of payout ratios, that is, as a percentage of earnings.

Cash Flow Approximation

Another reason for the analyst's interest in cash inflows is to determine the ability of the company to fund its growth internally—that is, from the cash it is able to generate from operations. A company cannot grow forever through increasing its leverage. The quality ratings of its debt will be downgraded, and the company will be forced to sell stock, diluting the growth in earnings per share. Thus, although some growth can be financed by debt, that debt can grow no faster in the long run than the growth of equity. Equity must grow largely from retained earnings if dilutive sales of stock are to be avoided. Since the growth rate of earnings has a major influence on the earnings multiplier, analysts must validate their projection of earnings growth with a cash flow analysis confirming the company's ability to finance the growth.

Revenues as a First Approximation of Cash Inflows

The cash flow concept can be better understood if considered in terms of the cash-to-cash cycle of the typical business enterprise. The operating cycle consists of buying raw materials, labor, and the like for cash and of subsequently receiving cash as a result of sale of output. Companies have very few nonmonetary transactions. Thus, cash, sooner or later, represents one side of most two-party transactions. Where do operating cash flows come from? Usually cash is received for outright sales or from exchange of goods and services for credit—accounts receivable, which are subsequently collected. Revenues can be used as a first approximation of the actual cash received from operations, since the cash payments on receivables from earlier periods may be about equal the absence of cash inflows from the uncollected receivables held at the end of the period.

Gross Cash Inflows

Dividends and growth are financed by the *net* cash inflows, of course. Cash revenues are not available for such uses except when they exceed cash expenses. However, analysts need the *gross* inflows from revenues and the outflows for expenses and losses for the same reasons that they need an income statement that shows both revenues and expenses. The primary use of the funds statement by stock analysts is to confirm or deny, over time, the amounts shown in the income statement. Having revenues and expenditures on a cash basis for comparison with accrual revenues and expenses permits the analyst to identify more specifically the *sources* of differences. Information about only the *net* cash inflows is deficient in that respect.

Example of a Gross Cash Inflow Comparison. Consider, for example, a company that reports growing accrual revenues but flat gross cash revenues. The difference may appear in the form of rising accounts receivable, since they can be sold. The revenue difference would initiate a series of questions in the analyst's mind:

- Has the company adopted a lenient credit policy?
- Is it selling to customers who are unable to pay?
- Has the company been "borrowing" sales from future periods?
- Is the company "parking" inventory in a financing transaction?
- Are cash sales down?

Some explanation is demanded to reconcile differences between cash revenues and accrual revenues, which in the long run must be the same. Information on only the *net* cash inflows might not raise those questions.

For similar reasons, analysts need to examine differences between accrual expenses and gross cash expenditures for operations. Those differences both raise questions and offer insights into the operating dynamics of a company. That such information has neither been available nor been demanded by users of financial statements is no reason to dismiss its potential usefulness. To the contrary, given the differences between analysts' and accountants' views of capital maintenance and income, the gross cash flows seem the most promising candidates to deal with the differences created by:

- Amortization of goodwill
- Treatment of other doubtful intangible assets
- Accretion or discounting of interest
- Physical capital maintenance difficulties
- Capitalization of interest

Method One: Unadjusted Indirect Calculations

Calculating Cash Flow the Indirect Way

The earlier method of calculating cash flow was to sum net income and depreciation. Depreciation was the only large noncash expense for most companies. The result was called "cash flow," and it began to take on a meaning of its own. Some still calculate it that way, for example, the *Value Line Investment Survey.*[1] Analysts and companies now calculate cash flow using a more complete version of the indirect method—adding net income, depreciation, increases in deferred tax liabilities, and other noncash charges from the income statement.[2] These other noncash charges include:

- Amortization of goodwill, patents, licenses, and the like
- Warranty expenses
- Amortization of bond discounts

[1] *How to Use the Value-Line Investment Survey—A Subscriber's Guide,* Value Line, Inc., New York, p. 30.

[2] Allen H. Seed, III, *The Funds Statement,* Financial Executives Research Foundation, Morristown, N.J., 1984, pp. 33–34. Seed found only two companies using the direct method in 1983: SafeCard Services, Inc., and Northrop Corp.

- Amortization of leasehold improvements

(Ideally, the credits, such as amortization of bond premiums, should be subtracted from the total.)

But Depreciation Isn't Cash Flow

Of course, if there were no sales for cash or receivables collected, there would be no cash inflow from operations. Analysts must keep in mind that depreciation and the like are not a source of cash, although if there is revenue, depreciation and noncash charges are expenses that generally do not require a concurrent cash outflow. That part of the cash inflow is a *net* inflow.

Flows and Capital Maintenance—Return of or Return on Investment?

All cash flows from operations represent either return *of* capital or return *on* capital. The amounts that are properly measured expenses are return of investment. Properly calculated depreciation represents the return of the investment in a building or a piece of equipment over its useful life. After all the proper expenses of a period have been recovered, any additional positive cash flows from operations are income, or return *on* investment. A major objective of security analysis is to measure this net income as accurately as possible through making appropriate adjustments to accounting net income. The adjustments include reallocation of some of the amounts that are stated on the books as "return of capital" to "return on capital," or the reverse. (Of course, the financial statements do not actually use the terms *return of capital* and *return on capital*.)

To the analyst, the return of capital is the amount of expense for the period necessary to maintain capital—to remain "as well off." The amount of return on capital, or income, is the residual after revenues and expenses have been brought to the analysts' estimate of *correct* levels. Many of the adjustments that the analyst makes to the income statement or to the balance sheet will also turn out to be appropriate adjustments for the funds flow statement.

Cash Flows—Independent of Accounting

A point worth repeating is that cash flow is the same in any accounting system. This is seen in the deferred tax example shown in Table 14.2 in Chapter 14. Notice that the calculated cash flow will be precisely the same *regardless of whether one uses the tax statements or the stockholder report* to measure the cash inflows. Cash flows are equal, in that example, to net income plus depreciation plus the increase (or minus the decrease) in the deferred tax liability.

Criticism of Method One

Dissatisfaction with the Funds Statement

Criticisms of Format and Implementation. The existing indirect method funds flow statement, which we shall call method one, has been criticized on a variety of grounds. Some have indicated that the format of current funds flow statements is so different from the income statement that it is difficult to relate the two. Others have pointed out that a variety of refinements should be made to the simple indirect formula so that a more accurate funds flow number is presented—regardless of whether the bottom line is changes in working capital or changes in cash and equivalent.

Working Capital as a Bottom Line. Another criticism is the vagueness of the concept of working capital flows. It is not easy to grasp exactly what that notion is. It is clearly not part of the cash-to-cash cycle previously described, and it can be argued that most changes in amounts of various working capital items are too loosely related to income and capital notions to be helpful as a check on the income statement.

The Bottom Line Is Not Important. It is quite easy to take a funds statement that reconciles to cash and reconstruct it to reconcile to working capital. Usually the information is shown in the funds statement itself and merely needs rearranging. If not, a bit of adding and subtracting of balance sheet items will permit that rearrangement. Thus, in terms of information, the argument for or against one or the other bottom line seems an arid debate.

Method Two: Adjusted Indirect Flows—An Easy Improvement

Custom and inertia are likely to perpetuate the prevailing indirect method for some time. However, its implied cash flows can be brought closer to actual cash flows by a series of adjustments that will bring it from a rough approximation to a reasonably close estimate.

The conventional indirect method assumes that there are no lags and leads between the times that accrual revenues and expenses are recorded and when cash is actually received or paid out. Clearly, that is not true. Accrual accounting deliberately moves revenues and expenses out of the periods in which the cash flows occurred. Some of the lags and leads are identifiable and can be used to the first approximation to make it a bit more accurate. For example, accounts receivable outstanding at the beginning of the year are usually uncollected revenues of the previous year or years. If the receivables are classified as "current" it is reasonable to assume that they fall due and are collected during the following year. The estimate of cash flows can be improved by adding to the revenues the accounts receivable outstanding at the beginning of the year.

Accounts receivable outstanding at the end of the year are amounts that were probably reported as revenue during the year but have not yet been collected. Thus, the revenues had a cash shortfall equal to the accounts receivable outstanding at year end. Making adjustments of this sort converts method one, the indirect method, into method two, an adjusted indirect method.

A wide variety of such adjustments can be made. Some are discussed below in connection with the third method. The point is that even the crude indirect method can be adjusted to improve the cash flow estimate. The analyst would still be dealing with *net* cash inflows, rather than the gross numbers. In that respect, the result is less than optimum, but the increased accuracy is worth the effort involved.

Method Three Is Preferred

A Direct Method of Estimating a Cash-Based Income Statement

Although the above-mentioned adjustments can be made to improve the net cash flow number provided by the indirect method, they can also be used to approximate the direct method. This cash flow statement focuses more closely on actual cash inflows and outflows and displays them in a format similar to an ordinary income statement.

A worksheet for this method is illustrated in Figure 15.1. The figure is a form that might be suitable for a manufacturing company that has revenues, a little interest income, and perhaps a foreign currency translation adjustment gain or loss arising from cash or equivalents.

Its expense categories include:

- Selling, general, and administrative costs (SG&A)
- Cost of goods sold (COGS)
- Depreciation and amortization

Cash Inflows from Ordinary Operations:
1. Revenues ....
2. Less Increase in Accounts Receivable ....
3. Plus Decrease in Accounts Receivable ....
4. Plus Interest Income ....
5. Less Noncash Interest Income ....
6. Plus Amortization of Bond Premium ....
7. Plus Dividends from Equity Method Investees ...
8. Plus Cash and Equivalent Portion of Foreign
    Currency Translation Adjustment Gain ....
9.   Total Cash Inflows From Operations ....

Cash Outflows from Ordinary Operations:
10. Selling, General and Administrative Expense ....
11. Cost of Goods Sold ....
12. Plus Increase in Inventories ....
13. Less Decrease in Inventories ....
14. Less Increase in Accounts Payable ....
15. Plus Decrease in Accounts Payable ....
16. Plus Increase in Prepaid Expenses ....
17. Less Decrease in Prepaid Expenses ....
18. Less Increase in Accrued Liabilities ....
19. Plus Decrease in Accrued Liabilities ....
20. Plus Increase in Other Noncash, Nontax
     Current Assets ....
21. Less Decrease in Other Noncash, Nontax
     Current Assets ....
22. Plus Cash and Equivalent Portion of Foreign
     Currency Translation Loss ....
23.   Total Cash Outflows for Expenses before
     Interest and Income Taxes ....

24. Net Cash Flow from Operations before Interest
    and Income Taxes (line 9 − line 23) ....

Cash Outflows for Interest Costs:
25. Interest Expense ....
26. Less Accretion of Interest Discount ....
27. Plus Interest Capitalized ....
28.   Total Cash Outflows for Interest Costs ....

Figure 15.1 Approximation of a cash basis income statement.

Cash Outflows for Income Tax Expense:
29. Income Tax Expense............................... _____
30. Less Increase in Deferred Tax Liability........... _____
31. Plus Decrease in Deferred Tax Liability............ _____
32. Less Increase in Income Taxes Payable............ _____
33. Plus Decrease in Income Taxes Payable............ _____
34.   Total Cash Outflow for Income Taxes.......... ==========

35.   Cash Flows from Operations Available for
       Dividends, Capital Expenditures, and Debt
       Repayment (lines 24 − 28 − 34)............... ==========

Investments:
36. Purchases of Plant and Equipment .... _____
37. Less Interest Capitalized .... _____
38. Less Net Disposition of Plant and Equipment.... _____
39   Total Investments................................. ==========

Cash Raised Through Financing:
40. Sale of Bonds................................. _____
41. Less Note Maturity............................... _____
42. Exercise of Stock Options.......................... _____
43. Less Decrease in Bank Loans....................... _____
44. Sale of Commercial Paper .... _____
45. Total Cash Raised by Financing.................. ==========

46.   Dividends Paid...................................... ==========

47.   Net Increase in Cash and Equivalent (lines
       35 −39 − 45 − 46)............................. ==========

Figure 15.1   (Continued)

Because the company borrows money, it has interest expense, some of which has been capitalized. The company has income tax expense, but part of that is deferred because of tax timing differences. The company makes investments in plant and equipment, sells off some used equipment, and even pays a few dividends to its stockholders.

The example starts with the accrual numbers from the income statement, and attempts to adjust each item from an accrual to a *cash* basis. If an income statement line item does not involve current cash flows, it is ignored. The intended result is a cash basis income statement. The model is like government accounting in that expenditures replace expenses.

A Parallel to the Income Statement

Figure 15.1 shows some similarity of format to the ordinary income statement, although differences exist. Information from the balance sheet, the present funds statement, the footnotes, and the 10-Ks is used. The outline of this particular format is:

Revenues and gains

 Less expenses and losses, excluding interest and taxes

Equals cash from operations before interest and taxes

 Less interest

 Less income taxes

Equals internally generated free cash

 Less cash spent for investments

Plus cash raised through financing

 Less dividends paid

Equals net increase in cash and equivalent

In the forthcoming paragraphs we will examine Figure 15.1 line by line, explaining the adjustments made, and reasons for them. Figure 15.1 is not a standardized form that would apply to every company. It is, instead, simply an example that sets forth certain assumptions, methods, and principles for adjusting line items to bring them closer to the actual cash flows. Yet, many industrial companies can be fitted into the form with little or no adjustment.

Cash Inflows from Ordinary Operations

Revenues and Gains and Their Adjustments. Figure 15.1 begins with the revenues as presented on the income statement. If all sales were made for cash, the revenue number would be exactly equal to the revenue cash flow. Most companies do not sell only for cash, but have a certain amount of accounts receivable from credit sales.

Accounts Receivable. The accrual revenues should also be adjusted for the accounts receivable outstanding at the beginning and the end of the year. Note that we have made assumptions about the accounts receivable, some of which will prove to be incorrect. For example, we assumed that the receivables outstanding at the beginning of the year would be collected during the year. In some cases, such as long-term contracting, such an assumption would be inappropriate and would be rejected by an analyst. The assumptions underlying the adjustments suggested for methods two and three are not heroic, and the reader will find them to be sufferable. They do not appear in practice to create significant errors.

The Accounts Receivable Shortcut. Since our procedure calls for us to add the accounts receivable held at the beginning of the year and subtract those held at the end of the year, our form uses a shortcut— only the changes in accounts receivable from the beginning to the end of the year are dealt with. If the change is an increase (line 2), it should be subtracted from accrual revenue to get the cash revenue number. Similarly, a decrease in accounts receivable (line 3) over the year results in an addition. The analyst may wish to review the allowance for doubtful accounts in Schedule VIII of the 10-K.

Interest Income. Line 4 shows that the company has interest income. Some interest income may not involve any cash during the period involved. If the company has bought bonds at a discount, the accrual interest income would include accretion of interest which is not a cash flow and would not be collected until maturity. Thus we should subtract any noncash interest income (line 5). Similarly, accrual accounting would amortize a premium paid for a bond, reducing the reported interest income to a level below the actual cash received. Thus, one should add back the amortization of bond premium (line 6).

Dividends. This company has some nonconsolidated subsidiaries accounted for using the equity method. The retained earnings are of no interest to us, since they do not represent a cash flow to the company. Thus, line 7 lists as cash income only the dividends actually received during the year—not the equity income from the income statement.

Gains. Line 8 calls for the addition of any increase in *cash and equivalent* that came about by foreign currency translation adjustment gains. (This statement treats such gains as revenues and such losses as expenses.) If a company operates abroad and holds variously denominated cash and equivalent, translation gains and losses are an ordinary and recurring result of its business.

Foreign currency translation gains and losses are as properly recorded in operating results as are transaction gains and losses, which also result from currency fluctuations. In addition, it does not seem fruitful to divide *translation* results among operating, financing and investing categories for the following reasons:

1. Similar *transaction* results are not divided among those categories.
2. The accrual income statement (with which this cash statement will be compared) makes no such adjustment.
3. The necessary information to make the separation is mostly unavailable.

It may very difficult for the analyst to estimate, but ideally the estimate is required because it represents a cash inflow.

Many other types of gains and losses may occur, some involving cash and others not. For example, provision for restructuring is often a loss that occurs prior to any cash outflows; a gain or loss on litigation is often accompanied by an immediate cash flow.

Cash Revenue. Summing these various revenue and gain items gives the total cash inflows from operations (line 9).

Cash Outflows from Ordinary Operations

Ordinary Cash Expenses. We now examine the income statement for those line items that include substantial cash outflows. Line 10 is Selling, General, and Administrative expense. Line 11 is Cost of Goods Sold.

Exclude Depreciation and Noncash Charges. Remember that depreciation, usually a noncash expense, may be shown as a single line item on the income statement, or it may be divided among SG&A, Cost of Goods Sold, and capitalized items. The analyst is advised to compare the depreciation number shown in the income statement with that in the funds statement, the footnotes, and in Schedule VI of the 10-K. Often this comparison provides clues as to the amount of depreciation that is in inventories or that is included under some other title in the income statement. If found, depreciation should be deducted from the appropriate line items of cash expense. The treatment of depreciation and interest under capital leases should be examined to determine that the cash outflows for rent are included in and apportioned properly between cash operating expense and cash interest expense.

Changes in Inventories. An increase in inventories represents an implied cash outflow in excess of the cost of goods sold. Thus, over the year, increases in inventories increase cash outflows (line 12), and decreases reduce cash outflows (line 13). (However, depreciation that is capitalized in inventory does not require a current cash outflow, as mentioned in the previous paragraph.)

Changes in Accounts Payable. If accounts payable have increased during the course of the year, expenses or losses have probably been recorded in the income statement but have not yet been paid for in cash; that is, they are not yet cash expenses. Thus, an increase in accounts payable (line 14) is assumed to reduce cash outflows, and a decrease (line 15) to increase cash outflows.

The analyst will recognize that all accounts payable do not arise from operations. Accounts payable could occur because of the purchase on credit of a new machine, which is part of investment activities rather than operations. Fortunately, that is the exception, and our assumption will be valid from a practical viewpoint.

Prepaid Expenses. If expenses are prepaid, cash has been paid out, but the expense has not yet been recorded in the income statement. Thus, a year-to-year increase in prepaid expenses is a net cash outflow (line 16), whereas a decrease (line 17) is a net cash inflow. In the latter case, an expense recorded during the period had been paid for in an earlier period.

Accrued Current Liabilities. If a liability has been accrued, an expense has been incurred but not yet paid for. Thus, an increase in accrued liabilities during the year (line 18) reduces cash outflows, whereas a decrease (line 19) increases them. Some authorities have recommended that prepaid expenses and accrued liabilities be associated with selling, general, and administrative expenses and that the inventory and accounts payable adjustments should be associated with cost of goods sold.[3] Although these relationships may often be correct the distinction doesn't seem worthwhile.

Other Liabilities. If other current liabilities increase, say, salaries payable, excluding taxes and borrowings, which are treated below, the assumption is that the increased liability was an avoidance of cash outflow for an expense. It should be subtracted from cash outflows (line 20).

[3]Robert Morris Associates, *RMA Uniform Credit Analysis*, I.M.D. Learning Systems, Inc., Oakland, Calif., 1982, pp. 26–30.

Similarly, decreases in other current nonfinancing liability accounts (line 21) are presumed to have incurred cash outflows that have not yet become an expense.

Many noncurrent liabilities other than long-term debt and deferred tax liabilities are financial rather than operating in nature. Often they are identified as such—for example, lease obligations—and therefore should not be considered reductions in cash expense. Further information may have to be sought from the company when the amounts are significant and the details sparse.

Foreign Currency Translation Adjustment Losses.   Having treated foreign currency translation adjustment gains from cash and equivalent holdings as cash revenues, losses from such holdings should be considered a part of cash expense (line 22).

Operating Cash Flows.   These expenses and their adjustments are totaled on line 23. When line 23 (cash expenses) is subtracted from line 9 (cash revenues), the result is cash flow from operations before interest and income taxes (line 24). This is a key number to compare with its counterpart—operating income—in the income statement, especially the total amounts over long periods.

Cash Outflows for Interest Costs

Interest cost is examined separately, as we consider it to be outside of operating expenses. We record first the interest expense shown in the income statement (line 25). However, if bonds were issued at a discount, a part of interest expense will be the bookkeeping accretion of the discount, which is not a cash outflow. Thus, on line 26 the accretion of interest discount is subtracted. (The amount would be added if it were amortization of a premium over par.)

Capitalized Interest.   A company which acquires plant and equipment that requires time for construction or acquisition is required to capitalize interest incurred during the acquisition period. This capitalized interest is normally a cash outflow (line 27) and, if so, should be added to interest expense to obtain (line 28) the total cash outflows for interest. (Note that the capitalized interest will later be eliminated from capital expenditures.)

Cash Outflows for Income Tax Expense

Income Tax Expense.   This number is taken directly from the income statement. However, this is not necessarily the amount paid to the government. If there were an increase in the deferred tax liability, that increase was not paid during the year, and should be subtracted from income tax expense. If deferred taxes (line 31) decreased, that amount would represent a cash outflow and should be added to taxes paid.

An increase in income taxes currently payable represents taxes owed but not yet paid, which is a reduction in cash outflow for income taxes (line 32). A decrease (line 33) should be added to tax cash outflows because it represents payments greater than the tax expense. Line 34 is the sum of all tax items resulting in cash outflows.

Line 35 is the cash inflows from operations after taxes and interest. It represents the cash flows available for dividends, capital expenditures, and debt repayment. This is another key line for comparison with the income statement.

Investments

Capital Expenditures. Acquisitions of plant and equipment are presumed to be cash outflows and are shown on line 36. These figures include capitalized interest that has already been recorded in the interest cash outflows, and therefore capitalized interest should be deducted here (line 37). In adddition, if the company has disposed of any of its plant and equipment, the net cash received is treated as a reduction in cash outflows for investment (line 38). We consider disinvestment to offset investment. Note that the gains or losses on dispositions are not cash flows and do not change the cash revenue or expense numbers. Line 39 sums the various investment cash flows.

Financing Activities

Financing transactions are almost by definition immediate sources or uses of cash. Thus, lines 40 through 45 are self-explanatory. Selling securities brings in cash. Retiring them requires a cash outflow. Care should be taken to include bond premiums as proceeds of sales, and discounts as reductions thereof.

Operating lease transactions should be treated as financings if the leased asset is treated as an investment. They do not ordinarily involve immediate cash flows (other than rent), and a case can be made for excluding both. Treat the leased asset and the lease obligation consistently. That is, they should be treated as one of the following:

1. A cash equivalent transaction, in which the asset is an investment and the lease obligation a borrowing

2. A noncash exchange (both items are left out of the table)

Although the arguments for either treatment seem fairly evenly balanced, we incline toward including both items because the rent expense will surely be included among cash expenses.

Dividends

Line 46 shows the dividends paid to preferred and common stockholders.

The Bottom Line

Line 47 sums up the cash flow results for the period. Ideally, this number will turn out to be precisely equal to the change in cash and equivalent shown on the balance sheet, but that seldom happens. If the difference is relatively small, it is easiest to put in a plug item increasing or decreasing the operating expense cash outflows. Errors and omissions are less likely in the revenues, financing and investing activities, or dividends paid.

The Customized Approach

Figure 15.1 presents an exercise in converting accrual numbers into cash numbers. It is a simple example with a deliberately brief explanation of the recommended approach that we could have complicated by adding other transactions. For example, if the company in the example used LIFO calculation and had had a liquidation of lower-cost inventories, the cost of goods sold would have been less, but cash outflow would not have been reduced. The analyst would reduce the calculated cash outflow for cost of goods sold by the amount of the layer invasion. Similarly, if there were a large increase in the reserve for doubtful accounts, the analyst would adjust the amount of increase or decrease in accounts receivable to indicate that the change had nothing to do with cash flows from revenues but was a matter of bookkeeping entries.

Our point is that no book could cover all the adjustments that might be needed. Preparing a table along the lines of Figure 15.1 is an exercise in financial analysis, not a set of inflexible rules. The general model is simply to:

1. Begin with those accrual items that imply cash flows

2. Make all logical adjustments to bring them closer to actual cash flows

Each company analysis is customized to reflect its particular mix of transactions.

The application of the general model begins with the assumption that ordinary revenues and expenses are cash flows. The familiar noncash expenses—depreciation, amortization, deferred taxes, and the like—are assumed *not* to be cash flows and do not enter into the model unless a cash flow is indicated. Here are a few reminders of a general nature:

1. The acquisition of any asset except cash is assumed to require a cash outflow.

2. The incurrence of a liability is a net cash inflow, because it is a borrowing, or it can be presumed to be an avoidance of a cash outflow.

3. Increases and decreases in asset carrying amounts are handled on a situational basis, because some of those changes result from changes in prices rather than cash flows (for example, certain marketable securities and noncash assets and liabilities of foreign subsidiaries using functional currencies other than the dollar).

4. The carrying amounts of other assets and liabilities may change as a result of changes in valuation accounts, such as the depreciation account. Such changes do not represent cash inflows or outflows and should be handled like foreign exchange rate changes.

5. Only the effect of foreign exchange rate changes on cash and equivalents should be treated as a cash inflow or outflow—not the entire translation adjustment.

Analysis of Funds Statements Prepared by Method Three

Compare Longer Periods of Time

The cash flow statements for perhaps a 10-year period should be added together, which eliminates by cancellation many of the leads and lags caused by the timing differences between accrual and cash accounting. When these numbers are compared with the numbers in a 10-year summation of the income statement, many of the major line items will be of the same general magnitude, giving the analyst some comfort about the income statement. Certainly, revenues, cost of goods sold plus selling, general, and administrative expense (excluding depreciation), financing, and dividends should compare well. Note that in a 10-year study, only the balance sheet changes from the beginning of the first year to the end of the last year are necessary. The intervening year-to-year changes cancel out.

The Comparison of Depreciation and Capital Expenditures

A comparison of depreciation (from the income statement) with cash capital expenditures has interesting implications. Perhaps the analyst's biggest challenge will be to determine what part of the capital expenditures over the 10-year period are to be considered replacement of departed capital—a counterpart of depreciation and amortization—and what part represents an increase in the capital base. Capital expenditures that increase efficiency or capacity are viewed differently than replacement of old capacity. The increases in the capital base are a part of income.

The leading question is "Did the capital expenditures improve earning power, hold it at the original level, or were they so inadequate as to permit earning power to decline?" Analysts who find an answer to that question can probably estimate an amount of the capital expenditures made that merely serve to replace the exhausted and obsolete plant. Those expenditures, like depreciation, assure maintenance of capital. Any additional expenditures for plant and equipment, unless they were somehow wasted, represent something akin to income—to being "better off."

Estimating Conventional Income from a Method Three Statement

Similarly, increases in working capital usually contribute to an improvement in the welfare of the company. In estimating conventional income from the cash-based statement, working capital increases should be included. The income estimated from the cash flow statement would be the sum of the following less net financing:

- Increase in cash items
- Dividends paid
- Capital expenditures (in excess of those needed for capital maintenance) and other investments
- Other increases in working capital

Estimating Distributable Income

However, if the analyst is seeking distributable income, that part of any increase in working capital that is needed to do a constant volume of business should not be included in income. (A variation of the distributable income idea would adjust for increases in the company's ability to borrow to finance the increased working capital needs.) The distributable income approaches have gained more attention from United Kingdom investors than those in the United States, perhaps due to greater exposure to the ideas.

At this point a comparison of the 10-year cash flow statement with the income statement can begin to focus on income from both perspectives. If the two statements tell widely disparate stories, the accrual income number cannot be considered to be confirmed.

Comparison of the Three Methods

Three approaches to a funds statement have been discussed in this chapter:

1. The conventional funds statement, using the indirect method
2. The indirect method adjusted to reflect the implied cash flows that are suggested by analysis of the two balance sheets and other data
3. The direct method that begins with the revenues and expenses in a quasi-income statement format and makes the same adjustments suggested for the second method

Method One Is Familiar and Relatively Labor-free

The conventional funds statement has the advantage of familiarity. It requires little or no labor, other than perhaps rearranging the numbers to fit the analyst's preferred format. Its disadvantage is that it cannot be put in a format that parallels that of the income statement and is therefore more difficult to compare with the income statement. The first method does not even attempt to deal with cash flows. Instead, it handles the accrual accounting numbers. The accrual system deliberately moves revenues and expenses away from the periods in which the cash flows took place, to the degree that such changes are needed to "match" revenues and expenses. To call the resulting funds flow a "cash flow" requires an assumption that exactly the same amounts of revenues and expenses were transferred in or out of the period under study. This could only occur by happenstance.

Methods Two and Three Seek the Actual Cash Flows

In contrast, the second and third methods are attempts to capture the actual cash flows that occurred during the period. To the degree that they succeed, the analysis will provide more reliable numbers, more understandable numbers.

Differences between the Second and Third Methods

In one respect, the second and third methods are the same: All adjustments that are appropriate for one are also appropriate for the other. The difference is just that the second method begins with the first approximation of funds flow by the indirect method and is an estimate of the net cash inflow: It adds net income to the expense items that are not cash outflows. It assumes that the net income and noncash expenses will equal the portion of cash revenues that are net cash inflows.

Method three, however, will reach the same net cash flow number but begins with the gross cash flows—the approximation of revenues and expenses on a cash basis. Taking that additional step has the advantages of

1. Ensuring that the revenues are actual cash flows so that the second method's assumption is fulfilled
2. Presenting the information in a format that is much more comparable to the traditional income statement format

The latter point is important because one of the major uses of the funds flow statement is to confirm, over time, the income statement. An additional advantage of method three is the ability to determine income on several different bases. For example, a cash income number can be derived based on:

- Conventional income notions from an analyst's viewpoint of the increase in net assets
- Distributable income notions
- Income on a liquidating basis

Method Three's Distributable Income Is Controversial

The distributable income notion associated with the direct method of calculating has been criticized because it excludes some of or all the increase in working capital. In a liquidation situation, an increase in working capital is an increase in net assets and in the expected liquidating value. For that analysis, of course, working capital changes are income items.

However, from the viewpoint of a going concern, changes in working capital are a part of management's deliberate operating decisions or a result of the operating environment in which the company does business. Thus, either the changes in working capital were necessary to achieve the operating results, or they were the casualties and windfalls of the operating environment. It appears logical to consider those working capital demands as part of operations when studying the cash flow dynamics of a company. At the same time, using a more conventional view of the ongoing firm, it seems appropriate to recognize in the analysis of income the benefits of those changes to overall profits.

Technical Difficulties of Methods Two and Three

Some have critized methods two and three because certain technical difficulties exist in their application. The most significant of these technical difficulties occurs when there is a change in the reporting entity, that is, when mergers, acquisitions, spinoffs, divestitures, and the like take place between the beginning and the end of the year. Those events do cause analytical problems, not only for the funds statement but for all other analysis of the surviving company. In most cases, there is enough information in the annual report and the 10-Ks for the analyst to cope with those problems.[4] The analyst may have to go to the company for additional information to complete the analysis, but regular company contact is a routine part of an analyst's activities.

Comparisons of inventory and cost of goods sold, particularly in LIFO layer invasion situations, are technically difficult, but, again, the same problems must be faced in the regular income statements.

---

[4]Ralph E. Drtina and James A. Largay, III, "Pitfalls in Calculating Cashflow from Operations," *The Accounting Review*, vol. 60, no. 2, April 1985, pp. 314–326.

Method Three Is Preferred

The analyst should use the direct method, if possible. No more work is involved in the third method than in the second, but the benefits of grossing up expenses and revenues for analysis gives the third method an informational advantage. Clearly, using the first method will avoid a considerable amount of effort on the part of the analyst. The analyst overburdened with responsibility for too large a number of companies may not have time to apply the third method, and the first method does provide useful information. However, in every case of analysis of underwritings, leveraged buyouts, speculative fixed-income financing, takeover and acquisition candidates, other similar analyses, and meeting due diligence requirements, the third method should be used.

Confusion between Income and Cash Flows

Cash Flow as a Substitute for Income

The heavy emphasis on cash flows (as opposed to earnings and income notions) by a few writers, analysts, and managements, especially in the real estate industry, has led some to believe that certain industries should not use depreciation in calculating earnings. That capital maintenance notion is unacceptable because it does not maintain the capital invested in the item to be depreciated. At the same time, one can understand the frustration of many in the real estate business because accounting does not fully reveal the values of their properties. Many companies in the real estate field present supplementary current value balance sheets and income statements, and we consider these to be helpful.

The Real Estate Industry Encourages a Cash Flow Focus

The problem in the real estate business is that the whole is often worth more than the sum of the parts. When a real estate development company builds a shopping center, initially it is worth just about what it costs for construction and land acquisition. However, when one combines that project with favorable long-term financing, a 95 percent occupancy rate with stable high-grade tenants and heavy retail traffic flow, the property suddenly becomes worth a good deal more than its mere acquisition cost. This additional worth, of course, is reflected in improving rentals and a high return on original cost. Many in the real estate industry, however, feel that some of or all the enhanced value should be reflected as income, preferably by excluding depreciation and certain other expenses from the income statement. Some would include the increased rents and also the unrealized gain on the value of the property that resulted from the increased rents. This is a sort of double counting.

Example. A booklet issued by Koger Partnership, Ltd., states:

> Cash flow is the accepted, professional measurement of the performance and value of income-producing real estate, used by lending institutions, tax assessors, appraisers and others engaged in the real estate field. Cash flow represents earnings before non-cash charges for depreciation, amortization of deferred property costs, provision for deferred income taxes, etc.
>
> Cash flow is a major consideration in the purchase, ownership and sale of commercial real estate.
>
> Cash flow is used for the payment of mortgage amortization, future expansion and other corporate purposes, and to make distributions to investors.
>
> Net earnings are not considered by real estate professionals as the important measure of results for income-producing properties. Ideally, real estate net earnings should approach zero, as the earnings are reduced by non-cash accounting entries and protected from taxes.

Example. The 1985 Annual Report of McCormick & Company, Inc., entitles a chart "Profitability" (p. 15). The vertical bars are described as "net income before financial charges, depreciation and amortization" with a footnote that they are also exclusive of loss from Mexican peso devaluations (1982). Its subsidiary, McCormick Properties, Inc., lists operational cash flow of $10.89 million for 1985, with a footnote as follows: "Operational cash flow is defined as net income plus depreciation, other non-cash charges and deferred taxes (excluding tax benefits from leveraged automobile leases) minus after-tax profit from improved property sales and scheduled mortgaged payments."

Is Depreciation a Necessary Cost?

To test the implication that depreciation is not a proper cost, see the data shown in Table 15.1 for the *Value Line Industrial Composite* from 1977 through 1986. The composite's comparative showing on a cash income basis (up 87.5 percent) is somewhat better than on the customary net income basis (up 47.5 percent). The issue is not the relative movement of the two but whether a cash income basis has a sound capital maintenance notion behind it. Cumulative capital expenditures during the 10-year period were $40.90 per share, or 89 percent of the total cash income. It is hard to imagine that a significant portion of those capital expenditures

Table 15.1. Per-Share Cash Income and Net Income from *Value Line Industrial Composite*

	1977 to 1986*	1977	1986*
Cash income	$45.82	$ 3.04	$ 5.70
Depreciation and amortization	21.06	1.21	3.00
Net income	24.76	1.83	2.70
Net worth		13.10	23.05

* The fourth quarter of 1986 is partly estimated.
NOTE: Cash income here is taken to be net income plus depreciation and amortization.
SOURCE: *The Value Line Investment Survey, Part 2, Selection and Opinion,* February 13, 1987, p. 691.

were not replacements of plant and equipment that was worn out or technologically or economically obsolete. If only half the expenditures were for replacement, rather than expansion or greater efficiency, the necessary depreciation would have been just about the $21.06 actually charged to expense using the conventional net income approach.

No one questions the importance of cash flow—it is required to service debt and finance future growth, and it is the best predictor of the future stream of dividends. However, we reject the notion that cash flows should be thought of as being the same as earnings.

16

Results of Subsidiaries, Affiliates, and Foreign Operations

Consolidation of Results

Affiliates and Subsidiaries Defined

A subsidiary is generally defined as a company controlled by a so-called parent company which owns more than half the voting stock. (Most subsidiaries, however, are 100 percent owned by the parent.) Affiliate is a less definite term. An affiliate may be a company effectively controlled—perhaps jointly with others—though ownership may be less than 50 percent. Or the relationship may exist through control of both companies by the same owning group or parent, with resultant close commercial or operating ties. In some cases a company may be called an affiliate but really be a subsidiary.

Provision of Consolidated Reports

The great majority of companies publish consolidated reports which include in the balance sheet and income statement the results and financial position of their subsidiaries. The earnings or net equity applicable to other stockholders, if any, are shown as a deduction of minority interests. Such consolidated reports usually have no reason to distinguish results attributable to one corporate unit or another. The matter may become important, however, when a company elects to publish an unconsolidated (or "parent company only") statement or when a so-called consolidated statement excludes certain important subsidiaries or affiliates.

Foreign Activities Are Sometimes Excluded

A large area for variation in reported results—and for possible correction or adjustment by the analyst—lies in the field of foreign operations, including those of subsidiaries and branches. For a number of our larger corporations such foreign operations are of major consequence, and their proper evaluation presents a challenge both of technique and of judgment to the securities analyst. We shall first discuss the treatment of domestic subsidiaries and affiliates, and then pass over to the foreign field.

Domestic Subsidiaries and Affiliates

Deduction of Minority Interest from Net Income

Where 50 percent or more of the voting stock of a subsidiary or affiliate is owned, the standard procedure is to consolidate the subsidiary, with a one-line entry on the balance sheet for the minority interest usually placed below other liabilities but above stockholders' equity. The minority equity in net income is shown as a one-line item in the income statement as a deduction, so that the amount shown as net income is the amount applicable to shareholders of the parent only.

Use of the Equity Method for Twenty to Fifty Percent Owned Affiliates

Where the parent owns less than 50 percent but as much as 20 percent of the voting stock, the equity method of accounting is normally used. Ownership of 20 to 49 percent of the voting stock presumably gives the parent significant influence over financial and operating policies.

The equity method shows in the income statement the proportionate interest, after taxes, in the net income of the affiliate. The investment in the affiliate is carried on the balance sheet also as a one-line item that is adjusted up or down to reflect the proportionate interest in retained earnings or in losses. The investor's net income and stockholders' equity are intended to be the same under the equity method as they would have been if the affiliate had been consolidated. Intercompany profits and losses are eliminated. If an investor's share of losses exceeds the carrying amount, the investor discontinues applying the equity method and the investment is reduced to zero. Any additional losses are ignored unless the investor has made financial commitments to support the affiliate.

Example. The Universal Leaf Tobacco Company, Inc., owns (1) *subsidiaries* in which there are minority interests and (2) *affiliates* in which the holdings are 20 percent or more. Table 16.1 is an abbreviated 1985 income statement showing the treatment of minority interests and equity income.

Table 16.1. Universal Leaf Tobacco Co., Inc. Condensed Income Statement, Year to December 31, 1985 (In Millions of Dollars)

Revenues	1,078.9
Costs and Expenses	1,030.3
Income before Income Taxes and Other Items	48.5
Income Taxes	13.3
	35.2
Minority Interests	0.2
Income from Consolidated Operations	35.0
Equity in Net Income of Unconsolidated Affiliates	10.9
Income from Continuing Operations	45.9
Income from Discontinued Operations	0.5
Net Income	46.4

The Universal Leaf Tobacco presentation is fairly typical of the income statement format used by most companies for their equity method investees. The company's accounts reflect that the presumption of influence can be overcome. Footnote 1 reads, in part, "However, due to the inaccessability of certain financial information and exchange controls which restrict the remittance of dividends, our affiliate in Zimbabwe is accounted for under the cost method. A Mexican affiliate is also accounted for under the cost method since the company does not exercise significant influence over its financial and operating policies." Universal's consolidation policies, however, are somewhat unusual. Although the parent company is primarily engaged in the tobacco business, it fully consolidates its Lawyer's Title Insurance Corporation subsidiary. The resulting balance sheet is somewhat difficult to analyze. The balance sheet is classified, showing current assets of $188.8 million and current liabilities of $148.8 million. The current ratio (current assets divided by current liabilities) is rather low for a company in the tobacco industry, but the details of the current assets and liabilities reveal the heavy influence of the current portion of policy and contract claims and of insurance customer advances and deposits. The apparent weakness in the net current asset position is more than offset by the presence of a $100.7 million investment portfolio which is shown as a noncurrent asset on the balance sheet, separate from the $47.4 million equity in net assets of and advances to consolidated affiliates.

Example. Schlumberger Ltd. includes the pro rata share of revenues and expenses of Dowell Schlumberger, a 50 percent owned oil field services business, in the individual captions in the consolidated statement of income. This presentation is uncommon. The balance sheet treatment of the subsidiary is on the equity method.

Cost Methods

Investments in less than 20 percent of the voting stock are assumed to be purely investments and are usually carried at the lower of cost or market value, or on the cost method, which does not recognize losses unless they are deemed permanent.

The cost and the lower of cost or market methods recognize only dividend income. Note that the retained earnings of an investment carried on one of the cost methods are not reflected in the investor's income, but it would be difficult to say that the investors are not better off for the existence of retained earnings than they would be without them. Some analysts add the retained earnings, if they are known, to the income of the investor, effectively converting those investments to the equity method for income purposes. In their view, control is not the central issue, nor is economic integration, and the earnings simply reflect fully the "better-offness." Other analysts—probably the vast majority—make no explicit adjustment but merely consider the retained earnings of an investment carried on a cost method to be a plus factor in deciding on the attractiveness of the company.

Economic Integration and Use of the Equity Method. When the business relationship between investor and the investee is a strong one, such as a supply arrangement, the analyst should place the income statement on the equity method. For example, oil companies often form joint ventures to build oil and gas pipelines or gathering systems. While the percentage holding might be small, the equity method seems more appropriate than the cost method in reporting the results of such integrated activities.

The Potential to Control. The analyst should look for the presence of potential control as well as existing control. When the parent does not wish to carry an investment on the equity or consolidated method, it is quite simple to have some other party own the nominal equity while the parent holds warrants, options, convertibles, or contractual agreements that ensure control whenever the company chooses to obtain it. Some abuses of accounting have occurred in recent years in such areas of nonconsolidation as start-up subsidiaries, grantor trusts, and research and development partnerships. Particular care should be given to the footnotes on related party transactions, which will usually reveal such matters as

- Interlocking directorates
- Business relationships
- Other evidence of economic interests and unity

In addition to the footnotes to the financial statements, information on related party transactions and business relationships is provided in prospectuses, the proxy statements, and in the 10-K and other SEC filings.

Exclusion of Domestic Subsidiaries' Results

In general, consolidated financial statements are considered more useful than a mere parent company statement. Many companies, however, do not consolidate certain subsidiaries because they are not homogeneous or because of other special circumstances. For example, it is not usual for a manufacturing company to consolidate financial subsidiaries such as

- Banks
- Finance companies
- Leasing companies
- Savings and loan associations
- Insurance companies

Inclusion or Exclusion of Finance and Leasing Subsidiaries—A Contentious Issue

Large makers and sellers of durable goods and capital goods often have subsidiary finance and leasing companies to handle installment sales and leases of such products. It is customary to include the full results of such operations as a single line item in the income statement but not to consolidate the individual asset and liability classes in the balance sheet.

On or Off the Balance Sheet?   The issue of consolidation or noncon solidation of finance subsidiaries is controversial. In general, the earnings of a wholly owned finance or leasing subsidiary are included in the net income of the parent company, barring extremely unusual circumstances. The disagreement lies in the proper handling of the balance sheet. If the subsidiaries are carried on the cost or on the equity method, ratios such as return on invested capital and return on total assets may appear to be higher than if there were full consolidation of the assets and liabilities on the balance sheet. At the same time, it is argued that finance companies have relatively huge liabilities to banks and others and that their inclusion in the financial statement of the parent would distort the normal credit ratios for manufacturing and distributing concerns.

Parent Guarantees of Subsidiary Debt—Is It Really Parent Debt?   Several points should be considered by the analyst. First, in most cases the parent gives substantial assurances to creditors of the finance subsidiary so that the debt of the subsidiary is effectively guaranteed by the parent. Most banks would not lend to highly leveraged finance companies without such guarantees. Thus, one of the issues is "off-balance-sheet financing," where the parent is obligated to see that payments are made but shows no debt on its balance sheet..

The parent's assurances to the lender may be expressed in terms that do not make the commitment an obvious liability. A guaranty that the parent will not allow the subsidiary's cash balance or its working capital to fall below a prescribed level is effectively a guaranty to pay the subsidiary's debt if the subsidiary fails to do so. The parent may also be obligated by circumstances, for example when it depends on the subsidiary's good financial health for distribution of products or to obtain critical parts or raw materials.

Comparability.   A second aspect is that comparisons between companies that do and do not consolidate are not possible on a truly comparable basis. However, companies with or without a finance subsidiary may (1) borrow from banks or the commercial paper market to finance their receivables or (2) simply sell their receivables, with or without recourse, to banks and other investors. The problem of comparability persists, regardless of the consolidation issue.

Captive Finance Companies.   The picture is further blurred by the differences in the activities of finance and leasing subsidiaries. General

Motors' Acceptance Corporation (GMAC) is a subsidiary of General Motors Corporation. GMAC is essentially a "captive" finance company, set up for the purpose of financing the inventories of the company's dealer network and the installment sales of its automobiles. It is integral to the automotive operations. At times General Motors has made interest-free loans to GMAC so that it can offer bargain interest rates to buyers of General Motors cars. This is a form of price cutting for purposes of increasing auto sales. Where the operations of the two organizations are so closely integrated, separation of the financial statements of the parent and the subsidiary can be considerably distorting and difficult to comprehend. Consolidation is needed.

Stand-Alone Finance Subsidiaries.   In other cases, such as General Electric Credit Corporation (GECC), the primary purpose of the finance subsidiary is not to finance the products of the parent, but rather to act as an independent financing and leasing company for purposes of generating profits and tax benefits . The case for consolidation of GECC is less clear than for GMAC, because GECC finances mostly products of other manufacturers.

A third example would be Sears, Roebuck Acceptance which finances a substantial part of Sears, Roebuck's durable goods retail sales but also finances the sales of other manufacturers and engage in other financial activities. In the case of Sears, the consolidation of retailing with such diverse financial activities as Dean Witter (a brokerage house), Sears, Roebuck Acceptance, Allstate Insurance, Coldwell Banker (real estate), and other financial services results in a balance sheet that is terribly confusing. Although the annual reports of Sears, Roebuck are outstanding in their efforts to reduce the confusion, the analyst faces a consolidated balance sheet for which determining the proper ratio of debt-to-equity, current ratio, interest coverage, or whether the cash position is adequate is impossible. About the only useful ratio that could be generated using Sears's balance sheet is return on equity, but that figure could be calculated if the financially oriented subsidiaries were carried on the equity method. There is something comforting in knowing that one has an "all-inclusive" balance sheet. The bothersome question in Sears, Roebuck's case is how to find any possible use for it.

Leasing Subsidiaries—The Same Consolidation Quandary.   For a variety of reasons, the activity of leasing buildings and equipment has grown dramatically in the postwar years in response to increasing capital needs caused by inflation, a desire to keep liabilities off the balance sheet, and the ability to transfer tax credits and tax deductions from one company or person to another. In addition, a manufacturer of durable goods that owns a leasing subsidiary may be able to place products more readily through leasing to some customers than through direct sales. Thus, many companies now have leasing subsidiaries, and in most cases they are accounted for by using the equity method rather than by being consolidated. The arguments for and against consolidating finance subsidiaries apply equally to leasing subsidiaries.

Recommended Procedure.   The analyst should consolidate most *captive* finance and leasing companies, if the needed information is available. Where the subsidiary is not a captive, integral to the parent's other operations, the analyst should make the decision on a case-by-case basis. This matter is discussed further in Chapter 23 on the analysis of fixed-income securities.

Treatment of Foreign Operations

Conditions for Deconsolidation

Over the past quarter century the diversity in practice concerning the consolidation of foreign operations has diminished considerably. Immediately after World War II, the foreign exchange markets were in turmoil. Many countries placed severe restrictions, if not absolute bans, on the transfer of foreign currencies across their borders. Those foreign currency difficulties have ameliorated considerably so that in recent years only occasional and short-lived restrictions occur, generally in the less developed countries. Today, a foreign subsidiary is rarely excluded from the consolidated statements except when:

- A similar domestic subsidiary would be excluded
- Genuine problems restrict the movement of currencies so that dividends and other payments cannot be remitted to the parent
- Serious political problems such as revolution, war, and nationalization are occurring

  Example.   In 1982 Carnation Company wrote off its Mexican subsidiary and, in 1983, deconsolidated the Mexican operations, although it continued to operate an evaporated milk facility. The reasons for the write-off were currency restrictions, price controls, and uncertainties about the supply of certain key raw materials. A footnote to the 1983 financial statements stated that any earnings would be reflected in the consolidated financial statements if and when dividends were received.

  Bear in mind that remittances received from abroad are in general subject to a U.S. income tax equal to the difference between our 34 percent rate and that imposed on the earnings by the foreign government, in accordance with tax treaties. Percentage differences will vary widely between different countries.

Deferred Taxes on Unremitted Foreign Earnings

Today the larger question for analysts relates to the company's provision, or lack of provision, for deferred income taxes on undistributed foreign earnings.

- Some companies do not provide for deferred taxes on the unremitted earnings of foreign subsidiaries, arguing that no tax will ever be paid because the company intends never to remit the profits. If that is the case, one could question whether the earnings should be consolidated, since apparently the earnings will never benefit the domestic stockholders.

- Some other companies maintain that there are legal ways to return the earnings without incurring any taxes and that no provisions for taxes should be made for that reason. That type of remittance sounds very much like the sort of tax loophole that Congress often becomes concerned about.

- Finally, some companies provide fully for the payment of taxes on the unremitted profits, regardless of whether they have any near-term plans for remitting them.

Example. In 1984 American Express Company sold a Canadian subsidiary and other assets at a gain of $42 million. The company also reported a related $42 million tax expense on undistributed earnings not previously provided for. Since the transaction was voluntary, it is a reminder that the tax cannot always be avoided by structuring the transaction in a particular way. Also, decisions of the past not to distribute foreign earnings can be reversed at any time.

Unremitted Foreign Profits and Related Taxes

The diversity in treatment of this item by corporations presents a problem for security analysts. Clearly, unremitted foreign profits should not be left out of reported net income. But should they be counted at full value, regardless of possible tax liability and transfer difficulties? We think not. Such profits should be taken in, after deducting the estimated taxes that their remittance will incur, only when reasonably assured that remittances can take place in an orderly fashion under the expected exchange control conditions. Such adjustments should be made, of course, only when appreciable amounts are involved.

In general, the analyst should adopt a consistent method of treating such unremitted profits that would not depend on the company's reporting procedure. In addition, the analyst should capitalize foreign earnings at rates which reflect political and exchange risks.

Subsidiaries' Losses

The Sum of the Parts

The matter of subsidiaries' losses raises a special question that can illustrate some of the finer logical points involved in security analysis. We have asserted that both the profits and losses of subsidiaries should be fully accounted for in the parent company's earnings. But is the loss of a subsidiary necessarily a direct offset against the parent company's earnings? Why should a company be worth *less* because it owns something—in this case, an unprofitable interest? Could it not at any time put an end to the loss by selling, liquidating, or even abandoning the subsidiary?

Treat Subsidiaries' Losses as Nonrecurring If the Subsidiary Is Separable. If good management is assumed, must we not also assume that the subsidiary losses are at most temporary and therefore to be regarded as nonrecurring items rather than as deductions from normal earnings? Some investors specialize in searching for "turnaround" situations. It is hard to imagine a more attractive turnaround situation than a company that could double its earnings by simply giving one of its subsidiaries to charity. Such a situation is even more attractive if the subsidiary can be sold, or can be gradually liquidated while generating positive cash flows.

Is Separability Really Feasible? There is no one simple answer to the questions of (1) including or excluding a subsidiary's losses in the parent's income and (2) valuing the unprofitable subsidiary as a going concern or a liquidation candidate. Actually, if the subsidiary could be wound up *without an adverse effect on the rest of the business,* viewing such losses as temporary would be logical. But if there are important business relations between the parent company and the subsidiary, e.g., if the latter affords an outlet for goods, provides cheap raw materials or supplies, or absorbs an important share of the overhead, then the termination of its losses is not so simple a matter. It may turn out, upon further analysis, that all or a good part of the subsidiary's loss is a necessary factor in the parent company's profit. It is not an easy task to determine just what business relationships are involved in each instance. Like so many other elements in analysis, investigating this point usually requires going well beyond the reported figures.[1]

Examine the Individual Parts Separately If There Are Losses. The analyst should consider the issue of separability of the unprofitable subsidiary in connection with the notion of normal earning power. If the parts appear separable, the total value of the parts may be greater than the value of the whole. Thus, some parts of a company might be valued on a basis of normal earning power while others were valued at zero or on a basis of whatever they would bring in liquidation.

Divisional Losses versus Subsidiary Losses

This subject could lead us into the much wider field of unprofitable divisions, departments, or products. The distinction between a subsidiary, with a separate corporate name and accounts, and a not-so-separate division is likely to be one of convenience and form rather than of substance. When the subsidiary is not 100 percent owned, the presence of the minority interest usually requires the publication of its separate results. Hence the analyst is made directly aware of the existence of losses from such a source. Much more frequent, however, are losses from a wholly owned subsidiary or from a company division; the extent of such losses is usually only hinted at by the management, if revealed at all in the segment reporting. However, a competent analyst, by inquiry and probing, can in most such cases obtain a fairly accurate idea of the drain on the company's profits. The possibility of terminating the drain should not be forgotten in the analysis. Action of this kind is clearly called for, is usually taken sooner or later—though a management shake-up may first be necessary, and, when taken, may transform the earnings picture and the value picture of the company's stock.

Example. In 1985, Acme-Cleveland Corporation sold the business, related fixed assets, and selected inventory of its Shalco Systems Division, its subsidiary LaSalle Machine Tool, Inc., and certain related activities for $12.8 million plus contingent payments and an $0.8 million pension plan asset reversion. These operations had operating losses after taxes of $4.2 million in 1985 and much larger losses in 1984 and

---

[1]For a discussion of two older examples illustrating this point, Purity Bakeries and Barnsdall Oil in the 1930s, see the 1951 edition of this book, pp. 159–160.

1983. The company's net income in 1985 was a loss of $1.90 per share, including the losses of the discontinued operations, but a profit of $0.70 per share from the continuing operations.

Recommended Treatment of Subsidiary's Losses.   To avoid leaving this point in confusion, we shall summarize our treatment by making the following suggestions:

1. In longer-term studies, deduct subsidiary or divisional losses.
2. If the amount involved is significant, investigate whether or not the losses may be subject to early termination.
3. If the result of this examination is favorable, consider all or part of such losses as the equivalent of a nonrecurring item and exclude the losses from the calculation of earning power.
4. Forecasts of future earnings should account for the availability of the proceeds of sale or liquidation of the unprofitable activity.

17
Effects of Income Taxes

Analysts Must Stay Abreast of Income Taxes

Tax Calculations Required for Analysts' Calculations

Chapters 10 through 16 have pointed out many occasions when a security analyst should change financial statements. When a nonrecurring item needs to be removed from the income statement, the tax results of that item also need to be removed. Most restatements of the financial accounts are pro forma, that is, presented as if something that happened had not happened, or vice versa. Clearly, if the accounts are to be presented as if a certain event had not occurred, the tax results of that event must be eliminated, or income will be distorted by an improper tax rate and the balance sheet also will be inconsistently presented. These tax adjustments require that the analyst be familiar with the tax rates and tax laws of at least the past 10 years as well as the current ones.

Judgment of Management's Tax Skills Necessary

An analyst must also know how well or poorly the company's management handles tax planning and implementation. Analysts do not have to be tax experts but should be familiar with the general characteristics of the U.S. tax laws and the specialized tax treatment of the industries in which the analysts have an ongoing interest.

Characteristics and Features of the Tax Laws

Taxes — A Moving Target

All security analysts should know a number of broad structural characteristics of the tax laws. The U.S. tax laws and regulations are changed nearly every year in some way. The practicing security analyst must stay abreast of new tax legislation when it is proposed and when it has passed, paying particular attention to the unique tax situation of the industries and companies followed. Some tax situations are very complex because various tax elements interact. In those cases, straightforward analysis and simple rules of thumb become quite unworkable.

The Effective Rate Often Is Not the Statutory Rate

We shall first consider why a given amount of *taxable income* on a corporation Form 1120 may not be taxed at the ordinary income tax rate of 34 percent. (The effective date of the 34 percent rate was July 1, 1987. Previously the rate had been 46 percent going back to January 1, 1980, and it was 48 percent for a number of years prior to that.)

Important Features of the U. S. Tax Code

Progressive Corporate Tax Rates.   Like the personal income tax, the U.S. corporate income tax is progressive. The following rates apply:

- Taxable income up to $50,000 is taxed at 15 percent.
- The next $25,000 is taxed at 25 percent.
- Above $75,000 is taxed at 34 percent.

For a corporation that earns $100,000 or more, the progressivity feature is gradually eliminated by a surtax of 5 percent of the excess income over $100,000. Thus when a corporation's taxable income has reached $310,000, it has become subject to a flat rate of 34 percent on its *entire* income. Nearly all corporations investigated by security analysts would have at least that income in normal years, so for all practical purposes the analyst may act as if ordinary income were taxed at a flat rate of 34 percent.

Alternative Minimum Tax.   The 1986 tax law introduced a minimum tax with real teeth in it. It is expected to raise $22 billion over the 1987–1991 period. A number of new tax preferences were added to those of the previous law. An interesting feature of the new alternative minimum tax (AMT) is that book income, that is, what is reported to investors and creditors, will enter into the determination of tax preference. Thus, 50 percent of the excess of book income over AMT taxable income is a tax preference item. The alternative tax is imposed at a 20 percent rate on the AMT income above $40,000 if that amount is greater than the normal tax calculation. In effect, all companies must calculate the AMT to determine whether they owe it. In selecting the tax preferences, Congress rounded up the usual suspects: accelerated depreciation, mining exploration and development costs, completed contract accounting, the last vestiges of installment method accounting, intangible drilling costs, tax-exempt interest on private activity bonds issued after August 7, 1986, and unrealized gain on charitable contributions of appreciated property.

All this will take place merely as a transition through 1989. After that, an undefined earnings and profits concept will come into play. Apparently, "earnings and profits" will be an adjusted book pretax income. Since most of the adjustments are to be determined by Congress in future years, that is not a very useful piece of information.

Because the 34 percent rate applies only to the second half of 1987, and the 46 percent to the first half of the year, the full year may be treated as if there were a flat rate that averages the two—that is, a 40 percent rate. In adjusting years prior to 1987, the 46 percent rate should be used from 1980 to 1985, and the 48 percent before 1980.

Tax-Exempt Interest.   Interest received on nearly all state, municipal, and other local government bonds is tax exempt and is thus excluded from taxable income. Under the 1986 tax act, tax-exempt bonds issued for private purposes such as industrial development bonds, bonds for sports stadiums, pollution control, and other private purposes became fully taxable for federal income tax purposes. Tax-exempt interest was the most important reason that many banks paid little or no federal income taxes and has been an important factor in the effective tax rate of insurance companies. A formula applicable to life insurance companies that would make tax-exempt interest partially taxable, was eliminated by the 1984 Tax Act.

Eighty Percent Dividend Exclusion.   Only 20 percent of dividends received by domestic corporations from other domestic corporations are taxable. Thus the effective rate is 34 percent of 20 percent, or 6.8 percent. In 1986 and prior years, the dividend exclusion was 85 percent, but at a 46 percent tax rate, the effective rate was 6.9 percent. Because of the low effective tax rate, preferred stocks have long been a favorite investment for insurance companies. Because of the tax advantage to corporate investors, preferred stocks provide yields that are below those of similar quality corporate bonds but above those of similar quality tax-exempt bonds.

Capital Gains.   Prior to 1987, capital gains realized on the sale of capital assets held more than six months (in excess of corresponding long-term capital losses) were subject to a tax rate of 28 percent. Capital gains now are treated as ordinary income.

Tax Credits.   Tax credits come and go with the whims of Washington, often promoting socially desirable but economically unjustified actions by business organizations. The appeal to Washington is that use of tax credits to accomplish political goals *reduces revenues* rather than increases expenditures. Thus, the subsidy is obscured from the voter's view. The chief distinguishing characteristic of a tax credit is that it is a direct reduction of taxes, whereas a tax deduction merely reduces taxable income and is therefore worth only 34 percent as much.

General Business Credit.   The general business credit is a group of tax credits that include:

- Low-income housing
- Energy investment (solar, ocean thermal, biomass, and geothermal)
- Certain rehabilitation expenditures
- Employee stock ownership plan (ESOP)
- Targeted jobs
- Research and development

Until the beginning of 1986, the investment tax credit (ITC) was a part of the general business credit and a major cause of effective tax rates on corporations well below the statutory rate. Repeal of the investment tax credit is expected to increase corporate taxes by $119 million over the 1987–1991 period, an average increase in corporate taxes of about $24 billion per year. Transition rules will permit certain types of property to receive the credit through 1991 if ordered before January 1, 1986. Farmers and the steel industry are allowed a 15-year carryback of the ITC. The ITC is not repealed for reforestation expenses, thereby aiding timber companies.

Importance of Investment Tax Credit.   Prior to 1986 the investment tax credit was given to corporations for acquiring qualified plant and equipment (but not land). The credit was given at the time the plant and equipment were first used. The amount of general business credit that can be taken is limited—85 percent of the income tax for the year. Any unused investment tax credit can still be carried forward for the subsequent 15 years. However, the amount of the carryforward is reduced to 82.5 percent in 1987 and 65 percent in subsequent years. For many companies, the investment tax credit was the major cause of the reduction of the effective tax rate.

Example. In 1985, Georgia Pacific Corporation had an effective tax rate of 33 percent. Ten percentage points of the reduction from the then 46 percent statutory rate were due to the investment tax credit, 10 percentage points for application of the capital gains rate to timber appreciation, and seven percent were increases due to state income taxes and other causes (46% − 10% − 10% + 7% = 33%).

Foreign Tax Credit. The foreign tax credit allows a corporation to subtract the amount of foreign income taxes paid from its U.S. income tax obligation. This credit is not available to foreign sales corporations (FSCs). The amount of foreign tax credit is limited by formula to the ratio of foreign income to total income multiplied by the U.S. income tax payable (with certain adjustments to the latter). Application of the formula has been made much more complicated by the 1986 tax bill. Foreign income must now be divided among a number of "baskets," each subject to a separate foreign tax credit limitation. These baskets include passive income, financial services income, oil and gas, shipping income, domestic international sales corporation income, foreign sales corporation income, and so on. This prohibits a company from "averaging" lowly and highly taxed income to maximize the foreign tax credit.

The new U.S. tax rate of 34 percent now places our rate among the lowest of the following corporate tax rates:

Australia	46 percent
Brazil	35 percent
Canada	46 percent
France	45 percent
Germany	56 percent
Italy	36 percent
Japan	43 percent
Korea	33 percent
Mexico	42 percent
Spain	35 percent
United Kingdom	35 percent

As a result, many companies will pay foreign income taxes in excess of the amount they can take as a credit against the U.S. 34 percent tax rate.

Allocation of U.S. Interest Expense. The 1986 tax law called for a new set of rules in the allocation of U.S. interest expense between U.S. and foreign income, based on the ratio of U.S. assets to foreign assets. These new rules were phased in over four years for debt incurred on or before November 15, 1985, the rule becoming applicable in 1987. Obviously, some companies must shift debt to their foreign subsidiaries by 1987 to avoid a potential double taxation of a part of their foreign earnings.

Foreign Remittances. The 1986 tax act also called for new "look-through" rules that will look to the earnings source of moneys transferred from the foreign subsidiary to the domestic parent or subsidiary. This emphasis of substance over form may cause problems for some companies.

Possessions Tax Credit. Corporations operating in U.S. possessions, including Puerto Rico and the Virgin Islands, may take a Section 936 credit in lieu of the foreign tax credit. The credit is the portion of the U.S. tax attributable to taxable income earned in the possession. The rules are complex, and some companies have found the benefits may be somewhat offset by (1) a lack of reinvestment opportunities in those locations and (2) inability to withdraw funds from the possession except under harsh conditions.

Net Operating Losses. Net operating losses usually may be carried back 3 years or forward 15 years. When a net operating loss occurs, it must be applied first to the earliest year of the previous three in which a taxable operating profit occurred, and then to the next succeeding year, and so on. Foreign expropriation losses cannot be carried back but can be carried forward either for a 10-year or for a 20-year period, depending on the country. Some financial institutions are permitted 10-year carrybacks. A substantial change of ownership may result in the disallowance of net operating loss carryforwards.

The 1986 tax law made major revisions in the rules for carrying over net operating losses and tax credits and deductions after a major ownership change (generally 50 percent or more over a three-year period). A Section 382 limitation may be applied, determined by multiplying the fair market value of the aggregate equity interest in the loss corporation immediately prior to the ownership change by the "long-term tax exempt rate." Potentially, a very large portion of tax benefits and deductions could be disallowed by this complex set of rules. Disallowance in full is also possible. Thus, the acquisition of a company to capture the value of its tax credits and tax loss carryforwards has become much more difficult and will be particularly risky in the second half of the 1980s during which the rules of the game are not well known or understood.

Recognition of Benefit. Accounting has taken a stern position on recognizing the benefits of tax loss carryforwards as assets or reductions in liabilities. In order to be in a carryforward position, a company must either (1) have had such a large loss in the current year that it exceeds the profits of the previous three years or (2), more often, have shown persistent losses for a number of years, and therefore have no profits from earlier years to offset with the current year's loss. As a result, the accounting rule demands that the realization of the tax loss carryforward be "assured beyond any reasonable doubt" for the benefit to be booked. When the benefit of an operating loss is realized, it must be reported as an extraordinary item.

Example. In 1984 Aetna Insurance Company had large underwriting losses. In the previous three years the company had little or no taxable income because of heavy investments in tax-exempt bonds. The SEC took the position that Aetna could not book the tax loss carryforward because it was not "assured beyond any reasonable doubt" that it would be able to realize the carryforward benefit. Yet, it was obvious that all Aetna needed to do was to sell its tax-exempt bonds, purchase higher-yielding taxable corporate bonds, and it would then have taxable income which it could use to gain the benefit of the operating loss carryforward. In fact, Aetna did so. An analyst who was familiar with the facts of the situation would accept the tax loss carryforward as a valid asset, properly belonging on the balance sheet, and thereby reduce the year's reported loss.

Match Operating Loss Against Deferred Taxes. Given that today's tax laws allow a 15-year carryforward period (versus much shorter periods at various times in the past), an analyst who has any confidence in the future of a company at all will probably conclude that some or all of its tax loss carryforwards are assets that will be realized.

Operating loss carryforwards, investment tax credit carryforwards, and foreign tax credit carryforwards can be realized and considered to be assets when the company has large deferred income tax liabilities on the balance sheet. In such cases, those book-tax timing differences which will reverse and trigger taxable income during the carryforward period—that is, the deferred taxes that will come due— should be offset by the various carryforward assets. Effectively the liability has been eliminated, for (1) if taxable income occurs, the carryforwards can offset it and eliminate the payment of taxes, or (2) if there is no taxable income after the timing reversal occurs, there will be no tax liability for it. In either event, having a carryforward assures that the reversing book-tax timing difference will not result in the payment of taxes.

Example. The 1985 Acme-Cleveland Corporation Annual Report's income tax footnote states "At September 30, 1985 the corporation has available for federal income tax purposes a net operating loss carryforward of $640,000 which expires in 1999, investment tax credit carryforwards of $1,300,000 which expire in 1998 through 2000, and foreign tax credit carryforwards of $1,160,000 which expire in 1986 through 1990." The amounts of carryforwards for financial statement purposes totalled nearly $25 million. However, the September 30, 1985, balance sheet showed a deferred income tax liability of $382 million, so there could be little question that the $3.1 million carryforwards of losses and credits could be used to reduce tax payments that might otherwise occur. The book carryforwards in excess of amounts available for income tax purposes should not be used to reduce real deferred tax liabilities, because they do not exist for tax accounting purposes.

Move Carryforward Benefit to the Loss Years. There is no justification for considering the tax saved by reason of a past loss or tax credit as part of the current year's earnings. The carryforward portion of reported income does not reflect in any sense the "normal results" of the year; obviously it cannot be projected indefinitely into the future as part of the company's earning power. The security analyst should treat such a tax saving as a nonrecurring item which should be excluded from the current year. To straighten out matters for purposes of projecting trends and the like, the loss carryforward or carryback should be applied to the year in which the loss occurred, not when the benefit was realized by offsetting impending tax payments.

Ignore Carryforwards in Projecting Earning Power. The loss and tax credit carryforwards remaining available at any date do, of course, have significance in the analysis, but not really as part of the future earning power. They represent a special or "windfall" value factor, which can add no more than the discounted present value of the *total possible tax saving* to the value found without benefit of such saving. In other words, the earning power should be projected without any credit from the loss carryforward, and the windfall value of the credit then should be added to the "ex-carryforward" value of the earnings.

Percentage Depletion. Percentage depletion is discussed in Chapter 14. The difference between annual report depletion and income tax depletion does not call for study and possible correction by analysts. They may be concerned, however, by the possibility of some adverse change in this tax privilege.

Portability of Tax Benefits. The tax deductibility of depreciation and amortization and the tax benefits of investment tax credits are transferable under certain circumstances. Transferability of tax benefits played a major role in the growth of the leasing industry, since these tax benefits can be kept, transferred to others, or used as a reduction in the rent charged the lessee.

Example. In 1985, Armco, Inc., sold certain investment tax credits and ACRS depreciation deductions for about $120 million at a profit of about $33 million. The sale complied with the rules for a "safe-harbor" leasing transaction and was therefore presumably structured as a sale and leaseback for tax purposes. The annual report referred to the transaction as a "sale of tax benefits," which is all that actually was sold. The related assets were oil field equipment, computers, steel equipment, and the Ashland caster, which remain on the books and will be depreciated for stockholder reporting purposes. Since Armco already had tax loss carryforwards of $775 million, taxes are not likely to be a problem for the company over the near term. Thus, the tax benefits of depreciation are not currently needed.

Transactions of this sort have been criticized, particularly when the lessor ends up paying little or no income tax. For example, General Electric (GE) has been criticized for "not paying its fair share" of taxes. Yet, the economics are that the lessor is often paying taxes through a conduit— the lessee. If the lessor takes the depreciation, the lessee will have increased taxable income because of the absence of the depreciation tax deduction. Perhaps GE is criticized for its tax planning because it is so good at it.

Industries with a Special Tax Status. The advantages of percentage depletion and other special tax treatment to certain industries have already been pointed out. Certain other industries also have been subject to special provisions in the tax law. Examples include: savings and loan companies, commercial banks, property and casualty insurance companies, and regulated investment companies.

Savings and Loan Companies. Savings and loan companies and certain other thrift institutions are allowed to deduct from income for tax purposes the dividends paid to depositors or holders of accounts. These thrift institutions also are allowed a reserve for bad debts based on (1) the experience method, (2) the percentage-of-loans method, such as commercial banks with assets under $500 million, or (3) the percentage-of-taxable- income method. For the reserve on their mortgage portfolio, they may use 8 percent (40 percent before 1987) of taxable income.

Savings and loans are not allowed to deduct the special premium reserves paid to the Federal Savings and Loan Insurance Corporation (FSLIC), although these reserves look remarkably like insurance premiums that should be expensed. Beginning in 1987, interest on borrowings to carry tax-exempt bonds is no longer deductible.

Commercial Banks. Prior to 1987, reserves for bad debts could be

- 0.6 percent at year-end, or
- The highest level previously reached, or
- A five-year moving average of the bank's own experience

Excess loss reserves are tax preference items for purposes of applying the minimum tax. Beginning in 1987, loss reserves are no longer permitted for banks with $500 million or more in assets. The specific charge-off method must be used. Interest expense for carrying tax-exempt bonds is no longer deductible. Prior to 1987, 80 percent was deductible.

Property and Casualty Insurance Companies. Property and casualty insurers were permitted, before 1987, deductions for increases in unearned premium reserves. Beginning 1987, only 80 percent of the increase will be deductible. In addition, income for the years 1986 through 1991 must include a ratable portion of an amount equal to 22 percent of the balance of the unearned premium reserve at the beginning of 1987.[1] The Tax Reform Act of 1986 also substantially changed the handling of loss reserves, including a requirement to discount loss reserves and loss adjustment expenses and to reduce the deduction for increases and loss reserves by 15 percent of tax-exempt interest and 15 percent of the dividends-received deductions, applicable to stocks and bonds acquired after August 7, 1986.

Regulated Investment Companies. A regulated investment company whose gross income is at least 90 percent dividends, interest, security gains, and the like, and which distributes 97 percent of its ordinary income and 90 percent of capital gains to its shareholders, and meets certain other requirements, is free from income taxes, except on its retained income. Like individuals, regulated investment companies will be able to deduct certain investment expenses (using the criteria of Section 212) only to the extent that they exceed 2 percent of adjusted gross income. The 30 percent limitation on profits from securities held less than three months was liberalized by the 1986 tax law to permit hedging with options, futures, and forward contracts. Real estate investment trusts (REITs) may also be taxed as a regulated investment company, but with a number of special rules and restrictions.

Oil and Gas Companies. Percentage depletion is permitted to small independent oil and gas companies but denied to the large integrated

---

[1]Apparently Congress adopted analysts' old practice of recognizing some profit when the policy is sold rather than waiting for underwriting results to confirm that a profit did indeed exist. Most insurance analysts have repudiated this practice in recent years, and we ardently hope that insurance companies will not adopt such a practice for accounting purposes.

companies. The 1986 tax law eliminated percentage depletion for lease bonuses, advance royalties, and certain other payments. The large integrated companies are required to capitalize 30 percent of domestic intangible drilling costs and amortize them over five years, straight-line, beginning 1987. The figure was 20 percent under the prior law. Intangible drilling costs incurred outside of the United States must be capitalized even by small independent producers and amortized over 10 years straight line, or alternatively, amortized as ordinary cost depletion. Oil and gas companies are subject to the windfall profits tax, which is technically an excise tax rather than an income tax. However, the tax is structured so that the rates apply entirely to amounts that are taxable income. Large oil companies are subject to taxes at rates varying from 30 to 70 percent of the excess of the price received for "old oil" over the base price for the class, with a limitation of 90 percent of net income attributable to each barrel sold. In 1980, when the law became effective, the base prices were far in excess of production costs, so the dollars exposed to this tax represented pretax income. Analysts interested in these companies should acquire IRS forms 720, 6047, and 6458, along with the related instructions.

Taxation of Specialized Industries. Specialized industry tax advantages and penalties of the type described above are extremely important to the companies and industries involved. Companies that enjoy a favorable tax environment are always subject to the hazard of adverse changes in the law or the regulations in the future, whereas companies bearing what seems an unfair burden of taxation may have more cheerful prospects that the levy may be reduced. Logically, the outlook for a change in the taxation of a company should be included in an appraisal of the value of its earnings. The analyst must read political trends as well as economic ones and may wish to incorporate in longer-term projections those tax changes that are deemed to be highly probable.

Difference Between Taxable and Reported Income

Management may at its option produce a difference between reported income and taxable income in a variety of ways. Other differences are mandated by differing treatment in the tax code and in the accounting rules. Some of the tax material is summarized here to present a unified survey of the tax consequences of corporate accounting methods.

Depreciation. The differences between reported and tax-return depreciation have been an important element in income account analysis. Formerly they were due to a variety of arbitrary practices by corporations, but at present they are pretty well confined to the use of the straight-line method in published figures versus tax reporting using these methods:

- Modified ACRS after 1986
- ACRS for assets acquired from 1980 to 1986
- Other permitted accelerated methods for pre-1981 assets
- 200 percent and 150 percent declining balance for qualifying assets acquired after 1986

This subject was discussed extensively in Chapter 14.

Unremitted Foreign Earnings. Earnings of foreign and U.S. possession subsidiaries ordinarily are not taxed until effectively remitted to the United States. Chapter 16, in its section on foreign earnings, recommends a method of dealing with the deferred tax provision for such earnings.

Amortization. Chapter 14 discussed the tax effect of various amounts amortized on tax returns but capitalized on the statements. Examples include: (1) intangible drilling costs of oil and gas producers and (2) exploration and development expenses of mines. First the analyst must see that a deferred-tax equivalent is set up against a benefit so obtained, and second, that the company's accounts are made comparable.

Capitalization of Interest. Interest costs incurred in acquiring plant and equipment that require a long acquisition period must be capitalized and amortized over the life of the asset. Companies have flexibility in determining the amount of interest capitalized. Current tax rules require that the capitalized interest be expensed over the shorter of 10 years or the life of the assets acquired. In a number of cases the period over which the company amortizes the capitalized interest for stockholder reporting purposes differs from the period over which the interest is amortized for tax deduction purposes. Therefore, there are deferred tax effects caused by these book-tax timing differences. There are currently no disclosure requirements for the pattern of amortization of capitalized interest. As a result, the analyst may seek that information by direct inquiry to the company.

From the analyst's viewpoint, capitalized interest and its counterpart, allowance for equity funds used during construction (AFUDC), should both be removed from the books, along with their tax effects.

Installment Sales. An important source of deferred profits for tax purposes has been installment sales. Prior to the 1986 act, the law permitted the profit to be taken in proportion with the receipt of payments; but, almost invariably companies report the full profit in their financial statements at the time of sale, and the difference between indicated and actual tax was disposed of by the standard deferred tax procedure. The 1986 act eliminated the use of installment sale reporting for tax purposes for publicly traded companies and for property sold on a revolving credit plan. The discontinuation of the installment method is a change in method of accounting for tax purposes with the resulting profit spreads over four years—15 percent in the first year, 25 percent in the second, and 30 percent in the third and fourth years. Certain installment sales of personal or real property by dealers and casual sales of real property fall under a *proportionate disallowance rule*. Analysts viewed most installment sales as true revenue all along, with certain exceptions such as abusive real estate transactions.

Bad Debt Reserves. The 1986 law (1) repeals the bad debt reserve method, which tended to smooth earnings, and (2) substitutes the specific charge-off method. Unless the accounting rules change, most companies will probably continue to use the bad debt reserve for stockholder reporting. We favor retention of the bad debt reserve because the receivables could not be sold without some discount for expected losses. However, in most cases adjusting the accounts will not be worthwhile.

Completed Contract Accounting. In the past, most contracting companies used percentage-of-completion accounting for stockholder reporting purposes and the completed contract method for tax reporting, thereby creating book-tax differences and the resulting deferred tax effects. The 1986 tax law allows 60 percent of income to be calculated on the completed contract method, subject to the alternative minimum tax, and sets up stricter cost capitalization rules, which will create a modified percentage-of-completion method for tax purposes. However, if the companies continue to report on their traditional percentage-of-completion bases, large book-tax differences will persist.

Analysts have never been entirely comfortable with percentage-of-completion accounting, since the profits reported depend so heavily on estimates, some of which are little better than guesses. Bad guesses and occasional manipulation have resulted in too many large write-offs, which raises the question whether companies using the method can be considered of investment quality.

Capitalization of Production Costs. The Tax Reform Act of 1986 brought a host of accounting changes for tax purposes. The new rules are being phased in over four years, beginning with 1987. GAAP accounting requires that at least some factory overhead be included in the cost of inventories. Most analysts feel that inventory costs already include too many period and overhead costs, thereby smoothing earnings unjustifiably. Congress seized the "full absorption" concept and raised it from a bad habit to the law of the land. For example, the following items must now be included in inventory:

- Excess of tax depreciation over book depreciation
- Warehousing costs
- General and administrative costs incident to the taxpayer's activities as a whole
- Property taxes and insurance
- Strikes, rework labor, scrap, and spoilage

We fervently hope that these items will continue to cause tax timing differences and not be adopted for financial reporting purposes. The analyst would have few tools to put companies' accounts in order, since little is revealed about what goes into inventories even today. Estimates are that these and other tax accounting changes will result in $60 billion of additional revenue over the period from 1987 to 1991.

Write-downs. Major write-downs and restructuring of unprofitable segments and product lines usually cause large book-tax differences. For example, in 1985 Mobil Corporation made a $775 million provision for restructuring its retail subsidiary Montgomery Ward. In connection with that transaction, the deferred tax liability was reduced by $227 million. The amounts suggested that part of the loss was expected to be ordinary income and part a capital loss. Under the new act both will be treated as ordinary income.

LIFO Pools. Timing differences arise when companies use different pools for LIFO inventory in reporting on the tax form and reporting to shareholders. This results in a tax timing difference that ultimately will reverse. If the difference is significant, the footnote reconciling the effective tax rate to the statutory rate should show a specific line item with an appropriate caption, such as "difference in inventory accounting."

Excessive Contributions.   Similar timing differences arise when a company makes contributions to a pension fund or to charities in excess of IRS limitations.

Goodwill.   Amortization of purchased goodwill is not tax deductible, but the goodwill is part of the tax cost basis when the subsidiary is sold or liquidated. Chapter 19 includes recommendations for removing goodwill and its amortization from the accounts for purposes of security analysis.

Early Extinguishment of Debt.   A gain on the extinguishment of debt is ordinary income, but solvent corporations can normally avoid the income by electing to reduce the tax attributes of depreciable assets. Thus, the tax is deferred but comes due through lower depreciation deductions in subsequent years. Losses on extinguishments are usually taken at once on the tax form.

Unexplained Discrepancies—Ask the Company.   Every now and then the analyst will find a discrepancy between reported income and the tax deduction for which no ready explanation is at hand. The effective tax rate will be clearly out of line with expectations based on the U.S. statutory rate and other rates of taxation to which the company is subject. In theory, at least, footnote disclosure will provide the explanation, but the analyst is unable to find an answer there. In such cases, the analyst interested in a thorough presentation should ask the company. An explanation will usually be forthcoming.

Deferred Income Taxes

Deferred Tax Deduction

Some argue that deferred income taxes are not liabilities, because they are taxes on taxable income that has not yet been earned and that therefore there should be no deferred tax liability or expense. However, failure to provide for deferred income taxes is inconsistent with modern accounting. Today's accounting model (sometimes imprecisely called "historical cost" accounting) has a fundamental tenet that the carrying amount of an asset must be a *recoverable amount* and that the carrying amount of a liability must be an amount at which the liability ultimately can be settled (ignoring accrual of future interest).

It can be demonstrated mathematically that if all the assets and liabilities of the company are collected or settled in cash *at their carrying amounts*, the deferred tax liabilities will at that point come due (that is, all book-tax timing differences will reverse). To say that the deferred tax is not a liability is to say that assets are being carried at amounts above the cash that will be recovered from them or that liabilities are being carried at amounts less than the amount necessary to settle them.

The Deferred Taxes Do Come Due. The taxable income will occur! For an example, see Chapter 14, Table 14.2, at the end of the third year: The recovery of the $150 carrying amount of the asset ensured that the $51 in the deferred tax account would become payable. Since no tax depreciation is deductible for the final three years, the entire $150 carrying amount, when realized, would become taxable income.

Most Tax Adjustments Are Made at the Ordinary Statutory Rate. In adjusting the income statement of a company for purposes of putting depreciation and other amortization expenses on a common basis, read the footnotes on income taxes carefully for any particular problems in calculating the related deferred tax provision. If the depreciation timing differences are only domestic, the analyst can approximate the related tax effect by multiplying the adjustment to depreciation by 34 percent, plus a bit more if necessary for state and local income taxes. (Calculations for years prior to 1988 would usually be made at the rate prevailing during that year. In the case of 1987, a blended rate of 40 percent would be used, with the 34 percent rate applying after June 30 and 46 percent before July 1.) The tax *expense* calculated by this method may call for an adjustment of deferred taxes in the income statement and the balance sheet, since the taxes paid remain unaffected.

Deferred Tax Liability

The provision for deferred taxes is a real liability, but it continues to be a source of problems for the security analyst. Some discomfort arises because deferred taxes seem to be liabilities that never require a cash outflow. Most companies are growing and regularly add new plant and equipment to replace the old. These new acquisitions create new tax timing differences to replace the old ones that are reversing. The result is that no cash outflow for taxes need occur. The deferred tax balance on the right side of the balance sheet continues to grow, and its nature is puzzling.

A Matter of Perspective. One problem is the way deferred taxes are measured. Most long-term receivables and payables that bear no interest, or bear an unreasonably low interest rate, must be discounted to their present value at the time they are placed on the books. Interest is accreted thereafter, resulting in either interest income or interest expense. But, for practical reasons, discounting is not required for deferred taxes.

Deferred Tax Issues for the Analyst. If no cash outflow will occur for many years—perhaps many decades—the analyst must wonder whether:

- The deferred tax account really is a liability with a present value near zero
- The tax deferred represents an interest-free long-term loan from the Treasury Department
- The deferred tax account is any different economically from retained earnings; it should be a part of the equity account

Clearly, capital is working for the benefit of the stockholders and not for bondholders or trade creditors. For purposes of comparison between companies, include deferred taxes in equity in calculations of return on invested capital and return on equity.

A final issue that the individual analyst must decide is whether deferred tax liabilities are sufficiently similar to shareholders' equity that *changes* in the deferred tax liability should be part of income in calculating those ratios.

Taxes and the Investment Overview

Concentrate on the Transaction

The frequency of tax changes may mesmerize the analyst into an attitude that the only problem is to make sure that the proper tax rate is used in making adjustments to the financial statements. This attitude carries two dangers. The most obvious is that concentration on the nature of the transaction may be subsumed or even lost. Yet, the centerpiece of financial statement analysis is the identification of the true nature of transactions. Without that, analysis becomes a mechanical and unthinking process that is unlikely to contribute much to investment success.

People Pay Taxes—Not Corporations

The second and more important danger is viewing tax changes as simple additions to or subtractions from the bottom line. That perspective says, in effect, that *corporations* pay taxes. But corporations are merely structures of human conception—a simple way for groups of people to act and organize. The analytical question when there is a tax change is *who will pay* the tax or receive the benefit of the reduction. There are only three choices—the shareholders, the employees, and the customers. One or more of these groups will reap the rewards or suffer the burden of a tax change. For example, the Tax Reform Act of 1986 eliminated the investment tax credit, reduced the benefits of accelerated depreciation, and lowered the rate on ordinary income. The simplistic view is that plant-intensive companies would suffer while companies paying the full rate, for lack of tax credits and deductions, would be the beneficiaries. The analysis must go much further. If the plant-intensive company is suffering stiff foreign competition, it will not be able to pass the tax on to customers. However, depending on its labor position, it may be able to shift part of a tax increase on to its workers. If it cannot, all the burden will go to the bottom line, and the stockholders will carry the full burden. If a company has an oligopoly position due to, say, patents and inelastic demand for its products, it may be able to pass all tax burdens on to its customers and retain all benefits for its stockholders. Admittedly, many companies will suffer a time lag before the tax burdens or benefits are shifted to specific groups of people—owners, workers, or consumers, but a good analysis of the relative bargaining position of each group will reveal the most likely ultimate taxpayers. *People* pay taxes, not legal fictions such as corporations.

18

Balance Sheet Analysis

The Balance Sheet

The balance sheet deserves more attention than Wall Street has been willing to accord it for many years. Following are six types of information and guidance that the investor may derive from a study of the balance sheet:

1. Information on how capital is invested and how the capital structure is divided between senior issues and common stock

2. Strength or weakness of the working-capital position

3. Reconciliation of the earnings reported in the income account

4. Data to test the true success or prosperity of the business, the amount earned on invested capital

5. The basis for analyzing the sources of income

6. The basis for a long-term study of the relationship between earning power and asset values and of the development of the financial structure

Presentation of the Balance Sheet

The conventional balance sheet lists all assets on the left side and the liabilities, capital, and surplus on the right. (In England the two columns are reversed.) Alternative and sometimes more informative methods of presentation are found occasionally in corporate statements, which seek to develop the figure for capital and surplus by subtracting the liabilities from the assets; they also supply a better picture of the working-capital position by listing current liabilities directly below current assets. In some corporate reports this presentation appears under the title of Statement of Financial Condition and is given in addition to the conventional balance sheet.

Although format is a matter of personal preference, we recommend that the analyst experiment with the one presented in Figure 18.1. We shall illustrate the method by restating the December 1985 balance sheet of Bristol-Myers Company, including therein our recommended elimination of $163.9 million of goodwill and restatement of the liability of preferred stock from the $1 par value to a more reasonable $50 liquidation value. Detailed items in the various categories are aggregated.

Capital funds:		
Funded debt		$ 114,200
Other liabilities		77,300
Deferred income taxes		81,700
$2.00 conv. preferred, par $1.00		
165,143 shares valued at $50		8,300
Total senior claims		$ 281,500
Common stock (138,048,132 shares outstanding)		2,278,800
Total funds		$2,560,300
Represented by:		
Current assets	$2,502,200	
Less current liabilities	997,000	
Working capital		$1,505,200
Intermediate assets, net		129,300
Fixed assets, gross	$1,482,400	
Less depreciation	(556,600)	
Fixed assets, net		925,800
Total		$2,560,300

Figure 18.1 Recast balance sheet of Bristol-Myers Company, December 31, 1985 (in thousands of dollars).

Current Assets and Liabilities

Since the reader is assumed to be familiar with accounting, we shall not discuss all the items in the balance sheet in detail but shall consider merely those aspects that may require special knowledge or, more often, a special viewpoint by the analyst.

The Definition of "Current"

Manufacturing, distributing, wholesaling, retailing, and some service companies have "classified" balance sheets, that is, assets and liabilities are classified between "current" and "noncurrent." Normally, electric utilities, banks, insurance companies, and other financial companies do not have a classified balance sheet. The word *current* encompasses assets and liabilities that are expected to be converted into cash or paid with cash within 12 months or over the operating cycle, whichever is longer. For example, cigarette tobacco is usually aged for about three years before sale. Thus tobacco inventories would be classified as "current." Similarly, wines and liquors that have to be aged, long-term construction projects, and the like, result in current assets that are not subject to conversion into cash in 12 months, but rather over some longer period. However, the prevailing practice is to use only the 12-month criterion for classifying liabilities, even when the liability is clearly a part of the operating cycle. For example, a liability for prepayment or deposit on a long-term construction contract would typically be classified as noncurrent.

Current Assets and Duration.   The classification of assets as current and noncurrent serves in a general sort of way to identify the speed with which the asset can be expected to be converted into cash in the ordinary course of business. Duration is a measure of risk, somewhat akin to maturity. The duration of accounts receivable may be a matter of days or a very few months. The duration of inventory may range from months to even several years. For fixed assets and long-term debt, duration is obviously measured in years and decades.

Duration and Risk.   The riskiness of long duration assets is obvious in the case of a holding of bonds, since the longer the bond the greater the price fluctuation resulting from a given change in interest rates. Although that risk may be less obvious in the case of plant and equipment, it is equally present. Plant and equipment sell at prices which tend to reflect the average discounted present value of future cash flows, just as a bond does. Current assets contribute to liquidity. The ratio of current assets to total assets is clearly a measure of risk. The longer the time before an asset will reappear in the form of cash, the greater the probability that something will go wrong. The analyst will therefore examine current assets, the ratio of current assets to total assets, and the current ratio from the viewpoint of risk evaluation as well as liquidity evaluation.

Current Assets

Cash Items.   Current assets include cash and cash equivalents, receivables, and inventories. Certain cash items, usually in the form of government bonds, are sometimes segregated by the company and shown elsewhere than in current assets. On rare occasions they are being held to meet liabilities not shown as current.

Example. At year-end 1985, IBM Corporation's balance sheet showed noncurrent "Investments and Other Assets." A footnote revealed that $503 million were U.S. fixed-income securities. Maturities were not given.

Include Portfolio Cash Items. When companies have a portfolio of investment securities, cash items may exist as part of the portfolio and be classified as noncurrent. There is no formal definition of the term *cash items.* We believe it is helpful to present as current assets actual holdings of cash, and the temporary investment of cash in high-quality, short-maturity investment media (so-called cash equivalents) if they are within the company's control.

Exclude Pension Assets. However, even if we had consolidated the company's pension fund into the company's balance sheet for purposes of certain calculations, we would *not* classify the cash items of the pension fund as current. Although a company could accomplish an "asset reversion" from excess pension fund assets, the process is complex, requires approval by the Pension Benefit Guaranty Corporation, and is subject to potential long delays. Because of this lack of ready access to these cash items, we do not believe that it would be helpful to include them with the company's other cash.

Compensating Balances May Be Unavailable. The analyst should be aware that cash in the bank is not always "available." Some bank loans include an agreement that the company maintain *at all times* "compensating balances" equal to, say, 10 percent of the line of credit plus an additional 10 percent of the actual amount of borrowings. The bank may even insist that these funds be kept in a non-interest-bearing certificate of deposit. In other cases the compensating balance requirement is merely that the company's average working balances remain at a certain level. In any case, cash that represents compensating balances cannot always be drawn upon for payment of obligations. Disclosure of the amounts and terms of compensating balances is improving.

Cash Value of Life Insurance. Cash surrender value of life insurance policies—at times a sizable item—was formerly shown as a current asset in most cases, but now it is almost always shown as noncurrent. The analyst may properly include such an amount, if important, in the current assets for the purpose of certain calculations, e.g., to find the current asset value of the stock.

Receivables. Trade or customer receivables, less allowances for losses, are shown as current assets, even though the period of payment may run well beyond a year, for example, in the case of installment notes. Such installment notes are often sold to finance companies, factors, or banks on a full or partial recourse basis, that is, the seller is, to some degree, responsible for nonpayment. The amount of such repurchase obligation and, if known, the uncollected balance will be shown in a footnote. Some analysts favor adding these amounts to both the receivables and the current liabilities, to get a clearer view of the company's financial position. Assume these circumstances:

1. The recourse provision is limited to, say, 10 percent of the receivables.

2. The bad debt loss experience of the company has been far less than 10 percent.

3. The owner of the receivables has no right to force the seller to repurchase them.

In this situation, we believe that only the expected recourse losses, or at most the 10 percent, should be recorded as an asset and a liability. Conservatism does not demand that liabilities be recorded when they can be avoided by simply saying "no."

But Never Show a Loss. Still other transactions are designed not to remove assets and liabilities from the balance sheet, but rather to *keep them on* to avoid recognition of a loss. Since transactions of this sort are designed to conceal rather than reveal, making appropriate adjustments for them should be considered an analytical triumph.

Adequacy of Loss Reserves. Where receivables play a large part in the company's business, special care should be given to the examination of the reserve for losses and collection expense. If the annual report provides inadequate information, the analyst should look to Schedule VIII of the 10-K. Comparisons should be made with other companies in the same field. In extreme cases, the true value of the receivables may prove to be badly overstated. Remember that credit losses are cyclical and that the losses will probably increase when a receivable comes due at the bottom of a recession and decrease in a business boom.

Example. Hilton Hotels Corporation, in its 10-K Schedule VIII, *Valuation and Qualifying Accounts*, showed the following information on its allowance for doubtful accounts:

Year	Charged to expense	Deductions from reserves
1985	$4,716,000	$2,679,000
1984	2,037,000	3,080,000
1983	2,055,000	4,856,000

The company's volatile collection experience was generated primarily by its casino operations. The company's expense understated its actual loss experience by significant amounts in 1983 and 1984 and partly made up for it in 1985. The expense number shows exactly the opposite trend from the actual pattern of losses, which was sharply downward. However, given the experience of rather large losses in 1983, the analyst would probably question whether the balance of the account at the end of 1984 (in the amount of $3,139,000) provided a safe margin. Apparently the company reached the same conclusion. At the end of 1985 the allowance for doubtful accounts had been raised to $5,174,000.

Inventories. Inventory amounts are increasingly being broken down into raw materials, goods in process, and finished inventory. This additional detail permits the application of new analytical techniques, including determination of the following:

- Turnover of finished goods (the only ones that are ultimately sold!)
- The company's raw materials acquisition policy
- The company's ability to anticipate price changes of raw materials
- Production economies or problems

Include the LIFO Reserve for Most Ratio Analysis. If inventories are carried on the LIFO method, the LIFO reserve should be added back for calculating such ratios as current assets per share, return on equity, return on invested capital, and physical turnover of inventory. However, in projecting a profit margin for next year's sales, or the effect of layer invasion on reported net income, the analyst will find it more helpful to keep the inventories on a LIFO basis.

Questionable Current Assets

The rules for classifying assets as current should be tightened up to exclude some of the more dubious items. For example, depreciable fixed assets such as bulldozers sometimes appear as current assets because they are being used on a long-term construction project, or a traditionally noncurrent asset will appear as a current asset because the company "intends" to sell it in the coming 12 months. If being part of the operating cycle is to continue to be one of the criteria for currentness, more specific guidance is needed on exactly what the operating cycle is. Obviously, many different cycles of varying lengths are going on at the same time. A defense contractor should not be allowed to keep the operating cycle open for 30 years just because it is continuing to sell spare parts for an airplane or a submarine!

Example. Tonka Corporation, in its annual report for the year ended December 29, 1984, reported in current assets "Assets Identified for Sale (Note 7) . . . $4.4 (million)." Note 7 said, in part, "During 1984, the Tonka Corporate Offices and Manufacturing facilities located in Spring Park and Mound, Minnesota were identified for sale." The buyer had a conditional right to rescind the transaction for a period of up to three years. The properties were, in fact, sold in February 1985 for approximately $5 million.

Off-Balance-Sheet Financing.   Companies prefer to get debt off the balance sheet. To do so, they must also remove assets. Be alert to a variety of structured transactions whose purpose is to remove debt, but which may also remove inventories or accounts receivable in the process. This activity has become so widespread that a whole new accounting vocabulary has grown up, including the following:

- Nonsub sub
- Tax-deductible preferred
- Collateralized mortgage obligations (CMOs)
- Collateralized automobile receivables (CARs)
- Nonsale sale

Current Liabilities

Current liabilities include all liabilities due within a year and, in theory but not in practice, those falling due during the operating cycle. They include the current year's maturities of a serial bond or note issue and, in some cases, the portion of a long-term bond issue due to be retired by sinking fund operation within the year. Certain intermediate term and off-balance-sheet liabilities should be reclassified as current by the analyst, if they are likely to be paid in a year or less.

Sinking Funds and Mandatorily Redeemable Preferred Stock.   Mandatory sinking fund payments on preferred stock represent the same probable cash outflow as bond sinking funds and maturities. If the amount is significant, the amount of preferred stock redeemable within 12 months should be added to current liabilities and subtracted from the preferred stock outstanding. Although the legal claim of a sinking fund preferred ranks far below that of debt maturities or taxes, the usefulness of the current classification of liabilities is enhanced by inclusion of all known cash outflows of the coming 12 months. If the cash outflow is probable, show the economic substance rather than the legal form.

Offsetting Taxes Payable with Tax Anticipation Notes. The large size of income tax liabilities gives rise to a device, designed partly to improve the current ratio and partly to help finance the usual Treasury deficit. Companies purchase large quantities of U.S. Treasury tax anticipation notes which bear below market rates of interest when held to maturity. The notes may be used at par for payment of federal taxes due on a date somewhat earlier than maturity, thereby providing a higher effective yield. As a result, corporations do not purchase tax anticipation notes unless they intend to use them for payment of income taxes. The notes are exact and legal offsets to the tax liability, and the tax notes must be used for payment of taxes to maximize the rate of return. However, the analyst should reverse the offsetting of the notes and the taxes due to enhance consistency through time and comparability of the current ratio of companies that do and do not use tax anticipation notes. The treatment suggested is controversial among analysts.

Noncurrent Assets

Plant, Property, and Equipment

Usually Carried at Conservative Figures. Fixed assets are referred to as the "plant account," "plant, property, and equipment," "PP&E," or the "property account." In nearly all companies they are now carried at a conservative figure. The usual basis is actual cost less depreciation. In view of the large inflation effect on the current cost of plant and equipment, the depreciated amounts of older plant and equipment are usually far below the cost of replacing the same equipment with used equipment—the depreciated replacement cost at current prices. This partially explains the willingness of acquiring companies to pay even 1½ or 2 times the book value for an acquiree company. Where the purchase method of accounting is used for the acquisition, the fixed assets of the acquired company are given a new carrying amount equal to "fair value," and in most cases the fair value turns out to be far above the previous carrying amounts.

Current Value Information. The changing prices information which was required of some 1200 companies, and provided voluntarily by many others, provides a current cost number that constitutes a measure of the degree of conservatism in the carrying amount of fixed assets. Long before that information was available, security analysts would make inquiries to management about the amount of fire insurance carried on plant and equipment. If the number of facility locations is small, tax assessments can be obtained and used to estimate the value of land and buildings.

Leaseholds. A leasehold is a right to the quiet enjoyment of premises for a stated period of time subject to payment of rent therefor. Such a right may be considered a valuable asset if the current rental value of the leased property is much greater than the rent called for in the contract. In past years, companies have sometimes set more or less arbitrary figures on such leasehold values and carried them as assets. In times of financial stress, the tenant's rights are usually limited to out-of-pocket damages. An asset of that type must of course be considered entirely intangible.

Leasehold Improvements as Tangible Assets. In many cases, however, companies have erected buildings on ground leased to them for a long period. At the expiration of the lease (and stipulated renewals) the building becomes the property of the lessor (the owner of the land). Technically, tenants (the lessees) do not own such buildings; they are part of the leasehold interest. To that extent such buildings, often designated in the balance sheet as "leasehold improvements," might accurately be called intangible assets; but it is more in accordance with substance to consider them as a tangible investment by the lessee and therefore as a tangible asset.

Intermediate and Longer-Term Assets

Intermediate-Term Assets. Intermediate-term items in general consist of noncurrent receivables, investments not treated as current marketable securities, and deferred assets. Claims for tax refunds may be intermediate assets or current receivables, depending on the expected date of their receipt. Some noncurrent receivables are due from officers, employees, or affiliated companies.

Long-Term Assets.

Investments. Most investments in subsidiaries are eliminated from the balance sheet by the use of a consolidated statement, but various types are exceptions to this rule. Some companies do not consolidate all their foreign subsidiaries; others do not consolidate subsidiaries of which less than 100 percent is owned. Most do not consolidate finance and leasing subsidiaries. These investment items may represent the ownership of a substantial amount of current assets. Advances to affiliates are usually eliminated in consolidation if the affiliates are consolidated. If not, they should be combined as "investments in and advances to subsidiaries" so that the dividends or equity earnings from those affiliates can be related to the total amount invested in them. The fact that interest is estimated on loans to equity method investees and disclosed as a related party transaction with affiliates carried on the investment method, permits the analyst a reasonable picture of the profitability of the relationship.

Marketable Securities. The *liquidity* of the company is enhanced by a portfolio of marketable securities, where the sizes of the holdings do not limit liquidity. Such securities may properly be included in current assets. For some purposes, such as determining the normal working capital requirements to support a dollar of sales of a manufacturing company, the portfolio of marketable securities should properly be excluded from current assets. In either case, analysts must decide whether to carry the marketable securities at market or at cost. Obviously, for purposes of determining liquidity, market value is more relevant. For purposes of calculating a return on investment that does not include in the numerator the market fluctuations of the securities portfolio, the lower of cost or market would seem more appropriate. Where working control is involved, it is doubtful whether the market value of the shares should enter directly into a balance sheet analysis of the owning company. In effect such a procedure would substitute earning power value for asset values with respect to an important part of the company's business and thus vitiate the purpose of balance sheet analysis, which deals with asset values as a separate factor in a company's valuation. An allocation of the underlying asset values—corresponding to an allocation of the controlled companies' earnings—seems more logical.

Example. Seagram Company, Ltd., owned 22.5 percent of E. I. Du Pont de Nemours & Company at 1985 year end. On March 29, 1986, a "standstill agreement" was signed which amended a 1981 agreement. The new agreement provides that Seagram will not purchase more than 25 percent of Du Pont except under certain dilutive conditions. Seagram will be permitted proportional representation on the Du Pont board of directors and its finance committee, to be accomplished by 1990. Du Pont will have the right to nominate two Seagram directors. The agreement extends to 1999, when it can be terminated with two years' written notice. Seagram carries the Du Pont holding on the equity method. The investment accounts for the majority of Seagram's earnings. Analysis of Seagram from the viewpoint of an asset play would surely suggest the use of the market value of the investment.

Prepaid Expense and Deferred Charges

Prepaid Expense. Prepaid expense represents amounts paid to other parties for services to be rendered by them in the future—rent and insurance paid in advance, for instance. The AICPA has suggested that such prepaid expense items be included in the current assets as the equivalent of accounts receivable, and they are now treated largely in this fashion. The analyst's view would be influenced by the nature of the company—an ongoing firm versus a liquidation.

Deferred Charges. Deferred charges, in contrast to prepaid expense, represent amounts paid or payable for which no specific services will be received in the future but which are considered properly chargeable to future operations. These include tax assets, some intangible operating rights, certain start-up costs, and other items. The cost of tools and dies for models not yet on the market, for example, is sometimes carried in this account. Companies usually charge off such items rather rapidly against actual sales. The analyst would consider many of these items doubtful for purposes of balance sheet analysis. In sum, the prepaid-expense and similar items are extremely varied in their character and their validity. The analyst may fortunately ignore most of them as unimportant. The larger ones may require rather careful scrutiny.

Concepts Statement 6, *Elements of Financial Statements*,[1] requires that all assets have "probable future benefits." Conceptually, this rejects the notion that assets are merely past expenses awaiting some future revenue to be attached to. We would anticipate a reduction in the more questionable deferred charges, some of which have been little more than dangling debits.

Example. IBM's 1985 annual report showed a somewhat condensed balance sheet which included a line item "Investments and other assets . . . $6,884 (millions)." Further on, a table provided a breakdown of this category into seven subcategories for the years ended December 31, 1984 and 1985. One of the lines could be described as a deferred charge. It was "program products, less accumulated amortization . . . $1,964 (millions)." Analysts (and accountants) are divided on whether computer programs should be capitalized or expensed. Another line item was goodwill, which nearly all analysts would write off. Still another line was U.S. Treasury securities, which everyone would agree are very solid assets. The analyst will need to do a good deal of searching simply to find the deferred charges and then must use judgment to decide whether they are real assets or items that should be charged to the income statement.

[1]Financial Accounting Standards Board, Statement of Financial Accounting Concepts No. 6, *Elements of Financial Statements*, December 1985, pp. 10–12, Stamford, Conn.

Intangible Assets.   The familiar types of intangible assets include

- Goodwill
- Patents
- Copyrights
- Trademarks
- Franchises
- Licenses
- Organization and development expense

These items are discussed in Chapter 19.

The Growing List of Intermediate Liabilities

In the past, few liabilities failed to fall in the categories of (1) current liabilities or (2) funded debt. Those that were of a general reserve nature belonged in surplus. The remainder were so small in amount that they could simply be added to current liabilities. The current situation requires the analyst to address a different set of problems. A sizable body of liabilities refuse to fall neatly into merely two classes. At least three areas need to be assessed:

- Off-balance-sheet financing
- Deferred taxes
- Preferred stock

Off-Balance-Sheet Liabilities

Off-balance-sheet liabilities include

- Operating leases
- Product financing arrangements
- Related party transactions
- Unconsolidated affiliates and related parties that are carrying parent company debt
- Contingent litigation liabilities
- Liabilities for pension and other postemployment benefits

The analyst must decide how to treat these liabilities. Those which properly belong on the balance sheet should be classified as current liabilities, long-term debt, or equity. For example, deferred nonrefundable fee income is not a liability and is best considered equity for purposes of calculating return on equity.

Operating Leases. The preference for *operating leases* over capital leases has two financial reporting reasons. First, operating leases are not shown as assets and liabilities on the balance sheet. In contrast, under a *capital lease*, the books show that an asset was acquired and a borrowing incurred. Second, the expense of an operating lease is simply the rental amount spread evenly over the life of the lease.

Expense under a Capital Lease. Under a capital lease, the asset is depreciated, usually using straight-line method. The interest component of the borrowing is reflected using the mortgage method. In the early years the interest component of a mortgage consumes almost all the payment, while in the later years the payment is practically all principal with very little interest. Thus, the total expenses under a capital lease (depreciation plus interest) are higher than an operating lease's rent in the earlier years and lower in the later years. Use of capital leases reduces the early years' net income and increases income in the later years of the lease.

Capital Leases Are Easily Avoided. The accounting rules to distinguish between capital and operating leases use arbitrary criteria, such as a requirement that the term of the lease not exceed 75 percent of the estimated economic life of the leased property or that the present value of the minimum lease payments at the beginning of the lease shall not exceed 90 percent of the fair value of the property. It is quite simple to convert a capital lease into an operating lease by structuring the terms appropriately. Thus two companies may operate precisely the same in economic terms, but the one with an operating lease will show fewer liabilities and earlier earnings than will the other that has a capital lease. The various ratios of profitability, stability, and financial risk will look better for the former company than for the latter. Yet the economic substance is identical.

The Old Rules-of-Thumb. Historically, most leased assets were real estate. Lease terms were long with extensive renewal options. The practice was for analysts to capitalize the lease by multiplying the annual rent by an arbitrary number such as 10 times or, somewhat later, 8 times. This technique solved a difficult analytical problem for those studying retail chains, in particular, but applied elsewhere. The calculation provided a good approximation of the value of real estate in those days of relatively low interest rates and permitted valid comparisons between those companies that owned their own properties and had debt on the balance sheet with those that rented and showed little or no debt outstanding.

Today's Leases—Shorter Term at Higher Interest Rates. Today, a much higher percentage of leases are short term in nature, covering computers, automobiles, machinery, and similar items having short useful lives. Thus, a multiplier of 8 or 10 times may overstate the asset and liability significantly. Fortunately, companies are required to disclose minimum lease requirements for each of the succeeding five years and the total for all subsequent years in a footnote. Many companies show the longer rentals in five-year brackets. This permits the analyst to estimate the asset and liability with more precision.

Two Leasing Disclosures. Table 18.1 provides a schedule of operating lease rentals for two companies—the data needed to capitalize the leases.

Tonka Corporation. The data clearly show that Tonka Corporation leases relatively short-lived items, and that some of the leases are expiring rather quickly. There is no difficulty in determining the present value of the Tonka leases, other than selecting an interest rate, since projecting future payment dates is unnecessary. All the payments are shown in the table. If an interest rate of 15 percent were selected, and the rental payments are made at year's end, the equation that follows

Table 18.1. Future Minimum Annual Rentals on
Operating Leases
(In Millions of Dollars)

Year (ending December 31)	Tonka Corporation	Mead Corporation
1986	0.6	28.9
1987	0.4	25.4
1988	0.4	17.8
1989	0.2	13.3
1990	0.1	10.5
Later years	0.0	285.6*
Total	1.7	381.5

* Through 2057.
SOURCE: From 1985 Annual Report.

would give the present value of Tonka's operating lease obligations at the beginning of 1986. The calculated value of the operating leases would be $1.301 million—about 3.7 times the average annual rental for the next five years and about twice the 1986 rent. Clearly, a multiplier of 8 or 10 would have severely exaggerated the liability and asset (figures represent millions of dollars):

$$\frac{0.6}{(1.15)} + \frac{0.4}{(1.15)^2} + \frac{0.4}{(1.15)^3} + \frac{0.2}{(1.15)^4} + \frac{0.1}{(1.15)^5} = 1.301$$

Mead Corporation. In the case of the Mead Corporation, long-term leases are involved, and at least one of them appears to have had a life of 72 years, since the payments continue through the year 2057. How should the analyst estimate the value of the Mead Corporation leases? First, the analyst would observe that some maturing leases or short-term leases (we don't know which) exist because the minimum annual payments drop fairly rapidly from almost $29 million in 1986 to a little over $10 million in 1990. As a rough estimate, the analyst might divide the number of years between 1991 and 2057 into the total lease payments for those years, giving an average annual rental of $4.26 million. An alternative is to divide the most distant known annual rent, 1990's figure of $10,500,000, into the total remaining rent of $285,600,000, which implies that payments would be completed in the year 2017. That would expire about 40 years too soon. Thus, as a compromise estimate, the analyst might decide to allow the annual rental to continue declining about $3 million a year for another two years, and then calculate the fixed amount that would equal the remaining rent from 1993 to 2057. Thus, the estimated schedule of remaining rent payments for Mead Corporation (in millions of dollars) would be as follows:

1991	10.5 − 3.0	= 7.5
1992	7.5 − 3.0	= 4.5
1993–2057	285.6 − 7.5 − 4.5	= 4.209 annually
	65	

Using our assumed maturity schedule and a 15 percent interest rate, the present value of Mead's leases would be $84.3 million. Assumption of a 12 percent interest rate would increase the present value to only $94.8 million, so our projection of Mead's pattern of interest payments does not result in a present value that is highly sensitive to changes in the assumed interest rate. Either number is only about one-fourth of the total operating lease rental payments ($381.5 million) for Mead. Assumption of a different pattern of rental payments could make a significant change in the number. Obviously, obtaining further details of the scheduled minimum rental payments from the company would give analysts more confidence in their calculations.

The Mead calculation illustrates that the old traditional multipliers of 8 and 10 times do not seem to give a very good answer in these times of high interest rates. The average annual minimum rental on operating leases for the first five years is $19.2 million, and a multiplier of 10 times would yield an estimate almost double either of the numbers that we calculated using a discounting technique. Our calculations came out with a multiplier of about 4 times.

Interest Component of Operating Leases. If the analyst capitalizes Mead's operating leases, both the asset and the liability must be shown on the balance sheet. To avoid distorting return on investment, an interest component of the rent must be added to the numerator to balance the presence of the lease liability in the denominator. What portion of the rent should be considered the interest component? We suggest that a reasonable solution is found in the present value calculation. Mead's total rental payments are $381.5 million. The present value is, say, $94.8 million. That is the principal part of the payments. The rest is interest. Thus, the fraction

$$\frac{381.5 - 94.8}{381.5} = 75.15\%$$

might be applied to the five-year average rent as an average interest component. If that figure seems unreasonable as a return on the lease liability, an up-to-date interest rate could be applied to the present value of the earlier expiring leases and an interest fraction, calculated as above, applied to the longer maturity leases.

Should Operating Leases Go on the Balance Sheet? The question remains whether the analyst should put these calculations on the balance sheet. For certain purposes, our answer is yes. Ideally, for calculating such ratios as return on investment, debt to equity, debt to plant, and plant turnover, both the asset and liability should be reflected in the balance sheet. In a liquidation study, operating leases should be excluded from the balance sheet. This asset is available only if the rent is paid, and the liability could be settled for far less than the present value of the asset.

Practical Difficulties. However, some difficulties may persuade the analyst that including operating leases on the balance sheet is not worthwhile. To be perfectly consistent with capital leases, the liability should be reduced each year using the mortgage method and the asset depreciated, probably using straight-line calculation. The calculations for a single lease would be extensive. In the typical case some leases expire each year and new ones are made. Calculating a reasonable depreciation number would require at a minimum viewing each year's expiration as a separate asset with its own useful life. That would require a great deal of labor, and (1) acquisition of information that is seldom available or (2) use of vulnerable assumptions.

The "One-Third of Rent" Rule Is Questionable. Since the interest and depreciation calculations would be complex, and probably subject to an uncomfortable amount of error, some authorities suggest the use of *one-third of the rental payment* as an estimate of the interest component. We are not entirely satisfied with that ratio for long-term leases in the early years. Rent for a lease on a building with a 50-year expected life will be largely interest, since straight-line depreciation would only be 2 percent a year.

What Method Should the Analyst Use? There is no altogether satisfactory solution to the problem of operating leases. Among the issues are the following:

Operating Lease Discounting Rates. Any estimate of the value of the asset and lease obligation will require an interest rate for discounting the stream of payments. Over the life of a lease, a calculation of the interest rate imbedded in the stream of payments will simply generate the interest rate that was assumed. Thus, when the interest rate is used as part of the return on investment, a high estimate of interest will result in a high return on a smaller amount of investment. A lower rate of interest will provide low return on a higher amount of investment. Some comparability could be achieved by using the same interest rate for all companies, but this may result in misleading return comparisons, since it provides the same answer for situations that are probably different.

Operating Lease Depreciation. Calculating a depreciation estimate requires assumptions about the *original* useful life of the asset. Large errors could occur in the depreciation estimate for long-term assets.

Rent as a Proxy. Use of the rent as a proxy for the sum of interest plus depreciation would not provide comparability with companies that lease property using capital leases. However, if the company has many leases that were initiated at various times, the rent may reasonably be assumed to be approximately the correct total of interest plus depreciation. In addition, this approach uses the interest rate assumption only for the allocation of the rent between the two expenses. Long-term leases are not terribly sensitive to moderate changes in the interest rate assumption, and short-term leases have a relatively small interest component in comparison to the amount of depreciation. Thus, a calculation of predepreciation return on capital using rent as the sum of depreciation and interest probably gives an answer that the analyst can live with.

Rules-of-Thumb Must Be Kept Up-to-Date. Use of rules-of-thumb is probably acceptable, although rough approximations of the interest component. We would suggest that if the analyst follows this route, the appropriate rules today are to use:

- One-third of the current year's rental payment for short leases
- One-half for leases in the 12 to 20 year range
- 60 percent for leases over 20 years

We suggest these numbers because they are in line with the interest component of a sample of capital lease disclosures where the length of lease and type of property were disclosed. These rules-of-thumb are based on interest rates inherent in leases that were outstanding in 1985 and the first half of 1986. These rules-of-thumb should be changed as interest rates change. We suggest that analysts who decide to use rules-of-thumb observe the interest rate component of capital leases, particularly of companies in similar industries.

Exclusion of Operating Leases from Return Calculations. An alternative is not to capitalize operating leases at all for purposes of calculating any return number. This approach uses the estimated lease obligation only in studies of the capital structure, the equity ratio, and similar calculations, but does not use the operating lease as part of the denominator of any calculation of return. However, treating operating leases differently from capital leases will often result in identical assets being treated differently. Many capital leases, after passage of a few years, would no longer qualify as capital leases if they were reclassified. They would be operating leases because the lease's life was no longer 75 percent of useful life, nor was present value any longer 90 percent of fair value. Conceptually, there is a good case for putting all these similar assets on the balance sheet.

Other Off-Balance-Sheet Liabilities

Most other types of off-balance-sheet financing require analysts to use judgment rather than fixed rules.

Product-Financing Arrangements

Return of Goods versus Goods on Consignment. Magazines are often sold to newsstands with an agreement to take back any unsold copies when the next issue comes out. In most industries, these would be considered goods on consignment, and the cash received from the customer would be considered a deposit rather than revenue because the returns are not readily estimable. However, those are not the product-financing arrangements that are a problem for analysts.

Inventory Parking. The more difficult inventory transactions are arrangements where inventory is "parked" with another party with the expectation that the buyer will exercise an option to return the goods and receive the original money back with interest. In effect, that is a secured borrowing transaction and should be accounted for as such.

Related Party Transactions. Many related party transactions do involve borrowing and lending between the reporting company and a related party. Related parties include people and organizations that often do not qualify for such terms as subsidiary or affiliate:

- Grantor trusts
- Nonsub subsidiaries whose stock is nominally owned by a third party or that essentially have no economic substance
- Joint venture partners
- Officers and directors
- Principal stockholders and their relatives

Such relationships are sometimes used to borrow in behalf of the company, without the borrowing appearing on the balance sheet. Even worse, the borrowing may show up on the balance sheet of the reporting company as preferred stock, common stock, or some other subordinated security. More often, nothing appears on the balance sheet, but the company has guaranteed the loan or offered other credit assurances through such devices as insurance or letters of credit. Unwinding and understanding some of these complex transactions can be a major task for the analyst.

Contingent Litigation Liabilities. Many contingent liabilities that involve litigation are excluded from the balance sheet on grounds that no reasonable estimate can be made of the outcome or that the outcome would be prejudiced by making such an estimate. These contingencies are usually revealed in footnotes, even though no estimate of the amount of loss may be given.

Is There an Asset?   The economic substance of some hidden liabilities is that the reporting entity is the primary obligor and prime beneficiary of a borrowing or guarantee. The analyst may conclude that a liability and possibly an asset should be placed on the books. Since the liability is usually well hidden, the analyst may uncover such situations more easily by finding the asset from which the company is benefiting.

Other Liabilities

Funded Debt

The characteristics of funded debt are discussed in depth in Chapters 23 and 24.

Pensions and Other Postemployment Benefits

These obligations were discussed in Chapter 12.

Pension Liabilities on the Balance Sheet

Sometimes a pension liability is shown on the balance sheet when in fact none exists economically. This may arise because the company has reached the limit of tax deductibility and chooses not to make further contributions to the pension fund until they become deductible. This can build a sizable liability on the balance sheet even though the pension plan itself may be significantly overfunded and no economic liability exists. The analyst should take the liability off the balance sheet and adjust pension expense, taxes, and equity over the years the overfunding occurred.

Pension Plan Terminations

Another complex pension situation has begun to arise recently. A company discontinues its old defined-benefit pension plan and replaces it with a new defined-benefit plan after purchasing annuities for all the obligations of the old plan and withdrawing cash from it. Any assets remaining in a plan that has satisfied its liabilities might properly be treated as an asset of the plan sponsor—the prepayment of pension expense, and certainly any liability remaining on the plan sponsor's books should be removed from the balance sheet.

"Book Reserve" Pension Liabilities

Most German subsidiaries did not until recently place money in trust for the payment of pension obligations. Instead, they merely showed a liability on the balance sheet—the "book reserve" method of pension accounting.

Deferred Taxes

The largest intermediate class of liabilities in terms of dollars must surely be the deferred tax liability. Deferred taxes were discussed in detail in Chapter 17; their cash flow effects were discussed in Chapter 15.

Preferred Stock Liability

Until recently, conventional balance sheets showed preferred stock as part of capital and surplus. Thus it was placed with the common stock, as if sharing in the ownership of the business, and was sharply separated from funded debt and other liabilities. (In 1985 the SEC began to require that mandatory redeemable preferred stock be shown outside of stockholders' equity.) The most useful balance sheet analysis will place preferred stock with the funded debt as making up the total prior claims against the capital fund. Bonded debt and preferred stocks may be designated together under "senior issues." However, in analyzing senior claims, the subordinate position of the preferred should be recognized. The proper carrying amount for the preferred stock liability is discussed in Chapter 19.

Preferred Stock Dividend Arrearages

When unpaid preferred dividends have accumulated, this amount should be shown clearly in the balance sheet and not be buried in a footnote. A good arrangement is to place the amount of such accumulation in parentheses immediately below the earned surplus figure, or else to add it to the preferred stock liability. From the viewpoint of the common stockholders such claims are liabilities.

19
Asset Values in Balance Sheet Analysis

Relation of Assets to Securities and Other Claims

The discussion of balance sheet affairs continues, giving attention first to asset values and their relationship to securities and other claims.

Asset Values

The Going Concern

The correct calculation of the asset values and their relationship to securities or creditors' claims depends on the purposes of the analyst. The novice investor is sometimes startled to learn that, say, the book value or net asset value for the common shareholders might legitimately be calculated several ways, depending on the question asked. We shall examine such a set of calculations shortly. Asset values are ordinarily not a critical "going concern" matter, because the assets are expected to be used, not sold. Analysts who are examining a company as a going concern are trying to determine the aggregate investment value of the firm. The earning power of the *assets in use* determines their investment value. Yet, asset values do play a role in analysis of going concerns because they are a measure of the capital employed. The various return-on-capital ratios are very powerful, for they indicate the efficiency with which capital is used.

Asset values may exceed the value based on earning power of some going concerns. In those cases the asset value represents a potential for favorable future developments and provides a margin of safety if earnings collapse. Even below investment value, the asset value is a definite positive factor that may limit the investor's potential loss if earnings fail.

Collateral Value

Viewed as collateral, the pertinent value of an asset is its potential sales price. Claimants and security holders are interested in the collateral and liquidating values of companies, particularly when full or partial liquidation is likely to take place or when there is some question about payment from earning power.

Merger and Acquisition Values

Companies with high liquidating values are often attractive acquisition candidates. Part of the acquisition price can be financed by borrowing against collateral value of the assets. Sometimes assets can be sold for amounts sufficient to repay the entire acquisition cost, leaving assets and earning power for the acquiror. Companies with large amounts of assets are more attractive purchase acquisitions, because there is less goodwill, which analysts ignore as an asset.

Companies that can be bought for substantially less than their asset values may be attractive acquisitions even though they are currently unprofitable. Some of or all the assets can be sold and the capital redeployed in other activities, one hopes in a fashion that will increase the investment value and ultimately the prices of securities.

As a Measure of Capital

The assets of a company are its true capital. Most security analysis tends to use the word *capital* to refer to the claims and interests of debtors and owners—those whose interests appear on the right side of the balance sheet. The right side of the balance sheet tells the *source* of the capital. The left side shows how that capital is allocated among types of investments, generally presenting those assets at the unrecovered amount invested in them.

As a Measure of Safety for Each Security Issue

One of the measures of safety of securities and the claims of creditors is the amount of assets, after deducting all prior claims, available for the particular security or class of claimants. A number of coverage ratios are calculated for purposes of determining the excess asset protection.

The Amount of Equity Claim

Shareholders are entitled to the residual assets after all prior claims have been satisfied.

Computation of the Equity or Book Value per Share

The book value per share of a common stock is found by adding up all the assets, subtracting all liabilities and stock issues ahead of the common, and then dividing by the number of common shares. Our balance sheet presentation of Bristol-Myers for 1985, as given in Figure 18.1 in Chapter 18, will lead readily to the book value per share. All that is necessary is to divide the number of shares into the indicated equity. In the case of Bristol-Myers, the figure is $16.51 per share.

Consider the Effects of Dilution

Dilution of book value should be examined if the analyst is looking to the book value per share in terms of

1. The company's potential for liquidation, sale of assets, acquisition as an asset play
2. Any fashion in which book value is considered a viable alternative to measuring value by capitalization of earnings

The analyst should calculate on a worst-case basis the various combinations of exercise of conversion privileges of convertible issues and of warrants and options so that dilution of book value per share may be assessed.

Treatment of Intangibles in Computing Asset Values

It is customary to eliminate intangibles in the computation of the net asset value, or equity, per share of common stock. The phrase *book value* is a little ambiguous; sometimes it means to include all the assets shown on the books, and, at other times, it means to exclude the intangibles.

When excluding intangibles entirely from book value, analysts often use the expression "net tangible assets per share." That phrase is not accurate for the book value number that we recommend, since we encourage the inclusion of any intangible assets which have a known or estimable market value or which have a direct stream of revenue, such as royalty income.

Example. The 1985 annual report of Philip Morris Companies, Inc., reported goodwill and intangibles of $4.457 billion. About $4.3 billion was goodwill which is being amortized on a straight-line basis over 40 years. About $3.9 billion of the goodwill came about as a result of the acquisition of General Foods. The net worth of Philip Morris at year-end 1985 was $4.757 billion. An immediate write-off of goodwill would virtually eliminate stockholders' equity.

Example. The proper treatment of a particular kind of intangible asset can change. Prior to the Motor Carrier Act of 1980, interstate operating rights were exclusive assets of motor carriers, originally acquired from the Interstate Commerce Commission or other licensing agency. Those operating rights could be sold to another trucking company. Prior to the act, transactions in motor carrier operating rights were frequent and at reasonably predictable prices. The Act deregulated the industry and made the operating rights worthless, since anyone could obtain identical rights at no cost beyond minimal paperwork. A previously valuable right had suddenly become worthless, wiping out the net worth of a number of the weaker trucking companies.

The intangible assets often seen on the balance sheet include such items as patents, franchises, operating rights, and purchased goodwill (the cost of acquisition of another concern in excess of the fair value of assets minus liabilities). Purchased goodwill acquired on or after November 1, 1970, is written off-in installments over not more than 40 years. Purchased goodwill that was acquired before November 1, 1970, need not be written off. That goodwill remains subject to management judgment about whether to amortize and over what period of time. A number of companies continue to carry their pre-1970 purchased goodwill and other intangibles at historic numbers and make no effort to amortize.

Example. The 1985 annual report of ITT Corporation describes its $51,788,000 of pre-November 1, 1970 purchased goodwill as "unamortizable," which is not accurate, and carries it in the plant, property, and equipment account.

Alternative Computation of Book Value

In most cases the book value may be computed readily from the liability side of the conventional published balance sheet. It is sufficient to add together common stock, at par or stated value, the various surplus items, and the translation adjustment. (Most intangibles must be subtracted from this sum.) This will give the total common stock equity, which is then divided by the number of shares. Adjustments may be desirable, to correct the stated liability for preferred stock, and to adjust the carrying amounts of any assets and liabilities that are improperly stated or are known but absent from the balance sheet.

Asset Values and Investment Values

Book Value Is Not Intrinsic Value

The calculation of an equity's book value is not intended to show the "true value" of the shares; if it were, the intangibles of many companies would have to be appraised at a very high figure. Book value is only one of many "values" that the analyst must deal with, and it clearly is not the market value of the stock, nor its intrinsic value, nor the liquidating value. It is, instead, accounting's net asset value, adjusted in a variety of ways by the analyst. It is but one step along the way to determining investment value or "intrinsic value." The very large premiums over book value paid in the acquisition of certain food companies, such as Nabisco and General Foods, is evidence enough that well-established brand names are true economic assets of considerable value. That value can be preserved by advertising, promotion, maintaining product quality, and other actions. The value may continue or even increase over the years. The *book value, asset value,* or *net worth,* discussed in this section, is merely a single factor in the entire value picture. For this limited purpose, we confine ourselves to the various categories of tangible assets and the few intangibles that have liquidating value or other measurable value. *The true value of goodwill, trade names, customer relations, and similar intangible assets is indistinguishable from the value of the earnings which they produce.*

Practical Significance of Book Value

The financial services regularly calculate from the published balance sheets the book value of common stocks, but it is seldom used in a direct way to measure value. This book value is limited to a few important generic situations:

- *Public utilities.* In the field of public utility stocks, the rates allowed by regulatory bodies, and the resultant earning power, may be largely governed by the assets, to the extent that they are included in the rate base. They are usually calculated at original cost, although in a few jurisdictions "fair value" is used.

- *Financial companies.* The assets of financial companies, such as banks, insurance companies, and investment companies, are nearly all so liquid that their value enters—to a varying extent—in investment decisions relating to their shares.

- *Return on equity.* Book value is useful in calculating the return on equity. To the degree that this is a stable number through time, the ratio, combined with the payout ratio, can offer some indications about the amount of growth that can be financed internally.

- *Asset plays and liquidating values.* Identifying takeover candidates known as "asset plays," and estimating liquidating values of companies requires use of book values to some extent. However, since the book values are largely based on recoverable investment on a going-concern basis, the book value is merely a first approximation. In addition to security analysts' usual adjustments, estimates of the current values of individual assets would be needed to improve the accuracy of the numbers.

- *Common-stock valuation models.* There are limited mechanical uses of book value in a few price models for common stocks, although the models are not widely used.

Asset Value and Earning Power Apparently Unrelated. For the great category known as "industrial companies" and for the railroads, book value does not appear to be widely used for direct valuation. Common stocks sell freely either at high multiples or at small fractions of book value and garner little notice. For example, Marion Laboratories, Inc., sold at 63 in April 1986, when its most recent recorded book value was $4.17 a share. At the same time, Datapoint Corporation was selling at 5½ with a book value of $14.92.

We agree with the prevailing viewpoint that asset values are not the primary factor in determining investment values. But this does not mean that it is wise or safe to lose sight completely of this element in the analytical picture. For discussion of this point, see Chapters 23 and 24 on bond and preferred stock valuation and Chapter 34 on the asset value in valuation of common stocks.

Preparation of Balance Sheet for Asset Value Analysis

Table 19.1 shows the adjusted capitalization of American Brands, Inc., at the 1985 year end.

Table 19.1. Adjusted Capitalization of American Brands, Inc., as of December 31, 1985

	Dollar value (millions)	Percent
Notes payable to banks..	243.2	6.6
Commercial paper..	138.7	3.8
Funded debt..	748.7*	20.4
Operating leases..	95.7†	2.6
Total debt...	1,226.3	33.4
Deferred income taxes	323.5‡	8.8
$2.75 Preferred stock, no par, stated at mandatory redemption price of $30.50 (4,507,528 shares).....................................	137.5	3.8
$2.67 Convertible preferred, no par, stated at $30.50 (preference amount in liquidation) (1,552,328 shares)...........................	47.3	1.3
Common stockholders' equity after subtracting $641.8 million goodwill..	1,930.0‡	52.7
Total capital structure...	3,664.6	100.0
Other current liabilities...	1,074.1¶	
Total capital and other liabilities......................................	4,738.7	

*Includes $8.2 current portion of debt and capital leases.
†Present value of minimum operating lease payments using a 12 percent discount rate. The pattern of payments beyond five years was estimated.
‡Adjusted to eliminate the effects of foreign currency translation adjustment losses arising from noncurrent items.
¶Not considered a part of capital structure but required for calculating coverage ratios.

Elimination of Intangibles

The company showed $641.8 million in goodwill resulting from business acquisitions. Net worth was reduced by that amount in full. No adjustment was made to the deferred tax account in this case because the company was considered to be an ongoing firm, the goodwill amortization is not tax deductible, and no tax benefit will be obtained from it until subsidiaries which gave rise to the goodwill are sold or liquidated. However, had we removed other intangibles which were deductible for income tax purposes, we would have reduced equity by only *1 minus the tax rate* times the amount of those intangibles and reduced the deferred tax liability by the remainder. In the case of a company that was expected to be liquidated soon, or which was expected to liquidate its investment in a subsidiary that had given rise to purchased goodwill, it would have been proper to make the tax effect adjustment.

Gains and Losses on Securities

The common stockholders' equity in the table included unrealized appreciation on investments in marketable equity securities of the

Franklin Life Insurance Company in the amount of $4.1 million. The Franklin Life Insurance Company is carried under equity method and is 100 percent owned; the latter fact justifies the inclusion of the $4.1 million in common stockholders' equity. If that unrealized gain represented American Brand's proportional interest in results of a 25 percent–owned affiliate carried on the equity method, the gain should not be used in a calculation of assets available to protect debt and preferred stock, because ready access to the unrealized gains would not exist.

Equity Method Investees

Similarly, one could argue that the *retained earnings* of a 25 percent–owned investee accounted for using the equity method should properly be excluded from this sort of calculation because the retained earnings are not readily accessibile.

Foreign Currency Translation Adjustments

For the reasons discussed in the foreign currency translation section of Chapter 12, stockholders' equity and the deferred tax liability were adjusted to reflect only that portion of foreign currency translation adjustment gains and losses that resulted from the effects of rate changes on working capital.

Carrying Amount of Preferred Stocks

American Brands has two preferred stocks outstanding, both without par value. Both are stated at a carrying amount of $30.50 per share. In the case of the $2.75 preferred, $30.50 is the mandatory redemption price. Both preferreds are entitled to $30.50 per share in liquidation. The $2.67 convertible preferred stock ranks equally with the $2.75 preferred, although the dividend amounts are slightly different. There is also a modest difference in the voting rights of the two preferred stocks, but neither has a prior claim over the other as to payment of dividends or payments in liquidation. As a result, we believe that they should be treated equally and carried at the $30.50 stated value, which is the best for both preferred stocks.

Deferred Taxes

The table shows that American Brands has accumulated a deferred income tax liability of $323.5 million, after our adjustment of foreign currency translation losses. That tax is not currently owed and will not be until certain book-tax timing differences reverse in future years. We have discussed deferred income tax items as a source of capital that works for the common stockholders. However, deferred taxes should not be ignored in calculating the asset protection for the long-term debt or the preferred stocks of American Brands. If the carrying amounts of the preferred stocks and common equity were realized, say in liquidation, the deferred income taxes would become payable and have a claim that would take priority over many debt issues. As a result, in calculating the coverage for the funded debt or the preferred, the deferred income tax liability must be covered too.

Pensions

The 1985 annual report of American Brands showed a modest deficit in its pension fund valuation as of January 1, 1984. The pension liability was $505.9 million versus net assets available for benefits of $484.2 million—a normal situation requiring no adjustment to net worth. However, if the company were in financial difficulty, we would be inclined to show the pension shortfall as a liability. Similarly, if American Brands had a large pension surplus, and it was deemed probable that the company would discontinue its pension plan to obtain the asset reversion, the net pension asset should be added to equity, after adjustment for deferred taxes at the ordinary income tax rate.

Operating Leases

For the reasons discussed in Chapter 18, operating leases were capitalized, using a 12 percent discounting rate.

The Structure of the Balance Sheet

The Capital Structure

Table 19.1 shows the major categories of the capital structure of American Brands:

- Short-term borrowings
- Current and noncurrent funded debt, including capital leases
- Operating leases
- Deferred taxes

- Preferred stock
- Common-stock equity

Ordinarily, those current liabilities other than the current portion of funded debt, notes payable, bank loans, and commercial paper are not considered a part of the capital structure. In some cases, the term *capital structure* is used to refer to long-term sources of capital only. To avoid confusion, use the term *permanent capital* or specify *long-term capital*, if that is what is meant. The treatment of other liabilities is situational. Capital leases would normally be included with the funded debt, but for non-interest-bearing liabilities, for which no interest rate can be assumed or calculated, the liabilities are best excluded from the capital structure to avoid distortions of the return on invested capital calculations. The treatment of deferred taxes varies depending on the objectives of the analysis; for discussion of the reasons to exclude deferred taxes from the capital structure for certain analytical purposes, see Chapter 17. The capital structure or capitalization structure is usually summarized by stating what percentage of the total each category represents.

The Working-Capital Position

Careful buyers of securities scrutinize the balance sheet to see if the cash assets are adequate, if the current assets bear a suitable ratio to the current liabilities, and if there is any indebtedness near maturity that may develop into a refinancing problem.

Cash Shortage Can Be Offset by a Strong Working-Capital Position. Nothing useful can be said here about how much cash a corporation should hold. The investor must decide what is needed in any particular case and how seriously to regard a deficiency of cash. A real shortage of cash rarely occurs unless the working-capital position as a whole is poor. With a good ratio of current assets to current liabilities a corporation can get the cash it needs by bank borrowing or sale of receivables.

Industry Current Ratio Standards. On the subject of the working-capital ratio, a minimum of $2 of current assets for each dollar of current liabilities was formerly regarded as a standard for industrial companies. In more recent years bankers have tended to deviate from the traditional 2-to-1 current ratio, because statistics are now available for individual industry averages. Those statistics indicate significant industry and company differences in the current ratios required for effective operations and reasonable conservatism. Such tables are published regularly by Robert Morris Associates and others, giving industry averages in total and by size of firm.

Bankers' Credit Standards. Analysts should be acquainted with the banking industry standards for credit decisions so that they can be alert to the possibility that a company may have its credit withdrawn. Because of defects in the definition of *current*, many accountants and others think the current ratio is meaningless. They are wrong on two counts:

1. Significant empirical evidence indicates that the current ratio, in combination with others, is highly predictive of bankruptcy and financial stress.[1]
2. Bank credit officers do think current ratios matter, and their decisions have practical consequences.

A Below-Average Ratio Does Not Mean Unsatisfactory. Some tend to believe that a company falling below the current ratio average of its group should be viewed with some suspicion. This logical fallacy necessarily penalizes the lower half of any group, regardless of how satisfactory the showing may be considered by itself. We are unable to suggest better figures than the industry average to use as a definite quantitative test of a sufficiently comfortable current ratio. Naturally the investor would favor companies that well exceed minimum requirements, but the problem is whether a higher ratio must be exacted as a condition for purchase, so that an issue otherwise satisfactory would necessarily be rejected if the current assets are below standard. We hesitate to suggest such a rule, nor do we know what new figure to prescribe.

Quick Ratio and Cash Ratio Standards. In earlier times, the "acid test" was the same as the "quick ratio": the ratio of current assets excluding inventories to current liabilities. With the passing of time, the term *acid test* gradually came to mean the *cash ratio*—that is, the ratio of cash and equivalent to current liabilities. Given that potential for confusion, we will use the expressions *quick ratio* and *cash ratio*. The accepted standard for quick ratio is that current assets exclusive of inventories must at least equal current liabilities. The cash ratio is not a very useful test: no universal standards exist to use as a guide, and the ratio itself is quite volatile.

Failure to Meet Either Current Ratio or Quick Ratio Criteria. Ordi-

[1] E. I. Altman, "Financial Ratios, Discriminant Analysis and the Prediction of Corporate Bankruptcy," *Journal of Finance*, September, 1968, pp. 589–609; there is a good discussion of Altman's studies and similar studies by others in George Foster, *Financial Statement Analysis*, Prentice-Hall, Englewood Cliffs, N.J., 1978, pp. 460–480.

narily the investor might well expect a company to meet *both* a current ratio test and the quick ratio test. The failure to meet either of these criteria would in most instances reflect strongly upon the investment standing of a common-stock issue—as it would in the case of a bond or preferred stock, and it would supply an argument against the security from the speculative standpoint as well.

Large Bank Debt.   Financial difficulties are almost always heralded by the presence of bank loans or other debt due in a short time. In other words, rarely is a weak financial position created solely by ordinary trade accounts payable. Bank debt is not, however, inherently a bad sign; the use of a reasonable amount of bank credit—particularly for seasonal needs—is not only legitimate but even desirable. But, whenever the statement shows bank loans or notes payable, the analyst will scrutinize the financial picture somewhat more closely than when the balance sheet is "clean."

Bank Loans of Intermediate Maturity.   Since the early 1940s, the *term loan* has developed as an important medium of financing by corporations. In general, such loans run from 3 to 15 years, and they are usually repayable in installments over their life—often with a larger than average maturity at the end (called the "balloon"). The lender is usually a bank, but sometimes is an insurance company. These term loans have been made for a variety of purposes:

1. To retire bond issues and even preferred stock
2. For additional working capital
3. To finance acquisitions of property or stock control
4. To finance a project or asset acquisition that will expire over the intermediate term

Debts Covenants and Dividend Restrictions.   In most term loan agreements, as well as other forms of borrowing, the borrower promises to maintain working capital at a prescribed figure and not to pay dividends except out of future earnings plus some limited figure. In effect, the greater part of the earned surplus is frozen until the loan is paid off. During that period, before the company has built up a cushion of retained earnings, company stockholders may face at least a temporary loss of divided income.

   From the standpoint of security analysis, term loans resemble the short-term notes that used to be sold to the public as a familiar part of corporate financing. They must be considered somewhat equivalent to both current liabilities and early maturing debt. They are not dangerous if either the current asset position is so strong that the loans could readily be taken care of as current liabilities or the earning power is so large and dependable as to make refinancing a simple problem. But if neither of these conditions is present, the analyst must view a substantial amount of intermediate bank debt as a potential threat to dividends or even to solvency.

Covenants in Term Loan Agreements. Term loan agreements are usually sensitive legal instruments because they often pick up both the normal protective provisions of an ordinary bank loan agreement and the traditional protective covenants of a long-term bond. The analyst should be familiar with the typical loan restrictions that exist on short-, intermediate-, and long-term borrowings and should assess the probability that any one of the three types might trigger a default, which in turn would probably trigger cross defaults, which, in theory, make all the debt payable immediately.

Current, Quick and Cash Asset Values per Common Share

In addition to book value per common share, we wish to suggest three other per share numbers of similar character: current asset value, quick asset value, and cash asset value.

Current Asset Value of a Common Stock

The current asset value of a stock consists of the current assets alone, minus *all* liabilities and claims ahead of the issue. This value excludes not only the intangible assets but also the fixed and miscellaneous assets. An occasional practice in Wall Street is to state the net current asset value of a common stock without deducting the senior securities from the working capital. We consider such a figure to be relatively meaningless and potentially misleading.

From time to time, when the market is deeply depressed, a large number of stocks will be available in the market at prices below their net current asset values. In effect, an investor can buy the company for its working capital, with the fixed assets thrown in for nothing. These conditions can exist for companies that are still profitable and for which no visible disaster lies ahead. A diversified portfolio of such companies will usually work out very well because of the low risk in the market price and the likelihood that sooner or later management will make the assets more productive. Also, such portfolios typically become available only in eras of extreme pessimism when stock prices in general are deeply depressed.

Cash and Quick Asset Values of a Common Stock

The quick asset value per share is the sum of cash and receivables, less all claims prior to the common, divided by the number of common shares outstanding.

The cash asset value of a stock consists of the cash assets alone, minus all liabilities and claims ahead of the common. Cash assets include:

- Certificates of deposit
- Call loans
- Commercial paper
- Bankers' acceptances
- Marketable short-term fixed income securities at market value
- Cash surrender value of insurance policies
- Cash itself

A somewhat more stringent calculation includes only the high-quality short-term fixed-income portion of the marketable securities.

Free Cash Asset Value

An alternative calculation of the cash asset value assumes that the current assets other than cash items are applicable to meet the liabilities ahead of the common. The cash assets are then reduced only by the amount needed to meet the balance of senior claims. The remainder of the cash may be considered as available for the common stock. This remainder may be called the "free cash," and the amount thereof per share of common may be called the "free cash asset value" of the common.

Table 19.2 shows an example of the computation of the 1985 asset values for Guilford Mills common stock. Guilford Mills's current assets should be increased by the amount of cash surrender value of life insurance. The analyst might estimate that at, say, $4 million. Thus,

Table 19.2. Guilford Mills, Inc. Condensed Balance Sheet
as of June 30, 1985
(In Thousands of Dollars)

Assets	
Cash items	$ 2,286
Accounts receivable	79,903
Inventories	58,258
Prepayments	3,303
Current assets	$143,750
Net plant account	68,382
Goodwill	7,122
Other, principally cash value of life insurance	5,680
Total assets	$224,934

Liabilities	
Current liabilities	$ 50,267
Long-term liabilities	11,860
Deferred income taxes	6,464
Other deferred liabilities	5,515
Stockholders' investment (7,858,442 shares)	150,828
Total liabilities	$224,934

working capital would be $143,750,000 plus $4 million less $50,267,000 current liabilities, or $97,483,000. From this must be subtracted the intermediate liabilities, which total $23,839,000, leaving $73,644,000 available for the common stock. This equals $9.37 for each of the 7,858,442 shares outstanding. To determine the amount of quick assets available for the common, the inventories of $58,258,000 must be deducted, leaving $15,386,000, or $1.96 of quick assets a share. Subtracting the $79,903,000 of accounts receivable produces a negative number, so there is no net cash and equivalent per share.

Calculations of Earnings via the Balance Sheet

An All-Inclusive Income

In some cases the true earnings over a period of years may be established more reliably by comparing the change in common-stock equity than by adding up the reported profits. These cases usually involve cases of foreign companies that send items directly to equity or an accounting change that has the same effect by adjusting the opening balance of the earliest year presented. The following equation may be used, when there are no complexities:

Earnings for period = Increase in earned surplus
+ gain on marketable securities
+ current portion of foreign currency translation adjustments
+ dividends paid

In an uncomplicated case, an equivalent calculation may be made by comparing the net assets per share at the beginning and end of the period and adding back the dividends paid. However, a balance sheet approach can become somewhat complicated in any of the following situations or circumstances:

- Mergers and acquisitions taking place during the period studied
- Dispositions of subsidiaries occurring, which remove a previously consolidated portion of earned surplus and replace it with a gain or loss in earned surplus resulting from the disposition
- Sale or repurchase of shares of stock by the company
- Extraordinary write-downs or write-ups of assets if they affect the earned surplus
- Stock dividends which may be charged to earned surplus in whole or in part
- Transfers from the earned surplus account to the capital account resulting from, say, an increase in the par value of the outstanding common stock

In all balance sheet comparisons over time, the analyst must trace through the charges and credits to earned surplus to see what items, if any, are to be excluded from the record of overall earnings.

Some Aspects of Stock Sales and Purchases

A basic tenet of accounting is that a company does not make money dealing with itself. As a result, sale or repurchase of stock does not result in income being reported. Yet, from the viewpoint of the long-term holder of the stock, judicious purchases and sales by the company of its own stock can result in increases in the book value per share. For the ongoing stockholder, a dollar of increase in book value per share that arises from the company's trading in its own stock is worth just as much as a dollar of retained earnings. It is simply one more dollar of capital working for each of the shares. It is true that such advantageous trading by the company must be disadvantageous for those investors on the other side of the company's transactions, since they must lose money in the aggregate in order for the remaining shareholders to gain anything.

Stock Repurchase Programs Can Help Long-Term Investors

The fundamental investor usually has a long-term horizon and is concerned with personal gains and losses—not those of other stockholders who come and go. Thus, a company which buys and sells its stock advantageously, thereby increasing both the book value per share of the remaining shareholders and, in particular, the earnings per share, has an attraction that goes beyond the basic earning power. In recent years many companies, such as Teledyne, Inc., General Foods, Washington Post, Ford Motor, Exxon, and Schlumberger have improved their per-share earnings by judicious purchases of their own shares, and in a number of cases they increased book value per share also. Usually, the announcement of the share purchase program by itself will result in an immediate upward move in the stock's price.

Not All Share Purchases Are Advantageous

If the share purchases are made when the stock is unduly high, perhaps to get rid of cash and discourage an unfriendly takeover offer, the analyst is given several incentives to recommend sale.

Long-Term Studies of Income and Balance Sheet Position

Chapter 20 considers the key relationships among invested capital, earnings, dividends, and market price that underlie our judgments as to the quality of a company's performance and the attractiveness of its securities. A comprehensive study of a common stock might well include comparisons of absolute amounts and key ratios that go back many years. Figures of this sort can give the analyst a long perspective and an adequate conception of both the company's vicissitudes and its rate and direction of change. Balance sheets and income accounts for selected years, spaced, say, 10 years apart, will do this job quite well for most purposes, especially when two or more enterprises are compared. A more complete study would include the aggregate earnings for the decades between the balance sheet dates, so that a few key ratios can be computed on the basis of successive 10-year performances rather than for the single years a decade apart.

20
Ratio
Analysis

The study of a given company's financial statements should proceed in the following logical sequence (chapter discussions are given in parentheses):

1. The analyst should make all adjustments to the financial statements needed to present true figures from an analyst's viewpoint and to make them comparable to other companies (Chapters 10 to 19).

2. True operating earnings and cash flows for the period under review should be determined (Chapters 10 to 17).

3. The analyst should examine the balance sheet and establish the working-capital position, the capital structure, and the amount of invested capital per share (Chapters 18 and 19).

4. The analyst should then develop a number of key ratios, which will throw light on the company's overall performance, the safety of its senior securities, and the attractiveness of its common stock for investment.

This chapter covers many of the more important ratios used in the analysis of financial statements. Some special ratios for analysis of senior securities are discussed in Chapters 25 and 26. Many other ratios are used by analysts when appropriate.

There are peculiar aspects in the use of ratios by security analysts. First, because various ratios can often be grouped together as essentially similar, within each group several may tell much the same story. Thus the analyst may pick one of several similar ratios and discard the others, depending largely on convenience and personal preference. For example, a calculation of return on assets tells essentially the same story as one of return on invested capital, because very little of the total assets is not funded by invested capital, and the two ratios tend to move up and down together. However, the analyst must use the same ratios, calculated the same way, for consistency through time and for comparisons between companies.

A peculiar aspect of ratio analysis is that the analyst may calculate a certain ratio one way for one purpose and another way for a different purpose. For example, the analyst may treat the deferred tax liability as part of equity for purposes of calculating return on equity but as a prior claim for purposes of calculating the book value of the common shares. These different uses merely reflect the analyst's attempt to answer different questions, using familiar terminology, such as "the common equity," but with different meanings for different purposes. As familiarity is gained with the use of the security analysts' terminology, the meaning usually becomes clear from the context of the analysis.

In our discussion of ratios throughout this chapter we will refer to the formulas in Figures 20.1, 20.2, and 20.4 through 20.7. The formulas are presented in a simplified form, referring to common terms such as *earnings* or *book value*. Since we assume that the analyst has already made all the appropriate adjustments to those items, we avoid long formula lines that would result if we were to express, say, earnings plus a long list of upward adjustments minus a long list of downward adjustments. Thus, our formulas are misleadingly simple for one who has not read Chapters 10 through 19.

Per-Share Figures and Related Ratios

The Per-Share Ratios

In Wall Street, it is customary to sum up the statistical data about a common stock in three salient figures: the earnings per share, the dividend rate, and the price. Although the price per share is a per-share ratio, it is not thought of as such because it is normally obtained directly from the market. Some analyses also include sales, cash flow, book value, and other items on a per-share basis.

Figure 20.1 shows formulas for calculating eight frequently used per-share ratios. These calculations are fairly straightforward. The numerator is whatever the ratio purports to show on a per-share basis. Where that item represents the results for the year, such as earnings, dividends, or cash flow, the denominator is the weighted average number of common shares outstanding. Where the ratio has a balance sheet figure in the numerator, representing the position on a particular date, the denominator is simply the number of common shares outstanding as of that balance sheet date.

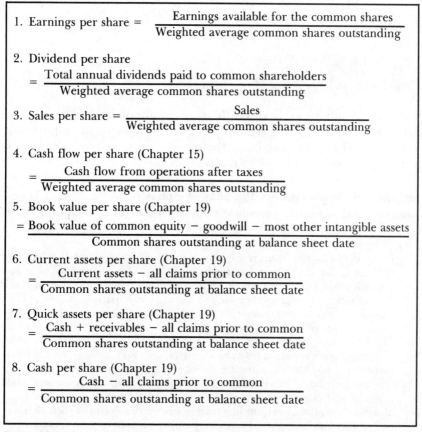

1. Earnings per share = $\dfrac{\text{Earnings available for the common shares}}{\text{Weighted average common shares outstanding}}$

2. Dividend per share
$= \dfrac{\text{Total annual dividends paid to common shareholders}}{\text{Weighted average common shares outstanding}}$

3. Sales per share = $\dfrac{\text{Sales}}{\text{Weighted average common shares outstanding}}$

4. Cash flow per share (Chapter 15)
$= \dfrac{\text{Cash flow from operations after taxes}}{\text{Weighted average common shares outstanding}}$

5. Book value per share (Chapter 19)
$= \dfrac{\text{Book value of common equity} - \text{goodwill} - \text{most other intangible assets}}{\text{Common shares outstanding at balance sheet date}}$

6. Current assets per share (Chapter 19)
$= \dfrac{\text{Current assets} - \text{all claims prior to common}}{\text{Common shares outstanding at balance sheet date}}$

7. Quick assets per share (Chapter 19)
$= \dfrac{\text{Cash} + \text{receivables} - \text{all claims prior to common}}{\text{Common shares outstanding at balance sheet date}}$

8. Cash per share (Chapter 19)
$= \dfrac{\text{Cash} - \text{all claims prior to common}}{\text{Common shares outstanding at balance sheet date}}$

Figure 20.1 Suggested formulas for calculating per-share ratios.

The meaning of each of the per-share ratios should be fairly straightforward, and we shall not dwell on them individually. Experience with calculating and using the ratios, detecting trends and variances, making comparisons, and similar analyses will give the analyst a "feel" for the numbers of the company under study and, over the years, greater depth of understanding of each of the ratios' meanings and limitations.

Per-Share Data Are Defective in Two Ways

Loss of Focus on the Company.   The convenience of per-share earnings figures leads inevitably to their widespread use. They have two drawbacks, however, which make them somewhat of a hindrance to serious analysis. The lesser defect is that they draw the investor's attention away from the enterprise as a whole involving magnitudes of

- Sales
- Profits
- Invested capital
- Aggregate market value of the firm

and concentrate it too much on the single share of stock. The greater defect is that a figure of earnings per share, accepted and emphasized without regard to the details of the income account from which it is derived, may easily give rise to misinformation.

Accountants Warn Against Per-Share Emphasis.   A significant statement on the dangers of a per-share emphasis was made by the Committee on Accounting Procedure of the AICPA:

> In its deliberations concerning the nature and purpose of the income statement, the committee has been mindful of the disposition of even well-informed persons to attach undue importance to a single net income figure and to "earnings per share" shown for a particular year. The committee directs attention to the undesirability in many cases of the dissemination of information in which major prominence is given to a single figure of "net income" or "net income per share." However, if such income data are reported (as in newspapers, investors' services, and annual corporate reports), the committee strongly urges that any determination of "income per share" be related to the amount reported as net income, and that where charges or credits have been excluded from the determination of net income, the corresponding total or per share amount of such charges and credits also be reported separately and simultaneously. In this connection the committee earnestly solicits the cooperation of all organizations, both governmental and private, engaged in the compilation of business earnings statistics from annual reports.[1]

A Technical Problem of Per-Share Figures.   A share is not a constant yardstick. That is, it does not necessarily represent a fixed percentage of the ownership of a company, nor is this year's share the same as last year's

---

[1] AICPA, *Accounting Research Bulletin No. 32*, December 1947, para. 32.

share in economic terms. As a result, a time series of per-share statistics can be subtly misleading if it is not examined thoughtfully and knowledgeably.

No similar objection applies to the use of per-share figures for the cash dividends paid in a given year. This can hardly be open to any misconception. There is frequently some doubt as to what the current dividend rate really is—mainly because of variations between regular and extra disbursements, but that is a difficulty of another sort.

Reported and Restated Earnings per Share

The analyst's intensive study of the income account will lead to occasional *restatement* of the reported profits to reflect the "true" operating earnings. These adjusted earnings will lead to a corresponding adjustment of the per-share earnings. Where the difference between the two amounts is substantial, analysts must point out that their corrected calculation presents a more serviceable picture of the results from operations. In the presentation of tables of historical per-share data, per-share columns can be shown both "As Reported" and "Adjusted," with footnotes explaining the types and amounts of adjustments for each year presented.

Allowances for Changes in Capitalization

Calculations of Earnings per Share (Ratio 1). Ratio 1 in Figure 20.1 shows the common method of calculating earnings per share for purposes of measurement and communication. Some of its complexities are discussed below. Like most other analysts' ratios, the calculation of earnings per share may be affected by what question the analyst is asking. Although the formula given is satisfactory for measuring the past, when estimating future earnings-per-share, the analyst would make the calculation based on the number of shares expected to be outstanding in the year for which the earnings per share estimate is being prepared. This same caveat applies to all other estimates of future per-share numbers.

Splits and Stock Dividends. In dealing with the past record, when data are given on a per-share basis, the analyst must follow the elementary practice of adjusting the figures to reflect any important changes in the capitalization which have taken place during the period. In the simplest case the changes will be only in the number of shares of common stock resulting from stock dividends, splits, etc. All that is necessary, then, is to restate the capitalization throughout the period on the basis of the current number of shares. For example, if the stock has been split 2 for 1, all previous per-share data must be divided by 2. (Some statistical services make such recalculations.)

Rights and Conversions.   When the change in capitalization results from sale of additional stock at a comparatively low price (usually through the exercise of subscription rights or warrants) or to the conversion of senior securities, the adjustment is slightly more difficult. Rights may be to purchase additional shares of the same issue, to purchase convertibles which may be exchanged for shares of the same issue, or to purchase other securities.

A Simple Method of Rights Adjustment.   To make a relatively simple adjustment that is applicable to all of these types of rights, simply obtain the market price of the stock and of the right to which it was entitled immediately after the stock went "ex-rights." The price of the rights is then divided by sum of the rights price plus the ex-rights price of the common stock to get a percentage that is the equivalent of a stock dividend. The per-share figures for all prior periods are then divided by 1 plus the percentage, just as they would be in the case of a stock dividend. This method is the same as used in apportioning the tax cost basis between the stock and the right by the Internal Revenue Service, and therefore historical data are available from the various published tax services, saving the analyst from doing all the individual calculations.[2]

Adjustment for Conversions.   When bonds or preferred stocks have been converted into common, the interest or dividend formerly paid, less any related tax credit, is added back to the earnings. The new earnings figure is then applied to the larger number of shares.

The Problem of Earnings Dilution

Analysis of Earnings Dilution

For the investor, three issues are raised regarding earnings dilution and its effects:

- The probability of dilution
- The timing of dilution
- The degree of dilution

[2]H. Levy and Marshall Sarnat, *Investment and Portolio Analysis,* John Wiley & Sons, New York, 1972, pp. 39–44.

This is an area for specific analysis rather than broad and somewhat arbitrary rules. We will contrast the accounting rules with some hypothetical situations to highlight the complexities.

Reported Earnings per Share

Primary Earnings per Share. The financial statements may present two earnings-per-share numbers; one is called "primary earnings," and the other "fully diluted earnings." The calculations use the concept of *common-stock equivalents.* Warrants and options are always considered to be common-stock equivalents. Convertible securities issued after February 28, 1982, are common-stock equivalents if at the time of issuance the convertible security had a cash yield (coupon divided by issue price) less than two-thirds of a certain interest rate—currently, the yield on Aa-rated corporate bonds. (The previous cash yield test had been two-thirds of the prime rate.) The accounting rule may be applied retroactively to convertibles issued prior to that date. Those convertible issues considered common-stock equivalents are treated as if they had been converted into common stock, with appropriate adjustments for the interest or preferred dividends and tax effects made to the earnings available for the common shares considered then to be outstanding. Warrants and options are assumed to be exercised, and the proceeds of exercise used to purchase treasury stock, thereby reducing the number of shares outstanding. If any exercise or conversion results in an *antidilutive* effect, it is eliminated from the calculation.

The Cash Yield Test Doesn't Work. It is interesting to note that articles in the academic literature have revealed that the cash yield test actually tends to identify the securities that will *not* be converted rather than those that will!

Fully Diluted Earnings per Share—A Valuable Warning. Fully diluted earnings is a calculation of the effects of full exercise and conversion on a worst-case basis, that is, the combination giving the greatest possible earnings dilution. If the number is much below primary earnings per share, it stands as a warning that there *may* be danger of dilution.

The Analytical Problem. One would not exercise a right to buy common stock at $40 a share when it could be bought in the market for $20. However, one may have expectations that the right will someday be exercised. The analyst's first step must be to evaluate the company and its prospects for growth to determine whether the future stock value will be greater than the $40 exercise price before the exercise privilege expires. The right will be exercised only when one of the following occurs:

1. The stock price is so far above $40 that the option value has

essentially disappeared, and the dividend from the common stock exceeds the cost of borrowing the $40 to exercise the right.

2. A valuable option is about to expire.

Estimating the Timing of Dilution. To estimate the timing of exercise of such a right, one must estimate that point in time when the dividend would exceed the cost of borrowing and when the stock would be selling at a sufficient premium over $40 so that the option value had essentially disappeared. As long as there is option value, it is more advantageous to sell the right and purchase stock at the market than to exercise. Thus, the analyst must estimate future price-earnings ratios, growth rates of earnings and dividends, payout ratios, interest rates, and similar elements. In the case of convertibles, the likelihood of the company calling the convertible instrument to force conversion has to enter into this enormous calculus. Two-thirds of a past interest rate is not a likely filter to capture such complexities.

What Gets Diluted—Earnings? Once the timing of the conversion or exercise has been estimated, how should this information be interpreted? What is it that gets diluted? Between today and the date that exercise or conversion is expected to occur, the company will pay dividends to its existing shareholders. Since the shareholders will not be expected to return any of those dividends, that part of earnings is not diluted.

Are Retained Earnings Diluted? Are the *retained earnings* diluted? Retained earnings, of course, become a part of book value. If the book value is projected to be $20 a share at the time of exercise or conversion, then we must compare this $20 per share with the dollars per share that the company will receive. If the company will get more than $20 for each new share created, the book value per share will rise rather than decline, that is, the effect would be antidilutive rather than dilutive. Thus, retained earnings may or may not suffer dilution!

Future Dividends? Perhaps the subsequent stream of dividends will be diluted by exercise or conversion. Dilution of future dividends will depend on the incremental rate of return earned on the funds acquired as a result of exercise or conversion, resulting in a dilutive or antidilutive effect on the stream of future dividends.

What Is the Price of Dilution? Assume, finally, that dilution of earnings per share will be 10 percent, beginning 10 years from now. How much does that change the price of the stock today? Assuming an earnings and dividend growth rate of 8 percent and a discount rate of 15 percent, the present value of the stock would be reduced by about 5 percent: 10 percent $\times (1.08/1.15)^{10} = 5.3$ percent. Thus the analyst must remember two important rules:

1. Dilution may not matter much if it is not going to take place for a long time.

2. Even if one expects immediate exercise or conversion, the results may be either antidilutive or dilutive.

What Steps Should the Analyst Take?

Determine If There Is a Problem—Then Calculate the Magnitude. First, the analyst should always look at the fully diluted earnings per share to see if there is a *potential* problem. If the fully diluted earnings are only 5 or 10 percent below reported earnings, there is no immediate problem. If the dilutive effect is greater, then the analyst must determine the timing, probability, and degree of dilution and discount the effects back to present value for a downward adjustment in the intrinsic value of the stock.

Normally Use Average or Projected Shares Outstanding. For the ordinary calculation of earnings per share, we recommend the use of (1) the weighted average number of shares outstanding for analysis of *past* results or (2) the number of shares expected to be outstanding for *prospective* calculations such as future earnings per share.

Adjust for Expected Conversion, If Significant. If there is an expectation of significant dilution from conversion, the analyst should calculate that per-share dilution on a worst-case basis for those issues which are expected to be transformed into shares of common stock.

Allowance for Outstanding Warrants and Stock Options

Use the Treasury Stock Method. In projecting future earnings, the *treasury stock method* normally should be used for any new funds expected to be received, that is, the cash proceeds of exercise are assumed to be used to purchase shares, and adjustment is made for the elimination of the interest or preferred dividends, with tax effects where appropriate.

Alternatively, Estimate the Return on the Proceeds of Exercise. The alternative to the treasury stock method is to estimate the earnings on the additional capital brought in by exercise of rights, warrants, or options. This is a more complicated procedure, but it may be justified if the expected incremental rate of return on investment is significantly higher or lower than is being earned currently by the company.

Formulas for Valuing Options.   Stock options granted to company employees and others have the same theoretical consequences as the warrants just discussed, but they do not have a market price. Their market price can be estimated using Black and Scholes's model or a variation thereof [3] or the *minimum value model*. The analyst can determine thereby roughly how much the option value exceeds the exercise price. That relationship is useful information on the *probability* of exercise, since a premium over exercise value inhibits exercise.

Minimum Value Formula.   The value of an option is never less than the current price of the underlying stock minus the present value of the exercise price and minus the present value of all dividends to be paid by the exercise date.[4] This is the *minimum value model*, and it is easily implemented by selecting a borrowing rate for discounting purposes, if the analyst has a satisfactory projection of future dividends.

Observe the Premium over Exercise Price.   At the same time, a fair sense of the likelihood of exercise is gained simply by observing the premium, if any, of the exercise price over the market price of the underlying stock. If they are far apart, the price of the stock must rise a great deal to trigger exercise. If they are close, say within 25 percent, applying the treasury stock method will give a quick picture of the seriousness of the dilution threat. Our 5 percent of net income rule should be used to judge whether the *cumulative* dilution effects require an adjustment of per-share numbers.

Conversion of "Class B" into Publicly Held Shares

A considerable number of privately owned companies have gone public through the sale of "Class A" common stock, whereas the interest of the former sole owners has been vested in "Class B" (sometimes plain "common") shares. Though the respective dividend rights of the two classes vary from company to company, they usually give some priority to the public shares. However, in virtually all cases the other issue has the

---

[3]Fischer Black and Myron Scholes, "The Pricing of Options and Corporate Liabilities," *Journal of Political Economy*, vol. 81, no. 3, May–June 1973, pp. 637–654.

[4] William F. Sharpe, *Investments*, Prentice-Hall, Inc., Englewood Cliffs, N.J., 1978, pp. 364–365.

right of conversion—share for share—into Class A stock. Occasionally, the conversion right is immediate and complete, but more often it can be done only in blocks over a period of several years.

In most cases, analysts make their calculations on the basis of full conversion, that is, assuming only one class of stock outstanding. In a few cases, when the analyst must decide about the Class B stock, the assumption would not be helpful.

A General Rule for Participating Interests

In calculating the earnings available for the common, the analyst must give full recognition to the rights of holders of participating issues, whether or not the amounts involved are actually being paid. Various types of bonds and preferred stocks have features which permit them to receive a share of income or a share of dividends paid on the common stock. These issues usually have claims to fixed payments which are made before the calculation of their participating or variable payments. The consequences of their existence are similar to those of convertibles and options, and thus the analyst must make appropriate adjustments to reflect in the per-share figures the claims of these instruments on the residual earnings of the company. In most cases the adjustment by the analyst will result in a hypothetical fixed-income security plus a number of shares of common-stock equivalents. Normally, the fully diluted per-share earnings shown in the annual report will signal the need for investigation of dilution.

Dividends per Share (Ratio 2)

Dividends per share qualifies as a ratio, but it is practically never calculated in any fashion other than to add the total dividends per share paid over the period in question, since dividends are normally declared on a per-share basis. Ratio 2 in Figure 20.1 would require that the shares outstanding be weighted by the dividends paid which is a fairly complicated way of calculating something that is available directly. Naturally, historical dividends per share would be adjusted for splits, stock dividends, rights, and the like.

Sales per Share (Ratio 3)

As shown in Figure 20.1, sales per share are calculated simply by dividing sales by the number of shares outstanding.

Cash Flow per Share (Ratio 4)

Cash flow per share is a useful measure of a company's general ability to leverage itself, to pay dividends, to convert "book earnings" into cash, and to enjoy financial flexibility. However, the cash flow does not "belong" to the equity holders in the same sense that earnings do. It may be committed to debt service or some other prior claim, such as rent. A ratio of "discretionary" cash flow per share requires making provision for these committed cash outflows.

Book Value, Current Assets, Quick Assets, and Cash per Share

Balance sheet data, when calculated on a per-share basis, are always the amounts outstanding as of the balance sheet date divided by the shares outstanding on that date. The common balance sheet per-share ratios are numbered 5 through 8 in Figure 20.1.

Price Ratios

A basic principle of finance is that no investment decisions regarding a common stock can properly be made except in the light of a specific price, which is usually the current market but may be some anticipated or calculated figure. The security analyst should compare the price with earnings, dividends, asset value, and—for a valuable additional insight—sales. Thus, the price ratios in Figure 20.2 are as follows:

Ratio 9 —price-earnings ratio

Ratio 10—earnings yield (the reciprocal of the price-earnings ratio)

Ratio 11—dividend yield

Ratio 12—sales per dollar of common, at market

Ratio 13—price-to-book value

These ratios are ordinarily calculated on the basis of the last full year's results or the latest balance sheet. However, the earnings may be an average for some suitable period of years. The earnings used for a price-earnings ratio may be for the trailing 12 months, the current fiscal year, or an estimate of the forthcoming 12 months. Some brokerage house letters give two price-earnings ratios, one using estimated current fiscal year earnings and the second using the ratio to the subsequent fiscal year's estimated earnings. One investment service publishes price-earnings ratios based on the latest three quarters of reported earnings plus an estimate of the earnings for the first unreported quarter. Since year-to-year earnings changes can be quite large, it is important that the earnings be identified as to the time period used and as to whether the figures are actual or estimated. The price may be a recent price, end-of-period, an average, anticipated, or a calculated price. These same problems can apply to other price ratios, and therefore the analyst must be aware what price and time period are being combined in any ratio. The analyst preparing a written report should take care that all ratios are properly explained, either in the text or in footnotes.

---

9. Price-earnings ratio (Chapter 19) = $\dfrac{\text{Price per share}}{\text{Earnings per share}}$

10. Earnings yield = $\dfrac{\text{Earnings per share}}{\text{Price per share}}$

11. Dividend yield = $\dfrac{\text{Dividend per share}}{\text{Price per share}}$

12. Sales per dollar of common at market value

$= \dfrac{\text{Sales}}{\text{Weighted average shares outstanding} \times \text{stock price}}$

13. Price-to-book value = $\dfrac{\text{Price per share}}{\text{Book value per share}}$

Figure 20.2 Suggested formulas for calculating price ratios.

Price-Earnings Ratios

Market Ratios and Multipliers

The main purpose of calculating earnings per share, aside from indicating dividend protection, is to permit a ready comparison with the current market price of the stock. The resultant *price-earnings ratio*, or *P/E*, is a concept that the working analyst will have to deal with extensively. The question of what price-earnings ratios are, and what determines them, must now be considered. Our treatment of the subject will fall into two parts. The first deals with the actual behavior of the market, that is, of investors and speculators, with respect to price-earnings ratios. The second part, reserved for a later chapter on valuation methods, will explore what the price-earnings ratio or multiplier *should be*.

Confusion Over Earnings Used

The statement that a common stock is selling at "N times earnings" is not without some ambiguity. The earnings referred to may be from the past year, from the current year, partly estimated, or next year's earnings, or even from the latest three months multiplied by 4. The phrase is sometimes amplified to read "N times anticipated earnings" for a stated period in the future, or "N times average earnings" for a stated period in the past, or even "N times trailing 12-months earnings." For the most part, however, the concept of the price-earnings ratio is applied to what is considered a current or quite recent full year's figure.

Diversity of P/E Ratios

When faced with a large assortment of price-earnings ratios, the analyst is likely to be bewildered by their diversity and inconsistency. Stock prices fluctuate over a wide range within a single year, which means that their ratios will vary correspondingly in that year. The average annual ratio for nearly every stock is likely to differ widely from one year to another. Finally, the ratios of different stocks when observed at the same moment cover a wide range. For example, in February 1987, Wheeling-Pittsburgh Steel sold as low as 1.3 times and International Banknote as high as 85 times the then current estimates by Value Line of earnings for the year ending March 1987. Surely, only price divided by normal earnings has any meaning or constancy.

Are There Any Understandable Patterns?

It seems almost impossible to make any degree of order out of this chaos. Nevertheless, one may discern some fairly well-defined and not irrational patterns in the price-earnings ratios, when they are viewed from the proper vantage. An effective method is comparing average price over a representative period of years with the average earnings during the same time. In Table 20.1 we show the resultant ratios for each of the 30 stocks in the Dow-Jones industrial average, taking the two 5-year periods, 1975 to 1979 and 1980 to 1984, and 1985.

Quality of Earnings.   For the vast majority of common stocks, the average relationship between price and earnings—as shown by this kind of computation—reflects the views of investors and speculators as to the quality and growth of the issue. A strong, successful, and promising company usually sells at a higher multiplier of current or average earnings than one that is less strong, less successful, and less promising.

Table 20.1. Average Earnings per Share, Prices, and Price-Earnings Ratios of Individual Stocks Constituting Dow-Jones Industrial Average (1975–1979, 1980–1984, and 1985)

Common stock*	1975 to 1979 Average			1980 to 1984 Average			1985		
	Earn- ings	Mean price**	Price- earn- ings	Earn- ings	Mean price	Price- Earn- ings	Earn- ings	Mean price	Price Earn- ings
Allied-Signal	$2.41	$33.9	14.1×	$4.88	$30.9	6.3×	$3.40	$41.0	12.1×
Aluminum Co.	3.48	23.8	6.8	3.18	33.6	10.6	1.32	35.3	26.7
American Can	5.51	36.2	6.6	3.50	37.4	10.7	5.02	56.6	11.3
American Express	1.79	17.7	9.9	2.75	27.3	9.9	3.55	45.5	12.8
American T & T	na†	na	na	na	na	na	1.43	22.2	15.5
Bethlehem Steel	2.12	25.6	12.1	(2.53)	22.9	nmf ‡	(2.45)	16.8	nmf
Chevron	3.26	19.9	6.1	5.62	38.1	6.8	4.19	35.1	8.4
Du Pont	4.08	41.1	10.1	4.98	43.2	8.7	5.04	58.5	11.6
Eastman Kodak	3.15	50.0	15.9	4.14	48.1	11.6	1.46	47.2	32.3
Exxon	3.29	24.3	7.4	6.06	34.8	5.7	7.43	50.2	6.8
General Electric	2.37	25.0	10.5	4.09	40.4	9.9	5.13	64.8	12.6
General Motors	8.86	60.3	6.8	5.14	56.9	11.1	12.28	75.2	6.1
Goodyear	2.59	19.0	7.3	3.28	23.8	7.3	2.81	28.1	10.0
Inco	1.75	23.4	13.4	(2.10)	17.0	nmf	0.28	12.9	46.1
IBM	4.48	63.5	14.2	7.79	85.1	10.9	10.67	138.1	12.9
International Paper	6.28	51.0	8.1	5.28	46.3	8.8	1.61	51.1	31.7
McDonald's	1.51	21.8	14.4	3.38	34.6	10.2	4.99	66.3	13.3
Merck	1.94	33.0	17.0	2.93	41.9	14.3	3.79	57.5	15.2
Minnesota M&M	3.84	55.5	14.5	5.77	66.8	11.6	6.02	82.6	13.7
Navistar	7.04	32.1	4.6	(13.48)	14.3	nmf	0.77	15.9	20.6
Owens-Illinois	3.56	23.2	6.5	3.76	29.6	7.9	5.23	46.9	9.0
Philip Morris	1.43	15.1	10.6	3.13	28.0	8.9	5.08	25.6	5.0
Procter & Gamble	2.77	42.7	15.4	4.57	46.6	10.2	3.80	61.1	16.1
Sears. Roebuck	2.38	28.1	11.8	2.86	26.0	9.1	3.53	36.0	10.2
Texaco	3.86	26.4	6.8	6.28	37.3	5.9	4.62	33.7	7.3
Union Carbide	2.27	16.6	7.3	2.15	17.3	8.0	.36	18.2	50.6
United Technolo- gies	2.13	17.4	8.2	3.63	28.4	7.8	4.58	40.5	8.8
U.S. Steel	2.60	34.8	13.4	2.01	25.3	12.6	1.71	28.7	16.8
Westinghouse Electric	1.50	9.1	6.1	2.61	18.1	6.9	4.30	36.5	8.5
Woolworth	2.36	10.8	4.6	1.88	13.6	7.2	2.75	24.8	9.0

*Adjusted for splits and stock dividends through 1985.
**Average of annual mean prices.
†na: Not available on a comparable basis.
‡nmf: Not a meaningful figure.

Certain Key Influences of P/E. The chief analytical elements governing the price-earnings ratio include

1. Those factors that are fully reflected in the financial data (tangible factors):

   - Growth of earnings and sales in the past
   - Profitability—rate of return on invested capital
   - Stability of past earnings
   - Dividend rate and record
   - Financial strength or credit standing

2. Those factors that are reflected to an indefinite extent in the data (intangible factors):

   - Quality of management
   - Nature and prospects of the industry
   - Competitive position and individual prospects of the company

The Intangibles Influence the Tangible Record. The five tangible factors may be studied by the analyst in the financial statements. The three intangibles do not, of course, admit of the same type of definite, quantitative calculation. Bear in mind that, typically, the incalculable factors have already exerted a strong influence on the reported results. In other words, the figures themselves will show, fairly clearly and comprehensively, how good a business is and how well the company is managed, unless the incumbent management has recently taken over or major new developments in the industry or in the concern make the past results irrelevant to the future. In the early stages of a highly dynamic industry—electronics, communication, semiconductors, computers, genetic engineering, drugs—expectations of future profits are often divorced completely from the actual accomplishments of the past. But those are not the usual cases.

Table 20.1 demonstrates another influence—the *Molodovsky effect.*[5] This is the tendency of a company suffering temporarily depressed earnings to sell at a high price-earnings ratio. The 1985 price-earnings ratios of Aluminum Company, Eastman Kodak, Inc., International Paper, Union Carbide, and Inco may reflect what the market perceives as a nontypical denominator. A casual scanning of the 1985 price-earnings ratios will show that some are two or more times the price-earnings ratios that prevailed in the 1980 to 1984 period. In fact, they look like the highly optimistic price-earnings ratios that are reserved for very high quality fast-growing companies. Examination of the particular companies sug-

---

[5]Nicholas Molodovsky, "A Theory of Price-Earnings Ratios," *Financial Analysts Journal*, November 1953, pp. 65–80.

gests that most of them are not growth stocks, and the quality of some is not especially high. Beware of using the price-earnings ratio to measure cheapness or dearness of the stock market. The *average* price-earnings ratio in 1985 is 75 percent higher than that of the 1980 to 1984 period, but a scanning of the individual stocks shows that the majority are up only 30 percent or thereabouts. The median of 12.6 times earnings in 1985 would probably give a much better indication of the cheapness or dearness of the market as a whole, and most of the high price-earnings ratio examples in 1985 (but not in the earlier periods) are probably results of the Molodovsky effect.

Key Ratios Pertaining to Tangible Factors

The tangible factors affecting the quality of a company may be measured by the use of key ratios and other calculations. In addition to the per-share and price ratios, five other groups of ratios give insight into the past record or "tangible factors":

Profitability ratios: margins and activity ratios

Growth rate

Stability ratios

Payout ratio (dividend policy)

Credit ratios

The previous section of this chapter discussed some of the shortcomings of per-share ratios, particularly distraction from analysis of the business as a whole. The best discipline is to focus on price and per-share data *last*, after a complete analysis of the above five groups of ratios. These five groups measure the performance and financial strength of the enterprise apart from the market valuation. Let us first discuss these various ratios in their proper sequence and then illustrate their use by applying some of them to a pair of chemical companies in Chapter 21 and to the grocery industry in Chapter 22.

Profitability Ratios

Management's Ability to Use Capital

The broadest measure of profitability is the ratio to total capital of the *final* net profit available for capital funds. The final net profit for capital reflects all recurrent items of profit and loss, including income tax, without deducting interest on funded debt and lease obligations, because interest is a part of return. The fundamental merit of the return-on-invested-capital ratio is that it measures the *basic* or overall performance of a business in terms of the total funds provided by all investors rather than a single class. The ratio is a measure of management's ability to employ assets profitably, independent of the method of funding the assets. The ratio can also be calculated *before income taxes*, which will provide a measure of profitability that is independent of both funding and how the company is taxed. The latter calculation is helpful in certain intercompany comparisons.

Several Useful Variations.   As a group, profitability ratios are perhaps security analysts' most powerful tools. They are calculated in a variety of ways, each telling a slightly different story from a slightly different perspective. Among these ratios are return on:

- Total assets
- Capital (variously defined)
- Long-term investment
- Equity

The latter may be the return on book equity, however stated in the accounts, or the return on net tangible assets attributed to the shareholders—the recommended method. In all cases, the return (numerator) must be consistent with the defined capital (denominator). For example, if short-term borrowings are excluded from capital, their interest should be excluded from return.

Average Capital or Beginning Capital.   A common error is to divide the return by capital as of the end of the period. For example, return on equity might be calculated, incorrectly, as the earnings for the year divided by the book value at the end of the year. The problem is that the capital referred to as "book value" was not at work either at the beginning of the year or throughout the year. It was simply the amount that had been accumulated or remained at the end of the year. The acceptable methods are return divided by (1) the average capital for the year (return on the average capital at work) or (2) the capital that existed at the beginning of the year (return on the beginning investment). Either figure is acceptable for analytical purposes, but the method should be identified and used consistently in comparisons. The first method has the advantage when capital has been infused or extinguished during the year. The end-of-year problem exists regardless of which profitability ratio is being calculated, so the above comments apply equally to return on assets, return on total capital, return on long-term capital, and others.

Return on Capital (Ratio 14). The most comprehensive gauge of the success of an enterprise is the percentage earned on invested capital (ratio 14 in Figure 20.3). The terms *invested capital, capital funds,* and *total capital* may be used interchangeably. Short-term borrowings, such as bank loans and commercial paper, and the deferred tax liability are included in the capital at work. Practice varies on the matter of operating leases, but we prefer to include them in invested capital. In theory, current accrued payables that are not interest bearing should be excluded because their interest component is not observable. As a practical matter, it is often more convenient to include them by calculating the return on (total) tangible assets, including the leased assets under operating leases. Either ratio, if consistently applied, is useful and provides comparability.

Adjustments. Certain adjustments should be made to the equity capital figure. In the case of companies that use LIFO inventory accounting, the LIFO reserve should be added back to equity. Goodwill and any other intangible assets which lack a going market price or an identifiable stream of revenues should be subtracted from the equity capital. Deferred taxes should be considered equity in return on equity calculations (but as debt when calculating capital ratios or book value per common share). The present value of operating leases should be inserted into the balance sheet both as an asset and a liability. This liability, of course, would be part of total capital but not, of course, of equity capital. The liability for other postemployment benefits should be recognized as additional debt, and equity should be reduced by that amount. Other hidden assets and liabilities may need similar treatment. Preferred stock dividend arrearages should be shown either as a liability or as an increase in the preferred stock claim, and an equal amount must be deducted from the common stock equity.

Our formula for the return on capital calculates the denominator from the asset side by subtracting from total assets the goodwill and any intangible assets that need removal, adding an asset for the asset leased under operating leases, and reduces the total by accrued payables. Accrued payables are viewed as current liabilities that do not bear interest, in contrast to bank loans, commercial paper, notes payable, and the like. The denominator could be constructed as easily from the right side of the balance sheet. Judgment may direct the analyst to make various other adjustments to the capital accounts. Similarly, adjustments may be made to the numerator of the equation. For example, if goodwill and other intangibles have been deducted from equity, their amortization, write-offs, and tax effects should be eliminated from earnings. If the present value of operating leases is included in the capital in the denominator, then the numerator must contain the appropriate interest component, tax adjusted, which is a portion of the rental paid.

Ordinarily, the return on capital should be calculated using the average capital at work during the year, which is often approximated by averaging the beginning and ending amounts of capital. Alternatively, the interim financial statements may be included in the average.

To make companies comparable, reduce the interest expense in the numerator by the appropriate income tax rate. This treats the interest as if it were not tax deductible, or the same as the earnings for the common, preferred stock or minority interest. Thus, companies with significantly different capital structures can be compared on a common basis in terms of the profitability of their capital. It also is helpful in presenting the trend of profitability over time for a company whose capital structure changed significantly.

Return on Capital—Indirect Calculation.   Return on capital may be either computed directly as shown in Figure 20.3, ratio 14, or as the product of capital turnover (ratio 15) times earnings margin (ratio 16).

Capital Turnover—An Activity Ratio (Ratio 15).   Capital turnover (ratio 15) is one of a family of ratios that is sometimes called "activity ratios" or "turnover ratios." These ratios are normally calculated as sales divided by the item mentioned. They often provide the earliest signs of change in a company and demand an explanation. This family includes:

- Total capital turnover (ratio 15)
- Asset turnover
- Inventory turnover (ratio 38)
- Equity turnover
- Plant turnover
- Accounts receivable turnover (ratio 39)
- Working capital turnover

Earnings Margin (Ratio 16).   Note that the *earnings margin* in ratio 16 is not the same as *margin of profit* as it is ordinarily used in accounting. The latter phrase refers to the direct operating results only and is figured before the income tax deduction and before nonoperating income and

---

14. Return on capital
$$= \frac{\text{Net income} + \text{minority interest} + \text{tax-adjusted interest}}{\text{Tangible assets} - \text{short-term accrued payables}}$$

15. Capital turnover $= \dfrac{\text{Sales}}{\text{Tangible assets} - \text{short-term accrued payables}}$

16. Earnings margin
$$= \frac{\text{Net income} + \text{minority interest} + \text{tax-adjusted interest}}{\text{Sales}}$$

17. Return on capital before depreciation
$$= \frac{\text{Net income} + \text{minority interest} + \text{tax-adjusted interest} + \text{depreciation}}{\text{Tangible assets} - \text{short-term accrued payables}}$$

18. Return on common equity
$$= \frac{\text{Net income} - \text{preferred dividend requirements}}{\text{Common equity} - \text{goodwill} - \text{most intangibles} + \text{deferred tax liability}}$$

Figure 20.3 Suggested formulas for calculating profitability ratios.

charges. Our figure is the ratio to sales of the *final* net profit and tax-adjusted interest available for the capital funds.

Turnover and Margin and Return on Capital. The turnover of capital and other activity ratios are very sensitive to changes in operations and the financial structure of a corporation. Examination of ratios 15 and 16 may offer a ready explanation for a change in the return on capital and an incentive for further investigation of the specific causes of the change.

Allowing for Differences in Depreciation Policy. The importance of depreciation has increased significantly in the postwar period, and at the same time marked differences in depreciation policies exist among companies. (See Chapter 14.) Thus, a comparative analysis of a number of corporations within an industry should consider the depreciation factor. This may be done in a number of ways, such as the ratios of depreciation to sales or to gross plant. In Table 14.4 of Chapter 14 an example of the latter sort of adjustment to the depreciation expense was shown for selected airline companies.

Return on Capital before Depreciation (Ratio 17). Return on capital before depreciation (ratio 17 in Figure 20.3) simply compares companies' returns on capital after eliminating the effects of different depreciation policies. Several warnings are in order in the use of this ratio. First, it represents neither a calculation of true return nor of cash flow. It is merely a ranking system that eliminates the effects of differences in depreciation. An assumption that the depreciation should be the same, relative to capital, is inherent in the ratio. Therefore, its use in comparing companies that are not relatively homogeneous is potentially misleading.

Return on Common Equity (Ratio 18).   The second most significant profitability ratio to investors is return on equity—ratio 18. Its fascination is proportional to the market's preference for common stocks over fixed-income securities. However, it is an important ratio with respect to management's use of the common stockholder's capital and the ability of management to leverage the rate of return on equity by incurring debt. The injection of financial leverage has the undesirable effect of increasing the variability of earnings for the common stock. Analysts use the trade-off between higher earnings and the increased variability of earnings to determine whether management has chosen the optimum amount of financial leverage.

Deferred Taxes as Equity Capital.   An area of some potential controversy is our decision to include the deferred income tax liability as a source of capital—particularly of equity capital. Although it is not "invested" capital in the usual sense, there is little doubt that when Congress creates rules that defer the payment of income taxes to a later date, the effect is the same as giving the company an interest-free loan. The absence of any capital cost (interest) causes the profits of using the assets funded by that loan to flow directly to pre-tax income, so the return on that capital is ultimately reflected as a part of the return on equity. Some companies have very large deferred income tax liabilities. For example, Exxon had over $11 billon of deferred tax liabilities at the end of 1985. Other companies have only trivial amounts. To compare Exxon's return on equity with a company that has no deferred tax liability or even has only deferred tax assets, would lead to an overly favorable assessment of the relative efficiency of Exxon's use of equity capital in comparison to the other company. Thus, to exclude the deferred tax liability would substantially destroy the comparability of return on equity calculations and convey a misleading impression to the user of such a ratio.

Are Deferred Taxes Earnings?   What is considerably more controversial in our view is whether changes in the deferred tax liability represent the equivalent of gains or losses that should be included in the numerator of the return on equity equation. The arguments for and against seem somewhat reasonably balanced, and the burden of that decision is placed upon the reader.

Other Quasi-Equity Items. Some companies have a significant amount of long-term liabilities that do not have financing characteristics and may be thought of in the same fashion as deferred taxes—that is, capital that is working essentially for the common shareholder. Most items that would qualify for that view are really deferred income and deferred gains. Unlike a true liability, these will not require a cash outflow. They are simply credits which accrual accounting is not yet ready to call income or gain. The best treatment is a matter for the individual analyst's judgment, since the choice of an appropriate method is a matter of some controversy. To think symmetrically, the issue should also arise on deferred losses which are carried as assets. No benefit will ever arise from them, and it can be argued that deferred losses should be subtracted from equity.

Profitability for Periods and for Individual Years. The profitability ratios should be examined in terms of both period averages and individual years. Thus the year-by-year fluctuations as well as the level of performance over a span of time may be appraised.

Growth Rates, Stability, and the Payout Ratio

Growth Rates

Ratios and Compound Annual Rates. The figures most frequently compared over time for company growth rates are sales, total return and earnings per share (ratios 19 through 21 in Figure 20.4). Although our suggested ratios merely compare levels, expressed as a percentage, many analysts express growth in compound annual growth rates by determining the number of years between the midpoint of the base period and the midpoint of the final period and using that as the exponent by which to reduce the overall change into an annual rate of change.

Many other growth rates are calculated by analysts, using both gross and per-share figures. They include:

- Cash flow
- Dividends
- Book value
- Plant account
- Physical data (such as units produced or capacity)
- Retained return on equity (a proxy for growth)

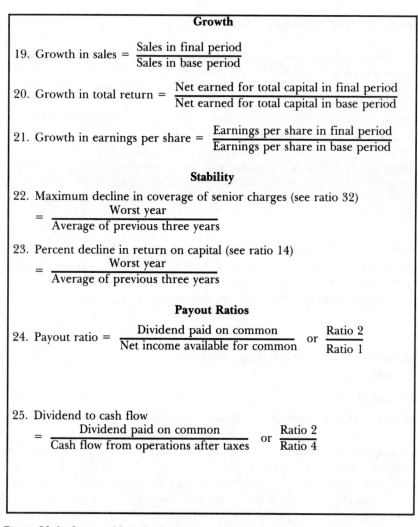

Figure 20.4 Suggested formulas for calculating growth, stability, and payout ratios.

Smoothing Cyclical Effects. The infrequency of *major* cycles since 1949 has often ruled out the smoothing of cyclical effects for analytical work. Instead the analysts have had to make trend comparisons over some conveniently long period, say 10 years. To diminish the effect of single-year variations we recommend that such a comparison be made between several-year averages, for example, 1983 to 1987 versus 1973 to 1977. Another technique uses statistical regression over time to obtain the trend.

Inflationary Growth.   The analyst must consider the source of growth and not be misled by growth caused partly by inflation. A company that shows annual sales growth of 5 percent in an era of 7 percent inflation is not even keeping up with inflation, and the analyst must determine whether the shortfall is due to a decline in units, a squeeze on profit margins, or other specific causes.

Industry Growth Rates.   The annual growth rates of various industries may be compared by this method, using a suitable group of companies as a sample of each industry. One difficulty that arises occasionally is the vast difference in size between the largest one, two, or three companies in an industry where the rest of the participants are relatively small. To get a better picture of the various growth opportunities for the smaller companies in the industry, create growth indices for each company and then average the growth indices so as to give equal weight to all companies. This may reveal that the significant growth opportunities that exist for some of the smaller companies are not large enough markets to make much impact on one of the larger companies. In other cases, where the industry's products are more homogeneous, the analyst may want the growth rate to be weighted by the relative size of the companies—a more conventional approach. Again, we have an example of devising a method of calculation that may depart from custom or the rules, but the analyst does so to find the right answer to the question at hand.

Stability

Treatment of an Earnings Decline.   The analyst can develop arithmetical indexes of the stability of earnings over a given period of years. For instance, select the lowest net income in, say, a 5- or 10-year period and calculate the ratio to the average of the preceding 3 years, as in ratio 22. This will indicate how serious was the effect of any temporary setback. A cumulative decline over several years also could be measured against a previous average period. We believe the effect of a "poor year" on earnings should always be measured against some preceding period and not against an average that includes subsequent years. If the later years show a large increase in profits, they (if used in such an average) would make the earnings appear arithmetically unstable, when in fact they are forging ahead.

Cyclical versus Secular Declines.   The last four decades have not seen a year of general business recession sufficiently marked to test out the inherent stability of all enterprises. In no year-to-year comparison did corporate profits decline as much as 25 percent, although some industries may have had severe changes in profitability. In some instances, a decline represents a drop from unusually high levels; in other instances, it represents a true business cycle decline in demand.

Thus in some companies and industries the postwar fluctuations have supplied a reasonably good test of the relative soundness or competitive position of the individual firm. However, for some companies (and industries) the analyst would need to go too far back in time for a comparable test. The remoteness of figures substantially reduces their usefulness, but in some cases it may not have been destroyed.

Stability and Growth.   Over short periods, say five or six years, stability may be measured by using the standard deviation, but this measure is not satisfactory when growth is rapid. In that case, departures from the trend line can be measured statistically or studied visually on log-linear graph paper.

Safety Considerations (Ratios 22 and 23).   Earning stability plays a large part in determining the quality of a bond or preferred stock. Simply calculate the *minimum* coverage of charges or of prior charges and preferred dividends shown during a substantial number of years in the past. It may be useful to test stability of coverage on a pro forma basis, as if the company had a similar capital structure and level of interest rates to those prevailing now.

In many cases the *minimum dividend* paid on the common stock over, say, a 10-year period will give a valuable clue to inherent stability as well as to management's attitude on this factor—of major importance for all but the acknowledged growth companies. (The dividend paid by a growth company in the past may have little bearing on minimum dividend expectations in the future or other determinants of its value.) Consequently, for the nongrowth company we suggest only two standard measurements of stability:

Maximum decline in coverage of senior charges (ratio 22)

Maximum decline in earnings rate on total capital (ratio 23)

Ratios 22 and 23 may be supplemented by measuring the maximum decline in the return earned on common-stock capital and in per-share earnings.

Payout Ratios (Ratio 24)

The percentage of available earnings paid out in common dividends often has a most important effect upon the market's attitude toward those issues not in the growth category. The payout of earnings may be calculated, quite simply, by dividing the earnings into the dividend (ratio 24 in Figure 20.4).

For issues paying stock dividends as well as cash, only the cash dividend should be included in the calculation of payout ratios. Stock dividends are like stock splits—the investor receives nothing that was not already owned, and the company gives up nothing of value. Some bookkeeping entries are made, and some paper is mailed out, but nothing of economic significance occurs.

Payout of Cash Flow (Ratio 25)

The percentage of cash flow paid out in dividends is a more stable number than the ratio of dividends to earnings. Thus, the past relationship of dividends to cash flow (ratio 25) is more useful in estimating future dividends than the conventional payout ratio (ratio 24).

Credit Ratios

Credit ratios (Figure 20.5) are a diverse group which attempt to capture liquidity, financial flexibility, capital structure, ability to service debt, cash-generating characteristics, and other credit tests.

The Current, Quick, and Cash Ratios (Ratios 26–28)

The significance of these ratios, along with the cash ratio (ratios 26 to 28) was discussed in Chapter 19, under "Working-Capital Position."

Equity Ratio (Ratio 29)

The surplus of assets over the claims of senior securities is indicated by the equity ratio—ratio 29. Essentially the same information is provided in two other ratios. One is the debt-to-equity ratio, also sometimes called the debt ratio. However, the term *debt ratio* is also frequently used for the ratio of debt to total capital. Since all three provide essentially the same information, the analyst or the investment organization should select a standard method and stick to it, with a footnote explanation of the ratio used for the benefit of outsiders and newcomers who might read the analyst's report. Note that deferred taxes are treated as debt in this calculation.

26. Current ratio (Chapter 19) $= \dfrac{\text{Current assets}}{\text{Current liabilities}}$

27. Quick ratio (Chapter 19) $= \dfrac{\text{Current assets } - \text{ inventories}}{\text{Current liabilities}}$

28. Cash ratio (Chapter 19) $= \dfrac{\text{Cash items}}{\text{Current liabilities}}$

29. Equity ratio $= \dfrac{\text{Common equity at book value}}{\text{Tangible assets } - \text{ accrued payables}}$

30. Equity ratio at market $= \dfrac{\text{Common equity at market value}}{\text{Tangible assets } - \text{ accrued payables}}$

31. Coverage of senior charges $= \dfrac{\text{Pretax earned for capital}}{\text{Senior charges}}$

32. Cash flow coverage of senior charges
$$= \dfrac{\text{Cash flow from operations after taxes } + \text{ senior charges}}{\text{Senior charges}}$$

33. Cash flow to total capital
$$= \dfrac{\text{Cash flow from operations after taxes } + \text{ tax-adjusted interest}}{\text{Tangible assets } - \text{ accrued payables}}$$

34. Total debt service coverage
$$= \dfrac{\text{Cash flow from operations after taxes } + \text{ rentals } + \text{ tax-adjusted interest}}{\text{Interest } + \text{ rent } + \text{ current maturities } + \text{ sinking fund payments}}$$

35. Defensive interval (days)
$$= \dfrac{(\text{Cash } + \text{ receivables}) \times 365}{\text{Total operating expenses } - \text{ depreciation } - \text{ other noncash charges}}$$

Figure 20.5 Suggested formulas for calculating credit ratios.

Equity Ratio at Market (Ratio 30)

The equity ratio at market (ratio 30) is calculated by dividing the total capital fund, at book figure, into the common stock component thereof at market value. That is, the common stock component is calculated as the number of shares outstanding multiplied by the price per share. An alternative method uses the same denominator but averages the market value of the equity, generally over a five-year period. The equity ratio at market indicates the market's view of the goodwill of the company. If the market value of the equity is far above book value, the company apparently could sell additional stock for purposes of reducing debt and not dilute the book value per share. Although investors would rather look to cash flows for payments on fixed-income securities, they may find it reassuring that the equity market offers another method of payment. They will feel less reassured when the market prices the company's asset value lower than the figures on the company's books.

Coverage of Senior Charges (Ratio 31)

Senior charges are defined most commonly as interest expense. The growth of leasing has seen the interest component of capital leases included in the definition, and interest on operating leases, total rentals, and preferred dividends may be included under some definitions.

The coverage of senior charges (ratio 31) is found by dividing the balance available for senior charges by the senior charges, which may be defined as some combination of the following:

- Interest on short- and long-term debt, including capital leases
- Interest expenses plus an interest component for operating leases
- Interest expense on short- and long-term debt plus rentals on both capital and operating leases
- Total fixed charges, rentals, and preferred dividends

Separate ratios may be computed for each type of coverage. These are key figures in determining the quality of a bond or preferred-stock issue. Their calculation and significance will be discussed in detail in Chapters 23 and 24. The quality of a common stock, and its resultant price-earnings ratio, are also influenced strongly by the margin of safety shown for the above senior charges.

It is our recommendation that the analyst define fixed charges to include interest and all rentals but not the preferred dividend requirements when the safety of the interest-bearing debt or the leases is a concern. However, if the issue is the safety of the preferred stock, then the calculation should include all the prior charges, including the preferred dividend. This latter definition is also desirable from the viewpoint of common-stock analysis, since all those claimants have a prior position over the common. The amount available for senior charges includes all the senior charges. For example, if the senior charges include rentals, then rentals should also be included in the numerator.

Most financial discussions assume that a company's credit indexes cannot be too strong. This plausible view ignores some real problems relating to the most advantageous corporate policies from the standpoint of its equity owners—the common stockholders. A company may have more cash than it needs, making for an impressive working-capital ratio and for excellent credit but maybe signifying a relatively unprofitable or inefficient use of the stockholders' capital.

Similarly, the best capital structure, in terms purely of credit standing and financial strength, includes no senior securities, that is, the "common-stock ratio" is 100 percent. However, the implication here is that no company should ever willingly issue bonds or preferred stock. This simply is not true. (See Chapter 33 for discussion of the optimal capital structure.)

Cash Flow to Senior Charges (Ratio 32)

Chapter 15 discussed methods of calculating cash flow. For purposes of calculating the relationship of cash flow to senior charges (ratio 32), the numerator should be the cash flow from operations less taxes paid with tax-adjusted interest added back.

Cash Flow to Total Capital (Ratio 33)

Cash flow to capital (ratio 33) focuses on the rate at which capital replenishes itself. If the ratio is 0.25, in theory at least, the company sees its capital in the form of cash every four years. In that sense, the figure is somewhat like an activity ratio, and, in every sense, the higher the number the better.

Total Debt-Service Coverage (Ratio 34)

The numerator of debt-service coverage (ratio 34) is the after-tax cash flow plus rentals and tax-adjusted interest. The denominator is the total debt-service requirements. These requirements include all interest, rent, current maturities of debt, and mandatory sinking fund payments. If the company is being studied from the viewpoint of the preferred stock, the preferred dividend requirements and sinking funds would be included with the senior securities' requirements. In general, bank credit officers consider the cash flow coverage of total debt service requirements to be more important than the more conventional coverage calculations that address only interest and rent.

Defensive Interval (Days) (Ratio 35)

The defensive interval (ratio 35) calculates the number of days of operating expenses that could be paid with only the currently available quick assets. The operating expenses should exclude depreciation and other noncash charges. This ratio is another worst-case test, since it assumes that operations continue at the current level, that no revenues come in, and that the only sources of payment of these out-of-pocket operating expenses are present holdings of cash and equivalent and the proceeds of collecting the accounts receivable. The ratio is best used as a series over time for an individual company and for comparing companies in the same industry.

Other Ratios

A few additional ratios of possible interest are shown in Figure 20.6. The ratio of depreciation to sales and of depreciation to gross plant, property, and equipment (ratios 36 and 37) are used primarily to compare companies in the same industry and with substantially similar property accounts. The ratios are designed to reveal the liberalism of or conservatism of depreciation policies, and in some cases to make adjustments to put the compared companies on essentially the same depreciation basis. In the case of capital intensive companies, depreciation may be a very large portion of total expenses. What seems a modest shift in the estimated useful lives may result in a significant shift in reported net income.

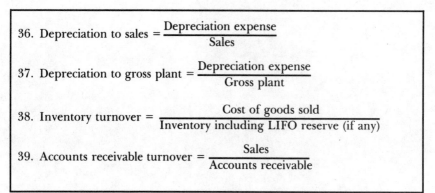

$$36. \text{ Depreciation to sales} = \frac{\text{Depreciation expense}}{\text{Sales}}$$

$$37. \text{ Depreciation to gross plant} = \frac{\text{Depreciation expense}}{\text{Gross plant}}$$

$$38. \text{ Inventory turnover} = \frac{\text{Cost of goods sold}}{\text{Inventory including LIFO reserve (if any)}}$$

$$39. \text{ Accounts receivable turnover} = \frac{\text{Sales}}{\text{Accounts receivable}}$$

Figure 20.6 Suggested formulas for calculating other ratios.

Inventory turnover (ratio 38) is simply the ratio of cost of goods sold to inventory, with the latter including the LIFO reserve if the company is on that basis. The resulting number shows the number of times the *units* of inventory are "turned over"—that is, sold and then replenished. A popular variation is to use the reciprocal of the ratio multiplied by 365 days. In that case, the inventory on hand is referred to as so many "days" of inventory.

Accounts receivable turnover (ratio 39) is simply the ratio of sales to accounts receivable and is sometimes a useful warning of credit or collection problems. Accounts receivable turnover is also sometimes expressed in days.

The ratios given in this chapter are the common garden varieties that will serve most of the analyst's needs. In a given analysis, the analyst will use only some of them. At times the analyst will run across printouts that may include a hundred or more general purpose ratios. Specialized industry ratios must bring the total available to more than a thousand, with perhaps that many in regulated industries alone (banks, insurance, railroads, utilities, airlines, etc.). Without a sense of perspective, an analyst can drown in ratios and in information overload. We suggest that the analyst stay largely within the 39 ratios suggested here, plus the ratios for senior securities in Chapters 23 and 24. Yet, at times the analyst will find or invent a ratio that gives just the exact answer needed for an important question. The area is one for judgment with an eye on consistency and comparability.

21
Key Ratios in Company Comparisons

Calculation of Key Ratios for Two Chemical Companies

To illustrate the key ratio technique, we have selected two chemical companies of roughly equal size but of with somewhat different financial and operating characteristics—Hercules, Inc. (Table 21.1), and Rohm & Haas Company (Table 21.2). The calculations are presented in separate columns, based on the averages of 1975 to 1979 and of 1980 to 1984 and also on the results of the single year 1985. All of the market value ratios are based on an average of the high and low price for each year. Table 21.3 shows separately the comparative market value ratios for Hercules Inc., and Rohm & Haas based on the price prevailing at the end of May 1986. (This date was selected on the assumption that by that time the analyst would have received the annual reports and have had the opportunity of analyzing the data.) For brevity's sake, not all the ratios discussed in Chapter 20 are used in this chapter. The subject here is the process of ratio analysis, not ratios themselves.

The Common-Stock Capital or Earning-Capital Base

In computing the return on common-stock capital, the analyst is concerned with the *earning-capital* as distinguished from the *equity* or *ownership base*. Thus the analyst measures the return on all the capital

Table 21.1. Hercules Incorporated

Data and ratios	1975–1979	1980–1984	1985
Basic data ($ millions)			
Sales	1,799.8	2,659.2	2,587.2
Depreciation and amortization	97.0	113.7	105.7
Tax expense	62.3	46.8	39.0
Net for capital (before tax)[a]	205.4	288.8	245.4
Net for total capital (after tax)[a,b]	123.0	203.7	162.0
Interest expense (including all leases)	40.9	83.8	96.6
Net for common	102.3	158.2	109.8
Common dividends	40.0	62.3	86.5
Total capital book value[c,g]	1,364.7	2,042.4	2,544.3
Deferred taxes[d]	95.3	190.5	212.0
Common-stock equity—book value[d]	794.8	1,218.0	1,496.8
Common stock at market value[e]	992.0	1,244.0	1,943.0
Average shares outstanding (millions)	42.9	46.7	54.1
Current assets (year end)			1,045.8
Current liabilities (year end)			415.9
Ratios (see Chapter 20):			
Profitability ratios			
14. Return on capital	9.0%	10.0%	6.4%
15. Capital turnover	1.3×	1.3×	1.0×
16. Earnings margin	6.8%	5.9%	6.3%
17. Return on capital before depreciation and amortization	16.1%	15.5%	10.3%
18. Return on equity[d]	11.5%	11.2%	6.4%
Growth ratios			
19. Ratio of sales to 1975–1979 base	100%	148%	144%
20. Ratio of net for total capital to 1975–1979 base	100%	166%	132%
21. Ratio of net per share of common to 1975–1979 base	100%	142%	85%
Stability ratios			
22. Maximum decline in coverage of senior charges—lowest year vs. average of three previous years[f]	−62%	−42%	−30%
23. Decline in return on capital—lowest year vs. average of three previous years[f]	−39%	−14%	−32%
Payout ratios			
24. Percent of earnings paid on common	39%	39%	79%
25. Dividends to cash flow	12%[f]	11%[f]	16%[f]
Credit ratios			
26. Current ratio	2.0×[f]	2.2×[f]	2.5×[f]
29. Equity ratio	59%	59%	58%
31. Coverage of senior charges	5.0×[f]	3.5×[f]	2.5×
31. Minimum coverage of senior charges	2.0×[f]	2.6×[f]	2.5×

Table 21.1. Hercules Incorporated (*Continued*)

Data and ratios	1975–1979	1980–1984	1985
Per-share figures ($)			
Price of common..................................	23.13	26.65	35.94
1. Earnings per share...........................	2.38	3.39	2.03
2. Dividend per share	0.95	1.33	1.60
3. Sales per share	41.95	56.94	47.82
5. Book value per share.......................	18.53	26.08	27.67
Market-price ratios			
10. Earnings yield................................	10.3%	12.7%	5.7%
11. Dividend yield	4.0%	5.0%	4.5%
12. Sales per dollar of common at market	$1.81	$2.14	$1.33
13. Price-to-book value.........................	1.3×	1.0×	1.3×

[a]Includes estimated interest component of rent on operating leases.
[b]Interest return has been reduced by pro forma tax effects, at a 46% rate after 1979 and a 48% rate during 1975–1979, for purposes of intercompany comparison.
[c]Includes deferred tax liability as part of equity.
[d]Based on average book value at beginning and end of years.
[e]Average of annual mean between the high and low prices, adjusted for stock splits, multiplied by average number of shares outstanding.
[f]These figures cannot be calculated from the basic data given.
[g]Includes estimated operating leases. Amounts are averages of beginning and end of year figures.

directly at work for the common stockholder, and whether or not the stockholder actually has legal title to all of this capital is somewhat beside the point. In this sense, the common stockholders' earning-capital base may be defined as total tangible assets less current liabilities and interest-bearing noncurrent debt. (The capital working for shareholders would thus include the reserve for deferred income taxes and similar items.) Approach this calculation from the right side of the balance sheet: Typically, the earning-capital base would consist of the following minus goodwill and other doubtful assets:

- Common-stock equity
- LIFO reserves and any hidden assets actively contributing to earnings
- Deferred tax liability

The computations which follow use this definition of earning-capital base.

Earnings Available for Total Capital

In this analysis, the earnings available for total capital are taken to be:

- Net income after taxes (subject to the analyst's adjustments)
- Interest on both current and noncurrent debt
- Interest on operating leases

Table 21.2. Rohm and Haas Company

Data and ratios	1975–1979	1980–1984	1985
Basic data ($ millions)			
Sales	1,174.1	1,871.2	2,051.0
Depreciation and amortization	77.6	93.9	111.0
Tax expense	37.6	77.0	86.0
Net for capital (before tax)[a]	128.1	234.9	189.1
Net for total capital (after tax)[a,b]	70.7	137.6	159.3
Interest expense (including all leases)	41.2	44.2	64.8
Net for common	49.3	113.7	124.3
Common dividends	18.0	36.1	49.3
Total capital book value[c,g]	972.4	1,254.8	1,490.1
Deferred taxes[d]	52.5	91.6	130.2
Common-stock equity—book value[d]	547.3	811.8	937.7
Common stock at market value[e]	619.4	1,035.5	1,572.6
Average shares outstanding (millions)	25.8	25.8	23.5
Current assets (year end)			924.0
Current liabilities (year end)			444.0
Ratios (see Chapter 20):			
Profitability ratios			
14. Return on capital	7.2%	10.9%	10.7%
15. Capital turnover	1.2×	1.5×	1.4×
16. Earnings margin	6.0%	7.3%	7.7%
17. Return on capital—before depreciation and amortization	15.2%	18.4%	18.1%
18. Return on equity[d]	11.7%	12.6%	11.6%
Growth ratios			
19. Ratio of sales to 1975–1979 base	100%	159%	175%
20. Ratio of net for total capital to 1975–1979 base	100%	195%	225%
21. Ratio of net per share of common to 1975–1979 base	100%	231%	277%
Stability ratios			
22. Maximum decline in coverage of senior charges—lowest year vs. average of three previous years[f]	−54%	−36%	−20%
23. Decline in return on capital—lowest year vs. average of three previous years[f]	−49%	−19%	−25%
Payout ratios			
24. Earnings paid on common	37%	32%	40%
25. Dividends to cash flow[f]	8%	10%	11%
Credit ratios			
26. Current ratio	2.4×[f]	2.6×[f]	2.1×
29. Equity ratio	56%	65%	63%
31. Coverage of senior charges	3.1×	5.3×	4.2×
31. Minimum coverage of senior charges[f]	1.6×	3.4×	4.2×
Per-share figures ($)			
Price of common	24.11	40.17	67.00

Tables 21.2. Rohm and Haas Company (*Continued*)

Data and ratios	1975–1979	1980–1984	1985
1. Earnings per share............................	1.91	4.41	5.29
2. Dividend per share	0.70	1.40	2.10
3. Sales per share	45.51	72.53	87.28
5. Book value per share.......................	21.21	31.47	39.90
Market-price ratios			
10. Earnings yield...............................	7.9%	11.0%	7.9%
11. Dividend yield..............................	2.9%	3.5%	3.1%
12. Sales per dollar of common at market	$1.90	$1.81	$1.30
13. Price-to-book value........................	1.1×	1.3×	1.7×

aIncludes estimated interest component of rent on operating leases.
bInterest return has been reduced by pro forma tax effects, at a 46% rate after 1979 and a 48% rate during 1975–1979, for purposes of intercompany comparisons.
cIncludes deferred tax liability as part of equity.
dBased on average book value at beginning and end of years.
eAverage of annual mean between the high and low prices, adjusted for stock splits, multiplied by average number of shares outstanding.
fThese figures cannot be calculated from the basic data given.
gIncludes estimated operating leases. Amounts are averages of beginning and end of year figures.

The interest on the debt is adjusted for the prevailing income tax rate: 48 percent in the years 1975 through 1979 and 46 percent in 1980 through 1985.[1] The interest expense includes the estimated interest component of rent paid on operating leases. Capitalized interest is also included in the return on capital and the amortization of capitalized interest is eliminated from expense. Interest is, of course, deductible for tax purposes, and earnings for common and preferred shares are fully taxed. To gain reasonable comparability between companies that are capitalized differently and use different instruments among their senior securities and borrowings—for example, operating leases, commercial paper, long-term bonds, and preferred stock—the interest must be reduced by the benefits of its tax deductibility. Using an alternative approach, the return on capital ratios may be calculated on a pretax basis. Both approaches are perfectly acceptable as methods to equalize the different tax treatment of interest and net income, but the after-tax approach has the advantage of treating taxes as an expense, which they are. Certain ratios are also calculated before depreciation in an effort to neutralize differences in companies' depreciation policies under comparison. Remember that depreciation is also an expense, and interpret those ratios accordingly.

The growth factor is measured by comparing 1985 and the 1980–1984 average with the 1975–1979 base. The data and ratios for the full analysis are presented in seven sections. Twenty-four key ratios, distributed in six topical sections, are identified by the ratio numbers used in

[1]The Tax Reform Law of 1986 changed the corporate rate on ordinary income from 46 percent in 1986 to a blended rate of 40 percent in 1987, and 34 percent thereafter.

Chapter 20. Whenever a substantial proportion (say, in the 50 to 60 percent range) of senior securities exists in the capital structure, as is the case in our example, the analyst may well find it desirable to compute all the profitability ratios on a common-stock, as well as a total capital, basis. Both of our sample companies spent at least part of the 1975–1985 period with their equity ratio in that range, but we have omitted those calculations and their discussion for purposes of brevity.

Details of the Adjustments

At the beginning of Chapter 20 we emphasized that the analyst must make all adjustments *before* calculating ratios, trends, averages, and other statistical or arithmetical processing. Thus it seems appropriate to relate here some of the adjustments that were made, some that would have been desirable but were not made, and some unusual adjustments which were based on analytical judgment rather than firm rules.

Eliminating Intangible Assets. Goodwill was eliminated from the balance sheet, reducing net worth by the full amount. No tax adjustment was made in the case of goodwill. Rohm and Haas had $60 million of patents and trademarks less an unknown amount of amortization. Details of these patents and trademarks were available for only the years 1983 through 1985, and the company was receiving royalties and related fees amounting to about 10 percent of the gross cost of those intangibles. It was decided that those intangibles had a reasonably identifiable earnings stream and that only the goodwill and its amortization should be removed from the accounts.

Other Postemployment Benefits. Rohm and Haas showed $25 million of expense for health benefits and insurance policies on 3100 retired and 8300 active employees. Since they were covered by a single policy, the company was unable to identify the portion attributable to retired employees. The liability for other postemployment benefits was ignored because (1) data were not available for earlier years and (2) the estimate of the amount of the benefit applicable to the retirees would be unreliable.

Operating Leases. Operating leases were capitalized for each year, estimating the pattern of rental payments beyond the fifth year, if necessary, and using a 10 percent discount rate. Note that the old rule-of-thumb of "one third of rent" as the interest component would have worked very well for Rohm and Haas. However, for Hercules, particularly in 1980 and subsequent years, when Hercules was leasing a considerable amount of office space, the one-third rule would have been only about half of an appropriate interest component.

Changes in Pension Assumptions and Methods. In 1985 both companies changed their actuarial cost methods to the projected unit credit method and made changes in certain assumptions. In addition, in 1984 Hercules changed some actuarial assumptions. Rohm and Haas reduced pension expense from previous amounts around the $30 million level to zero for 1985; Hercules reduced pension expense by about the same amount for 1984 and 1985 from the levels which had prevailed over the previous decade. Is is reasonable that Rohm and Haas' workers earned large pension benefits in 1985 but the company recorded no cost for them? A more realistic view would say that pension expense had been overstated in prior years when gains were shown in the company's portfolios and on other actuarial assumptions and that some reasonable adjustment should be made by the analyst. In the case of Rohm and Haas we estimated the correct pension expense at $30 million pretax, reducing 1985 earnings by $16.2 million after tax. The $30 million was then used as a reduction in past pension expense, spread over the previous 10 years in equal amounts. A similar adjustment was made for Hercules, but pension expense was increased in both 1984 and 1985 and the cost thereof was spread over the previous nine years. These steps also required balance sheet and tax adjustments.

LIFO Reserves. Both companies use LIFO figures for substantial portions of their inventories. For purposes of calculating the capital at work, the after-tax amount of LIFO reserve was added to equity, and deferred taxes for the gain were set up based on the prevailing tax rate for the year. Changes in the LIFO reserve were not added to the income for the year.

Foreign Currency Translation. Rohm and Haas is unusual in that it uses the dollar as its functional currency for all overseas operations. Thus, no foreign currency translation adjustment arises in its accounts. The gains and losses shown in income are from all monetary assets and liabilities denominated in foreign currencies which changed relative to the dollar during the period. Hercules uses local currency in a number of overseas locations. Information was available in the 10-K to eliminate the effect of foreign currency rate changes on plant and equipment. For comparative purposes, eliminations of the gains and losses from the plant account would put Hercules on almost the same basis as Rohm and Haas, with the exceptions of inventories and a few other minor nonmonetary assets and liabilities. Thus, the gains and losses arising from land, plant, and equipment were eliminated from Hercules accounts, both in the balance sheet and the income statement.

Capitalized Interest. The effects of interest capitalization on the plant account were removed.

Analysis of Financial Statements

Depreciation and Amortization.   Depreciation and amortization were adjusted to eliminate the amortization of goodwill, amortization of capitalized interest, and some other intangibles.

Extinguishment of Debt.   In 1982 Hercules recorded an extraordinary nontaxable gain of $11,553,000 as a result of exchange of 2,038,000 shares of common stock for $50 million principal amount of 6½ percent convertible subordinated debentures. This transaction was not a conversion but rather a special exchange offer of about $38 million of stock for the convertibles. We do not believe that an economic gain occurred, and therefore we eliminated this item from the income statement and stockholders' equity. The transaction does have tax consequences, but the amount did not justify making an adjustment.

Estimations.   It was necessary to estimate a number of needed figures and, as indicated in the discussion of the pension situation above, to spread certain numbers in an arbitrary fashion. This is a common problem for security analysts, and the only answer is to apply common sense to the facts that are known. Our examples were deliberately based on published information only. In an ongoing analytical situation, the analyst would have frequent contact with the company, permitting more knowledgeable adjustments.

Ratio Comparisons

Note that the figures and ratios in the first five sections of the comparison relate to the performance and position of the two *companies*. Thus they supply indications of the quality of the enterprise as a whole and, presumably, of its management. In nearly all the ratios developed in the first three sections, Rohm and Haas fared better than Hercules, although not by a large margin.

The fifth section, on credit ratios, shows that Rohm and Haas had the better current ratio from 1975 through 1984, and the poorer one in 1985 due to heavy stock repurchases. Rohm and Haas has had a more conservative equity ratio over the past six years and somewhat better interest coverage. With a small edge to Rohm and Haas, the credit standing of the two companies is about the same.

The final section of the tables offers ratios that depend on the market price of the common stock. At its *average price* Hercules has offered more sales, earnings, dividends, and net assets per dollar invested than Rohm and Haas. This correlated with the historical record, which showed the advantage in profitability, growth, and stability to be in favor of Rohm and Haas. Hercules' per-share progress shows the negative effects of dilution, whereas Rohm and Haas benefited from repurchase of shares.

A Comparison at Current Prices

Table 21.3 shows the relations of price to earnings, dividends, and assets of the two stocks, using the end-of-month price for May 1986. The table shows that Hercules' 1985 earnings were sharply depressed from the level of the previous five years. Rohm and Haas's 1985 earnings were off from the 1984 peak but up from the 1980 to 1984 average. Hercules is the cheaper stock in terms of assets, yield, and adjusted earnings for recent years but not in terms of 1985 earnings. Our key ratio technique can carry the analyst to the point of demonstrating that Rohm and Haas has been a more profitable and more dynamic business than Hercules, but this advantage may be offset by Hercules' lower price. Whether the advantage is in fact offset cannot be demonstrated by any mathematical operations. The answer must be given in the form of an opinion emanating from the informed judgment and perhaps the prejudices of

Table 21.3. Market Value Ratios, for Two Companies

	Hercules	Rohm and Haas
Market price on May 31, 1986..	50⅛	100½*
1985 sales per dollar of common at market.........................	$0.95	$0.87
1985 earned per dollar of common at market†	4.05%	5.26%
1980–1984 average earned per dollar of common at market†	6.76%	4.39%
Dividend yield..	3.2%	2.4%
Price-to-book value using 1985 year-end net assets..............	1.81×	2.52×

*Before 3-for-1 split payable June 12, 1986.
†Adjusted earnings from Tables 21.1 and 21.2

the analyst. The determination of the respective merits or attractiveness of the two common stocks *at their prevailing market prices* is the final and most difficult stage of a full-scale comparative security analysis. This is a matter of common-stock valuation, and our observations on the subject belong to a later section of this book. But prior to reaching a conclusion as to value in relation to price, the analyst will draw a number of deductions from the key ratios developed in our comparative table. Let us discuss these in some detail, to illustrate what we may call the "intermediate" or "dissective" state of security analysis.

Profitability and Turnover Ratios

Table 21.4 offers a possible explanation of the more rapid growth shown by Rohm and Haas from the mid-1970s to the mid-1980s. The first ratio, capital turnover, is an activity ratio. It shows that Rohm and Haas increased the turnover of its capital significantly from the first period to the second. Hercules did not. Both companies suffered a modest decline in margins before depreciation (but mixed results after depreciation). Those differences were minor. The third line, the return on capital before depreciation, is simply the product of the first two lines. Clearly the factor that increased Rohm and Haas's return was the increased capital turnover. Both companies showed a decline in the ratio of depreciation to sales, but Rohm and Haas's decline occurred in part because sales outgrew capital. When that element is factored in, the two companies' depreciation policies appear roughly the same. The decline in the relationship of depreciation to sales aided the return on total capital after depreciation for both companies.

Table 21.4. Profitability and Turnover Ratios for Two Companies

	Hercules		Rohm and Haas	
	1975–1979	1980–1984	1975–1979	1980–1984
Capital turnover	1.32	1.30	1.21	1.49
Earnings margin before depreciation and amortization	12.2%	11.9%	12.6%	12.3%
Return on capital before depreciation and amortization	16.1%	15.5%	15.2%	18.4%
Ratio of depreciation and amortization to sales	5.4%	4.3%	6.6%	5.0%
Return on capital	9.0%	10.0%	7.2%	10.9%
Return on equity	11.5%	11.2%	11.7%	12.6%

Finally, the difference in the pattern of return on total capital from the return on equity shows that Rohm and Haas used a smaller amount of leverage somewhat more effectively than Hercules did in providing an improved return to the common stockholders.

The numbers in Table 21.4 would lead the analyst to an investigation of segment and product line data to determine what changes over the decade led to Rohm and Haas's improved activity ratio, and whether further improvements seem likely.

Progress Ratios

Each of the three ratios pertaining to growth favor Rohm and Haas by a significant margin. However, the 1985 figures for Hercules are probably not as bad as they seem. High start-up costs, production problems at certain new plants, and a significant strike had a hopefully nonrecurring negative impact on sales and earnings. The sales numbers in 1984 and 1985 were also significantly reduced by the formation of a 50-percent-owned joint venture at the end of 1983 to take over sale and manufacture of polypropylene resin products and certain other lines of business. That joint venture, HIMONT, Inc., had sales of over $900 million in both 1984 and 1985. Since the joint venture is carried on the equity method, some significant amount of Hercules' sales and capital were effectively deconsolidated for the years 1984 and 1985.

A comparison of the return on total capital to the return on equity for Hercules in 1985 demonstrates that company's vulnerability to its relatively larger financial leverage.

Indexes of Stability

The measures of stability in Tables 21.1 and 21.2 tend to give an edge to Rohm and Haas but demonstrate the inherent volatility of the chemical industry. An almost universal law of security analysis is that, within any industry, the units with better profit margins show smaller percentage profit declines in recession years. Similarly, those with the least financial leverage show smaller percentage declines in earnings for the equity. Rohm and Haas has been increasing its margins after depreciation and reducing its financial leverage. Hercules has improved in after-depreciation margins but has not reduced its leverage.

Payout Ratios

Rohm and Haas consistently had lower payout ratios of earnings and cash flow than Hercules. (The figures for 1985 should be considered nonrepresentative, since both companies had depressed earnings in 1985 relative to 1984.) Rohm and Haas's lower payout ratio permitted it to finance a larger portion of its growth from internal sources, and this permitted the company to improve its equity ratio. Hercules, however, was able to maintain its equity ratio only by increasing the number of shares of stock outstanding, thereby diluting the rate of growth of earnings, dividends, and book value per share. Average shares of Hercules outstanding in 1985 were 26 percent more than the average for 1975 to 1979, whereas Rohm and Haas had a 13 percent reduction for the same period.

Credit Ratios

The credit ratios for both companies are in satisfactory condition, and both companies should be considered financially strong. Rohm and Haas has improved its coverage of senior charges and Hercules' coverage has been well maintained. Rohm and Haas has had a slightly superior current position except in 1985. However, most of that reduction in the current ratio is due to repurchase of over 8.5 million shares of common stock in 1984 and 1985.

Per-Share Figures and Price Ratios

Note in Tables 21.1 and 21.2 that the purchaser of Rohm and Haas at the average price from 1975 to 1979 was buying *more* dollars of sales and net assets and *less* earnings and dividends than could have been obtained by investing the same money in Hercules. However, on average during 1980 to 1984 the Rohm and Haas investor's stock was selling at a price 66 percent higher than its purchase price, versus 15 percent for Hercules investors. The Rohm and Haas investor would also have received an average dividend of 5.8 percent in the 1980 to 1984 period, the same as the Hercules investor. If the figures were brought up to date through May 1986, the superior investment results obtained in Rohm and Haas would be even more dramatic, with the common stock increasing from $24.11 to $100.50—a gain of over 300 percent in market price; Hercules slightly more than doubled from $23.13 to $50.12. Hindsight clearly shows that the accolades go to Rohm and Haas in terms of both dividends and price appreciation. The bulk of the explanation is found in the per-share figures, which show far superior growth in sales, earnings, dividends, and book value. The superior return to Rohm and Haas investors is attributable to the substantially greater growth in earnings. It is the earnings growth that permits the growth of dividends and a rising yield on cost. It is earnings that cause the stock price to rise if the multiplier remains constant. And it is superior earnings growth that can justify an increase in the multiplier from the level of the average stock to a level that includes a premium for growth.

Note that an investor who early in 1980 could observe only the figures for 1975 to 1979 in Tables 21.1 and 21.2 might well have chosen Hercules in preference to Rohm and Haas. The profitability numbers gave Hercules better marks on four out of the five ratios shown. The measures of stability, payout, and credit were by and large a standoff for that period of time. The growth in earnings from the previous peak to 1979 favored Hercules, as did the price-earnings ratio and the yield offered. The investor who had a firm conviction that Rohm and Haas was the more attractive stock would not have been able to make a strong case based on the historical record alone and would have had to justify that position by correctly forecasting a more rapid rate of growth in earning power for Rohm and Haas than for Hercules. The additional information for the years 1980 through 1985 in Tables 21.1 and 21.2 give a clear statistical advantage to Rohm and Haas but pose for today's investor the same question of which stock is more attractively priced, based on such price data as that presented in Table 21.3.

Emphasis Is on Quality

The foregoing analysis of key ratios for the full period from 1975 to 1985 showed that the qualitative factors clearly favored Rohm and Haas and the pricing measures now make Hercules appear the cheaper stock. The comparative investment results for the period of the analysis show that in spite of its higher price Rohm and Haas was by far the better buy. This conclusion confirms the accepted view in the market regarding to the purchase of *quality* shares. Remember, however, that (1) at some point even the best common stock can be overpriced and (2) anticipation of an improvement in the quality of a below-average share can result in an excellent investment opportunity. In the latter instance the investor is certain to enjoy an increase not only in earnings and dividends but also in the multiplier.

Improved quality can be the result of numerous factors; changes in management and in product mix are among the most prominent. At an early stage in the proceedings, anticipating with reasonable accuracy either the results of such changes or the length of time that may be required to bring them to fruition is no easy task. But the rewards for successfully doing so can be substantial.

Analysis Related to Physical Data

Analysis of a company's results should not be confined to dollar figures but should extend to those physical data that lend themselves to analytical study. The material usually considered, whenever it is available, includes the following.

Physical Reserves

The category of physical reserves is significant for all companies dependent on a wasting asset, such as oil and gas producers and mining companies, and possibly also for a transportation concern which depends on the reserves of its main shippers or suppliers, such as a railroad transporting chiefly coal or an oil or gas pipeline.

Metal, mineral, and oil reserves are often found in less developed and/or politically unstable parts of the world. Analysts will typically discount the value of such reserves to reflect expectations of nationalization, oppressive taxation, or wars and insurrection.

Many companies limit their development to only a few years' reserves because local taxes would be greatly increased if they reported that more ore was being developed. In addition, companies with wasting assets generally anticipate the exhaustion of present bodies by property purchases or leases. Thus, it is quite unusual for an important company of that type actually to go out of business because its reserves have been exhausted.

In estimating reserves, the analyst should consider the quality as well as the quantity. If a mining company has mainly low-grade ore in reserve and is presently mining high-grade ore, its future earning power must be viewed conservatively. There is similar significance in the ownership of less valuable oil reserves as against the more valuable high-gravity, low-sulphur oil.

The analyst must treat figures of reserves with circumspection. They do, of course, have some informative value. Other things being equal, a company with large developed reserves is preferable to another with small reserves.

Example. The 1984 annual report of AMAX, Inc., included the data on its molybdenum reserves shown in Table 21.5. Similar details were provided on the company's other major metal and mineral reserves. Detailed production figures for each product were also provided.

Table 21.5. Reserve Data from the 1984 Annual Report of AMAX, Inc.

	Molybdenum (millions of tons)				
	1984	1983	1982	1981	1980
Colorado					
Climax	408	413	413	418	433
(% molybdenum disulfide)	(0.31)	(0.31)	(0.31)	(0.31)	(0.31)
Henderson	240	246	246	230	239
(% molybdenum disulfide)	(0.38)	(0.38)	(0.38)	(0.42)	(0.42)
Canada					
Kitsault	115	115	115	105	105
(% molybdenum disulfide)	(0.19)	(0.19)	(0.19)	(0.19)	(0.19)

Example. Exxon Corporation's 1985 annual report includes required information on the "standardized measure of discounted future net cash flows relating to proved oil and gas reserves." Table 21.6 shows the worldwide figures for 1985 and the causes of changes in the figures. The total disclosure was far more extensive than this sample.

This standardized measure is not an appraisal of the oil and gas reserves. It is simply a calculation, using a discount rate of 10 percent, of the present value of the future net cash inflows from sale of *proven* oil and gas reserves, with consideration given to the costs, taxes, method of production (e.g., secondary or tertiary recovery), and the like. *Probable* reserves are not included, nor is the value of *possible* oil reserves on lands

Table 21.6. Condensed Disclosure on Oil and Gas Reserves from the 1985 EXXON Annual Report

Standarized measure of discounted future net cash flows	
	Total worldwide ($ million)
As of December 31, 1985	
Future cash inflows from sales of oil and gas	217,131
Future production and development cash costs	84,562
Future income tax expenses	63,843
Future net cash flows	68,726
Effect of discounting net cash flows at 10%	37,904
Standardized measure of discounted future net cash flows	30,822

Changes in the standardized measure	
	1985 ($ million)
Value of reserves added during the year	
Extensions, discoveries, other additions and improved recovery, less related costs	3,916
Changes in value of previous year reserves	
Sales and transfers of oil and gas produced during the year, net of production costs	(12,065)
Development costs incurred during the year	4,205
Net change in prices and production costs	(3,252)
Revision of previous reserves estimates	831
Accretion of discount	6,268
Other changes	(1,210)
Net change in income taxes	2,180
Total change in standardized measuring during the year	873

NOTE: The complete disclosures included details for 1983–1985 and data for six geographic areas.

held under lease. Interestingly, although the information was not received with much excitement on Wall Street when it first became available, subsequent acquisition prices of oil companies tended to confirm that the standardized measure was not too bad an estimate of the takeover value of oil reserves, and oil analysts began to pay considerably more attention to it.

The calculation of oil reserves (including the liquid content of gas reserves) has made a great deal of technical progress in recent years, and most companies now supply estimates by their own staff or by consulting geologists. Use of reserve figures in analyses and comparisons of oil companies is common—in general a certain dollar value is set on the oil in the ground and then the book figure for the other assets, net, are added to find a total valuation. Observe that, in the field of oil and mining companies, more emphasis is placed on appraised value of the assets than in the case of manufacturing and trading concerns.

Capacity

Most producers and processors of basic materials have a definite capacity expressible in physical units, for example, tons of steel ingots; bags of sugar, both raw and refined; barrels of oil put through refineries; or barrels of cement. The capacity figure changes, of course, through plant additions or abandonments, but it helps describe the position of the company at the time of analysis. How much weight capacity figures deserve will vary greatly with circumstances.

Production in Units

Production in units is a basic figure for intensive analysis; when compared with capacity it indicates

- Possible need for future expansion
- Potential increase in output
- Breakeven point

When a company produces a *homogeneous product*, e.g., copper, sugar, or cement, and when unit figures of production are published, the analyst can calculate

- Selling price
- Cost of production

- Margin of profit per unit
- Share of market

These are useful for comparative analysis and for calculating the effect of price and cost changes on the individual company.

Some productivity ratios and capacity utilization ratios should be used with caution. Capacity utilization figures for the textile industry have long been based on operating two 8-hour shifts, with Sundays and holidays off. In war time, the industry typically operates around the clock, seven days a week, indicating that the true capacity to produce goods is about twice the number normally used for purposes of measuring plant capacity.

In the coal industry, the total of tons produced per worker day was long considered the measure of a coal mine's efficiency. Early in the 1980s an industry group investigated how companies were calculating this number. They found huge disparities. Some companies counted only underground production workers, excluding shift leaders, inspectors, and others. Other companies included anyone vaguely associated with coal production, including those involved in washing, cleaning, sizing, and transporting the coal, overseers, and the like. Recalculations on a common basis established that some mines long considered to be among the most efficient in the country actually had an unenviable standing in the rankings.

For many years the retail trade industry put great emphasis on the statistic "sales per square foot of retail floor space" for comparable stores. Again, there were definitional problems concerning which floor space should be included and which excluded. With some grocery chains now staying open 24 hours a day, seven days a week, comparisons of grocery chains' sales per square foot must be done with a great deal of care.

Production by Divisions

Many manufacturers turn out a variety of products, which fall into several categories or industrial divisions. To study the company from the standpoint of industry analysis, clearly the analyst wants to know how the firm's products are divided, in unit terms and by dollar value. Companies now provide segment data in considerable detail, although the allocation of overhead continues to lack comparability. A typical disclosure would include the following items for each major product group:

- Sales
- Operating profits

- Equity in earnings of affiliates
- Identifiable assets at year end
- Investment in affiliates
- Depreciation expense
- Capital expenditures

Concentration and Geographical Location of Sales

Businesses dependent on one or two major customers are considered somewhat more vulnerable than are those with a large number of less important accounts. The former situation is found often among the makers of automobile parts, defense contractors, and in companies manufacturing almost exclusively for a large mail-order or chain-store organization. A large, successful company normally will have a substantial foreign business in addition to its domestic sales, but a heavy dependence on exports—especially to a single geographical area—must be viewed as an added hazard. Analysts must consider these matters and allow weight in their valuations according to their own judgment.

22
Ratios in Industry Analysis

Comparing Companies with Related Groups

Securities can neither be analyzed nor valued in a vacuum. The analytical function requires that a company be compared both with companies of a similar nature and with stocks in general to determine the characteristics and attractiveness of the individual issue. In general, individual companies are grouped together by

- Traditional industry definitions, such as soft drinks or automobiles
- Economic sectors, such as consumer nondurable goods
- Sensitivity to some economic factor, such as interest rates
- Market sector, such as low-priced stocks or growth stocks

Before making any forecast, the analyst must understand how the company makes money. Profit comes from adding value to the inputs (labor, raw materials, etc.). The value added arises from increasing the utility through changing the form, location, size, convenience, appearance, or some other characteristic of the original inputs in a way that makes the product or service more desirable.

Thus, the analyst must understand the workings of the industry in which the company operates and competes. A company's competitors must be understood, for they are a part of the operating environment. Analysts tend to compare stocks in a "peer group," such as an industry, with others in the group to a greater degree than with the market as a whole.

Before the valuation the analyst will try to determine which companies have done better or worse than the group, and more important, why. It is a great convenience to devise some measure of what has been "normal" or average performance for the group, as a yardstick against which each company can be compared. Because of the difference in the size of the companies, ratio analysis has become the most common tool for measuring the tangible record of the companies and the industry on a basis independent of size. The modest objectives of this chapter are to provide sample displays of industry data, and to discuss some of the uses of averages, indexes, and other techniques, along with some of their disadvantages.

Analysts face many challenges in preparing the data for a company so that its ratios are consistent through time and comparable with other companies under consideration. In addition, preparing an industry "average" or benchmark ratio against which to compare the other companies presents some technical complications.

Seven Grocery Chains

Ratio Tables

To provide a basis for discussion of alternative techniques and their strengths and weaknesses, a number of tables of ratios have been prepared on seven grocery chains. The grocery industry was chosen because of its homogeneity and because all readers should be generally familiar with its retailing activities. The list of companies includes very large and very small companies, some with high profitability and others with low, and companies of disparate qualitative characteristics.

Original Data Adjusted for Operating Leases

In preparing the data for industry ratio analysis, each company was treated in accordance with the recommended adjustments discussed in Chapters 10 through 19. The rent schedules of operating leases were projected and discounted at a 10 percent rate. The resulting present value was capitalized as an asset and a lease liability. The present value is *principal* and the remainder of the operating lease rental payments is *interest*. The ratio of this interest component to the total rental payments was assumed to be constant for all years, and therefore, the interest expense for operating leases for each year was calculated as the interest ratio multiplied by the year's total operating lease rental expense. These steps put the equity ratio and the return on total capital on a more comparable basis than would be the case if the operating leases were not capitalized. Some error is introduced on an absolute basis because of the estimated discount rate, but on a *relative* basis the picture is improved because the bias is in the same direction for all companies.

FIFO Inventories

At the beginning of the 10-year period studied, only a minority of the companies were on a LIFO basis, but at the end of the period all seven companies used LIFO. Because discontinuity would exist if no adjustment were made, and proper information is not available to adjust to LIFO for the early years, all companies were placed on a FIFO basis for the years studied.

Other Adjustments

Where interest had been capitalized, it was expensed, and estimated amortization and tax effects eliminated from the accounts. A few unusual and nonrecurring items along with their tax effects, were eliminated or moved to years other than the ones in which they had been reported. Goodwill was eliminated, along with its amortization. Only one company had foreign currency translation adjustments, but inadequate information was available for the recommended analytical adjustment.

Other than the capitalization of operating leases, most of the adjustments for these companies turned out to be sufficiently small so that they could have been ignored. However, the analyst seldom knows whether the aggregate sum of the adjustments is large enough to make a material difference until the adjustments have been calculated.

The Industry Is Changing

A few decades ago, grocery chains were mostly homogeneous in their activities and characteristics. A variety of standardized ratios for the industry were used to discover the reasons for differences in profit margins, sales growth, and the like. These included such data as sales per store, square feet of retailing space per store, sales per square foot of retailing space on a "comparable stores basis," and the like. In more recent years, nearly all grocery chains have added drugs as a product line; some acquired drug stores and others introduced a drug department into the grocery store. In addition, some have gone for superstore and combination store concepts, handling as many as 20,000 items versus 10,000 three decades ago. The old-fashioned neighborhood supermarket may now have grown to more than an acre of retailing floor space, be located in a huge shopping mall, and offer such durable and luxury goods as lawn and garden furniture, power tools, or several brands of videocassette recorders. Sales per square foot no longer seem to mean very much when one company tends to operate on the traditional Monday through Saturday store hours while another is open around the clock year-round. Although the ratios continue to tell the analyst that something is happening, more digging is required of the analyst today to understand why a grocery chain is successful or not.

Profitability

The Profitability Ratios

Table 22.1 shows the conventional profitability measures of the seven grocery chains. We reemphasize our belief that the percentage earned on total capital is the best measure of the success of any company and should be the starting point for the analysis. Because of our bias favoring investing in common stocks over bonds, the table also includes the return on common stockholders' equity for the seven companies. Five-year averages are also shown for 1976 to 1980 and for 1981 through 1985.

Technical Issues

Weighted versus Unweighted Industry Averages. The table introduces the first of our technical issues in calculating industry averages. The industry ratios could be calculated by setting up an aggregate industry income statement and industry balance sheet, and then calculating the desired ratios for each year. The advantage of this calculation is primarily in comparing the success of one industry with that of another. Such aggregate calculations do a very good job of showing the overall results of the industry, regardless of whether it has many small participants, some small and some large, or only a few large participants.

However, in the case of our seven grocery chains (which represent only a small part of the entire grocery industry) Kroger and Safeway would have accounted for 62 percent of sales and would have a similarly large influence on each of the ratios. For practical purposes, the calculated ratios would essentially reflect what happened to those two companies, and the results of the other five companies would be largely obscured. Comparing the five smaller companies with a weighted industry average would simply indicate how each of the five companies did relative to Kroger and Safeway. This would deemphasize the rankings of performance of the individual companies.

Table 22.1. Profitability Measures

Years	Unweighted industry average	Albert-son's Inc.	Borman's	Food Lion	Lucky Stores	Kroger	Safeway Stores	Super-markets General
			Percent Earned on Capital					
1985	9.9	10.6	8.0	13.3	7.6	7.4	9.4	12.9
1984	9.3	11.2	3.2	13.9	8.1	7.5	8.7	12.8
1983	7.8	11.0	−5.5	12.7	9.0	7.4	8.3	11.4
1982	10.1	11.5	8.0	12.8	8.7	8.2	8.1	13.4
1981	11.0	11.7	1.3	14.9	10.1	8.8	6.9	12.9
1980	10.6	11.9	7.5	13.6	11.1	9.2	7.5	13.5
1979	11.2	11.9	6.7	15.0	13.2	8.5	8.5	14.7
1978	10.9	11.9	9.4	14.6	12.2	7.5	8.9	11.7
1977	9.3	10.4	4.3	12.7	10.7	6.9	7.6	12.4
1976	10.2	9.2	6.6	14.4	9.0	6.4	12.3	13.6
Average								
1981–1985	9.6	11.2	5.2	13.5	8.7	7.8	8.3	12.7
1976–1980	10.5	11.1	6.9	14.1	11.2	7.7	9.0	13.2
Difference	−0.9	0.1	−1.7	−0.6	-2.5	0.1	-0.7	−0.5
			Percent Return on Equity					
1985	15.7	16.7	15.9	22.6	12.4	11.8	12.5	18.2
1984	13.6	18.2	−1.7	24.3	13.9	11.5	11.6	17.4
1983	9.5	18.7	−29.6	23.1	16.6	10.9	12.4	14.2
1982	16.5	20.9	13.6	21.4	16.1	12.8	12.4	18.0
1981	13.9	23.3	10.8	20.1	20.0	15.4	8.7	17.4
1980	18.0	24.8	13.4	16.4	23.1	15.6	10.8	22.2
1979	20.6	26.5	10.8	17.5	29.2	15.2	13.8	31.0
1978	19.6	26.3	19.8	16.4	25.9	14.0	15.2	19.9
1977	15.6	21.3	1.9	15.1	22.9	11.1	11.9	25.0
1976	16.1	17.0	8.8	18.6	19.5	9.5	12.3	26.8
Average								
1981–1985	14.0	19.6	−1.9	22.3	16.8	12.5	11.5	17.1
1976–1980	18.1	23.8	10.9	16.8	24.1	13.1	12.8	25.0
Difference	−4.1	−4.2	−12.8	5.5	−7.3	−0.6	−1.3	−7.9

Thus, for purposes of comparing individual companies, an unweighted industry average was chosen. That is, the ratio was calculated for each company, the ratios for the year added, and the sum divided by 7. These are the columns entitled "Unweighted industry average." Although this method was chosen for its simplicity and because the five-year averages would tend to ameliorate some of the technical problems, the analyst should be aware that the unweighted industry figures for a single year may be misleading. The most obvious example is the industry return on equity for 1983. It includes Borman's negative return of 29.6 percent of equity, which pulls the industry average down sharply, even though

Borman's represents only about 2 percent of the revenues and assets of the seven companies sampled.

Dealing with Outliers.   One technique for handling the Borman's problem is to eliminate the highest and lowest observation in each sample as being atypical, and simply average the remaining five. The elimination of Borman's and Food Lion, the worst and the best return on equity for 1983, would give a more characteristic 14.6 percent average for the industry sample. An objection to that technique is that throwing out the high and low observations each year means that a different mix of companies is represented in the industry average in each year, and therefore not exactly the same companies are being presented through time.

Borman's 1983 loss was so large as to draw the analyst's attention to the possibility that some highly unusual and nonrecurring event had taken place during that year. No other number in the table comes anywhere close to it. The analyst, upon investigating Borman's situation, would find that the company had left itself vulnerable to a price war (initiated by competitors who were enjoying lower labor costs due to protection of the bankruptcy courts), and was exposed because of its geographic concentration in the State of Michigan, circumstances which do not justify treatment of the figures as unusual or nonrecurring.

Averaging Ratios.   Although it is not the common practice, from a mathematical viewpoint the preferred procedure in averaging ratios is to take the geometric mean rather than the arithmetic mean. However, this method does not work where negative numbers may be involved. To use a geometric mean requires that the negative numbers be excluded from the sample or that other techniques be used that are mathematically quite complex. The practical answer seems to be to use the arithmetic mean, perhaps with removal of outliers.

Decomposition of Return on Capital

Table 22.2 shows the return on total capital decomposed into its two components, the earnings margin and capital turnover. The three companies with the highest return on total capital all enjoy superior earnings margins and in general stood up well in capital turnover.

The surprise in the picture is the remarkably high turnover of Borman's, which has suffered a weak and erratic earnings margin. In seeking the explanation for Borman's rapid capital turnover, inventory turnover figures were also included in the table. Unfortunately,

Table 22.2. Decomposition of Return on Capital

Years	Unweighted industry average	Albert-son's Inc.	Borman's	Food Lion	Lucky Stores	Kroger	Safeway Stores	Super-markets General
			Earnings Margin					
1985	1.9%	2.3%	1.0%	3.0%	1.5%	1.7%	1.9%	2.2%
1984	1.9	2.3	.4	3.1	1.6	1.8	1.7	2.2
1983	1.7	2.3	− .6	2.9	1.9	1.7	1.6	2.0
1982	1.8	2.3	.9	2.6	1.7	1.6	1.6	2.2
1981	1.9	2.2	.2	3.4	2.0	1.8	1.3	2.1
1980	2.0	2.2	1.0	3.5	2.2	1.7	1.4	2.2
1979	2.1	2.3	.9	3.7	2.4	1.6	1.6	2.4
1978	2.1	2.2	1.3	3.7	2.2	1.6	1.7	2.1
1977	1.9	2.0	.6	3.3	1.9	1.5	1.5	2.4
1976	1.9	1.8	1.0	3.3	1.7	1.3	1.7	2.7
Average								
1981–1985	1.8	2.3	.4	3.0	1.7	1.7	1.6	2.1
1976–1980	2.0	2.1	.9	3.5	2.1	1.5	1.6	2.3
			Capital Turnover					
1985	5.3×	4.7×	8.1×	4.4×	5.0×	4.3×	4.9×	5.8×
1984	5.5	4.8	8.9	4.5	5.1	4.2	5.2	5.8
1983	5.4	4.7	8.6	4.4	4.9	4.4	5.1	5.7
1982	5.6	5.1	7.6	5.0	5.0	5.2	5.2	6.0
1981	5.6	5.4	7.8	4.3	5.0	4.9	5.3	6.3
1980	5.6	5.3	7.8	3.9	5.1	5.4	5.2	6.3
1979	5.5	5.2	7.5	4.0	5.5	5.2	5.2	6.1
1978	5.4	5.4	7.3	3.9	5.5	4.8	5.2	5.7
1977	5.2	5.3	6.9	3.8	5.5	4.7	5.2	5.2
1976	5.5	5.1	6.8	4.3	5.2	4.8	7.2	5.0
Average								
1981–1985	5.5	4.9	8.2	4.5	5.0	4.6	5.1	5.9
1976–1980	5.4	5.3	7.3	4.0	5.4	5.0	5.6	5.7
			Inventory Turnover					
1985	8.4×	10.3×	9.2×	7.5×	7.7×	7.7×	7.9×	8.5×
1984	9.0	10.9	10.5	8.0	8.8	8.3	8.0	8.3
1983	8.8	10.6	10.4	7.5	7.9	8.7	8.3	8.5
1982	9.4	10.6	10.3	8.0	8.3	10.4	8.4	9.6
1981	9.4	10.9	11.1	8.7	7.9	9.3	8.7	9.3
1980	9.7	11.2	10.1	10.1	8.1	9.3	9.3	9.7
1979	9.7	11.5	10.8	10.0	8.0	8.6	9.1	9.8
1978	9.8	11.3	10.9	10.0	7.5	8.7	9.0	11.2
1977	10.1	12.5	12.4	11.1	8.3	8.4	9.4	8.5
1976	10.1	12.5	12.5	11.6	7.5	8.8	9.7	8.3
Average								
1981–1985	9.0	10.7	10.3	7.9	8.1	8.9	8.3	8.8
1976–1980	9.9	11.8	11.3	10.6	7.9	8.8	9.3	9.5

they do not appear to offer a full explanation of Borman's capital turnover. The analyst would have to look to the company's other assets, probably to the depreciated carrying amounts of the stores themselves, for an explanation of Borman's high capital turnover rate.

The manufacturing of house brands is a significant activity for some but not all grocery chains. Manufacturing, of course, requires capital investment in plant and inventories, and the turnover in manufacturing is far below that of ordinary food retailing. Thus, those companies that are vertically integrated would be expected to have lower turnover rates. The analyst would also investigate whether this would offer an explanation of Borman's high turnover rate in comparison with the other companies.

The Effects of Leverage

Table 22.3 offers some explanation of the difference between companies in bringing down to equity a disproportionately large or small portion of the return on total capital, as found in Table 22.1. Leveraging a company increases the return on equity above what would be obtained if the company did not borrow. The leveraging will work as long as the after-tax cost of the borrowing is less than the return on total capital. In the case of Borman's, the equity ratio was consistently the lowest in the industry sample. However, because, in some years, Borman's did not earn a sufficient return on total capital to cover its interest expense, the heavy leverage served to reduce rather than increase earnings in those

Table 22.3. Equity as a Percentage of Total Capital

Years	Unweighted industry average	Albert-son's Inc.	Borman's	Food Lion	Lucky Stores	Kroger	Safeway Stores	Super-markets General
1985	38	50	29	43	36	29	40	39
1984	38	48	25	49	36	33	38	38
1983	37	44	26	42	35	31	41	41
1982	38	43	34	45	34	35	36	41
1981	38	37	30	55	35	32	37	38
1980	40	36	29	71	34	35	40	36
1979	40	33	28	73	36	36	40	33
1978	39	30	30	78	32	32	41	31
1977	39	34	26	76	37	31	40	26
1976	37	30	30	68	33	34	41	24
Average								
1981–1985	38	44	29	47	35	32	38	39
1976–1980	39	33	29	73	34	34	40	30

years. The analyst should examine the interest rates paid by Borman's on short-term bank borrowing, funded debt, leases, and the like to determine whether the company had been paying inordinately high interest rates on some of its debt, and when those high interest rate instruments are due to mature. The effects of leverage are influenced by the ratio of total debt to capital, and by the interest rate paid on debt.

Growth by Leveraging

The relatively modest leverage of Food Lion makes its recent return on equity all the more remarkable. However, the analyst would notice that a significant contributor to Food Lion's high and growing profitability has been the reduction from an ultraconservative 73 percent equity ratio in 1976 to 1980 to a moderate 47 percent ratio in the more recent five-year period. Thus, the increase in the return on equity from the earlier five-year period is in part due to increased borrowing. Although the company's equity ratio remains conservative, one would not expect a great deal more improvement in return on equity once the company's ratio reaches the industry average.

Supermarkets General shows an opposite pattern from that of Food Lion, having moved from a highly leveraged position to a level approximately equal to the industry average. This reduced leverage has been a cause of the company's decline in return on equity from the level of the earlier five-year period.

Although we chose to show only the equity ratio as a measure of leverage, a more detailed industry analysis could include a table of average interest rates on borrowings, including leases. Changes in interest rates may also give useful explanations of changes in the return on equity of leveraged companies.

Indexes—Base Period versus Base Year

The use of indexes is a convenient way to escape the difficulty of comparing trends of companies whose data vary significantly in size. Most government indexes use a single base year, setting the index at 100 at that point. That is workable in economics because most economic statistics on the broader aspects of the economy are fairly stable. Results of individual companies tend to be much more volatile, and therefore, it is usually a better practice to use a period of several years as the base, rather than a single year.

Table 22.4. Growth Indexes, 1976–1980 (Base = 100)

Years	Unweighted industry average	Albert-son's Inc.	Borman's	Food Lion	Lucky Stores	Kroger	Safeway Stores	Super-markets General
			Sales Index					
1985	246	224	123	565	193	214	156	248
1984	220	210	128	445	190	199	156	211
1983	193	190	125	355	172	190	147	171
1982	176	175	125	287	164	184	140	157
1981	148	154	118	202	148	141	131	145
1980	133	135	125	165	133	129	120	127
1979	116	118	113	126	119	113	109	115
1978	98	100	98	91	96	98	100	100
1977	81	80	86	66	80	84	89	84
1976	72	66	78	52	72	76	83	74
Average								
1981–1985	197	191	124	371	173	186	146	186
1976–1980	100	100	100	100	100	100	100	100
			Total Cash Flow before Interest Index					
1985	259	255	139	574	199	200	189	257
1984	219	233	97	422	182	195	188	217
1983	179	203	22	330	175	186	158	176
1982	162	176	139	247	161	128	143	163
1981	161	148	93	213	162	237	125	152
1980	134	132	125	161	130	144	115	133
1979	111	119	93	132	127	102	109	97
1978	105	106	126	96	106	93	105	102
1977	75	79	68	62	75	74	85	85
1976	74	64	89	48	63	87	87	83
Average								
1981–1985	196	203	98	357	176	189	161	192
1976–1980	100	100	100	100	100	100	100	100
			Total Earned for Capital Index					
1985	235	235	129	480	137	237	190	238
1984	200	230	49	390	142	226	164	200
1983	152	205	−84	291	150	206	152	146
1982	161	184	123	207	133	187	139	152
1981	131	156	21	196	141	163	108	129
1980	133	141	126	161	135	140	109	119
1979	121	126	106	133	134	118	112	119
1978	103	104	132	95	100	97	107	89
1977	73	73	56	62	73	80	83	86
1976	69	56	79	49	58	64	89	87
Average								
1981–1985	176	202	48	313	141	204	151	173
1976–1980	100	100	100	100	100	100	100	100

Table 22.4. Growth Indexes, 1976–1980 (Base = 100) (*Continued*)

Years	Unweighted industry average	Albert-son's Inc.	Borman's	Food Lion	Lucky Stores	Kroger	Safeway Stores	Super-markets General
			Earnings per Share Index					
1985	205	232	157	426	103	137	151	231
1984	160	221	− 15(d)*	363	109	124	129	192
1983	91	195	−311(d)	265	121	104	128	134
1982	151	172	148	196	107	166	121	144
1981	109	161	− 79(d)	191	122	162	83	120
1980	133	144	139	162	123	143	99	123
1979	126	129	107	132	130	123	118	146
1978	109	104	172	93	99	102	118	78
1977	67	71	15	64	82	73	84	78
1976	64	51	67	49	66	59	81	74
Average								
1981–1985	143	196	− 20(d)	288	112	139	122	164
1976–1980	100	100	100	100	100	100	100	100

*(d) = deficit.

In Table 22.4 we have selected the average results for the years 1976 through 1980 as 100, the base for our index. Note that for the sales index, excepting Food Lion, setting the year 1978 as our base year would have made little difference. However, when we create an index for such a volatile number as earnings per share, 1978 would have been a poor one to use as a base for measuring progress.

Several of the companies were very consistent in bringing down a constant portion of sales to cash flow and to the total earned for capital, but some fell considerably short in bringing a proportional amount down to earnings per share. The analyst would investigate the causes of these shortfalls, which could range from dilution due to sale of additional shares, to poor margins, or to high interest rates.

Interest Coverage—Cash Flow Is the Key to Quality

Table 22.5 shows the cash flow coverage of all interest expense. That ratio is one of many used to measure the quality of the company's debt instruments. It is a maxim of this book that if debt of a company is of unsuitable quality for purchase, no one other than a speculator should purchase the equity. Thus, all analytical studies should include at least some measures of the quality of a company's debt.

The reader may be interested in comparing the relative standing of these companies in terms of interest coverage with the Table 22.2 data on capital turnover. In general, rapid capital turnover is viewed as a

Table 22.5. Cash Flow Coverage of All Interest

Years	Unweighted industry average	Albert-son's Inc.	Borman's	Food Lion	Lucky stores	Kroger	Safeway stores	Super-markets general
1985	5.8×	4.6×	3.1×	12.3×	6.4×	6.9×	4.4×	2.8×
1984	5.7	5.0	2.3	11.6	7.6	4.8	5.6	3.1
1983	6.4	5.2	4.0	12.4	6.7	6.3	6.5	3.4
1982	6.3	4.9	2.7	13.8	6.9	5.8	5.8	3.9
1981	6.0	5.0	3.4	12.3	5.9	6.6	4.9	4.1
1980	6.3	5.2	2.7	12.7	6.0	9.1	4.3	3.8
1979	5.6	5.2	4.2	12.2	5.5	3.7	4.5	3.8
1978	4.8	5.7	0.7	8.9	5.2	4.3	4.7	4.1
1977	5.3	6.1	2.9	9.4	5.4	4.4	5.1	4.0
1976	5.6	7.3	3.9	9.0	5.8	4.4	4.6	4.1
Average								
1981–1985	6.0	4.9	3.1	12.5	6.7	6.1	5.4	3.5
1976–1980	5.6	5.9	2.9	10.4	5.6	5.2	4.6	4.8

highly desirable characteristic, but it is sometimes accompanied by low depreciation expense, perhaps because stores are old and have low acquitision costs. This tends to reduce cash flow. Although Food Lion and Kroger had rather unimpressive capital turnover, both had very good cash flow coverage of interest. Food Lion's interest coverage is easily explained by its wide earnings margin and conservative capital structure. The explanation for Kroger's interest coverage is not obvious from these tables, so the analyst would review Kroger's cash flow statement to determine whether the favorable coverage came about from above-average depreciation or perhaps from high deferred taxes. If the answer were not found there, it might be derived from low interest rates. Whatever the answer, the important point is that comparative ratio analysis not only tells a variety of useful stories about companies and industries, it also indicates areas which should be investigated by the analyst. Thus, the anomalies make a unique contribution to security analysis.

Per-Share Growth Rates

Comparisons of Averages

Table 22.6 presents a convenient mechanism for comparing the growth in per-share attributes for the seven grocery chains from the first five-year period to the second. The five-year averages are assumed to represent the normal cash flow, earnings, dividends, and book value for the companies. Thus, the percentage change from the first five-year period to the second five-year period represents the *total* growth from

Table 22.6. Per-Share Growth Attributes

	Unweighted industry average	Albertson's Inc.	Borman's	Food Lion	Lucky Stores	Kroger	Safeway Stores	Supermarkets General
			Cash Flow per Common Share					
Averages								
1981–1985		$ 3.77	$ 2.89	$ 0.93	$ 4.18	$10.57	$ 8.17	$ 3.03
1976–1980		1.96	2.97	0.27	2.67	7.71	5.71	1.60
Percent change 1976–1980 to 1981–1985	80	92	−3	244	57	37	43	89
			Earnings per Share					
Averages								
1981–1985		$ 2.26	$−0.24	$ 0.59	$ 1.94	$ 4.21	$ 3.09	$ 1.32
1976–1980		1.15	1.21	0.20	1.72	3.04	2.52	0.81
Percent change 1976–1980 to 1981–1985	42	96	nmf*	180	12	38	64	63
			Dividend per Share					
Averages								
1981–1985		$0.60	$0.03	$0.05	$1.15	$1.85	$1.44	$0.37
1976–1980		0.26	0.08	0.01	0.86	1.00	1.18	0.17
Percent change 1976–1980 to 1981–1985	87	126	−63	286	34	85	22	117
			Book Value per Share					
Averages								
1981–1985		$12.95	$12.13	$2.46	$11.64	$28.50	$25.40	$7.21
1976–1980		5.23	11.19	1.19	6.69	19.75	18.85	3.23
Percent change 1976–1980 to 1981–1985	77	148	8	107	74	44	35	123

* nmf = not a meaningful figure.

the midpoint of the first five years to the midpoint of the second five years. To obtain the *annual* rate of change, one would add 100 percent and take the fifth root of that sum. For example, the earnings per share growth from the 1976–1980 period to the 1981–1985 period for Albertson's, Inc., was 96 percent. To get the annual growth rate, one would add 100 percent to the total and express the result as a decimal: 1.96. The natural logarithm of 1.96 is 0.673. That divided by 5 is

0.13459, the antilog of which is 1.144. Thus the annual growth rate from midpoint to midpoint was 14.4 percent.

Growth Rates Using Indexes

An alternative measure of the growth in earnings per share would be to use the index shown in the final section of Table 22.4. A simple calculation from the beginning to the end can provide a growth rate estimate. First divide the beginning index of 51 (1976) into the final index of 232 (1985). Using the same logarithmic method described above, the index would give a rate of 18.3 percent growth in earnings per share for Albertson's, reflecting the unduly low index number for the beginning year, 1976. Note that earnings per share doubled from 1976 to 1978 (the index moved from 51 to 104). Which growth rate better characterizes the company's history is a matter for analytical judgment and consideration of many factors. In any event, the important growth rate lies ahead. The central issue of the growth aspect of valuation is whether the future growth of the company will be in some ways similar to that of the past, or in some ways different.

The index numbers can also be used with other techniques to estimate an annual rate of historic growth, e.g., a linear regression of the years versus the index numbers. The values found on that regression line give a compound growth rate of 17.1 percent, whereas log linear regression gives an 18.6 percent growth rate.

With such a large range of calculated growth rates, the analyst must pay close attention to choosing between the use of a series or averages. Averages have the advantage of muting the outliers. Individual years give a longer history, but at the cost of some accuracy. The analyst's judgment will lead to one or the other approach, in a given situation, as having greater potential usefulness in estimating the future growth rate.

Stock Price Comparisons—Attributes per Dollar Invested

Table 22.7 shows certain key data on a basis of the investment of $1 in a stock. The first data line is based on the stock price as of December 31, 1985. Ordinarily we would have selected a date somewhat later—in the year 1986—so that the annual report would be available when the analyst was making the purchase or sale decision. However, in the first half of 1986 three of these grocery chains were rumored to be takeover targets, and the prices reflected that speculative possibility. The dollars of sales, cash flow, earnings, dividends, and book value shown on the

Table 22.7. Stock Data on a Per-Dollar-Invested Basis

Company	Stock price	Sales	Cash flow	Earnings	Dividend	Book value
Albertson's Inc.						
1985	32.50*	4.69	0.15	0.08	0.02	0.53
1981–1985 Average	22.50	6.32	0.17	0.11	0.03	0.59
Borman's						
1985	12.00*	29.35	0.39	0.16	0.00	1.11
1981–1985 Average	6.93	58.42	0.50	(0.05)	0.01	2.04
Food Lion						
1985	21.75*	1.61	0.07	0.04	0.00	0.17
1981–1985 Average	11.00	2.18	0.09	0.06	0.00	0.24
Kroger						
1985	47.88*	8.19	0.19	0.09	0.04	0.59
1981–1985 Average	35.09	11.99	0.34	0.13	0.05	0.85
Lucky Stores						
1985	25.00*	7.35	0.19	0.07	0.05	0.53
1981–1985 Average	18.10	9.33	0.23	0.11	0.07	0.65
Safeway						
1985	36.88*	8.83	0.24	0.10	0.04	0.77
1981–1985 Average	23.56	14.84	0.36	0.13	0.06	1.13
Supermarkets General						
1985	50.50*	2.81	0.08	0.04	0.01	0.19
1981–1985 Average	11.82	11.34	0.31	0.13	0.04	0.73

*Price as of December 31, 1985; other data on this line are for the year 1985.

first data line are the actual figures for 1985. Since some of those numbers may not have represented normal conditions, most analysts would use an average or an estimate of what was normal rather than the actual figures for the year. The first line is designed to show what the investor could have bought with $1 invested in each of the seven stocks on December 31, 1985. The 1985 data were used in preference to the five-year data because of the strong growth trends of three of the companies.

The second data line shows the average stock price for the period 1981 through 1985 and the average amounts of the various data items for the five-year period from 1981 to 1985, calculated as amounts that would have been obtained by investing $1 in the stock at the average price for the five years. Comparing the two lines gives a notion of what could be bought at the end of the period versus what could have been bought at the average price.

The calculated results, in this case, show that if the 1985 figures are representative, investors would have obtained much less of each attribute at the December 1985 price than they had been able to obtain at the average price for the previous five years. This is not particularly startling, since all the stocks were up sharply from their five-year average price. However, some of the attributes rose sharply also.

Tables such as 22.7 help provide a sense of perspective. They indicate what the analyst can obtain today versus what was obtainable on average over a reasonably long previous period. They bring together the data for a number of companies that are reasonably similar in their business activities. They emphasize how much the investor is giving up to obtain a rapid rate of historical earnings growth and how much can be gained in past attributes for the investor who is satisfied with lower-quality issues.

Although Table 22.7 may help the investor decide which of the seven stocks is the most attractive growth stock and which is the most attractive yield stock *in historical terms,* the industry-oriented table provides no information about whether grocery stocks are cheap or dear relative to the rest of the stock market. This comparison requires industry data and some broad measure such as Standard & Poor's 400 industrials stock index, for which similar data can be obtained.

Table 22.7 is a good example of the techniques of combining ratios to produce new ratios. The sales per dollar of market value ratio is simply the ratio of sales per share to price per share, and the other ratios to market value are calculated similarly.

The examples of useful tables and techniques in this chapter have used only historical data, but a real study of an industry would include projections of the future for both the companies and the industry composite. The orderly comparison of the past record of a homogeneous group of companies is a sound basis for detecting and understanding what is "normal" for or characteristic of that group. Individual companies' departures from the norm tell something of the individual company's characteristics. All that information is good background for forecasting the future.

The reader may find it useful to spend some time comparing the price data of Table 22.7 with the various data found in the other tables. What factors correlate best with the pricing of these stocks at year-end 1985 or during the 1981 to 1985 period? Profitability, growth, stability, leverage, yield, or creditworthiness? How much more important is the current record than the distant past? Which measure of the growth record or of earning power seems the best technique in explaining the stock prices?

Tentative answers to such questions can be formed, but pricing anomalies will continue to leave one with a feeling that the stock prices are not fully explained by the past record, regardless of technique. That feeling is correct. Expectations about the future are the dominant factor in stock pricing. The correlation of stock prices with the past is largely a reflection of the persistence of past company and industry characteristics through time. That continuity exists to a greater degree in stable industries, such as the grocery chains, than in cyclical or technology industries. Even in the stable industries, blind extrapolation of past data is a poor substitute for analysis.

Price comparisons between companies, such as those found in Table 22.7, are among the analyst's most powerful tools for determining relative values. They are used in the final steps of the investment decision, for price is the analyst's greatest ally.

PART 3

Analysis of Fixed-Income Securities

23

The Bond Investing Environment

Martin L. Leibowitz

The U.S. fixed-income markets have undergone a remarkable transformation in both structure and style. In the years before the 1970s, the maturity of the instrument dictated its application. A traditionalistic buy-and-hold philosophy prevailed, and the yield to maturity was the reigning gauge of investment value. The very certainty of the cash flows laid the foundation for a certain type of highly structured approach to investment. Long-term bonds were held for long-term investment periods. Bonds were predictable, even somewhat dull.

The current market, in contrast, places enormous emphasis on liquidity and flexibility. Investment goals vary much more widely from one institutional investor to another, and the portfolio objectives of any one fund can change quite radically from one day to the next. The financial activities of market participants are more attuned to the competitive pressures of the day. With the long-term prospect so volatile and uncertain, naturally a greater emphasis is placed on adapting to short-term needs. At the investment level, this emphasis has led to increasing focus on short-term rate of returns and to a sizable premium for portfolio flexibility.

However, even in today's hectic marketplace, the investor still looks to a portfolio's fixed-income component for the reliable achievement of certain specific objectives, although these objectives are now more likely to be characterized in terms of short-term requirements for both adequacy of return as well as flexibility for revision. The trend in bond investment is toward new forms of structured management that can reliably provide more targeted results, at least in relative terms. This search for closely targeted outcomes, even in the short term, can derive only from the promised long-term cash flows that are the distinguishing hallmarks of the fixed-income market.

Chapter 23 traces some of the key historical developments that led to the new management styles, the new structured strategies, the enormously increased range of new vehicles that form today's bond market, and the resulting analytical judgments required of the security analyst.

Buy-and-Hold Management

In the United States prior to 1970, the fixed-income market functioned largely as a primary market. The issuance of bills, bonds, notes, and "placements" raised funds for government and corporate entities and simultaneously served to help fund the future liabilities of financial institutions and individuals. In these early days, the *intention* of most bond investors was to keep the bonds, clip the coupons, and ultimately reap the redemption payment at maturity. Although statistics are scanty, bonds were mostly held to maturity, and interim sales occurred only in extraordinary circumstances.

The accounting techniques at most financial institutions certainly encouraged this buy-and-hold approach. Bond investments were kept on the books at amortized purchase cost. If the current market rate was higher than the purchase yield, a sale would generate an immediate book loss. However, if the current rates were lower than the purchase rate, then the sale would create a capital gain tax liability as well as lead to a decline in the overall book yield. All these outcomes were generally viewed as undesirable. Clearly, these attitudes led to only one course of "action"—continued holding.

Yield Maximization

In such a buy-and-hold world, bond investors measured their success by how high a yield they could obtain—in terms of overall portfolio yields, yield on annual investments, or the yield they could obtain in an "acceptable" bond purchase. Naturally, this led to stretching for yields within certain "acceptability bounds." The security analyst's assignment was to define those bounds, to avoid downgradings of credits, and to aid the search for additional fractions of 1 percent in yield as a reward for making less conventional or more complicated bond investments.

Investing solely by yield maximization risked certain pitfalls, for example, acceptance of lower credits; uncertain liquidity; and less desirable characteristics in terms of call features, sinking funds, covenants, etc. These potential problems were controlled to some extent by the high degree of market segmentation that prevailed in these times.

Segmented Investing

Long-Term Corporate Securities

Prior to 1970, by far the highest yielding bonds were corporate securities (see Figure 23.1). High-grade industrial and utility issuers were primarily interested in selling 25-year and 30-year bonds that matched the lifetime of the capital project that they funded. Consequently, the preponderance of high-grade corporate bonds were long-term maturities (see Figure 23.2). Thus, as they reached for higher yielding but still acceptably high-grade bonds, pension funds and insurance companies found themselves largely focused on long-term corporate securities. These long-term purchases seemed to fit into the nature of these

Figure 23.1 Time chart of yield levels: long U.S. Treasuries versus new long AA utilities.

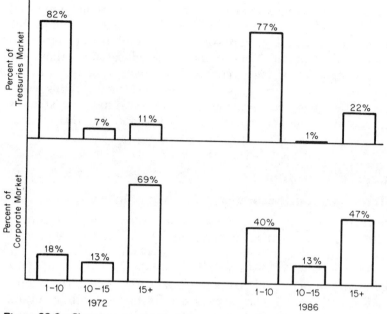

Figure 23.2   Changing maturity structure.

institutions' liabilities in a general sort of way. There were often very specific limitations on the credit-rating structure of the overall portfolio, for instance, no more than 10 percent A or no more than 60 percent AA. In the "old days," a bond's credit rating was more stable than in these days of "event risk," so this quality structuring by rating probably had greater validity and relevance.

Given the limited choice of market sector, the yield maximization styles of our predecessors made some sense. This style certainly had a more reasonable basis than one might believe from a current vantage point. This may be yet another example where modern people's scorn of their ancestors' practices is itself rooted in ignorance: The old timers were acting in a perfectly rational fashion within the framework of what was relevant in their time.

Treasury Securities

There were other market segments. The short-term market existed primarily in the form of Treasury securities (T-bills). Certificates of deposit (CDs) and commercial paper started to become a major market in the 1970s. The U.S. Treasury and various departmental agencies were of course issuing short- and intermediate-term notes as well as long bonds. However, notes were fewer than 7 years in maturity, whereas long Treasury bonds had maturities of 25 or 30 years. Thus, even the Treasury yield curve was spotty and had large gaps. Moreover, a law prohibited the U.S. Treasury from issuing "bonds" with a coupon rate exceeding 4.25 percent. (This quaint law is *still* on the books, but a sequence of special exemptions was passed by Congress starting in 1973.) As rates rose beyond this level in the mid-1960s and stayed there, all long Treasury bonds became deep discounts. In itself, this turned the long Treasury market into a relatively moribund secondary market. However, the "moribund" turned into the "morbid" as these long 3.5 and 4.25 percent Treasury bonds began trading on their special value for payment of estate taxes. Simply put, these long Treasuries could be used to pay estate taxes at their full *par* values. Since the higher market rates meant that these bonds could be purchased at a substantial discount, the about-to-become-deceased investor could pay off $1 of estate taxes by purchasing 70 cents of these so-called flower bonds. This rather specialized application soon dominated the market for long Treasuries, causing them to sell at higher prices (and hence lower yields) than their coupon rates would justify.

Taken together, this relatively low-yielding, purely secondary market in long Treasuries was properly deemed unacceptable by healthy long-term investors of both the individual and the institutional variety (see Table 23.1). This market segmentation and the buy-and-hold approach characterized the bond market prior to 1970. This fairly rigid structure led to managers focusing solely on yield improvements through the purchase of new corporate issues from the flow of new funds that they *had* to invest.

Table 23.1. Changing Portfolio Structures
(In Billions of Dollars)

	1970		1985	
	Treasuries	Corporates*	Treasuries	Corporates*
Private pension funds	2.1	29.4	134.1	97.1
State and local retirement systems	5.1	35.1	78.5	114.9

*Includes privates and convertibles.

Forces of Change

In the years after 1970, these bond market traditions were stretched and shattered by the impact of many new forces:

• The onslaught of inflation and the associated rise in interest rates

- The renewed issuance of long-term U.S. Treasury bonds as a result of the lifting of the 4.25 percent maximum coupon restriction in 1973
- The unbelievable growth of the U.S. deficit and the concomitant explosion in the U.S. Treasury securities market (see Figure 23.3)
- The deregulation of interest rates within the financial system
- Internationalization of the credit markets and of all the capital markets
- The delinking (in the corporate area, at least) of capital project lifetimes with the maturity of the debt instruments used to fund these projects
- The changing attitude toward financial leverage by corporate and governmental issuers
- The explosion of liability management (a battle that was so thoroughly won that most people today have forgotten there ever was any controversy about the need to manage the liability side of a financial institution)
- The development of new interest-rate-sensitive products in the insurance, banking, and thrift areas
- The increased volatility of liability costs within financial institutions
- The transformation of many financial institutions from primary investors to wholesalers and repackagers

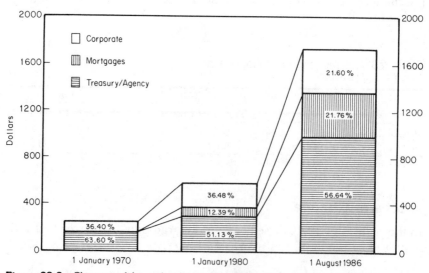

Figure 23.3   Change in debt market structure: public issues – amount outstanding.

- The explosion of private and public pension funds
- The transformation of the investment and management business from a "relationship" business to a largely stand-alone competitive business based on short-term rate-of-return performance (first in the equity markets and then transformed investment practices in the debt markets as well.

These basic changes in the financial system were mirrored over the years by changes in investment styles, by the development of new investment techniques, and of course by the emergence of a whole new array of fixed-income vehicles.

Fundamentally, all these changes can be summed up in one word—*flexibility*. The environment changed from a traditional segmented market characterized by a crusty buy-and-hold mentality to one with an enormous appetite for flexibility by both investors and suppliers of credit instruments. All participants in these changed markets have found themselves vulnerable to eroding margins, to more volatile liabilities, to a changing business environment, and to a far more competitive market for their products (both domestically and internationally). Capital market participants now require an unbelievably flexible range of vehicles, instruments, and styles to keep step with the competitive pressures that they face on a daily basis.

Emergence of Active Bond Management

The evolution of bond investment strategy must be viewed from the framework of the changes in interest rates that accompanied this process. Figure 23.1 traces the yields of new long AA utility bonds from 1960 to 1986. In this rather hidebound environment, the range of management activities was relatively limited. The traditional market segmentation was so strong that managers would typically have few strategic considerations. Funds were put into a well-defined market sector; managers did not hoard cash, at least not for very long, nor did they go back and forth between long-term and short-term areas of the maturity spectrum. Nevertheless, on some occasions bonds would be traded, usually in response to some developing credit consideration or concern or to pick up yield. For the most part these trading decisions were based on assessments of factors related to a specific issuer or a rather narrow sector. The analyst would identify candidates for downgrades and upgrades in agency ratings or other measures of creditworthiness before the market realized the changes. Indeed, for many years, active management was considered equivalent to carrying out "bond swaps." The very term *bond swap* reveals the highly tactical nature of this early activity in the fixed-income area.

The Pure Yield Pick-up Swap

The granddaddy of all bond swaps is the pure yield pick-up swap. The ideal form of this swap would be a 1-for-1 exchange of a portfolio holding for a bond that matches the held security in all important characteristics and yet, for some reason, has a higher yield to maturity in the marketplace. The purpose here is to increase the total contractual yield over the bond's life.

The pure yield pick-up swap seems so obvious and irresistible that one wonders how such opportunities could arise in an efficient and competitive marketplace. The answer to this question provides a highly revealing insight into how traditionalistic rigidities can create market inefficiencies. With the passage of time and with market movements, these inefficiencies can lead to sizable and clear-cut opportunities. In turn, the very obvious character and magnitude of the trading opportunity then stimulates a powerful drive toward greater flexibility. Ultimately, this struggle to realize the obvious benefits from enhanced flexibility overcomes traditionalism, arbitrages out most of the market inefficiency, and then feeds on itself to generate a far greater appetite for flexible active management.

A major source of opportunities for yield pick-up swaps was the combination of the secular rise in interest rates that began in the mid-1960s with the various accounting restraints that limited funds' ability to realize book losses. These constraints forced many funds to carry positions of low-yield bonds far beyond the point where they represented appropriate holdings for their portfolio. However, to the extent that such issues did become available for trading, their very discount nature often had a special appeal for certain types of fresh investors. For example, the older long-term U.S. Treasury bonds were priced at the lower-than-market yields (and hence higher prices) because the specialized demand from flower bond buyers who were looking to estate tax value as an overriding inducement. In other cases, corporate bonds with sinking funds that required periodic mandatory retirements often sold at higher prices than comparable current coupon issues. Deep discount bonds, because of the favorable capital gains tax treatment at this time, had special appeal for certain classes of taxable institutions, especially if a large reservoir of losses could be used to offset any capital gains liability.

In each of these cases, the original purchasers found that their portfolios now contained bonds that were of far more use to someone else than to them. In concrete terms, the market was willing to pay a higher price, that is, a lower yield, for the security. In turn, the investors could sell these particular bond holdings at their lower yields and take the proceeds and invest them in a higher coupon issue of comparable credit or maturity and achieve a significant increase in yield.

As rates moved even higher, the incentives for such pure yield pick-up activity became ever more compelling. Of course, taking advantage of this seemingly irresistible opportunity required some weakening of the absolute prohibition against book losses. This weakening started in the late 1960s and continued apace during the early 1970s. Various types of special accounting offsets were developed for dealing with the book loss problems. Many state legislatures actually enacted special rules that allowed their retirement systems to incur book losses provided that they could be "made up" by the additional yield generated from the bond swap within a specified number of years.

A number of other doors were opened to enable large funds to take advantage of these yield pick-up opportunities. A veritable garden of accounting fictions sprang up reflecting various formulas for determining loss recovery times and/or for amortizing realized losses as a charge against the portfolio's future income stream. Ingenuity bordered on the bizarre. Many of the formulas were inconsistent or flawed from a true investment point of view. For example, they often failed to deal correctly with the coupon reinvestment and compounding process. Nevertheless, virtually all these loss recovery formulas could be satisfied with a sufficiently large improvement in yield to maturity. The preceding years of total loss constraint ensured that many portfolios contained ample opportunities for the needed sizable yield improvements. This led to increasing levels of pure yield pick-up swapping. Some older pension funds spent years moving out of their massive accumulated holdings of low-yield Treasury and corporate bonds.

From an economic point of view, the key point is that the funds began actively to seek out trading opportunities—especially the irresistible ones. As a corollary, managers began to realize that the very actions of the market could take what had been a perfectly legitimate set of portfolio holdings and transform them so that they no longer fit the needs of the fund. In other words, the passage of time and the market movement itself could render a portfolio in need of management activity just to keep it freshly attuned to sponsor's goals.

Management for Short-Term Returns

The movement toward recognition of the need continually to freshen a bond portfolio contributed to an atmosphere in which active management could take some beginning steps. This trend was further enhanced by changes in the stable traditional relationships that had long characterized the professional investment management community. Such changes had long been underway in the equity markets, and the equity markets had also led the race toward total return performance measurement as a hallmark of the modern management process. For competitive equity managers, total return held a particular appeal as a natural measure of management activity.

The bond market was much slower to accept the total return yardstick. Undoubtedly, the natural traditionalism of the bond market was reinforced by bonds' other measure—long-term yield—that had seemed to suffice for many years. However, as the new breed of bond managers sought to establish their credentials, they embraced the short-term total return measures. The combination of these trends in portfolio management and in the investment management community opened up a new dimension in the world of tactical bond activity—the substitution swap.

The Substitution Swap

In the early 1970s, interest rates were relatively stable. The new breed of bond managers were eager to take advantage of the highly liquid marketable bonds that formed the fixed-income component of pension portfolios. The new managers recognized that the cost of this liquidity was generally lower yields, and they were determined to make this liquidity pay for itself on an ongoing basis. The managers focused on short-term trading activity and on the substitution swap in particular.

In substitution swaps, the portfolio manager tracked the yield spread (or price spread) relationship among groups of substitutable bonds. When the spread between any two bonds within the same group reached some extreme limit, a swap was executed in the hope of obtaining a prompt, profitable reversal as the spread later returned to more normal levels. In essence, the substitution swap amounted to selling overpriced bonds and buying underpriced bonds. Because the bonds were so similar, a substitution swap usually involved little or no change in maturity, credit, or sector exposure.

Portfolio managers hoped that the under- or overpriced condition was a temporary aberration and that the swap would profit from a relatively quick return to a more normal relationship. Because of the institutional dominance of the bond market, such temporary market imbalances were not unusual for a host of reasons.

The rewards from any single substitution swap would naturally be fairly limited. However, a reversal could be a very clear-cut demonstration of management success. Thus, swaps from A into B and then from B back to A could be quite dramatic when the portfolio reestablished its original holding, having accumulated extra funds in the process. For many managers, a cleanly executed string of substitution swaps paved the way for even greater investment flexibility. Of course, the security analyst had to be able to certify to no loss of investment quality. If the spread opened because someone else had recognized a deterioration in creditworthiness, profitable completion of the round trip was in jeopardy.

Sector Management

Sector Swaps

By 1972, this drive for flexibility and performance had begun to manifest itself in the rise of sector swapping. Basically, this bolder form of active bond management focused on rearrangements of the sector distributions within a portfolio. Thus, the manager in a sector swap would try to capitalize on changing value relationships between distinguishable market sectors. For example, the manager might swap from utilities into industrials or from Canadians to U.S. agencies. Sectors could be defined in many ways—by type of issuer, as in the preceding example; by coupon, for example, from discounts to current coupon bonds; by credit rating, to upgrade from single A's to double A's or vice-versa, for example.

Sector swapping was greatly facilitated by the broader trends in the fixed-income marketplace. The upsurge in yields over the preceding few years had clearly distinguished the current coupon bonds from the older discount bonds. Increased issuance of nonutility corporate debt (straight industrials and finance paper) provided a wider choice of sectors. The beginning of the mortgage security market with the introduction of the Government National Mortgage Association (GNMA) pass-throughs represented a major opportunity for sector swapping—a veritable magnet for such activity which has continued for a number of years.

In fact, the GNMA pass-through provides several classic illustrations of a sector swap. For example, in the fall of 1973, the yield on GNMA pass-throughs rose to unprecedented levels relative to both corporates and other agency issues. The underlying cause was clear—the natural initial purchaser of these instruments, the thrift institutions, had basically run out of investable funds. (The GNMA pass-throughs were intended to tap the pension fund market. However, this goal had not yet been reached because pension fund managers were put off by the GNMA's apparent complexity and the associated accounting problems.)

As the GNMA yields continued to rise to ever higher levels over corporates, a certain number of alert corporate bond investors began to take notice. The pension fund managers who undertook these sizable sector swaps into the pass-throughs reaped considerable rewards, as the spreads did narrow relative to corporates in the course of the next several months.

By their very nature, sector swaps involved major percentages of the portfolio. Consequently, they had a larger impact on the structure and performance of a bond portfolio than did 1-for-1 substitution swaps.

Rate-of-Return Performance Measurement

This narrowing of yield spreads was particularly important in light of the increased application of rate-of-return performance measurement. The first rate-of-return index for the bond market was introduced in 1972 by Salomon Brothers—the High-Grade Long-Term Corporate Bond Rate-of-Return Index. At the time, it served as a benchmark for the natural baseline investment of most bond managers in the pension fund area. In later years, as the view of the natural hunting ground for bond managers expanded across the maturity spectrum and moved toward a capital market orientation, more broadly based rate-of-return indexes became popular, for example, the Shearson Lehman Government/Corporate Index, the Merrill Lynch Bond Index, and the Salomon Brothers Broad Index (see Figure 23.4). The combination of sector swaps and rate-of-return measurement led more bond portfolio managers to turn from a focus on yield to a focus on "value." The best rate of return over short-term periods would not be achieved by continuing the ancient policy of reaching for the highest-yield security. Rather, it was the bond and/or bond sector that appreciated most in relative price that mattered over the short term. These swings in relative price would swamp the short-term effects of greater yield. Managers sought the current best value, and they would pursue this "cheap sector" even if it meant giving up (that is, moving down in) yield. Thus, yield maximization ceased to be the sacred cow of the bond market and gave way to short-term performance.

Rate Anticipation: Maturity Management

By and large, the sector swap tended to preserve the maturity structure of the original portfolio: The long portfolio remained a long portfolio; the intermediate portfolio remained an intermediate portfolio. Sector-

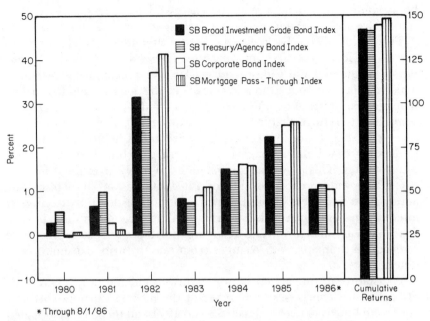

Figure 23.4   Historical returns over calendar years (through August 1, 1986).

independently of the direction of interest rates. Bond portfolio managers of a pension fund or insurance company still felt that their natural
investment habitat was the long market, and that was where they put
their funds. Apart from the temporary accumulation of new investable
funds for slightly longer periods, these managers did not really try to
base major investment decisions on their forecast of the direction of
interest rates.

All this began to change in 1973. By this time, performance measurement was quite entrenched. Starting in early 1973, interest rates began
a rise that continued through most of 1974 and led to a devastating
erosion in the value of the typical bond portfolio. This erosion was often
as large as 25 percent, and the devastation afflicted all bond managers:
the substitution swappers, the sector swappers, the passive managers,
the insightful managers, and so on.

There were a few exceptions. Certain managers who by insight or
great luck were able to foresee the continuing rise in rates took bold
action and put substantial portions of their portfolios into short-term
securities. These few managers preserved the market value of their
portfolios and enjoyed huge performance advantages. Needless to say,
the results of this maturity strategy attracted great attention within the
swapping focused on relative values that existed (to a large extent)

Analysis of Fixed-Income Securities

bond community, especially as the successful managers were (understandably) not shy about marketing their spectacular results.

This 1973–1974 debacle was hardly the first adverse cycle for bond prices, but it was the first time that such horrendous results were *fully visible* because of the widespread tracking of portfolio performance. This visibility led to a dramatic change in the style of bond portfolio management. First, it demonstrated that a fortuitous maturity structure could lead to returns that far exceeded any benefits from even the most successful substitution or sector swaps. Second, it helped to foster the impression that bond managers could anticipate broad movements in interest rates. This powerful combination led many investment managers to the widespread adoption of rate anticipation strategies. Rate anticipation managers focused primarily on forecasting the direction of interest rates and then making corresponding changes in their portfolios' maturity structure. The resulting portfolio restructurings were often quite dramatic, with changes from one maturity extreme to the other.

The stature of rate anticipation was further enhanced by two rounds of back-to-back successes: A number of the new anticipators correctly anticipated the rate rise during 1973 and 1974 and then correctly called the turn when rates plunged during 1975 and 1976. This second round of successes naturally heaped fuel on an already strongly burning fire. Active bond management soon became equated with rate anticipation. The gifted active managers widely believed that interest rates could be predicted and that the only useful role for bonds was to seek the maximum return through such maturity strategies. It is interesting that these beliefs were widely held even by fund sponsors who fully embraced the efficient market theory as it applied to their equity portfolios. Timing was generally thought to be impossible in terms of choosing direction of the equity market, but the pejorative word *timing* was virtually never applied to the growing ranks of rate anticipators within the bond market.

The bloom came off this rose relatively slowly. As interest rates proceeded on one roller coaster ride after another throughout the 1970s and into the early 1980s, the markets themselves may have changed. With the increasing deregulation and the huge buildup of the credit flows from many different sources (see Figure 23.3), reasonable estimates of the factors affecting bond market movements became more difficult to obtain. In addition, the very growth of ever more anticipatory investment funds seeking to capitalize on any prospective change in the direction of rates helped to create a much more volatile and more unpredictable market. A fully anticipatory market is obviously the most difficult one for anticipators.

Whatever the reasons, it seemed to become harder and harder to maintain an unblemished record of rate anticipation for one cycle after another. One by one, the heroes of the rate anticipation movement seemed to stumble. These missteps proved costly. The rate anticipators' portfolio shifts were extremely radical, and hence their returns suffered all the more when they proved wrong. With clearly more difficult markets and consistency problems among the well-known rate anticipators, sponsors' faith in rate anticipation began to erode.

Duration: The Search for More Deliberate Risk Control

By the early 1980s, sponsors were clearly seeking ways to exercise greater control over the interest rate sensitivity of their bond component. Rather than leave such key decisions to the discretion of an anticipatory manager, sponsors began to seek ways for the management of their bond portfolio to serve the larger purposes of the fund. This trend took place in an environment of historically high interest rates, which spawned a spectrum of new tools and new vehicles. These new tools proved to be well-suited to the sponsor's emerging needs for better control of rate sensitivity. The most basic of these tools was the *duration* measure.

The concept of duration began to be broadly used as a gauge of price sensitivity during the late 1970s. In the new world of rate-of-return measurement, changes in the market value of portfolios dominated all other considerations. For bond portfolios, the key became the price sensitivity of individual securities to changes in a common interest rate. In earlier days, the maturity of individual bonds or a portfolio's average maturity would have sufficed as rough sensitivity gauges, but the new investment environment required a more refined level of control. A manager's short-term performance might be carefully scrutinized quarter by quarter or even month by month. A given manager's returns would be compared with other managers' results as well as with the returns from bond market indexes. Bond portfolio managers now needed to know how their interest rate sensitivity compared with that of their peers and the major indexes.

For these purposes, a bond's maturity was far too crude a tool. The price sensitivity of a bond is derived from its *total* cash flow—coupon payments, sinking fund payments, as well as the maturity redemption. All these components of the cash flow enter into the equation that determines the present value (its price) of a bond for a given discounting rate (its yield). The maturity reflects only one component of this total cash flow. Indeed, for longer instruments, the maturity payment may be a relatively minor part of the bond's present value. Clearly, a more reliable guide would apply the present value formula to all cash flows and then mathematically derive an expression for the percentage price change associated with small changes in the discount rate. This expression is termed the bond's *duration*.

The duration concept was particularly intriguing because it could be interpreted in two seemingly different ways. On the one hand, it was indeed a better measure of average life. On the other hand, it provided a useful measure of "tangential" price sensitivity (Figure 23.5). At first glance, price sensitivity and average life would appear to be quite different concepts. Upon reflection (or simple mathematical manipulation), one can see that these two characteristics are virtually identical for fixed-income instruments.

As a measure of price sensitivity, duration had a number of advantages: It could be easily computed for individual bonds; by using market value weighting, a bond's duration could be combined with other bonds in a portfolio to arrive at an overall portfolio duration value; the differences in duration between two portfolios was a useful gauge of the subsequent differences in their price behavior.

However, duration was still far from a perfect measure for these purposes. It was accurate in a strict sense only for infinitesimal interest rate movements—the kind that never happen! For large interest rate

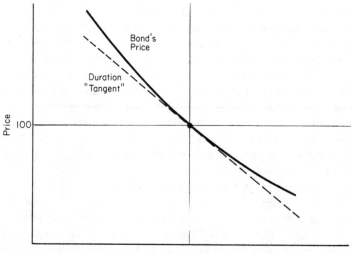

Figure 23.5   Duration of a bond.

movements, duration would lead to only approximate answers whose accuracy would erode with the size of the yield move. More seriously, these duration errors would depend on the direction of interest rate movements. In general, the errors became much more severe as interest rates declined. In a portfolio context, the duration approach depended on a common interest rate affecting all bonds. This assumption was clearly compromised by changing sector spreads and market movements that reshaped the yield curves across maturities.

These problems with the duration concept were further aggravated by the optional features embedded in many bond portfolios. These optional characteristics create a so-called convexity problem that severely limits the effectiveness of duration as a guide to price response. For example, most corporate bonds (as well as many agency and long-term Treasury bonds) are subject to refunding calls as of some specified future date. In essence, this is an option that the issuer retains to "call in" the bond should the outstanding interest rate drop sufficiently below its coupon rate. Consequently, as interest rates decline below a bond's coupon rate, the bond's price response is increasingly dampened by the threat of such refunding calls. A similar but far more complex phenomenon affects mortgage securities where the cash flow can be accelerated through prepayments of refunding-oriented mortgagors.

These effects lead to a radical curtailment in the price sensitivity of fixed-income portfolios in lower-interest environments. The pro forma duration of such portfolios based on maturity dates cannot capture this "adverse convexity effect." However, in the high-interest markets of the late 1970s and the early 1980s, these low interest rate problems had a low priority in the bond manager's consciousness; this helped the simple duration tools to find widespread applications as a measure of portfolio price sensitivity.

Immunization of Returns

Duration had another source of appeal in this environment. Just as maturity was an unacceptably crude gauge for price sensitivity, the bond's yield to maturity was an inadequate guide to the return that could be captured over a span of time. Thus, in a time of high interest rates, certain bond portfolio managers sought to lock up high yields for a prescribed period of time. Traditional coupon-bearing instruments could not be used for these purposes in the normal buy-and-hold mode because of the problem of coupon reinvestment: Future coupon payments had to be reinvested at whatever interest rates then prevailed. Since this future reinvestment rate could conceivably be far lower than the initial yield level at which the bonds were purchased, it followed that no satisfactory yield lockup could be achieved by simply buying and holding coupon-bearing bonds.

A new technique based on the duration concept, *bond immunization,* allowed for this lockup (within certain limits). For example, suppose that in a 14 percent interest rate environment a manager wished to provide a fully compounded return of 14 percent over a five-year period. The problem is how to overcome the reinvestment problem, that is, having to reinvest coupon payments at a rate below 14 percent should the general level of interest rates decline. Clearly, five-year 14 percent coupon bonds will not do. However, if a zero-coupon five-year bond at an interest rate of 14 percent were available, the problem would be immediately solved. Unfortunately at the time, a wide range of zero-coupon bonds had not yet become available. (Even now, the full maturity spectrum of zero coupons is available only at the lower rates embedded in the U.S. Treasury yield curve.) To achieve this high degree of return lockup with coupon-paying bonds, the reinvestment of those coupons must be "immunized" against changes in future interest rates. In 1952, the British actuary F. M. Redington developed a very clever scheme for achieving this immunization.[1]

The central idea was to create a portfolio of assets whose value coincided with the present value of the scheduled liabilities and whose interest rate sensitivity exhibited the dominance pattern illustrated in Figure 23.6. In other words, under a prescribed set of interest rate changes, the market value of the assets would always remain greater than the present value of the liabilities. This dominance pattern would ensure that as interest rates changed the changes in reinvestment income and capital gains would always compensate. Thus, under lower rates, the reduced reinvestment income would be offset by increased capital gains.

The basic mechanism for immunization relies on several measures based on present value. First, an asset's present value (usually taken as the market value) must match the present value of the liabilities. Second, the assets and the liabilities must have the same average life when weighted by the present value of their respective flows—this is just the duration measure of average life. Thus, the duration model is the first key to the immunization procedure. (However, additional second-order conditions are required to ensure the dominance pattern of Figure 23.6—even under relatively simple changes in interest rates.)

Immunization inherently requires portfolio changes over time. This need for continuing changes in immunized portfolios is derived from

[1] F. M. Redington, "Review of the Principles of Life-Office Valuations," *Journal of the Institute of Actuaries,* vol. 78, no. 3, 1952.

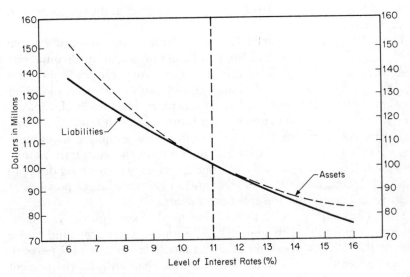

Figure 23.6 The immunization concept.

the need to preserve the dominance pattern over time. However, each cash inflow or outflow disrupts this pattern and requires some rebalancing of the immunized portfolio. These forced rebalancings are an intrinsic part of the immunization process.

Immunization of returns was an intriguing idea and quickly caught the attention of the bond community, although it seemed to be discussed more than applied. The problem was that some limited purposes truly demanded an exact lockup of a prespecified return. Immunization and related techniques did not really take off until they were embedded in the framework of the pension fund's liability schedule, which began with the rise of corporate interest in dedicated bond portfolios.

Dedicated Bond Portfolios

The early 1980s saw explosive growth in the development of specialized bond portfolios *dedicated* to funding a prescribed set of corporate pension payouts over time. The techniques used in constructing these specialized portfolios were referred to in various ways—dedication, immunization, cash matching, horizon matching, combination matching, and so on. The fundamental objective of all these techniques was to reduce the uncertainty of long-term investment results as they related to the fulfillment of specific liabilities. Such reductions of uncertainty, in turn, led to a number of direct and indirect benefits at the corporate and institutional level.

These benefits were particularly large with market interest rates at levels materially higher than the pro forma or actuarial discount rate used to value the liabilities. At this time, many corporations found their profit and cash flow levels under considerable pressure, and their pension contributions had risen to a particularly onerous level. Concurrently, interest rates had risen to such historically high levels that many corporate sponsors felt that bonds represented a unique investment opportunity—at least for the long term, if not for the short term as well. This confluence of events led corporate sponsors to (1) a strong desire to reduce pension costs and (2) a willingness to allocate larger portions of their overall assets into the fixed-income area.

The dedicated portfolio fitted these needs like a glove. The basic motivation is depicted in Figure 23.7. Suppose a pension fund had a class of liabilities on its books at an actuarial return rate of 7 percent. When discounted at this rate, these liabilities had an actuarial present value of around $128 million. Suppose further that they could be fulfilled, almost dollar for dollar, in a relatively assumption-free way with a cash-matched dedicated portfolio that cost $88 million at the 14 percent market yields that were available in the early days of dedication. Moreover, suppose this procedure was so assumption-free that the firm's actuary would have no problem accepting it.

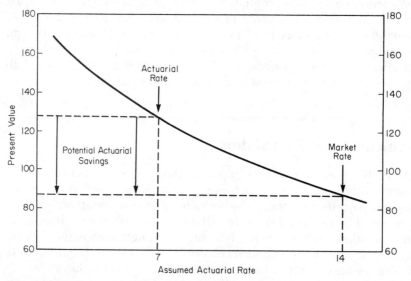

Figure 23.7   Present value of retired-lives liability.

The $40 million gap between these two figures translated into a 31 percent reduction in the fund's pro forma liability costs. This reduction would be realized on an amortized basis over time. The appeal of such a technique is clear—it was, in effect, a rather significant funding deferment.

This was the original motivation behind the dedication trend. In subsequent years, the role of dedication in pension funding has expanded considerably, both in terms of the purposes and in the financial situations of the corporations that have embraced its use. Dedication is no longer the sole province of the cash- or earnings-stretched company. Many leading actuaries have accepted dedication (in at least some forms), and it has become a fairly standard tool in the corporate pension planners' kit bag. Many of the recent applications have been by a variety of corporations with the highest possible financial standing. In fact, it is becoming increasingly used by corporations with *overfunded* pension funds.

From a bond investment viewpoint, the problem is again one of yield lockup. However, the objective target has moved from a compounded return target to the fulfillment of a prescribed schedule of pension fund payouts that can stretch over many years. Obviously, bond credit losses are not acceptable in this kind of a program, and the security analyst must be satisfied as to the quality of individual issues.

The terms *dedication* and *immunization* are often used interchangeably. However, it is more fruitful to distinguish the individual techniques by such specific terms as *cash matching, immunization,* and *horizon matching.* This reserves *dedication* for a more encompassing description of all these formalized techniques for bond portfolios *dedicated* to servicing a prescribed set of liabilities.

Cash Matching

The simplest dedicated approach is cash matching. The typical cash-matching problem begins with a liability schedule such as that depicted in Figure 23.8. The declining series of liability payouts represents the retired-lives component of a pension system.

The objective of cash matching is to develop a fixed-income portfolio that will provide a stream of payments from coupons, sinking funds, and maturing principal payments that will "match" the prescribed liability schedule. More precisely, the problem is to receive sufficient funds in advance of each scheduled payout so as to have full assurance that the payouts will be met from the dedicated portfolio alone.

The portfolio in Figure 23.9 represents the theoretical case of an exact

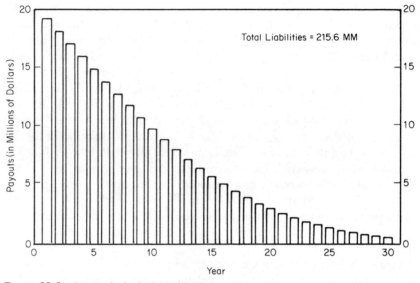

Figure 23.8   A prescribed schedule of liabilities.

match. With the exact match, each dollar of coupon and principal receipts on a given date is immediately used to support the required payout on that same date. This would seem to be the ideal fit for a cash

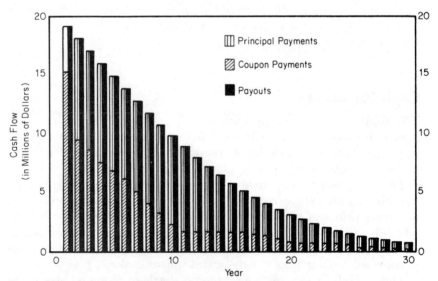

Figure 23.9   An exact-match portfolio.

flow matched portfolio. However, it turns out that such an exact match portfolio—even when possible—would usually not be optimal!

In practice, there will be a much larger universe of acceptable bonds that have coupon and principal payments on dates other than the exact payout dates of the liability schedule. In general, this larger universe will contain acceptable bonds with higher yields than their exact maturity counterparts. The inclusion of such higher-yielding securities naturally results in lower portfolio costs. When such bonds are used in a cash flow matching portfolio, the coupon and/or principal receipts must be accumulated for a period prior to their use on the payout date. Under such circumstances, these prior receipts must be reinvested at some rate until they are needed.

In practice, cash-matching portfolios are subjected to a variety of constraints imposed by both the logic of the problem and the degree of conservatism sought by the fund's sponsor. These constraints relate to call vulnerability, quality, type of issuer, diversification across type and individual issuer, the utilization of holdings from preexisting portfolios, and so on.

Considerable incremental savings could be extracted through energetic management of a cash-matched portfolio. At the same time, cash matching was a relatively stringent and tightly constrained period-by-period approach to the problem.

Immunization of Liability Schedules

To achieve greater flexibility and perhaps somewhat lower costs, portfolio managers need a procedure for funding scheduled liabilities without being constrained at the outset to match each individual payout, especially the relatively uncertain ones in later years. It turns out that the concept of immunization has a natural extension for dealing with this problem of scheduled liabilities.

In this application, immunization requires that the stream of liabilities be expressed in terms of their present value and their duration. Once again, by maintaining a match between the present values and durations of assets and liabilities, immunization can be achieved. The key difference here is that the asset flows and asset sales must be used to meet the cash outflows required by the liability schedule. This somewhat complicates the immunization process, as shown in Figure 23.10.

With the immunization concept, the portfolio structure can take on many forms as long as the interest rate sensitivity meets the several conditions required to achieve the dominance pattern of the asset curve over liability curve. This provides a high level of flexibility in choosing

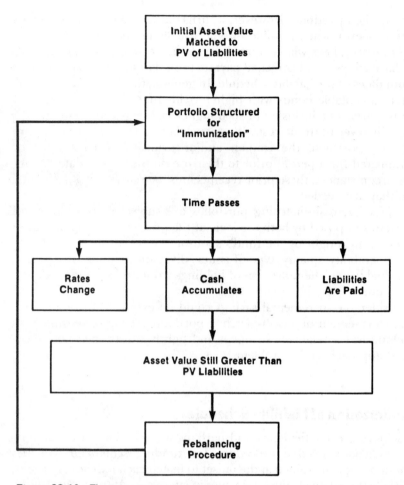

Figure 23.10   The immunization process.

an immunized portfolio, but it also means that the ultimate fulfillment of the liabilities depends far more upon the specific assumptions that underlie immunization theory. Unfortunately, the actual behavior of the fixed-income markets has sometimes violated these assumptions, parallel movements in the yield curve, constant sector spreads, etc.

For instance, Reddington's initial proposal required that interest rates be restricted to a flat yield curve subject only to parallel movements. Although modern techniques have enabled immunization to address a wider range of yield curve behaviors, immunization procedures still remain vulnerable to certain sequences of market movements.

Horizon Matching

The preceding discussion of cash matching and immunization revealed that a properly balanced combination of these two tools could lead to a very desirable new technique. A number of such combinations were explored. In 1983, the concept of horizon matching was introduced. Horizon matching provides just such a valuable blend—one that incorporates the best features of both techniques.

The central concept of horizon matching is illustrated in Figure 23.11. Essentially, the liability stream is divided into two segments by the selection of an appropriate horizon. Then, a single integrated portfolio is created that simultaneously fulfills the two liability segments in different ways. In the first segment, the portfolio must provide a full cash matching of the liabilities that occur up to and including the specified horizon date. This cash-matched portion will be subject to the same stringent constraints that would apply to any cash-matched portfolio.

For purposes of illustration, the horizon is assumed to be five years. For these first five years, the sponsor will have full assurance that the horizon-matched portfolio will provide cash flows adequate to meet the specified payouts. The liabilities beyond the fifth year will be covered through a duration-matching discipline that is based on immunization principles.

Figure 23.11 illustrates the types of cash flows generated by a horizon-matched portfolio with a five-year horizon. In this case, the first five years are shown to be almost perfectly matched on a year-by-year basis. However, in the duration-matched period from the fifth year on, the asset flows can depart—even radically—from the pattern of the liability schedule. However, these asset flows are structured so that the overall system satisfies the interest rate sensitivity requirements (that is, the duration match of asset and liabilities) as well as a number of second-order conditions.

This structure should allow more room for elective management, and the portfolio will serve its function even if it remains passive for the first five years. Thus, theoretically, the sponsor can simply pay out the liabilities as needed during the first five years and not worry about the passage of time. Even with such a passive stance, the dominance condition will be maintained throughout the course of the initial horizon period as long as interest rate movements fall within the broadly prescribed range.

One problem with the practical application of immunization had to do with nonparallel movements of the yield curve. This vulnerability to yield curve reshaping is largely eliminated in a horizon-matched port-

Analysis of Fixed-Income Securities

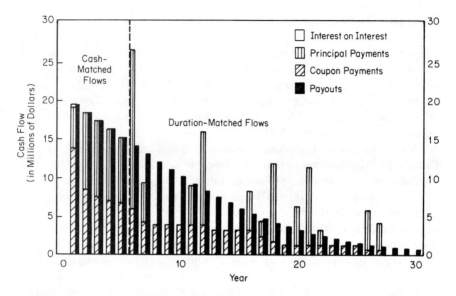

Figure 23.11 Horizon-matched portfolio.

folio with horizons of three to five years or more for the simple reason that the most severe yield curve reshapings occur in the shortest maturities.

The benefits of horizon matching do entail the acceptance of some degree of additional risk. The horizon-matched portfolio, by definition, will have a lower asset value than the fully cash-matched portfolio with its far tighter constraints. Consequently, there can be no assurance that the horizon-matched portfolio can be transformed into a fully cash-matched portfolio at any given time. Moreover, although the portfolio will retain its cash-matched characteristics through the horizon period without any further rebalancing, certain types of market movements could lead to shortfalls in the duration-matched portion once the horizon period has passed. Thus, horizon matching would fall somewhere between optimal cash matching and pure immunization in terms of both cost and the risk of potential shortfalls.

An additional advantage of horizon matching lies in the fact that the outer years of the liability schedule are often conservatively stated at the outset. Hence, the demands are likely to be relaxed with the passage of time. Horizon matching enables the portfolio to obtain cost efficiency by fully matching the more definite near-term liabilities without being hostage to specific pro forma liabilities that are likely to change in amount and time over the years.

Contingent Immunization

It has long been recognized that immunization procedures that stretch for the highest possible portfolio yields in a given market environment also incur the greatest risk of future shortfall. By the same token, economists have also observed that a "cushion" below this maximum rate provides additional comfort as well as flexibility to any immunization procedure. This concept of cushion flexibility can be extended to allow a significant degree of active management within a conservatively structured portfolio framework.

As interest rates rose to unprecedentedly high levels in 1981, minimum returns that were *well below* the maximum possible market rate became acceptable. Thus, when the market rate was 15 percent, a minimum return of 14 percent seemed to be a highly satisfactory level of return. For this 100-basis-point *cushion spread* (from 15 to 14 percent), a certain degree of portfolio flexibility could be obtained. In fact, cushion spreads of 100 to 200 basis points create a surprisingly large latitude for the pursuit of active management. With these cushion spreads, there could be a series of repeated adverse movements—the traditional "whipsaw" nightmare of every portfolio manager—and the portfolio would still retain some residual cushion above the promised minimum rate. It was this realization of the degree of flexibility afforded by reasonable cushion spreads that motivated the concept of contingent immunization.

The key idea is that managers can pursue active strategies as long as they retain a positive safety cushion. Should the market erode this safety cushion, the move is triggered to an immunized portfolio and the originally promised minimum floor return will still be achieved.

Suppose, for example, that a portfolio manager was strongly optimistic and wished to hold a portfolio of 30-year, 15 percent par bonds. The duration would then be seven years—far longer than the five-year horizon. This portfolio would clearly not be immunized. In fact, the least adverse movement (i.e., upward move in rates) would immediately violate the required assets line for the 15 percent target rate. However, if the fund is willing to accept the lower 14 percent floor rate as a minimum return, a wide range is tolerated in the subsequent price behavior of 30-year bonds.

If yields declined, the active strategy would have proved successful, and the safety margin of excess assets would rise with the superior performance of the 30-year bond portfolio. This successful move would enable the portfolio to generate five-year returns well in excess of the original 15 percent market rate. However, should interest rates rise, the safety margin would decrease, and the portfolio's assets would approach the minimum required asset level. In fact, the value of 30-year bonds would decline to the required asset level after an upward rate move of about 350 basis points. At this point, the safety margin would have been totally eroded, and the portfolio would have to be immunized to ensure fulfillment of the 14 percent floor rate. In this example, the portfolio can tolerate adverse market movements of more than 350 basis points even after having adopted the longest possible maturity stance in the par bond market.

How does contingent immunization compare with classical immunization? Classical immunization carries a high opportunity cost: the forgone potential profits of successful active management. Contingent immunization restores this profit potential in exchange for the spread between the immunized rate and the floor return. More generally, in the dedication context, contingent immunization incurs a somewhat higher initial portfolio cost to gain the flexibility for potential takeouts. With successful active management, these takeouts could significantly reduce the effective cost of funding the entire liability schedule.

New Fixed-Income Vehicles

The drive for flexibility on the part of both the investor and the issuer of debt securities led to an entirely new spectrum of investment vehicles in the late 1970s and the 1980s. Together with the new portfolio strategies described above, these new instruments enabled market participants more precisely to fulfill their objectives in the increasingly volatile and competitive environment.

The Treasury Yield Curve

With the special exemptions to the rule prohibiting long Treasuries above 4.25 percent, the U.S. government began in 1973 to issue bonds along the entire yield curve. This was accompanied by increasing budget deficits that fueled huge increases in the net issuance of treasury securities of all maturities. The Treasury market came to realize, in *practice*, its natural *theoretical* role as a benchmark for virtually every area of the fixed-income market. All bond spreads in every sector came to be measured relative to the Treasury yield curve level for that maturity.

Floating-Rate Instruments

The late 1970s witnessed the successful introduction of a whole new class of fixed-income securities that represented a hybrid between ensured long-term financing and an economic sensitivity to short-term interest rates. *Basically*, the floating-rate bond has a coupon payment rate that is determined as a specified function of the value of some interest rate index when the coupon payment becomes due. Thus, the coupon payment "floats" with the level of interest rates. Floating-rate notes first became popular with international banks as a way of obtaining long-term financing with interest rate costs geared to the floating-rate character of their loan portfolios. With the onslaught of high interest rates and high volatility in the debt market, floating-rate notes soon found a far wider audience among issuers who wished to ensure long-term financing at current market rates without locking into the high rates that prevailed at the time of issue. Since typical floating-rate notes offered a significant yield spread advantage to actual short-term instruments (at least in the U.S. markets), they quickly found a strong appetite among investors who wished to remain in the short-term end of the maturity spectrum.

Futures and Options

In 1975, the first interest rate future—based on the GNMA pass-through—was introduced on the Chicago Board of Trade. This was soon followed (January 1976) by a Treasury bill futures contract on the Chicago Mercantile Exchange. The T-bill contract quickly became a highly successful and intensively traded futures contract. It was followed in 1977 by the Treasury bond future on the Chicago Board of Trade, which has become the most successful contract in the history of exchange-traded futures. Other futures contracts in the United States include CDs, Eurodollar CDs, Treasury notes, and municipals. Futures exchanges in other countries have introduced interest rate contracts based on U.K. gilts, Japanese government Yen bonds, and Eurodollar CDs.

The initial appetite for the U.S. futures contracts was provided by many of the speculators (or "locals") that traded commodity futures. However, traditional bond market participants soon learned how to use futures as effective hedging vehicles, and they began to spread to an ever-widening circle of applications. Dealers and commercial banks were among the first to use them to hedge their inventory positions. Recently, pension funds and, to a certain extent, insurance companies have utilized futures contracts to shape their interest rate sensitivity or to help in achieving transitions between changing asset allocations. In the latter applications, futures serve as a sort of highly liquid bridge that enables the fund to lock in its desired allocations until the actual cash security transactions can be more comfortably implemented. Recently, the role of futures has expanded to include the new dynamic hedging procedures that have recently become popular among corporate pension funds.

Options on Treasury bonds futures were introduced on the Chicago Board of Trade in 1982. These options became popular and found a number of applications among institutional investors. Options can serve as protection for issuers who wish to lock in current interest rates for a span of time and are willing to pay the associated insurance "premium." On the asset side, options can protect the value of an investment portfolio over a limited time. They have been integrated into certain forms of dynamic hedging. The exchange-traded options contracts are often supplemented with a series of over-the-counter forward contracts on interest rates, sometimes in the form of *caps* or *floors*.

Many conventional fixed-income securities have embedded options that the investor implicitly grants to the issuer. For example, corporate bonds usually carry an explicit schedule of prices where the bond can be "called in" and redeemed prior to maturity. These call features are really a complex series of options that convey a definite economic benefit to the issuer under a sufficient decline in rates. Similarly, in mortgage securities, the ultimate mortgagor retains an option to pay off the loan under a wide variety of circumstances. Exchange-traded options can often be combined with conventional securities having embedded options to produce a package with a more desirable payoff pattern. For example, in the lower rate environment of 1985 to 1986, many such "synthetic" packages were constructed that used exchange-traded call options to offset the prepayment risks associated with high-coupon mortgage pass-throughs.

Original Issued Discount Bonds

Moderate original issue discount bonds (OIDs) had long been in various markets, as the prices of new bond issues were adjusted slightly away from par in order to bring them into alignment with the current market. Actually, the tax-exempt market had seen some issuance of *nickel bonds* carrying the near-zero coupon rate of 0.05 percent. (These nickels were small tail components in a package of serial maturities that comprised a single municipal underwriting.) However, in 1980, a new wave of taxable OIDs surfaced. These issues carried coupon rates that were significantly lower than market yields and hence were issued at prices ranging from 35 to 85. They were harbingers of a whole new family of first low-coupon and then zero-coupon securities that have had a profound impact on the bond market as a whole.

The initial motivation for the early OIDs sprang from certain tax advantages that became attractive in a higher interest rate environment. The issuers of such securities obtained a significant benefit from the then available tax regulations which enabled them to deduct computed interest on a straight-line basis (this rule has been subsequently changed). Investors were attracted to such securities because, at high interest rates, the OIDs afforded extraordinary call protection and a high duration with the associated protection from lower reinvestment rates over the bond life. This combination of motivations led to its ultimate realization in the form of a zero-coupon security where the only interest payment consisted of a lump-sum payment at maturity. Many corporate and international issuers came forth with such securities and they were quite popular in the marketplace for a period of time. Security analysts must include the accrual of discount as an interest item in their measurement of debt service coverage. Cash outflows will, of course, be concentrated in the maturity year.

Zero-Coupon Bonds

Since the zero-coupon bond provided no interim payments until maturity, the credit of the issuing entity was emphasized. This naturally led to a strong interest in obtaining zero-coupon instruments based on U.S. Treasury securities. By "stripping" the coupons from a U.S. Treasury bond, one could obtain individual coupon payments (and of course one maturity payment) that would act as such single-payment instruments. These so called "stripped treasuries" were available from time to time, but the supply was limited because U.S. Treasury regulations discouraged their formation.

In 1982, in conjunction with changes in tax rules that rationalized their tax treatment, the U.S. Treasury lifted these restrictions. Investment dealers immediately began to create various forms of single-payment instruments derived from stripped Treasury bonds. These instruments were immensely popular, and large proportions of certain Treasury issues were transformed into these specialized securities. These instruments were given an amusing set of acronyms, all depicting different species of the feline family: *TIGERS* (Treasury Investment Grade Receipts), *CATS* (Certificates of Accrual for Treasury Securities), etc. These new securities developed into a relatively liquid market with pure single-payment instruments that spanned the entire yield curve. At long last, the academic's dream of having market-determined discount rates for virtually every point in the future was now at hand (subject to a few mild distortions that always seem inevitable in any real capital market). Any fixed income security could—in theory—be decomposed into its individual cash flows, and then these flows could be valued relative to the corresponding maturity point on the "spot rate" yield curve.

In practice, these single-payment vehicles were used in a host of applications in the new high interest rate environment. For the investor who wished to lock up yield over a specified period, they provided the ideal vehicle. For the rate-of-return investor who wished to obtain a precise duration instrument, these single-payment bonds provided the answer. For the dedicated portfolio that needed to fit additional dollar flows into precise periods in the future, the single-payment bond was the perfect "plug."

The various packagers of such securities waged a considerable battle until the U.S. Treasury decided to get directly into the act in 1985. At this point, the U.S. Treasury announced that it would henceforth allow for strips to be created out of Treasury bonds at the instigation of the holder. In essence, the U.S. government would perform the role of stripping dealer by dismembering a Treasury security into its component cash flows and registering each of the components separately. This "strips" market continued to flourish on this new basis until the appetite for single-payment instruments abated during the lower interest rate periods that followed the great rallies of 1984 and 1985 to 1986.

Interest Rate Swaps

Another phenomenon of the 1980s has been the quiet marketplace explosion of interest rate swaps. An interest rate swap is basically a contract in which one party agrees to pay a series of fixed-rate coupon payments in exchange for the receipt of floating-rate coupon payments from a second party. There is no exchange of principal payments. Thus, in an interest rate swap, an investor who holds a fixed-rate instrument can agree to swap its coupon flows for the flows that would be received from a floating-rate instrument.

Interest rate swaps can be used either for investors such as thrifts and insurance companies (asset-based swaps) or for issuers (liability-based swaps). Interest rate swaps can be struck across many maturities and with a wide range of counterparties. They are powerful weapons in the battle for greater flexibility for both investors and issuers, and they have a very wide range of applications: The swap market grew from a standing start in 1982 to over $200 billion by 1986!

Issuers can use interest rate swaps to achieve important savings in financing costs. For example, suppose a given issuer wishes to obtain floating-rate financing, but the issuer represents a more attractive credit to investors as a long-term issuer in certain markets. The issuer can proceed to issue long-term debt at the preferential rates, then executed an interest rate swap with a counterparty into a more attractive floating-rate exposure than could have been obtained by going directly to the floating-rate market. As another example of a liability-based application, suppose an issuer of outstanding long-term debt feels that rates may be heading lower. Participation in that decline can be achieved by swapping the currently outstanding long-term payments for floating-rate payments.

On the investment side, interest rate swaps can be used to transform the cash flow of a fixed-payment portfolio to that of a floating-rate portfolio or vice-versa. Moreover, since the floating rate component acts as a proxy for future short-term rates, the floating-rate side can be used as a hedge against arbitrage financing costs or against the costs of future cash borrowings. By entering into an interest rate swap that substitutes floating-rate payments for a series of fixed payments, investors also significantly lower the duration of an existing component of their portfolios. Note that interest rate swaps can often have accounting advantages. For example, by acting as a counterhedge to an existing investment position, swaps can reduce the interest rate exposure of existing bond holdings. The use of swaps can materially alter the interest rate sensitivity and cash flow characteristics of a portfolio without incurring the adverse tax and accounting consequences of an outright sale.

In today's world, the drive for flexibility has become paramount, and the interest rate swap is indeed a powerful tool. From this brief sampling of its many applications, one can see why the interest rate swap market has so quickly grown to its current size.

The corporate borrower who issues floating-rate obligations or engages in interest rate swaps makes life difficult for the security analyst seeking to project borrowing costs. There is no practical alternative to selecting some arbitrary but reasonable average rate.

The Move Toward Structured Management

The 1980s have seen a vast change in the goals and styles of bond portfolio management. In some ways, it has been a disappointing period of lowered expectations. In other ways, it has laid the foundation for a better-defined and more realistic appraisal of the entire role of the bonds component within various institutional funds.

Investors have become considerably disenchanted, perhaps predictably, with the ability of bond managers to consistently "time" the swings in the bond market and to reap excess returns through rate anticipation. The return statistics from the early 1980s indicated that the majority of active managers failed to outperform the broad market rate-of-return indexes. Bond managers found themselves in need of a credible new approach that could ensure more reliable performance results.

Bond dedication appeared to be *the* solution for a while. As one fund after another elected to construct a dedicated portfolio, a massive transition seemed under way from fully active management to this highly structured form of bond management. Bond dedication did indeed eliminate many of the problems associated with the recent adverse experience with unfettered active management. However, dedication derived much of its appeal from the high interest rates and the wide actuarial spreads that prevailed in the early 1980s. Bond dedication could not serve as bond strategy for *all* times and for *all* purposes.

With the decline in rates from the highs of 1981, a clear need developed for structural approaches other than dedication to bond management.

The key element of any structured approach was the disciplined control of rate risk. By controlling the portfolio's interest rate sensitivity relative to some benchmark index, professional bond managers could pursue a series of active strategies based on relative value, and their results would no longer depend totally on an explicit (or implicit) bet on the direction of interest rates. Two major benefits resulted: (1) Managers could focus on professional insights in pursuit of incremental *relative* returns, and (2) sponsors could begin to expect *total* returns that had a certain degree of consistency relative to the bond market as a whole.

As more bond managers began to measure their performances against the broad market indexes as well as against each other, and as they sought to avoid the timing problems of the past, the range of returns achieved by managers began to close in around broad market index returns. Managers began to use a series of structural techniques to bring themselves within specified proximity to these index returns. These techniques included various forms of closet indexing and duration control relative to the index. Finally, as fund sponsors began to seek basic market returns with minimum management costs (especially those sponsors with very large funds), money began to flow into *explicit* bond index funds, first in 1985 and then much more significantly in 1986.

At this point many fund sponsors basically want to achieve returns from their bond component that coincide with the broad market indexes. Pension fund money continues to be directed toward bond index funds that simply mimic this broad structure of the fixed-income market. The fixed-income area is following an evolutionary trend in management styles that is similar to that which occurred several years earlier in the equity area. A considerable degree of commitment to some form of active bond management remains, but such active management is increasingly subject to various explicit forms of structured risk control. The structure of risk control may take various forms. For example, the portfolio may be required to have returns that must approximate those of an explicit index. There may be carefully controlled departures gauged so that the portfolio returns cannot fall more than a certain tolerance limit below the index returns. Or the control structure may take the related form of a duration target which is set jointly with the sponsor. This target may differ from index control if the chosen duration is significantly shorter or longer than the index duration. Recently, the techniques of *dynamic hedging* have been applied to risk control in the bond market. Dynamic hedging is a procedure that changes the portfolio duration in accordance with a well-defined discipline to achieve an option-like return over a specified period. Thus, the first response to the disenchantment with all-out timing forms of active management has been to cluster around a broad index of the fixed-income markets or to enter into some highly specialized structured portfolio such as dedication. Peering into the future, one might expect that the greater concern with liabilities would lead to bond management styles that more directly address the asset and liability problem.

To a certain extent, the liabilities certainly did thrust themselves on the bond managers' consciousness during the heyday of bond dedications. However, a much more generalized approach can be envisioned in terms of a spectrum of active strategies structured around baseline indexes that are directly related to liabilities. A continuum of departures from the pure matched-funding strategy, entailing various degrees of risk, could minimize the risk of fulfilling the specified liabilities. The key ingredient would be a baseline index that captures the interest rate sensitivity and other risk characteristics of the liabilities and establishes a customized target for each fund. In such a context, active managers would be able to pursue their professional insights in search of improved returns relative to this baseline target, thus retaining active management within a structure that is directed toward the ultimate goals of the fund.

The ability to readily define such a baseline index is certainly more characteristic of the fixed-income markets than of the equity markets. (In fact, this may be an important distinguishing feature of bonds as an asset class.) Managers and fund sponsors alike should take advantage of this natural opportunity that the fixed-income markets afford.

24

Selection of Fixed-Income Securities

The selection of fixed-income securities to meet investors' objectives proceeds from financial statement analysis to the security analyst's steps in the appraisal of a company's creditworthiness and the attractiveness of its bond and preferred stock for investment. Indeed, financial statements are the principal source of any such judgments.

Systematic Evaluation

A principal objective of the systematic evaluation of fixed-income securities is the obvious goal of making superior selections in the search for those financial assets which offer the most desirable characteristics to the investor seeking a predictable contractual return on capital. To identify the improving or deteriorating creditworthiness of the firm from some defined level of safety is the primary assignment of the analyst in this selection process. A collateral task is to exercise discrimination among the types and terms of individual issues.

A second reason for carefully appraising the financial position of a company is the equity investor's need for a meaningful measure of the riskiness of the enterprise. The risk component of the rate at which future equity returns are discounted is clearly derived from the same sources that the fixed-income investor investigates in the search for a reliable credit evaluation.

The third objective of systematic analysis is the determination of a company's capacity to finance future growth with debt or with debt and equity combined. Any meaningful forecast of future growth in earnings available for total capital implies access to some or all sectors of the capital market in which expansion can be financed without incurring excessive costs or burdensome restrictions on corporate discretion.

Unused Borrowing Power

By definition, the largest sum a company can borrow without unduly restrictive terms is exactly the amount lenders will be prepared to lend without insisting upon such requirements. Thus determining the level of debt which a company can comfortably carry and which lenders will be eager to lend at rates prevailing for securities of investment quality is essential.

The difference between a company's existing debt position and the defined level of borrowing power is the measure of the unused capacity to borrow. A major weakness of many common-stock analyses is the failure to account for the terms on which future growth can be expected to be financed. The calculation of unused borrowing power as illustrated in Chapter 25 is designed to provide a specific response to this question. No appraisal of a company's prospects can be relied on unless it includes an analysis of the means by which future periods will be financed by combinations of debt and equity. The appraisal must also consider contractual debt repayments, lease obligations, and planned repurchases of equity securities.

A Certificate of Confiscation?

In the rampantly inflationary years of the 1970s, bonds earned the opprobrium of being "certificates of confiscation." The bond buyer was seen as the dullard who bought a contract whose terms ensured a loss from inflation that would exceed the promised return. The subsequent years of extraordinarily high real total returns (as measured by coupon income plus or minus price change less change in the Consumer Price Index) from corporate bond investments, amounting to almost 18 percent per annum in excess of the inflation rate, have obliged investors to modify this negative verdict.

Clearly, the bond contract is inherently unattractive. In exchange for limited rights to share in future earning power, the bondholder obtains a prior claim on cash generated by the borrower and a definite promise of repayment at a stated date. Profitable growth will bring comfort and confidence to the investor but no material increase in return. The deterioration of profitability, however, will bring both anxiety and a downward market valuation of the issue.

The call feature of corporate bonds, moreover, ensures that the investor loses the winners and retains the losers in a bond portfolio. For example, an investor bought a high-quality bond like a Southern Bell Telephone 12⅞ percent debenture due October 5, 2020, when the issue came to market in 1980. In the following year, the investor saw his bond sell as low as 75⅛ as interest rates rose sharply. (The high investment quality of the bond never came into question.) In early 1986, declining interest rates came along to provide a handsome profit. The January 1986 market rate of 10¾ percent gave the 12⅞ percent issue a value of 119.21. Unfortunately, this was not the outcome, because the company sold 10¾ percent debentures due in 2025 to redeem the 12⅞ percent issue at its 110.61 call price. In contrast, the investor who bought in August 1963 the company's 4⅜ percent debentures due in 2003 saw them sell down almost to 30 in 1981 and recover only to 62 in late 1986 and can look forward to another 17 years of 4⅜ percent interest payments. Protection from call is obtained by the purchase of discount bonds, frequently at the cost of some return. The maturity yield of the Southern Bell 4⅜ percent bond at 62 was 8.85 percent when an 8¼ percent bond due in 2016 at 91 offered a yield of 9.13 percent.

Nevertheless, investors face circumstances in which fixed payments of interest and principal are essential to achieving a logical asset-liability relationship. This very need requires that each bond selection provide specific and convincing factors of safety to ensure payment in accordance with the terms of the issue. To obtain less than this assurance while giving up participation in profits is to make a very bad bargain indeed: no significant participation in gains but full participation in losses from unanticipated inflation. To sustain credit losses in addition is inexcusable.

Avoidance of Loss

Since the chief emphasis in bond investing is avoidance of loss, bond selection is primarily a negative art. It is a process of exclusion and rejection rather than a search and acceptance unless the investor is equipped to assemble a broadly diversified portfolio of issues of questionable safety for which the yield differential is generously rewarding. (See discussion of "junk" bonds in Chapter 25.)

The penalty for mistakenly rejecting a bond offering is unlikely to be significant, but the acceptance of an unsound issue will be costly. In the selection of bonds for *investment*, therefore, rules of exclusion, expressed in quantitative tests, are both logical and essential. In the application of such rules, creditworthiness must be seen as a corporate appraisal. Safety is measured by the issuer's ability to meet *all* its obligations under adverse economic and financial conditions, not by the contractual terms of the specific issue.

Corporate Debt in Perspective

For many decades, total outstanding debt of nonfinancial borrowers in the United States bore a stable relationship to current-dollar gross national product (GNP) (see Table 24.1).

Table 24.1. Outstanding Debt of U.S. Nonfinancial Borrowers Expressed as a Percentage of GNP

Year	Total	Federal government	State and local government	Nonfinancial business	Households
1960	137.6	45.2	13.7	37.9	40.9
1970	136.4	28.4	14.2	47.8	46.2
1980	138.1	25.7	10.6	50.6	51.2
1981	135.8	25.7	9.8	50.3	50.0
1982	142.5	28.4	10.0	52.9	51.0
1983	146.7	32.9	10.3	52.1	51.4
1984	149.8	34.1	10.1	53.2	52.4
1985	161.4	37.3	11.5	56.6	56.0

SOURCE: Board of Governors of the Federal Reserve System, Division of Research and Statistics, and *Federal Reserve Bulletin*, August 1986, pp. 511–524.

The spectacular increase of nonfinancial corporate debt in recent years, especially the increase for the years 1984 and 1985 of $358 billion (31.2 percent in two years), is a clear signal that security analysts should adhere strictly to their rules of exclusion. Loss of confidence in borrowers is a contagious disease not only because one firm's payables are another's receivables but also because lenders and investors raise their standards as even isolated instances of financial distress occur.

In 1985, net bond financing by nonfinancial corporations totaled $73.9 billion (compared to an average of $26.3 billion in the preceding five years), and equity retirements amounted to $77 billion. Acquisitions, leveraged buyouts, restructurings, and share repurchases combined to produce this unprecedented reduction in corporate net worth, offset only in part by retained earnings. Financial leverage, therefore, was rapidly increased and so was the market expanded for the lower-quality and subordinated debt instruments which made this possible. High-yield bond funds became one of the most popular products of the mutual fund industry. In 1985, corporate bond funds, largely in the high-yield category, increased their net assets by almost $9.5 billion to a total of $24 billion. The increase in this category came to $17.5 billion in 1986. Financial institutions such as savings and loan associations and insurance companies were also large buyers.

Interest Coverage

Interest Charges

The traditional measure of coverage of interest charges by net income before interest and taxes is still central to the evaluation of a company's creditworthiness. The standard of adequacy must be adjusted, however, to account for the radical change in the level of interest rates. A simple illustration makes the point. Industrial Company XYZ has net income before interest and taxes of $20 million with $100 million of debt bearing a composite rate of 4 percent. The times interest charge coverage ratio is 5 times and, on this basis, the bonds are clearly entitled to an investment rating. Two decades later, Company XYZ has grown and prospered. It now earns $60 million before interest and taxes but has only doubled its outstanding debt to $200 million. But rolling over old issues and selling new have changed the average rate to 10 percent. Interest coverage has shrunk to three times ($60 million available to pay $20 million of interest), and on this measure alone Company XYZ has sustained a substantial loss of investment merit. (In passing, observe that the economic advantage of financial leverage has substantially declined.)

Historical records of interest coverage have, then, lost much of their value as test measures. Moreover, they were never an adequate substitute for a true measure of debt service coverage, that is, coverage of the total cost of interest plus retirement of principal (assuming that earning power, rather than the liquidation of assets, is expected to service debt). In the Company XYZ example, if both the 1966 and the 1986 outstanding debt were scheduled to be retired in 10 equal annual installments, coverage of debt service can be measured as in Table 24.2. On this basis, it is evident that, as common sense told us, when a company expands 200 percent while financing only one-half of the expansion with debt, its creditworthiness has increased, and its bonds should rank higher in quality as a result of the increase in the margin of safety. If the 1966 debt

Table 24.2. Debt Service Coverage

	1966	1986
Debt service		
Tax-deductible interest	$ 4.0*	$ 20.0*
Annual sinking fund on a pretax basis†	20.8	37.0
	$24.8	$ 57.0
Sources of funds for debt service		
Net income before interest and taxes	$20.0	$ 60.0
Depreciation, amortization, deferred taxes, and other noncash		
charges	20.0	60.0
Total cash flow	$40.0	$120.0
Cash flow coverage of interest	10.00×	6.00×
Cash flow coverage of debt service	1.61×	2.11×

*Dollar amounts in millions.
†The step-up fraction to calculate the pretax equivalent of the debt retirement charge, 100/(100 − tax rate), assumes that Company XYZ had a tax rate of 52 percent in 1966 and 46 percent in 1986.

were charged with a rate closer to those of the past decade, of course, the comparison would be even more favorable to Company XYZ in its 1986 dimensions.

Debt Service

Shifting the focus from interest coverage alone to total debt service coverage does not eliminate the sensitivity of ratios to imbedded interest rates. As a practical matter, the problem of achieving comparability among borrowers and for the same borrower across time has no general solution. Each fixed-income security analysis has to address this problem and to determine a "normal" debt service to minimize the instability of coverage ratios. The adjustment of reported interest payments to a 10-year moving average for A-rated new bond issues will serve as a normal interest rate for this purpose, setting aside for the purpose of appraising creditworthiness the gains or losses from the accidents or good management of timely trips to the capital markets.

A more recent problem is the large volume of variable-rate bonds. Bank term loans have frequently presented the same problem. Since none of us can reliably predict interest rates for the next decade or more, the analyst must simply make a sensible assumption, one not unduly favorable to the borrower, and proceed to the quantitative tests. If only the low end of the scale of rates permits classification as of investment quality, rejection is the correct decision. This is particularly true because the bond investor is already taking the market risk of a rise in rates.

To judge the trend of an individual company's creditworthiness over a span of years, the simple ratio of total debt to net income after taxes is useful and provides a figure for years required to pay debt. Since interest charges are ignored except as they are deducted from net available for equity capital, changing rates have little effect on the meaning of the ratio.

A General Standard of Creditworthiness

The ability to meet all obligations of the business as they mature with a margin of safety which ensures that ability even in periods of adversity entitles a company to full access to the capital markets on reasonable terms. A determination of the adequacy of that margin of safety relative to the risks of the business constitutes the security analyst's assignment. Clearly, the analyst must look at the business as a whole to form an opinion of its stability and profitability.

Assets as the Source of Payment

The capacity of a company to pay debt from the liquidation of assets is a useful measure only when asset values are, to some significant degree, independent of the value of the business. A captive finance company like General Motors Acceptance Corporation is not expected to pay its debts out of earnings. In a prosperous year like 1985, net income amounted to only 1.4 percent of total debt. The margin of safety is to be found not in earning power but in the excess of collectible receivables over total borrowings. At the year's end, cash and receivables in billions showed the following coverage of debt. All assets other than receivables are ignored. Payables to the parent are included as subordinated debt.

$$\frac{\text{Cash and receivables}}{\text{Senior debt}} = \frac{\$66.64}{\$60.34} = 1.10 \text{ times}$$

$$\frac{\text{Cash and receivables}}{\text{Total debt}} = \frac{\$66.64}{\$65.79} = 1.01 \text{ times}$$

Another measure is the equity cushion expressed in these terms:

$$\frac{\text{Net worth} + \text{subordinated debt}}{\text{Senior debt}} = \frac{\$10.60}{\$60.34} = 17.6 \text{ percent}$$

$$\frac{\text{Net worth}}{\text{Total debt}} = \frac{\$ 5.15}{\$65.79} = 7.8 \text{ percent (a debt-equity ratio of 13 }\times)$$

Other instances in which assets are the source of debt repayment are:

- Natural resource production payments
- Installment receivables generated by product sales
- Transportation equipment such as railroad rolling stock, airplanes, and oil tankers
- Petroleum pipelines backed by take-or-pay contracts
- Leased capital equipment such as data processing, communication, and production equipment
- Real estate mortgages

The significant factors for analysis are the quality of the collateral and the creditworthiness of the user.

The analyst's judgment of a bond issue's creditworthiness, then, relies on the terms of the commitment to repay. The financing of an airline's fleet, for example, need not be secured by a lease, conditional sales agreement, or chattel mortgage to protect the lender, if the loan agreement has a strong negative pledge clause to deny other creditors access to the fleet. Modern equipment, well-maintained, is marketable and provides good collateral to bolster the frequently weak credit position of airlines.

In periods of a surplus of oil tanker capacity, the collateral value of a tanker may decline so far that it provides little security, but a bareboat charter to a major international oil company will make the financing of high-investment quality. This is the typical case in which the appraisal of creditworthiness applies to the asset user's ability to service the debt. Industrial revenue bonds are now a major capital market instrument for the security analyst's discipline. The credit of a little known municipality or county is immaterial; only the obligor to that entity, frequently a major business enterprise, needs analytical scrutiny.

A lien against property owned and used in the borrower's business turns out to add little value to most debt instruments. Specialized properties used in the business have value primarily because of their contribution to corporate earning power. Profitability of the operation is, therefore, the real source of creditworthiness. Claims on assets have also lost value as the evolution of reorganizations in bankruptcy has persisted in the direction of restructuring to continue in business rather than to liquidate and pay debts in accordance with their legal priorities. Mortgage foreclosures can be deferred for extended periods under the

Bankruptcy Act, and delays in enforcing claims reduce their potential value. The primary aim of the bond investor, therefore, must be to avoid trouble rather than to seek protection in the event of trouble.

Thus if the junior debt of a company lacks safety, the senior debt is unlikely to be a suitable investment. Stated conversely, if a company is creditworthy, the investor should buy the higher yielding issue, which would presumably be the junior or the subordinated obligation. To restrict investment only to the senior security is a vote of no confidence in the appraisal of the company's credit standing.

One qualification needs to be made of this sweeping conclusion in favor of the junior security: If the senior position does not cost more than a small sacrifice of yield, the modest protection against the unforeseeable and the unpredictable may be worth having. If the investor has a concern over the liquidity of the bond, moreover, selection of the senior issue is logical in the expectation that it will be subject to less price variability.

Earning Power as the Source of Payment

For the bulk of corporate bonds, the investor looks to earning power for the source of payment. To be sure, an electric power company serving a growing territory will retire one issue by selling another, but it is the record of earnings which makes the refunding feasible in the marketplace. For capital-intensive industrial companies, the retirement of individual bond issues is expected, even though total outstanding debt may be increasing with growth of the enterprise.

Look at the record of bond defaults in Table 24.3: Chronologically, with a modest time lag, the default rate has risen in periods of recession or depression.

Table 24.3. Incidence of Default in Publicly Issued Corporate Bonds

Period	Total corporate default rate (%)
1900–1909	0.90
1910–1919	2.00
1920–1929	1.00
1930–1939	3.20
1940–1949	0.40
1950–1959	0.04
1960–1967	0.03
1968–1977	0.16
1978–1985	0.10

SOURCE: The historical data are presented as rearranged and updated by Edward I. Altman and Scott A. Nammacher in *Investing in Junk Bonds*, John Wiley & Sons, New York, 1987, p.107.

Table 24.4. Distribution of Defaulting Issues by Rating

Original rating	One year prior to default	Six months prior to default
BBB	22.4%	7.8%	1.4%
BB	19.8	11.3	7.9
B	40.5	42.6	41.1
CCC	17.3	33.3	41.1
CC	.0	5.0	8.5
	100.0%	100.0%	100.0%

SOURCE: Edward I. Altman and Scott A. Nammacher, *Investing in Junk Bonds*, John Wiley & Sons, New York, 1987, p. 131.

A more meaningful measure may be the default rate on lower-quality issues, but some defaults occur in investment-grade issues. For example, Table 24.4 shows the distribution of defaults by rating grade during the 1970–1985 period.

The breakdown of bond defaults by industry in the 1970–1985 period in Table 24.5 demonstrates that growth and profitability of an industry by no means ensure that all entrants will have satisfactory performances. Indeed, there is some suggestion that a favorable industry environment may influence investors to let their guard down and to accept specific

Table 24.5. Corporate Bond Defaults, 1970–1985, by Industry

	Total number of borrowers	Total debt ($ million)
Industrial (58.6%)		
Retailers	14	669.9
General manufacturing	18	573.4
Computer, electronics, communication	21	574.4
Oil and gas	18	1101.4
Real estate, construction	12	209.4
Miscellaneous	17	737.2
	100	3865.6
Real estate investment trusts (5.7%)	12	379.2
Financial services, leasing (8.8%)	10	579.0
Transportation (26.9%)		
Railroad	9	1291.3
Air	6	303.0
Other	6	181.1
	21	1775.5
Total (100.0%)	143	6599.3

SOURCE: Edward I. Altman and Scott A. Nammacher, *Investing in Junk Bonds*, John Wiley & Sons, New York, 1987, p. 133.

risks which would otherwise be considered unacceptable. The story of Viatron Computer Systems is an illustration. The company offered, but was unable to deliver, a low-cost, efficient system for small business firms of the type which eventually became highly successful. Viatron, however, was in bankruptcy within a year of the offering of its convertible debentures.

The so-called three Cs of creditworthiness as identified many years ago are *collateral* (assets as a source of debt repayment), *capacity* (earning power as a source of debt repayment), and *character*. The third *C* is too frequently taken for granted and inadequately evaluated. We need not go back to Ivar Kreuger and International Match Corporation to find instances of the absence of integrity in business and financial affairs. Equity Funding, Flight Transportation, Itel, Saxon, U.S. Financial, and Westgate contributed 6 percent of the bond default dollars tabulated in Table 24.5, and the losses to investors were ultimately greater.

What constitutes adequate earning power to ensure a satisfactory bond investment depends on basic strengths, both business (trade position, customer loyalty, new product development, marketing, and general management, for instance) and financial (liquidity, capital adequacy, pricing, cost controls, and profit planning, for example) as well as the economics of the industry. Even this abbreviated list suggests that the factors are highly company-specific. Nevertheless, are there any guidelines which we might use in measuring the adequacy of earning power protection? Efforts to predict corporate bankruptcies are a fertile field for such guidelines, because they seek to identify financial ratios which might, in general, act as early warning signals of prospective failure.

The leading work of Beaver and Altman[1] provides an abundance of evidence that financial ratios, individually or in combination with others, can distinguish with a fair amount of leadtime companies which are likely candidates for bankruptcy. Altman's Z-Score has been enhanced in the development of the ZETA model which is commercially marketed by Robert Haldeman as ZETA Credit/Risk Evaluation.[2] The seven financial ratios employed in arriving at a score rank in this order of contribution:

---

[1]William Beaver, "Financial Ratios as Predictors of Failures," *Journal of Accounting Research*, January 1967, and Edward I. Altman, "Financial Ratios, Discriminant Analysis and the Prediction of Corporate Bankruptcy," *Journal of Finance*, September 1968. For a comprehensive review of the entire area, see Edward I. Altman, *Corporate Financial Distress*, Wiley, New York, 1983.

[2]Zeta Services, Inc., 5 Marineview Plaza, Hoboken, N. J. A ZETA score and changes in it are calculated for more than 4800 companies.

1. *Cumulative profitability.* The ratio of balance sheet retained earnings to total assets

2. *Stability of earnings.* A measure of the standard error of estimate around the 10-year trend of earnings before interest and taxes in relation to total assets

3. *Capitalization.* A five-year average of the market value of the common equity as a ratio of the total capitalization taking senior securities at par or liquidation value and common stock at market

4. *Size.* Total tangible assets

5. *Liquidity.* The current ratio

6. *Debt service.* Interest coverage ratio

7. *Overall profitability.* Earnings before interest and taxes in relation to total assets

Average ZETA scores for individual companies with senior debt rated by Standard & Poor's were as follows in February 1987:

S&P rating	Average score	S&P rating	Average score
AAA	8.78	BB	1.47
AA	6.82	B	−0.59
A	5.19	CCC	−8.36
BBB	2.87	Not Rated	0.41

SOURCE: Zeta Services, Inc., *Analysis Book*, Hoboken, N.J., Winter 1986–1987, bond rating analysis table, p. 1.

These analyses, in addition to identifying possible candidates for bankruptcy, provide a running measure of creditworthiness trends and assist the analyst in identifying candidates either for upgrades or for downgrades in the opinions of investors. ZETA scores declining below 2.9 suggest an impending loss of a BBB or better investment rating.[3]

Significance of the Record

The actual record of performance is the primary source for determining the adequacy of protection for fixed-income securities. The capacity which the analyst seeks to measure to determine the margin of safety is

[3]For a useful discussion of ratings, see David F. Hawkins, Barbara A. Brown, and Walter J. Campbell, *Rating Industrial Bonds*, Financial Executives Research Foundation, Morristown, N.J., 1983.

that which has already been demonstrated and proved reliable for the future. Taking chances on favorable future developments is the business of junk bond buyers and common-stock risk takers.

In selected cases of exceptionally strong borrowers, the analyst need not go beyond reported earning power and liquidity to satisfy the need for a margin of safety in an unfavorable economic or industry environment. In the usual case, however, the balance sheet and income statement as restated for analysis are the only valid sources. Part 2 has completely addressed the kinds of adjustments that need to be made.

The record, especially when purged of arbitrary or artful efforts to improve its appearance, is also the best source of insights into the effects of current and prospective developments. The most recent evidence of sensitivity to macroeconomic and competitive factors is frequently a better guide to future prospects than results in the remote past. Without becoming obsessed with short-term developments of limited significance, analysts can gain many insights gained by close observation of a company's response to the vagaries of product markets.

Amplitude versus Stability of Debt Service Coverage

The buyer of investment-grade fixed-income securities is normally prepared to take some interest rate risk, especially in longer-term issues but does not intend to take a credit risk and does not receive compensation for doing so. A consistent modest margin of safety is preferred over a higher average coverage of debt service characterized by wide fluctuations.

Characteristics of the industry (and secondarily the company) should determine the analyst's standards of adequacy for capacity to pay debt. A very modest margin of safety can be satisfactory if the business is inherently stable in its ability to generate cash. Electric power companies have provided many examples of good-quality fixed-income securities because of the low variability of their revenues. Even so, the new technology of nuclear power introduced major changes in some companies' historical growth rates and stability. This experience is a forceful reminder that forces of change are constantly destroying comfortable reliance on history.

Restructurings

The restructuring of a company, whether by radical changes in the mix of businesses or by major revisions in the corporate financial position, makes necessary completely different employment of the past record. When that record can be focused on an individual business sector, there may well be enough continuity to make the record relevant. In other situations, the analyst must construct future financial statements with ingenuity and imagination controlled by a healthy skepticism about the new mix.

If the restructuring is largely financial, the analyst is well prepared for the assignment. In the case of a leveraged buyout, for example, the major difference may be that the management, lacking unused borrowing power, can develop the business only along somewhat prescribed lines. Restraints on capital investments are likely, and a span of time is required to earn out the liquidation of equity positions. A modest substitution of debt for equity in the capital structure will not normally have such consequences.

Definition of Creditworthiness

For both corporate financial policy making and lender or investor decision making, a broad definition of creditworthiness is useful. For stocks and bonds to be judged of investment quality (where investment rather than speculative factors dominate the investor's experience), the analyst must be satisfied on three main points:

1. The company's ability to sustain its operations without serious losses or drastic cutbacks in periods of adverse economic and industry conditions

2. The company's ability to meet current liabilities and to service its fixed obligations under adverse conditions for a reasonable time

3. The company's ability to access new sources of funds under adverse conditions to modify or expand critical areas of its lines of business

Given the uncertainties associated with such judgments, a margin of safety is essential in the projected size and stability of the cash flows needed to meet these tests.

25

Specific Standards for Bond Investment

Systematic application of the negative art of bond selection requires some uniformity in standards of creditworthiness. Exceptions to general rules may be fully justified, but the starting point must be some definite standards for excluding issues from consideration for investment. Efforts to legislate such standards for financial institutions have failed because the standards were expressed in terms of historical and mechanical ratios that may not reflect the basic economic and industry factors which will govern future operations.

A classic example of such an effort was the 1929 relaxation of earnings standards for railroads in the definition of bonds legal for savings bank and trust fund investment in New York State. On the eve of serious deterioration in the economics of rail transportation, the volume of railroad bonds eligible for "safe" investment was enlarged by 64.3 percent. Of those added to the legal list, 22 percent defaulted in the next decade of the Great Depression.

Nevertheless, specific quantitative standards force the analyst to pay special attention to any proposed exceptions from them.

Standards of Safety

Nature of the Business

The financial record clearly shows the extent to which a business is characterized by dynamic growth, stability, sensitivity to the business cycle, or political (noneconomic) factors.

Capital Turnover. The stability of any such characteristics across different cycles can readily be observed by comparing the capital turnover ratio (sales divided by total capital) from year to year.

Example. American Home Products has a long history of stable growth with little sensitivity to technological change or business cycle developments. The first half of the last decade saw a remarkable stability in the capital turnover ratio, but a change occurred in the second half of that period:

1976	2.49×	1981	2.50×
1977	2.59×	1982	2.49×
1978	2.60×	1983	2.32×
1979	2.57×	1984	2.15×
1980	2.58×	1985	2.04×

The analyst's questions in the 1980s are: Is the business maturing? Is the company accumulating redundant capital? Was the earlier stability an artifact created by stating sales in current dollars and total capital in historical units? The company has been answering those questions in the affirmative. Divestment of the household products business in 1984 (10 percent of 1983 sales) was one response. More activity in acquisitions and new drug product development are other responses, accompanied by a 3.2 percent share repurchase program in 1984–1985, to be followed by a second one of equal size. Widely known and appreciated as the "analyst's best friend," the capital turnover ratio provided a reliable clue to a change in the nature of the business.

One would anticipate a lower return on total capital as a result of a decline in capital turnover, but return did not decrease in the American Home Products case, because the earnings margin increased enough to improve the return from 29 to 30 percent in the late 1970s and to 31.3 percent in 1984 to 1986. The analyst would always prefer to see such improvement come from capital turnover because of its presumably greater continuity, but of course a widening of the earnings margin may signify commendable gains in efficiency.

Profitability. The second useful measure of the nature of the business is its profitability. A year-by-year comparison of the return on equity (although not as valid as the frequently unavailable return on total capital) with the return on net worth for the Standard & Poor's 400 industrial stock index provides a record of profitability adjusted to account for inflation and cyclical factors. Investment information services provide data by industries which permit useful comparisons of the level, growth, and stability of earning power. This aspect of fixed-income security selection is nearly identical to that employed in common-stock valuation (Part 4).

Location. Location of the business may also be relevant if overseas political risks are a factor. In general, the U.S. investor should assume that physical plants or natural resources of domestic companies located abroad are subject to extra risks. Debt instruments backed by such assets are essentially unattractive and unable to provide the margin of safety of a domestic enterprise. Location within the United States may be an economic factor of more than marginal significance if not favorable in relation to resource availability, product markets, transportation, labor supply, and regulatory attitudes; but such deficiences, if they exist, will presumably be already reflected in the level of profitability.

Growth. The measurement of historical increases in the business shows a demonstrated capacity to deliver goods and services. As previously emphasized, such data are not for extrapolation into the future but may be useful for estimating the development of markets. The end point sensitivity problem emerges in any such measures. For most purposes, peak-to-peak and trough-to-trough calculations are adequate without going to the refinement of log least-squares trend lines to avoid sensitivity to the choice of starting and ending dates.[1]

The more serious problem stems from the inflation of the 1970s. Deflating by use of the gross national product (GNP) deflator, producer price indexes, or other measures is essential to escape the money illusion in looking at historical growth when unit data are not available in consistent form. For the 15 years from 1970 through 1984, American Home Products logged reported earnings increases of 12 percent a year with extraordinary consistency on a rate of growth in sales of less than 11 percent. What does that mean? How does one account for an irregular but persistent inflation rate of nearly 7 percent as measured by the producer price index for finished consumer goods? Should one advert

---

[1]The correct procedure for avoiding the problem is illustrated in Chapter 2, Figure 2.2.

to a *real* growth rate of 4 percent? But surely nominal, not real, dollars should be used to measure the capacity to pay debt stated in nominal dollars.

A more significant aspect of expectations for future growth is the implication for capital demands. The stability of the capital turnover ratio, absent major changes in the nature of the business, greatly assists the analyst in estimating possible requirements and methods of funding them. The adequacy of unused borrowing power to meet such needs requires appraisal in the course of passing judgment on existing or soon-to-be-offered fixed-income securities.

Stability of Earning Power. The continuity, consistency, and stability of earning power are key factors in determining creditworthiness. Consider the choice between Company A earning its debt service an average of twice, with no year less than 1.75 times, and Company B with an average coverage of 3 times, with variations from 4.5 to 0.5 times; the investor should favor Company A on the basis of this measure. Company B may never be in real danger of default, but if investors lose confidence in subsequent recovery, the price of the issue will materially suffer. As previously emphasized, the avoidance of price variability from a perception of financial weakness is a major objective of bond selection.

Recurrent cyclical instability is of less concern because of the assumption that an unfavorable trend will be reversed. Political factors and the winds of technological change, in contrast, may be presumed not only to continue but also to become more powerful with the passage of time. The same may be said of competitive forces in the marketplace. On some occasions, the prospects of a competitor may be as germane to the analysis as any information about the company under study.

In addition to these external influences on the characteristics of the business, some internal elements relate to the economics of the industry. The high operating leverage of an airline, when compounded by financial leverage in financing equipment, makes investment quality for its debt instruments an elusive goal. The analyst's reading of the financial record can identify at least a rough division between a company's fixed and variable costs. Should operating leverage be a critical factor, then the analyst must update those calculations to reflect changes in product mix and the addition or subtraction of financial leverage.

No quantitative measure of stability can be prescribed for the exclusion of fixed-income securities as candidates for investment. The general rule that failure to earn debt service in a period of adversity should result in rejection of the security needs qualification. The analyst must be aware of the factors which created adversity and the likelihood of their recurrence.

Size

Larger companies, as measured by tangible assets, are likely be more creditworthy than smaller firms, simply because of their greater market presence, broader product lines, and easier access to credit markets. To set a minimum size for fixed-income investment securities is inevitably arbitrary. American Motors with $4 billion in sales and more than a billion dollars in capital is a small company in the automobile industry. J. M. Smucker Company, however, with less than $300 million in sales and $100 million in net worth, holds a leading position in the market for jams and jellies and has a record of many years of profitable growth to support its evident credit worthiness.

The Great Depression and prior periods demonstrated that substantial size affords an element of protection against the instability of capacity to pay debt to which industrial companies are subject. The record of the period from 1900 through 1943 compiled by W. Braddock Hickman shows, by size of obligor, the proportions of industrial bond offerings going into default prior to 1944 (see Table 25.1).

Table 25.1. Industrial Bond Offerings in Default, 1900–1943

Asset size of obligor	Percent defaulted
Under $5 million	38.0
$5 to 99 million	25.3
$100 to 199 million	17.2
$200 million and over	3.4

SOURCE: W. B. Hickman, *Corporate Bond Quality and Investor Experience*, Princeton University Press for the National Bureau of Economic Research, Princeton, 1958, p. 495.

The greater vulnerability of the earning power of smaller companies to recession is illustrated by the recent record of the 1981–1982 period. Table 25.2 shows the decline in annual rate of return on net worth after taxes for all manufacturing companies from the third quarter of 1981 to the third quarter of 1982.

Although there is logic to measuring size relative to industry leaders, setting a numerical minimum size is also useful. To be sure, size alone is not a guarantee of profitability and financial strength, but its established relevance to creditworthiness argues for a minimum obligor size of $50 million five-year average market net worth. This simple computation is the sum of the high and low stock prices for the preceding five years divided by 10 and multiplied by the number of shares outstanding at the

Table 25.2. Decline in Annual Rates of Return on Net Worth
(In Percentages)

Asset size	1981	1982	Change
Under $5 million	16.1	9.1	−43.5
$5 million to $10 million	14.6	8.0	−45.2
$10 million to $25 million	11.4	10.4	−8.8
$25 million to $50 million	10.6	7.8	−26.4
$50 million to $100 million	13.0	5.0	−61.5
$100 million to $250 million	12.5	7.4	−40.8
$250 million to $1 billion	12.2	6.8	−44.3
$1 billion and over	13.6	10.0	−26.5
All manufacturing corporations	13.4	9.2	−31.3

SOURCE: Federal Trade Commission, *Quarterly Financial Report for Manufacturing, Mining, and Trade Corporations*, third quarter 1982, p. XXIII.

end of the period. There appears to be no need to set any minimum size for regulated industries like electric power, telephone, and gas distribution.

An industrial company meeting these minimum size standards might typically have bond issues outstanding in the range of $10 to $25 million. No minimum size of issue is prescribed, since this may affect marketability but has no relevance to the analytical process.

Terms of the Issue

Terms of a bond issue which expose it to, or protect it from, the consequences of interest rate fluctuations merit the portfolio manager's attention. The security analyst has a descriptive function for such features of an issue, making sure that the investors fully understand their and the issuer's options. In addition, analysts must determine whether protective provisions are present and whether they may be meaningful in providing security and enhancing the suitability of a bond for investment.

Early Maturity. A short maturity, representing the right to repayment fairly soon after purchase, is considered an advantageous feature from the standpoint of safety, presumably because there is less time for things to go wrong. Consequently, investors have been prone to be less exacting in their standards when purchasing notes or bonds due in a short time than in their other bond selections.

This distinction is unsound. A near maturity is a problem of refinancing for the company as well as a repayment privilege for the investor. The bondholder cannot count on the mere fact of maturity to ensure that repayment. The company must have either cash available or an earning power and financial position which will enable it to raise new funds. Corporations have frequently sold short-term issues because their credit was too poor at the time to permit sale of a long-term issue at a reasonable rate. In short, draw no distinctions between long- and short-term issues by relaxing standards of safety in the selection of issues of short maturity.

Secured Obligations. As previously stated, analysts should not give predominant weight to the pledging of assets for security. To be sure, transportation equipment, store locations, rental cars, and other assets which produce revenues make good collateral when profitable to a user. The lender looks to that earning power, however, not to taking possession of physical assets, for assurance that the bond contract will be met on schedule.

Although the holder of senior securities must rely primarily on the earning power of the issuer to provide the element of safety, the obligor should be bound by reasonable rules of financial housekeeping designed to prevent corporate acts injurious to the investor's position, to strengthen the company's creditworthiness, and to afford remedies in case of unfavorable developments. It is not feasible or even desirable to reduce these guidelines to precise rules, but they undoubtedly safeguard the position of the senior security holder.

The terms of subordinated debt and of senior securities deserve special review because there may be no limit on the issuance of senior claims and only weak protection against dilution of the subordinated claim. The almost exclusive reliance on earning power is most explicit in this case, and the investor will look in vain for other sources of meaningful protection.

Protective Provisions. Some fairly common protective provisions for senior issues include:

- *Prohibition of prior liens.* Other things equal, a provision in a mortgage bond indenture prohibiting the placing of any new prior lien on the property is both common and desirable.

- *Equal-and-ratable-security clause.* When a bond is unsecured, provision should be made that no mortgage lien shall be placed on all or certain of the company's properties without equally and ratably securing the issue.

- *Purchase money mortgages.* It is customary to permit without restriction the assumption of purchase money mortgages on property subsequently acquired.

- *Limitations on the creation of additional amounts of the issue or of other debt.* Many bond issues have protection against both dilution of the specific claim of the issue and the increase of debt relative to equity. Customary provisions require capital additions in the case of public utilities and satisfactory earnings in the case of industrial companies. The practical importance of these safeguards is less than might appear, however, because in the ordinary case the provisions would need to be met to come successfully to market with an additional debt issue.

- *Working-capital requirements.* Provisions for maintaining net current assets in relation to total debt appear only in industrial issues. The required percentages vary as do the penalties for noncompliance. In most cases, the result is a prohibition of dividends or restrictions on investment in plant and equipment until the required level or ratio of net current assets is restored. The prohibition of dividends and share repurchases under such conditions is sound and practicable, but the more stringent penalty which terms a working-capital deficiency "an event of default" is not likely to prove effective or beneficial to the bond holder. The fact that bankruptcy harms rather than helps creditors applies with particular force in this connection. Limited waivers of such provisions are common in directly placed issues and bank term loans.

- *Sinking funds and serial maturities.* The benefits of a sinking fund are twofold. The continuous reduction of the size of the issue makes for increasing safety and the easier repayment of the balance at maturity. Also important is the support given to the market for the issue through the repeated appearance of buying demand. Under some circumstances, a sinking fund is absolutely necessary for protection, for example, when the chief backing of the issue is a wasting asset. A sinking fund provision which is related to earnings may be particularly desirable. When American Sugar Refining retired its 7 percent preferred stock, it made payment in part with 5.30 percent subordinated debentures due in 1993. The indenture provided for a sinking fund of the lesser of 10 percent of consolidated net income or an amount sufficient to retire the entire issue at maturity. Earnings have been more than adequate, and the last 23 percent of the issue was being rapidly bought in by the sinking fund. The bond, which sold at 81 in mid-1986, was redeemed at 101½ in January 1987. The enforcement of sinking fund provisions presents the same problem as that involved in securing compliance with working-capital covenants. Failure to make a sinking fund payment is regularly characterized in the bond indenture as an event of default, which will permit the trustee to declare the principal due. This provision is almost never

enforced. Bondholders are generally willing to agree to the postpone-
ment of sinking fund payments, especially on subordinated debt,
rather than precipitate insolvency in legal terms.

Because of cross-default and other provisions, analysts must look at
the terms of all the company's borrowings and lease obligations, not just
at those of a particular issue under analysis. Frequently, bank loan
agreements will contain the tightest restrictions, but they may be
renegotiated or the loans paid off long before the bond issue matures.

Call provisions and sinking fund requirements which are important to
the portfolio manager in tailoring a portfolio to specific needs and
objectives have entirely different significance to security analysts. They
are concerned with such terms only as they affect the borrower's ability
to meet debt service without unduly restricting its capacity to move
ahead on new projects and new opportunities.

Record of Profitability

The simple ratio of balance sheet retained earnings to total assets seems
like a hopelessly naive standard, but it does contain significant information about the record of (1) profitability, (2) age (seasoning), and (3)
growth of the company. Its significance in predicting bankruptcy cannot
be ignored. Ordinary caution should be exercised in the use of the ratio
to make sure that it is not distorted. For example, a very successful
company which paid large stock dividends over a period of years could
show (because of transfers from retained earnings to stated capital) a
level of retained earnings which greatly understates its history of
profitability.

No minimum figure is set as a requirement, but ratios of 40 percent or
more suggest a long history of profitability. For capital-intensive companies, 25 percent or better can be equally positive. Percentages below
these should stimulate the analyst to take a closer look at the record. This
measure of a company's profitable record is preferred to the less reliable
reference to the record of dividend payments.

Asset Protection

Liquidity. Except for capital-intensive industries such as materials processing, public utilities, transportation, forest products, and others characterized by low capital turnover ratios, net current assets should equal
100 percent of total long-term debt. The alternative ratio of total current
assets to total liabilities is equally informative.

For liquidity, the conventional working-capital ratio still has its place.

More efficient management of current assets may well be reflected in a lower standard than the traditional 2 to 1, but 1.75 to 1 should be required of financially strong companies, with the exceptions as noted.

The quick ratio (current assets minus inventories divided by current liabilities) is the best liquidity measure and in general applies to all industries. It should be close to 1-to-1 to support a strong credit rating, despite the extent to which companies have developed techniques to economize on holding cash assets. The trend of these ratios is more significant than a particular year-end figure.

Example. Monsanto Company showed the ratios shown in Table 25.3 for 1985 and 1984. The deterioration in these ratios reflects the purchase of G. D. Searle & Company during 1985. The company's

Table 25.3. Monsanto Company Ratios

	1985[†]	1984[†]
Working capital ratio		
Current assets[*]	$3497	$2830
Current liabilities	2378	1202
Ratio	1.47:1	2.35:1
Quick ratio		
Current assets less inventories	$2180	$1758
Current liabilities	2378	1202
Ratio	0.92:1	1.46:1
Coverage of total liabilities		
Current assets[*]	$3497	$2830
Total liabilities	5470	2739
Ratio	0.64:1	1.03:1

[*]Adjusted to restore LIFO reserve after tax.
[†]Dollar amounts in millions.

statement in its 1985 annual report (p. 35) is explicit on the subjects of liquidity and capital structure: "To restore debt levels and financial ratios to acceptable levels after the Searle acquisition, the Company advanced the program to dispose of several businesses and assets.... Monsanto's current ratio... was 1.4:1 at year-end 1985, compared to 2.2:1 in 1984. Management believes a 2.0:1 ratio is desirable." Noting that long-term debt was 38 percent of total capital as compared to 18 percent in 1984, the 1985 annual report goes on to say, "Management believes the long-term debt to total capitalization should approximate 33 percent over time." This statement makes clear to the analyst that corporate financial policy contemplates meeting standards which ensure the unquestioned creditworthiness of company obligations.

Equity Cushion.   The plant account of a public utility company, as recognized in its rate base, affords a significant indication of the protection existing for the bond issues. This is hardly true in the case of transportation and industrial concerns. For the latter, one should use a different measure of *equity cushion* on which the bondholder relies to absorb the shocks of adversity. This equity is the going-concern value of the enterprise rather than the book value of the assets. Before paying full prices for the bonds of any enterprise, the investor must be convinced that the business is worth much more than it owes.

For a sound industrial bond, the value of the enterprise should be three times the total debt. The equity cushion should be 200 percent of the face amount of the debt of an industrial or transportation company if its obligations are to provide strong assurance of creditworthiness. To require that the analyst make a complete valuation of the equity for this purpose as presented in Part 4 of this book, however desirable, might well require more time and effort than justified by the bond investment decision. We recommend as a substitute, not without diffidence about relying on the vagaries of the marketplace, the five-year average market value of the equity.

By this measure, Monsanto Company had a large amount of unused borrowing capacity at the end of 1984, when the five-year average market value of the equity was 382 percent of total debt. Reflecting the Searle acquisition, the equity cushion shrank to 168 percent at the end of 1985 but has since been rebuilt by debt reduction. To be sure, a 200 percent equity cushion is a demanding test of bond quality, but it is consistent with a one-third debt component in an industrial company's capital structure. If the average market value of the equity comes to only 133 percent of book value, a 40 percent debt component of capitalization at book would still pass this test. The Value Line industrial composite of over 900 industrial, retail, and transportation (excluding rail) companies produces a capital structure of 32 percent debt, 2 percent preferred stock, and 66 percent common stock at book values at the end of 1985. On that date, the ratio of market to book was 1.58.[2] The equity cushion test is a supplement to, not a substitute for, the earnings coverage test.

Earning Power Protection

As discussed in the preceding chapter, times interest covered by net income before interest and income taxes presents real problems because of the wide variations in interest rates over the last decade. A moving

[2]Value Line, Inc., *The Value Line Investment Survey*, New York, July 25, 1986, pp. 951–954.

average for the 10 years ended in 1986 of 12 percent for new corporate bond issues of investment quality (rated A) can be used to calculate a pro forma interest coverage which may be more meaningful. Capitalizing lease rentals on the same basis may also be desirable to avoid the distortions created by especially good or bad timing of new financing.

When there is no significant distortion of the interest charges, a pretax minimum of five times average coverage for industrials and three times for public utilities will provide strong assurance of safety. (For these calculations, total interest obligations are used, without deduction of interest capitalized or for public utilities the sometimes large item of allowance for funds used during construction.) A poorest-year test of twice interest coverage for most borrowers, based on operating earnings, is sufficient to deal with cases of characteristically wide swings in earning power.

The period of observation and calculation of coverage averages should be sufficient to include a full business cycle or two, which may require 5 to 10 years. The 1980 and the 1981–1982 recessions, for example, provided reasonably demanding tests, but certain industries have had protracted recessions of their own, farm equipment, steel, and nonferrous metals, for example. The use of a poorest-year coverage minimum requirement is designed to capture any signs of chronic instability in earning power.

The preferred measure of earning power protection, however, is the coverage of total debt service. This ratio of net income before interest and taxes plus other noncash charges to the recurring level of interest on total debt plus debt retirement payments stepped up to a pretax basis should average two times and not drop below once in the poorest year. Lease obligations are of course included, but the portion attributed to repayment does not need to be stepped up because it is tax deductible just like the interest component. The variability and trend of this ratio are as important as the absolute level of coverage and deserve careful analysis.

Net cash generation in relation to total capital is used in the electric utility industry; 6 percent or higher is viewed as acceptable for long-lived assets such as its permanent capital. This turnover in the investment base also provides insight on the utility's ability to finance investment from internal sources.

Summary

The minimum quantitative requirements for investment-grade bonds are as follows:

1. Retained earnings equal to 40 percent of assets, except in capital-intensive businesses where 25 percent may be adequate

2. Positive trends in growth and profitability relative to trends in the economy and in the company's industry

3. Reasonable stability of earning power, with no or infrequent loss years

4. A minimum size of $50 million as measured by the five-year average market value of the borrower's net worth

5. Reasonable protection against excessive dilution of the priority of claim on earning power

6. Net current assets equal to 100 percent of total long-term debt

7. A working capital ratio of at least 1.75:1

8. A quick ratio of 1:1

9. An equity cushion of 200 percent of total debt as measured by the five-year average of the market value of the borrower's net worth

10. Interest charges earned an average of five times before taxes for industrials and three times for public utilities, with a poorest-year minimum of twice

11. Total debt service coverage averaging twice and not below once in the poorest year

Exceptions to any one of these standards can be made for valid reasons in specific cases, but the burden is on the analyst to make that case. An especially good record on one standard may justify accepting another's marginal reading.

Securities of Questionable Creditworthiness

Subordinated Debt

In the case of creditworthy issuers, subordinated debt may be of satisfactory investment quality. The danger involved is that very large prior or equally ranking claims will be issued to dilute the existing participation in earning power. Special covenants dealing with working capital, debt-equity ratios, dividend payments, and share repurchase restrictions are all desirable. Senior debt covenants may also protect subordinated debt.

Sinking funds to provide for orderly retirement are essential, even though they are unenforceable in the event of serious problems. As a practical matter, they can be related to earnings and serve their purpose well by making the subordinated debt less of a potential problem by active retirement in good years.

Fallen Angels

Bonds once regarded as high-grade that are encountering serious adversity have earned the label of *fallen angels*. Major electric utility systems such as Consumers Power, Long Island Lighting, and Public Service of New Hampshire and major airlines and steel companies have contributed to the large volume of these once acceptable or even strong credits. These represent risky but potentially profitable speculations on the future. The provisions of individual issues of such borrowers repay the most careful study.

Many holders of such issues find it inconvenient, excessively risky, and uncomfortable to retain such securities in their portfolios. As a consequence, prices may be depressed far below salvage value. Time and effort in such situations may well repay those with expertise and experience. Price is the analyst's ally; delay is the analyst's worst enemy.

Unseasoned Borrowers

The fixed-income securities of unseasoned borrowers going through the high-risk years of their start-up period are fundamentally unattractive as straight debt. No bearable interest rate is likely to compensate for the risks involved. Some form of equity participation in the form of a conversion feature or stock purchase warrants affords the only means of striking a fair bargain between borrower and lender.

With a generous "equity kicker" included in the terms of unseasoned issues, a diversified portfolio can be constructed with a reasonable potential for returns commensurate with the risks taken. Diversification must, however, be across time as well as across economic sectors and industries. In times of general optimism bordering on euphoria large quantities of unseasoned issues come to market, and investor experience is dismal if not disastrous. The aftermath may provide opportunities, but in most instances the risk taker might better buy the depressed shares of common stock.

Junk Bonds

The label of *junk bonds* has been especially applied to large issues of subordinated notes and debentures issued in leveraged buyouts and corporate restructurings. Since the analyst should look to the value of the enterprise as a whole for the security of its debt, there is no way that such issues can be found of investment quality. Almost by definition, the price paid for the company was its investment value plus a control premium. Even if undervalued in the marketplace, a 25 to 50 percent premium paid in the transaction must have greatly reduced the extent of the undervaluation.

Among promising candidates for leveraged buyouts are fairly solid, reasonably stable companies which do not require heavy infusions of capital and produce a positive cash flow for debt retirement. The introduction of substantial financial leverage, the familiar practice of trading on the equity, may provide sound investment opportunities for lenders, but only on condition that they accept a security which is, in reality, part debt and part equity. In this perspective, one might consider a junk bond as composed of two parts: a debt instrument of marginal safety plus a piece of paper which, if all goes well, may turn into a recognizable debt instrument. It is a contingent claim not unlike a warrant or other means of participating in the future of an enterprise. The analyst's assignment is to judge the relative size and riskiness of the debt and equity components of the junk bond.

The absence of a significant margin of safety for debt service at the outset is the reason for a risk premium in the junk bond interest rate pending the hoped for earnout of senior debt. The adequacy of that risk premium is a major consideration of the investor to which the analyst must contribute a careful evaluation of the risk of failure.[3]

Only the future will tell whether the wave of junk bond flotations was soundly based on the disciplined application of security analysis. The conviction of the authors is that the perceived urgency of "making a deal" has distorted judgment and that there will be many difficult situations to work out, with consequent losses of economic value. Equity cannot be made into unused borrowing power by labeling it as such; only the underlying economic and financial realities can so produce equity. Excessive financial leverage has always taken its toll of security values, and we are not convinced that this episode will be an exception.

---

[3]For an excellent study of the anatomy of this market and of risk premiums in it, see Edward I. Altman and Scott A. Nammacher, *Investing in Junk Bonds*, John Wiley & Sons, New York, 1987.

26

Selection of Preferred Stocks

Another major category of corporate fixed-income securities is preferred stock. Because of their major differences from bond investments in characteristics and in the application of selection standards, preferred stocks are given separate treatment in this chapter. The primary focus is on industrial issues, which represent the most broadly representative problem in security analysis.

Characteristics of the Security

The Tax Factor

As long as the 80 percent intercorporate dividend received deduction persists, there will be active investment interest in preferred stocks. A corporation subject to the 34 percent federal income tax rate, therefore, pays an effective rate of only 6.8 percent on dividend income. Corporate cash reserve mutual funds have been marketed in large volume, and there has been active issuance of variable rate instruments to tap this market. Commercial banks have been active in selling adjustable rate preferred stocks which are designed to shift the interest rate risk to them.

The tax benefit to a corporate taxpayer, as anticipated, has a pronounced effect on market prices and yields. High-grade issues, although junior to senior and subordinated debt and lease obligations, frequently sell at lower yields than the same company's bonds. For example, at year-end 1986 two companies showed these yields:

	Bond yield(%)	Preferred stock yield (%)
E. I. Du Pont de Nemours	8.65	7.00
General Motors	8.80	6.98
Standard & Poor's High Grade Industrials	9.31	7.15

It follows that individuals and entities not taxed like corporations should not invest in preferred stocks but should prefer the interest-paying obligations of creditworthy companies. Exceptions are limited to the appropriateness of a perpetual instrument because of its long duration or special features like conversion rights. From an analytical perspective, of course, the presence of preferred stock in a corporate capital structure raises questions as to its suitability.

General Position

In an industrial corporation's capital structure, preferred stock represents a portion both of the equity ownership of the company and of the equity cushion for its debt. From the perspective of the common shares, however, its prior claim on earnings and assets makes the preferred stock an expensive senior security, given the nondeductibility of its dividend for income tax purposes. To sustain an investment-quality rating for debt issues and some leverage to enhance the growth in earnings for the common shares, however, preferred stock may still perform a useful function.

The preferred stock contract is fundamentally unsatisfactory, since it does not provide the holder either with an enforceable claim to interest and principal at maturity that attaches to a standard bond or with the right to residual profits that inures to common stock. Nevertheless, preferred stocks can constitute sound and well-protected investments of the fixed-income type if their contractual weakness is offset by the strength of the issuing company. Basically, the same elements of protection which ensure the safety and relative stability of a high-grade bond can do the same for a strongly entrenched preferred issue. But as a class, preferred shares are distinctly more vulnerable to adverse developments than are bonds. Hence investor experience with them as a whole over past decades has been less satisfactory than with bonds. It follows that preferred stock selection is even more of a negative art. In addition to their vulnerability to adverse business and financial developments, the longer duration of straight preferred stocks, those with no provision for retirement, contributes to their much greater price volatility in reflection of interest rate changes.

Present Status of Preferred Stocks

Most industrial corporations have ceased to issue investment-quality preferred stocks, because, financially, they do not make sense. If such an issue is really of investment grade, the company must be strong enough to assume a debt obligation of equivalent amount, with consequent saving in net annual cost. The use of the subordinated debenture provides whatever flexibility is needed for present or future borrowing. The existing supply has been considerably diminished by the operation of sinking funds, and many preferred issues have been retired and replaced by bond issues. Only regulated utilities, which in effect pass through the corporate income tax to the rate payer, have continued to use preferred stock on a regular basis.

For new ventures and those in which borrowing capacity is severely limited, preferred stocks of less than investment quality continue to be issued. For the most part, such securities, even in a broadly diversified portfolio, can be expected to produce a poor return after taking capital losses fully into account. An investor in this sector of the capital market is well advised to insist upon some form of participation in the earning power that may be generated beyond the conventional dividend preference.

Claim for Dividends

The preferred-stock holder has a claim on earnings and assets which is preferential to that of the holder of common stock only. Investors have insisted that the dividend claim be cumulative, that is, all dividends on preferred shares accumulated since date of issuance must be paid before any dividends can be paid on common shares. In corporate reorganizations, preferred shares issued to creditors may be cumulative to the extent earned, but this feature in itself signals that the security is backed by inadequate and uncertain earning power.

During the Great Depression, when the preferential dividend claim of preferred stocks was put to its severest test, in almost half of the instances of the passing of common dividends, preferred dividends were passed within a year. In nearly one-quarter of the cases, the preferred dividend was not continued for more than three months. In this protracted period of economic adversity, perhaps two-thirds of all the preferred stocks that accumulated dividend arrears would have paid interest in full had they been in the form of bond issues. The form of the contract, therefore, can be a real disadvantage to the holder of preferred shares as compared to the bondholder.

The record for 243 industrial preferred stocks of general market interest outstanding in the decade of the 1930s shows that 41 percent paid their full dividends in every year. Another 24 percent paid up arrears in cash within a reasonable time, but the remaining 35 percent addressed dividend arrears only in recapitalizations or not at all.[1]

The discretionary right of directors to omit preferred dividend payments accounts for this kind of record. With primary allegiance to common shareholders, it is not surprising that, when adversity dictates to directors that they pass the common dividend, suspension of payments on the preferred soon follows. Applying cash receipts to plant modernization, new product development, debt repayment, and other good purposes may indeed be in the long-term best interests of the preferred stock, but all these ultimately benefit the common equity without limit. In essence, interest-free loans from preferred-stock holders can be obtained without burdensome repayment terms by the simple step of passing the preferred dividend even when earned.

As a result, the holder of preferred stock faces the hazard of interruption of income, an exposure not present in a similarly situated bond. Such a hazard automatically disqualifies the preferred issue as a fixed-income investment, because it is the essence of such investments that the income must be considered highly dependable. Also, any preferred stock subject to a real danger of a dividend reduction or suspension will fluctuate widely in market price. Whenever a dividend which could be continued is instead withheld "for the stockholders' future advantage," the quoted price suffers a severe decline, indicating that the investment market does not agree with the directors as to what is really in the best interests of the preferred stock.

Voting Rights

The typical preferred stock has no voting rights except in the event that dividends are unpaid for four, six, or eight quarters. In such circumstances, the holders may elect two or more directors but almost never a majority of the board. The right to vote separately as a class on mergers or restructuring may also be provided, but none of these provisions is meaningful. Delay in obtaining the vote and inability to exercise any real

---

[1]Roger F. Murray, "Preferred Stocks of Industrial Corporations," Ph.D. dissertation, Graduate School of Business Administration, New York University, 1942, p. 46.

measure of control over company affairs make voting rights of little practical value. Giving the holders of preferred stock the right to elect the entire board of directors in the event of nonpayment of dividends for one year might be effective, but as a group these shareholders are seldom well-equipped to recruit a new board independent of corporate management. An analysis of preferred stocks for investment purposes must assume that the investor cannot rely on the voting rights for the protection of preferential interests.

Claim on Assets

A preferential claim on assets would appear to imply at least full realization of liquidation value on sale of a company before any return to the common shares. As a practical matter, this may be turn out to be an empty promise.

Example. Liggett Group 7 percent noncallable preferred stock of $100 par value, entitled to eight votes per share on all matters, was selling at 60¼ in April 1980 as a consequence of high interest rates. The 103,231 shares outstanding supposedly had a preferential claim of $10,323,100 on the proceeds of a takeover bid of $606,957,000. The tender offer accepted 39.8 percent of the shares at $70 per share, which was also the price in the subsequent merger. The directors found the terms "in the best interests of the Company and its stockholders" and that "the prices being paid for the shares were fair." The investor's perceived preference of at least $100 per share turned out to be worth $70 because sale of the enterprise was not regarded by legal minds as a liquidation. A small number of shareholders sought to exercise their Delaware appraisal rights but, with one exception, gave up at the prospective cost and delay involved. They settled three years later for $73.50 per share plus interest and modest legal expenses. The fair value of the preferred stock clearly should have been evaluated on the basis that it was noncallable, a valuable provision over and above the par value preferential claim on assets. The company, in previous years, had recognized the value of that feature by paying prices far in excess of $100 per share to retire much of the original issue. Clearly, the Liggett Group directors who bargained hard for the common stock felt no such responsibility to the senior "owners" of the company.

Given the problems in asserting a preferential claim on assets, investors have been entirely logical in seeking orderly retirement provisions through sinking funds. The analyst must determine whether the provision is merely preferential or a defined obligation of the issuer. The investor in Cleveland Cliffs Iron Company 4½ percent preferred, observing a sinking fund of 15 percent of consolidated net income for each year, could buy shares at a 5¼ percent return in 1961, when long-term governments yielded 3.85 percent, and have them redeemed at 101½ in 1975 when U.S. Treasury bonds provided an 8⅜ percent yield.

The failure of investors to take the trouble to study sinking fund terms can afford exceptional opportunities. Crown Zellerbach had been retiring its $4.20 preferred shares for a number of years until the amount outstanding was no longer substantial. The shares were selling at 63 in January 1979 and were redeemed at 102½ on April 2, 1979 for a substantial gain.

Qualifications of High-Grade Preferred Stocks

Given the inherent weakness of the preferred stock contract, a well-protected issue must meet all the minimum requirements of a safe bond. It must also exceed these minimum requirements by an added margin of safety to offset the discretionary feature in the payment of dividends, that is, the margin of safety must be so large that the directors will be expected to declare the dividend as a matter of course. Finally, the stipulation of the inherent stability of the business itself must be more stringent than in the case of a bond investment, because a company subject to alternations between large profits and temporary losses is likely to suspend preferred dividends during the latter periods even though its average earnings far exceed the annual requirements.

Standards of Safety

It is unnecessary to repeat in detail all the general and specific standards presented in Chapters 24 and 25 for the selection of bond investments. All are applicable but some need extra emphasis for industrial preferred stocks.

Nature of the Business

The financial record and all other evidences of profitability, growth, and stability are critical factors. Size and competitive position are equally relevant because of their contribution to the continuity and consistency of earning power. For investment-quality issues, in short, the investor must look to large, strong, and well-established firms.

The continuity and stability of earning power, however, deserve special attention. The dividend record for preferred stocks in an industry is useful background for the appraisal of an individual issue. There were no surprises in the dividend records of industries during the Great Depression's severe test. The following scores for groups of industries represent the fraction of all preferred dividends paid from 1931 to 1940[2]:

Growing industries   88%

Consumer goods industries   84%

Cyclical industries   48%

Declining industries   32%

For recent years, the last 5 or 10 for example, the record of common dividends should be relevant. An industry which does not generate a growing stream of dividends for the common equity is unlikely to provide preference issues of good quality, except possibly for the special case of the small issue of a company with little or no debt. More important than dividend records, however, is the same thorough understanding of the nature of the business described previously for bond investing.

Terms of the Issue

Like their bond counterpart, the subordinated debenture, preferred stocks typically are junior to a variety of debt and lease obligations. Provisions which limited the issuance of senior or equally ranking securities used to be commonplace. Also, common dividends and the repurchase of common shares were frequently limited to amounts earned after the issuance of the preferred shares. Since many or most of these protective provisions are no longer included in preferred or preference shares, the analyst must look carefully at the terms of outstanding debt for meaningful safeguards of the preferential position. The reservations about relying on protective provisions outlined in Chapter 25, however, apply even more persuasively to preferred stocks.

If a company is badly managed, preferred shareholders are best advised to join common shareholders in changing that management. If the business is declining because of external conditions beyond the control of management, protective provisions will be of little or no help and may even be a hindrance.

[2]Murray, "Preferred Stocks," pp. 90–91.

Record of Profitability

A ratio of balance sheet retained earnings equal to 40 percent or more of assets (or 25 percent or more in the case of capital-intensive businesses) applies as well to preferred stock analysis as to bonds (see Chapter 25). Balance sheet adjustments are not necessary for these calculations except to include off-balance-sheet liabilities and corresponding assets. Because this measure is independent of capital structure, either bonds or preferred stocks can be analyzed.

Asset Protection

Liquidity.   The liquidity measures applied to bonds in Chapter 25 are equally appropriate when preferred stock at par value, or liquidation value if higher, is added to the total of debt. Net current assets should equal at least 100 percent of the total, with the exceptions noted. The current ratio should be 1.75 to 1, and a quick ratio of 1 to 1 is equally desirable. The analyst should be especially strict on the level and trend of these liquidity ratios because of the discretionary nature of preferred dividend declarations.

Equity Cushion.   When deferred income taxes are a significant item, their treatment materially affects asset coverage ratio calculations. Using the data in Table 19-1 for American Brands, the book value of tangible assets coverage of total debt and preferred stocks is 2.11 times if deferred taxes are included as a liability, which they presumably would be in the course of liquidation. On a growing-concern basis, in which the deferred tax is treated as an addition to net worth, the ratio would increase to 2.60 times.[3]

A shift to the five-year average market value of the common equity produces an equity cushion of 272 percent of long-term debt and preferred stocks:

$$\frac{2796.4}{748.7 + 95.7 + 137.5 + 47.3} = 2.72 \times$$

---

[3]In this and the preceding ratio, other current liabilities are deducted from total assets and liabilities. The two calculations are:

$$\frac{3664.6}{1734.6} = 2.11 \times \text{ and } \frac{3664.6}{1411.1} = 2.60 \times$$

This is comfortably in excess of the 200 percent equity cushion safety standard. In the case of American Brands, the average market value of the common equity was 145 percent of the year-end 1985 tangible book value, which suggests that brand names are perceived in this instance to have substantial economic value.

Capital Structure. That the absence of funded debt is a desirable feature for a preferred stock goes without saying; it is an advantage like that of having a first mortgage on a property instead of a second mortgage. It is not surprising, therefore, that preferred stocks without bonds ahead of them have as a class made a better showing than those of companies with funded debt. But it does not follow that all preferred stocks with bonds preceding them are unsound investments. For example, in the severe test period from 1931 to 1940, up to 30 percent of industrial corporate capitalizations in preferred stock could frequently be serviced without interruption if not preceded by debt in excess of 5 percent. In contrast, if debt exceeded 15 percent of the capital structure, dividend continuity was threatened except in strong companies in growing or stable industries.[4]

Obviously, capital structure is not the only factor to consider. Operating leverage, even without magnification by financial leverage, makes investing in preferred stock questionable; the combination of both kinds of leverage almost invariably makes the preferred stock unsuitable for investment.

Earning Power Protection

Measurement. The adequacy and consistency of earning power are especially important for a satisfactory investment experience with an inherently weak form of contract like a preferred stock. Measurement of that earning power protection, therefore, is the analyst's primary assignment. From the record, the only useful measure of dividend coverage is pretax income divided by interest plus preferred dividends converted to a pretax basis.[5] The step-up fraction of 100/(100 − tax rate) works out to be 1.5 times, using a 34 percent tax rate.[6]

The coverage of interest and dividend charges in a typical case would be calculated as follows:

---

[4]Murray, "Preferred Stocks," p. 100.

[5]Reported earnings per share of preferred is a totally useless and potentially misleading calculation happily no longer in widespread use.

[6]The reader will observe that the reduction in the corporate tax rate from 46 to 34 percent reduced the step up from 1.85× to 1.5×, thus enhancing the position of preferred shares relative to bonds in the corporate capital structure.

	Millions	Times earned
Net income before interest and taxes	$200	—
Senior bond interest	20	10.0×
Subordinated debt interest	5	8.0×
Preferred dividends—10 × 1.5	15	5.0×

Clearly, when a company meets high standards of dividend coverage, it is inevitably meeting even higher standards for its debt. The analyst knows that if a company's bonds show marginal creditworthiness, a preferred issue is sure to fail the tests.

Adequacy. Just as the coverage of total debt service is the best measure of earning power protection for bonds, the preferred stock standard requires an equal margin of safety. The calculation follows:

$$\frac{\text{Net income before interest and taxes} + \text{noncash charges}}{\text{Debt interest} + 1.5 \times \text{debt ret. pay't.} + 1.5 \times \text{pfd. div.} + 1.5 \times \text{pfd. s/f}}$$

This coverage should average two times and not drop below once in the poorest year.

Stability. The extra emphasis in preferred-stock analysis is on the stability and consistency of earning power. Experience clearly shows that after some minimum level, coverage does not matter. Indeed, modest coverage combined with stability is better evidence of investment quality than high average protection with occasional bad years. The record may be quite informative as to the sensitivity of earning power to the economic environment. Changes in the product line, management, and financial structure may, however, require that the analyst adjust the information derived from the past to new circumstances. Qualitative factors are likely to be dominant in framing expectations for the long future.

The best measure of the stability of earning power, without any influence from the presence or absence of financial leverage, is the variability of the return on total capital. The ratio of the worst year to the average of the preceding three years is the kind of a measure which can be used across industries. To capture the additional effects of capital structure, an additional calculation of the ratio of the worst year's coverage of total senior claims to the average for the preceding three years is also relevant.

Obviously, a combination of adequacy and stability provides investment standing to a preferred stock. Stability at a fairly good level is always preferable to instability at a very good average level. An issue of investment grade must pass both tests.

Summary of Standards

The minimum quantitative requirements for investment-grade industrial preferred stocks are as follows:

1. Retained earnings equal to 40 percent of assets, except in capital-intensive businesses, where 25 percent may be adequate

2. Positive trends in growth and profitability relative to trends in the economy and the company's industry

3. Reasonable stability of earning power, with no losses from operations

4. A minimum size of $100 million as measured by the five-year average of the market value of the issuer's common equity

5. Net current assets equal to 100 percent of total debt plus preferred stock at liquidation value

6. A current ratio of 1.75 to 1

7. A quick ratio of 1 to 1

8. An equity cushion of 200 percent of total debt plus preferred stock at liquidation value as measured by the five-year average market value of the issuer's common equity

9. Interest charges and preferred dividends on a pretax basis earned an average of five times, with a poorest-year minimum of twice

10. Total debt and preferred service coverage averaging twice but not less than once in the poorest year

Exceptions to these standards should be made only after very careful study in view of the inherent weakness of the preferred stock contract.

Preferred Stocks as Equity

In cases of business failure, whether economic or legal, the preferred stock may turn out to be the real equity, if any, and the common stock becomes the equivalent of a warrant or other form of contingent claim. In such an event, preferred shareholders must organize through a committee or board representation to protect their interests in reorganization or recapitalization.

Despite the long delays in resolving such situations, a few of them repay careful study. When extremely low market prices prevail, preferred shares tend to become materially undervalued relative to the common. On occasions, too, such companies rise, phoenix-like, from the ashes of a pyre of excessive debt.

PART 4

Valuation of Common Stocks and Contingent Claims

27

Common-Stock Investment in the Late 1980s: The Security Analyst's Assignment

Common-Stock Component in Portfolios

Previous editions presented the following arguments for inclusion of a common-stock component in typical investment portfolios: (1) A representative group of common stocks bought at a *reasonable price level* can be counted on to provide a higher total return than bonds. (2) The probability of inflation has removed many of the safeguards inherent in bond investment and requires a significant holding of common stocks as a protective measure. Clearly, the safety and attractiveness of common stock investing would be jeopardized if stocks were bought at an excessively high general market level or too much was paid for the promising prospects of favored issues.

Is the foregoing advice appropriate today? As the facts set forth below establish, arguing for the inclusion of common stocks in investment portfolios is no longer necessary. However, the importance of a standard of value for buying stocks at a reasonable price level remains.

It is well-known that common stocks are now a widely accepted investment vehicle—to what extent is established by the results of a survey of 37 companies.[1] The normal level for the common-stock component of their pension and profit-sharing funds was 57 percent. (The normal level is that mix which would exist if all the asset classes were considered properly priced relative to one another, that is, if security markets were in equilibrium.) Although differences in portfolio objectives will dictate a wide range of asset mixes, there is substantial adherence to a two-thirds common-stock exposure for long-term investment portfolios.

This chapter examines three aspects of current practices in the management of common-stock portfolios: (1) the forces of change making equity management so dynamic, (2) styles of portfolio management, and (3) categorization and consideration of basic investment approaches from the standpoint of the security analyst's inputs.

Forces of Change

There are four major stimuli to innovation and change in common stock portfolio management. First, the marked growth and present size of institutional funds (such as pension and endowment funds) and the resulting development of multimanager structures. The assets of the 1000 largest employee benefit systems totalled over $1.339 trillion as of September 30, 1986.[2] Because most large funds are now characterized by multimanager structures, the definition of style is receiving increased emphasis. Now, sponsors rank style almost as important as performance record in selecting a manager. Consideration of style is a dominant factor in establishing an optimum mix of managers. In response to this, managers seek to define explicitly their styles and to exercise special care to assure consistency of execution.

The second stimulus is the rising level of sophistication among sponsors. In this connection, the growing interest in managers' styles has been a strong stimulus to the development of quantitative, as distinguished from qualitative, evaluation of style.

The third force making common-stock portfolio management dynamic is the intense competition among investment organizations for the management of institutional funds. Accordingly, managers, in seeking

---

[1]Survey conducted in 1982 by FRS Associates, Los Altos, California. The pension fund and profit-sharing assets for the 37 companies totalled over $86 billion.

[2]Reported in *Pension & Investment Age*, Jan. 26, 1987, p. 1.

to improve performance and control risk, are devoting much attention to finding that style most suited to their operational capabilities. This includes establishing a system of monitoring portfolio characteristics to exercise quality control and to assure conformity to style.

The fourth stimulus is progress in investment technology, particularly as evidenced in the establishment of quantified investment objectives, performance measurement, performance attribution, risk analysis, and the definition of normal portfolios.

In combination, these four factors have caused investment management to become increasingly an integrated and focused process for selecting and timing the purchase of common stocks. This process (style) may be classified from two standpoints—portfolio management and security analysis.

Investment Styles and Portfolio Management

From the standpoint of portfolio management, an investment organization's specific process or style can be classified as either passive or active management. Passive management seeks to replicate the performance of a predetermined stock index (for example, the S&P 500) or other identifiable objective standards appropriate to the investment assignment (for instance, a group of preselected growth stocks). A passive manager has no need for a security analyst and uses various statistical and market techniques to build an index fund.

In contrast, active management seeks to outperform a selected standard. There are four principal active common-stock investment styles: diversified, undiversified, rotator, and module manager. The characteristics of each style are summarized below.[3]

A *diversified* manager will hold all industries of significance and have no strong and continuing bias toward any single industry or sector. In addition, the normal industry holding of a portfolio will be the market weight when the manager considers the outlook for the industry to be neutral. Value is added entirely by selecting relatively undervalued stocks in each industry or sector.

The *undiversified* category covers every type of specialized manager (or "concentrator") whose portfolios always have a strong bias toward one or more sectors of the market. Examples are organizations concen-

---

[3]There are alternative style categories. Trust Universe Comparison Services uses the following six : growth, growth-small, diversified, value, sector, and market timer. Reported in R.L. Knisely, Jr., "Performance Evaluation: How Do You Compare Management Styles?" *Pension World*, October 1985, pp. 19–21.

trating their investment activities in such major sectors as large capitalization growth stocks, quality oriented stocks, small companies, special
situations, or income stocks.

The *rotator* type of manager lies in between the diversified and
undiversified manager. The rotator is similar to the diversified manager
in that the organization invests in all sectors of the market and industries
with no continuing bias toward any sector or industry. However, the
rotator differs from the diversified manager because the market weight
of a sector or industry is not considered a neutral position. The rotator
does not choose to hold any stocks in a sector or industry unless it is
appraised as attractive. Thus, at points, the portfolios might have
pronounced growth, income, quality, or size weightings.

The *module* manager represents a recent approach to portfolio
management. A module is a group of stocks that because of their
economic, financial, or other characteristics can be considered comparable from an investment standpoint (for example, high-growth stocks,
income stocks, or foreign issues). With a full set of modules, a manager
can create portfolios concentrated in either selected sectors or in all
major sectors. Thus, the manager could be in either the diversified or
specialist category.

Investment Approaches and Security Analysis

The four active investment management styles could use the same
company and industry analytical inputs. However, the following practices can be appropriately designated as basic "approaches" to selection
and timing, rather than as styles. Viewed from this perspective, the
required inputs of security analysis are not identical:

1. The cross-section approach
2. The anticipation approach
    a. Short-term selectivity
    b. Growth-stock selection
3. The margin-of-safety approach
    a. Values at market bottoms and midlevels
    b. Individual issue values

Cross-section Approach

This approach is known as passive management. It subordinates selectivity to diversification. When measured in terms of an index such as the S&P 500, the object of this approach is to make sure that the investor fares as well as major U.S. business corporations. This approach eliminates the need for security analysis.

Anticipation Approach: Short-Term Selectivity

The recommendation of common stocks in Wall Street, and presumably their purchase by both investors and speculators, are too frequently based on near-term anticipations. This is not a value approach; instead, the focus is on relative earnings. According to this approach, stocks with the greatest quarterly earnings momentum will provide the highest return and, when the rate of change in earnings peaks, it is time to sell. Much analytical effort goes into appraising near-term prospects for the next 6 or 12 months. Volume, selling prices, and costs are carefully estimated, often with the aid of field studies. The attention paid to these short-period anticipations is often justified by the assertion that forecasts for more than a year ahead are not really dependable.

Despite this plausible argument, the weight so frequently accorded to the near term is still regrettable. The value of a stock does not depend on what it is going to earn this year or next but on its expected average earning power and dividends over a fairly long time and on its general prospects over the longer future. The chief fallacy in buying stocks on the basis of their immediate prospects is that the price of the issue may already have anticipated the very improvement or misadventure that the buyer or seller is counting on. In many such cases, little or no attention is paid to the price of the stock and whether it has already fully reflected the favorable earnings outlook. Moreover, there is no floor of value to protect the buyer on the downside.

Emphasis on the near term is also reflected in the action of some professional investors. The 1986 turnover rate of reported share volume on the New York Stock Exchange (share volume divided by average shares listed) was 64 percent compared to a 23 percent turnover rate in 1976.[4] The upward trend in this exchange's turnover rate can be noted by the following tabulation of three-year averages:

[4]*New York Stock Exchange Fact Book,* New York Stock Exchange, Inc., New York, 1987.

Years	Turnover (%)
1975–1977	22
1978–1980	30
1981–1983	42
1984–1986	56

The extent of the near term emphasis is also indicated by portfolio turnover. A survey of 778 money managers by CDA Investment Technologies, Inc., revealed that, for the four-quarter period ending in December 1986, 141 major investment organizations had portfolio turnover in equities at annual rates in excess of 100 percent.[5] Another report notes that in 1983 portfolio turnover averaged 62 percent for pension funds compared with 21 percent 10 years earlier.[6] Clearly, the holding period has been reduced significantly, in part because fund sponsors tend to measure and judge managers in terms of their quarterly performance.

Anticipation Approach: Growth-Stock Selection

Selectivity based on near-term prospects may be criticized as a criterion of common-stock investment on the grounds that it deals too much with the transient and superficial. This criticism does not apply to long-term prospects, which not only are relevant to the investment value of any security but also may well embody the most important determinant of ultimate worth. In the past a number of favored concerns have grown and prospered far beyond the average. Such growth companies have come to be considered particularly suitable media for long-term investment.

Obviously, the investor who can successfully identify growth companies when their shares are available at reasonable prices is certain to do extremely well. Some investors are undeniably capable of making such selections with impressive accuracy, and they have benefited markedly from their foresight and good judgment. Can careful and intelligent investors as a class follow this policy with fair success? The question has three parts: (1) What is meant by a "growth company?" (2) Can the

---

[5]*Spectrum Turnover Report*, Dec. 31, 1986, CDA Investment Technologies, Inc., Silver Spring, Md.

[6]"Will Money Managers Wreck the Economy?" *Business Week*, Aug. 13, 1984, pp. 86–93.

investor identify such companies with reasonable accuracy? (3) To what extent does the price paid discount the expected growth?

What Is a "Growth" Company? We know of no universally accepted definition of a *growth company*. For purposes of this book, a growth company is defined as one in growth product or service markets which has had an annual average growth in earnings of at least 12 percent over perhaps 5 or 10 years and is expected to continue at this rate. This rate is 60 percent higher than our secular projection of 7.5 percent for the S&P 400 stock index.[7] The 12 percent criterion is not intended to be applied to companies whose earnings had merely been depressed (due to business cycles or otherwise) and are currently enjoying a recovery. Such companies are not within our definition of a growth company; rather, the recovery of such stocks represents examples of price converging on value.

Can the Investor Identify Them? Our natural enthusiasm for excellent records and for especially favorable industry prospects is tempered somewhat by a sobering consideration. Viewed historically, even the most successful companies generally follow a well-defined life cycle—the traditional S-shaped growth curve. It consists of first a series of struggles and setbacks; second, a halcyon period of prosperity and persistent growth; third, a final phase of maturity, characterized by a slackening of expansion and perhaps a loss of leadership or even of profitability. Thus, a company that has enjoyed a very long period of increasing earnings may for this reason be nearing its own saturation point because its sustained profitability will stimulate competition.

Hence the seeker for growth companies faces a dilemma. If newer companies with a short record of expansion are chosen, the problems of small companies set forth below are encountered. If, in contrast, enterprises that have advanced through several business cycles are chosen, this apparent strength may be the harbinger of coming maturity or even weakness.

Smaller companies in the early stages of their life cycle present a number of special problems in valuation. First, financial analysis has its limitations when (1) there is no meaningful record of accomplishment for analysis, (2) competitive factors are difficult to evaluate, (3) growth strains on both financial and managerial resources (including a lack of managerial depth) present major obstacles to success, and (4) technological or other nonfinancial developments dominate the uncertain future.

Second, growth for such emerging companies is unlikely to occur in a smooth pattern of accelerating or decelerating volume. Rather, success,

[7]See this projection in Chapter 32, "Capitalization Rate for Earnings and Dividends".

if realized, is likely to form a series of steps as breakthroughs into markets are achieved. The timing of these steps is extremely important for the valuation process.

The financial picture of achievement can perhaps be sketched out for some point in the future, say, in three or five years. A model of the company in the position of having completed its next phase, generating expected levels of volume and financial requirements, can present a rough picture of a going concern with the potential for growth as an established enterprise. In calculating the present value of such a firm, the discount rate should reflect the risk that such a venture entails.

The security analyst may not be able to refine such estimates of the future sufficiently to arrive at a meaningful valuation. This fact is important and useful information because it tells investors that they are making a bet on some process and some people which cannot be subjected to a reliable analytical judgment of the appropriate odds. But if a systematic valuation can be made with reasonable confidence, the exercise is likely to be rewarding.

What has been described as the "small company effect" is the promise that a diversified portfolio of selected smaller companies will provide superior long-term returns to the investor, after allowance for their volatility, than will a diversified group of larger, more mature companies. This pure size effect appears to be the result of systematic undervaluation of small companies and is a denial of market efficiency notions.

The small company effect can be measured historically by an index like the Wilshire 5000 tracked on a market value weighted and an equally weighted basis. A comparison follows for periods ended December 31, 1986 (volatility is measured by the standard deviations shown in parentheses):

	1 year	2 years	5 years	10 years
Wilshire 5000 equal-weighted price index (without income) %	21.2	30.8	26.3 (18.0)	24.7 (15.1)
Wilshire 5000 value-weighted total return index (including income) %	16.1	24.1	18.4 (9.7)	14.9 (13.0)

This comparison of the Wilshire 5000 value-weighted, total return index to the equal-weighted price index reveals that even excluding dividends, the small capitalization stocks significantly outperformed the large capitalization stocks. If the equal-weighted index were based on total return, its performance differential would be even greater.

The identification of a growth company or a growth industry is not as simple a matter as it may first appear. It cannot be accomplished solely by an examination of the statistics and records but requires a considerable supplement of special investigation and business judgment.

Does the Price Discount Potential Growth?   The third source of difficulty is perhaps the greatest. Assuming a fair degree of confidence that the company will expand in the future, what price is the investor justified in paying for this attractive element?

An evaluation that rests heavily on future anticipations—in the form of the long-term continuation of a significantly above-average performance—inevitably embodies a wide possibility of error. To avoid this, we suggest (1) that the high-growth rate be projected out not more than seven years and (2) that in estimating value, the analyst use the projected earnings or dividend figure for the fourth year (equivalent to an average of the seven years). Irrespective of the analytical methodology adopted, the investor must be convinced that the price is fair, considering the risk involved and the growth expected. Thus, the price should be justifiable on a quantitative basis.

This discussion has put more emphasis on the pitfalls of investing in growth stocks than on its advantages. Nevertheless, if the analysis of growth companies is pursued with skill, intelligence, consistency, and diligent study, it yields satisfactory overall results. Consistent records of good performance are being compiled by many experienced growth-stock investors.

Selection Based on the Margin-of-Safety Principle

The third approach to common stock investment is based on the margin-of-safety principle. Analysts who are convinced that a stock is *worth more* than is being paid for it and are reasonably optimistic as to the company's future would regard the issue as a suitable component of a group investment in common stocks. This approach lends itself to two possible techniques. One is to buy when *the general market is low*, measured by quantitative standards of value. Presumably, the purchases would then be confined to representative and fairly active issues. The other technique would be to discover *individual* issues which are under—or at least within—a conservative value range. Such stocks are presumably available even when the general market is not particularly low. In either case, the margin of safety resides in the fact that the stock is satisfactorily priced in terms of its intrinsic value as measured by the analyst. That is, by conservative standards, the investor is getting full money's worth. But with respect to the hazards and the psychological factors involved, the two techniques differ considerably. They are discussed below.

Values at Market Bottoms.   At the low levels of general market swings it is usually possible to identify undervalued primary issues by using the valuation process applied to individual stocks or to a composite group such as the Dow-Jones Industrial list or the S&P 500 or 400. Here the cross-section approach and the value approach converge, because at historically low market levels most common stocks prove to be under-valued when subjected to appraisal.

From late 1974 to mid-1982, the persistent undervaluation of corpo-rate earning power in the marketplace brought value investing back in style. The unprecedented wave of mergers, acquisitions, and buyouts was the inevitable response of corporate financial managers and investors who searched for such undervaluations of earning power. We view these merger and acquisition transactions as confirmation of the benefits of a value approach to investing.

Values at Market Midlevels.   When the stock market is at more or less neutral levels, leading issues selling at demonstrably bargain prices are hard to find. The field of undervalued securities would then be confined largely to depreciated bonds and preferred stocks and to certain sec-ondary common stocks. In most cases the latter will appear cheap from the *quantitative* angle, but their prospects for the future will be no better than average. This can result in an attractive quantitative showing—in relation to price, of course—with a mediocre qualitative position.

Consequently, some enterprises that are long-established, well-financed, important in their industries, and presumably destined to stay in business and make profits indefinitely in the future, but lacking in growth appeal, will tend to be discriminated against by the stock market. This is especially true in years of subnormal profits; they will sell for considerably less than they would be worth to private owners. This last criterion—a price substantially less than value—constitutes the touch-stone for the discovery of true investment opportunities in common stocks.

Individual Issue Values.   The security analyst seeks out individual se-curities that are attractively priced relative to a conservative value esti-mate. The procedure is to recommend for investment a group of issues which currently sell at prices either under or within a calculated range of value. Although the idea of formally appraising individual securities to arrive at their intrinsic value is no longer novel, it was put aside by many for the growth-stock fad of the 1960s and early 1970s. This was the era of the "one-decision stock"—that is, buy-and-hold growth stocks without regard to price. The result was a two-tier market in which the preferred growth issues—the "nifty fifty"—received valuations of two-to-three times the market multiple. It was not until after the protracted market decline of 1973–1974 and the concurrent collapse of growth stock prices that investors turned again to the value concept. This renewed attention is particularly evident in the search for merger and acquisition candidates.

Fighting the Last War

The standard criticism of the military is that they are likely to be preparing to fight the last war. Investment strategists are victims of the same tendency. The hazards and opportunities of the past market cycle are clear, in hindsight, and so are the defenses not developed and the strategies overlooked. Even after the 1973–1974 major decline in stock prices, when excellent investment opportunities were unfolding, market timing became very popular. Those investors still convinced it was imprudent to be in the market were unable to think in terms of long-term growth.

The recovery from August 1982 to June 1983 was led by technology, emerging growth, and unlisted issues. The NASDAQ Over-the-Counter Composite Index was bid up 105.8 percent compared to an appreciation of 66.9 percent for the S&P 500. Just as this phase of the market was peaking, the IPO (initial public offering) market thrived, and venture partnerships were inundated with funds.

From June 1983 to July 1984, however, the NASDAQ Index declined 31.5 percent, and the S&P 500's price decline was limited to 13.6 percent. "Value investing in the Graham and Dodd tradition" was a prominent 1984 theme in reaction to the correction of high-market multiple NASDAQ stocks in the second half of 1983.[8]

What is noteworthy of these examples is that after each phase of promise and profit, the less successful money managers tended to adopt the strategies of the more successful money managers at a time where these strategies ceased being effective.

---

[8]The ensuing two years turned out to be favorable for virtually all groups of stocks.

Passive Management

Passive management in the form of an index-matching portfolio comes back in style after each contraction of the small company effect. In general, active investors do not own holdings in proportion to their market weightings but lean toward more equally weighted portfolios. When large seasoned companies lead the market, therefore, active managers are likely on average to turn in inferior total returns. When the environment favors smaller, less mature companies, active management is going to perform relatively well, even after adjustment for an increase in volatility.

There are, of course, other reasons for going to passive management, such as very large concentrations of assets, interim lack of conviction about market sectors, and emphasis on market exposure rather than individual security returns. Programs of portfolio insurance, for example, are designed to work most efficiently with an indexed portfolio which closely tracks a futures contract. Option writing across an equity portfolio is also likely to work well when an option manager focuses on the fair value of the option contracts rather than the valuation of the underlying equities. Advocates of indexing an international equity portfolio advance the additional argument that financial reporting in many countries does not permit the successful application of fundamental analytical techniques.

The ebb and flow of funds in and out of passively managed pools tend to be influenced more by the experience of the recent past than any other factor. This is almost inevitable. Seldom can we anticipate whether active management in general is likely to be superior in the next market move. The conviction by the two generations of authors of this book is that across a market cycle, with all the divergent trends at work within it, consistent application of valuation principles will produce good results without exposure to serious risk of loss.

Emphasis on Value

The wider swings in stock prices since the late 1960s have brought spectacular gains and losses to investors. Diversification is back in style, and the thought of seeking a margin of safety related to intrinsic value is more widely accepted. Performance measurement in absolute terms, not just in relation to peer groups, also has recovered its place in investment thinking.

Such trends are gratifying to advocates of fundamental analysis of the value of companies, industries, and sectors. But this is not the whole story. In the long spans of market strength since August 1982, attention has been frequently diverted from specific companies to the market for stock certificates (or book entries) and arithmetic artifacts called indexes, averages, and composites, which are designed to conceal or cancel individual differences. The huge volume of daily transactions recorded on the books of a depositary trust company reflect arbitrage activity, block positioning too large for specialists and market makers to handle, portfolio exposure hedging, and a myriad of efforts to control market risk in all its forms. A minor portion of this sometimes frenzied activity reflects investment decisions based on the systematic valuation of corporate enterprises.

Concern for the efficiency of our securities markets as allocators of scarce capital resources should give observers of the scene cause for serious misgivings. For analysts faithful to the application of discipline to the evaluation of specific companies as going concerns, however, the diversion of their competitors' or other investors' attention from the serious business of security analysis spells exceptional opportunities to identify not just mispricings of individual companies but also undervaluations of whole industries and sectors. With these opportunities, moreover, comes the assurance that fundamental values will inevitably take over the direction of capital flows for investment.

28

The Pros and Cons of the Valuation Approach

The practical objective of security analysis in the common stock field is to assist the investor in selecting attractive issues. How does the analyst conclude that a given stock is attractive?

At this point in our 1962 edition we stated that, although much progress had been made, many individual company studies by Wall Street brokerage houses rested on a too-abbreviated forecast of earnings covering generally only the next 12 months. The balance of the typical study was mainly qualitative in character, relating to the standing and prospects of the enterprise.

Now, as a result of use of the dividend discount model and advances in analytical practices, a longer projection span is getting more attention. At the same time, company studies have been made somewhat more quantitative, and a move toward more specific value or return estimates has developed so that a stock is "cheap" or "attractive" according to the relationship of its calculated value or return compared to the current market price.

The Valuation Approach in Perspective

Analysts can do a more dependable or professional job of passing judgment on a common stock if they can determine some objective value (as discussed in Chapter 4), independent of the market quotation, with which the current price can be compared. The analyst could then advise the investor to buy when the price is at or below value—or, at least, when the current price lies within the indicated range of value—and to sell when the price is well above value. This is undoubtedly a good idea if it will work. Obviously it must have difficulties and limitations; otherwise it would have become standard practice long ago. We recognize these difficulties, but we believe that the valuation or appraisal idea is nevertheless basically sound.

From the most general standpoint we consider that common-stock valuations can help the investor choose issues that will yield satisfactory dividends and maintain an earning power commensurate with the price paid. If such results are obtained, the overall experience of stock market behavior should not be unsatisfactory. But the market price factor is the hardest of all for the security analyst to foretell or to control. One basic trouble is that the shares which appear most attractive from the standpoint of value analysis usually do so precisely because they are relatively unpopular in the market. The market's "momentum" is against them, and there is no assurance that the unpopular will become popular within a measurable time.

Let us state our position in another way. The valuation approach cannot be counted upon for a quickly gained stock market profit; indeed it is doubtful that any approach or method can deliver this brand of goods. Successful common-stock investment extends over many years and usually involves many separate commitments. Its results are measured by the aggregate dividend return received and by the movement of aggregate market value, preferably from an earlier point to a later point similarly situated in the stock market cycle. Common-stock investments based in the first instance upon the valuation method, and if possible buttressed by a substantial indicated margin of safety, are more likely to work out well over the years than those based on superficial analysis, market popularity, or business anticipations for the short term.

Practical Application and Utility of the Valuation Method

To determine how useful the results obtained by the appraisal process are, several issues need to be addressed:

What kinds of valuations have been made in the past, and how dependable were they?

2. What kinds of common stocks lend themselves best, and what kinds least, to valuation?

3. To what extent does the utility of the valuation approach depend on the additional factors of margin of safety and diversification?

4. Is an imperfect valuation better or worse than none for the investor? Is a valuation that is imperfect in absolute terms but right in relative values adequate?

Past Valuations—Legal

Up to the present the largest collection of formal and complete valuations of common stocks are to be found in legal proceedings. Legal valuations may be divided into three classes: those made (1) for purposes of estate and gift taxes; (2) as a basis for reorganization, recapitalization, and merger or other intercompany plans; and (3) for the purpose of determining amounts payable to dissenting stockholders under the appraisal statutes of the various states.

Legal appraisals, however, are made not because the common stocks involved are best suited for valuation but because some corporate or personal events make a determination of value necessary. In fact, most legal valuations deal with rather unsuitable material. The typical gift or estate tax case involves shares in a "closed corporation," which is usually of less than major size and would be considered in Wall Street terms as being exposed to a more-than-average degree of future uncertainties. Corporate reorganizations grow out of insolvency, which suggests considerable vulnerability to business vicissitudes. To some extent this is true also of recapitalization plans designed to clear up large amounts of preferred dividend accumulations, which are in themselves a mark of subnormal past performance.

The extensive body of securities litigation, however, has, in general, accepted the security analyst's process of arriving at value. Such cases frequently involve a determination of the existence and the amount of damages for the misrepresentation or omission of financial information. The analyst is called on to define those facts which a reasonable investor would consider important in reaching a decision. Such a definition inevitably leads to a valuation of the company involved on the assumption that the true facts were fully known.

Value Based on Future Earning Power

A historical review of valuation work shows that since the 1930s some important changes in the judicial view of "value" have brought it closer to the thinking of the experienced investor. Earlier valuations, made mainly for tax purposes, often followed a rigid formula based on past earnings and on the balance sheet equity. It was assumed either that future earnings would repeat those of the past or that—most impractically— only the past earnings and the assets counted in determining value. The Supreme Court has long held that the value of a company for purposes of reorganization depends primarily on its expected earning power.[1]

Similarly, in tax and appraisal cases the standard of value is the price at which a willing and informed buyer would do business with a willing and informed seller. In ordinary instances, where a business is to be valued primarily on a going-concern rather than on a liquidating basis, this criterion coincides with the judgment of the Supreme Court; and both would also represent the accepted view of sound value in investment circles.

In sum, judicial valuations and investment valuations now follow the same principles and face the same problems. Security analysts have an advantage denied the courts—they can choose to some extent the types of common stocks they will value.

Issues Suited and Unsuited for Valuation

Good judgment must be used in distinguishing between securities and situations that are better suited and those that are worse suited to value analysis.

A working assumption is that the past record affords at least a rough guide to the future, since typically there is a continuity in corporate affairs. However, when this is not the case, the record and other underlying evidence become more questionable as guides to the future and thus security analysis becomes less valuable. Hence, this technique is more useful when applied to senior securities (which in certain respects are protected against change) than to common stocks, more useful when applied to a business of inherently stable character than to one subject to wide variations, and finally more useful when carried on under fairly normal general conditions than in times of great uncertainty and radical change.

---

[1] For example, see *Consolidated Rock Products Company et al. v. du Bois*, 312 U.S. 510 (1941). *Case* v. *Los Angeles Lumber Products Company, Ltd.*, 308 U.S. 106 (1939). *Group of Institutional Investors and Mutual Savings Bank Group* v. *Chicago, Milwaukee, St. Paul & Pacific Railroad Company*, 318 U.S. 523 (1943). *Ecker* v. *Western Pacific Railroad Corporation*, 318 U.S. 448 (1943).

A Company Well-Suited to Analysis. Dayton Hudson Corporation, which operates chains of department, apparel, specialty, and book stores, illustrates that continuity and consistency in performance which make possible effective intrinsic value analysis. The data in Table 28.1 demonstrate this continuity over the span from 1976 through 1985:

- The compound annual growth in sales for the second half of the 10-year span (16.9 percent for 1981–1985) was comparable to that for the first half (19.5 percent for 1976–1980).
- The net profit margin was nearly identical for each 5-year span (3.5 percent and 3.3 percent), and the range in the annual figures was very limited.
- The return on total capital was very close for each 5-year period (11.2 percent versus 11.7 percent).

Table 28.1. Dayton Hudson Corporation Data

Year	Net profit margin (%)	Return on total capital (%)
1976	3.5	10.9
1977	3.8	11.9
1978	3.3	10.6
1979	3.7	11.6
1980	3.4	10.9
1981	3.2	11.1
1982	3.5	11.6
1983	3.5	12.1
1984	3.2	12.3
1985	3.2	11.6
1976–1980 average	3.5	11.2
1981–1985 average	3.3	11.7

SOURCE: Value Line, Inc., *The Value Line Investment Survey*, March 6, 1987, p. 1639.

A Company Not Well-Suited to Analysis. Arrow Electronics, Inc., a large distributor of electronic components and computer products and a secondary refiner of lead, illustrates performance that is extremely difficult to evaluate in terms of an intrinsic value approach. Using the same measures as Table 28.1, the data for Arrow Electronics are in Table 28.2.

- The compound annual growth rate in sales for 1981–1985 was 8.7 percent compared with 32.2 percent for 1976–1980.
- Comparative five-year averages cannot be computed for the net profit margin because of losses in 1982 and 1985, but it is clear from the

Table 28.2. Arrow Electronics Data, Inc.

Year	Net profit margin (%)	Return on total capital (%)
1976	0.7	4.5
1977	3.6	11.0
1978	3.1	11.5
1979	2.1	7.4
1980	2.3	10.9
1981	0.3	5.0
1982	loss	loss
1983	0.9	6.2
1984	1.7	8.8
1985	loss	0.8

SOURCE: Value Line, Inc., *The Value Line Investment Survey*, Feb. 6, 1987, p. 1032.

annual data that in profitable years the margin varied widely from 3.6 percent to 0.3 percent.

- The return on total capital measure of profitability is subject to the same difficulties. Note that in profitable years the return ranged from 11.5 percent to 4.5 percent.

A further qualitative problem was the December 1980 tragic loss of 13 key executives, including the chief executive, in a hotel fire which destroyed the continuity of the management group.

Best Industries for Valuation.   Public utility common stocks appear to have qualities of stability and predictability which make them ideal for formal appraisal. In theory, the mere factor of variability in earnings would not be a bar to a worthwhile valuation, provided that one could reasonably ascertain what the *earning power* would prove to be. But in practice, the more a company's results are subject to fluctuation, the less predictable becomes the earning power. Thus the best industries for valuation are those which do not show large profit declines in periods of recession. Such industries would include, in addition to public utilities, life insurance companies, food processing companies, medical supplies companies, beverage companies, distilling and tobacco companies, household products companies, drug stores and others.

Using return on net worth as a measure of profitability, Table 28.3 illustrates that, over the six-year span, the eight industries shown were characterized by stable returns. The fact that the three geographical groups of electric utilities had identical returns in each year is to be noted. However, in the last year or two, companies constructing nuclear plants have had write-downs that severely affected their profitability.

Table 28.3. Comparative Return on Net Worth for Stable Industries, 1980–1985

Industry	Percent earned on net worth					
	1980	1981	1982	1983	1984	1985
Electric utility—east	10.1	11.0	11.7	12.7	12.9	12.8
Electric utility—central	10.1	11.0	11.7	12.7	12.9	12.8
Electric utility—west	10.1	11.0	11.7	12.7	12.9	12.8
Beverage	16.8	18.3	16.4	17.1	18.0	16.2
Distilling and tobacco products	18.1	17.3	16.5	16.6	18.5	17.2
Drugstore	16.5	17.1	16.2	16.4	17.5	15.9
Food processing	14.8	14.5	13.9	14.2	15.4	15.6
Household products	16.2	16.3	15.8	16.3	15.3	13.2
Life insurance	12.7	12.8	10.9	11.5	11.9	12.2
Medical supplies	16.1	16.4	16.9	16.7	16.2	14.1

SOURCE: Value Line, Inc., *The Value Line Investment Survey*, editions published March 29–June 7, 1985 and January 2–March 27, 1987.

Many rather unstable industries include a few favorably situated members which have a strategic or management advantage over the rest, and which turn in a good performance even in bad times. Such companies have a stability of their own that makes them suitable for valuation.

Let us make the point here, however, that while the future earnings of the strong and stable companies (for, say, a seven-year period) may be estimated with some degree of confidence, this very fact may lead to overpricing so excessive that they become unattractive for investment. Issues which combine resistance to depression with good records of growth tend to become so popular with investors that they sell at excessive multipliers of their past earnings and dividends and of any reasonable projection of expectable earnings and dividends. Thus we face the familiar dilemma that common stocks of investment quality often sell at speculative prices. Thus the successful choice of common stocks for investment is a much more difficult matter than the mere identification of "good companies."[2]

Margin of Safety and Diversification as Aids to Practical Valuation

If a high price can turn an investment issue into a speculation, can a low price turn a speculative issue (the shares of a secondary company) into

[2] Benjamin Graham, "The New Speculation in Common Stocks," address before the Annual Convention of the National Federation of Financial Analysts Societies, May 1958. Reprinted in *The Intelligent Investor*, by Benjamin Graham, 4th ed., Harper & Row, New York, 1973, p. 292.

an investment? This question implies, in valuation language, that even though a company may be subject to a more-than-average amount of uncertainty and fluctuation, its shares may still have a minimum valuation which is so conservative as to be reasonably dependable and is significantly above the market price. This situation exists for the great majority of issues when the market is at depression levels. It also exists at most other times for individual issues which are suffering from unpopularity or mere neglect. Therefore, the answer to the question is "yes."

When the price is well below the indicated value of a secondary share, the investor has a margin of safety which can absorb unfavorable future developments and can permit a satisfactory ultimate result even though the company's future performance may be far from brilliant. This margin of safety corresponds to that which we have found to be essential in the purchase of bonds and preferred stocks for investment. It serves the same purpose in common stocks as in bonds but with the added advantage for common stocks that it will often permit a substantial profit to be reaped out of the initial discrepancy between price and indicated value.

In our opinion, a margin of safety—in the form of an excess of estimated intrinsic value over current market price—is prerequisite to investing in secondary shares. But, is it equally essential in the purchase of primary issues?

Obviously, it is highly desirable also to have a substantial "protective cushion" between the estimated intrinsic value and the price paid for an investment-quality stock. However, this may prove difficult to find except at low levels of the general market. Does this mean that the analyst must give up the margin-of-safety concept for standard issues? We think not. Rather it is sought in a different form: in an excess of expected dividends for a period of years over the income which would result from a normal interest return. For example, the investor who purchased Abbott Laboratories in 1976 received a current return of less than 2 percent (10¾ cent dividend on a purchase price of $5.75), but the growth in dividends to a $0.84 rate in 1986 brought the current return up to more than 14 percent on the 1976 price.

A margin of safety—either a price or a yield differential (or both)—does not *guarantee* an investment against loss; it merely indicates that the probabilities are against loss. Therefore a single issue—whether a primary or secondary stock—purchased with a margin of safety may still "go sour" for some special reason and produce a loss.

A group of, say, 20 or more common stocks will usually average out the individual favorable and unfavorable surprises. For this reason, the diversification or group approach is an integral and essential part of the valuation concept. Clearly, analysts will have much more confidence in their projections of the future earnings and dividends of a representative list of common stocks, taken together, than in any of their individual estimates and over time rather than for any single year.

Valuation versus Alternative Procedures for the Analyst

Assume that a run-of-the-mill common stock is not particularly well suited to a formal valuation because there are too many uncertainties about its future to permit the analyst to estimate its earning power with any degree of confidence. Should analysts reject the valuation technique in such cases and form their opinions about the issue by some other approach? A common stock that cannot be valued with confidence cannot be analyzed with confidence. In other words, buying or selling recommendations that cannot be related to a reasonably careful valuation are not based on analysis proper but on what might be called "pseudo-analysis" or "quasi-analysis." In such situations the underlying interest in both the analyst's and the investor's mind is likely to be the probable market action of the stock in some relatively short period in the future. The analytical work done, which may be quite comprehensive, will thus serve as an adjunct to an essentially speculative decision—disguised though it may be under some other name.

Another alternative is to do whatever everyone else is doing, even though the price of a stock appears high; this is the so-called greater fool theory. This theory is applied on the basis that "I know I am a fool to pay such a high price for a stock but I know that a greater fool will come along and pay me an even higher price."

The soundness of a common-stock investment, in a single issue or a group of issues, may well depend on the ability of the investor or the analyst-advisor to justify the purchase by a process of formal valuation. In plainer language, a common-stock purchase may not be regarded as a proper constituent of a true investment program unless some rational calculation will show that it is worth at least as much as the price paid for it.

Tests Measuring Results of Intrinsic Valuation Approaches

To have practical value, the appraisal approach must produce satisfactory investment results. How should such "satisfactory results" be measured? In recent years much attention has been given to performance measurement and attribution. Measurement determines *how* a portfolio did. Attribution seeks to determine *why* a portfolio performed as it did.

Various objective tests may be used to check whether the valuation approach produces satisfactory results. For example, a purchase at a 20 percent discount from the central value—the center or midpoint of the valuation range—may be taken as the "justified purchase price." The top of the range—say, 20 percent above the central value—could be taken as the "justified selling price." It should be reached within a reasonable period of time, such as the next four years. Under normal conditions, central value would grow over the four-year period, presumably at the rate at which the company's earning power was growing. An investment purchased at a 20 percent discount and sold at a 20 percent premium to intrinsic value provides more than a mere 50% gain. The investor will also receive dividends and growth of the intrinsic value. If one assumes (1) a 4 percent dividend, (2) 6 percent growth, and (3) a 4-year holding period, the annual return would be over 20 percent, or a doubling of the investment in 4 years.

The success of the valuation technique could be judged by the percentage of issues purchased below their central value that actually reached a premium to the central value within four years. The result must be adjusted, of course, to eliminate the effect of action of the market as a whole. The measurement of excess return on the stock (of which price is a major component) is always relative to the market (S&P 500) adjusted for the stock's beta.

Value-Oriented Approaches Compared to the S&P 500

In this performance measurement process, there are many tests of different valuation approaches. Some examples of value-oriented management records follow:

	Compound annual total return 1981–1985 (%)
First Manhattan Capital Management	21.7
Prudential Equity Management Associates	19.6
Trinity Investment Management	21.1
Windsor Fund	22.6
Standard & Poor's 500	14.6

To be sure, this 1981–1987 period was a favorable one for value-oriented managers, but the results were achieved with a generally lower level of volatility, as measured by the standard deviation of returns.

In addition to such portfolio performance results, a useful measure can be to compare analysts' rankings of stocks in order of attractiveness against subsequent three- to five-year realized returns. The Value Line Timeliness Rankings cited in Chapter 2 are an example, for a shorter time horizon, of determining whether the rankings add to the returns subsequently earned by investors.

Price-Earnings Ratio Rankings

Another simple test uses the price-earnings (P/E) ratio as the chief criterion of relative value. Those stocks selling at the lowest P/E ratios are presumed to be undervalued as against those selling at high ratios. Various studies have been made along this line. One of the earliest was 1960.[3] Critics of these early studies have held that other factors in addition to P/E ratios were influencing the results—for example, small size of the firm, risk, and infrequent trading. A recent study "was designed to determine whether portfolios of low P/E stocks, constructed so that non-P/E-related biases were controlled for, could achieve excess rates of return."[4] Stocks were put into five P/E groups (portfolios)—with the lowest P/E stocks in group 1. There was quarterly rebalancing for 42 quarters from the beginning of 1970 to mid-1980. The results were as tabulated below:

P/E portfolio	Annualized risk-adjusted returns (%)
1	10.89
2	3.69
3	0.69
4	−5.35
5	−9.91

The study confirms the findings of others and shows that over time the return on low P/E stocks outperforms that on high P/E issues. There will

[3] S.F. Nicholson, "Price-Earnings Ratios," *Financial Analysts Journal*, July/August 1960, pp. 43–45.

[4] D.A. Goodman and J.W. Peavy, III, "Industry Relative Price-Earnings Ratios as Indicators of Investment Returns," *Financial Analysts Journal*, July/August 1983, pp. 60–65. The sample consisted of 40 stocks from each of three industries—electronics, paper container, and food. P/E relatives based on an index of the P/E ratio of a stock relative to its industry were used.

be limited periods, of course, in which this will not be true, notably after there has been an extended compression of P/E ratios.

Undervalued versus Overvalued Issues

A fundamental of security analysis—supported reasonably well by overall experience—is that most of the wide discrepancies between price and value will be corrected by the market itself so as to produce satisfactory results for the investor who (using publicly available information and the tools of security analysis) has the ability to identify these discrepancies.[5] However, there is an important limitation. Both the nature of the stock market and the psychology of investors tend to confine these satisfactory results more to the purchase of undervalued issues than to the sale of overvalued ones. The intrinsic value approach provides a discipline that can be helpful in parting with overvalued winners.

Many such overvaluations are shown by "glamor" companies which tend to sell much above what conservative valuations would warrant. These issues are refractory material for analysis. To advise their sale may prove as embarrassing as to advise their purchase. After all, a potential loss is limited to 100 percent of the investment, but a gain can develop to many times the original outlay.

The valuation technique is undoubtedly useful in showing that many of the new stock offerings in bull markets are priced much too high and so also may be the prices for cyclical secondary stocks in a favorable market environment. The valuation may show that the investment component of a share price is small relative to the speculative fraction of the total.

The Value Approach in Investment Timing

The intrinsic value approach proposed in this book is but one of several methods for determining both the absolute and the relative attractiveness of common stock issues. Those who practice this approach will use their conclusions as a basis for selecting issues to make up a common-stock portfolio and for recommending the sale of holdings that appear definitely overpriced or the replacement of less attractive by more attractive stocks.

---

[5] Clearly, if such wide discrepancies were obvious, the market would already have adjusted the price. The existence and full extent of a discrepancy are usually obvious only after the fact.

If classifying individual stocks as selling above or below their value range is feasible , then the same should be true of the market as reflected in a comprehensive index. Thus the adoption of the intrinsic value approach for single issues logically implies its application to the market as a whole, with necessary consequences as to overall holdings of common stocks. For example, if the prices of individual issues are above the value range and no attractive values are to be found, it logically follows that the market as a whole is overpriced. The reverse would, of course, be true of the market if many individual stocks are considered to be underpriced.

The distinction should be clear between this application of a standard of value to the level of the market and a forecast of the stock market's future behavior. Identification of a range of fair values is not a prediction of whether or when that channel will be breached in either direction. Nor does such a conclusion violate the classic advice to persons required to form judgments about the future: "Don't be afraid to predict the possible tops and bottoms of the stock market and don't be afraid to predict the timing of tops and bottoms; but *never* predict both together!"

29

Significance of the Earnings Record

Time Horizon, Reinvestment Rate, and Investment Value

Chapter 28 discussed a common-stock valuation approach based ordinarily on projected earnings and dividends for perhaps the next 5 to 10 years. This method has not been the standard procedure on Wall Street, which has, in fact, tended to use both shorter and longer periods for earnings projections. For the usual company—that is, one not designated as a "growth" enterprise—it has been popular to estimate earnings only for the current and perhaps the coming 12 months. By contrast, to justify the high multipliers of earnings sometimes commanded by growth stocks, rapidly expanding earnings are projected quite far into the future. When speculative enthusiasm abounds, the many analysts who favor companies of this type find no difficulty in making such far-reaching forecasts.

Present Value Formula

Growth Stocks. A well-established financial principle states that the investment value of a common stock equals the present worth of all its future dividends.[1] To apply this principle would require dividend pro-

---
[1] John Burr Williams, *The Theory of Investment Value*, Harvard University Press, Cambridge, Mass., 1938, p. 55.

jections for, say, between 40 and 50 years.[2] We do not believe that estimates for so remote a future can be made with enough dependability to be really useful. The investor may, however, assume a permanent or "built-in" growth rate *for common stocks in general,* derived basically from the reinvestment of undistributed earnings and buttressed by the country's history of long-term growth in corporate profits. In contrast, for *high-growth stocks,* the specific projections of earning power should be limited to, say, four years (the midpoint of a seven-year projection span), and the attractive longer-range prospects should be allowed for, less definitively, in a higher-than-average multiplier.[3]

Slow Growers. For companies with significantly below-average rates of return, it is hard to argue that stockholders and directors will tolerate such conditions indefinitely. Sooner or later liquidation will be demanded, or a new management will take over, or the old management will feel the pressures to reorder the affairs of the company, leading ultimately to a more typical growth rate than that which appears likely over the near to intermediate term.

Fungibility of Actual Dollars of Earnings

Clearly, an *actual* dollar of earnings of growth stocks is worth no more than an actual dollar of earnings of nongrowth stocks. Consequently, if a completely accurate estimate of the total earnings (and dividends) of a growth and a nongrowth share over the life of each corporation were possible, the *same* capitalization rate—or discount factor—would be appropriate for each. Using the same discount rate for the dollars of earnings produces a different multiplier for earnings of different companies, depending on the particular company's growth rate. The analyst should be willing to forecast normal earning power, say, four years into the future but may have expectations for further growth at an above-average pace beyond the fourth year. This would justify the analyst using a higher multiplier for the four-year-out normal earning

---

[2] Beyond 40 to 50 years the present value of all future dividends becomes relatively inconsequential. The present worth of $1 payable 50 years hence, discounted at 12 percent, is less than four-tenths of a cent. The marked decline in the present value of earnings to be received in the distant future means that, on a 12 percent basis, the present worth of an annuity of $1 per year for 25 years is 94 percent of the present worth of a like perpetual annuity.

[3] Except in the case of very high assumed growth rates, a trend projection of four years is representative of the *average* level for seven years. For example, assuming a 10 percent growth rate, a four-year projection would show an increase of 46 percent. On average, the earnings over a seven-year period would have been 49 percent above the beginning level.

power for the ongoing growth company than the multiplier that would be appropriate for the nongrowth company. For example, an analyst might be willing to pay 12 times the estimated earning power four years hence for the average company but 18 times the estimated future earning power of a company that is expected to continue to grow at a relatively high rate. The analyst should be aware, however, that the justification of a 50 percent premium in the multiplier would require an assumption that the growth stock would grow *more* than half again as fast as the nongrowth stock for the full seven years. Alternatively, the period of rapid growth would have to be extended further into the future than the seven-year time horizon suggested by this book. Many companies have put together persistent growth records over periods of five, ten, or even twenty years. The issue is the probability that past rapid growth will continue for another extended period. History indicates that only a small percentage of the companies with fine past records succeed in enjoying continued rapid growth for such long periods. A 50 percent premium in the multiple removes any margin of safety due to under-valuation. Thus the premium for nonspecific growth should be rather modest.

Retained Earnings Are Not Fungible

As discussed, the actual dollar of earnings is worth the same whether it is earned by a growth company, or a nongrowth company. That is entirely true in the sense that a dollar in hand is worth the same to anyone because anyone can spend it and obtain the going purchasing power of the dollar. The statement of equality is also true for a dollar of dividends paid by a company. The dollar of dividends paid by the finest growth company spends no better than the last liquidation dollar of a bankrupt company. Yet, in the valuation of securities, a dollar of retained earnings in the hands of a company which has opportunities to invest it at a higher rate of return has an *investment value* much higher than a dollar of retained earnings in the hands of a company that has only poor opportunities for reinvestment. In fact, if a dollar of retained earnings could be reinvested at the same reinvestment rate for an indefinite period of time, its investment value would be directly proportional to its reinvestment rate.

Reinvestment Rates and Investment Value

To illustrate the notion of differing values of retained earnings, we will examine a simple hypothetical case of two companies, each of which earns $2 per share and has a 50 percent payout ratio. The appropriate discount rate is assumed to be 10 percent for both companies. Company A can reinvest all retained earnings perpetually at a 20 percent annual rate, whereas Company B has opportunities to reinvest its retained earnings at only a 10 percent annual rate. We assume for simplicity that investors are equally satisfied with dividends or capital gains, and therefore no weighting system is necessary to differentiate the investment value of the dividends from the value of the capital gains. For both companies, the dividend will be $1, because the payout is 50 percent of $2. In each case the investment value of the dividend is $10, because the discounting rate for both companies is 10 percent.

However, the value of the $1 of retained earnings of A, the growth company, is $2, the investment value of $1 of retained earnings that will earn 20¢ perpetually—whle the $1 of retained earnings of the less profitable company, B, is worth only $1 because it will earn only 10¢. Put another way, $1 of retained earnings of the growth company is as productive of future earnings as is $2 of retained earnings of the more stable company. This simple description works for a single-period analysis or when the incremental earnings are all paid out as dividends. However, if the growth company maintained a 50 percent payout ratio and the 20 percent reinvestment rate, it would be worth even more in a multiperiod analysis because of the impressive compounding effect on the growth in dividends. A key point here is that although the actual dollars of earnings of the two companies are no different, the difference in opportunities for reinvestment results in different investment values for those dollars of earnings and make the payout ratio a critical issue in management's efforts to optimize the value of the company.

If the dollar of retained earnings of company A is the equivalent of $2 of B's retained earnings, then A's retained dollar's investment value should be twice as much, and the argument can be made that the investment value of A should be based on $3 of earnings—$1 of dividends and $2 of B-equivalent retained earnings. A would properly sell at $30 and B at $20, which places both on a 10 percent return basis. Obviously, this overly simple case is designed to make a philosophical point—that the multiplier is influenced by the amount of retained earnings and their reinvestment rate—rather than to offer a direct valuation method.

Choice of Projection Period—Arbitrary

The actual choice of the projection period must—of necessity—be arbitrary. The span from 5 to 10 years, which we have suggested, is based in part on the concept of including the good, bad, and average years of one or more full business cycles. Moreover, it is comparable to the period for which most intelligent business managers are accustomed to looking and planning ahead. And incidentally, it tends to correspond to the period of *past* earnings which the analyst ordinarily will scrutinize with particular care.

Longer Forecasts—More Difficult but More Useful

Although their number is decreasing rapidly, some analysts still hold that it is difficult enough to estimate the coming year's results with any accuracy and that therefore to extend the forecast through the next 5 to 10 years is foolhardy. The trouble with this approach is that it emphasizes the easier thing rather than the more important and more useful. For the investor, next year's profits are of real importance only if they can be viewed as indicative of the longer-term *earning power*. Thus to use a year's results intelligently, the investor and the analyst must have at least a background idea of the probable earnings level for a number of years. Seldom does a single year's result turn out to be representative of the results over a full business cycle. The analyst may choose to identify a business cycle that includes the estimated year, average those years, and then apply the growth rate from the midpoint of the period to the end of the period to get the end-of-period level of earning power. A personality trait of the successful security analyst is a willingness to forecast the future, knowing beforehand that the forecast will often be wrong. Those who can't make decisions or can't stand the embarrassment of making mistakes suffer miserable lives during their brief careers as security analysts.

Projection of Earnings

Earning Power and Projected Earnings

In estimating the *earning power* for a target date, such as five years ahead, the procedure follows this order:

1. The economic forecast
2. An earnings estimate for the Standard & Poor's 500 or other broad index
3. Sector and industry earnings forecasts
4. Company earnings estimates

These projections extend at least as far into the future as the target date.

A Check on Analysts' Estimates

An interesting sidelight is the comparison of the sum of individual company earnings estimates and the aggregate estimate for an index, such as the Standard & Poor's 500 (S&P 500). Large investment organizations use these comparisons as a discipline on the analytical process, since initially the estimate for the index will be for an increase of, say, 5 percent, whereas the sum of the estimates made by the analysts for the individual companies will show perhaps a 15 percent earnings increase. This disparity reflects the bright hopes of the analyst, augmented by the eternal optimism of management. At the industry level, the numbers can be used to remind the analyst that not all companies in an industry can gain share of market next year, nor can all industries do better than average.

Macroforecasting versus Microforecasting

The number of variables involved and their constantly shifting influence make it impossible to establish definitive, teachable techniques for successfully forecasting financial developments. Consistently successful work here must be attributable to superior ability to discern and appraise the key factors which determine earnings in any period. Nevertheless, in security analysis, projective work inevitably starts with an examination of the actual record of the past. The extent to which that past average or trend may be counted on to continue determines the relative value and importance of such an examination. In general, the broader the segment of the economy analyzed, the more gradual will be the change and the closer the probable relationship between the past and the future. Thus a projection of gross national product—the basic measure of the nation's final output—is likely to prove closer to the mark than a projection of earnings of common stocks as a whole, and the latter forecast is likely to be more accurate than similar projections for sectors, industries, and then, the least accurate, individual companies.

Projection of GNP and Corporate Profits

The GNP projections should be made in considerable detail if they are to be helpful to the security analyst. For example, the housing component of gross private domestic investment should be accompanied by statistics on single family and multifamily housing starts, sources and amounts of mortgage money available, mortgage interest rates, average price of houses, and cost and labor factors. In their absence, the analyst will have to spend more time gathering such data and less time analyzing individual companies.

The economic forecast will normally include a forecast of corporate profits, which is partly reported in the net domestic product of corporations accounts. The unremitted foreign earnings component of corporate profits is not included in domestic product and must be estimated separately.

There is a strong link between corporate profits as developed in economic forecasts and the aggregate profits of a broad index of publicly held companies, such as the Standard & Poor's 400 Industrials Index. One cannot, however, forecast the Index earnings well by simply multiplying the corporate profits forecast by a factor, for several technical reasons:

- Frequent substitutions of the companies in an index

- Mergers, acquisitions, and recapitalizations

- Dilutive and antidilutive sales of stock

- The absence of small companies

- Heavy use of tax accounting and economic accounting ideas in the GNP corporate profits.

Chapter 6 discusses an approach to forecasting earnings of a market index, but many other approaches are in use.

A specific forecast of earnings for a broad market index may be disaggregated to a modest degree by the economist or investment strategist, but it is doubtful that much is gained by it. The analyst is in a much better position to estimate company and industry profits. The relationship between analyst earnings and the broader picture of index earnings can be rationalized by good communications between those who do economic and strategy work on the one hand and the analysts on the other.

Projection of Earnings of Individual Stocks

The earnings estimates for most common stocks will, of course, relate to the growth rates assumed for the economy and particularly total earnings for all common stocks. However, no type of solely mechanical projection, or formal approach, will produce results sufficiently dependable to be made the basis of investment choices. If the analyst's work is to have significant value, any mechanical approach must be supported by considerable knowledge of the profit-making factors present in the company. These will be discussed later in this chapter.

Mechanical Estimates

Every projection has a mechanical basis in that it starts with a consideration of past results—including average, variance, and trend. A frequently employed shortcut projection is to estimate future growth at the same rate as in some past period. How good is such an approach? Let us apply it to the stocks in the Dow-Jones Industrial Average in a manner that permits some evaluation of its usefulness.

Table 29.1 first shows for each stock the percentage change in earnings from the 1973–1975 average to the 1978–1980 average. (Three-year periods are preferable to single years, since they reduce the impact of nonrecurrent conditions.) Next the table shows projected earnings for 1983–1985 assuming the same rate of change in the second as in the first five-year span. For contrast, we add an even more naive projection, which assumes the same 67 percent growth rate for each stock as was recorded for the average stock in the group from 1973–1975 to 1978–1980. Finally, the actual 1983–1985 average earnings are listed and the percent change from 1978–1980.

Several conclusions emerge from the figures in the table. First, neither the company's past rate of increase nor the flat application of a 67 percent growth factor produced sufficiently accurate estimates of 1983–1985 earnings to encourage reliance on this approach. The results of this simple exercise reinforce belief in the futility of almost any naive extrapolation of earnings. If there is one thing certain in life, it is that the future will differ from the past in a variety of ways. The chances of those differences offsetting one another are poor, particularly at the microeconomic (company or industry) level. Second, the across-the-board advance of 67 percent was nearer actual earnings in more instances than the application to each company of its own past performance. Here, we begin to see more the influence of economywide developments on the individual stock. No company is totally free of the influences of what happens in the economy at large to prices, wages, unemployment rate, taxes, interest rates, and the like.

A casual pairing of companies in the same industry is highly suggestive that careful study of industry prospects would have provided valuable guidance on the potential for individual companies. The steel industry turned unprofitable, and both Bethlehem and U.S. Steel suffered with the rest of the industry. Electrical equipment did well, and both General Electric and Westinghouse Electric showed above-average earnings. The basic chemical companies generally did poorly. Union Carbide felt the full force of the unfavorable environment, but diversification reduced the impact on Eastman Kodak and Allied Signal.

Table 29.1. Mechanical Estimates of Per-Share Earnings for Selected Stocks in the Dow-Jones Industrial Average

Company	Earnings per share 1973–1975	Earnings per share 1978–1980	Change (%)	Estimate based on Individual change ($)	Estimate based on Group change of 67% ($)	Actual 1983–1985 earnings	1978–1980 to 1983–1985 change (%)
Alcoa	$1.68	$6.05	+260	$21.78	$10.11	$ 2.27	− 62
Allied Signal	2.90	2.80	− 3	2.72	4.68	4.20	+ 50
American Can	4.41	5.58	+ 27	7.09	9.33	4.42	− 21
Am. Express	1.10	2.41	+119	5.28	4.03	2.96	+ 23
Beth. Steel	6.04	4.74	− 22	3.70	7.92	−4.36	d*
Chevron	2.54	5.16	+103	10.47	8.62	4.76	− 8
DuPont	2.85	5.55	+ 95	10.82	9.27	5.13	− 8
E. Kodak	2.61	4.21	+ 61	6.78	7.03	2.51	− 40
Exxon	3.01	4.82	+ 60	7.71	8.05	6.66	+ 38
G.E.	1.62	3.04	+ 88	5.72	5.08	4.87	+ 60
G.M.	5.31	6.54	+ 23	8.04	10.92	12.78	+ 95
Goodyear	2.32	2.66	+ 15	3.06	4.44	3.27	+ 23
IBM	3.05	5.53	+ 81	10.01	9.24	10.16	+ 84
Inco Ltd.	3.22	1.65	− 49	.84	2.76	−1.14	−169
Int'l Paper	4.83	7.29	+ 51	11.01	12.18	3.07	− 58
McDonald's	.77	2.10	+173	5.73	3.51	4.40	+ 110
Merck	1.37	2.45	+ 79	4.39	4.09	3.40	+ 39
MMM	2.52	5.40	+114	11.56	9.02	5.99	+ 11
Navistar	3.53	1.75	− 51	.86	2.92	−4.90	d
Owens-Il. Gl.	2.74	.40	+114	11.56	9.02	5.99	+ 11
Philip Morris	.79	2.02	+156	5.17	3.37	4.30	+ 113
P. & G.	1.93	3.50	+ 81	6.34	5.85	4.70	+ 34
Sears	1.81	2.44	+ 35	3.29	4.08	3.78	+ 55
Texaco	4.55	5.98	+ 31	7.83	9.99	4.50	− 25
U. Carbide	2.19	2.74	+ 25	3.43	4.58	1.03	− 62
United Tech.	1.28	2.83	+121	6.25	4.73	4.24	+ 50
U.S. Steel	6.24	1.56	− 75	.39	2.61	−.52	d
Westinghouse	.67	2.03	+203	6.15	3.39	3.03	+ 49
Woolworth	1.44	2.61	+ 81	4.72	4.36	2.28	− 13

NOTE: Earnings adjusted for stock splits and dividends.
* d = deficit.

Dominant Companies Control Their Destinies

Several companies represent dominant players in their particular fields, and were able to control their earnings trends well—examples are IBM, McDonald's, and Philip Morris. Thus projections must necessarily analyze the future at at least three levels—the economy, the industry or sector, and the particular company—to obtain reasonably successful estimates of company earnings. And even there, the analyst must be satisfied with success in relative more than in absolute terms.

A huge amount of effort is devoted to predicting earnings for the next quarter or the next year. This focus on reported earnings, as opposed to the overall ongoing earning power of a company, can be an unfortunate distraction. Analysts may find the greater fascination in the market's reaction to announcements of reported earnings rather than in focusing attention clearly on the determination of investment value and other fundamental issues associated with a longer-term time horizon.

Two Other Tests of Earnings Projections

To pursue our investigation further, let us now examine two other types of forecast of future changes in earnings. The first type is the forecast implicit in the stock market's valuation of different issues. It is fair to assume that, in general, the higher the market's multipliers of current earnings are, the more optimistic its view as to what the expected growth will be. The second type consists of forecasts of earnings made by large investment organizations on the basis of a study of individual company potential.

The Price-Earnings Ratio as a Forecaster

Table 29.2 lists again the companies in the Dow-Jones Industrial Average, this time in order of their average 1978–1980 price-earnings ratios. The table also shows the actual percentage gain—or decline—in average per-share earnings for each company from the 1978–1980 period to the 1983–1985 one. If the price-earnings ratio indicates expected future growth, the correlation between the market's growth expectations and the growth that actually occurred in the next five years appears to be a positive but weak relationship. The 10 stocks with the highest price-earnings ratios had positive earnings growth in all but two cases, and five of the six highest growth rates were among those 10 stocks. The bottom 10 stocks for which data are presented included only 2 stocks with positive growth and included four of the six worst performers. The relationship is positive, but it is not reasonable to think that this relationship provides analysts with any information that the market does not already have. Since these forecasts were already reflected in the prices that created the price-earnings ratios, one could hardly expect the stock market to reward the investor a second time for information it had already reflected. Abnormal profits and losses come

Table 29.2. Price-Earnings Ratios and Change in
Per-Share Earnings

Company	Average P/E ratio 1978–1980	Change in earnings per share from 1978–1980 to 1983–1985
Inco Ltd.	14.2×	d**%
Merck	13.6	+ 39
IBM	12.3	+ 84
Procter & Gamble	11.6	+ 34
MMM	10.3	+ 11
McDonald's	10.2	+110
Eastman Kodak	9.1	− 40
Philip Morris	8.9	+113
General Electric	8.4	+ 60
Sears	8.1	+ 55
United Technologies	7.6	+ 50
Allied Signal	7.5*	+ 50
DuPont	7.5	− 8
American Express	7.0	+ 23
U.S. Steel	6.7†	d
American Can	6.5	− 21
Exxon	6.2	+ 38
International Paper	6.2	− 58
Goodyear	6.1	+ 23
Chevron	5.7	− 8
Texaco	5.6	− 25
Bethlehem Steel	5.5	192
General Motors	5.3†	+ 95
Westinghouse	5.3	+ 49
Union Carbide	5.1	− 62
Owens-Illinois Glass	5.0	− 7
Alcoa	4.5	− 62
Woolworth	4.5	− 13
Navistar	4.4†	d
AT&T	‡	‡

* A year of nominal earnings excluded.
† Loss year excluded.
‡ Comparable data not available.
** d = deficit.

about when the investor holds and acts on a different view from that
held by the market.

Professional Analysts' Forecasts

The forecasts of earnings by an investment organization are set forth in
Table 29.3. The 1983–1985 earnings projections of 29 Dow-Jones shares

made by Value Line in 1980 are compared to the actual results. Nineteen of their estimates for individual companies missed the actual results by more than 25 percent—again, estimating the absolute levels of earnings of individual business enterprises is very difficult. Before the

Table 29.3. Value Line Earnings Estimates
Compared with Actual Results

Company	1980 Value Line estimates for 1983–1985	Actual 1983–1985 earnings per share
Alcoa	$ 7.75	$ 2.27
Allied Signal	7.20	4.20
American Can	8.50	4.42
American Express	5.64	2.96
Bethlehem Steel	9.00	−4.36
Chevron	10.00	4.76
DuPont	8.70	5.13
Eastman Kodak	7.47	2.51
Exxon	10.00	6.66
General Electric	5.20	4.87
General Motors	13.00	12.78
Goodyear	6.50	3.27
IBM	9.90	10.16
Inco Ltd.	5.25	−1.14
International Paper	9.20	3.07
McDonald's Corp.	4.55	4.40
Merck	4.60	3.40
MMM	9.25	5.99
Navistar	13.00	−4.90
Owens-Illinois Glass	8.00	4.14
Philip Morris	4.35	4.30
Procter & Gamble	6.53	4.70
Sears, Roebuck	4.20	3.78
Texaco	9.40	4.50
Union Carbide	4.17	1.03
United Technologies	5.25	4.24
U.S. Steel	8.30	−0.52
Westinghouse	3.63	3.03
Woolworth	5.75	2.28

reader concludes that Value Line did a poor job of estimating earnings, we hasten to mention that a large portion of these estimation errors were caused by the worldwide decline in basic commodity prices such as oil, steel, nonferrous metals, paper, rubber, and chemicals. At the time of the estimates, 1980, the conventional wisdom was that commodity prices would rise, with oil leading the way. Thus, a substantial portion of the errors must be attributed to economics and to sector and industry factors for which the analyst is responsible only in part. A common and probably valid excuse for why analysts do not forecast earnings very well is because economists do not forecast the economy very well.

Projection of Earnings by Analysis of the Business

The figures set forth in Tables 29.2 and 29.3 lead to two conclusions: (1) Table 29.3 demonstrates that even the most carefully developed forecast may go wide of the mark, especially when it is confined to a single company. (2) Table 29.2 is one more piece of evidence that to obtain creditable results, the analyst cannot follow mechanical methods but must bring specialized knowledge and skill to bear on the problem. In other words, the job is to analyze the business *itself*. To do so, the analyst must also probe carefully the performance and prospects of the industry (or industries) of which the company is a part. There are two approaches to a company analysis and projection, and they can be used separately or together: the *explicit* method and the *return-on-investment* approach.

The Explicit Forecast

The *explicit method* of projecting future earnings develops the figure from estimates of units, prices, sales, the individual operating and nonoperating expenses, and taxes. The sales figure is derived usually by relating it to expected economic and competitive conditions in the industry. The expenses may be worked out by categories—labor costs, material costs, services (say, utilities), overhead, and so on, or they may be covered by a single estimate of the *profit margin*.

Explicit forecasting requires sources of information that reach beyond regular contact with company sources. Some items, such as depreciation expense, can be calculated from historic numbers plus knowledge of the company's depreciation policy and the new plant and equipment added to the plant account. However, labor costs are sometimes best obtained from the company and at other times from observation of labor settlements generally, settlements in the particular industry, conversations with union leaders, or other sources. The best source of information about the cost of raw materials may be from other analysts, companies, and trade associations in those particular raw materials industries.

Changes in technology play a major role in security analysis. This is not merely a matter of the development of new products, but includes the development of new materials, and new processes. Technological change can be overwhelmed by other influences, such as changes in social values, demographics, alternative life styles, and foreign competition. It may be true that if you make a better mousetrap, the world will beat a path to your door, but the rule simply did not apply to buggy whips when the world no longer wanted to ride in buggies.

In the 1970s and 1980s, Americans relearned their lessons about the strength or weakness of the dollar and the effects on foreign competition. Many analysts spent a great deal of time determining which of the domestic producers was the most or least efficient in the domestic industry, when the real issue was whether any of them would survive the onslaught of foreign competition.

The Management Factor

Over the longer term, forecasting increasingly depends on a correct appraisal of the competence and integrity of management. In the case of medium-sized and smaller companies, management depth is a serious issue, and loss of one or two key people may represent disaster or a golden opportunity for the company. In larger companies, management sometimes becomes top heavy and ineffective despite individual skills. Several sources of information about management can be helpful. First, the company's record demonstrates what ongoing management has accomplished and is the primary source of judgment about the quality of management. Second, insights can often be gained from competitors, who often know more than one would expect about the knowledge, skills, strategies and tactics, organization, character, and personal habits and problems of the managements against which they compete. Although such sources may at times reflect favorable or unfavorable personal relationships, envy, sour grapes, or other bad information, they also provide factual information. Talking to the managers of one company about the managers of another may also tell much about the management of the first company. If they do not understand what the second company is doing or why, they are simply not on top of things.

The analyst will usually be exposed to a financial public relations person who is intelligent, charming, friendly, and helpful. Such a person, in turn, will introduce to the analyst those in the top echelon of management who will leave the best impression of management. Any unattractive geniuses will be hidden. Management people are *likable*, because they could not have risen to the top if they had not been. They can and will turn on the charm. The only advice we can offer to the analyst is to seek *specific* information from contacts and judge management by its stated plans and strategies—how well or poorly those plans and strategies were executed and how successful they were.

Keep in mind the advantages or disadvantages management faces. Very few managements can obtain superb results in an industry that has unfavorable economics, such as heavy foreign competition. Nearly all managements in fast-growing industries seem to be geniuses—until the growth rate slows.

For all corporations, the management factor enters into the picture in a special way when *major* changes have recently taken place in the top personnel. In such cases the past record of the company may afford little clue as to the quality of the new management, and thus it must be gauged in some other way—preferably by direct interview concerning plans and strategies.

The Return-on-Investment Method

The forecast of per-share earnings will usually be more accurate if derived from the estimated earning power of the enterprise as a whole, that is, from its ability to earn on its total capital. Thus the per-share estimate should be developed from an analysis and prediction of the earnings available to total capital rather than from an estimate of only the earnings available to the common-stock equity. In other words, the rate of return earned on the total capital is the basic test of profitability and the factor of primary initial concern.[4]

There are several reasons for employing the rate of return on total capital as the criterion of earning power. First, through the use of a rate of return—rather than actual dollar amount of earnings—we make allowance for changes in the capital investment and thus obtain a more satisfactory measure for reviewing the long-run earnings performance of a business. Second, unlike earnings on net worth or common-stock capital, earnings on total capital are not affected by changes in capital structure and thus provide the most consistent long-run measure of performance. Third, because the earnings rate on total capital minimizes the influence of differences in capital structure, its use provides a sound and common basis for comparative examination of the earning power of companies.

In dealing with a specific future span of years, the analyst's objectives are to

[4] Comparisons of operating performance are made more exact by deducting from reported earnings on total capital any tax saved because of funded debt.

1. Select that earnings rate which will be most representative of *average* performance

2. Estimate the *average* total capital investment

In this connection, the return-on-total-capital technique may be used in either a broad-brush or a detailed manner in projecting future earnings. In the first approach, the analyst may derive the estimate of the average rate of return for a future period simply from an analysis of earnings rates for selected past periods, and the estimate of average total capital simply from the anticipated amount of retained earnings and borrowings. In the more thorough approach, the analyst would base the rate-of-return estimate on a careful investigation of the primary determinants of the rates of return in past periods. For example, since the earnings rate is a product of the earnings margin (earnings available for total capital divided by sales) and capital turnover (sales divided by total capital), the principal factors behind changes in these ratios should be carefully analyzed. A careful projection must be made of the amount of capital, since the overall results are as dependent on the denominator as they are on the numerator. Future capital structure and its tax effect should be projected, and if possible, confirmed by discussions with management. The amount of capital outstanding may be influenced by sale or purchase of additional stock, above or below book value; changes in short- and long-term debt; and in off-balance-sheet financing. Conversely, the analyst might base the estimate of total capital on a careful projection of sales and estimated capital turnover as well as on a projection of retained earnings.

The use of both the explicit and the return-on-total-capital techniques—although they are not entirely independent throughout—provides a helpful check on estimated earnings.

Questioning or Rejecting the Past Record

Forecasting future earnings includes, as we have pointed out, a careful study of the past record, with a presumption that this record is of substantial value for the subsequent projections. In various cases, however, the analyst will reject the past record (or parts of it) as a guide to the future. The major elements that produce the operating results of an enterprise are volume, price received, and costs. If developments have occurred or are to occur that will significantly change the company's position in any of these categories, the analyst must be sure to account for them. If they are likely to make the past record irrelevant for future prognoses, the past must be rejected as a guide, and some more reliable basis must be found for the estimate of value. Changes *are* constantly under way in all three of the major components of the earnings statement, but in the typical case these changes are not sufficiently drastic to break the continuity of the operations for purposes of analysis. The developments that we have in mind are discussed in the sections that follow.

Product Line Change. Changes in the product line come about in a variety of ways. For reasons of diversification, some companies enter new fields by acquisition or direct investment. In either case, past financial information on the new activity may not be available. Major new products may arise out of internal research or purchased licenses and royalties. Again, past financial information will be unavailable, and future financial statements will take on a new complexion, with different trends, ratios, averages, and the like. Product lines may be discontinued for lack of profitability or simply because management finds them boring or mystifying. Whatever the cause, the problem is a discontinuity in the financial statements that will downgrade the usefulness of past financial statements in projecting future earnings and capital.

Example. At the end of World War II practically all of U.S. cigarette companies were nondiversified. With increasing public concern about health issues involving tobacco, and a trend toward large product liability litigation awards, the companies began diversification efforts, with the pace accelerating in the 1970s and 1980s. By 1985, American Brands (formerly American Tobacco) had reduced tobacco products to 61 percent of sales; Philip Morris had reduced its tobacco sales to 46 percent of the total.

American Can reduced its emphasis on containers to 37 percent of sales and USX Corporation (formerly U.S. Steel) reduced its steel activities to 33 percent of the total. In both cases, the companies did not view the long-range outlook for their existing product lines as being favorable, and therefore, diversified by acquisitions in areas they believed were more promising.

Manufacturing or Sales Policy Changes. Sales and manufacturing changes might include the abandonment of highly unprofitable operations. Research and development might produce new and improved manufacturing processes. Equally dramatic changes can happen when a company decides to buy parts instead of making them or to move manufacturing operations abroad to reduce labor costs. Sales policies can change in a variety of ways: The service component of a product can be increased or reduced. The method of distribution can be shifted from an internal sales staff, to a dealer organization, to manufacturers' representatives, to mail order, or to a part-time door-to-door sales staff. Sales policies may be for cash only, or for credit only; leasing or other financing facilities may be included or removed. The analyst's problem is to define what the new financial statements will look like after the policy change has been effected.

Example. In the early years of television, most of the domestic radio manufacturing companies entered the field and produced television sets in the United States made almost entirely of parts manufactured in the United States. Many of these companies continue to distribute televisions bearing their brand names, but much of the manufacturing has been contracted out to manufacturers in Southeast Asia. Some that have continued manufacturing have moved their operations to the Far East or Mexico. The few manufacturing operations located in the United States are heavily automated assembly lines processing foreign parts. Since these companies are primarily providing distribution and sales rather than manufacturing, and because of stiff competition worldwide, the profit margins in the television activities of the domestic companies have narrowed dramatically. In fact, the entire income statement shows a different character, as depreciation of highly automated machinery replaces the previous high labor costs and the value added from parts manufacturing is now replaced by purchased parts.

A Drastic Change in Management. Past financial statements may have provided some insight into the quality and characteristics of the company's management, but a drastic change in management means that the past financial statements will offer no insight into the quality of management. In addition, expect significant changes in policy, reorganization, and rationalization of the company, and future financial statements that reflect the nature of the new management rather than the old one. But, since financial statements for short periods are not characteristic of normal operations, several years may pass before sufficient financial statements are accumulated for the analyst to make forecasts with any confidence.

Example. Gulf & Western, Inc., was built into a highly diversified conglomerate under the leadership of Charles Bluhdorn. The company had over 100 manufacturing subsidiaries and was perhaps the most diversified company on the New York Stock Exchange. As a result, Wall Street considered it unanalyzable, a company without a clear sense of direction. On the death of Mr. Bluhdorn, the stock rose 8 points. The new management simplified its activities into three clearly understandable areas (entertainment, financial services, and publishing). The new management's strategy was simply to restructure the company so that it was more manageable and certainly more understandable (*rationalized* is the British term).

The Loss of Some Special Advantage. Some company advantage may be lost through expiration of patents or sales contracts, exhaustion of ore bodies, and the like. Perhaps the simplest example of such a break with the past is found when a mining company which is nearing the exhaustion of its old mine is planning to transfer operations to another property. Here the former earnings are clearly irrelevant in the future, since the analyst is dealing virtually with a new and different enterprise. A similar effect appears when a mining company exhausts high-grade or low-cost ore, with a subsequent significant lessening in its profit margin. Conversely, the development of a new ore body can move a mining company's basic position in the opposite direction.

Example. Johns Manville is a company going from special advantage to special disadvantage. In its heyday, the company had a virtual monopoly on high-quality asbestos reserves and dominated the industry. It was one of the United States' unquestioned monopolies. Upon the discovery of the health hazards of working and living in an atmosphere containing asbestos, and the proof that asbestos exposure resulted in deaths and other damage to health, the company was driven to the protection of the bankruptcy courts by literally billions of dollars of litigation claims.

Example. Industrial Rayon was for many years the prime producer of synthetic apparel materials and tire cord, until new products of superior characteristics made their product obsolete. The one-time industry leader disappeared.

Example. In December 1981, 4530 oil drilling rigs were active in the United States. Oil and gas prices were near their peak, and everyone *knew* that oil prices would double again to $80 a barrel or more within 10 years. Since the worldwide explosion of drilling was fairly successful in bringing forth new supplies of oil to compete with the OPEC oil cartel, the world soon had a surplus of oil. By mid-1986 the number of rigs actively drilling had fallen almost to 600. With hindsight, it is clear that profits in the oil drilling and service industries were temporarily bloated by circumstances which would not continue. Whether it is reasonable to believe that an analyst should have anticipated the temporary nature of those earnings is a matter of debate. Clearly most people in the industry did not think their prosperity was temporary, since they borrowed heavily to make huge investments in drilling rigs as a bet on the continuation of their good times. In 1985 and 1986 the oil patch was terribly depressed, and many participants in the drilling boom had visits to the bankruptcy courts, write-offs, forced mergers, and the all the other horrors of overexpansion. Large gains are to be made and losses avoided for the analyst who can identify temporary booms and busts and time their reversals.

Problems of Projecting for Diversified Companies

Diversification and the Conglomerates

Growth Through Acquisition. During the 1950s a number of entrepreneurial financiers acquired control of companies and began a process of expanding by acquisitions. Most of the acquisitions were of common stocks of companies in highly diversified industries, with the parent exchanging a variety of securities, often convertible preferreds. The latter securities came to be known as "Chinese money," a pejorative term. Much of the apparent growth in earnings per share came about through the use of pooling of interest accounting. Under that accounting it was possible to "grow" the reported earnings per share through well designed acquisitions, even for a company which had a declining trend of earnings in every one of its divisions!

Mixed Results. The results of these acquisitions were rather mixed. In some cases the acquisition was picked purely for its impact on earnings per share over the short term, without regard to the fundamental longer term earning power being acquired. In some cases, under the new management, a sleepy old company that was rich with assets but employing them inefficiently, was upgraded to a highly profitable and growing enterprise. In other cases, managements were simply going into businesses they did not understand, and the subsequent operating results were most unfavorable.

The False Growth Is Revealed. Since the conglomerate trend came along when Wall Street was turning its attention to growth, the growth in earnings per share of conglomerates initially made them glamorous favorites. Wall Street raved over the "synergy" of each new acquisition, which was sure not only to do well on its own, but to bring new opportunities to the rest of the company. As with most Wall Street fads, the stock prices were driven far too high, and when it was demonstrated that the geniuses had feet of clay, and that accounting growth is not nearly as good as growth in true earnings, the conglomerate balloon crashed. Most of the companies remained quite depressed for a considerable time, and ultimately many of them offered some engaging bargains.

Lessons for the Analyst. The history of the conglomerates had many lessons for security analysts. Diversification into areas about which management knows nothing usually turns out poorly—unless good management comes with the acquisition and is kept on. The best diversification seems to occur when the company keeps within the industries or areas with which it is already familiar. Growth through acquisition and the resulting accounting peculiarities require that the analyst search carefully for the underlying growth in earnings to determine whether it parallels what is being reported as earnings growth. A company must at all times have a clear identity in the minds of investors so that they can have some confidence that they understand it well enough to make reasonable forecasts of its future. Companies that are not understandable are usually avoided by investors and fail to fulfill their market potential.

Not Like Portfolio Diversification.   Diversification within a company does not accomplish the same result as diversification of investments in a portfolio. Diversification within a portfolio permits upward stock price fluctuations to offset, to some degree, downward price fluctuations and results in less volatility of investment performance of the portfolio. Although this offsetting takes place in earnings for a diversified company, it does not take place in the stock's price, since there is only one stock being traded.

Two Plus Factors.   Two favorable aspects of diversification are (1) the ability to transfer capital from a less favorable area of the company to one with better prospects of future earnings and (2) an operating base from which to restructure a company in an industry which has less than favorable long-term prospects. For example, USX Corporation's acquisitions of Marathon Oil in 1982 and Texas Oil and Gas in 1986 was considered by much of Wall Street as less an effort to get *into* the oil business, than an effort to get *out* of the steel business. Parallel developments in many other industries have been viewed the same way by Wall Street.

Divestment Opportunities.   For highly diversified companies, the late 1970s and the 1980s were years of divestment, in which unsuccessful and unmanageable affiliates and subsidiaries are liquidated, sold to others, bought out by the management, or otherwise disposed of. In too many cases, the bright prospects of 5 or 10 years earlier have simply proved that it is possible to lose money in a large variety of industries.

Lack of Continuity and Comparability.   The vogue of diversification has created some other difficulties for the security analyst. As mentioned, the past results may appear of little value for study if the operations of future years will be radically different. However, if the acquisitions are long-established firms for which financial information is available, this obstacle may be overcome at least in part by combining the figures of past years to create a pro forma record of performance. (This will not always be possible.) The use of segment data has been particularly helpful when a segment of one company is purchased by another company. This permits a rough pro forma history to be created, even in the absence of complete financial statements of the acquiree company. A separate problem of classification occurs when a company crosses industry lines so substantially that it can no longer be placed in the single category of "steel," "department stores," or some other grouping. Valid comparisons with other companies in the same industry—a favorite analytical tool— then become well-nigh impossible.

Caution Regarding Temporary Factors in Earning Power

A competent analyst is always alert to discover elements in the past earnings picture that are unlikely to continue in the future. These are similar in their significance to the nonrecurring gains and losses that the analysts should eliminate from their presentations of the "actual operating results" of a given year. But they differ from nonrecurring items, in the technical sense, because the latter represent transactions that can and should be separated from the company's ordinary operations, whereas those we now consider are *discontinuities* rather than extraordinary items.

30

Projections of Earnings and Dividends: The Concept of Earning Power

Earning Power

Two Approaches

The concept of earning power has a definite and important place in investment theory. It combines a history of actual earnings performance over a period of years with a reasonable expectation that the past level or trend will be approximated in the future, unless extraordinary conditions supervene. This performance may be measured in terms of either (1) the earnings per share of common stock or (2) the rate of return earned on the common-stock equity. In fact, analysts may use both methods to check their results. When using the rate-of-return approach, first compute the return on total capital, take this as the basic measure of company performance, and then derive from it the return on the common-stock equity. This suggested approach ensures that proper attention is paid to changes in the capital structure and in the costs of senior capital.

A Long Enough Record to Smooth the Bumps

Whatever earnings yardstick is employed, the record must cover a number of years. This is essential for two reasons: first, because a continued or repeated performance is always more impressive than a single occurrence, and second, because the results for a fairly long period—either a trend or an average—will tend to absorb and equalize the distorting influences of the business cycle and any industry or sector cycle.

Return on Equity or on Capital. In our opinion the use of a period average is nearly always appropriate when the rate of return is being analyzed; it may or may not be appropriate in the analysis of per-share earnings. Whenever an average is used, the analyst must distinguish between an average that is the mere arithmetical resultant of an assortment of disconnected figures and an average that is "normal" or "modal," in the sense that the annual results show a definite tendency to approximate the average. The contrast between the two types of earning power may be clearly seen from the three examples in Table 30.1.

Earning Power of PSA, Inc.. In the case of PSA, Inc., which operates Pacific Southwest Airlines, the variance of the earnings per share figures in the individual years from the period average is so great and so erratic that the 10-year average is of no practical assistance to the analyst in predicting the future *level* of earnings. In 1 of the 10 years, the company happened to earn exactly the $2.23 average per share, but in the other 9 years the earnings results were not within 50 percent of the average. In the case of PSA's return on equity, two years were very close to the average, but the rest were quite scattered, and the return on equity applied to the most recent book value per share would not have provided any useful estimate of earning power. Clearly in a case of this sort, the analyst must take the explicit approach of forecasting volume and prices to get revenues and individual line items of expense to obtain an earnings estimate. Even then the result would likely be an estimate for a single year rather than an estimate of normal earning power. It is characteristic of speculative companies that normal earning power is almost beyond estimation.

Earning Power of Sierra Pacific Resources. In contrast with PSA, note how closely in each year the per-share earnings for Sierra Pacific Resources cling to the 10-year average of approximately $1.80. Such a consistent record is ordinarily of decided help in making earnings

Table 30.1. Comparative Earnings per Share and Return on Equity for Three Companies, 1976–1985

	McDonald's Corp.	Sierra Pacific Resources	PSA, Inc.
	Earnings per Share* ($)		
1985	$3.32	$1.95	$3.88
1984	2.93	2.11	(0.90)
1983	2.55	1.70	(2.95)
1982	2.22	1.82	3.56
1981	1.94	1.48	6.19
1980	1.63	1.56	3.58
1979	1.39	1.96	5.28
1978	1.19	1.83	2.23
1977	1.00	1.90	0.61
1976	0.81	1.69	0.86
10-year average	1.90	1.80	2.23
	Return on Equity* (%)		
1985	20.9	12.5	13.3
1984	21.0	13.9	—‡
1983	20.8	11.2	—‡
1982	20.7	12.3	10.1
1981	21.0	9.9	20.4
1980	21.1	10.0	14.2
1979	21.6	12.7	25.3
1978	22.6	12.2	12.9
1977	23.4	13.2	3.8
1976	23.4	12.3	5.5
10-year average	21.7	12.0	13.2†

* Extraordinary items omitted.
† Average of the eight profitable years.
‡ No meaningful figure available.
SOURCE: Annual reports.

projections, but it is not an infallible guide to the future. Many other utility examples could be presented that would appear similar to Sierra Pacific Resources, but which, due to rate regulation, escalating cost of plant construction, plant abandonments, and other circumstances, have shown abrupt departures from their apparent normal earning power—generally departures on the downside. Note that the average return on equity of Sierra Pacific Resources also appears to hold promise for the calculation of normal earning power.

Earning Power of McDonald's Corp. McDonald's Corporation is an interesting example of another way in which average earnings per share can be a misleading indicator of earning power. It is true that McDonald's was earning around $1.90 at the midpoint of the 10-year history, but earnings at the beginning and end of the period were quite far away from the average. Clearly, the company's earnings have grown persistently, and the analyst would be inclined to put much greater emphasis on the more recent years than on the average. Given the stability of the growth rate and of earnings around the trend line, one could argue easily for using the results of the latest known year as the best estimate of earning power.

However, an examination of the return on equity may prove to be more useful in estimating earning power. The company's return on equity has consistently been close to the average, but the analyst would find it useful to observe the slight downward trend in return on equity. At the beginning of the period, the return on equity was above 23 percent, and in more recent years, it has been a bit under 21 percent. An analyst using a return on equity approach, giving consideration to the trend and the estimated average amount of equity capital at work during the year 1986, might multiply a return on equity of 20.5 percent times a book value of $18.50 and achieve an earnings estimate of $3.79. This could be viewed either as an earnings estimate *for* 1986 or as a point estimate of the company's normalized earning power at mid-1986. It is interesting that Value Line *Investment Survey* estimated 1986 earnings per share at $3.80 in its edition of July 4, 1986. We would hope our McDonald's example would not mislead the reader into believing that determination of normal earning power should in real life be carried out in such a simple mechanistic way. Even for an excellent growth company with a record such as that of McDonald's, the entire record of the company and all the external facts known must be brought together in the earnings projection process.[1] In a few cases they will not lead the analyst to further adjustments, but in most cases they do.

In the case of McDonald's, the rapid growth of the U.S. fast food industry must be considered. Certainly, one must assume that all participants attempted to select the best locations first and that additional locations will tend to be less desirable. At some point, saturation must set in as the high profits of the earlier successful participants attract more and more competition. Changes in the company's leverage would suggest that greater attention should be paid to return on total capital than to return on equity. And, of course, the implications of the company's rising payout ratio as a signal of possible reduced growth opportunities would draw the analyst's attention.

---

[1] A. Briloff, " 'You Deserve a Break': McDonald's Burgers Are More Palatable Than Its Accounts," *Barron's*, July 8, 1974, p. 5.

Supplementing Quantitative Analysis with Qualitative Considerations
In studying earnings records, an important principle of security analysis must be borne in mind.: *Quantitative data are useful only to the extent that they are supported by a qualitative survey of the enterprise.*

In nearly all cases a long record of stable earnings, under varying economic conditions, will prove a good indication that the business is inherently stable. An examination of the nature of the business will usually indicate the qualitative factors on which such stability is based. There are a number of exceptions, of course. Two illustrations, Caterpillar, Inc. and Enterra Corp., are shown in Table 30.2

Table 30.2. Fluctuations in Per-Share Earnings

	Caterpillar Inc. ($)	Enterra Corporation
1985	$2.11	$(0.73)
1984	(2.60)	(1.29)
1983	(3.12)	(1.94)
1982	(2.04)	3.17
1981	6.64	5.78
1980	6.53	3.28
1979	5.69	2.42
1978	6.56	2.34
1977	5.16	1.74
1976	4.45	1.37
1975	4.65	1.13
1974	2.67	0.73
1973	2.88	0.51
1972	2.41	0.34
1971	1.50	0.27

NOTE: Extraordinary and nonrecurring items excluded.

Caterpillar, Inc.'s Earnings Record. Prior to 1982, Caterpillar, Inc., had a long history of steady growth and resistance to the business cycle that made it an institutional favorite "blue chip." The flattening of the earnings growth and the subsequent deficits were due partly to labor problems but mostly to the strong dollar which damaged the company's price competitiveness in world markets.

Enterra Corporation's Earnings Record. Again, the record of Enterra Corporation is included to display the suddenness with which a long and persistent record of growth can be reversed—often without warning, or with such modest signs of foul weather that they are obscured by the lovely past.

Trends versus Average of Earnings. It is our opinion that a *permanent* growth rate exists in investment-quality common stocks in general. This growth might be estimated at 7½ percent per annum, based on the factors discussed in Chapter 32 in connection with our valuation of the stock market as a whole. We, therefore, favor use of a trend approach in projecting per-share earnings of the typical industrial concern. Note two facts: (1) In the early editions of this book we suggested that the analyst use *averages* of per-share earnings for selected *past* periods as indicators of future earnings. (2) The analyst must not use a projected per-share figure higher than that already achieved. Those views were presented in the context of lower levels of inflation and of lower historical growth rates of earnings per share than have been the experience in more recent decades. In addition, outright refusal to project an upward trend in earnings can force investors to remain on the sidelines with their funds uninvested for extended periods, if the market itself is priced on a basis of expectations of future earnings that do exceed the previous peak earnings.

Average the Past, Trend the Future.   In accepting the trend approach, we are not suggesting the complete abandonment of the use of averages. A straight average fails to take into account what may be a significant trend in per-share earnings, but this does not mean that a growth economy makes the use of averages obsolete. In fact, we believe the reader may be surprised at the number of companies whose per-share earnings—principally as a result of cyclical fluctuations—do not readily lend themselves to trend treatment. In those instances, a comparison of averages for selected periods may be a more effective tool—than fitting traditional trend lines—for arriving at growth rates and making earnings projections.

Selecting a Suitable Period.   Whether one is dealing with averages or with trend lines, the results will be heavily influenced by the period of time from which data are taken. The problem comes about partly because of the volatility of earnings. The inclusion or exclusion of a particularly good or bad year can have considerable impact on the average for the period, unless the period is extremely long. If a trend approach is taken, the beginning and ending years are of the utmost importance, regardless of whether the calculation is based only on those two years, or whether a regression is performed to obtain a statistical trend. An example might be the growth rate of the earnings of the Value Line Industrial Composite from 1972 through 1981. If only the beginning and ending years are used, the growth rate is 11.5 percent. If the same calculation is performed for the years 1973 through 1982, merely shifting the years one year forward, the growth rate is only 4.8 percent. Analysts measuring the trend by linear regression rather than the beginning and ending points would have found a growth rate of 13.9 percent for the 1972–1981 period and 12.1 percent for the 1973–1982 period.[2] The superiority of using statistical regression to obtain trend lines is thus demonstrated, but even the best statistical methods cannot avoid the influence of the time chosen. For example, 1982 earnings for the Industrial Composite were slightly below those of 1978, and choosing the 1978–1982 period, regardless of method, would have produced a negative rate of growth in earnings of the Industrial Composite. This decline did not have anything to do with the *secular growth rate* of corporate profits, but rather with where the economy was in the business cycle at the beginning and end of the period under study. Keep in mind that earnings for individual companies are much more volatile than those for an index, and therefore the task of measuring growth is more formidable.

Domination of Short-Term Trends by the Business Cycle. It is clear that a trend over a short period of time is likely to be dominated by the business cycle, or in some cases the industry cycle. As a result, it is present custom to use longer periods such as 10 or 15 years for trend analysis. Even for these long periods, the terminal dates selected remain most important. In addition, the longer the period selected, the more likely that the earlier years are no longer relevant to the present situation.[3]

Danger of Overemphasis of Trends. Valuations based on trend projections of per-share earnings obey no mathematical rules and therefore may too easily be exaggerated. All too frequently a proposed trend— particularly if pronounced—proves deceptive, and the error then becomes the more costly because so much of the conclusion as to the value has depended on the trend projection and so little on past earning power. For growth companies, the trend is most tempting as a measure of future earning power—and the most disastrous if the trend falters, because both the earnings and their multiplier will fall short of expectations.

Conflict of Averages and Trends. There is indeed a fundamental conflict between the concepts of the average and the trend, as applied to an earnings record. In the simplified example in Table 30.3 it may be seen that, although each firm had the *same earnings* in the current year (year 7), Company A had a pronounced upward trend and, in relation

---

[2]Actually, log-linear regression is theoretically the preferable method, but for periods as short as 10 years the difference in the calculated growth rates is small.

[3]In the early 1960s earnings growth for a period as short as five years was generally considered sufficient to establish the enterprise as a growth company. This was notoriously true in the case of new offerings of shares of smaller companies. (A ¾-page advertisement in a well-known eastern newspaper with the caption, "Our Approach to Growth Stock Investing," stated, "We project earnings on the basis of a 3-to 4-year historical trend.")

Table 30.3. Earnings per Share in Successive Years

Company	Year 1	Year 2	Year 3	Year 4	Year 5	Year 6	Year 7 (current)	Average of 7 years	Trend
A	$ 1.00	$ 1.35	$ 1.85	$ 2.50	$ 3.30	$ 4.50	$ 6.00	$ 2.95	Excellent
B	6.00	6.00	6.00	6.00	6.00	6.00	6.00	6.00	Disappointing
C	11.00	10.00	9.00	8.00	7.20	6.50	6.00	8.25	Bad

to current earnings, a low seven-year average. In contrast, Company C had a downward trend and a seven-year average much higher than the current earnings figure. Company B, with constant per-share earnings—a horizontal trend—lay between the other two companies. These hypothetical figures bring out two important facts:

1. The better the trend in per-share earnings of a company, the lower will be the period average in relation to current earnings.

2. The poorer the trend, the higher will be the average in relation to current earnings.

The foregoing study raises an important question in regard to the theoretical and practical interpretation of earnings records. Is not the trend at least as significant for the future as the average? Concretely, in judging the probable performance of Companies A and C over the next five years, would not the analyst find more reason to think in terms of their trends—an increase of approximately 35 percent per year for A and a decline of about 10 percent for C—than in terms of past averages? In other words, A's future earnings pattern would be assumed to be $8.09, $10.90, $14.70, $19.81, and $26.71 rather than the seven-year average of $2.95, whereas C's earnings would be taken at $5.42, $4.90, $4.43, $4.01, and $3.62 rather than the seven-year average of nearly $8.25.

The answer to the problem derives from common sense rather than from formal or *a priori* logic. The favorable trend of Company A's results must certainly be accounted for, but not by a merely automatic projection of the 35 percent growth rate into the distant future. On the contrary, remember that the normal economic forces militate against the indefinite continuance of unusually rapid growth. Remember that past *levels of earnings* are quantitative information, but *past records of earnings growth* are both quantitative and qualitative in character. The occurrence of growth changes the environment for future growth. Competition, regulation, the law of diminishing returns, and so on are powerful foes to unlimited expansion, and in smaller degree, opposite elements tend to operate to check a continued decline. Hence instead of taking the maintenance of a pronounced trend for granted—as the stock market is often inclined to do, the analyst must approach the matter with caution, seeking to determine the causes of the superior showing and to weigh the specific elements of strength in the company's position against the general obstacles in the way of continued rapid growth.

Money Is Made by Unpopular Opinions. Where a trend exists in the record, everyone who is interested in the company knows about it. To the degree that the market makes naive extrapolations, the trend is fully reflected in the stock price. If the investor (1) believes that the trend will continue and (2) knows that most other investors following the stock hold that same belief, then even being correct about the trend does not offer an unusual opportunity to take money in the market. The stock is probably fairly priced, but only if the trend continues. *Superior returns are not achieved by buying fairly priced stocks,* but by buying stocks at prices well below the intrinsic worth of the company. In general, the investor will buy in circumstances of disagreement with popular opinion. The market thinks the stock is fairly priced, or it would change that price. Investors buy that stock because they believe it to be underpriced—an unpopular view. For stocks whose prices are influenced heavily by trends—either upward or downward—the contrary opinion is generally an opinion that the trend is about to change. Detecting change earlier than the rest of the market and acting promptly on the conviction of change are the critical steps to exploiting mispriced securities.

The Detection of Change. Because the detection of change is such a key element in security analysis, the analyst devotes a great deal of time thinking about change and its causes. Some leading questions are:

- How long can this go on?
- What factors will most likely change the trend?
- What is the status of each of those factors?
- What evidence of change should one look for?
- Where can one find such evidence that will tell when a causal factor or event is coming into play?

A Changing Ratio May Be Evidence. Chapter 20 was devoted to ratio analysis, but without a discussion of this emphasis on change. The initial reaction of many is that ratio analysis is a lot of dull, arithmetical pencil pushing, and in the old days the slide rule and the pencil were the analyst's professional insignia. The reason the analysts were willing to go through those arduous labors, which now can be done so quickly on a personal computer, was that when the numbers begin to change, ratio analysis makes that fact stand out. The discipline of calculating ratios, trends, and averages forces the analyst to ask questions about the evolving patterns.

With experience, the analyst begins to learn how companies and people act under circumstances of change. If a company has been growing at 20 percent a year for decades and then gradually begins to see its growth rate slip, management typically does not quite believe what it is seeing and tends to offset the slippage in some fashion, perhaps by whittling a few expenses here and there, such as research and development, training programs, or advertising. Offsetting can also be achieved by accounting changes, with the company gradually adopting more and more liberal accounting techniques to keep the earnings on the trend line. As the accounting options run out, contrived transactions may begin to appear in the record, accelerating the timing of the reporting of earnings. It is remarkable how often ratio analysis will disclose such sequences of events. Unit sales stop growing at 20 percent and drop to 18 or 15 percent, but reported earnings continue on the 20 percent track. For that to happen, something in the numbers has to change—perhaps the depreciation rate is declining because the company has adopted longer useful lives for its fixed assets, or some other expense has been arbitrarily reduced to aid the profit margin. The company will be able to stay on the growth trend for a while, but clearly the quality of earnings will be declining all along. The ratios will shower the analyst with clues.

Growth Stocks

Rules for Projecting Rapid Growth

If a qualitative study leads to a favorable verdict about a continuation of a growth trend—as frequently it should—the analyst should limit possible unjustified enthusiasm. In this regard, we have three suggestions to make:

1. A projected rapid growth rate for earnings should not exceed the growth rate already achieved by the business—giving consideration to the years of abnormal and normal profits. We suggest this limitation because, in our opinion, investment values can be related only to demonstrated performance, so neither an *expected* higher rate of increase nor even the past results under conditions of abnormal business activity may be taken as a basis for projecting growth. As we pointed out earlier in this chapter, because of the brevity of the period from which a trend of earnings is typically derived, the results

for a single year—if abnormally good or abnormally bad—can distort the figures. The analyst seeks either to develop the trend from those earnings figures which are considered to be most representative of the company's earning power, or to establish it by an independent appraisal of future prospects.

2. We propose that the projection for growth be limited to seven years, with the valuation based on normal earning power at the midpoint— the fourth year. Longer projections are suitable, of course, for purposes other than valuation.

3. Also of primary importance, we suggest that the growth rate assumed, except in the most extraordinary circumstances, *should not exceed 20 percent per annum.*

Note that a compound rate of 20 percent represents more than a doubling of earnings in a four-year span and a 258 percent increase over seven years. Moreover, this aggregate growth for the four years exceeds by three times that which would result from the use of our conservative rate of 7½ percent for the overall growth of industrial corporate per-share earnings (see Chapter 32). Finally, a check of the per-share earnings growth of more than 800 shares covered in Value Line's *Investment Survey* reveals that over the five years ending in fiscal 1985, only 8 percent had growth rates of 20 percent or higher, and of those companies, only about half had such growth extending as far back as 10 years. A number of the companies that had growth rates averaging 20 percent for 10 years achieved most of the growth in the first five years and were below 20 percent during the second five years. Most of the companies that achieved 20 percent over two consecutive five-year periods were small high-technology companies. Earnings patterns of the individual companies revealed many situations in which a recovery of earnings from a deeply depressed level accounted for the favorable growth rate, rather than true growth characteristics.[4]

Limiting the Earnings Multiplier of Growth Companies

We suggested in the previous edition of this book that if the valuation were to be kept within investment limits, the maximum multiplier should be held to about 20 times the projected earning power four years

---

[4]Similar studies mentioned in the fourth edition of this book showed much smaller percentages of companies achieving a 20 percent annual growth rate over the 1950s, but revenues in those days had not been accelerated by inflationary forces to the degree that has occurred in the decade ending 1985. Thus the proportion of shares exceeding our maximum growth rate appears to be very small.

hence. The crash in growth-stock prices in the early 1970s demonstrated that such a limitation can fail to protect the investor from overpaying for growth stocks. The principal deficiency was that the formula permitted both four years of rapid growth and a premium in the multiple based on that growth.

Consider a different decision rule that would prohibit paying more than two times an appropriate market multiple for current earning power. This *market multiple* is appropriate for the stock market as a whole or, say, for Standard & Poor's 500 stock index. In Chapter 32, which discusses the valuation of the stock market, a market price-earnings multiple of 12.3 is developed. If we apply the two times market multiple to Company A, the growth company in Table 30.3, the maximum price would be $2 \times 12.3 \times \$6.00$ of current earnings, or $147.60. The Fourth Edition's investment value limit was 20 times earnings four years hence. If one assumed a 20 percent earnings growth rate, it would have permitted a price of $\$6.00 \times (1.20)^4 \times 20$, or $248.80. Thus, a limit tied to the *market multiple times current earnings* can certainly temper growth-stock enthusiasm—but is two times an appropriate limitation? Perhaps a discussion of the speculative component of growth stocks will provide guidance.

Investment versus Speculation. If investment is defined as paying only for the demonstrated record and speculation as any amount paid in excess thereof, even a double-the-market-multiple rule would permit inclusion of more than 50 percent speculation in the price. That occurs because our 12.3 market multiple is already based on a 7.5 percent growth assumption for the average stock.

If a company has earned $6 in the past, it seems quite reasonable that the $6 level of earnings should have some or even considerable influence on the analyst's estimate of earning power. Replication of the earnings depends only on circumstances being as favorable as they were in the past. To the degree that current earning power is based on information taken from the financial history of a company, it is demonstrated as "do-able" because under a given set of circumstances in the past it was in fact done. Remember that the $6 of earnings used by the analyst is what remains after elimination of unusual and nonrecurring effects. Thus, no miracle is necessary to achieve actual earnings equal to the analyst's normal earning power estimate. The portion of the price paid for a stock that is based on past accomplishment may be considered an *investment* component. The payment for anything more than that is a *speculative* component; it depends on the company's capacity to:

- Produce and sell more units

- Sell them at higher unit prices
- Sell to customers who have not bought in the past
- Reduce unit costs below the levels of past experience
- Develop successful new products

In short, the speculative component depends on the company's developing new capacities to do things which the company has not previously done. That portion is based on projection, conjecture, extrapolation, hopes, and even dreams.

A second component of the speculative risk is in the multiple applied to *future earnings*. If a premium multiple of, say, 20 times is applied to projected earnings four years hence, that multiple has implications about expectations that will exist four years in the future. It implies, for example, that four years from now, the market will believe that the *subsequent* period will have continued growth at a high rate—high enough to justify 20 times the current earning power of that year. Otherwise, in four years the stock will sell at a price that is lower than today's presumably "justified" price!

What is the proper relationship of the multiple for the investment component and the multiple suited to the obviously more risky speculative component? If the speculative aspect is twice as risky as the investment part, then one might consider paying only half as much for it. A stock which was half investment and half speculation would lead to a price limit of possibly 1½ times the market multiple, applied to current earning power.

Expressed another way, if both the estimate of earnings growth and the premium multiplier turn out to be wrong, the investor is left with the demonstrated *investment* value as a likely market price. The loss will be the speculative component, which we would hope to limit to no more than a third of the capital invested in the stock. If the company has been "borrowing" earnings from the future, through liberal accounting and earnings-accelerating transactions, part of the perceived investment value may not exist, and the loss may be even more. There is no margin of safety in such cases. Instead it is quite the opposite, for if there is a large speculative component, there is an unduly large margin of *risk* rather than of safety.

Our Suggested Limit on Growth Stock Multipliers. The 1973–1974 collapse of growth-stock prices suggests that we should adopt a more restrictive decision rule than "20 times normal earnings four years hence": *Our recommendation today is to limit the multiple for a growth stock's current earnings to 1½ times the market multiple.* Using the multiple of 12.3 developed in Chapter 32, the present limit is about 18½ times the current normal level of earnings. We are aware that nearly all growth stocks would fail this test today. The reader may disagree with our recommended formula and yet agree that some arbitrary limitation is needed.

We accept the view that our mossback conservatism will indeed keep the investor out of many growth stocks in which huge profits will be made by others. We believe that there are few geniuses on Wall Street, but that most security analysts have reasonable amounts of common sense—the principles and techniques urged in this book require only diligence and common sense, and discourage investment ventures which demand either flashes of genius or very good luck.

Declining Stocks

Attitude of the Analyst When the Trend Is Downward

Where the trend has been definitely downward, as was that of Company C, analysts will assign great weight to this unfavorable factor. They will not assume that the curve *must* turn upward, nor can they accept the past average—which is much higher than the current figure—as a normal index of future earnings. Analysts should be equally chary about any hasty conclusions to the effect that:

- The company's outlook is hopeless
- Its earnings are certain to disappear entirely
- The stock is therefore without merit or value.

Here, again, a qualitative study of the company's situation and prospects is essential to forming an opinion whether *at some price*, relatively low, of course, the issue may not be a bargain, despite its declining earnings trend. Once more we identify the viewpoint of the analyst with that of a sensible businessman looking into the pros and cons of some privately owned enterprise.

Some Earning Power Must Be in Sight. The analyst's viewpoint should be similar to a business manager considering an acquisition. Remember that the business manager will have direct control over the assets and liabilities and therefore the ability to restructure the company to maximize its value. The analyst is essentially helpless in this respect and must depend entirely upon whatever management exists in the future to stabilize the downtrend and turn the company around. Given that caveat, the first question is always the survivability of the company. This is an urgent question if the company is already recording losses. If that is the case, determine first whether they are temporary in nature, such as losses of operations which have since been or will shortly be discontinued. There should be some underlying earning power, that is, some profitable divisions that could be separated from the rest of the company and continue to produce postive results, for the company to have any place in an investment portfolio. Without that, it is a pure speculation that can be valued only by conjecture.

Positive Cash Flows after Debt Service. The second aspect of survivability is the question of positive cash flows in amounts sufficient to service at least the near-term obligations for creditors, short-term debt, interest payments, rent, and the like. A careful analysis must be made of protective covenants of debt issues and provisions of loan agreements to determine if there is any danger of default.

Assets—A Basis for Turnaround. Once the analyst is satisfied that the company will survive, the leading question becomes "Are there elements in place which can become the basis for a turnaround of the company?" These elements are often strong working capital, valuable plant and equipment capable of being sold or liquidated, LIFO reserves, hidden assets such as excess pension assets, and the like. Identification of those assets with a particular division is important, since the divisions of low profitability or unprofitability must be examined for possible disposal to obtain assets for debt repayment, reinvestment in other activities, and similar purposes.

Find the Reasons for Decline. A third area of essential information is the list of causes of the company's deterioration. Leading questions include

- Are those events or factors ongoing?
- When will they end?
- Are they controllable?

The investigation will usually convince analysts that the risks are too great and that they should avoid the declining company. In a small number of cases, an analyst will discover that very little is wrong with the company that cannot be corrected in the course of time. The problems may be simply a sleepy management doing a poor job of managing a basically sound and profitable business. The company may be financially strong and asset-rich but merely need to dispose of some unprofitable subsidiaries and to get costs under better control in certain other divisions or affiliates. If the company can be bought with confidence that a certain level of earning power exists, that the price is cheap, and that a decent dividend will be paid while the investor awaits an ultimate turnaround, the situation can be potentially quite rewarding. Just as the glamour growth stock risks the danger of both a disappointment in earnings and price multiple, the well-selected company with a mediocre record has the potential of both significant earnings improvement and multiple improvement. A diversified list of such holdings in a portfolio can enhance performance considerably—for the patient investor who does not expect instant rewards.

Deficits—Qualitative, Not Quantitative

When a company reports a deficit for the year, it is customary to calculate the amount in dollars per share or in relation to interest requirements. For example, it was reported that in 1983 Armco Steel suffered a net loss after taxes of $672.5 million or $10.27 per share. The company was said to have "earned" the interest on its long-term debt a "deficit 3.6 times." Such figures, when taken by themselves, have no quantitative significance, and their value in forming an average or a trend may often be open to serious question.

Let us assume that Company X lost $5 per share of common in the last year, and Company Y lost $7 per share. Both issues sell at 25. Is this an indication of any sort that Company X stock is preferable to Company Y stock? Obviously not; for assuming it were so, it would mean that the more shares there were outstanding, the more valuable each share would be. If Company Y issues two shares for one, the loss would be reduced to $3.50 per share, and on the assumption just made, each new share would then be worth more than an old one. The same reasoning applies to bond interest. Suppose that Company X and Company Y each lost $1 million, and X had $4 million and Y $10 million of 5 percent bonds. Company X would then show interest earned "deficit five times" and Company Y would earn its interest "deficit two items." These figures should not be construed as an indication of any kind that Company X's bonds are less secure than Company Y's bonds. For if so, it would mean that the smaller the bond issue, the poorer its position—a manifest absurdity.

In general an average of past earnings must include deficits as well as income figures, but the predictive value of an average containing deficit figures is necessarily less than in other cases. This is true because any average based on individual figures with wide variability must be viewed as an accidental rather than a descriptive figure.

Intuition

In the absence of indications to the contrary, we accept the past record as at least a starting basis for judging the future, but the analyst must be on the lookout for any indications to the contrary. Here we must distinguish between vision or intuition on the one hand, and ordinary sound reasoning on the other. The ability to see what is coming is of inestimable value, but it cannot be expected to be part of the analyst's stock in trade. (With such an ability, one could dispense with analysis.) The analyst can be asked to show only that moderate degree of foresight which springs from logic and from experience intelligently pondered. It was not to be demanded that the security analyst foretell well in advance the formation of the OPEC oil cartel, the rise of Moslem fundamentalism, the war between Iran and Iraq, and many of the other factors that have had such great influence on energy prices worldwide. Similarly, the analyst should not be expected to forecast far in advance the dramatic shift in the work force resulting from increased participation by women nor to predict foreign exchange fluctuations that have influenced so greatly the nation's trade balance. Of course, as developments begin to appear, the analyst must consider them and extrapolate from them within reasonable bounds. Analytical reasoning with regard to the future can only be penetrating—not prophetic.

Intertype Corporation—An Unimpressive Earning Record

The following examples (from the third and fourth editions of this book, respectively) are recounted here as illustrations of accurate common-stock valuations that were current at the time of selection and that involved no advantage of hindsight.

Example. Intertype Corporation's stock was selling at $8 per share in March to July 1939. This old, established company was one of the leaders in a relatively small industry (line-casting machines for the printing trade). At that time, its recent earnings had not been favorable, nor did there seem to be any particular reason for optimistic expectations as to the near-term outlook. The balance sheet was impressive, however, as it showed net current assets available for the stock at almost $20 per share. The ten-year earnings, dividend, and price record of the common stock was as shown in Table 30.4.

Table 30.4. Intertype Corporation

Year	Earnings per share ($)	Dividend paid ($)	Price range
1938	0.57	0.45	12¾–8
1937	1.41	0.80	26¼–9
1936	1.42	0.75	22¾–15
1935	0.75	0.40	16–6⅛
1934	0.21	—	10–5⅝
1933	0.77d*	—	11¼–1⅞
1932	1.82d	—	7–2½
1931	0.56	1.00	18½–4⅝
1930	1.46	2.00	32–12
1929	3.05	1.75	38⅞–17
Average, 1934–1938	0.87		
Average, 1929–1938	0.68		

*d=deficit.

Most analysts would have found this record unattractive because of earnings volatility and the absence of a favorable trend, but the essential question was whether the company could be counted on to remain in business and to participate at about the same level as before in both good times and bad. The industry, the company's prominent position in it, and the strong financial setup clearly suggested yes, leading to the conclusion that the shares could be bought at 8 with very small chance of ultimate loss and with every indication that under the next set of favorable conditions the value of the stock would double. (In 3 out of the 5 years previous to 1939 and in 6 out of the 10 years preceding 1939 the stock had sold between two and four times the July 1939 price.)

This type of analytical reasoning does not emphasize accurately predicting future trends, but rather reaching the general conclusion that the company will continue to do business pretty much as before. Wall Street is inclined to doubt that any such presumption may be applied to companies with an irregular trend and tends to consider that it is just as difficult and hazardous to reach a conclusion of this kind as to determine that a "growing company" will continue to grow. But in our view the Intertype form of reasoning has two definite advantages over the customary attitude, which at the time (1939) preferred a company such as Coca-Cola at 142 (24 times recent earnings and 35 times its asset value) because of the virtually uninterrupted expansion of its profits for more than 15 years.

Sequel

The fourth edition illustrated that the selection of Intertype would have been a good one. The comparative results are given in Table 30.5 based

Table 30.5. Comparative Results for Intertype
and Coca-Cola

	Harris-Intertype*	Coca-Cola
Market price, December 31, 1959	$ 98†	$150
Cost	08	142
Realized appreciation	$90	$ 8
Total cash dividends	35	102
Total return	$125	$110

*Intertype merged with Harris-Seybold Company in 1957 through an exchange of 6 shares of Intertype for 5 shares of Harris-Seybold.
†After allowing for stock dividends and splits.

on the following:

1. Intertype was purchased in 1939 at 8 and Coca-Cola at 142.

2. Stock dividends and splits were held.

3. Both issues were sold out at the closing price on December 31, 1959.

The return over 20 years on the investment of $8 in Intertype would have been 19.9 percent per annum, compounded, versus 4.1 percent for Coca-Cola. A more reasonable scenario is that Intertype would have been sold by the time it quadrupled (1946). Sale at the average 1946 price would have given a compound annual return of 29.2 percent.

The Intertype example is classic in a number of respects. The earnings history of Intertype from 1929 to 1938 was essentially a reflection of extreme business conditions. Losses were shown even by sound companies at the bottom of the Great Depression. Purchase of working capital at a discount is among the great but infrequent bargain opportunities, and the desirability of buying a stock at prices well below previous high prices in the company's not-too-distant history are both bases for sound decision rules. The mediocre return from Coca-Cola resulted in part from paying too much for a growth stock and in part from the lack of earnings growth from 1939 to about 1956.

Ratio of Price to What Earnings?

Current Earnings as a Basis of Market Prices

In considering the role of current earnings in stock prices, our objective is not to undertake intensive research into stock price formation but rather to set forth some general views on the subject. Current earnings play neither a readily definable nor a constant role in stock prices. That is, the stock market does not always give the same weight to current earnings. (This is not to imply that it should. Current earnings should be valued in relation to whatever is considered to be "normal.") The contrasting experiences of the post–World War II market illustrate well this point.

The average price-earnings ratio during the 1940s was near 12 times earnings, but by 1949 it had become so depressed as to fall below 8 times. The 1950s averaged about the same but ranged from less than 7 times earnings to over 20. From about 1958 to 1972 the market averaged about 17 times earnings, but during each year had a range that often exceeded 20 and touched 15. In the 1974 to 1984 period price-earnings ratios spent most of their time under 10 and were under 7 times earnings in 1979. After a market bottom in 1982, price-earnings multiples climbed during a major market move to a level around 15 in mid 1987.

Current versus Future

If the historical record of price earning ratios is meaningful at all, there seems little doubt that *at the extremes* the market is not much influenced by current earnings and is heavily influenced by expectations of earnings over the years to come. At other times, price-earnings ratios tend to stay on a plateau, perhaps plus or minus 20 percent, and give the impression that the current level of earnings is thought to be representative of future earnings.

Despite the repeated disregard of current earnings, as indicated by various stock market averages, substantial fluctuations in individual stock prices have often accompanied announcements of current earnings and changes in current earnings prospects. A considerable part of the activity of Wall Street analysts—as reflected in the advisory publications of financial services and in brokerage-house reports—is devoted to the effort to forecast near-term changes in earnings. Furthermore, many of their conclusions as to the dearness or cheapness of individual shares (other than growth stocks) appear to be based on a capitalization of the profits and dividends expected in the next 12 months or so. This is a recognition of the fact that *announcements* of the latest earnings do influence stock prices—at least in the short run.

The effect of announcements of earnings on value is likely to be insignificant, unless the earnings announcement itself signals a change in the outlook for the future. The long-term value investor recognizes that purchasing a stock accomplishes the acquisition of existing assets and liabilities, regardless of where they came from or when they were acquired. Since the past cannot be changed, it is not an issue in the purchase decision. What is an issue in the purchase decision is the future earnings that the investor will obtain by buying the stock. It is the ability of the existing assets and liabilities to create future earnings that determine the value of the equity position.

The distinction between price and value becomes more vivid once analysts understand that events such as earnings announcements can affect price in the short term without changing the underlying value by even a penny.

Cyclical and Temporary Earnings

Clearly, for individual stocks, current earnings which have been unduly depressed by temporary factors such as a long strike or a deep business recession have only modest market influence. For that reason, a cyclical company is often found selling at price-earnings ratios that would be high even for the finest growth company. That is, if normal earnings of $2 per share are imbedded in the market's thinking and earnings temporarily decline to $0.10 per share, a price earnings ratio of 100 could easily be the result. If the extremely depressed earnings are a result of temporary business conditions, the investor probably does well first to buy a cyclical company when its price-earnings ratio is high relative to current earnings but low relative to normal earnings and then to sell the stock when earnings are booming and the price-earnings ratio is low.

Seasonal Earnings Effects. Note that during the course of a year the earnings of various years may influence the market's thinking. In January, the market may still be heavily influenced by its estimate for the full previous year and only modestly influenced by the estimate for the current year. By the middle of the year, the current-year estimate may dominate, but some influence will be shown by expectations for the subsequent year and the actual results for the previous year. Toward the end of the year, the previous year may no longer matter, the current year may be the larger influence, and the subsequent year estimate beginning to have increasing influence. Some investment organizations have attempted to introduce a three-year earnings approach and calculate weighting factors on a seasonal basis in an effort to identify the "normal" way that price-earnings ratios act. Such studies have shown apparent seasonal influences, but the proper seasonal weights do not appear to be stable, perhaps because at times the market is willing to project the future many years ahead, and at other times seems to lack the conviction necessary to estimate more than 12 months ahead.

Anticipating Price Movements versus Value Investing. There appear to be at least two styles of investing that are based on differing views about current earnings or those that are immediately foreseeable. Some investors note that individual stock prices react to current earning reports and near-term earnings estimates, and they view such information as the primary objective of their activities and the principal causal factors for buying and selling stocks. This investment approach demands a very short-term time horizon, rapid portfolio turnover, and high commission costs. Such a trading strategy demands great estimation accuracy, fast information sources, and the ability to act with speed.

In contrast, *value investing* places only minor emphasis on the short-term earnings outlook and focuses on the fundamental factors that will influence the long-term trends and levels of earnings and dividends. Whether a fresh earnings report or estimate results in a change in value is simply an analytical question. The stock price movements that result from short-term earnings developments are usually viewed as useful opportunities to buy underpriced shares or sell those that are overpriced.

Professional security analysts must choose between the two approaches—a decision of vital importance to their careers. We recommend the long-term-value approach strongly, as by far the sounder and more rewarding of the two.

Dividend Projections

The estimate of expectable dividends is ordinarily related closely to the projection of earnings. This explains the paradox that, although for most companies the dividend payments may be basically more important than the earnings, the bulk of the analyst's attention is likely to be focused on earning-power factors. Earnings are the most variable component of cash flows, and cash flows are the dominant factor in the dividend decision. In considering the dividend question separately, the analyst will be guided by the company's past payout policy, by consideration of its financial position, by the cash flows needed to finance the projected growth, and by an appropriate allowance for the impact of new conditions.

A subtle but most important point is that dividends tend to have been determined by the cash flows available over the short run, and there is a better correlation between dividends and cash flow than between dividends and earnings. Thus, the most useful payout ratio is the percent of cash flows paid as dividends. However, over longer periods of time, say five or ten years, dividends must be related to true earnings. If dividends exceed true earnings, the company is liquidating part of its equity, and, if the policy persists, the company must ultimately go out of business. As a result of this apparent contradiction, the analyst will predict each year's dividend based on the projection of cash flows but will examine the longer-term relationship of dividends to earnings by taking the sum of dividends paid over 5 or 10 years and dividing that amount by the total earnings for the period. This technique will be used both to examine the past and to gain insight into the reasonableness of projections.

We hope that in future years both managements and stockholders may gain a better understanding of the merits of an overall dividend policy geared in principle to the earning power and intrinsic value of the equity, rather than to the arbitrarily determined "needs of the business." (Such a policy should permit the legitimate needs of the business for *large* amounts of additional capital to be financed by sale of securities on satisfactory terms.) For growth companies, the adoption of a clearly formulated and consistently followed stock-dividend policy would permit sufficient flexibility in the payout with more confidence, and the stockholders might be able to count on more equitable and favorable treatment.

At the present time, however, the dividend policy of many companies is not closely related to the past or estimated future earning power. Consequently the dividend factor, as an element of *value independent of earnings*, often plays a major role in common-stock valuation. In the next two chapters we deal with what at bottom may be called "the problem of disparities between earnings and dividends."

31
The Dividend Factor in Common-Stock Valuation

Dividend-Paying Capacity versus Earning Power

The return for an investor in a common stock is the cash dividends received during the period held plus or minus any price change between purchase and sale. Where the holding period is infinity, the value of a stock is the discounted present value of its prospective dividend stream, because the stock will presumably never be sold.[1] On this basis, value is a function of a company's dividend-paying capacity.

Future earnings, however, are generally perceived as the long-term determinant of a company's ability to pay future dividends. This link between earnings and dividends allows a view of value as a function of future earning power. This fact has led to controversy as to the relative importance of earnings and dividends as sources of value. It has also resulted in the existence of two basic types of valuation models: dividend discount models (DDMs) and earnings capitalization (price-earnings

---

[1]If the stock is to be sold at the end of some shorter period, N, its sale price will be the discounted present value of the then remaining dividends (from year $N + 1$ to infinity), which gives the same total present value as the perpetual model. Thus, the perpetual model is the one usually used unless the investor holds beliefs about changes in the discount rate in year N.

ratio) models. To us, the two estimates of future earning power and future dividend-paying capacity are indistinguishable. One cannot adequately estimate one without the other. Since earnings are the source of dividends and since the dividend payout rate (the earnings retention rate) must be considered in predicting the growth of earnings, appraisal and prediction of the dividend-paying capacity of a corporation must be an integral part of a careful and thorough estimation of a corporation's earning power. Accordingly, either of the two basic models can be used. The security analyst must forecast both earnings and dividends even if the organization is using solely a DDM for valuing stocks.

Dividends and the Payout Ratio

A discussion of corporate dividend policy provides both an appropriate starting point and perspective in considering dividends and the payout ratio from the investor's standpoint.

Corporate Dividend Policy

Investors have never expected companies to pay out the full amount of their earnings. It is considered sound corporate policy, and thus in the interests of the shareholders, to retain an appreciable part of an average year's earnings for various protective and constructive purposes such as (1) strengthening the liquidity and capital position—that is, the ratio of current assets to current liabilities, or of stock equity to debt; (2) modernizing the plant for greater efficiency; (3) providing capital for expansion and new products; and (4) building up a surplus for "rainy-day" contingencies and to maintain the dividend rate in low earning years. This heterogeneous list supplies no clue in itself as to what portion of the earnings of a given company should best be withheld from the stockholders.

Table 31.1 provides figures that show how actual payout practice developed over the 50-year span from 1936 through 1985. In the 1936–1945 span, the average was about two-thirds payout and one-third retention. This ratio was roughly comparable to historic experience before the severe depression of the 1930s. (The 1871–1930 average was 64 percent.) In the 1946–1970 period, need for funds for corporate expansion, aggravated by price inflation, held down dividend disbursements to the 50–60 percent range. Since 1971, as the result of intensified inflation until recently, the payout ratio has been in the 40–50 percent range. As a result of inflation, true earnings—in terms of the maintenance of productive capacity—were being overstated. Clearly, the

Table 31.1. Payout Rates of Standard & Poor's
Composite Stocks in Five-Year Spans, 1936–1985

Period	Percent
1936–1940	71
1941–1945	64
1946–1950	52
1951–1955	55
1956–1960	56
1961–1965	57
1966–1970	55
1971–1975	46
1976–1980	41
1981–1985	49

SOURCE: Compiled from Standard & Poor's Statistical Service,
Security Price Index Record, New York 1986, pp. 118–121.

historic dividend payout of two-thirds of earnings is no longer the
standard and a much lower "normal" has been adopted during this
inflation-affected period.

The Case for Liberal Dividends

Before taking up concepts that favor low payout ratios for particularly
successful and rapidly growing companies, let's examine the reasons
behind investor preference for liberal dividends. This preference is
based on more than the natural liking for good dividend checks, and on
more than the practical view that a corporation is in business to earn
profits and to pay commensurate dividends to its stockholders. The
need for corporations to demonstrate dividend-paying ability is also a
factor. Moreover, investors know that the larger the dividend component of total investment return (since dividends fluctuate so much less
than stock prices) the lower the variability of their shares will tend to be.
The lower this variability is, other factors being equal, the higher the
earning power will be valued in the marketplace. The security analyst
must observe investors' partialities, as expressed in the market itself, in
evaluating the dividend factor, mindful that if investors are irrational in
their partialities, resultant mispricing of the security will afford opportunity.

Retained Earnings Not Reliably Available.   On the more negative side,
long experience has taught investors to be somewhat doubtful of the

benefits claimed to accrue to them from retained and reinvested earnings. In many cases a large accumulation has failed either to produce a comparable increase in earnings and dividends or to ensure the continuance of the previously established dividend rate. This important point can be illustrated by examples from the steel and aerospace/defense industries.

Example 1: Armco Inc. The lack of relationship between retained earnings and subsequent dividends is well exemplified by figures for the nation's fifth largest steel company for the 20-year span from 1962 to 1981:

Net income available for common stock	$2,370,500,000
Cash dividends paid	1,013,200,000
Undistributed earnings	$1,357,300,000

The payout ratio averaged 42.7 percent over the 20 years, and retained earnings were built up to $1,862,000,000 by the end of 1981. However, when losses were encountered in the third and fourth quarters of 1982, dividends were reduced from 45 cents (paid for the prior four quarters) to 30 cents. As a result of continuing losses in 1983 and 1984, dividends were drastically cut and in the third quarter of 1984 completely eliminated.

Example 2: Fairchild Industries, Inc. Over the 14 years, 1970 through 1983, Fairchild had aggregate earnings per share of $18.74 and paid cash dividends of $4.88—a payout ratio of 26 percent. Retained earnings increased from $14 million to $194 million. From the third quarter of 1984 through the second quarter of 1985, the company had a loss. In the third quarter of 1985 dividends were cut from 20 cents per share, which had been paid since the first quarter of 1981, to 5 cents.

Retained Earnings Not Reflected in Market Price. The fact that retained earnings may not be fully reflected in price can be illustrated with the data for Brad Ragan in Table 31.2.[2] The dividend payout was exceedingly low in both five-year periods. The low 1980–1984 payout resulted in retained earnings increasing average book value per share in the first period from $15.65 per share to $19.57 in the second period. However, the 1980–1984 price averaged only $12.21 or 62 percent of book value. For every dollar of retained earnings, the investor received a modest $0.57.[3] Clearly, retained earnings were far from being fully

---

[2]Brad Ragan, Inc.. is the largest retreader of tires for off-the-road vehicles used in mining, construction, and earth moving. The company maintains service centers in 25 states and operates stores in the Carolinas which retail tires, auto accessories and appliances for home use.

[3]The change in price ($2.24) divided by the change in book value ($3.92) shows that retained earnings were not worth a dollar in market price: $2.24 ÷ $3.92 = $0.57.

Table 31.2. Book Value and Price Per Share
Brad Ragan Inc.—Five-Year Averages

Per-share data	1975–1979	1980–1984
Earnings	$5.34	$ 3.71
Dividends	.50	.60
Payout ratio	9.4%	16.2%
Book value (average)	$15.65	$19.57
Price*	$9.97	$12.21
Price/book value	.64×	.62×
Return on equity (book value)	34.1%	19.0%

*Average of annual high and low prices.
SOURCE: Compiled from Value Line, *The Value Line Investment Survey*, September 27, 1985, p. 135.

reflected in market price in that kind of a market environment. Moreover, the earning power of the business failed to maintain the return on equity at previously high levels.

Retained Earnings Remain at Risk. *Retained earnings are equivalent to a fully subscribed preemptive rights offering made on behalf of all share-holders.* Whether this form of raising equity capital is advantageous to the shareholder's investment position is the question to be answered. It is to be emphasized that cash dividends are certain whereas retained earnings are at risk. If the purpose of retained earnings is primarily defensive, the retention is impelled by competitive pressures rather than free choice looking toward enlarged earning power. These retained earnings reflect such factors as inadequate depreciation and obsolescence, and thus are not true economic earnings. They are retained to prevent deterioration of the firm's competitive position. Consequently, such compulsory reinvestment cannot be expected to add much to the stockholder's real equity. In these instances, the analyst would conclude that dependable earnings are those paid out in dividends and that the retained portion should be valued at a substantially discounted rate because it is not reliably available and remains at risk. The following section provides the logic and examples favoring reinvestment.

The Case for Reinvestment

For purposes of this discussion, assume that a successful company is defined as one that is expected to earn a return on its common-stock equity that is above the earnings yield on the market price of its stock. This differential is sufficient to produce an average market price for the stock in excess of the book value. Furthermore, assume that this level of return can be maintained on a large amount of reinvested profits. The logical deduction from these assumptions is that, in terms of return, it is to the investor's advantage if *all* profits are reinvested by such companies up to the point where diminishing returns vitiate the superior marginal reinvestment rate.

Retained Earnings Reflected in Market Price.   A large proportion of important U.S. industrial corporations have sold for many years above their book values as illustrated in Table 31.3, which provides a 25-year record for the relationship of price as a percentage of book value for the Standard & Poor's 400 (S&P 400) Industrial Stock Index. This broad

Table 31.3. Market Price to Book Value for Standard & Poor's 400, 1961–1985

Year	Average price ($)	Average book value ($)	Average price/ average book value
1961	69.99	34.29	2.04
1962	65.54	35.60	1.84
1963	73.39	37.27	1.97
1964	86.19	39.20	2.20
1965	93.48	41.87	2.23
1966	91.08	44.55	2.04
1967	99.18	46.69	2.12
1968	107.50	49.00	2.19
1969	107.10	50.96	2.10
1970	91.29	52.18	1.75
1971	108.40	53.97	2.01
1972	121.80	56.81	2.14
1973	120.50	60.59	1.99
1974	92.91	65.33	1.42
1975	96.54	69.33	1.39
1976	114.30	73.55	1.55
1977	108.40	79.24	1.37
1978	106.20	85.97	1.24
1979	114.80	94.22	1.22
1980	134.50	103.51	1.30
1981	144.20	112.20	1.29
1982	133.60	117.35	1.14
1983	180.56	120.46	1.50
1984	181.26	122.80	1.48
1985	207.78	124.74	1.67
1961–1985 average			1.73
1976–1985 average			1.38

SOURCE: Standard & Poor's Statistical Service, *Security Price Index Record*, 1986, pp. 110, 237; *Current Statistics*, November, 1986, p. 30.

index shows that on average over the full 1961–1985 span the investor received $1.73 for every dollar of earnings reinvested. Over the last 10 years the average has dropped to $1.38. This recent decline in price/ book value suggests, but does not prove, that recent incremental dollars reinvested had a value of less than $1.00.

Data over the 15-year span from 1971 to 1985 for three leading stocks—IBM, Hewlett-Packard, and General Electric—support more strongly the case for reinvestment (Table 31.4). All three companies have a conservative capital structure, and there was no significant change in capital structure over the period, so that financial leverage was not an important factor in the return earned on the book value of the common stock. Since return on equity (ROE) was well-maintained, new

Table 31.4. Net Available Common Equity Divided by Average Common-Stock Book Value, Earnings Yield, and Market Price to Book Value, 1971–1985

	IBM			Hewlett Packard			General Electric		
	NACE/* book value†	NACE/ market price	Price/ book value	NACE/ book value	NACE/ market price	Price/ book value	NACE/ book value	NACE/ market price	Price/ book value
1971	17.2	2.9	5.9	10.5	2.2	4.7	17.3	4.6	3.8
1972	18.8	2.9	6.5	14.6	2.2	6.8	18.1	4.5	4.1
1973	19.3	3.6	5.4	16.2	2.2	7.2	18.2	4.9	3.7
1974	19.5	6.2	3.2	20.9	4.3	4.8	17.2	7.0	2.4
1975	18.5	7.0	2.7	16.4	3.4	4.8	15.0	7.5	2.0
1976	19.9	6.2	3.2	14.8	3.3	4.4	18.2	7.7	2.4
1977	20.7	6.9	3.0	16.0	5.5	2.9	19.5	9.2	2.1
1978	23.9	7.8	3.1	16.6	6.8	2.4	19.6	10.7	1.8
1979	21.2	7.3	2.9	18.0	6.6	2.7	20.3	12.4	1.6
1980	22.7	9.9	2.3	19.2	6.0	3.2	19.5	12.5	1.6
1981	19.1	9.4	2.0	18.0	5.6	3.2	19.1	12.0	1.6
1982	23.2	9.6	2.4	17.8	5.2	3.4	18.9	10.3	1.8
1983	25.4	7.7	3.3	16.3	4.1	4.0	18.9	8.5	2.2
1984	26.5	9.5	2.8	16.9	5.6	3.1	19.2	9.3	2.1
1985	22.4	7.7	2.9	13.0	5.6	2.3	17.7	7.9	2.2
1971–1985 avg.‡	21.2	7.0	3.4	16.3	4.6	4.0	18.4	8.6	2.4
1976–1985 avg.	22.5	8.2	2.8	16.7	5.4	3.2	19.1	10.1	1.9

*Net available common equity (NACE) divided by book value is equivalent to ROE except when preferred stock exists. When there is preferred stock in the capital structure, use net available to common equity (NACE) rather than earnings per share.

†Average (rather than end-of-year) book value is used, as we advocate. Market price is the high and low average for the year.

‡Ten-year period average given for purposes of comparison to the S&P 400 price/ book value 10-year average (Table 31.3).

SOURCE: Earnings, book value, and market price are taken directly from *The Value Line Investment Survey.* February 6, 1987, pp. 1013, 1099, 1102. Book value numbers include some amounts of intangibles that were not material for these companies.

equity financing did not dilute the position of shareholders. The price/book value ratios for IBM and Hewlett-Packard, two growth stocks, make the case for a low payout ratio.

Companies with High Return on Equity. The higher the ROE for a company (which will be reflected in the average multiplier of earnings) the greater the proportion of earnings that should be retained. Presumably the rate of return on reinvestment will substantially exceed, in the typical case, what the stockholder could earn on the same money received in dividends. A good corporate earnings picture and opportunities for profitable expansion generally go together. For such companies, particularly those in technological fields, in theory at least, low dividends and high reinvestment would appear the best policy for the stockholders. Carried to its logical conclusion, this analysis would suggest that nearly all really successful companies should follow a program of substantial reinvestment of profits, and that cash dividends should be paid only to the extent that opportunities for profitable expansion or diversification are not present.

The inferences drawn above are stated in a provisional and qualified manner. There is no certainty that the rate of future return on additions to capital can be equated with past returns or calculated by the analyst with true dependability. This very real uncertainty will make it more difficult for stockholders in general—and their alter ego, "the stock market"—to abandon their ingrained preference for cash dividends in favor of the theoretical advantages of retained profits.

Cashing In. The fact that some owners need cash income from their shares is not a valid argument against complete reinvestment of profits, for presumably these dollars will have a premium value in the market when reinvested. Hence shareholders will fare better by selling off corresponding amounts of their holdings than by receiving the money in dividends. Such cashing in where needed could be readily facilitated by the company through paying periodic small stock dividends to represent the profits plowed back.

Example. Citizens Utilities Company has its common shares divided 64 percent in Class A and 36 percent in Class B. The only difference between the two is that Class A dividends are paid in stock equivalent to the cash paid on Class B. All shares sell at the same price, with A shares convertible into B shares on a share-for-share basis. This unique arrangement accommodates two clienteles: (1) the investor who wants to reinvest dividends and to defer taxes on their recognition and (2) the investor who wants a current cash dividend equal to about 80 percent of per-share earnings. The Internal Revenue Service is not about to approve this substitutability of dividends for other companies.

Conclusion

The data presented in support of liberal dividends and for reinvestment suggest that a fundamental difference exists between the appropriate payout policy for average or subaverage companies and that for above-average or growth companies. In theory, this conclusion should point to complete retention by companies with a well-above-average earning potential, since it would be hard to establish any percentage figure beyond which the payment of cash dividends becomes inherently more advantageous.[4]

Dividend Discount Models

The role of dividends in the valuation of common stocks has changed greatly in recent years as a result of the development and increasing use of the dividend discount model (DDM). The DDM requires an explicit forecast of dividends over a span of years. Consequently more attention must be given to how much a company can be expected to pay out from earnings than under a P/E ratio model. Although the DDM has become a prominent valuation method for about the last 10 years, the theory was set forth by J. B. Williams in the late 1930s.[5]

The Structure of Dividend Discount Models

The concept of discounting future cash flows to arrive at their present value is a standard tool of most financial and economic analysis. The essential idea is that a future stream of dividends (D) has a present value when discounted at a selected rate (K):

$$\text{Value} = \frac{D_1}{(1+K)^1} + \frac{D_2}{(1+K)^2} + \frac{D_3}{(1+K)^3} \cdots + \frac{D_n}{(1+K)^n}$$

The structure of DDMs and their key parameters may be best understood by focusing first on the simplest model. A common stock extends into perpetuity. Thus the stream of dividends that the analyst

[4]For an instructive review of the dividend controversy and new research results, see Terry A. Marsh and Robert C. Merton, "Dividend Behavior for the Aggregate Stock Market," *The Journal of Business*, January 1987, pp. 1–40. The authors conclude that stock prices lead dividend changes with consistency and serve as a better forecaster than accounting earnings.

[5]J. B. Williams, *The Theory of Investment Value*, North Holland Publishing Company, Amsterdam, 1938.

must predict is infinite. Meaningful dividend forecasts on a year-by-year basis into the indefinite future are impossible, and some simplifying assumptions are therefore necessary. These assumptions can take several forms. One reduces the forecast to a single number, representing a continuous average growth rate. This model of the DDM is known as the *constant growth* (one period or one stage) model. It is illustrated by the following equation:

$$\text{Value} = \frac{D}{K - g}$$

D = Expected dividend for next 12 months
K = Discount rate
g = Rate of growth in normalized earning power

The above form of the DDM constitutes an oversimplification. It involves loss of information in regard to the future growth pattern of a company that is needed in its evaluation.

It is logical and typical practice to employ a multiperiod model, particularly a three-period model. Such a model provides more information relative to the growth pattern of a firm and, at the same time, provides some simplifications that bring the forecasting task within manageable limits. The first period is the *growth* stage. Depending on the model, analysts forecast dividends either at a constant growth rate or on a year-by-year basis for a duration that they decide.

The second period is the *transition* stage in which the earnings growth rate slows (or rises) and the payout ratio adjusts to the rate expected for the third period—the long-run *steady state* stage. The analyst forecasts, ordinarily within some designated limits, the duration of the transition period. The pattern of the decline (or increase) can be linear or exponential. Although some models provide the analyst with the option to use one or the other, many analysts use a linear pattern for simplicity.

In the third period, it is usually assumed that a company will grow at the same rate and have the same payout ratio as the average firm for an infinite time span. However, a few organizations recognize that in rare instances there may be justification for the analyst's estimating a higher or lower rate.

In moving from a one-period model to a three-period model, the input requirements from the analyst are materially increased. As a result, a more extensive analysis of industry and firm characteristics is required. As stated, the objective is, of course, to gain information. The three-period model allows the analyst to forecast explicitly the future growth pattern and thus to develop a more meaningful value estimate.

By segmenting future time into three discrete periods, future time patterns for dividends can be flexibly developed and evaluated using a limited number of parameters. Thus, a DDM can calculate value using a modest number of inputs that analysts are able to forecast.

Two Basic Types of Dividend Discount Models

Individual users tend to add their own features to the dividend stream structure, and thus a wide variety of dividend discount models are in use. However, all these models are of two basic types: One discounts the projected dividend stream at some prespecified rate to obtain an estimated investment value that can be compared to the current market price. The other derives that discount rate which equates the present value of the projected dividend stream with the current market price (the implied discount rate or internal rate of return). This implied rate is then compared with some prescribed total return rate objective— usually a rate that is adjusted for the risk of the stock. Most DDMs are of the latter type. The choice between setting the discount rate and solving for price versus the reverse procedure is often a matter of internal convenience. However, more judgment is involved in selecting the discount rate which requires looking at the rate on fixed-income securities and adding an appropriate risk premium. Given the term structure of interest rates and the greater uncertainty of far distant growth in dividends, a case can be made for using different discount rates in each period; but this refinement is seldom introduced.

The Dividend Discount Model in Perspective

The DDM has a number of attractive characteristics. It provides a structured approach to the valuation of common stocks; it provides for the systematic processing of data; it requires the production of explicit data inputs. As a result of these characteristics, it is possible, when mistakes in inputs are made, to determine the nature of these mistakes and decide how to correct them.

Much research has been devoted to understanding the DDM and its behavior.[6] This research has produced two schools of thought. One

[6]For example, see R. O. Michaud, "Another Look at Dividend Discount Models," paper presented at Institute for Quantitative Research in Finance, Key Biscayne, Fla., May 1985; S. G. Einhorn and P. Shangquan, "Using the Dividend Discount Model for Asset Allocation," *Financial Analysts Journal*, May–June 1984, pp. 30–32; W. M. Bethke and S. E. Boyd, "Should dividend discount models be yield-tilted?" *Journal of Portfolio Management*, Spring 1983,

holds that the DDM has structural valuation biases that favor high-yield stocks (called the "yield tilt") and low P/E stocks—causing them to look unduly attractive against growth stocks. Thus there is an antigrowth stock bias. The other school holds that the model is neutral and has no significant structural biases. It contends that the performance biases observed are in the analytical inputs and in the market itself. In regard to inputs, the bias results in part from simplifying assumptions—such as that all stocks have the same growth rate and payout in the steady state stage—and from the natural tendency of analysts to be conservative in projecting the growth rate for high-growth companies.[7] In regard to the market, the existence of a bias that values low-yield growth stocks much higher than high-yield low-growth stocks is well known.

We endorse the dividend discount model particularly when used for established companies with consistent earning power and when used along with other valuation models. It is our view that, in any case, an investor should employ more than one model.

pp. 23–27; R. O. Michaud, "Should Dividend Discount Models Be Yield-tilted? Comment," *Journal of Portfolio Management*, Summer 1984, pp. 85–86; R. O. Michaud and P. L. Davis, "Valuation Model Bias and the Scale Structure of Dividend Discount Returns," *The Journal of Finance*, May 1982, pp. 563–573; J. D. McWilliams and James Wei, "Some Like To-matoes and Some Like To-matoes," *Journal of Portfolio Management*, Summer 1981, pp. 43–47.

[7] If capacity to pay dividends, rather than dividends themselves, were used as an input, this antigrowth bias might be eliminated.

32

Capitalization Rate for Earnings and Dividends

As indicated in preceding chapters, there are two principal methods for valuing common stocks—through capitalizing earnings or dividends. This chapter examines both methods and, in each instance, proposes a capitalization rate for the market. The economic and capital market assumptions underlying the proposed capitalization are specified in the discussion, and the economic assumptions are in accord with those in the chapters dealing with the projections of earnings and dividends. To provide a basis for judging the capital market assumptions used, the range of forecasts developed through a survey of several major investment managers and brokerage firms is provided.

Two-Step Approach

Just as analysts examine the past to estimate future earnings and dividends, so should they study the past in selecting a capitalization rate—accepting or modifying it as rational considerations would dictate. This involves consideration of the price-earnings ratio (multiplier for earnings) or discount rate for dividends of the specific share, not only in terms of its own historic record but also in terms of its relationship to that of the general market.

It is our suggestion that a capitalization rate (multiplier for earnings or discount rate for dividends) for a company be arrived at by two major steps: First, establish a *basic capitalization rate* for common stocks in general, that is, a comprehensive group of companies, such as those in one of the well-known market indexes. Second, develop a multiplier or discount rate for an individual issue which is related to this basic rate but which also reflects appraisal of the record, quality, and long-term prospects of the specific company. This twofold approach provides a consistent valuation procedure.

Basic Capitalization Rate for the Market

Choice of Market Indexes

There are a considerable number of common stock indexes or "averages," but most studies of the earnings, dividends, prices, and other market relationships of cross-sectional groups use the two Standard & Poor's series—Composite Index of 500 Stocks (S&P 500) and the 400 Industrial Stock Index (S&P 400).

Earnings and dividend data are calculated quarterly and prices daily. In July 1976, the composition of the comprehensive S&P 500 index was changed significantly. It had consisted of 425 industrial, 60 utility, and 15 rail stocks. The revised index consists of 400 industrial, 40 utility, 20 transportation, and 40 financial stocks. In addition to earnings, dividend, and price data for the indexes, Standard & Poor's supplies an index figure for the book values of the Industrial Stock Series.

The present Standard & Poor's index goes back to 1926, but the S&P 500 is linked to the Cowles Commission indexes which commence as early as 1871. It is possible, therefore, to make continuous studies of certain common-stock relationships extending over a 115-year span. (The data in the years prior to 1900 are much more fragmentary and less reliable than those for subsequent years.)

Prices, earnings, and dividends are reported for the indexes calculated by the *base-weighted aggregative* method: The current value is related to the average value for the 1941–1943 base period, which is set equal to 10.

In the following pages, more attention is given to the S&P 400 than the S&P 500, because Standard & Poor's provides book value data for the former series, allowing calculation of return on equity and price/book value ratios for the S&P 400 but not for the S&P 500.

The Historical Market Multiples of Earnings

We want to develop a basic multiplier for the market which can be considered appropriate for use in terms of the future. In seeking a guide to the future, a prudent person always begins by consulting the past. Thus Table 32.1 provides a substantial amount of data bearing on the relationship between selected average earnings and prices for the Cowles Commission—S&P 500 Index and the S&P 400. The latter series begins in 1926.

The relationships shown by the record summarized in Table 32.1 appear highly variable when studied in the form of five-year averages, and they would of course be much more so if considered for single years. For the Cowles Commission—S&P Composite series over the 115 years from 1871 to 1985, the mean of the sixteen 20-year averages is 13.8 times, or an earnings-price ratio (earnings yield) of 7.2 percent.

Table 32.1. Average Price/Earnings Ratios for Selected Indexes, 1871–1985

Period ending	5-year period S&P 500	5-year period S&P 400	10-year period S&P 500	10-year period S&P 400	20-year period S&P 500	20-year period S&P 400
1880			11.2×			
1890			16.0		13.6×	
1900			16.1		16.1	
1910			13.2		14.7	
1920			9.7		11.5	
1930	14.7×	14.5×	12.3		11.0	
1935	18.0	18.9	16.4	16.7×	14.4	
1940	13.5	14.5	15.8	16.7	16.7	
1945	11.7	13.7	12.6	14.1	14.5	15.4×
1950	10.1	10.6	10.9	12.2	13.3	14.4
1955	10.7	11.5	10.4	11.1	11.5	12.6
1960	15.3	15.8	13.0	13.7	11.9	12.9
1965	18.8	18.8	17.1	17.3	13.7	14.2
1970	16.5	16.2	17.7	17.5	15.3	15.6
1975	14.2	14.8	15.3	15.5	16.2	16.4
1980	8.9	9.2	11.5	12.0	14.6	14.7
1985	10.3	11.0	9.6	10.1	12.5	12.8
Average	13.6	14.1	13.5	14.3	13.8	14.3

SOURCES: Standard & Poor's Statistical Service, *Security Price Index Record*, 1986, pp. 118—121; Graham, Dodd, Cottle, *Security Analysis*, 4th ed., McGraw-Hill, New York, 1962, p. 509.

572   Valuation of Common Stocks and Contingent Claims

Data for the S&P Industrial Stock Series cover the 60-year span from
1926 through 1985. The comparative range and mean for the twelve
5-year periods for the two S&P series are:

	S&P 500	S&P 400
High	18.8×	18.9×
Low	8.9	9.2
Mean	13.6	14.1

Across time, the multiples for the two series have been reasonably
comparable, but the market has continued to favor slightly the S&P 400.
For example, the 1961–1985 average for the S&P 500 was 13.8 times
and that for the S&P 400 was 14.0 times.

Rather than examining earnings multiples in terms of set periods of
time, such as five years, they can be viewed in terms of levels for
different periods. For example, the postwar record of multiples for the
two indexes is as follows:

Period	Price/earnings multiples	
	S&P 500	S&P 400
1947–1957	10.1×	10.5×
1958–1972	17.6	17.7
1973–1985	10.1	10.5

The differences in multiples that existed reflect the higher growth
expectations for the S&P 400. Although this difference is limited, it is
sufficiently persistent to justify a multiplier higher by one-half (0.5) for
the S&P 400.

Dividend Capitalization for the Market

The essential projected stream of dividends is the product of a chain of
economic and capital market projections. The following pages spell out
these projections and our assumptions in regard to them are stated.

Economic and Capital Market Projections.   To project dividends, you
first must project earnings and the dividend payout ratio. The profitability of corporate America depends on the level of economic activity in
the United States. Accordingly, the underlying forecasts are projections

of the nation's output of goods and services, real gross national product
(GNP) and the inflation rate (GNP deflator). With these inputs it is possible
to project nominal GNP and aggregate corporate profits and, in turn,
earnings for the S&P 500 and S&P 400. Since the return expected from
stocks is affected by the return expected for bonds, the next step is to
project the interest rate for Aaa industrial bonds and an equity risk
premium.

Specific Underlying Projections.   Table 32.2 sets forth the assumptions
on which our valuation of the S&P 400 is based. The secular economic,
earnings, and dividend projections were discussed in earlier chapters.
Considering the expected inflation rate of 5.2 percent, the secular level
of Aaa industrial bonds is projected at 8.5 percent. The equity risk
premium forecast is 2.75 percent. Thus, the expected return for the S&P
400 is 11.25 percent, of which 7.5 percent would be from capital appreciation due to growth in earnings and dividends. The balance of 3.75
percent is the dividend yield. The return on equity of 14 percent approximates the 1976–1985 average of 13.8 percent.

Table 32.2. Secular Projections for Standard
& Poor's Industrial Stock Index
(In Percentages)

Real GNP growth	2.7
Inflation—GNP deflator increase	5.2
Nominal GNP growth	8.0
Corporate aftertax profits growth	8.0
Index earnings growth	7.5
Dividend payout ratio	46.0
Dividend growth	7.5
Interest rate—Aaa industrial bonds	8.5
Equity risk premium	2.75
Total return expected	11.25
Return on equity	14.0

   Our multiplier for earnings may be derived from the projections in
Table 32.2. The equation $V = D/(K-g)$ provides the basis for the
calculation. In other words, value (V) is equal to dividends (D) divided by
the required discount rate (K) (11.25 percent), less the growth rate in
dividends (g) (7.5 percent). For ease of illustration, assume that normal
index earnings in the current year are $1 and dividends are 46 cents
(payout ratio 46 percent), so that:

$$\text{Value} = \frac{\$0.46}{0.1125 - 0.075} = \$12.27$$

This computation has provided for the S&P 400 both the divisor for dividends of 3.75 percent (0.1125 − 0.075) and a multiplier for earnings of, say, 12.3 times ($12.27/$1.00 of earnings).

To provide a basis for appraising the assumptions in Table 32.2, we have surveyed several institutions and brokerage houses to determine current opinions on the longer-term outlook for the factors listed. The following indicates the range of our findings:

	Growth rates (%)
Real GNP	2.0– 3.0
Inflation—GNP deflator	4.5– 6.0
Nominal GNP	7.0– 8.5
Corporate profits after taxes	7.0–11.0
Index earnings	6.5–10.5
Dividend payout ratio	40.0–47.0
Dividends	6.5–10.5

The interest rate projections and risk premiums of those institutions surveyed were not comparable to our projected rates because their forecasts were for differing fixed-income securities. Thus, our assumptions in Table 32.2 are within the range of current professional thinking.

Resultant Valuation of the Market

Standard & Poor's Industrial Stock Index. Using the capitalization rates developed above and normal estimated earnings, we can now calculate value estimates for the S&P 400. On the basis of a normal earnings estimate of $19.50 for 1987 and a multiplier of 12.3 times, the estimated value at year-end 1986 is 240 or, say, between 220 and 260. The market price of the S&P 400 was 270 or about 12 percent above the midpoint of the estimated value range.

Assuming a 46 percent payout rate, dividends in 1987 will be increasing to a $9 annual rate during the year, equal to a 3.75 percent current return on the estimated value of 240. How does this compare to the record? The following tabulation of five-year averages reveals that our forecast 3.75 percent yield is below those for two recent five-year periods, but well above those for two preceding five-year spans:

1966–1970	3.2%
1971–1975	3.3
1976–1980	4.7
1981–1985	4.5
1986	3.2

The lower dividend yield is to be expected, in view of the decline in interest rates. Over the 1976–1985 period, the yield on Aaa industrial bonds was as high as 15 percent, and the average was 11.1 percent. By year-end 1986, the yield had dropped below 9 percent.

Price-to-Book Value Ratio. The value estimate may also be viewed in perspective by examining the price-to-book value ratio. The ratio resulting from an S&P 400 valuation of 240 is 1.76 times. Note from the following tabulation that the ratio is well above those for the 1976–1985 period but below those for the preceding 1961–1970 decade.[1]

Period	Price-to-book value ratio
1946–1950	1.16 times
1951–1955	1.34
1956–1960	1.76
1961–1965	2.00
1966–1970	2.00
1971–1975	1.74
1976–1980	1.28
1981–1985	1.38
1986	1.97

Standard & Poor's Composite Stock Index. As stated earlier in this chapter, the earnings multiplier for the S&P 500 should be slightly lower than that for the S&P 400. Accordingly, a multiplier of 11.8 times is suggested. On that basis and accepting the consensus estimate of normal earnings, our valuation estimate for the S&P 500 is 213 (11.8 × 18.00). The market price at year end 1986 was 242 or nearly 14 percent above our intrinsic value estimate.

[1]Very large write-offs by basic industrial companies in 1985 and 1986 have depressed the rate of growth in book value. Also, replacement cost book values, in general, would be higher than those compiled from historical costs. Our valuation's ratio to book value, therefore, probably overstates the premium. By the same token, our projected 1987 return on average reported book value of 14.7 percent would be lower if deferred income taxes were included in equity as would be appropriate for the S&P 400.

Another way to judge our valuation of the S&P 500 is to examine the projected total return of 11.25 percent (3.75 percent dividend yield plus growth of 7.5 percent) in terms of the record. The average annual return for the entire postwar span (1946 to 1985) is 12.6 percent. If the high returns for the 1980–1985 period are eliminated, the 1946–1979 average is 11.5 percent, or slightly above our projected total return. The following tabulation o9f five-year period averages reminds us of the volatility in common-stock returns:

Period	Total return (%)
1946–1950	10.7
1951–1955	25.1
1956–1960	10.3
1961–1965	14.0
1966–1970	4.1
1971–1975	5.9
1976–1980	14.8
1981–1985	15.5

SOURCE: R.G. Ibbotson Associates, Inc., *Stocks, Bonds, Bills and Inflation: 1985 Yearbook*, Chicago, 1985, pp. 90-91.

Importance of Market Valuations

It is important that the reader understand just what we have and have not attempted to do in the preceding discussion. This has not been a mathematical or "scientific" calculation of exact value of the two stock indexes in late 1986. But, for consistency in security valuation, analysts need some idea of the proper or justified level of common stocks in general. We have shown how we would go about determining such a level or valuation.

In 1962, there was criticism of our position, taken in the fourth edition of this book, as to the importance of valuing the market. At that time, we stated, "Many analysts claim that the whole idea of 'valuing the averages is passe, and worse than useless.'" A defense of our position is no longer needed. The necessity of valuing the market is now widely accepted, since what happens to the market will be a primary determinant of the price performance of individual issues.

Intelligent investors will have a smaller proportion of their resources in common stocks at high levels of the market than at low or normal levels. To implement such a policy, it is necessary to form a careful view as to whether the market level is or is not excessive. Satisfied that the level is not excessive, an investor is free to make selections of individual issues as extensively as analytical talents permit.

Defining the Range of Multipliers

We suggest that analysts confine their range of multipliers within somewhat narrower limits than the market has done. It is a basic assumption of this book that the processes of the stock market are both psychological and arithmetical. This produces the well-known tendency of stock prices as a whole to go to extremes in either direction, as optimism or pessimism holds sway. It produces a tendency for favored stocks to sell at unduly high prices while unpopular stocks sell at unduly low prices. This characteristic shows itself in an extraordinarily wide dispersion of the market's capitalization rates when applied to current or past average earnings.

If the range of multipliers is to be limited, these limits must be somewhat arbitrarily set. For reasons which can be explained in broad terms—but which are difficult to defend in detail—we favor a range from about 6 to 18. These multipliers would be applicable to current "normal" earnings. Having selected 12.3 as the multiplier for average industrial shares of investment quality (e.g., S&P 400), this figure could be taken as representative of the center of the valuation range. In Chapter 30 we suggested that, for a top-quality growth share, the analyst restrict the premium paid for the above-average growth potential to not more than about 50 percent of the price considered appropriate without it. Using 12.3 as the base, this would mean not paying more than about 18½ times the current estimated normal earnings—except under most unusual circumstances.

In theory the minimum multiplier could drop to practically nothing. However, it is doubtful that a stock which in today's investment climate warranted a normal multiplier of less than 6 times normal current earnings would come within the category of common stocks suitable for the value approach. The use of a minimum multiplier of 6 would mean that approximately the same proportional difference would exist between the capitalization rate for the average investment-quality share and the lowest investment-quality stock that exists between the average and the top-quality growth share.

Capitalization Rate for Individual Issues

The choice of the specific multiplier will need to be made by the analyst without benefit of a definite formula. It will reflect the qualitative factors, discussed in previous pages, which are expected to influence the long-term prospects. It is possible, of course, to develop a rating system that will convert "marks" given for growth prospects, inherent stability,

---

578 Valuation of Common Stocks and Contingent Claims

and quality of management into a final figure for the multiplier. To suggest a specific way of doing this—even for purely illustrative purposes—might lead the reader to ascribe more authority to such a formula than it would merit.

Evaluating Intangibles

The factors that appear to influence greatly the attitude of security buyers and sellers toward any company are (1) the quality of management and (2) industry prospects. The vital importance of both factors cannot be gainsaid, but neither lends itself particularly well to the processes of security analysis.

Quality of Management.   The problem of appraising the management factor in reaching an investment decision is twofold: First, how does the analyst form a dependable judgment of management's ability or lack of it apart from the actual results obtained in the past? Second, assuming management may properly be considered a plus or minus factor separate from the actual financial results achieved by it, how does the analyst or investor translate that factor into an appropriate price-earnings ratio?

Caveats Concerning Industry Studies.   Chapter 9 set forth two basic points pertaining to industry studies: (1) Industry information has an essential role to play in the evaluation of individual companies. (2) Analysts should beware of industry studies which represent a warm-over of readily available data with which the public is already fairly familiar and which has already exerted a substantial influence on market quotations. To make a worthwhile contribution to security analysis and to common-stock investing, industry studies should have sufficient depth to generate new information and to reveal more fully than before the anatomy of the industry. To the extent that such studies produce insights into important factors that will operate in the future and are insufficiently appreciated by the current market, their value will be substantial.

Techno-Financial Analysis.   Along with manufacturing, marketing, and management skills, the area of research and development has become one of the major determinants of success in a number of industries. Substantial increases in research and development (R&D) expenditures indicate this factor's impact on the industrial scene. Product life cycles are becoming measurably shorter in high-research industries, and the sales of new products constitute a growing proportion of corporate sales. Through intensifying the technological obsolescence of both products and processes, R&D has injected a dynamic element into business which requires the pronounced attention of the analyst.

Industry studies must now become more penetrating techno-financial analyses. Financial projections will remain the all-important end product; reliable projections based on detected change will require a broader and deeper study of the company's position. Careful consideration must be given to (1) growth opportunities arising from product developments and process improvements and (2) threatening competition resulting from industry shifts and changes. Furthermore, widening diversification among corporations—which will also be accelerated by R&D—will force closer interindustry analysis to appraise more fully the possible attractiveness of significant corporate moves into different fields.

The Future and the Price Paid. In forecasting the relative long-term prospects of an industry, the analyst must consider that where the chance of error in the prediction appears to be least, the chance of profit therefrom may also be least. Current market prices most probably already reflect (or "discount") these confident expectations. Thus the analyst may be right about the future but wrong about the price paid for the issue. It is also possible to be wrong about the future as well as about the price.

Working Backward from the Answer. A frequent procedure of security analysts is to form a favorable opinion of the long-term prospects of a certain industry, based on their general knowledge and judgment, and then make an intensive study of the available materials to find confirmation of those views. Research which (albeit unintentionally) represents "working backward from the answer" is of questionable worth. One of the dangers is that the readily available and familiar figures will prove—at least at first blush—quite encouraging, since the analyst was very probably attracted to the industry in the first place by optimistic on-the-surface indications. As a consequence, the analyst is greatly inclined to rest the case there without probing deeply below the surface.

Beware Idols of the Marketplace. Studies in depth can reduce, though not eliminate, the hazards involved in forecasting the relative long-term prospects of an industry. Up to a point, the judgment factor in any long-term projection should become sharper and more dependable as it becomes better informed. Nevertheless, such long-run industry prospects as the caliber of management must still be considered a qualitative factor in security analysis.

In envisaging industry prospects, the analyst must beware of worshiping what may prove to be, in Francis Bacon's phrase, the "idols of the market place." The payment of an exceedingly liberal price for expected future improvement—in the form of a very high multiplier of past or current earnings—is hardly a business-like procedure. The investor should expect to be rewarded for good judgment when the anticipated improvement is realized, but if the price paid today already reflects tomorrow's performance, the best that can be hoped for is not to lose. In view of the hazards of the future, that would be a bad bargain.

Promising companies, mainly in promising industries, are bound to sell at more liberal prices than unpromising ones. The analyst, while accepting this fact, must be careful to set modest limits to the premiums paid for prospects. The market's general failure to do this has served at times to turn some of our best and strongest common stocks into speculative and risky vehicles.

Stock Market versus Security Analysis Valuations

In recommending attractive common-stock purchases, analysts will prefer issues selling at a lower percentage of estimated value to those selling at a higher percentage. With due consideration to the stability factor, analysts normally compose an investment list of diversified issues giving the most "value" for the price paid. One of the limitations of this approach derives from the necessarily inherent shortcomings of all investment decisions based largely on estimates of future earnings and on a more or less subjective choice of the multiplier to be applied to these expectations.

Analysts must also understand the inherent opposition between stock market valuations and security analysis valuations. The stock market tends to recurrent extremes, in its general bullishness and bearishness, in its marking up of investment and speculative favorites and its marking down of unpopular issues. The analyst seeks for a middle ground in viewing common stocks in general and tends to narrow somewhat the huge spread which the market has established between the valuation rates for popular and unpopular issues. This attitude provides what is, on the whole, a sound corrective for the excesses of the stock market, and it produces over the long haul a more satisfactory investment result than comes from "following the crowd."

This attitude and the related valuation techniques tend to exclude from the analyst's investment list the shares of those companies with the most impressive record of past growth and the best promise of future growth, except in periods of depressed market prices. For it is precisely such shares that are valued most liberally by the stock market and hence that in most periods command prices above the maximum value which the analyst could justifiably assign to them. But any one of such issues contains the possibility of a substantial further advance in market price, either because its subsequent growth rate exceeds the analyst's conservative expectations or because the market itself persists in an unrealistically high multiple for its special favorites. Our contention is that in such cases there exists an essentially speculative corporate development and price advance which the analyst is not equipped to foresee and foretell with a sufficient degree of confidence to recommend these issues.

33
Capital
Structure

In our discussion of key ratios in statement analysis in Chapter 20, we commented briefly on the relationship of common-stock equity to total capital funds: Other things being equal, the higher this ratio, the better the credit standing of the company, the higher in turn the "quality" of the stock issue, and the higher the multiplier to be applied to earnings per share. However, an all common-stock capital structure was not necessarily the most advantageous for the owners of the business. This subject is now returned to, as part of our discussion of factors governing the multiplier of per-share earnings and dividends. Two questions arise:

1. What should be, in theory, the effect of variations in capital structure on the multipliers for earnings and dividends?

2. What average relationship actually prevails in the markets between one factor and the other?

The second question is more important to the analyst than the first. For clarity of exposition, the theoretical issues are discussed first, then relevant material drawn from the stock market itself is presented, and finally our conclusions are set forth in terms of both valuation procedure and corporate policy.[1]

---

[1]Two excellent collections of papers on this subject were edited by B. M. Friedman and published by the University of Chicago Press: *The Changing Roles of Debt and Equity in Financing U.S. Capital Formation*, 1982, and *Corporate Capital Structures*, 1985.

Theory of Capital Structure

One of the most controversial issues in the field of corporate finance over the last 25 years has been the effect of capital structure on the market value of a corporation. The controversy began with a theory developed by Modigliani and Miller in 1958 which contended that the market value of a corporation is independent of its capital structure (relative proportions of debt and equity).[2] This original thesis, which assumed no income taxes or other market imperfections, was subsequently modified by the authors to provide for taxes.[3] Since then there has developed extensive theoretical literature on optimal capital structures. The extent of the academic interest in this subject is highlighted by the fact that in the last four years two presidential addresses at the Annual Meeting of the American Finance Association have been devoted to capital structure considerations.[4]

The controversy continues. However, the preponderance of academic opinion and empirical data support the position that typically the appropriate use of debt will maximize the market value of a corporation. In other words, there is an optimum capital structure, and leverage does affect value.[5] Thus a corporation's capital structure will, indeed, impact its market value, and an optimum capital structure will maximize the value of the firm.

Hypothetical Results from Variations in Capital Structure

Assume three similarly situated industrial companies, A, B, and S (S standing for speculative)—each of which has $10 million of capital funds and earns $1.6 million before interest and income taxes. Company A's only securities are 100,000 shares of common stock, without par value. Company B has the same number of common-stock shares, plus $3 million of 10 percent bonds. Company S has the same common-stock issue, plus $8 million of 10 percent bonds.

Example 1. For our first approach, assume that, regardless of capital

---

[2]F. Modigliani and M. H. Miller, "The Cost of Capital, Corporation Finance and the Theory of Investment," *American Economic Review*, June 1958, pp. 261–297.

[3]F. Modigliani and M.H. Miller, "Corporate Income Taxes and the Cost of Capital: A Correction," *American Economic Review*, June 1963, pp. 433–443. For a further discussion see M. H. Miller, "Debt and Taxes," *Journal of Finance*, May 1977, pp. 261–278.

[4]F. Modigliani, "Debt, Dividend Policy, Taxes, Inflation and Market Valuation," *Journal of Finance*, May 1982, pp. 255–273; and S. C. Myers, "The Capital Structure Puzzle," *Journal of Finance*, July 1984, pp. 575–592.

[5]For a comprehensive examination of this subject, see J. C. Van Horne, *Financial Management and Policy*, Prentice-Hall, Englewood Cliffs, N.J., 1986, pp. 275–307.

Table 33.1. Computation of the Effects of Capital Structure Constant
Multiples and Par Price for Bonds
(Dollar Amounts in Thousands)

Capital structure	Company A	Company B	Company S
Bonds – 10 percent	0	$ 3,000	$ 8,000
Book value of common	$10,000	7,000	2,000
Total capital funds	10,000	10,000	10,000
Net before interest and taxes	1,600	1,600	1,600
Interest	0	300	800
Balance	1,600	1,300	800
Income tax (34 percent)	544	442	272
Balance for common	1,056	858	528
Value of common at 11.6 times earnings	12,250	9,953	6,125
Value of bonds at par	0	3,000	8,000
Total value of company	$12,250	$12,953	$14,125
Times interest earned before taxes		5.3×	2.0×
Return on equity	10.6	12.3	26.4

structure, the market is willing to pay 11.6 times earnings for each
common stock and that the bonds would be worth par. The figures
would work out as shown in Table 33.1

These results, if actually realized in the market, would be extraordinary. Company A would sell at a premium of 22.5 percent over the
amount invested, Company B, for 29.5 percent more, and Company S,
for 41.2 percent more. These differences in the enterprise value would
be due solely to variations in the capital structure, including the
differing tax burdens. If our postulates as to price relationships were
valid, stockholders obviously would gain most by issuing the largest
possible amount of bonds, and the much-praised "clean" capital structure would be a costly mistake. Of course, our assumptions are not
correct. The common stocks of all three companies would *not* sell at the
same multiplier of earnings, nor would both the bond issues sell at the
same price.

Example 2.   Let us now make an alternative assumption. Since all the
companies are in exactly the same position as to the total amount of
capital invested, earnings before interest and taxes, and prospects,
assume that they sell at the same aggregate enterprise valuation, except
to the extent that interest charges reduce the tax burden. Thus we
assume that the three companies sell at the same multiple of total
earnings on capital after taxes (earnings available common plus interest).
For simplicity, assume further that the bond issues sell at par. The
resultant company valuations are set forth in Table 33.2.

Table 33.2. Computation of the Effects of Capital Structure
Constant Multiple for Total Earnings after Taxes and Par Price for Bonds
(Dollar Amounts in Thousands)

	Company A	Company B	Company S
Earnings after taxes	$ 1,056	$ 858	$ 528
Interest	0	300	800
Earnings after taxes plus interest	1,056	1,158	1,328
Assumed multiplier for common	11.6×	11.6×	11.6×
Value of company	$12,250	$12,953	$14,125

In accordance with the assumptions, the company value increases as the bond component rises, because of the tax savings.

A More Realistic Market Reaction

Table 33.3 presents the valuation picture more realistically in terms of the market's probable reaction to the capital structures of the three companies. Company B is considered to have an appropriate amount of debt in its capital structure. The debt is 30 percent of total capital, and interest coverage before taxes is 5.3 times. Both are within the upper limit of conservative borrowing for a typical industrial concern. For such a company, the advantage to the equity investor of the conservative leverage with its tax savings should result in the multiplier for earnings being an edge above that for a similar company without bonds (Company A).

Using a multiplier of 11.6 times for Company A and 12.0 times for Company B and carrying the debt at par produces a total value of $12,250,000 for A and $13,296,000 for B. The company with a moderate debt proportion has a value advantage of 8.5 percent over debt-free Company A.

Table 33.3. Computation of the Effects of Capital Structure
More Realistic Market Prices for Bonds and Stock Issues
(Dollar Amounts in Thousands)

	Company A	Company B	Company S
Assumed price of bonds		100	70
Resultant value of bond issue		3,000	5,600
Assumed multiplier of common stock	11.6×	12.0×	6.0×
Resultant value of stock issue	12,250	10.296	3,168
Market value of company	$12,250	$13,296	$8,768

Reason for the Higher Multiple. The initial reaction to the higher multiple for Company B may be suspicion. One effect of leverage is greater variability of earnings—to which the market is known to be averse. Considered alone, an increase in variability should result in a reduction in the multiple. However, the more important effect of leverage, properly applied, is an increase in the return on equity. Company A earned $1,056,000 on equity capital of $10 million, or 10.6 percent. Company B earned $858,000 on $7 million, or 12.3 percent. Company B can reinvest retained earnings at the higher rate if it maintains its leverage through small additional borrowings each year. This means that B can grow faster than A at a given payout ratio or can pay higher dividends at the same growth rate. The effect of reinvestment rates on investment value was discussed in Chapter 29.

Other Important Considerations. It is understood, of course, that the terms of the borrowing, including the interest rate, are the major factors in determining the advantage of financial leverage. With respect to making adjustments in the multiple, where debt (and/or preferred stock) is conservative and earnings are stable, the security analyst should adjust the earnings or dividend multiplier upward only slightly. In these instances, senior securities can virtually be disregarded in selecting the capitalization rate. Finally, the implications for corporate financial policy are discussed later in this chapter—usually stockholders will be better off if the company has a moderate amount of debt than if it has none.

Company S: A Case of Excessive Debt. Let us now consider Company S which was taken as an extreme case. Company S clearly has a speculative capital structure, with consequent instability and even possible insolvency. Since the interest payment is covered by a narrow margin (only 2 times before taxes), the issue is obviously unsuitable for conservative investment. For this reason the bond issue would normally sell below par, and the common stock would sell at a relatively low multiplier of its average or current earnings. One of the effects of a highly leveraged capital structure is to make the market value of the company largely unpredictable. In a favorable financial climate, Company S might be valued at a premium above the $10 million invested, but when sentiment is adverse, or even indifferent, it might just as easily sell at a discount from book value. At such times the hazards created by the excessive bond component could more than offset the impressive financial leverage and tax savings. Hence the assumption made in Table 33.2—that Company S will sell at the same multiple of total earnings as the other two companies—has no sound basis. The oversimplifications for Company S were merely for purposes of demonstration and clearly are not realistic.

Avoidance of Formal Valuations of Speculative Companies.   The analyst will find it exceedingly difficult to select an appropriate multiple for Company S's projected earnings and dividends for purposes of valuation. Our selection of 6 times in Table 33.3 is based on the arbitrary assumption that these earnings are entitled to a multiple about one-half of those of Company A. The capital structure itself throws Company S into the speculative category, just as uncertainties about the future of the business would for other industrial concerns. As we have stated before, the analyst should avoid placing major reliance on formal valuations of essentially speculative enterprises.

In a speculative market, investors will pay more attention to Company S's high return on equity and the implied growth prospects than to the high risk, and Company S's multiplier could exceed those of Companies A and B.

Capital Structures and Actual Earnings Multiples

Our position equates with the conclusions drawn as to the desirability of Company B—or a conservatively leveraged type of capital structure. Let us now examine the actual common-stock equity-to-total capital ratios and earnings multipliers for electric companies and debt-to-total capital ratios and earnings multipliers for other selected industries to determine what support or rejection of our view may be found.

Operating Electric Company Data

Although they may differ considerably, operating electric companies present enough homogeneity when studied in quantity to suggest that if actual capital structures have an appreciable effect on actual multipliers, the data should support our thesis. Table 33.4 summarizes the figures for 1984 on 102 electric utilities.[6]

Common-stock ratios of the 102 companies are strongly concentrated in the 36 to 47 percent range. Within this large modal group, using the median as an appropriate measure, the P/E ratio declines by only one multiple—from 6.6 times to 5.6 times—as the common-stock equity proportion of the capital structure drops from 45.5 percent to 37.5

---

[6]Compiled from *The Value Line Investment Survey*, Value Line, Inc.: January 23, 1987, pp. 701—749; March 6, 1987, pp. 1715—1733; March 27, 1987, pp. 175—210. After 1984, there were a rash of completions of nuclear power plants which caused severe rate problems, resulting in major diversification moves by a number of utilities. Consequently there is now far less industrial homogeneity.

Table 33.4. Capital Structures and Earnings Multipliers for One
Hundred and Two Electric Utility Companies

	Price-earnings ratios			Number of
Stock equity ratios	High	Low	Median	companies
Under 36 percent	8.7×	4.5×	5.0×	8
36–39 percent	9.4	2.2	5.6	27
40–43 percent	12.4	2.0	6.0	32
44–47 percent	8.4	5.6	6.6	26
48 percent and above	11.1	4.7	6.7	9

percent (midpoints of class intervals). This corroborates our earlier
suggestion that for those companies with conservative capital structures,
analysts should make very modest, if any, adjustment in the multiplier
for the debt factor.

Industry Data

Table 33.5 sets forth the average percentage that long-term debt
constituted of total capital over the 1982–1985 span and the average
price-earnings ratio for each of 25 major U.S. industries.[7] (The debt
ratios are based only on long-term debt as set forth on company balance
sheets and do not include short-term debt and off-balance-sheet financing.) The industries are ranked by P/E ratios. Two facts stand out: First,
there is no close relationship between capital structure proportions and
the P/E ratios of the individual industries. Second, the use of long-term
debt is modest; in only 3 instances did it exceed 35 percent of total
capital. For 5 industries it was less than 15 percent. The average for the
25 industries is 24.3 percent.

If, instead of taking the ratio of long-term debt to the book value of
total capital, we used the market value of the common stock, the debt
ratios of most major industrial enterprises would be lower. For example,
using the S&P 400 industrial stock index as representative of the major
industrial companies covered in the Value Line industries, the
1982–1985 average price-to-book value ratio was 143 percent. On this
basis the foregoing debt ratio of 24.3 percent would drop to 17.0
percent. It would therefore appear that, using market value, many large
companies, say three-fourths, have a debt ratio of less than 20 percent.

[7]Data compiled from Value Line, Inc., *Value Line Investment Survey*: January 2, 1987,
p. 334; January 9, 1987, pp. 401, 446, 500; January 16, 1987, p. 551; January 23, 1987, p.
812; January 30, 1987, pp. 851, 912, 954, 974; Febrary 6, 1987, pp. 1001, 1027, 1078,
1118; February 13, 1987, pp. 1240, 1250; February 27, 1987, p. 1451; March 6, 1987, pp.
1621, 1632; March 13, 1987, p. 1829; March 27, 1987, pp. 113, 127, 138, 147, 211.

Table 33.5. Comparison of Debt–Total
Capital Ratios and Earnings Multipliers, of
Twenty-Five Industries—1982–1985 Averages
(Ranked by Multipliers)

Industries	Long-term debt as % of total capital	Price-earnings ratio
Electronics	19.6	20.7×
Precision instruments	12.0	17.9
Petroleum producing	51.3	17.5
Home appliances	17.3	16.1
Medical supplies	21.0	15.1
Building	31.4	13.7
Auto parts (replacement)	17.5	13.6
Computer and peripherals	14.5	13.4
Chemical (specialty)	21.3	12.3
Packaging and containers	29.2	12.3
Drugs	11.8	12.2
Office equipment and supplies	21.8	12.0
Chemical (basic)	30.1	11.7
Natural gas (diversified)	46.4	11.7
Electronic equipment	10.0	11.0
Retail stores	39.4	11.0
Toiletries, cosmetics	24.2	10.9
Furniture, home furnishings	16.1	10.7
Household products	19.2	10.7
Tire and rubber	25.7	10.3
Textile	26.7	10.0
Food processing	25.1	9.9
Aerospace, defense	14.6	9.5
Distilling, tobacco	32.7	8.4
Petroleum (integrated)	29.0	6.7

Our conclusion from these data is that for the bulk of common-stock issues the actual debt ratios do not have a noticeable effect on the earnings multipliers, because for most industries (1) the debt ratio is well within conservative limits and (2) the large majority of companies have capital structures that fall within a comparatively narrow band which reflects the current financial standards for that industry. The difference between the lower and upper limits of these ranges is not large enough to affect the multiplier to any substantial degree. Moreover, its minor influence is typically offset by the powerful factor of the expected growth rate.

Theory and Actual Multipliers—
Conclusion

The findings of these studies of actual experience do not seriously oppose our thesis that companies with moderate debt are likely to have a larger enterprise value than are the same type of company without debt. This would certainly be true if the common-stock multipliers for moderate-debt companies are generally no lower than those of lower-debt or no-debt companies. Most of the available data indicate just such a condition. These findings confirm our recommendation to the analyst that, within a reasonable range of sound indebtedness, little or no adjustment of the earnings multipliers is needed for variations in the debt ratio.

Corporate Capitalization Policy

The foregoing discussion leads naturally from the field of arithmetical calculations and common-stock appraisals into that of corporate policy. Our conclusions that Company B will have a larger enterprise value than Company A, *merely because its capital structure is more suitable,* suggests that the stockholders of Company A would be better off if that concern were capitalized with 30 percent in bonds instead of having only common stock outstanding. Many corporate managements and experienced investors may disagree with this conclusion. It has been traditional to regard corporate debt as something inherently unfavorable and to view a "clean balance sheet"—that is, an all common-stock capitalization—as a praiseworthy achievement by management.

In Defense of Debt

That excessive debt is damaging needs no argument, and the history of the railroads points this up only too well. But it would be naive to assume, from such examples, that all corporate debt is bad and to be avoided. If that were so, the only companies that would deserve good credit would be those that never borrowed. Furthermore, how would it be possible to identify *conservative* investment with bond investment—as is done by life insurance companies, savings banks, and trust funds—if the very contraction of a bonded debt meant that the company had taken a dangerous and unwise step? Obviously, the objection to debt capital per se is more of a cliché than a serious principle of corporate finance.

In our view the question whether corporate borrowing is desirable or undesirable is to be decided not as a matter of general principle but by reference to the circumstances of the case. For some companies owing more than a nominal amount is dangerous, and not enough money could be soundly borrowed to make the transaction worthwhile. For most public utility companies, substantial debt is warranted by the inherent stability of their operations, and the gain to the stockholders from the use of low-cost money (after tax saving) is essential to make their own investment profitable. It is customary to consider a representative utility structure as consisting of about 45 to 50 percent debt, 10 percent preferred stock, and 40 to 45 percent common stock and surplus.

In the case of nonutility enterprises, the soundness of the debt structure cannot be judged by reference to the book value of the stock equity, since there is no assurance that earnings will be commensurate with the book investment. (The railroads appear to offer the opposite and melancholy assurance that earnings will *not* support the asset values.) Thus the primary criterion of sound borrowing is not necessarily the balance sheet but may be primarily the income account over a number of past years and a business-like appraisal of the hazards of the future.

Principle of the Optimal Capital Structure

The criteria developed in Part 3 for sound bond selection may be taken also as criteria of sound bond financing by corporations. In most enterprises a bond component no more than—and not too far below—the amount that careful financial institutions would be ready to lend, at the going rate for sound risks, would probably be in the interest of the owners and would make for what may be called an *optimal capital structure*. The bond component for industrial concerns might typically be set at about 30 percent of total capital.

When interest rates are high, the effect of a given amount of leverage on earnings variability is high. At some point the cost of incurring debt must exceed the pretax return on capital, which would mean that issuing new debt would have a negative effect on return on equity. At times, equity capital is cheaper than senior securities and should be used in place of them. Clearly, the optimal capital structure changes with movements in the markets and alterations in the tax law.

Factors Favoring a Bond Component

As stated above, an industrial company of good size and reasonable earnings stability should have a bond component of conservative but appreciable size, because the favorable income tax status of the bond interest charge effectively reduces the cost of bond money by 34 percent in most instances and brings its net cost well below that of common-stock capital. In our Company B example, the $300,000 of earnings before taxes was worth $3 million on a bond basis, whereas the remaining $1.3 million of net before taxes was worth only $9,953,000 on a stock basis (Table 33.1). This is a differential of 1.3 to 1 in favor of bond money.[8]

In practice, one area for applying the principle of an optimal capital structure is companies with a good financial position, including little or no debt, and with insufficient return on capital. Their common stocks are likely to sell persistently at market prices below book value. For such companies, acquisition of other enterprises with significant earning power, through issuance of senior securities, is very likely to prove of real benefit to the stockholders. Alternatively, companies may borrow to repurchase stock to create a better balanced capital structure.

[8] At this writing, stocks sell at a P/E ratio of 16× which is an earnings yield of 6.25 percent. New issue bonds yield about 8.75 percent, or cost the company 5.8 percent after taxes. Therefore the cost of debt financing is currently only slightly below that of common-stock equity financing.

34

The Asset Value Factor in Common-Stock Valuation

Chapter 19 gave techniques for calculating net asset value per share and certain related per-share calculations. Chapter 34 considers the significance of such calculations in valuing and selecting common stocks.

Renewed Focus on Asset Values

In 1962 we stated: "The basic fact is that—except in certain limited parts of the common stock universe—asset values are virtually ignored in the stock market." Since then, there has been a modest shift toward greater use. The rash of mergers and acquisitions has focused attention on asset values, particularly when a portion of the acquired company may be sold off. Computations of return on total capital (ROTC) and return on equity (ROE) have also caused analysts to examine company assets more closely. Finally, another measure of growth in earnings now being used is the earnings retention rate times ROE. This analytical step leads to an examination of assets. To illustrate, assume a dividend payout rate of 40 percent of earnings, and thus a retention rate of 60 percent, and an ROE of 20 percent. The growth rate of book value is 12 percent ($0.60 \times 0.20 = 0.12$). If ROE remains at 20 percent, earnings will also grow at 12 percent.

Asset values have long been recognized as important in such industries as public utilities, financial companies, forest products, oil and gas, and mining. These industries are briefly discussed at the end of this chapter.

Illustrative Data

We believe that the ratio of price to book value merits increased consideration in the analysis of industrial enterprises. Data on the relationships between market price and book value for 596 large U.S. industrial companies are shown in Table 34.1. Almost 60 percent of the companies had a March 21, 1986 price-to-book value ratio in excess of 200 percent, and 10 percent sold above 500 percent of book.

Table 34.1. Relationship between Market Price and Book Value

Ratio of price-to-book value	Number of companies
50 to 100 percent	45
100 to 200 percent	196
200 to 500 percent	295
500 to 1000 percent	48
Over 1000 percent	12
Total	596

SOURCE: Compiled from "The 1000 Largest U.S. Companies Ranked by Stock-Market Valuation," *Business Week*, Special Issue, April 18, 1986, p. 62.

Table 34.2 compares the average annual price and book value for 1971 and 1985 for 28 out of the 30 issues comprising the Dow-Jones Industrial Average. This compilation indicates the wide range of the price-to-book value ratio within a group of comparable major companies. In 1971 the ratio for Coca-Cola (835 percent) was almost 18 times that for USX (formerly U.S. Steel) (47 percent). In 1985 the range was much less extreme, the ratio for Coca-Cola (332 percent) was 5.5 times that for Texaco (60 percent). The average price-to-book value ratio for the 28 companies declined from 290 percent in 1971 to 164 percent in 1985.

Table 34.2. Price-to-Book Value Ratios for Twenty-Eight DJIA Companies, 1985 and 1971

	Average book value 1985	Average price 1985	Price/book value ratio 1985	Price/book value ratio 1971
Allied Signal	$33.00	$ 40.95	124.1%	99.5%
Alcoa	40.12	35.30	88.0	95.5
American Can	22.80	28.80	126.3	91.7
American Express	21.59	45.45	210.5	460.9
Bethlehem Steel	17.58	16.80	95.6	54.8
Boeing	26.73	44.50	166.5	50.3
Chevron	44.31	35.05	79.1	97.2
Coca-Cola	7.40	24.55	331.8	835.0
duPont	50.84	58.50	115.1	238.8
Eastman Kodak	29.82	47.20	158.3	571.8
Exxon	38.33	50.20	131.0	144.6
General Electric	29.07	64.75	222.7	368.0
General Motors	83.74	75.15	89.7	248.9
Goodyear	31.11	28.55	91.8	156.7
IBM	47.61	138.10	290.1	564.3
International Paper	66.32	51.05	77.0	142.9
McDonald's	15.91	44.20	277.8	757.1
Merck	18.21	57.05	313.3	800.3
MMM	33.94	82.60	243.4	532.0
Philip Morris	18.35	41.80	227.8	276.1
Procter & Gamble	30.96	61.10	197.4	400.2
Sears, Roebuck	30.64	36.00	117.5	342.9
Texaco	56.10	33.65	60.0	139.6
Union Carbide	21.56	18.15	84.2	146.3
United Technologies	30.81	40.50	131.5	83.3
USX	44.58	28.70	64.4	47.0
Westinghouse	21.22	36.10	170.1	202.5
Woolworth	17.57	24.80	141.1	168.0

NOTE: American Telephone and Telegraph and Navistar are excluded due to lack of comparability.

SOURCE: Compiled from Value Line, Inc., *The Value Line Investment Survey*, editions published from January 9, 1987–April 3, 1987.

The Stock Market's Treatment of Net Assets

The Asset Factor in Private Business

The asset factor is a primary consideration in valuing most privately owned businesses. The private owner often has no better measure of the value of the business than book value. Hence, the private owner usually starts with this figure and often ends with it—any adjustment made will be in the direction of adding a tentative increment for goodwill, which is calculated along conservative lines.

Publically Traded Common Stocks

This procedure is not followed for publically traded, marketable common stocks. However, by studying the actual behavior of issues in the market, we can infer some ruling relationships between the valuation of tangible assets and of goodwill. The basic ratios are the opposite of those obtaining in the field of privately owned business. This would necessarily be true if we made the plausible assumption that the market's multipliers for common stocks tend to vary more or less in proportion to the percentage earned on capital, that is, stocks with a high ROE sell at high price-earnings ratios. The arithmetical consequences of this market attitude can be shown in Table 34.3, which is based on certain oversimplified assumptions.

The conditions represented by Table 34.3 occur in a market in which earning 10 percent on equity is just enough for a stock to sell at book value. Stocks earning more than that are given a goodwill premium by the market—their market prices reflect intangible values not shown in the tangible equity. The most significant factor is the negative goodwill (attitude of potential investors rather than potential customers toward the enterprise) created by the low profitability of Company C. In other words, companies earning a low return on invested capital tend to sell at a discount from asset value.

Table 34.3. Hypothetical Influence of Book Value on Stock Prices

	Company A	Company B	Company C
Tangible equity per share	$100	$100	$100
Rate earned on equity	10%	14%	8%
Assumed multiplier of earnings	10×	13×	8×
Resultant market price	100	182	64
Resultant goodwill component	0	82	−36
Earnings attributable to			
Tangible assets @ 10 percent	$ 10	$ 10	$ 10
Goodwill @ plus or minus 5 percent	0	+4	−2
Total earnings	$ 10	$ 14	$ 8

Emphasis on Profitabililty or Future Growth. The reader may object that the calculation, which derives the multiplier exclusively from the rate earned on capital, is inconsistent with our repeated statements that stock market multipliers are governed mainly by the assumed rate of future growth. The contradiction is only apparent, however, because high profitability and good growth tend to go together.

Assets as a Negative Factor in Value.　A more serious objection to our type of calculation is that it makes a large asset investment less valuable than a small asset investment—and thus, in a sense, turns assets into liabilities. For if Company C had an equity of $57 per share instead of $100, it would earn 14 percent on capital, be entitled to Company B's multiplier of 13, and thus sell at $104 per share instead of $64. Does this mean that the additional $43 per share of Company C's assets actually functions as a negative factor, or virtual liability, of no less than $40? If so, could not Company C benefit its stockholders by marking down its assets and, by a stroke of the pen, increase substantially its profitability and add 47 percent to its market price?

This is perhaps an intriguing idea, but usually not practical.[1] Security analysts tend not to be led astray by such blatant financial juggling. Furthermore, as already explained, the test of profitability rests on the comparative margin of profit on sales as well as on the indicated rate of return on capital.

Small Company Initial Public Offerings.　In spite of theoretical objections to the market's ignoring of asset values, analysts may accept this attitude but should remain alert to situations in which asset values do play a role of some significance in determining market price. One set of harmful results is seen in the flotation of new common stocks of relatively small companies—particularly high-technology enterprises. Here the discrepancy between private business valuations and stock market valuations produces its most spectacular and ominous results.

In the distant past the main dividing line between shares deemed eligible and ineligible for initial distribution to the public was the size of the enterprise. Among the millions of small businesses in operation, it was never difficult to find a considerable number which had high ROE and good growth over several past years. These favorable results are more readily attainable by a small business with an investment perhaps under $1 million than by large enterprises with a formidable amount of capital to figure earnings against. Responsible investment banking houses disqualified small companies from public distribution because of special hazards growing out of their limited size. Beginning in the 1960s a flood of little companies began to inundate the market. For most of them the

---

[1] Moves of this kind were actually made in the 1930s by some companies which marked down their plant values to $1. Their chief purpose, however, was to relieve the income account of depreciation charges.

high returns on capital plus apparently impressive growth rates (generally for only a few recent years) permitted an offering price equal to several times the net equity and a subsequent market price well above that.

The purchase of such issues at a price several times their book value must carry substantial risk for the buyers as a whole, and these risks are related directly to the asset situation. In past periods of similar offerings—always in the higher ranges of bull markets—the invariable sequel was for most of these unseasoned issues to fall below their asset values. They were then, belatedly, recognized as unsuitable for public ownership because of their inadequate size, and their shares found buyers in the market only on a bargain basis. This meant that, instead of valuing them more generously than from a privately owned ("Main Street") viewpoint, Wall Street now considered them to be worth a good deal less to their buyers than their value to a private owner.

Asset-Value Factor in Larger Companies. High ratios of market price to book value occur, of course, in major prosperous companies as well as in the small concerns discussed above. It would be difficult to develop from experience any proof that a high price-to-book ratio in the case of a leading company will per se make its purchase hazardous and unwise. The danger, if any, would seem to be associated more clearly with a very high multiplier of current or average earnings—that is, with an over-generous discounting of future prospects. By the nature of the market's valuation process, the two ratios tend to go together.

Quantitative Adjustments
for Asset Values

There are plausible reasons for giving separate weight to the asset factor in all analysts' valuations and thus for penalizing the intrinsic value calculation when value based on other factors reaches a high multiple of net worth. One reason is that asset values are never ignored in legal valuations, which are made for a variety of purposes. Asset values are sometimes given as much as 25 percent weight. The assets increase the potential of companies which sell at a discount from net worth and which for that very reason are often candidates for merger or sale. The opposite effect may be visibly produced for "high-premium" companies with high returns on capital. Economists believe that high returns on capital attract competition, which ultimately forces down the rate of profit. Since high market multipliers of book value and of earnings require many years of growth and superior profitability for their vindication, this economic "law" may prove more significant than short-term prospects would suggest.

High-Premium Companies—Small Asset Values. We have always hesitated to lay down any hard and fast rule for evaluating the asset factor in the case of premium companies. In earlier editions we suggested, quite tentatively, that analysts might deduct one-quarter of the amount by which the earning power valuation exceeded twice the asset value. This formula imposed no penalty on an asset deficiency up to 50 percent of the basic appraisal. To use an extreme illustration, consider a company assigned a 20 percent growth rate for the next four to seven years for which we have posited our maximum recommended multiplier of 18 times current profits. Such a concern might easily be earning 20 percent on its invested capital, and hence our indicated value would be 3.6 times its net worth. If analysts then apply the asset-value "deflator" suggested in this paragraph, they would take off about one-ninth of the earning power valuation, reducing the multiplier to 16.

Very few practicing analysts would favor any such reduction. A premium over asset value is implicit in the whole growth-stock concept. The reader must decide whether to accept all, or part, or none of our suggestion. At bottom the issue is between conservatism and optimism.

Valuations Equal to Asset Value. In only a minority of cases will the standard methods of appraisal, based mainly on expected earnings and dividends, produce a value approximating stated book value. If a valuation range is used, the wider the range, the greater the chance, of course, that the asset value will fall within it. In such cases the appraiser may take the net worth itself as a convenient and somehow satisfying measure of "best" value. In so doing, analysts will be in harmony with the practice often followed in formal or legal valuations and will also associate themselves with the time-honored private, or "Main Street," point of view. Such a value would be far below the historical "Wall Street" value, since the price-to-book ratio has averaged nearly 1½ times over the past 100 years.

Sub-Asset Common Stocks. In schematic opposition to the many companies selling well above asset value is the inglorious array of those that cannot earn enough to carry their book value in the market. The reasons for these inadequate earnings are various. They may be inherent in the industry, such as the substantial losses suffered by the integrated steel industry in the 1982–1985 period. One study of the industry stated that "Low demand for steel and steel products, excess worldwide capacity,

Table 34.4. Comparative Ratios for Diversified Chemical Companies, 1983–1985

| | Per-share figures | | | Ratios | | |
| | Sales | | Book | Average | Price/ book | Earnings/ book | Price/ |
Company	($ million)	Earnings	value	price	value	value	earnings
MMM	7530.3	5.99	$33.14	81	244%	18.1%	13.5
Millipore Corporation	330.6	.94	7.90	17	215	11.9	18.1
Dexter Corporation	606.6	1.19	8.69	15	173	13.7	12.6
American Cyanamid	3642.8	3.47	34.01	49	144	10.2	14.1
Ethyl Corporation	1655.8	.87	5.71	8	140	15.2	9.2
First Mississippi	249.1	.79	8.26	11	133	9.6	13.9
Air Products	1733.0	2.12	18.26	24	131	11.6	11.3
Cabot Corporation	1572.7	2.31	21.03	26	124	11.0	11.3
International Minerals	1540.7	3.49	38.82	40	103	9.0	11.5
W. R. Grace	6046.8	2.83	44.42	43	97	6.4	15.2
National Distillers	2374.3	1.75	30.13	28	93	5.8	16.0

SOURCE: Sales and per-share figures based on Value Line's annual figures; ratios based upon these three-year averages. Earnings and book value are adjusted for preferred stock. *The Value Line Investment Survey*, December 12, 1986, p. 1886.

noncompetitive labor costs, antiquated plant and equipment, and ruinous pricing have contributed to making the last four years steel's worst in memory."[2]

The rate of return on equity often varies widely among companies in the same industry, producing correspondingly diverse relationships between price and asset value. To illustrate this point, Table 34.4 presents a condensed comparative analysis of 11 diversified chemical companies. The companies are ranked in descending order of the 1983–1985 average price-to-book value ratio. Note that a good general correlation exists between the ROE and the ratio of price-to-book value. The price-earnings ratio does not coincide with profitability to the same extent as price-to-book value, as we suggested would be a logical expectation. In some instances the P/E ratio reflects the market's belief that normal earning power is well above or below the three-year average. There is no correlation between the size of these companies and their performance.

Our concern is whether the possession of net assets is a factor for analysts to consider apart from the inadequate earnings on these assets. Clearly, in the extreme case the assets must be given some consideration. A company with no earnings, and even with no definite prospect of earnings, will not sell for zero in the market. For the same reason a truly marginal company, with very small earning power, will usually sell

[2] Value Line, Inc., *The Value Line Investment Survey*, May 23, 1986, p. 140.

at a large multiplier of its microscopic earnings—the Molodovsky effect.[3] In such cases the investor is paying for the assets which are expected in some way to produce a satisfactory result for the buyer who gets them at a low fraction of their book value—either by being made more productive, or by bulk sale to, or merger with, some other enterprise, or—very rarely indeed—by piecemeal liquidation.

The sale or merger of a "subasset" company is a far from negligible possibility. The number of such transactions has greatly increased in recent years. The acquiring enterprise is able to obtain tangible assets at well below their reproduction cost less depreciation, plus a certain added volume of sales, plus at least some worthwhile personnel. One might say that the longer and the farther a company sells below its net worth, the greater the pressure is on management from various sources to improve its operating results or to sell or merge. In a merger the net assets are bound to receive serious consideration in arriving at the terms of the deal.

It would be logical, therefore, to suggest to analysts that they assign some plus value for an appreciable excess of net assets above the valuation based on earnings and dividends. We have not done so in the past because of conservatism and the absence of clear-cut statistical evidence, but the growth of merger and acquisition activity makes the case for a quantitative recognition of excess assets somewhat stronger than before. We might suggest, again tentatively, a formula somewhat parallel to that given for the opposite situation—premium companies. That is, analysts give weight to ordinary net worth only when it exceeds 150 percent of the earning power value. They might arbitrarily add one-third of the amount by which two-thirds of net worth exceeds the earning-power appraisal. For example, say a company has estimated earning power of $3 and book value of $100 per share, and the earnings and dividends warrant a value of $30. If analysts follow this formula they would add one-third of the difference between $67 and $30, making the final valuation $42. However, such an adjustment should not be made if the liquidating value of the assets is thought to be much below their carrying value. Of course, the investor seeks to buy the stock well below the valuation.

Net Current Asset Value

Those cases in which the market price or the computed value based on earnings and dividends is less than the net current assets applicable to the common stock are more clear-cut. (The reader will recall that in this

---

[3] See the discussion in Chapter 20 of how the intangibles influence the tangible record.

computation we deduct all obligations and preferred stock from the working capital to determine the balance for the common.) Experience teaches that the purchase of a diversified group of companies on this bargain basis is almost certain to be profitable within a reasonable period. One reason for calling such purchases "bargain" issues is that usually net current asset value may be considered a conservative measure of liquidating value. As a practical matter most such companies could be disposed of for not less than their working capital, if that capital is conservatively stated. It is a general rule that at least enough can be realized for the plant account and the miscellaneous assets to offset any shrinkage sustained in the liquidation process. (This rule would nearly always apply to a negotiated sale of the business to some reasonably interested buyer.) By using the working-capital value as the equivalent of "minimum liquidating value," we can now discuss the relationship between the price of a stock and the realizable value of the business.

The historical development of this relationship provides perspective. Before the 1920s, common stocks selling under current asset value were practically unknown. During the twenties, when prime emphasis was placed on prospects, to the exclusion of other factors, a few issues in *depressed* industries sold below their working capital. In the Great Depression of the early 1930s, this phenomenon became widespread. Our computations show that about 40 percent of all industrial companies on the New York Stock Exchange were quoted at some time in 1932 at less than their net current assets. Many issues actually sold for less than their net cash assets alone. Writing about this situation in 1932, Benjamin Graham stated that the market prices as a whole seemed to indicate that U.S. business was "worth more dead than alive."[4] It seemed evident that the market had carried its pessimism much too far—to compensate, no doubt, for its reckless optimism of the 1920s.

Ratio of Sub-Current-Asset Stocks a Key to Market Levels

At the top of the ensuing bull market, in 1937, this situation had all but disappeared, but, in the following recession about 20 percent of all industrials sold on a "sub-current-asset" basis. For a number of years thereafter the variations in the number of such issues on the New York Stock Exchange could have been taken as a fairly dependable guide to the technical position of the stock market. When the number was large,

---

[4] See three articles by Benjamin Graham on this subject, in *Forbes Magazine* on June 1, 1932, June 13, 1932, and July 1, 1932.

the market had reached a buying range; when it was very small, the market was dangerously high.

For example, in May 1946 it was difficult to find any sub-current-asset issues. In 1947–1950, however, we witnessed a new and more extraordinary phase of this phenomenon. Sustained high earnings built up working capital for many companies at a rapid rate, but the prevailingly cautious attitude toward the future prevented stock prices from moving up in the same proportion. The result was not only that many issues persistently sold in those years at less than their working capital, but, more strangely, that this relationship was largely due to the very fact that the companies had been showing such large earnings. In earlier years a low price in relation to current assets almost always indicated unsatisfactory current earnings. But between 1947 and 1950, if it reflected anything other than the market's heedlessness, it must have indicated only a distrust of the future in the face of a highly satisfactory current performance.

A characteristic of depressed markets is an abundance of stocks which can be purchased for less than their working capital. The bear markets of 1974 and 1982 are cases in point. In those years there was no difficulty in finding profitable companies with small likelihood of failure which could be bought for less than working capital. Even in average markets a diversified portfolio can be constructed. As this is written, in early 1987 with the Dow at 2400, few such stocks can be found. From the vantage (or disadvantage) point of our experience we are inclined to regard the drying up of these bargain opportunities as an indication that the general market has reached a hazardous level. Based on their earning power, there are always some companies which are worth less than their book value, and when their book value is largely made up of working capital they are worth less than working capital—on a going concern basis. A stock market that is so priced that no viable companies are found at prices below working capital is probably overpriced across the board. Of course, the market may stay overpriced for years based on "new era" thinking.

Cash Assets—Special Factor in Valuation

Some companies sell at too low a price because their cash assets are too large. This paradoxical statement can be true because cash assets bring in no earnings—or very little. Market price depends chiefly on earnings. A company with nothing but cash in the bank cannot be earning enough to support a market price equal to its cash-asset value. It has been by no means unusual to find companies so rich in cash that they are necessarily poor in earning power as related to book value.

Tax Aspect of Sub-Asset Situations

The reader may reflect on the fact that the 34 percent partnership held by the U.S. Treasury in the profits of earning companies carries with it an equivalent 34 percent interest in most types of losses. Operating losses are carried backward against prior years' profits or forward against later years' profits. Under certain conditions, they can be availed of by a profitable company which takes over another with tax losses to its "credit." In somewhat the same way a decline of enterprise value to a figure well below its net worth (presumably its tax base) may possibly be recouped to the extent of one-third. This would be done by the realization of the indicated loss under circumstances which permit it to be offset against equivalent operating profits of the same or another company. The purpose of this cryptic utterance is to indicate that somewhat the same kind of tax advantages, which have recently been stressed so much in the case of concerns "blessed" with carry-forward losses, may exist with respect to companies valued in the market at well below their asset values, even though operating losses are absent. Sale of the assets at the price indicated by the stock price would create losses that might be carried back or forward.

Stockholder-Management Problems

In quite a number of instances, companies selling below working capital have had disappointing records. Either they have lost money or they have earned less than enough to justify a price equal to the working-capital figure. Under such conditions the current assets alone could not establish investment value in excess of the market price. They are not necessarily "bargain issues," but these issues supply an interesting problem of another sort. Why should the stockholders permit matters to continue on so unsatisfactory a basis? This issue will be discussed in Chapter 36.

Adjustment for Net Current Assets

We have suggested an arbitrary reduction of the earning power value when it exceeds twice the asset value. A similar adjustment in the opposite direction may properly be made when the net-current-asset value alone exceeds the earning power value. Our suggestion is that one-half of such excess be added to the earning power value to give the final appraisal figure.

Industries Where Asset Values Are Important

Public Utilities

The chief characteristics of *public utilities* are their regulated rate environment and asset-oriented rate base as the determinants of earnings. The rate base usually includes virtually all balance sheet assets, although some may be disallowed as "imprudently incurred costs." Some assets in rate bases are no more than bookkeeping entries, such as the "allowance for equity funds used during construction," and some of the earnings reported are the same fluff. Public utilities do not sell at book value because "allowed rates" of return on the rate base are not as high as market rates, nor are the achieved rates equal to the allowed rates.

Financial Companies

In most groups of *financial* enterprises, the asset value factor has exerted a greater influence than in industrial companies. Since their assets are mainly cash, investments, and receivables, their stated net worth is taken to be fairly representative of their actual liquidating value—subject to certain adjustments, such as allowance for an equity in unearned premiums of insurance companies. The closest relation to asset value is, of course, open-end investment funds. This is the necessary consequence of their fixed policy of issuing and redeeming shares at about current liquidating value. The closed-end companies, which do not redeem shares on demand, are subject to significant variations between asset value and price. Yet the range tends to be much narrower than for industrial companies.

Until recent years, the price-asset ratios for banks and property and casualty insurance companies had a tendency to bunch within a fairly narrow area, which varied with the times. Somewhat surprisingly, the modal figure stayed below 100 percent for a long period—which called into question the basic profitability of these important enterprises. It was quite rare to find issues selling at more than twice or less than half of asset values. A greater scattering of ratios was discernible among the various types of finance companies. Also, a goodly number of life insurance stocks—as distinct from the casualty companies—have sold at many times their stated asset values.

The valuation of life insurance companies is somewhat specialized, chiefly because of actuarial complexities. It has become customary in this field to ascribe a definite value to the insurance in force—at so much per

$1000 of face value—the rate varying between the different forms of policy. These policy values are included with the tangible assets in figuring the *adjusted book value* of the shares, and the increase in the policy values for a given year is added, by some analysts, to the reported earnings to give *adjusted earnings* for the year.

The latter treatment is fundamentally unsound. Increases in capital values can be presented in the guise of capitalizable earnings in many ways. Investors must guard against them, and analysts must oppose them.

Natural Resources Companies

Primary producers of raw materials usually own substantial reserves which can be valued on the basis of their quantities, locations, and grades, for example, those producing metals, oil and gas, lumber, sulphur, and many other minerals. Analyses of such enterprises will often assign a monetary value to their developed reserves and use this value as at least one of the tests of the attractiveness of the shares at current market. We have seen this method applied most often among the oil and gas companies and also fairly regularly for timber companies with large forest reserves. For the latter, a value per thousand board feet of standing timber owned or controlled may be used. For oil and gas companies, the standardized measure of discounted future cash flows (discussed in Chapter 21) suitably adjusted for political risk, or other appraisals of oil and gas reserves, play a role in longer term earnings projections. In general, the value of reserves is given more attention in oil and gas stock prices than in the prices of industrial stocks. The value of reserves in undeveloped acreage is usually not computed separately from their book cost, but it can exert a determining influence on the market price ultimately reached by the shares.

Hidden Values of Small Companies

In the early 1960s a rather paradoxical situation developed in the oil and gas group. Many small companies sold out to larger ones. The price netted by the shareholders was usually quite high in relation to their earnings and sometimes several times the market price ruling before the negotiations. In effect, all these smaller companies proved to have a realizable value for their owners considerably higher than that paid in the market for either the comparable earnings or the comparable stated reserves of the larger and presumably stronger units. Such transactions are not possible under the efficient market hypothesis.

Another example of the hidden values of small companies is found in the acquisition of small ("country") banks at prices more than twice book value by large banks seeking to enter new markets. Country banks not considered to be acquisition targets continue to sell around book value.

35

Contingent Claims: Convertibles, Warrants, and Options

Investor Experience with Convertibles

Before addressing the analysis and valuation of convertible bonds and preferred stocks, it is useful to reflect briefly on the investors' experience over many years with this type of security.

A Record of Disappointment

No comprehensive historical study has been made of bonds and preferred stocks with conversion features, but none is really needed to learn from experience. On a day in late January 1987, for example, *The Wall Street Journal* reported transactions in the convertible bonds of 169 issuers listed on the New York Stock Exchange and the American Stock Exchange. Substantially all of them were originally purchased at 100 by investors who were prepared to give up a material fraction of current income return in exchange for a call on the issuer's common stock. How had these investors fared after 3½ years of a sustained bull market in both bonds and stocks? Did most convertible bonds sell above 110 to afford at least some modest appreciation as an offset to the below-market interest rate? The dismal answer is in the negative. Only one-third of the issues were selling above 110 (57 out of 169). Another 47 were selling between 100 and 110, but 65 were quoted below par, and of these losers 16 showed depreciation of more than one-third in price.

There is, of course, a bias in this sample, since a number of winners had been eliminated by redemption and profitable conversion into equity. Nevertheless, 112 distinctly unprofitable investments after such a protracted advance in stock prices is a sobering record for the investor to study. Almost two losers for each winner among the survivors in a very favorable capital market is enough to daunt even the most confident analyst. The overall performance record of convertibles has been so inferior over such long periods that one writer was moved to title an article on convertible preferred stocks "The Triumph of Hope over Experience."[1]

With a fixed-income "floor" to provide downside protection and current income while the conversion feature offers participation in stock appreciation, convertibles appear to offer the best of both worlds: opportunities for gain with limited exposure to loss. The old warning comes to mind: "If a security offering sounds too good to be true, it probably isn't." Convertibles sound so attractive that investors on average pay much too high prices for issues of good quality. They also purchase marginal offerings which should be rejected on grounds of inadequate safety because the floor cannot stand shocks of adversity. In the latter cases, promising future growth proves an inadequate substitute for a margin of safety in the foundation for the floor.

The Timing Problem

The volume of convertible security offerings tends to expand at its most rapid rate during a protracted period of rising stock prices and optimistic expectations. The absence of credit restraint leading to favorable interest rates and borrowing terms is the other positive stimulus to new convertible financing volume.

Example. With earnings, dividends, and share prices at the highest levels in 15 years, USX (then U.S. Steel) came to market in mid-1976 with a large issue of 5¾ percent subordinated debentures due in 2001. With the stock selling in the low 50s, the debentures were made convertible at 62¾, a price last seen in 1959. After the four-year stock decline following the offering, highs from 1981 to 1986 did not reach 36. Investors, entranced by a view of the recent past, paid a substantial premium over the investment value of a 5¾ percent USX subordinated debenture for a stock appreciation potential that did not exist.

---

[1] Borrowed from Boswell's *Life of Johnson*—this was the great lexicographer's response to Boswell's inquiry as to his opinion of second marriage.

Many chief financial officers wish that their market timing matched that of USX in 1976, especially if they did not plan to come to market again for a decade or two. When good bond and stock markets coincide, the volume of new convertible offerings expands to meet the favorable environment. The good deal for the borrower is by definition a poor one for the investor. A naive, but not illogical, rule for the buyer might be: Never purchase a new issue at the offering. Exceptions to the rule would be limited to offerings at or near market bottoms accompanied by tight money, that is, when new offerings are least likely to be made.

Short of such a broad rule against new issues as a class is the familiar injunction that there is no such thing as a free lunch. Avoid paying too much for the fixed-income component, for the conversion feature, or for both. These components may, of course, be available at bargain prices in protracted periods of gloom. Inefficient pricing of convertibles makes them, after all, precisely what the analyst is searching for.

The selection of attractive investment opportunities in convertible bonds and preferred stocks, then, starts with the same analysis of the issuer required for any investment decision. The firm's creditworthiness must be ascertained to establish the floor value of the convertible as a straight fixed-income security. The conversion value is based, of course, on the valuation of the common stock relative to the conversion price. It is self-evident that *both* components must be fairly priced relative to value for a successful investment outcome.

Outright purchase of the common stock is the logical and preferable alternative if it is undervalued in the market.[2] Paying a reasonable conversion premium for the floor may be appropriate for capital protection purposes, provided the stability and reliability of that floor are established not too far below the security's price. Periodic review is necessary to determine what is happening to the issue. Have changes in interest rates affected the protective floor? Has the conversion premium become a larger or smaller proportion of the total price? In short, has the mix of debt and equity components been materially altered since the original investment was made?

That success can be achieved over an extended time is indicated by the record of a large ($825 million in assets) mutual fund in convertible security selection. Table 35.1 is Putnam Convertible Income-Growth Trust's record of total returns for periods ended October 31, 1986. The most recent returns, greater than for straight bonds but less than for

---

[2]An exception can be made if (1) the stock is an attractive investment, (2) the convertible security has a sufficiently higher current return to amortize any modest premium over conversion value, and (3) call protection is adequate. Under these conditions, the investor is buying the common stock with the prospect of a higher current return.

Table 35.1. Putnam Convertible Income-Growth Trust's Total Returns
(In Percentages)

	1 year	3 years	5 years	10 years
Putnam Convertible	25	55	138	387
S&P 500	33	69	151	284
Shearson Lehman Government–Corporate Bond Index	20	61	135	176

SOURCE: Putnam Convertible Income-Growth Trust, *Annual Report*, October 31, 1986. Fund returns are after all expenses except sales load.

stocks, represent what might be expected, that is, ranking between bond and stock indexes in both variability and return. Prior to 1981, when the fund was much smaller and exceptional opportunities were available, the fund exceeded expectations based on conventional capital market assumptions.

The fertility of the convertible security field for disciplined security analysis makes it a logical point at which to bring together discussions of fixed-income security selection and common-stock valuation—both of which are essential to avoid the pitfalls which so many investors have experienced.

Warrants

Characteristics

A warrant offering the holder the opportunity (not a requirement) to purchase common stock from a company at a specified price for a specified period can be thought of as a contingent claim: The holder has the right to exercise an option to acquire shares during a future period if the purchase is advantageous. It is a call that can be exercised at any time prior to expiration at a strike price. The elements of value in such a warrant are principally the exercise price, the term to expiration, and the likelihood that the optioned security will sell above the exercise price.

An illustration can be provided from the marketplace. The common stock of Intel Corporation, a leader in the technology of semiconductors and computer memory components, in late 1986 sold at 21½, down from a 1983 high of 46½. An investor wishes to take a long-term position in this technology leader and must choose between outright purchase of 1000 shares at 21½ in the over-the-counter market for a $21,500 investment or purchase of 3500 warrants at 6 net at a cost of $21,000. The warrants entitle the holder to purchase shares from the company at any time in the next eight years and five months to May 15, 1995, at a price of $40 per share.

In about seven weeks of strong markets, Intel advances to 36½, a 68.6 percent increase in price while the warrant rises to 11, an 83.3 percent enhancement. Between the two alternatives, the choice of the warrants proves advantageous as the stock price comes closer to giving the warrant some exercise value. If Intel's shares should return to the 1983 high of 46, the warrant choice would be even better, because the warrant holder would have 3½ times the participation in each point of rise above 40. An unfavorable price trend, one should hasten to add, brings home the full impact of leverage when price moves in the opposite direction.

Our example illustrates the attractive features of a warrant, which can be thought of as a means of economizing on the use of scarce capital. The investor who wants only to invest in the success of Intel as represented by the prospective intrinsic value in excess of $40 per share should be glad to pay a good price for the warrant which provides that contingent claim. The alternative of borrowing to buy shares involves interest costs, possible margin calls, and the requirement of a greater equity in the transaction. These costs can be avoided by the premium paid for the long-term call on Intel stock at 40 in the form of a warrant price.

Warrant Valuation

The valuation of warrants has been the subject of many studies over the years, and from them come some rough rules of thumb that are serviceable, even if not elegant, for the security analyst.[3]

Giguère. The simplest expression for a warrant valuation, developed by Guynemer Giguère, is $W = P^2/4A$, where P is the price of the stock and A is the exercise price of the warrant W. In our December 1986 Intel example, the figures are

$$W = \frac{(21.5)^2}{4 \times 40} = \frac{462.25}{160} = 2.89.$$

The result is a characteristically low value (only 48 percent of the market price of 6) for out-of-the-money warrants. The valuation seven weeks later was

$$W = \frac{(36.25)^2}{4 \times 40} = \frac{1314.06}{160} = 8.21$$

[3] A comparison of several valuation formulas and those used here are well covered in John P. Shelton's two-part article "The Relation of the Price of a Warrant to the Price of Its Associated Stock," *Financial Analysts Journal*, May–June 1967, pp. 134–151 and July–August 1967, pp. 88–100.

The $8.21 is almost 75 percent of the market price of 11. In general, the Giguère valuation parabola produces very low values at which warrants can seldom be purchased in the market.

Kassouf.　A more helpful, and equally simple, valuation formula was developed by Sheen T. Kassouf. Using the same notation, his expression is

$$W = \sqrt{A^2 + P^2} - A$$

For Intel, then, the figures would be

$$W = \sqrt{1600 + 462.50} - 40 = 5.41$$

Since this formula assumes only average volatility, and Intel's beta coefficient is 1.45 (indicating a volatility 45 percent greater than the S&P 500), the warrant at 6 was undervalued by this method.[4] The valuation of 13.98 seven weeks later would suggest that the warrant was an attractive alternative to owning the stock directly.

Shelton.　A formula designed to also account for shorter terms to expiration, dividends on the underlying shares, and listing on a national securities exchange was developed by John P. Shelton.[5] His result for the two dates would be warrant valuations of 8¼ and 13¼.

A Range of Value.　Also of interest would be the valuations if the warrant were at the money, that is, if $A = P$:

Giguère　　10
Kassouf　　16⅝
Shelton　　15⅜

These rough valuations take no account of the capital which would result from the exercise of warrants. The 5.9 million warrants represent 5 percent of the 117 million shares outstanding and if exercised would add 18.5 percent to the 1986 year-end net worth. Another factor not reflected here that would enhance the warrant value is the presumed much higher volatility of Intel shares relative to the market. The obvious

---

[4]This is a material simplification of Kassouf's basic model as presented in his Columbia University doctoral dissertation, "A Theory and Econometrics Model for Common Stock Purchase Warrants," New York, 1965.

[5]Shelton, "Price of a Warrant," *Financial Analysts Journal*, July–August, 1967, pp. 90–99.

difficulty in seeking to express this factor in the valuation is the uncertainty of any estimate for volatility over extended periods.

Imbedded Warrants

Few warrants are traded independently of other securities. Most are imbedded in bonds and preferred stocks and carry the label of a conversion feature. The analyst's task is to value the two components of the convertible issue, the warrant and the fixed-income security, to reach a conclusion as to the fairness of the price for an alternative to owning the common stock directly. This process is supplementary to the basic assignment of valuing the enterprise as a whole with a view to arriving at a judgment of the creditworthiness of its debt and the value of its equity.

Example. Burlington Industries has outstanding $75 million 8¾ percent subordinated debenture issue due September 15, 2008, and convertible into 20.62 common shares per bond, or at $48.50 each. The debenture sells at 110 with the stock at 44. Using the Kassouf formula provides a warrant value of 16.98. The hypothetical value of the debenture, then, is

20.62 imbedded warrants at $16.98 each	$ 350
8¾ percent subordinated debenture at 10.25 percent maturity yield	870
	$ 1220

Since this "value" of 122 substantially exceeds the market price of 110, one might well conclude that imbedded warrants are worth less than separately traded instruments.[6] This is logical, since they are not detachable and borrowing out the fixed-income security component may be costly. Furthermore, the company's right to redeem the debenture in whole or in part prior to maturity could materially shorten the warrant's term to expiration. An offset is that the bond component is only worth 87 but will have a value of 100 for exercise of the warrant (conversion). If the warrant component (conversion feature) is given its full 35-point value, leaving 75 for the bond component, the yield to maturity at that price is 12 percent. This is a generous return for an investment quality-issue and could represent a reasonably solid floor unless interest rates were to rise sharply.

Compare this issue with the same company's 5 percent subordinated debenture due September 15, 1991, and convertible into 25.64 shares at

---

[6]The Giguère formula would produce a warrant value of $206 and a debenture value of $1076.

39. This issue sells at 113. A similar valuation process produces this result:

25.64 imbedded warrants at $19.80 each	$ 507
5 percent subordinated debenture at 10.25 percent maturity yield	811
	$ 1318

The market discount from calculated value reflects a lesser time value in the warrant and a much greater risk of call for redemption.[7] The debenture is selling right at its conversion value (25.64 shares at 44 = 112.82). A Giguère valuation of the warrants would also give the debenture a value of 113.

One might conclude that the 8¾ percent issue is preferable for a three- to five-year commitment because of the higher floor and superior current return. For a short-term position, the more immediate participation in the equity through a call at 39 instead of 48½ is the main attraction. Also the floor will be rising steadily as the 5 percent debenture approaches maturity. Beyond this narrow comparison of terms lie the fundamental questions of the value of the firm in relation to the current price, the creditworthiness of the fixed-income component, and the interest rate risk in the floor even if credit quality is maintained. Only these analytical steps offer a chance of convertible security investments turning out to be profitable commitments instead of frustrated hopes.

Adjustment for Volatility

The preceding warrant valuation rules of thumb, as has been emphasized, do not account for expected volatility of a particular share price. For the Burlington Industries example this is not a significant problem, because that stock has an average or slightly below-average price variability. But we know from research in option valuation that the expected probability distribution of future share prices is, quite logically, a major ingredient of warrant value. The case of a volatile glamor stock illustrates the point. Datapoint Corporation convertible 8⅞ percent 2006 came to market at par in late May 1981. The subordinate debentures were convertible at 83 with the common selling at 65. Valuing the imbedded warrant by Shelton's method, Table 35.2 compares average calculated values to the average prices at which the debentures actually sold.

---

[7]A Shelton valuation which picks up the short term to expiration would value the warrant component at $380 and the debenture at $1190.

Table 35.2. Datapoint Corporation Convertibles

	Stock price	Fixed-income security value	Warrant value	Total value	Market price
July 1981	51	55½	24½	80	87
September 1981	44	53½	22	75½	82
November 1981	46	55¾	22¼	78	84
January 1982	51	53½	24½	78	87
March 1982	22	53½	10½	64	65
April 1982	22	53	10½	63½	63

The volatility premium shown in the first four observations evaporated when Datapoint reported a sharp decline in prospective earnings for the 1982 fiscal year and high-growth expectations were dashed.

Because meaningful volatility estimates for three- to five-year periods are so difficult, this factor cannot be accounted for in warrant valuations with the precision frequently possible in option pricing for relatively short periods. Nevertheless, a judgment is clearly necessary, and the security analyst must interpret indications of under- and overvaluations with care.

The Option Alternative

Characteristics and Uses

Calls. The listed call option traded on a national securities exchange has the same investment characteristics as a warrant: a term to expiration (measured in months rather than years) and a strike price (usually one of several traded). Two options with identical strike prices and expiration dates will differ in value because of their relation to the price of the underlying stock, the dividend it pays, and its volatility. These elements of the value of the contract are the principal ingredients of the Black-Scholes option valuation model.[8]

With Intel at 36¼, the pattern of option prices for one- and two-month calls was

Strike price	1 month	2 months
35	3¼	4¼
40	1⅜	2⅛

---

[8]Fischer Black and Myron Scholes, "The Pricing of Options and Corporate Liabilities," *Journal of Political Economy*, May–June 1973, pp. 637–654. See also Robert A. Jarrow and Andrew Rudd, *Option Pricing*, Richard D. Irwin, Homewood, Ill., 1983; and Gary L. Gastineau, *The Stock Options Manual*, 2d ed., McGraw-Hill, New York, 1979.

The time value of two months in a 40 call contrasts with the more than eight years in the warrant selling at 11. Options, then, relate to prices over relatively short spans, but provide much greater leverage.

For example, in late December 1986, when Intel traded at 21¼, calls expiring in February with a strike price of 22¼ could have been purchased at 1 (that is, $21,000 for calls on 21,000 shares at 22¼). When Intel sold at 36¼ seven weeks later, the call contracts were approaching expiration with a value of $288,750, representing a $13.75 gain on each of 21,000 shares, compared with $38,500 in the hypothetical case of an equal dollar investment in warrants. Such exercises in the might-have-been world, illuminated by brilliant hindsight, lead people to pay exorbitant prices for out-of-the-money calls which expire without value. Such prices are set, of course, not by fundamental factors affecting the company, which takes no part in the transactions, but by security dealers and speculators who wish to transfer risks for short periods of time.

The uses of calls to reduce risk include the following:

- Covered call writing on a portfolio is recognized as a method of creating a bond alternative.

- A short sale no longer has an unlimited loss exposure if protected by ownership of a call contract. For example, a person believing that Intel was vulnerable to unfavorable industry developments or a general market decline could sell short at 36¼, purchase a two-month 40 call at 2¼, and know that the maximum loss exposure was limited to 6 points (40 − 36¼ + 2⅛ = 5⅞).

- A nervous Intel investor could acquire a fiduciary call, one in which the exercise price is placed at interest in escrow. Instead of having $3625 at risk in 100 shares of stock, the person would have $3500 in cash and own a two-month 35 call at 4¼ for a total investment of $3925, but any loss would be limited to the cost of the call less any interest earnings.

Puts. Put options, which represent the right to deliver 100 shares of a stock to the seller (writer) of the contract at a specified price at any time during a specified period, are the mirror image of a call option. Their usefulness can be illustrated by a specific case.

Example. An executor receives large blocks of Chevron, Exxon, and Mobil on April 22, 1980, portions of which will have to be sold for the payment of estate taxes the following December and January. Believing that these shares are undervalued at 34¼ , 29¼, and 36¼ respectively, the executor buys puts for downside protection. There is a modest subsequent rally in international oils, and the necessary sales are made at 36⅜ , 35, and 39¾. The puts expire or are sold for nominal amounts.

On holdings of $695,000, price protection costs $15,500, but permits realization of $73,600 in gains by deferring the sales as long as possible.

By buying a put, the investor's position can be insured at modest cost. In the conviction that Company A is undervalued, but with reservations about market levels in general, the investor buys 1000 shares at 52¼ and 10 seven-month 50 put contracts at 2¾. The total investment is now $55,000 in price protected shares with full upside potential. (In contrast, a two-month 35 put for Intel shares selling at 36¼ is logically more expensive to reflect Intel's greater volatility. The premium for shorter protection is 2⅞.)

A Synthetic Convertible

The analyst can create the convertible security of choice by buying calls plus Treasury bills. A commonly used mix is 10 percent calls and 90 percent money market instruments. Units of $1000 of Treasury bills plus purchased slightly out-of-the-money calls are synthetic convertible debentures with a fixed floor having neither interest rate nor credit risk. Rolling up or down the calls adjusts the conversion terms to current market levels. How much better investors would have done with this combination instead of the USX convertibles! Rolling over the calls costs the time values, but convertibles which produce no appreciation in the first three years of a holding period or less are unlikely to prove to be profitable investments. Liquidation or conversion into the common stock should occur within some such time span.

The use of synthetic convertibles permits the investor to own issues of selected companies at the times chosen. If the valuation work has been well performed, the best opportunities should be those created by analysts, not by corporate financial officers and their investment bankers seeking to sell overpriced merchandise in a favorable market.

Adjusting Positions

Limit orders and stop-loss orders have long been used in executing judgments about equity securities. In some respects, option contracts can be seen as a means of getting paid for doing what one intended to do anyway. Having seen Company X shares appreciate from 40 to 60, from under- to overvaluation, the investor is thinking of letting someone else have the next 20 points—but the company is still doing well. Writing a 60 call is tantamount to making the sell decision but accepting an additional 4 points in premium. Selling deep-in-the-money calls may be a device to save brokerage commissions.

If an investor would be glad to buy Company Y shares at 25 but they are selling at 28, accepting a premium of 1¼ for writing a seven-month put at 25 would be logical. Such a transaction is like being paid to enter a limit order below the market and the net cost becomes 23¼.

In general, security analysts are allergic to option writing or buying on stocks which they cover, because an option strategy is very specific about price anticipations, indeed much more specific than a good analyst is prepared to be. Factors directly related to the firm under analysis are the analyst's responsibility, but the industry, sector, or general market factors which may determine the outcome of a holding period as short as an option's term to expiration are not. As a consequence, a covered call writer may never talk with anyone specifically involved in stock selection, be forbidden to let stocks be called away, and be judged entirely on skill in writing overpriced options.

PART 5

Impact of Security Analysis

36
Corporate Governance

The knowledgeable, experienced security analyst is uniquely qualified to advise investors on the wide range of corporate governance issues. Rights and responsibilities of equity ownership in U.S. companies should never be ignored or passed on to others.

Analytical versus Legal-Political Issues

The field of corporate governance also involves the legal profession and the political process, although here we address neither of these dimensions. Our concern is purely with the security analyst's role and functions in reacting to events and practices which affect the valuation of corporate securities and therefore investment results. Common-stock values are, of course, the most sensitive to the terms of security ownership on which investors participate in the U.S. business system.

Our analytical emphasis brings us directly to questions about security values rather than to profound issues of property rights. Nevertheless, broad questions of the fiduciary responsibilities of corporate directors to stockholders engage close attention because unresolved conflicts of interest, waste of corporate assets, and absence of accountability destroy investment values.

The persistent elimination of the rights of share ownership over the decades has created the situation described in the Berle and Means classic of more than a half-century ago:

The shareholder in the modern corporate situation has surrendered a set of definite rights for a set of indefinite expectations. The whole effect of the growth of powers of directors and "control" has been steadily to diminish the number of things on which a shareholder can count; the number of demands he can make with any assurance that they must be satisfied.[1]

The familiar ring of these sentences demonstrates their relevance to the late 1980s. The separation of ownership from control in the hands of management has, of course, proceeded in the decades since Berle and Means so clearly identified it.[2]

Euthanasia of the Shareholder

Elimination of Shareholder Rights

Historical terms of the shareholders' contract included:

- Limitations on lines of business
- Definition of a permitted capital structure
- Preemptive rights to subscribe to new equity issues
- Control over the issuance of securities which would alter the sharing of assets and income (including options and warrants)
- Operational limits to "blank check" stock authorizations (both preferred and common shares)

These provisions of corporate charters, designed to protect the contractual position of shareholders, were being eliminated at the time of the Berle and Means study. Since then, especially since the late 1940s, corporate lawyers and investment bankers have earned large retainers by showing management how to "increase flexibility" by authorizing huge amounts of preferred and common shares while eliminating preemptive rights.

At the same time, management's control of the board of directors through use of the proxy mechanism has been strengthened by elimination of cumulative voting, adoption of staggered boards, and requirement of supermajority votes to remove directors. Calling shareholder meetings without corporate notice and holding meetings by mail are excluded to prevent actions not under the direction of corporate

---

[1]Adolf A. Berle and Gardiner C. Means, *The Modern Corporation and Private Property*, rev. ed., Harcourt Brace & World, New York, 1968, p. 244. The original volume was published in 1932.

[2]See also the prefaces and appendixes to ibid. and Professor Berle's *Power without Property*, Harcourt Brace, New York, 1959.

management. Even shareholder resolutions regarding the location of annual meetings have been vigorously opposed on the ground that the board of directors is best able to make such decisions. The idea of polling shareholders on the subject has apparently not appealed to the managements of major public companies.

Absence of Shareholder Representation

Ostensibly, the creation of board of directors' nominating committees ensures a succession of independent directors. In practice, of course, management has an influential role in identifying congenial candidates. Interlocking directorates are not necessarily undesirable, but they raise questions about independence. When Director A sits on the compensation committee of Company X and passes on Chairperson B's bonus, we can rest assured that B, sitting in judgment on A's incentive compensation, is unlikely to be niggardly.

The typical proxy statement reflects unanimous votes on many subjects. If directors never dissent on complicated subjects, are they really doing their homework or are they passively assenting to whatever management proposes? The credibility of directors' independence, in the view of shareholders, has to be almost nil.

In contrast is the disinterested director defined in the regulations of the Securities and Exchange Commission (SEC) under the Investment Company Act of 1940. With responsibility clearly defined for the terms of a contract with an organization managing a regulated investment company (mutual fund), the disinterested directors have an explicit assignment from the fund shareholders to pass upon the terms of the management contract, expenses, performance, distribution, and shareholder services. The definition of *disinterested* is strict independence from the management or its affiliates and a traditional concept of undivided loyalty. The accountability of management to this kind of a board is clear and explicit, unlike the case of the typical corporate board. Clearly the concept of the mutual fund disinterested director works and works well.

Finally, the absence of dissents, protests, and resignations from many thousand board members inevitably raises questions about the system. The Corporate Governance Project of the American Law Institute is an example of the recognition by responsible leadership of the need to review and rethink some of the legal principles involved. In some instances, however, directors have taken over critical situations to restructure a company or its management. Such examples as Chrysler in the early 1960s, Penn Central, and several major bank problems in the 1970s and 1980s illustrate that boards can act effectively if a situation becomes desperate, but this occurs long after investors have sustained serious losses. The effectiveness of the U.S. business system depends on the promptness with which those in executive positions are held accountable. To be sure, the market for company securities is the ultimate discipline, but it lags, rather than anticipates, performance disappointments.

The Need for Independent Directors

The obvious questions about management's role in the design and execution of compensation plans are frequently the topic of discussion by critics of the system. Do compensation committees obtain independent studies of competitive salaries and benefits? Are executives present for board deliberations? Do they vote on their own terms of employment? Proxy statements do not disclose the answers.

Less visible, but more substantive, are the elements of compensation structures which relate directly to shareholders' equity interests. Some examples are:

- *Performance measures.* Performance units awarded for increases in per-share earnings are one example. High earnings retention and leveraging the balance sheet facilitate growth as measured by shares outstanding. Return on average total capital would be a more meaningful measure.

- *Stock appreciation rights and phantom shares.* Recipients have a full participation in potential appreciation, but, unlike shareholders, recipients have no exposure to capital loss. A qualified option (incentive stock option), after all, is a very substantial form of compensation. It should be worth at least 40 percent of the price of a share of stock. If the stock declines, the executive can make the equivalent purchase in the market and remain fully protected against an advance.

- *Rights offerings.* A privileged subscription offering of equity or convertible securities by giving rights to shareholders, it can be argued, makes the timing and pricing of new issues much less consequential. "Benefiting" present shareholders by a rights offering at a below-market price is perfectly legitimate and perhaps even desirable. Executive compensation geared to stock price, however, will suffer as a consequence. Dividend reinvestment plans, of course, represent a continuous preemptive rights offering, with or without a discount to the market. They represent almost the only form of rights offering being made.

- *Employment contracts.* Holding an unwilling executive in the company by the terms of a contract is unlikely to be a productive arrangement. The benefit, if any, may be to the executive, as is clearly the case in a "golden parachute" which assures the employee of substantial compensation (perhaps two or three years') in the event of termination of employment following a change in control. What became of the case for generous salaries and benefits based on the absence of job security?

These and similar issues are resolved in most cases through the exercise of good sense and good judgment by all parties. In the final analysis, superior management is a bargain at fully competitive levels of compensation. Overreaching in particular instances may give the system a bad name, but what shareholders really need is not a pay cut but replacement of mediocrity in the executive suite. Security analysts are well positioned to appraise the level of achievement based on their in depth study of industry conditions and competitive factors.

The role of independent directors is critical not just to arbitrate compensation issues, to evaluate key members of management, and to ensure orderly management succession, however important these responsibilities may be; the board must address the more fundamental questions about the productiveness with which capital is being employed. Absent persuasive evidence to the contrary, every divestment of a previous acquisition, every restructuring in response to external pressures, every major write-off of assets, and every takeover may well be signs of failure attributable to the directors' stewardship of shareholders' investment. To reach such judgments on an informed basis, the counsel of experienced security analysts is an essential and underutilized resource for board members in search of means to maximize the value of the enterprise.

Raiders Are Welcome

If directors are captives of management or if they fail to recognize deficiencies in corporate performance, shareholders are left with the option of dumping their stock, presumably at a low price, or of banding together to bring about change. As a practical matter, only a person or group with substantial resources can mount such an effort. Such a "dissident," "raider," or rival firm will find using the proxy mechanism to effect change a difficult assignment.[3] As a consequence, a tender offer

---

[3]Management was the victor in more than 40 percent of the cases in the 1981–1985 period, but another sizeable fraction was settled. See Ronald E. Schrager, *Corporate Conflicts: Proxy Fights in the 1980s*, Investor Responsibility Research Center, Washington, D.C., 1986; and James E. Heard and Howard D. Sherman, *Conflicts of Interest in the Proxy Voting System*, Investor Responsibility Research Center, Washington, D.C., 1987.

for a substantial fraction of the outstanding shares becomes the principal method for obtaining results.

Some individuals and groups making such tender offers are expected to break up companies, liquidate major segments, milk the continuing operations, and use the proceeds to pay down the debt created for acquisition. This process makes no positive contribution to economic development and is a predator's destructive strategy. Whether the investor likes such a process or those who execute it is not the real issue. The process appears to be the only way some less productively employed capital can be redeployed for greater efficiency. Each painful instance of a successful raid, moreover, reminds officers and directors that they had better control costs, build markets, increase profitability, and raise the dividend as regularly as possible. Despite some of their tactics, raiders deserve the good will of shareholders who might otherwise be unable to stir lethargic managements into action.

The independent security analyst, familiar with the raider's past record and the state of affairs in the target company, is the logical source of advice on whether there is a feasible alternative to the raider's tender offer. The proposed price is presumably no more than the last sale plus a premium sufficient to trigger a rush of acceptances. The analyst's assignment is to judge the price offered as it relates to the intrinsic value of the firm plus a reasonable control premium.

A Productive Alternative

The long process by which shareholders have been relieved of the rights and responsibilities of ownership has transferred to boards of directors and from them to management most decision-making power. The shareholder has become an ineffectual nuisance to be pacified by self-congratulatory reports and increasing dividends. Only raiders, and of course the media, can call management to account unless true disaster strikes or regulations of the SEC are violated.

Security analysts can make find their opinions effective in investor portfolio decisions and in the marketplace, but most frequently the analysts are following the Wall Street rule "if you cannot support the management, sell the stock." A tender offer, a leveraged buyout proposal or financing, or a merger plan, however, need not be the stimulus to expert analysis of the earning power and value of the enterprise. Without such changes in control, large stockholders or creditors may logically look to such analytical support for bringing about constructive change while continuing an investment position. Out of the public eye and without confrontations, there is frequently a place for this kind of dialogue with management on corporate strategies as a rational and productive alternative to the raider's frequently destructive course of action.

Disenfranchisement of the Shareholder

Increasingly, "in the interest of flexibility and to save the expense of a special meeting of shareholders" (standard explanations for eliminating participation in major decisions), the right to vote has degenerated to the privilege of ratifying the slate of directors and the selection of independent auditors. Approving incentive plans for executives and limiting director liability remain as matters on which shareholders are permitted to vote affirmatively. Because decisions regarding mergers and being acquired remain as fundamental shareholder rights, the trend of the 1980s was to induce shareholders to relinquish these rights and responsibilities of ownership for such matters.

Election of Directors

One Share, One Vote.   The creation of multiple classes of stock with unequal voting rights is a longstanding device to ensure control of the board of directors. Dow Jones, Wang Laboratories, New York Times, Hershey Foods, and McCormick are some companies to do so.[4] A novel provision adopted by Potlatch Corporation in 1985 was to provide four votes per share for all shares held for 48 months or more. Thus the holder of shares, assured of being outvoted on almost any issue, has effectively no vote at all. The New York Stock Exchange's historical stance in favor of a one-share–one-vote rule is no longer heeded.

Cumulative Voting.   Shareholders frequently had the right to cumulate their votes in favor of a single board candidate. Cumulative voting has been widely eliminated since World War II. A rare instance of restoration by Burlington Industries is the special case where there is a 40 percent shareholder, presumably involved in a takeover.

Staggered Boards.   If only one-third of the board is up for election each year, the right to vote has been effectively reduced by two-thirds. Fre-

---

[4]Of the *Fortune* 500 companies, 30 have unequal voting rights. This and subsequent data on this group of large companies is from Virginia K. Rosenbaum, *Takeover Defenses: Profiles of the Fortune 500,* Investor Responsibility Research Center, Washington, D.C., 1987. This study has profiles of 424 of the 500 companies.

quently companies with staggered boards have provisions to prevent removal of directors except for cause, action of other directors, or a supermajority vote. By May 1986, 223 of the *Fortune* 500 had classified boards.

Limitations of Shareholder Rights

No action by written consent, no right to call special meetings, and supermajority votes (frequently 75 to 80 percent) to change bylaws are recent curtailments of shareholder rights adopted by 222 *Fortune* 500 companies.

Takeover Defenses

In addition to these dilutions of voting rights, the full arsenal of "shark repellents" includes the weapons described in the following sections.

Supermajority Vote. Setting the requirement for a shareholder positive vote at 75 or 80 percent for a merger not approved by the board of directors in effect gives the board a veto over the decision of a majority of shareholders.

Fair Price Provisions. Charter provisions requiring a bidder to pay all shareholders a fair price, adopted by 158 of the *Fortune* 500, are intended to prevent two-tier tender offers which may be abusive. As such, they appeal to considerations of equity. They also, of course, threaten to increase the cost of an acquisition. Typically, this provision may not apply to a board-approved transaction.

Blank-Check Preferred. Frequently these authorizations of preferred stocks for which directors have complete discretion in setting terms are longstanding and are designed for acquisitions rather than as antitakeover weapons. When 362 of the *Fortune* 500 companies have secured these authorizations by mid-1986, clearly this has been the most widely used and most easily obtained antitakeover security issuance provision. After bemused Schlumberger stockholders authorized a blank-check preferred issue of 200 million shares (compared with 285 million common), the company was sufficiently embarrassed to volunteer some restrictions on possible issuance.

Common-Stock Authorization. Huge amounts of authorized but unissued common shares can be made available for antitakeover purposes.

With the recision of preemptive rights, an option on shares can be granted to a favored acquiring company, and blank-check preferred can be made convertible. A knowledgeable security analyst is best equipped to express an opinion on whether a requested share authorization is genuinely needed for corporate purposes or only as a shark repellent.

Poison Pill. Largely since 1983, 143 *Fortune* 500 Companies have issued rights to subscribe on exceedingly favorable terms, usually 50 percent of the market price, to shares of the company or the new entity in the event of takeover.[5] This right would make acceptance of a tender offer unattractive unless the acquiring company was prepared to raise its bid substantially, that is, ready to swallow the poison pill. Issuance of the rights does not require shareholder approval, and typically it is not requested.

Greenmail. *Greenmail,* the purchase of stock from a raider at a premium over the market price, developed as a means of turning away an unwelcome tender offer. Prohibiting greenmail is logically supported by shareholders, who see it as unfair and as a waste of corporate assets, and by some corporate managements who believe that it will deter some potential bidders. Some 37 *Fortune* 500 companies have adopted rules against greenmail.

Golden Parachutes. Liberal severance agreements in the event of a change of control are obviously an added cost to an acquiring company, but such cost may not be material. The absence of any shareholder approval of such arrangements is customary but again reminds shareholders of their lack of voice in decisions. "Silver parachutes," those which cover very large numbers of employees or even all, cause less unfavorable reactions and may be even more effective. A pension parachute provides for any fund surplus to go to employees' benefits.

Cumulative Results. The cumulative effect of this array of shark repellants is to take from shareholders their right to determine the future of their company and to transfer it to a board of directors whose independence is open to question. To be sure, nonmanagement directors may be given a special voice, and an investment banking house may be retained to pass upon terms, but the record is not altogether reassuring. In some instances, a management buyout has been recommended to shareholders only to have outside bids come in at appreciably higher levels. For ex-

---

[5]This is the number as of May 1986, with additional pills subsequently adopted. A tabulation of the Investor Responsibility Research Center in February 1987 identified some 370 public companies with poison pill plans.

ample, a Stokely–Van Camp buyout at $55 per share was recommended by participating management, but competitive bids eventually produced a price of $77.[6]

The shareholder has been disenfranchised in these instances, but possibly not disadvantaged. If, in a generally depressed market, raiders seek to acquire companies at cheap prices for the purpose of breaking them up and liquidating them at a profit, it may be advantageous to hold them at bay and to afford management the opportunity to add value for all the shareholders in a more favorable environment. For this purpose, suspending the right to vote on takeover bids may be the only way to prevent arbitrageurs, seeking a quick profit, from exercising control of the situation.

The making of a tender offer in compliance with regulations can seldom be stopped by management, directors, or shareholders except by making the terms unattractive to the bidder. Again, arbitrageurs will be the first to tender their shares to the highest bidder. For many shareholders, especially fiduciaries, it is difficult to refuse a bid well in excess of the recent market price. The security analyst would have to conclude that the shares were very materially undervalued and that the tender offer is still so far below intrinsic value that even the control premium being offered does not bring the price to a reasonable estimate of value. For most institutional investors, moreover, realization of a control premium is almost a duty, since they own securities for investment and not for the exercise of control. Indeed, they do not own "control"—they owe it to their beneficiaries to realize that value when they find themselves joint owners of control in a takeover contest.

Under all the circumstances, the investor must make difficult decisions. Must a premium be realized when offered, or may long-term investment opportunities be preserved? Should not a new management or new corporate strategies be afforded time to be brought to fruition for the existing body of shareholders? A strong case can sometimes be made by experienced security analysts that even better values can be realized by keeping the existing corporate structure and management in place. The logical outcome, however, would be not perpetual antitakeover provisions but those which would expire in three to five years. Affording this kind of interim or transitional immunity from takeover threats could

---

[6]For a perceptive discussion of this problem, see Bevis Longstreth, "Management Buyouts: Are Public Shareholders Getting a Fair Deal?" reprinted in Richard F. DeMong and John W. Peavey III, eds., *Takeovers and Shareholders: The Mounting Controversy,* Financial Analysts Research Foundation, Charlottesville, Va., 1985.

serve shareholders well. Unfortunately, such restraint and accountability have not been accepted by corporate managements and their advisers.

Implications for Valuation. The analyst faces a legitimate question: Does the adoption of effective antitakeover provisions reduce the value of a company? Should the multiplier be reduced because the management has secured immunity from the discipline of the marketplace? Empirical studies have produced somewhat mixed results, but some loss of market value seems to have followed adoption of a full panoply of shark repellants. Such studies of average experience are not really responsive to a specific case. It seems logical to expect that barring a potential bidder for a company cannot possibly add to its value but may subtract. How large might be the subtraction is surely a function of the specific ingredients of prospective value without such a bidder in the picture.

If the analyst can identify real elements of potential value to be developed from mergers with other companies, the possibility still exists that a favorable deal can be made voluntarily as so many have been made in the past. In any event, success and rising share prices are the ultimate defenses against raids and make repellants superfluous.

The Future

At long last, institutional investors are taking an interest in corporate governance issues. They increasingly recognize that the stakes are too high for complacency and inaction to prevail. At one time, private pension funds, invariably supporting managements' proposals, earned the epithet of "silent partners." Security analysts were equally uninterested. As the issues have emerged more clearly, leaders of the investment management business have recognized their significance and have become more outspoken.[7]

Fiduciary responsibilities under the Employee Retirement Income Security Act of 1974 (ERISA) appear to require careful attention to shareholder voting and other issues of corporate governance.[8] Wherever these new expressions of interest may lead, clearly, silent partners are now speaking out and are prepared to take an active part in shaping the future.

[7]See DeMong and Peavey, *Takeovers and Shareholders*, pp. 68–102 for discussion among William S. Gray, Robert J. Kirby, Dave H. Williams, and Dean LeBaron.

[8]See James E. Heard, "Pension Funds and Contests for Corporate Control," *California Management Review*, Winter 1987, pp. 89–100.

Index

654

Royal Dutch/Shell Transport Group, 123*n.*
Royalties, on oil, 231–232
Rudd, Andrew, 23, 619*n.*

Safety:
    assets as measure of, 316–317
    standards of, 454–465, 474–479
Safeway, 386
Sales:
    of assets, 158–160
    concentration and geographical location of, 382
    installment, 287
    per share, 343
    of stocks, 330–331
    variables affecting, 30–31
Sales policy, 527–528
Sales-profit margin, 77–78
Salomon Brothers, 14*n.*, 74, 107, 414
Sarnat, Marshall, 338*n.*
Savings and loan companies, special tax status of, 283
Savings flow, 75
Saxon, 449
Schlumberger, Dowell, 266
Schlumberger Ltd., 266, 331
Scholes, Myron, 342, 619*n.*
Schrager, Ronald E., 629*n.*
Seagram Company, Ltd., 118, 302
Searle, 462
Sears, Roebuck, 269
Sears, Roebuck Acceptance, 269
SEC (*see* Securities and Exchange Commission)
Sector analysis, 4, 87–94
    defined, 87–88
    FRS industrial groups and, 91–94
    ratios in industry analysis, 383
    SEI homogeneous groups and, 88–91
Sector management, 413–414
Sector swaps, 413–414
Secular average projections, 56
Secured obligations, 459
Securities:
    allowance for, 171–172
    array, 11–14
    asset value analysis and, 322
    balance sheet and, 302
    corporate, 12–14
    (*See also specific types of securities*)
    exchanges, 12

Securities (*Cont.*):
    groups of, 11–14
    marketable, 171–172, 302
    of questionable creditworthiness, 465–467
    rates of return for principal classes, 82
    safety of, 316–317
    senior, 16–17, 36–37
    Treasury, 406–407
Securities and Exchange Commission (SEC), 12*n.*, 34, 35, 95, 97*n.*, 98–104, 100*n.*, 101*n.*, 102*n.*, 103*n.*, 106, 134*n.*, 152, 218*n.*, 627
    EDGAR, 106
Security analysis, 4, 33–40
    anticipation approach to, 38
    assignment, 483–495
    discipline of, 8–10
    economic analysis and, 58–66
    extent of, 114
    functions of, 35–40
    future and, 127–128
    intrinsic value approach to, 38–39
    investment approaches, 486–493
    market and informational challenges and, 34–35
    perspective, 9–10
    relative value approach to, 39
    scope and limitations of, 29–40
    stock market valuations versus, 580
Security markets:
    behavior of, 14–23
    efficient market hypothesis and, 23–27
Seed, Allen H., III, 242*n.*
Segment reporting, 103
Segmented investing, 405–407
SEI Corporation homogeneous groups, 88–91
Senior charges, 361–362
Senior securities:
    second-grade, 16–17
    valuation of, 36–37
Settlements, pension, 192
Shangquan, P., 567*n.*
Shareholder rights, 626–628, 631–635
Sharpe, William F., 25*n.*, 342*n.*
Shaw Data Services, Inc., 109
Shearson Lehman Brothers, 71, 108, 414, 614
Shelton, John P., 615*n.*, 616
Sherman, Howard D., 629*n.*
Sierra Pacific Resources, 534–535
"Silver parachutes," 633

GROWTH RATIOS

21. Growth in earnings per share *(Chapter 20)*

$$= \frac{\text{Earnings per share in final period}}{\text{Earnings per share in base period}}$$

STABILITY RATIOS

22. Maximum decline in coverage of senior charges (see ratio 32) *(Chapter 20)*

$$= \frac{\text{Worst year}}{\text{Average of previous three years}}$$

23. Percent decline in return on capital (see ratio 14) *(Chapter 20)*

$$= \frac{\text{Worst year}}{\text{Average of previous three years}}$$

PAYOUT RATIOS

24. Payout ratio *(Chapter 20)*

$$= \frac{\text{Dividend paid on common}}{\text{Net income available for common}} \quad \text{or} \quad \frac{\text{Ratio 2}}{\text{Ratio 1}}$$

25. Dividend to cash flow *(Chapter 20)*

$$= \frac{\text{Dividend paid on common}}{\text{Cash flow from operations after taxes}} \quad \text{or} \quad \frac{\text{Ratio 2}}{\text{Ratio 4}}$$

CREDIT RATIOS

26. Current ratio *(Chapter 19)*

$$= \frac{\text{Current assets}}{\text{Current liabilities}}$$

27. Quick ratio *(Chapter 19)*

$$= \frac{\text{Current assets} - \text{inventories}}{\text{Current liabilities}}$$

28. Cash ratio *(Chapter 19)*

$$= \frac{\text{Cash items}}{\text{Current liabilities}}$$

29. Equity ratio *(Chapter 20)*

$$= \frac{\text{Common equity at book value}}{\text{Tangible assets} - \text{accrued payables}}$$